Illustrator 8 Bible

Illustrator 8 Bible

Ted Alspach

Foreword by Pierre Bézier

IDG Books Worldwide, Inc.
An International Data Group Company

Foster City, CA ✦ Chicago, IL ✦ Indianapolis, IN ✦ New York, NY

Illustrator 8 Bible

Published by
IDG Books Worldwide, Inc.
An International Data Group Company
919 E. Hillsdale Blvd., Suite 400
Foster City, CA 94404
www.idgbooks.com (IDG Books Worldwide Web site).

Library of Congress Catalog Card Number: 98-75151

ISBN: 0-7645-3269-3

Printed in the United States of America

10 9 8 7 6 5 4 3 2 1

1B/QS/RS/ZY/FC

Distributed in the United States by IDG Books Worldwide, Inc.

Distributed by Macmillan Canada for Canada; by Transworld Publishers Limited in the United Kingdom; by IDG Norge Books for Norway; by IDG Sweden Books for Sweden; by Woodslane Pty. Ltd. for Australia; by Woodslane (NZ) Ltd. for New Zealand; by Addison Wesley Longman Singapore Pte Ltd. for Singapore, Malaysia, Thailand, Indonesia, and Korea; by Norma Comunicaciones S.A. for Colombia; by Intersoft for South Africa; by International Thomson Publishing for Germany, Austria, and Switzerland; by Toppan Company Ltd. for Japan; by Distribuidora Cuspide for Argentina; by Livraria Cultura for Brazil; by Ediciencia S.A. for Ecuador; by Ediciones ZETA S.C.R. Ltda. for Peru; by WS Computer Publishing Corporation, Inc., for the Philippines; by Unalis Corporation for Taiwan; by Contemporanea de Ediciones for Venezuela; by Computer Book & Magazine Store for Puerto Rico; by Express Computer Distributors for the Caribbean and West Indies. Authorized Sales Agent: Anthony Rudkin Associates for the Middle East and North Africa.

For general information on IDG Books Worldwide's books in the U.S., please call our Consumer Customer Service department at 800-762-2974. For reseller information, including discounts and premium sales, please call our Reseller Customer Service department at 800-434-3422.

For information on where to purchase IDG Books Worldwide's books outside the U.S., please contact our International Sales department at 650-655-3200 or fax 650-655-3297.

For consumer information on foreign language translations, please contact our Customer Service department at 1-800-432-3422, fax 317-596-5692, or e-mail rights@idgbooks.com.

For information on licensing foreign or domestic rights, please phone +1-650-655-3109.

For sales inquiries and special prices for bulk quantities, please contact our Sales department at 650-655-3200 or write to the address above.

For information on using IDG Books Worldwide's books in the classroom or for ordering examination copies, please contact our Educational Sales department at 800-434-2086 or fax 317-596-5499.

For press review copies, author interviews, or other publicity information, please contact our Public Relations department at 650-655-3000 or fax 650-655-3299.

For authorization to photocopy items for corporate, personal, or educational use, please contact Copyright Clearance Center, 222 Rosewood Drive, Danvers, MA 01923, or fax 978-750-4470.

is a trademark under exclusive license to IDG Books Worldwide, Inc., from International Data Group, Inc.

ABOUT IDG BOOKS WORLDWIDE

Welcome to the world of IDG Books Worldwide.

IDG Books Worldwide, Inc., is a subsidiary of International Data Group, the world's largest publisher of computer-related information and the leading global provider of information services on information technology. IDG was founded more than 30 years ago by Patrick J. McGovern and now employs more than 9,000 people worldwide. IDG publishes more than 290 computer publications in over 75 countries. More than 90 million people read one or more IDG publications each month.

Launched in 1990, IDG Books Worldwide is today the #1 publisher of best-selling computer books in the United States. We are proud to have received eight awards from the Computer Press Association in recognition of editorial excellence and three from Computer Currents' First Annual Readers' Choice Awards. Our best-selling ...For Dummies® series has more than 50 million copies in print with translations in 31 languages. IDG Books Worldwide, through a joint venture with IDG's Hi-Tech Beijing, became the first U.S. publisher to publish a computer book in the People's Republic of China. In record time, IDG Books Worldwide has become the first choice for millions of readers around the world who want to learn how to better manage their businesses.

Our mission is simple: Every one of our books is designed to bring extra value and skill-building instructions to the reader. Our books are written by experts who understand and care about our readers. The knowledge base of our editorial staff comes from years of experience in publishing, education, and journalism — experience we use to produce books to carry us into the new millennium. In short, we care about books, so we attract the best people. We devote special attention to details such as audience, interior design, use of icons, and illustrations. And because we use an efficient process of authoring, editing, and desktop publishing our books electronically, we can spend more time ensuring superior content and less time on the technicalities of making books.

You can count on our commitment to deliver high-quality books at competitive prices on topics you want to read about. At IDG Books Worldwide, we continue in the IDG tradition of delivering quality for more than 30 years. You'll find no better book on a subject than one from IDG Books Worldwide.

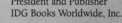

John Kilcullen
Chairman and CEO
IDG Books Worldwide, Inc.

Steven Berkowitz
President and Publisher
IDG Books Worldwide, Inc.

*Eighth Annual
Computer Press
Awards ≥1992*

*Ninth Annual
Computer Press
Awards ≥1993*

*Tenth Annual
Computer Press
Awards ≥1994*

*Eleventh Annual
Computer Press
Awards ≥1995*

IDG is the world's leading IT media, research and exposition company. Founded, in 1964, IDG had 1997 revenues of $2.05 billion and has more than 9,000 employees worldwide. IDG offers the widest range of media options that reach IT buyers in 75 countries representing 95% of worldwide IT spending. IDG's diverse product and services portfolio spans six key areas including print publishing, online publishing, expositions and conferences, market research, education and training, and global marketing services. More than 90 million people read one or more of IDG's 290 magazines and newspapers, including IDG's leading global brands — Computerworld, PC World, Network World, Macworld and the Channel World family of publications. IDG Books Worldwide is one of the fastest-growing computer book publishers in the world, with more than 700 titles in 36 languages. The "...For Dummies®" series alone has more than 50 million copies in print. IDG offers online users the largest network of technology-specific Web sites around the world through IDG.net (http://www.idg.net), which comprises more than 225 targeted Web sites in 55 countries worldwide. International Data Corporation (IDC) is the world's largest provider of information technology data, analysis and consulting, with research centers in over 41 countries and more than 400 research analysts worldwide. IDG World Expo is a leading producer of more than 168 globally branded conferences and expositions in 35 countries including E3 (Electronic Entertainment Expo), Macworld Expo, ComNet, Windows World Expo, ICE (Internet Commerce Expo), Agenda, DEMO, and Spotlight. IDG's training subsidiary, ExecuTrain, is the world's largest computer training company, with more than 230 locations worldwide and 785 training courses. IDG Marketing Services helps industry-leading IT companies build international brand recognition by developing global integrated marketing programs via IDG's print, online and exposition products worldwide. Further information about the company can be found at www.idg.com.   10/8/98

Credits

Acquisitions Editor
Andy Cummings

Development Editors
Kathryn Duggan
Philip C. Wescott, Jr.

Technical Editors
Steven Frank
Sandra Alves

Copy Editors
Christine Schultz-Touge
Richard H. Adin
Anne Friedman

Project Coordinator
Susan Parini

Graphics and Production Specialists
E. A. Pauw
Chris Pimentel
Mark Yim

Quality Control Specialists
Mick Arellano
Mark Schumann

Proofreader
Laura L. Bowman

Indexer
Ty Koontz

About the Author

Ted Alspach is the author of many books on desktop publishing and graphics, as well as hundreds of articles on related topics, including *Illustrator 7 Studio Secrets*, *Illustrator 7 Bible*, *Photoshop Complete*, *Kai's Power Tools Studio Secrets*, and *Illustrator Filter Finesse*. He is a contributing editor to *Adobe Magazine*.

To the furry creatures who allow us to share their lives:

Linus *Felis orangeris*

Murphy *Equus stubbornis*

Toulouse *Felis monstrositis*

Pyro *Felis whinyis*

Yote *Canis lazyis*

Static *Felis obnoxious*

Sage *Felis affectionis*

Foreword

Around 1960, engineers and technicians in the European car industry were divided into two groups: those who worked on mechanical parts and those who worked on car body parts.

For the mechanical group, the surfaces that could be manufactured were clearly defined with dimensions and limits — there was no place for haggling or bargaining at inspection time, and the verdict was simple: GOOD or SCRAP.

For the body-design group, things were far from being simple. From the stylist's small-scale mock-up to the full-scale drawing of the "skin," to the clay model, to the final drawing, to the master model, to the stamping tools — each rendering was supposed to be in accordance with the preceding one. Designers used French curves, sweeps, and lathes (plastic splines), but small discrepancies could not be avoided at each step. These minor errors added up, to the detriment of the final product.

Although these problems had been experienced for decades, people were not satisfied and still looked for a solution. They believed, as Plato said, that "Number is the expression of everything," and, as Lord William Kelvin said, that "No one can claim to have mastered a phenomenon as long as he has not been able to express it with figures."

By 1960, a small number of people believed that the computer could provide an acceptable solution to the problem of discrepancies in measurements. The aircraft industry was probably the first industry in the United States to use computers, but the automotive industry rapidly followed suit.

At this time, two solutions were considered. The first solution was to keep the general process of manufacturing and, with the help of computers (CRT or numerically controlled machine tools), improve one or two steps. The second solution was to forget the existing scheme and start from scratch to take full advantage of the computer's capabilities. This step entailed greater risks but also had greater advantages.

For those who chose the latter solution, the first task was to build a list of requirements that included the following:

> ✦ Creating or adopting a mathematical system that could be easily understood and operated by draftsmen, designers, and methods people. The system needed to describe space curves — not only conics and surfaces — and to

provide an accurate, complete, and distortion-free definition of the curves. It needed to be easily transmitted between offices, shops, and subcontractors.

✦ Providing the body- and tool-drawing offices with full-scale drawing machines, controlled completely by computers that work in interactive mode, such as those capable of tracing curves at a speed of one foot per second.

✦ Equipping the drawing offices, not the tool shops, with rapid milling machines that could carve large portions of a car — the top, the hood, and so on — in a soft material, such as Styrofoam, urethane foam, or plaster.

✦ Devising the relevant software.

✦ Equipping the tool shops with heavy NC milling machines for manufacturing stamping units.

In 1960, the mathematical theory was based on the use of conics — nonrational polynomials with vector coefficients. Mathematical theory now includes B-splines and NURBS, but mathematicians still search for other solutions.

By the end of the 1960s, some simple systems were operative, but a complete system was not fully operative until the end of the 1970s. Since that time, many basic improvements in car design have been developed, including color, reflection lines, perspective viewing, animation, finite elements, crash simulation, aerodynamics, stress and strain, vibration and noise, and so on.

No doubt, the advent of CAD/CAM has been one of the most important changes that took place in the automotive industry during the present century. Of course, it is not necessary for the lay user to master the complete theory — one can play basketball without referring to Galileo, Newton, Keppler, or Einstein — but students and engineers who take part in the development or improvement of a system will find plenty of food for thought in this book.

Pierre E. Bézier

Pierre Bézier is the creator of Bézier Curves, a unique mathematical system used for defining curves. Bézier Curves were adopted by Adobe when they created the PostScript page description language. Illustrator is very much a "front end" for PostScript, and the software would undoubtedly be quite different today if not for Bézier's (unknown at the time) contribution. Pierre Bézier lives in Paris, France.

Preface

You are holding in your hands the biggest, most thorough, and most helpful guide to Adobe Illustrator you'll find anywhere.

Gives you a bit of a rush, doesn't it?

This is the fourth edition of the best-selling *Illustrator Bible*, the first book I had ever written, and still my favorite (well, I'm also partial to the original version of *The Stand*, but Mr. King probably won't let me take credit for that . . . especially since I was only about 9 when I first read it).

The *Illustrator Bible* is the book I wrote because I couldn't find the book I wanted about Adobe Illustrator. Now I have it, and believe it or not, I'm constantly using my own book for a reference. I'd love to tell the world, "sure, I know that," without putting them on hold while I search my own index for the "Reset Tracking to 0" key command (Command-Shift-X, by the way). There's just too much about Illustrator for any one person to keep in his or her head at one time; the *Illustrator Bible* gathers all the Illustrator information you can't remember and makes it more available and easier to follow than the plot twists on *Melrose Place*.

If you're at your local bookstore looking at the different Illustrator books to choose from, don't just pick this one because it weighs the most (sorry about that . . . I get more thank-you letters from chiropractors who've stayed in business because of this monstrosity . . .) or because it works great as a booster seat for your two-year-old nephew. Instead, take a look-see through these pages, which are stuffed to overflowing with in-depth Illustrator information that you just won't find anywhere else. And then there's the CD-ROM — packed with chapters that didn't fit in the book, tons of images and software, as well as two fully functional, free plug-ins from Extensis and Cytopia.

What's New in This Edition

Illustrator has gone through a serious makeover with version 8. So has this book. I've reorganized the chapters into a leaner, meaner book. Okay, it's not any leaner, but it is meaner, in a good way.

Illustrator 8 has added many very cool new features as well as revamping some of the old standby tools. In this edition, you'll find complete coverage of the new tools and features and extensive explanations on how these new features work. Adobe has enhanced some of the drawing tools to our delight. They have taken in the users' comments and given us what we want.

To accommodate all the Illustrator for Windows users, I've included a sidebar to summarize what's new and/or different in each chapter since version 7.

There's stunning new art in the color section, as well as a handy Pantone color reference chart for process-based Pantone Colors, making the color section more of a tool than you'll find in any other similar color pages. The CD-ROM contains all the Illustrator images you see in the book, labeled by figure number, including the images in the color section. Finally, and most important, in addition to the free distortion filter Doodle Jr., Extensis has graciously given me the exclusive rights to distribute a fully working version of VectorFrame, a frame-making plug-in from their VectorTools set of plug-ins (covered in Chapter 14).

Is This the Illustrator Book for You?

I've been to bookstores. I've seen the other Illustrator books out there. Some of them are quite good. Some of them are fairly awful. But none of them can match the *Illustrator Bible* for thoroughness, usefulness, or completeness. I've left no vector-based stone unturned.

Here are more reasons the *Illustrator 8 Bible* is the best overall book on Illustrator:

The most complete coverage of Illustrator. This book isn't big because I wanted to hog all of the retail book space to myself (of course, that's not a bad idea) but because I've included every possible thing you'd ever want to know about Illustrator. From learning the basics of drawing to creating outstanding special effects with vectors and rasters, it's all here.

Fun, original, different artwork to illustrate the techniques and capabilities of Illustrator. When I say *different*, I'm not talking about the type of "art" where there's a naked guy in a room sitting on a stool reciting the first few lines of the Declaration of Independence over and over and over again (that's supposedly "performance art," heh), but instead, I mean that each technique is created with a different piece of artwork. Some of it is simple and some of it is complex, with each piece showing not only a particular feature but other Illustrator capabilities as well.

Clean artwork without those annoying jaggies. This is vector software. When you think of vectors, you probably think of smooth, flowing paths that don't look like someone filled in a bunch of squares on a sheet of graph paper. So instead of using screen shots for paths shown in this book, each path was painstakingly drawn in Illustrator. I think you'll appreciate the difference.

Top-notch technical prowess. Once again, the *Illustrator 8 Bible* has gotten the best possible person to do a technical review of the book. Previous editions were technically reviewed by Eric Gibson, the lead technical support engineer for Illustrator, and Andrei Herasimchuk, who designed and implemented the Illustrator 7 interface and was behind such useful new features as the visible transformation origin point. This edition was tech edited by Steven Frank and Sandra Alves.

Perfect for teaching. If you know Illustrator inside and out, you'll find the *Illustrator 8 Bible* the best teaching tool available for Illustrator, with examples and explanations that perfectly complement a teaching environment. Most computer training companies teaching Illustrator use this book, as do schools and universities.

The most in-depth coverage of filters and plug-ins. Filters and plug-ins are an integral part of Adobe Illustrator, so I've devoted an entire section of the book to covering native filters and third-party plug-ins such as Extensis VectorTools. There's even a section on how you can make your own plug-ins.

Real-world examples and advice. Illustrator doesn't exist in a vacuum. Instead, it is often used in conjunction with other programs, in a variety of different environments and situations. Some people use Illustrator to create logos, others create full-page advertisements, and still others create entire billboards with Illustrator. Throughout this book, various real-world situations and examples are presented that truly add to your understanding of each topic.

A CD-ROM with artwork and exclusive plug-ins. The CD-ROM contains Illustrator artwork from this book, as well as several software and plug-in demo files. In addition, Doodle Jr. and VectorFrame are included free on the CD-ROM. As if that weren't enough, fully functional plug-ins from Adobe that they don't want anyone to know about are on the CD-ROM for your use in Illustrator.

The best information for upgrading from previous versions. Appendix D, Shortcuts for Illustrator 8, indicates different and new shortcuts. Appendix C, What's New in Illustrator 8, lists each and every new feature, as well as changed features, with cross- references to supporting material throughout the book.

You don't need to be an artist or a computer geek to learn Illustrator with this book. No matter what your level of Illustrator experience — from the person who calls tech support for help getting the #$@&#!! shrinkwrap off the box to the person who puts the frustrated party on hold at Adobe — you'll undoubtedly find new things to try, and learn more about Illustrator along the way.

How to Get the Most Out of This Book

There are a few things you may want to be aware of before you dive too deeply into the mysteries of Vector-based graphics, Adobe style:

Versions. When you see the word Illustrator, it refers to all versions of Illustrator. When I stick a number after the word Illustrator, it's relevant to that version only. Version numbers in the software industry change faster than time slots for *Murder One*, so Version 8.0 may become Version 8.0.1, 8.1, 8.2, or some other number before you know it. When I'm talking about Version 8, I'll be referring to 8.*x*, where *x* is any number at all. When Adobe releases Version 9 or the next major upgrade, there will be a new version of this book to help you through it.

Menu and keyboard commands. To indicate that you need to choose a command from a menu, I write something like MenuName ⇨ Command. For instance, File ⇨ Save. If there is a command nested in a submenu, it is MenuName ⇨ Submenu ⇨ Command, like Filter ⇨ Distort ⇨ Roughen. If a command has a keyboard command, I mention that as well for both Macintosh and Windows versions. For instance, Save uses "Command-S," on the Mac, which I'll put here as ⌘-S (the ⌘ corresponds to the ⌘ symbol on your keyboard). The other Mac keys are spelled out — Option, Shift, Control, and so forth. Save uses "Ctrl+S" in Windows (corresponds to the Ctrl key on your Windows keyboard).

This is not a novel. As much as I'd like you to discover plot intricacies, subtle characterizations, and moral fabric woven into the story, none of those things exist in this book (if they do, be sure to let me know about them). There are two really good ways to use this book:

1. Look up what you're interested in the Table of Contents or the Index, and refer to that section. Rinse and repeat as necessary.

2. Slowly, calmly work your way through the entire book, trying out examples (the funky Steps that are almost everywhere) and techniques as you run across them. The book is designed to be read this way, each chapter building on the previous chapter.

Have fun. This book is a pretty straightforward, serious tome, although I have managed to include many bad puns ("rotate the image as far as you're inclined to") and terrible jokes — How many FreeHand users does it take to draw a light bulb? Three. One at the computer, one on hold to Macromedia tech support, and the other back at the computer store, trying to exchange the software for Illustrator. Of course, I show you how to draw a realistic-looking light bulb in Chapter 10, with an abbreviated version in the color section.

What's a Computer Book Without Icons?

Nonexistent, for the most part. I'm not exactly Dr. Icon, but I've included several throughout this edition that may make reading this book a little more enjoyable and helpful.

Tip

These icons indicate some sort of power user secret you absolutely need to know to be able to illustrate with the big kids.

Note

Did you know that the third edition of this book was the best-selling book on Illustrator 7? Interesting tidbits like this are noted by this icon. Sort of like having Cliff from *Cheers* rambling on about something every few pages. Slightly interesting, but they won't increase your Illustrator skills. Just something I thought you might want to know.

Danger Will Robinson!!! If Robby the Robot used Illustrator, he'd be reading about all the nasty things that can happen and how to avoid them.

These icons indicate what's brand new in this version of Illustrator.

What's Inside the Book

Part I: Introducing Illustrator. This section has me pointing out points and helping you get a handle on paths. You learn how to color things, how to uncolor things, and how to delete the things when you don't like their color. I even show you how to customize Illustrator to work better and faster.

Part II: Putting Illustrator to Work. This section puts you to work learning about type and how to fine-tune those paths you drew in Part I. Part II also contains a healthy dose of the hard stuff — like compound paths, masks, blends, gradients, patterns, and graphs.

Part III: Filters and Plug-Ins. Here's where the fun begins, as you start distorting and coloring using the native Illustrator filters and plug-ins. Then there's a whole chapter on VectorTools (Chapter 14), one on other third party filters and plug-ins like CADtools, VectorEffects, and another on Photoshop filters.

Part IV: Mastering Illustrator. This is the section that contains the nitty gritty — and I don't mean the band. Hot topics such as using Illustrator on the Web, printing, and techniques for creating fantastic graphics are presented.

Appendixes. The six appendixes contain information on installing Illustrator, using the CD-ROM, what's new in Illustrator 8, shortcuts, context-sensitive menus, and troubleshooting. There's also a handy guide to all sorts of useful Illustrator resources.

Yo, Ted!

Send any comments you may have about the book to:

    IB8@bezier.com

(IB8 is my own personal mis-ordered acronym for the *Illustrator 8 Bible*.)

I get tons of e-mail from my loyal, intelligent readers, and I try to answer each and every message. However, due to time constraints, it may appear that I'm blowing you off. Please be assured that I do respond to e-mail when I can, although there are times when I'm holed up with a deadline of some sort for weeks and just can't respond. Either that or I'm perpetually napping. . . .

Help Make Illustrator Better

Okay, you know by now that I just love Illustrator. But there are always things that can be done to make the program more user-friendly, more functional, and just plain better.

If you have such an idea, please send an e-mail to:

suggestions@adobe.com

Send me a copy of your e-mail, too (IB8@bezier.com). I'd love to know what features you want to see in future versions, and if and when they're implemented.

Adobe does listen to its users, and the more readers that ask for a feature, the more likely that feature will get into a future version of Illustrator. The Illustrator product managers are eager for any and all suggestions.

Help Make VectorTools Better

You've also figured out that I really really like VectorTools (love is such a strong word). If you can think of a way to make an existing component better, or if you have a plug-in you'd like to see implemented, send an e-mail to:

suggestions@extensis.com

Copy me on it as well (IB8@bezier.com).

Acknowledgments

Whew. As I write these acknowledgments, I'm just about finished with the total revamping of this gigantic book. And while I'm just plain exhausted, I know I'd be much more tired if it were not for the help and support of several key people. This list is by no means exhaustive, but the individuals named here are the ones most responsible for getting this book out the door.

The most important person is the most important person. Jennifer Alspach took it upon herself to make sure this book was up to date and as accurate as possible.

Andy Cummings at IDG Books Worldwide, Inc., who withstood my whining about this and that, as well as considerable delays.

Dave Burkett and Michael Hopwood at Adobe, the folks who are most directly involved with the Illustrator 8 product as you know it.

Thanks to everyone at Extensis who was involved with creating VectorTools, the best plug-in set for Illustrator the world has ever seen.

Contents at a Glance

Contents

Part II: Putting Illustrator to Work   231

Chapter 7: Fine-Tuning Illustrator Artwork...233

Introducing Illustrator

The first time you run Adobe Illustrator, you may be overwhelmed by the number of tools and palettes that you have to choose from. And then there are those menus. Fifty tools, 13 palettes (more if you count all those swatch palettes), and 7 menus (containing more than 200 menu items). It's almost enough to drive you to pixels. And if that weren't bad enough, each Illustrator session starts with an artist's nightmare: a giant white virtual canvas staring him or her in the face.

Part I dispels the apprehension and fear of learning Illustrator. This part includes such basic concepts as drawing, painting, and how Illustrator works with files. I've included samples and interactive lessons throughout so that you can try out the concepts that are being introduced.

Illustrator Basics

Not too long ago, artists and illustrators worked by hand, not on computers. It may seem hard to believe, but artists spent hours and hours with T-squares, rulers, French curves, and type galleys from their local typesetters.

Now, of course, artists and artist wannabes spend hours and hours with their computer, a mouse, a monitor, and onscreen type that they set themselves. Some traditional artists are still out there . . . although they seem to be a dying breed. Eventually, most serious computer artists come face to face with Illustrator, the king of PostScript drawing programs. And they're frightened by what they see.

The Learning Curve

Quite a few years ago, I was setting type with PageMaker at the service bureau where I worked. I noticed that the specifications called for type to be set at a 15° angle. In those days, type at any angle on the computer was a big deal because none of the desktop publishing programs had that capability. PageMaker 3 had more options and menus than almost any other software on the market, and I spent considerable time searching for "rotate" or something similar. No such luck. I got so desperate that when I spied the manual out of the corner of my eye, I began to reach for it.

"What troubles you, young Skywalker?" asked my boss.

Out of instinct, I punched ⌘-S on my keyboard. (The boss, a former soldier, had this thing about saving often; his method of enforcement was a lightning-fast flick of my Mac's power switch.) "I can't find where you rotate type in PageMaker," I replied sheepishly.

He nodded. And then he spoke two simple, forceful words: "Adobe Illustrator."

Thus began my journey into the land of Illustrator, and my subsequent PageMaker productivity slide.

Figuring out how to rotate type wasn't too difficult, but then I started playing with some of the other tools and features of the software. Confusion ensued. Hours of staring at an Illustrator document and wondering "Why?" took up most of my time in those days. I didn't understand Fills and Strokes; I didn't understand how to make things certain colors; and I didn't understand why what I drew was so different from what I printed (see Figure 1-1).

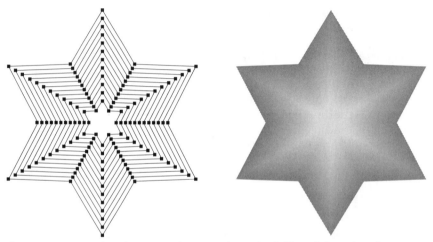

Figure 1-1: Artwork as it appears in Artwork mode (left) and the printed result (right)

Even my boss couldn't help me much with Illustrator; questions to him resulted in a knowing nod and the customary tilt and swivel of his head toward the Illustrator manual. I went through the tutorial three times, but when I tried to mask anything but those darn fish, it wouldn't work. I was convinced that the Pen tool was Satan's pitchfork in disguise. Patterns made about as much sense as differential equations (those I'll *never* understand, much to my math-teaching mother's chagrin). Then there were things like flatness (huh?), miter limits (yeah, right), and splitting paths (I wouldn't know a clue if I was sitting on one) — all subjects that may as well have been written in a third-century Chinese dialect.

I had never used or seen software as *different* as Illustrator.

That Was Then, This Is Not Then

The version of Illustrator that I was introduced to in 1988 was an incredible improvement over Illustrator 1.1, but still not a user-friendly piece of software. Version 3, introduced in 1990, was a little better, but most of its improvements were in functionality, not user interface. In the summer of 1993, Illustrator 5 was introduced, with a full load of new features and better ways for people to access those features. In 1997, Illustrator 7 arrived, which equalized the program's features for both Windows and Macintosh platforms. The upgrade for Windows users was quite a leap; for Macintosh users it was more of an enhancement, offering fluidity between Adobe's programs.

Finally, Illustrator 8 came to us in 1998. Adobe has made Illustrator much more compatible with its Adobe counterparts, Photoshop and PageMaker. It is as if Adobe realized how many users work between programs and has made working between all of their programs intuitive and a smooth transition. Illustrator 8 is chock full of new features as well as incredibly enhanced old features. Like Illustrator 7, it is easier for beginners to use, but with more features being added, the intermediate and advanced areas are still beyond the scope of the majority of users.

Techniques for Learning More

There are a number of ways you can get to know Illustrator faster than the average Joe D. Designer:

✦ **Playing, the right way:** I used to hate the term *playing,* which has been typically used to describe trying out new features and areas of the software you aren't familiar with. Normally, the word is said in a negative way, although if done correctly, it can be the most important and valuable time spent while learning software. When playing with Illustrator, follow these rules for the most effective playtime:

• Create something that you want to keep, like a business card, a new logo (especially if your company currently has a hokey one designed in the 1970s by the owner), a letterhead, or a graphic masterpiece.

• Even if you don't like what you're doing, *don't* delete it. It may look awful, but it could be a starting point for another illustration in the future. Save it.

• Print everything. After an hour of playing, you will (1) feel better about the time your coworkers and boss think you spent playing with new software and (2) have a file of stuff you did that you can review in the future. I love going back to artwork I did three months before and remembering a feature I used for that art that I've just plain forgotten about since then. (Imagine if you had years' worth of this stuff—you'd have a treasure chest full of Illustrator experiments at your fingertips that could save you lots of time and effort in the future.) Or, if you'd like to take the high-tech route, save the paper and add the Illustrator files to your favorite Portfolio catalog.

- Don't do real-life projects during playtime. Real-life projects are artwork you are doing for someone else, which has to be perfect, and artwork you are doing for yourself, which—surprise!—also has to be perfect. Either way, you will invariably delete quite often, and hardly ever print anything but the final product. Try to separate real life from playtime. (I'm currently just trying to distinguish what exactly *is* real life, so you're already a step ahead of me.)

- Don't do too much in one sitting. The more you do at one time, the more you'll forget. More than a couple hours of play at one time starts becoming detrimental.

✦ **Dissect existing illustrations:** "How'd they do that?" You can figure out all but the most complex artwork by opening it up in Illustrator and selecting different pieces. You can discover techniques that you probably would never have come across on your own.

Note

The *Illustrator 8 Bible* CD-ROM contains much of the artwork that you see here in the book. Just open up the folder called Artwork, and find the chapter and figure number you're looking at. You can see how the artwork that graces these pages was created by dissecting and examining it.

✦ **Talk to other Illustrator users:** By talking to other users, you can discover ways they approach similar illustrations or learn of their pitfalls before they become yours. One of the best places to do this is at the frequent Illustrator Conferences sponsored by Thunder Lizard Productions (1-800-221-3806), where hundreds of top-notch Illustrator users gather for several days of talks and seminars about every aspect of Illustrator. Another great place to "talk Illustrator" is to check out the Vector Special Interest Group on America Online. You'll find many questions answered in their message boards (keyword "Illustrator").

✦ **Attempt the impossible:** If you successfully use Illustrator to create a replica of the ceiling of the Sistine Chapel, including the proper shading and discoloration associated with aging, you will undoubtedly master the software in the process. Realistically, if you try something that you believe is beyond either your skills or the capabilities of the software, you may be surprised at what you know and what Illustrator can do with you in the driver's seat. And, in the process, you'll probably also come up with new techniques and procedures for creating similar, simpler artwork.

✦ **Read the entire *Illustrator 8 Bible:*** Just because you never understood masking before, and never thought you would need it in the future, doesn't mean that nothing else in the chapter on masking is of interest to you. Throughout this book, I try to show new and exciting ways of doing everything, from the basics of drawing a line and creating a simple closed shape to reversing gradients and accessing the Convert Direction Point tool while using a pressure-sensitive brush.

Note   The *Illustrator 8 Bible* CD-ROM tutorials are arranged in the same order as this book, with each section corresponding to a book chapter.

Mousing Around

Illustrator requires the use of a mouse for selecting items, pulling down menus, moving objects, and clicking buttons. Learning to use the mouse efficiently requires a great deal of patience, practice, and persistence (the three-*ps*). In most programs, you can master using the mouse quickly, but using the mouse with Illustrator's Pen tool takes those *p*'s to a new extreme. If you're unfamiliar with using a mouse, a fun way to get used to working with one is by playing a mouse-driven game, such as *Eric's Ultimate Solitaire* from Delta Tao. After several hours of play (providing you don't get fired by your employer or kicked out of the house by your irritated spouse), you'll become Master of Your Mousepad, King of Your Klicker, and so on.

The mouse is used to perform five basic functions in Illustrator:

✦ **Pointing,** which is moving the cursor around the screen by moving the mouse around your mousepad.

✦ **Clicking,** which is pressing and releasing the mouse button in one step. Clicking is used to select points, paths, and objects, and to make windows active. (Windows users: *Clicking* means left-button clicking.)

✦ **Dragging,** which is pressing the mouse button and keeping it pressed while you move the mouse. You drag the cursor to choose items from menus, select contiguous characters of text, move objects, and create marquees.

✦ **Double-clicking,** which is quickly pressing and releasing the mouse button twice in the same location. Double-clicking is used to select a word of text, select a text field with a value in it, access a dialog box for a tool, and run Illustrator (by double-clicking its icon in the Finder).

✦ **Control-clicking [right-clicking],** which displays a context-sensitive menu when you press Control and click. (Windows users: Simply press the right mouse button.)

Cursors

When I refer to a cursor, I don't mean someone whose favorite phrase is "@#&*%!!"—although this is a popular saying for people who are using Illustrator for the first time.

The cursor is the little icon (usually an arrow) that moves in the same direction as the mouse. (If the cursor seems to be moving in the opposite direction from the mouse, check that the mouse isn't upside down, or, heaven forbid, that you aren't upside down.)

In Illustrator, the cursor often takes the form of a tool that you are using. When the computer is busy—doing whatever it is a computer does when it is busy—an ugly little watch takes its place. Figure 1-2 shows many of the standard cursors that appear in Adobe Illustrator.

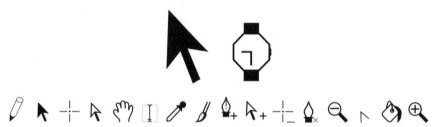

Figure 1-2: An assortment of Illustrator cursors

Keyboard Commands

Keyboard commands are shortcuts for common activities that you perform in Illustrator. Ninety percent of the shortcuts use the Command key (the one with the cloverleaf symbol ⌘ and the on a Macintosh; the Ctrl key in Windows) in combination with other keys.

Many of the Illustrator menu items have keyboard shortcuts listed next to their names. Pressing the key combination does the same thing as choosing that menu item from the menu. Some menu items do not have keyboard commands; usually, you have to choose those items from the menu.

On a Macintosh, common keys that are used with the Command key are the Option key (located handily next to the Command key) and the Shift key. The Control key had been used in Versions 5, 5.5, and 6, but since Illustrator 7, the Control key is used only to simulate the right mouse button that Windows users have. You hold down these keys while you press another key or click the mouse. Figure 1-3 shows these four modifier keys.

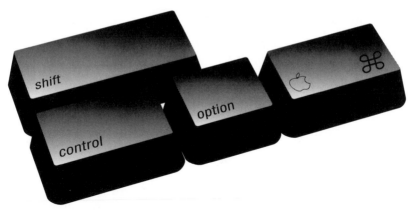

Figure 1-3: The four keyboard-modifier keys for Macintosh

On a Windows system, the Ctrl key is used along with the Alt and Shift keys. If you press certain combinations of these keys while pressing another key or clicking the mouse, special things happen.

A complete listing of key commands for Macintosh and Windows systems can be found in Appendix D.

Keyboard commands are as important to an Illustrator artist as the mouse is; with a little practice, you can learn them quickly. Besides, many keyboard commands are the same from program to program, which will make you an instant expert in software that you haven't used yet!

Illustrator Terminology

The language of Illustrator users sounds kind of funny to normal people and FreeHand users.

Sometimes Illustrator users, in their enthusiasm, start spouting off all manner of ungodly terms, such as *RAM, Pantone colors, megabytes, PostScript Level 3, dpi,* and *Option[Alt+7]-clicking.* Then there are the power users, who are into *megahertz, gigabytes, Bézier curves, line screens,* and ⌘*-Option-Shift-clicking* [Ctrl+Alt+Shift+clicking]. In this book, such terms are discussed as they come up.

A word of advice: Don't use Illustrator language in front of people who have never used (or never plan to use) Illustrator. You might get put away in one of those places where the walls are soft and so is the food, as should anyone who spouts off, "Thank God for RGB support!" at the drop of a bitmapped hat.

ASK TOULOUSE: Commanding Attention

Mrs. C: Do you know the "Illustrator Alphabet" commands?

Toulouse: Sure. A is for Select All, B is for Paste Behind, C is for Copy, D is for Transform Again.

Mrs. C: Wait, D is for Transform Again? What happened to T?

Toulouse: T is for the Character palette.

Mrs. C: Oh.

Toulouse: O is for Open.

Mrs. C: I see.

Toulouse: I shows and hides the color palette; C, as I said before, is for Copy.

Mrs. C: You and . . .

Toulouse: Hide. New Document.

Mrs. C: Why . . .

Toulouse: Preview and Artwork toggle.

Mrs. C: Heyyyyyyy!

Toulouse: What, are you Fonzie? You know, I know the Command-Shift alphabet as well.

Mrs. C: Sometimes I really wish Brooklyn Bridge had stayed on the air.

Fonts

Fonts are a big deal to Illustrator users.

For the seasoned graphic artist, the thousands of typefaces that are available for the Mac provide a typesetting heaven on earth. For a newcomer to Illustrator and typesetting, fonts can be overwhelming. Illustrator ships with about 300 Adobe PostScript Type 1 fonts; others are available for purchase at costs that range from about $2 per face to hundreds of dollars for a family.

Fonts for the Macintosh come in various formats, each format having advantages and disadvantages over other formats. Fonts fall into the following categories:

   ✦ Bitmap fonts, also known as screen fonts

   ✦ PostScript fonts, also called Type 1 or Type 3

   ✦ TrueType fonts

Bitmap Fonts

A bitmap font is a font that is made up of a series of dots inside a grid pattern. Bitmap fonts were the original computer fonts. They worked well both onscreen and on the dot-matrix printers that were prevalent at the time that they were introduced.

Each character in a bitmap font has a certain number of square black dots that define its shape. Some bitmap fonts include different point sizes, with the smaller point sizes having fewer dots than the larger point sizes. The larger the point size of the bitmap fonts, the more detail is available, and the better the letter looks.

A problem arises when a point size is specified for which no corresponding bitmap font is available. Then dots from the point size that is closest to the specified size are scaled to the new size. The result is usually large, blocky-looking letters. The larger the size specified, the larger the "blocks," as shown in Figure 1-4.

Geneva   Geneva   Geneva

12 pt.   24 pt.   48 pt.

Figure 1-4: Different point sizes of bitmapped type

Because bitmap fonts were originally designed for a computer screen, the dots in a bitmap font are set at 72 *dpi* (dots-per-inch). When you print a bitmap font on a laser printer, which has a resolution of at least 300 dpi, the letters look blocky, even when their sizes are supported by the typeface. A typical viewer of such a font might be heard to say, "bitmapped . . . too jaggy . . . must find outline font."

PostScript Fonts

PostScript fonts are the most popular font format (see Figure 1-5), but they also are the most confusing and frustrating fonts to use because they have two parts: the screen fonts (which are really bitmap fonts) and the printer fonts.

Garamond   Eras   **Poplar**

Figure 1-5: Three PostScript typefaces

For the computer to recognize a PostScript font in the different programs you use, its corresponding screen font must be installed. If the printer font is installed but the screen font is not installed, you can't use the font at all. Screen fonts for PostScript fonts are usually in little suitcases. Double-clicking the suitcases reveals the bitmap fonts inside the suitcase, and each point size has its own file. Double-clicking a bitmap font displays a screen with that font in that point size and a sentence that contains all the letters in the alphabet. This makes for sentences that are pretty bizarre. Nothing like reading "How razorback-jumping frogs can level six piqued gymnasts!"

Printer fonts are needed, as their name implies, for printing. Printer fonts consist of outlined shapes that get filled with as many dots as the printer can stuff into that particular shape. Because these printer fonts are mathematical outlines, and not a certain number of dots, they make characters look good at any point size. In fact, PostScript printer fonts are *device independent,* meaning that the quality of the type depends on the dpi of the printer (which is device dependent). The higher the dpi, the smoother the curves and diagonal lines look. If printer fonts are missing, the printer either uses the corresponding bitmap font or substitutes another font whose printer font is available (usually Courier . . . yuck!).

PostScript fonts were developed by Adobe, which, just by coincidence, created the PostScript page description language, which is also, just by coincidence, based on outlines instead of dots. Adobe also created typefaces in PostScript format, called Type 1 format. They released a set of specifications for third-party manufacturers to use in creating other fonts, called Type 3 fonts. The advantages of Type 3 fonts over Type 1 fonts are that the outlines of these fonts can be Stroked, not just Filled, and that they can be filled with various shades of gray instead of just black. However, Type 1 fonts are easier to program and to test, and they also have *hinting* (a method for adjusting type for better viewability at small point sizes at low resolutions). Then Adobe released the specifications for Type 1 fonts, and third-party manufacturers have been creating fonts in the Type 1 format ever since.

Things wouldn't be so bad if printer fonts were needed only for printing, but they are also needed for drawing good fonts on the screen at any point size. If the Adobe Type Manager (ATM) control panel is installed, the screen font information is supplemented by the printer font outline. (Illustrator's built-in font engine replaces the need for ATM — that's what CoolType lib is.)

Since the rise of desktop publishing, the font standard has been PostScript. In 1990, Apple developed a new font format called TrueType, and licensed it to Microsoft.

TrueType Fonts

The greatest advantage of TrueType fonts is that they have only one component. Screen and printer fonts are not separate — there is just the TrueType font. Actually, many TrueType fonts do include screen fonts because hand-tuned screen fonts at small sizes tend to look better than Filled outlines at screen resolution.

The difference is that both the TrueType font and the bitmap are contained in the same suitcase. Believe me, when you are used to finding two of everything, this idea of one font, one file, and so on, is a godsend. The quality of TrueType fonts is comparable to, if not better than, that of PostScript typefaces. Apple includes TrueType fonts with every new computer it sells. There are some potential quality advantages to TrueType fonts, such as the Quadratic curves used to draw TrueType outlines and the supposedly superior hint capability.

Why, you ask, haven't the high-quality type vendors (like Lino, ITC, and so forth) jumped on the TrueType bandwagon? My sources tell me that TrueType fonts are harder to engineer and draw. The comparison is this: TrueType font-creation environment feels more like an engineering environment, and the Type 1 environment feels more like a design environment. Obviously, we are talking about the high end here. A program such as Fontographer uses the same interface to create both TrueType and Type 1 fonts. But the high-end folks go in and hand-tune everything to the *n*th degree, and the difference shows.

Battles between the two formats are still raging, but PostScript appears to be winning the war. In this case, competition isn't really better for the consumer, just confusing.

Fonts and Adobe Illustrator

Adobe makes PostScript. Adobe makes Illustrator. What type of fonts should you use when using Illustrator? Although PostScript is the obvious answer, Illustrator also supports the use of TrueType fonts. One thing that Illustrator does *not* support, however, is having two fonts with the same name, one in PostScript and one in TrueType. If this event should occur, you may end up with some strange results, such as invisible type.

Make sure that you have only one type of font format per typeface.

Adobe Type Manager

Adobe Type Manager (ATM) is to computer screens what PostScript is to printers. ATM is a sort of link between the screen fonts and the printer fonts. If the point size that you choose is unavailable for a certain typeface, the screen font references the printer font for its outline and fills the outline with dots. The result is a smooth character, whatever the point size onscreen.

Because of screen-resolution limitations (72 dpi), type smaller than 8 points can be hard to read, even with ATM. When type gets below this size, many software applications use *greeking,* which changes small type into gray bars, saving the application a great deal of processing time. (They figure that if you can't read it anyway, no reason exists to put all those dots in the right places.) And remember that in the smaller point sizes, it is better to have the hand-tuned bitmap font installed.

If you start a Macintosh with extensions off (by pressing Shift until the "Welcome to Macintosh" screen appears), ATM will be disabled, and you can see bitmap fonts in all their glory (this isn't recommended for those with weak stomachs). Oddly enough, the fonts will still print correctly to a PostScript printer, which doesn't use ATM to generate font outlines.

Note   TrueType automatically renders type at various point sizes without the use of ATM.

ATM 4.0 is automatically installed with Adobe Illustrator. The most important feature in 4.0 is that type can be set to appear anti-aliased (smooth-edged). You can turn on and off the Smooth Type option in the ATM 4.0 control panel (located in your Control Panel folder).

Multiple Master Fonts

Multiple Master fonts, again from Adobe, provide an impressive, if not somewhat complex, way to vary typestyles. Normally, a typeface may come in several weights, such as bold, regular, light, and black. But what if you want a weight that is between bold and black? Usually, you're out of luck.

The theory behind Multiple Master fonts is that a font has two extremes — black and light, for example. Multiple Master technology creates any number of in-betweens that range from one extreme to the other. Multiple Masters don't stop with weights, though. They also work to step between regular and oblique, wide and condensed, and serif or sans serif.

Multiple Master font capabilities are built into many high-end graphics applications, such as Illustrator, Adobe PageMaker, and QuarkXPress. Since Illustrator 7, a special Palette was added for adjusting multiple master fonts.

PostScript and Printing

Up until the mid-1980s, computer graphics were, well, crusty. Blocky. Jagged. Rough. If we saw graphics that were done on computers in 1981 and printed to a black-and-white printer, we'd laugh so hard we couldn't breathe, stopping the laughter only when we realized that we couldn't breathe. Of course, in 1981, the world was gaga over the capabilities of computers and computer graphics. Those same pictures were admired, and the average person was generally amazed (the average designer, on the other hand, shuddered and prayed that this whole computer thing wouldn't catch on).

Desktop publishing was pushed to a level of professionalism in 1985 by a cute little software package called PageMaker. With PageMaker, you could do typesetting *and* layout on the computer screen, seeing everything on the screen just as it would eventually be printed. Well, almost. Aldus was the company that created PageMaker. In 1994, Adobe swallowed Aldus, and now PageMaker is "made" by Adobe as well.

The worst acronym this planet has ever seen was coined at this time: *WYSIWYG*, pronounced the way it reads (wizzy-wig), and standing for "what you see is what you get." Oddly, a more accurate term would have been *WYSISSTWYGIYGIAL*, (pronounced wizzys-twiggy-guyal), meaning "what you see is somewhat similar to what you get if you get it at all." The screen representation was poor, and the likelihood that anything remotely complex would actually print was even poorer. Figure 1-6 shows a common response to these silly acronyms.

Figure 1-6: What you see here is just another unnecessary acronym

Problems aside, PageMaker would not have been a success if the laser printer hadn't handily arrived on the scene. Even so, there were problems inherent with laser printers, too: at 300 dpi, there were 90,000 dots in every square inch. A typical 8½ x 11-inch page of type had 8.5 *million* dots to put down. Computers were finally powerful enough to handle this huge amount of dots, but the time it took to print made computers pretty much useless for any real work.

Several systems were developed to improve the printing process, and the one standout was PostScript from Adobe Systems. Apple licensed PostScript from Adobe for use on its first LaserWriter, and a star was born. Installed on every laser printer were two things from Adobe: the PostScript page description language, and the Adobe base fonts, which included Times, Helvetica, Courier, and Symbol.

PostScript became fundamental to Apple Macintosh computers and laser printers and became the standard. To use PostScript, Apple had to pay licensing fees to Adobe for every laser printer it sold. Fonts were PostScript, and if there ever was a standard in graphics, the closest thing to it was PostScript (commonly called *EPS,* for Encapsulated PostScript).

Today, the majority of fonts for both Macintosh and Windows systems are PostScript, and almost all graphics and desktop-publishing software can read PostScript in some form. However, technically speaking (I'm supposed to speak technically, aren't I?), there are actually a greater number of TrueType fonts available.

What PostScript Does

A typical graphic object in painting software is based on a certain number of pixels that are a certain color. If you make that graphic larger, the pixels get larger, giving a rough, jagged effect to the art (see Figure 1-7). To prevent these *jaggies,* two things can be done: Make sure that there are enough dots-per-inch in the image so that when the image is enlarged, the dots are too small to appear jagged; or define graphics by mathematical equations instead of by dots.

Figure 1-7: A bitmap image at normal size (left) and enlarged by 300% (right)

PostScript is a mathematical solution to high-resolution imaging. Areas, or *shapes,* are defined, and then these shapes are either *Filled* or *Stroked* with a percentage of color. The shapes are made up of paths, and the paths are defined by a number of points along the path *(Anchor Points)* and controls off those points *(Control Handles,* sometimes called *curve handles* or *direction points)* that control the shape of the curve. Figure 1-8 shows a PostScript outline around a bitmapped image and the enlarged outline Filled with black.

Figure 1-8: A PostScript outline surrounds the original bitmapped image

Because the Anchor Points and Control Handles have real locations on a page, mathematical processes can be used to create the shapes based on these points. The mathematical equation for Bézier curves is quite detailed (at least for someone who, like me, fears math).

PostScript is not just math, though. It is actually a programming language and, more specifically, a *page description language*. Like BASIC, Pascal, and C, PostScript is made of lines of code that are used to describe artwork.

Fortunately, the average user never has to use PostScript code; instead, the average user uses a simplified interface, such as Illustrator. Software that has the capability to save files in PostScript or to print to a PostScript printer writes this PostScript code for you. Printers that are equipped with PostScript then take that PostScript code and convert it to dots on a printed page.

Why PostScript Is So Cool

That most applications can handle EPS files and that most printers can print PostScript are of great benefit to users, but the strength of PostScript is not really in its widespread use.

If you create a 1-inch circle in Photoshop or any other pixel-based drawing software and then enlarge that same circle in any application, the circle begins to lose detail.

A 300-dpi circle at twice its original size becomes 150 dpi. This makes those jagged edges more apparent than ever.

If you create a 1-inch circle in Illustrator, you can enlarge it to *any size possible* without losing one iota of resolution. The Illustrator circle stays perfectly smooth, even enlarged to 200% because the circle's resolution depends on the laser printer or imagesetter that prints it. That means that a perfect 1-inch circle has the potential to be a perfect 2-foot circle (providing you can find a printer or imagesetter that can print a 2-foot x 2-foot diameter circle).

But scaling objects is only the beginning. You can distort, stretch, rotate, skew, and flip objects created in Illustrator to your heart's content, and still the object will print to the resolution of the output device (see Figure 1-9).

Figure 1-9: The original PostScript mouse (we'll call him Theme) is in the upper-left corner. The other mice are, appropriately, variations on a Theme.

ASK TOULOUSE: Capital *S*?

Al's Diner: So, what's up with the capital *S* in the middle of PostScript?

Toulouse: I believe it was a creative way to establish a trademark, considering the word "postscript" is quite common. Adobe's normally pretty conservative about that sort of thing. They didn't do "IllusTrator" or "PhotoShop" or "StreamLine" or "DimeNsions" or "PreMiere."

Al's Diner: That's the best you could come up with?

Toulouse: Oh, and the name of your restaurant was thought up by a team of marketing whizzes?

Al's Diner: What about PageMaker?

Toulouse: Aldus did that. It's too late to change it, really.

Here's an example: A company wants its tiny logo on a 3-foot wide poster. If you use conventional methods, the edges will become fuzzy and gross looking, pretty much unacceptable to your client. Your other conventional option is to redraw the logo at a larger size or to trace the blown-up version — a time-consuming proposition either way.

Illustrator's solution is to scan the logo, trace it either in Adobe Streamline or with the Auto Trace tool, touch it up, and build your design around it. Afterward, output the illustration on a printer that can handle that size poster. There is no loss of quality; instead, the enlarged version from Illustrator will often look better than the scanned original.

Paths

The most basic element in Illustrator is a *path*. A path in Illustrator must have at least two Anchor Points, and there will be a line segment between those two Anchor Points (see Figure 1-10). Conceptually, there is no limit to the number of Anchor Points or segments that can be in any one path. Depending on the type of Anchor Points that are on either end of a line segment, the segment may be straight or curved. A path really must have two Anchor Points because without two Anchor Points, there is no place to draw a path segment (the line between the points). A single Anchor Point will never print anything.

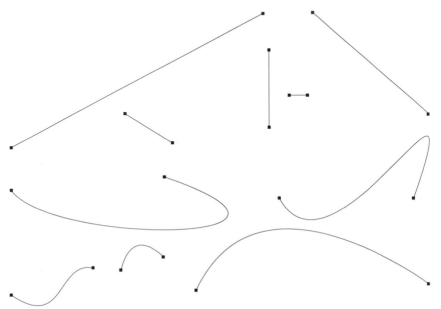

Figure 1-10: Paths consisting of two Anchor Points with a line segment between them

There are three major types of paths:

✦ **Open paths** are paths that have two distinct End Points, with any number of Anchor Points in between.

✦ **Closed paths** are paths that are continuous. There are no End Points and no start or end to a closed path — it just continues around and around.

✦ **Compound paths** are paths that are made up of two or more open or closed paths. (For a detailed look at compound paths, see Chapter 9.)

When you work in Illustrator in Artwork mode (View ➪ Artwork), only paths are visible. In Preview mode (View ➪ Preview), Fills and Strokes applied to paths are visible. Unless a path is selected in Preview mode, that path (Anchor Points and line segments) isn't visible.

Paths in Illustrator can be Filled with color, a pattern, or a gradient. Closed paths always use the color to Fill the *inside* of the shape they form (see Figure 1-11).

Artwork
Preview
↓
Close path
always use
Color

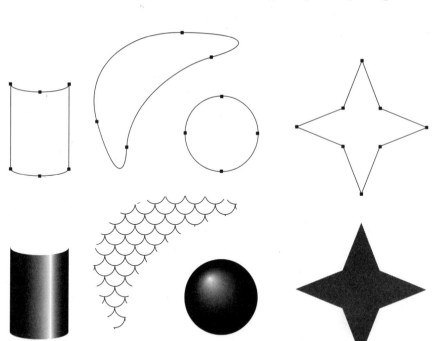

Figure 1-11: Closed paths with different Fills: The top row is how they appear in Artwork mode (⌘-Y) [Ctrl+Y], while the bottom row shows what they look like in Preview mode (⌘-Y) [Ctrl+Y] (Artwork and Preview are the two different viewing modes that can be toggled between using the same keyboard shortcut.)

Open paths also can be Filled; the Fill goes straight across the two End Points of the path to enclose the object. Figure 1-12 displays different types of Filled open paths. Filling an open path is usually not desirable, although in some circumstances it may be necessary.

Figure 1-12: Open paths with different Fills: The top row is how they appear in Artwork mode, while the bottom row shows how they appear in Preview mode

Caution Filled two-dimensional line mistake: In PostScript, when a Fill is specified but there are only two dimensions to an object (a straight line), it prints (rasterizes) at one "device pixel." At 100% onscreen, the Filled line looks exactly like a 1-point Stroked line (72 dpi = 1 device pixel = $\frac{1}{72}$ inch and 1 point = $\frac{1}{72}$ inch). When you zoom in to 200%, the Stroked line scales by 200% but the Filled line stays the same (1 device pixel or $\frac{1}{72}$ inch). When you print this line to a laser printer, one device pixel is as tiny as $\frac{1}{300}$ or $\frac{1}{600}$ inch. By the time you print to a typical Imagesetter, one device pixel will be $\frac{1}{2570}$ inch, making it too small to be visible in most situations.

Besides Filling paths, you can also Stroke paths with any tint of any color or a pattern. These Strokes can be any weight (thickness), and the width of the Stroke is equally distributed over each side of the path. Open paths have ends on the Strokes; these ends can be cropped, rounded, or extended past the end of the Stroke by half the width of the Stroke. Several different paths with Strokes are shown in Figure 1-13.

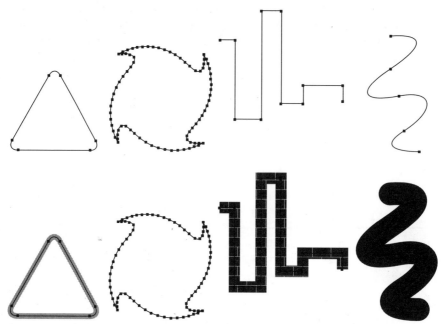

Figure 1-13: Various paths with different Strokes applied to them

Caution
A single point is also considered a path, but single points in Illustrator can have no printable qualities. This isn't readily noticeable because you can assign a Fill or Stroke color to a single point, although it can't be seen in Preview mode or when printed. When the document is color separated, it will cause a separation of the color to print even if nothing else on that page is using that same color, and the separation will be blank. If you think you may have individual Anchor Points floating around your illustration, you can select all of them at once by choosing Filter ➪ Select ➪ Select Stray Points and then delete them.

Fills and Strokes in Illustrator can be colors or an opaque white, which knocks out any color underneath. Fills and Strokes may also be *transparent*, in which case the Stroke or Fill will not be opaque. Transparency in Illustrator is commonly referred to as a Fill or Stroke of None.

Anchor Points

Paths are made up of a series of points and the line segments between these points. These points are commonly called *Anchor Points* because they anchor the path; paths *always* pass through or end at Anchor Points. There are two classes of Anchor Points:

✦ **Smooth Points** are Anchor Points that have a curved path flowing smoothly through them; most of the time you don't know where a Smooth Point is unless the path is selected. Smooth Points keep the path from changing direction abruptly. There are two linked *Control Handles* on every smooth point.

✦ **Corner Points** are a class of Anchor Points in which the path changes direction noticeably at those specific points. There are three different corner points:

  • *Straight Corner Points* are Anchor Points where two straight line segments meet at a distinct angle. There are no Control Handles on this type of Anchor Point.

  • *Curved Corner Points* are points where two curved line segments meet and abruptly change direction. There are two *independent* Control Handles on each Curved Corner Point.

  • *Combination Corner Points* are the meeting places for straight and curved line segments. There is one independent Control Handle on a Combination Corner Point.

Figure 1-14 shows the different types of Anchor Points in Illustrator.

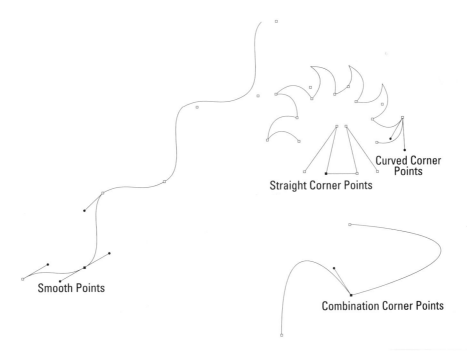

Figure 1-14: The different types of Anchor Points in Illustrator

Anchor Points, Control Handles, and Control Handle Lines do not appear on the printed output of your artwork. In fact, they only appear in Illustrator and Photoshop, never on artwork imported into other applications.

Bézier Curves

Not knowing all that much about geometry (or maybe not remembering that much . . . it was eighth grade, after all), I find the very concept of creating curves by using math frightening. But most of the curve creation in Illustrator takes place behind the scenes in the PostScript language code we almost never see.

PostScript curves are based on *Bézier* curves (pronounced *bez-ee-ay*), which were created by Pierre Bézier (see Figure 1-15) in the early 1970s as a way of controlling mechanical cutting devices, commonly known as Numerical Control. Bézier (see the Foreword) worked for Renault (the car manufacturer) in France, and his mission was to streamline the process by which machines were controlled.

A mathematician and engineer, Bézier developed a method for creating curves using four points for every curved segment. Two of these points lay at either end of the segment (we call them Anchor Points in Illustrator), and two points just floated around the curve segment, controlling the shape of the curve (Control Handles). Using these four points, a person could conceivably create any curve; using multiple sets of these curves, one could create any possible shape. The two PostScripteers, John Warnock and Chuck Geschke of Adobe, decided that Bézier curves were the best method for creating curves in a page description language, and suddenly those curves became a fundamental part of high-end graphic design.

Bézier curves are anything but intuitive. I believe that Bézier curves represent the most significant stumbling block to learning to use Illustrator well. After you've mastered the concept and use of these curves, everything about Illustrator suddenly becomes easier and friendlier. Don't try to ignore them, because they won't go away. You'll find it easier in the long run to try to understand how they work.

You already know half of what a Bézier curve is: two Anchor Points. Here comes the hard part (brace yourself).

Figure 1-15: Pierre Bézier, who laid the groundwork for PostScript and, thus, Illustrator

Control Handles and Control Handle Lines

If an Anchor Point has a Control Handle coming out of it, the next segment will be curved. No Control Handle, no curve. Couldn't be simpler.

Control Handles are connected to Anchor Points with *Control Handle Lines*. Figure 1-16 shows what happens when an Anchor Point with no Control Handle and an Anchor Point with a Control Handle are connected to another Anchor Point.

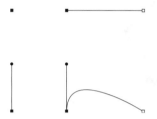

Figure 1-16: An Anchor Point without a Control Handle (top left) and an Anchor Point with a Control Handle (bottom left) are connected to new Anchor Points, resulting in a straight line segment (top right) and a curved line segment (bottom right)

The Control Handle Lines themselves really have no function other than to show you which Anchor points the Control Handles are attached to. You cannot select a Control Handle Line. The only way to move a Control Handle Line or change the length of a Control Handle Line is by moving its corresponding Control Handle. Figure 1-17 displays how Control Handles and Lines work with curves and Anchor Points.

Adjust control Handle to change line.

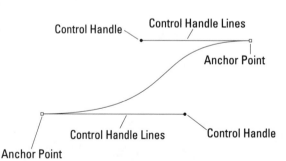

Control Handle — Control Handle Lines

Anchor Point

Control Handle Lines — Control Handle

Anchor Point

Figure 1-17: Anchor Points, Control Handles, and Control Handle Lines along a path

The basic concept concerning Control Handles is that Control Handles act as magnets, pulling the curve toward them (see Figure 1-18). This presents an interesting problem because there are usually two Control Handles per curved line segment. Just as you might suspect, the Control Handle exerts the greatest amount of force on the half of the curved segment nearest to it. If there is only one Control Handle, then the segment is curved more on the side of the segment with the Control Handle than the side with no Control Handle.

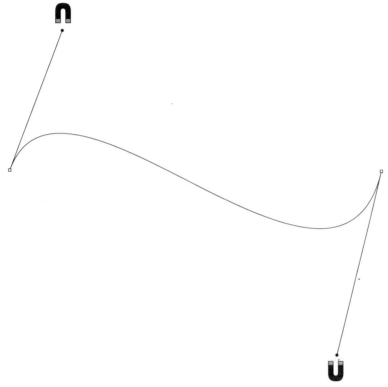

Figure 1-18: Control Handles act as magnets, pulling the curve toward them

The greater the distance between a Control Handle and its corresponding Anchor Point, the farther the curve (on that end of the curve segment) pulls away from an imaginary straight segment between the two points (see Figure 1-19). If the Control Handles on either end of the segment are on different sides of the curved segment, the curved segment will be somewhat S-shaped, as the bottom path in Figure 1-19 shows. If the Control Handles on the ends of the curved segment are on the same side, the curve will be somewhat U-shaped, as shown in the top path of Figure 1-19.

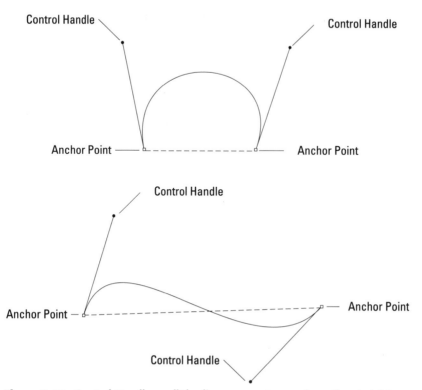

Figure 1-19: Control Handles pull the line segment away from the straight line that would normally exist between them. The bottom path is an *S* Shape because the Control Handles are being pulled in opposite directions.

Control Handle Lines coming out of an Anchor Point are always *tangent* to the curved segment where it touches the Anchor Point, regardless of whether the Anchor Point is a Smooth Point, a Curved Corner Point, or a Combination Corner Point. Tangent refers to the angle of both the Control Handle Line and the angle of the curved segment as it crosses the Anchor Point (see Figure 1-20).

Chapter 3 teaches you how to use the Pen tool for drawing with Anchor Points, Control Handles, and Control Handle Lines. Rules are also given to help you determine the placement, length, and angle of the various points and Control Handle Lines that are encountered using this tool.

Figure 1-20: Control Handle Lines run tangent to the path where the path meets the Anchor Point

ASK TOULOUSE: Curves Are Tough

Potsie: I'm having trouble with curves.

Toulouse: What kind of trouble?

Potsie: Moving the Control Handles around is really difficult.

Toulouse: You know, there's an easier way . . . but it's not quite as accurate.

Potsie: Tell me! At this rate, I'll never finish my drawing of Jennie Piccolo.

Toulouse: Wow. Lots of curves there. Looks like you might need to add a few extra Anchor Points. . . .

Potsie: (blush)

Toulouse: To adjust the curves without moving the Control Handles, just click the curve and drag it.

Potsie: Wow!

Toulouse: Keep in mind that you're changing both Control Handles at once with that, and it's very imprecise. Sort of like your occasional musical outbursts.

Potsie: Was I really that bad?

Toulouse: Ever notice the lack of work after the series ended?

Clear, Cut, Copy, and Paste

In most software, including Illustrator, many of the most basic functions of the Edit menu work the same way. If you have used the Edit menu in QuarkXPress or Microsoft Word, for example, you should have no trouble using the same functions in Illustrator because the menu options are located in the same place in each program.

Clear

The most simplistic of these commands is Clear, which in Illustrator works almost exactly like the Delete key on the keyboard. When something is selected, choosing Clear will delete, or get rid of, what is selected.

You're probably asking yourself, "If the Delete key does the same thing, why do we need Clear?" or "Why didn't they just call the Clear command *Delete?*" Ah, the makers of Illustrator are a step ahead of you in this respect. Note that I said "almost" the same way; there actually is a subtle yet important difference in what the Clear command does and what the Delete key does, due to Illustrator's abundant use of palettes since Version 7.0.

If you are working on a palette and (1) have just typed a value in an editable text field, (2) tabbed down or up to an editable text field, highlighting text, or (3) dragged across text in an editable text field, highlighting text, then the Delete key (1) deletes the last character typed, or (2) and (3) deletes the highlighted characters. In all these situations, the Clear command deletes anything that is selected in the document.

Cut, Copy, and Paste

The Cut, Copy, and Paste commands in Illustrator are very handy. Copying and cutting selected objects places them on the Clipboard, which is a temporary holding place for objects that have been cut or copied. After an object is on the Clipboard, it may be pasted into (1) the center of the same document, (2) the same location as the cut or copied object, or (3) another document in Illustrator, Photoshop, Dimensions, or Streamline.

Choosing Cut (⌘-X) [Ctrl+X] from the Edit menu deletes the selected objects and copies them to the Clipboard, where they are stored until another object is cut or copied or the computer is shut down or restarted. Quitting Illustrator *does not* remove objects from the Clipboard. Cut is not available when no object is selected.

Choosing Copy (⌘-C) [Ctrl+C] from the Edit menu works like Cut, but it doesn't delete the selected objects. Instead, it just copies them to the Clipboard, at which time you can choose Paste and slap another copy onto your document.

Choosing Paste (⌘-V) [Ctrl+V] from the Edit menu places any objects on the Clipboard into the center of the document window. If type is selected with the Type tool or copied from another application to the Pasteboard, either a Rectangle type, Area type, Path type, or Point type area must be selected with the Type tool. Paste is not available if nothing is in the Clipboard or if the contents of the Clipboard were copied there from another application.

Now, the really cool part: Just because you've pasted the object somewhere doesn't mean it isn't in the Clipboard anymore; it is! You can paste again and again, and keep on pasting until you just get plain bored, or until your page is an indecipherable mess, whichever comes first. The most important rule to remember about Cut, Copy, and Paste is that whatever is currently in the Clipboard will be replaced by anything that subsequently gets cut or copied to the Clipboard.

Cut, Copy, and Paste also work with text that you type in a document. Using the Type tools, you can select type, cut or copy it, and then paste it. When you're pasting type, it will go wherever your blinking text cursor is located. If you have type selected (highlighted) and you choose Paste, the type that was selected is replaced by whatever you had on the Clipboard.

You can cut or copy as much or as little of an illustration as you choose; you are only limited by your hard disk space. A good rule of thumb is that if you ever get a message saying you can't cut or copy because you are out of hard disk space, it is time to start throwing out stuff on your hard drive that you don't need or simply get a bigger hard drive.

Note

Thanks to the Adobe PostScript capability on the Clipboard, Illustrator can copy paths to other Adobe software, including Dimensions, Streamline, and Photoshop. Paths created in those packages can be pasted into Illustrator. With Photoshop, you have the option of pasting your Clipboard contents as rasterized pixels instead of as paths.

Tip

Since Illustrator 7 and Photoshop 3.0.4 and later, you have the ability to drag Illustrator artwork from an Illustrator document right into a Photoshop document. In addition, because Adobe goes both ways, you can drag a Photoshop selection from any Photoshop document right into an Illustrator document.

The Clipboard

You can view the contents of the Clipboard by going under the Edit menu to Show Clipboard. Unfortunately, the only thing you'll usually see in Illustrator is (1) the PostScript logo with the number of objects you have selected and the layers those objects are on or (2) copied text. To see text in the Clipboard, you must copy it using the Type tools. Type that is cut or copied using the selection tools does not appear as type, but instead as an *object*. When you view type, it usually does not look like the type you selected; the words are there, but the font and style information isn't. Instead, the type is displayed in Geneva, at either 9 or 12 points, depending on what you copied prior to copying your text.

Selecting Show Clipboard from the Edit menu opens a window that shows the current contents of the Clipboard. You can keep this window open and put it anywhere on the screen, but it will always be behind all palettes and the active document once you click within any of the palettes or the document. When a portion of the Clipboard is visible behind the palettes or document window, clicking the visible part of it brings it back to the front (of course, you can also just select Show Clipboard from the Edit menu again).

You can't do anything to the Clipboard by displaying the Clipboard window. You can only resize the window and move it around your screen for the sole purpose of displaying what you copied last. The Clipboard can be resized with the box in the lower-right corner, toggled between the current size and the full screen with the box in the upper-right corner, and closed with the box in the upper-right corner. The only way the contents of the Clipboard window can be altered is when something is cut or copied. Figure 1-21 shows two examples of how the Clipboard can look when different things are copied.

Figure 1-21: The Clipboard when several objects on different layers were copied or cut (left), and the Clipboard when text selected in a Type tool was copied or cut (right)

Selecting Hide Clipboard from the Edit menu hides the Clipboard. This option is available only if the Clipboard window is *active* — that is, in front of all open documents.

Undo and Redo

In most applications, you can undo the last thing done by choosing Undo from the Edit menu. That works in Illustrator, but Adobe has taken the undo concept just a little further: You can keep undoing in Illustrator up to 200 times, providing your system has enough memory and you have enough patience. After you have undone, you can redo by choosing Redo, which is found right below Undo in the Edit menu. And, guess what — you can redo up to 200 times as well.

Choosing Undo (⌘-Z) [Ctrl+Z] from the Edit menu undoes the last activity that was performed on the document. Successive undos undo more and more activities, until the document is at the point where it was opened or created or you have reached the undo limit, which was set in the Units and Undo Preferences dialog box (File ➪ Preferences ➪ Units and Undo).

The default minimum number of undos is 5. To change the minimum number of undos, go to the Units and Undo Preferences dialog box (File ➪ Preferences ➪ Units and Undo) and type in the minimum number of undos that you want. You *can* set the minimum undo levels to 0, but I wouldn't recommend it; this will disallow any undo or redo operations. If you *do* set the minimum number of undos too low and later realize you want to undo more actions, the cold, hard truth of the Undo levels box will raise its ugly head: You can't increase the number of undos after you have run out of them.

Caution Undos are the chief source of Illustrator's occasional memory woes. All those undos are being kept track of in the Illustrator RAM partition; when it fills up, you are presented with a dialog box to get rid of the oldest undos. Never do this. Instead, click the Cancel button and manually change the number of undos to a smaller amount and try again. This way you can control the number of undos Illustrator has available at all times.

Choosing Redo (⌘-Shift-Z) [Ctrl+Shift+Z] from the Edit menu redoes the last undo. You can continue to redo undos until you are back to the point where you started undoing or you perform another activity, at which time you can no longer redo any previous undos.

If you undo a couple of times and then *do* something, you won't be able to redo. You have to undo the last thing you did and then actually do everything again. In other words, all the steps that you undid are gone.

It is fine to use the Undo feature to go back and check out what you did, but after you have used multiple undos, don't do anything if you want to redo back to where you started undoing from. Got that?

ASK TOULOUSE: The Undoables

Not Opie: I think my Undo command is broken.

Toulouse: Uh-oh. Are you sure it's not set to 0 in your preferences?

Not Opie: Yeah, it's set to 10. Most of the time it undoes fine, but every once in a while . . .

Toulouse: What types of things can't you undo?

Not Opie: Well, my receding hairline, for one thing. Why do you think I'm *behind* the camera now? I can't undo my saves either.

Toulouse: Ah-ha! Saving has no impact on Undo or Redo. Saving is not considered to be an option that can be undone, or done again, so it's very existence is ignored by Undo and Redo. After you save, you'll undo the last thing you did before you saved.

Not Opie: Oh. Well, I can't undo my zooms or scrolls either.

Toulouse: Two more things that Illustrator ignores when it comes to undoing and redoing. Sorry.

Not Opie: Anything else I should look out for?

Toulouse: Undo and Redo only work on actions that actually change your document. Zooming and scrolling don't affect your document. Neither do changing tools or selecting or deselecting things.

Not Opie: I guess my hairline doesn't affect my documents either. . . . (sigh!)

Artwork and Preview Modes

Gone are the days of working blind, having to wait to see what you were illustrating until you chose Preview and then not being able to work again until you chose Artwork. I'm being sarcastic, of course. FreeHand has enabled artists to work in Preview for many years (since 1989, to be exact), and Adobe finally included this capability for Windows users in 1992, and for Macintosh owners in 1993.

Artwork Mode

Many artists who have used Illustrator in the older versions (1.1, 88, and 3.2) actually *like* working in Artwork mode because it's faster, you can see every path in the document (and select those same paths), and the Anchor Points and Control Handles stand out more. Artwork mode is much closer to what the printer sees: paths that define the edges of the objects you are working with.

Artwork mode seems to be a misnomer. *Wireframe* mode would be more descriptive—or maybe *Paths* mode. The only things visible in Artwork mode are the paths that make up the objects, and all paths are always visible.

Note Since Illustrator 5, Artwork mode has worked slower than in previous versions. The reason is that layers can be colored via the Layers Palette, and selected points and paths reflect those colors. To give that little extra boost of speed back to Artwork mode, install the Artwork View Speedup Plug-In from the Extra Plug-Ins folder in your Illustrator folder (by placing it in the Plug-Ins folder). When installed, all points and paths will be black, not their layer colors. This speed difference is determined by the difference in redraw times between 1-bit (black and white) and 8-bit (256 colors) color.

Preview Mode

In Preview mode, you see onscreen what your illustration really looks like when it prints (with the exception of displayed paths, which don't print). Figure 1-22 shows Illustrator art in both Artwork and Preview modes.

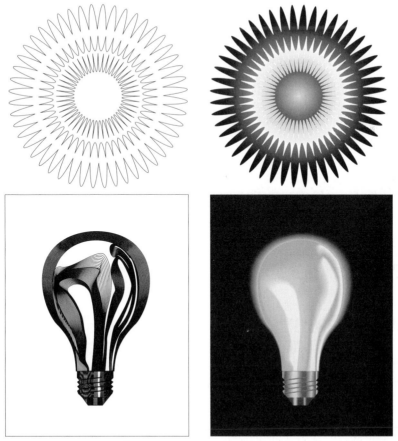

Figure 1-22: Art from Illustrator shown in Artwork mode (left) and Preview mode (right)

[handwritten margin note: All about selecting certain pts a path]

Caution Illustrator can't show overprinting when previewing. To see overprinting, open, paste, or drag the artwork to Photoshop.

Instead of selecting a path by clicking it, you can select entire paths by clicking the inside of those paths in a Filled area. It becomes a little more difficult to select certain points on paths because the Strokes on those paths are also visible. Sometimes there is so much stuff on your screen in Preview that you don't know what to click. The option that allows to select an entire path by clicking in a Filled area is called Area Select, which is activated by a check box (turned on by default) in the General Preferences dialog box (⌘-K) [Ctrl+K].

Note The inside of a compound path is considered a Fill for Area Select functionality. It may look transparent, but you can't directly select an object appearing behind the transparent portion of a compound path. When Area Select is on, clicking the transparent portion of a compound path results in the compound path being selected.

The major drawback to Preview mode is not the inability to select paths or parts of paths, but the amount of time it takes for certain types of Fills and blends to redraw accurately on your screen. The first time a slow redraw takes place in your document, you hardly notice it; you are too busy looking at how that object appears now that it has, say, a pattern Fill. After that, though, you may not be working with that object but others, and you still have to wait for that pattern-filled object to completely redraw every time you change views, move that object, or move something in front of that object.

Fortunately, Illustrator has a saving grace that makes this slowness almost acceptable. Whenever the screen is in this redraw mode, you can do other things. While your patterned, Filled object is redrawing, for example, Illustrator lets you go to the Type menu to change the typefaces you selected; when you are done selecting the type, the image finishes redrawing. This process is called *interruptable redraw,* and it is a godsend for Illustrator users.

Tip You can quickly toggle between Artwork and Preview modes by pressing ⌘-Y [Ctrl+Y].

Illustrator's Menus

Adobe's main products — Illustrator, Photoshop, PageMaker, Premiere, Dimensions, and Streamline — all have a fairly consistent interface, including menus, palettes, and dialog boxes. Adobe listened carefully to their end users and has made certain that Illustrator is not so *different* anymore in almost all respects.

Some general rules apply to Illustrator menus:

✦ To select a menu item, pull down to that item and release the mouse button (Macintosh) or click on that item (Windows). If the cursor is not on that item, but it is still highlighted, the command will not take effect.

✦ Whenever an *ellipsis* appears (three little dots that look like . . .), choosing that menu item brings up a dialog box where you must verify the current information by clicking an OK button, or enter more information and then click OK. If there is no ellipsis, the action you select takes place right away.

✦ Anytime there is a *key command* listed on the right side — usually the Command (⌘) symbol and a character for Macintosh or Ctrl plus a character for Windows, but sometimes the ⌘ symbol [Ctrl] or another modifier key plus a character — instead of using the mouse to pull down this menu, you can type this key command. Using key commands for menu items works just like clicking the menu bar and pulling down to that item.

✦ If you see a little *triangle* next to a menu item, it means there is a *pop-up menu* associated with it. Items in the pop-up menu can be chosen by pulling over to the menu and then pulling up or down to select the menu item needed. Pop-up menus usually appear on the right side of the menu, but due to space limitations on your monitor, they may appear on the left side for certain menus.

Using Menus Effectively

If you can never remember what is on which menu and you are constantly holding down the mouse button while slowly running along the menu bar, reading every menu item, and looking for a certain command, you have a disease. Every year millions of people become afflicted with Menu Bar Scanning Syndrome (MBSS): the need to continually search and hunt for special menu items that they just can't remember the locations of. MBSS is a disease that can be treated fairly easily, but it wastes valuable production time, costing companies billions of dollars a year. Don't be surprised if the next time you flip to *60 Minutes,* Steve Kroft is doing an inside investigation into the mysteries of MBSS.

MBSS is deadly not only because it wastes time, but because the user is forced to read every single menu and pop-up menu. Sure, in the File menu you *know* that Document Setup is where to go to change the size of the page, but as you work your way over, things begin to get a little fuzzy. By the time you get to the Filter menu, your mind is mush. You see the Distort category and figure that all the pop-up menu items in there are legal functions. If you can manage to get to the Windows menu, thewordswouldjustruntogether, making no sense whatsoever. If Figure 1-23 looks familiar, then you're probably one of the millions of afflicted computer users.

Figure 1-23: MBSS in the later stages

You can help prevent MBSS by doing three things:

✦ **Memorize what is in each menu.** This is the hardest thing to do, but a few hours spent memorizing each menu item and where it goes will eventually prevent countless MBSS-related searches. Make sentences out of the first letter of each menu item, if it helps. The File menu is either, "New, Open, Close, Save, Save As, Save a Copy, Revert, Place, Export, Document Info, Document Setup, Print, Preferences, Color Settings, Quit" or "Nine Old Cats See Some Silly Retired People Eating Damp Danish Pieces of Pruned Cauliflower Quiche." (I know, I know. You're not supposed to eat pruned cauliflower quiche when it's damp. That's why these retired people are *silly*.)

✦ **Use the menus as little as possible.** Instead, memorize key commands. Most of the menu items have them (if you don't include the Filter menu, more than half do), so now you only need to go up to the menu bar when a menu item doesn't have a key command.

✦ **Create buttons for menu commands with VectorTools' VectorBars.** VectorBars can be a serious timesaver if used properly. See Chapter 14, "VectorTools," for more information on using Extensis' VectorTools.

Palettes versus Windows

If there is a trend in graphics programs, it's the trend toward using palettes for everything possible. It started being noticeable with Fractal Design Painter, which has 12 palettes that can be on the screen at the same time. QuarkXPress soon followed with a half-dozen palettes, and Photoshop has scads of them. Illustrator 8 has even more palettes than Version 7, all of which can remain open while you work on your document (providing you can still see your document through all those palettes!).

Technically speaking, a palette is a window. Everything on the Mac and in Windows is a window except (I think) the desktop. Movable Modeless Windows (palettes) are a variation on windows.

In many respects, palettes are like windows. They have a title bar that can be clicked and dragged to move the palette. There is usually a close box in the upper-left corner of the palette, and in the upper-right corner there is often an autoresize box, which makes the palette smaller or larger than its original size. Occasionally, a manual resize box is located in the lower-right corner for dragging the palette to a new size. Options for hiding and showing palettes are even located under the Window menu. Figure 1-24 shows the Character palette with all its parts labeled.

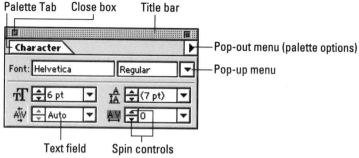

Figure 1-24: The Character palette

Palettes are unlike windows in several ways. Palettes seldom have scroll bars, although the Layers palette is an exception. When you hop from one program to another, palettes automatically hide, while windows remain visible.

Unlike windows, palettes are never really active. Instead, the one you are working in is in the front, and if it has editable text fields, one is highlighted, or a blinking text cursor appears. To bring a palette to the forefront — bring it into focus — simply click it anywhere.

Note

Beginning with Illustrator 7, palettes can be linked together in different ways called tabbing and docking. Each palette (except for the toolbox) has a tab on it. Clicking the tab of a palette brings it to the front. Dragging a tab from one palette to another moves that palette into another palette. Dragging a tab out of a palette makes the palette separate from the previous palette. Palettes can be docked together by dragging the tab of one palette to the bottom of another palette; when the bottom of the other palette darkens, releasing the mouse button will "dock" the moved palette to the bottom of the other palette. Now when the other palette is moved, the docked palette will move with it.

The Document Window

Prior to Illustrator 7, you had to resize your document window if you had a monitor that was a different resolution than 640 x 480. Now, the Illustrator window automatically resizes to match the resolution of your monitor.

The Pasteboard

Probably the worst thing that can possibly happen when you are using Illustrator is for you to lose everything you've worked on. "Where'd it all go?" you cry, along with the expected vulgarities. You can make this happen very easily in Illustrator by clicking a few times on the gray parts of the scroll bars at the bottom of the document window. When you click those gray parts, you are moving about half the width (or height) of your window with every click, and three clicks later, your page and everything on it is no longer in front of you. Instead, you see the Pasteboard, a vast expanse of white nothingness.

The Pasteboard measures 120 x 120 inches, which works out to 100 square feet of drawing space. At actual size, you only see a very small section of the Pasteboard. A little lettersize document looks extremely tiny on a Pasteboard that is this big. If you get lost on the Pasteboard, a quick way back is by choosing View ⇨ Actual Size. This puts your page in the center of the window at 100% view, at which time you should be able to see at least part of your drawing. To see the whole page quickly, choose View ⇨ Fit In Window, which resizes your page down to where you can see the entire page.

This assumes, of course, that you have actually drawn artwork on the defined page. I used to get frantic calls from people who had double-clicked the Zoom tool and all their artwork would disappear. It took me a while to figure out that they had drawn their artwork way off on the side of the Pasteboard.

Tip   VectorTools to the rescue again! VectorNavigator is a floating palette that shows you all of the artwork in the document and where you are in relation to that artwork. You can even move around your document by clicking in the VectorNavigator preview. See Chapter 14 for more on VectorTools and VectorNavigator.

The Artboard

In the center of the Pasteboard is a black-bordered box called the Artboard. The Artboard represents the largest area that will actually print out of Illustrator. If you are taking your Illustrator artwork into another application, such as Photoshop or QuarkXPress, the size of the Artboard is irrelevant; your entire illustration appears in most other software applications even if that artwork is larger than the Artboard.

The dotted lines on the Artboard represent the area that will print and the size of your printer's paper, referencing the printer options you chose in Page Setup for this information. There are two sets of dotted lines on the Artboard, although you can normally only see the inside line. The inside line represents what will actually print; the outside line is the size of the paper you chose in Page Setup.

The dimensions of the Artboard can be changed by choosing File ⇨ Document Setup and typing in different values in the width and height text fields of the Document Setup dialog box.

The Page Tool

The Page tool changes how much of your document will print by moving the printable area of the document, without moving any of the printable objects in the document. Clicking and dragging the lower-left corner of the page relocates the page to the place where you release the mouse button.

Tip

Page tool is useful when your document is larger than the biggest image area your printer can print. The tool enables you to *tile* several pages to create one large page out of several sheets of paper. *Tiling* is the process whereby the image consists of several pieces of paper arranged in a grid formation. A portion of the image is on each page, and when fitted together, the image can be viewed in its entirety. This is really only good for rough laser prints, as there will be ¼ inch around the edge of each paper that will need to be manually trimmed.

Miscellaneous Window Stuff

Illustrator windows act like windows in most other programs. The close box is in the upper-left corner, and the manual resize box is in the lower-right corner. The box in the upper-right corner toggles between your current window size and full-screen size.

The title bar at the top of the window is used to move the window around your screen. On the title bar is the name of the document (if you have not yet saved your document, the name of the document is Untitled Art 1, with the number changing for each new document you create). Next to the title of the document is the current viewing zoom percentage relative to actual size.

The scroll bars on the right side of the window let you see what is above and below the current viewing area. The scroll bars at the bottom of the window control panning from side to side. The arrows on each scroll bar let you see just a bit more with every click; holding down the mouse on an arrow slowly scrolls to other parts of the document. Dragging the *elevator box* in the scroll bar takes you to another part of the document, relative to the direction you are dragging. Clicking at either side of the elevator box in either bar changes your view by chunks of about half the width or height of your window.

In the lower-left corner is the status bar, which tells you all sorts of neat information you just can't get anywhere else. The default is usually set to display the name of the tool you are working with.

The Toolbox

Beginning with Illustrator 7, the toolbox incorporates the (Version 6) Plug-in Tools palette tools, eliminating any need for a Plug-in Tools palette. The toolbox can grow as additional tools are added to it (via plug-ins such as VectorTools Magic Wand).

The Illustrator 8 toolbox has also added some new tools and features since Version 7:

✦ New tools have been added including a Free Transform Tool and a Gradient Mesh Tool (see Figure 1-25).

✦ A tearoff option to tools has been added so you can make any tool with a pop-up menu a separate palette (see Figure 1-26).

The toolbox appears on top of your document window, covering up part of your illustration in the upper-left corner. The toolbox has no close box; to close it you must choose Window ⇨ Hide Tools. To show the toolbox, choose Window ⇨ Show Tools; it will appear. You can also press the Tab key (which hides *all* palettes, not just the toolbox).

The toolbox has two columns of tools, with the tools in each section related to each other. The viewing tools — the Hand tool and the Zoom tool, for example — are next to each other. The transformation tools — Scale, Rotate, Reflect, and Shear — are together in one section. However, the middle two sets of tools are more a miscellaneous grouping than anything else.

To choose a tool, click the one you want to use in the toolbox and release the mouse button. You can use this tool until you click another. You can also choose tools by pressing a key on the keyboard; for instance, pressing P selects the Pen tool. The keys to press for each tool are listed in Figure 1-25.

Many tools have additional *pop-up* tools — tools that appear only when you click and hold down the mouse on the default tool. The default tools that have pop-ups are located in the right column and are indicated with a little triangle in the upper-right corner of the tool. To select a pop-up tool, click and hold on a tool with a triangle until the pop-up tools appear; then drag to the pop-up tool you want. The new pop-up tool replaces the default tool in that tool slot.

Any tool with a pop-up option also has a tearoff option. When you select the tearoff option, those tools become a free-floating palette as seen in Figure 1-27.

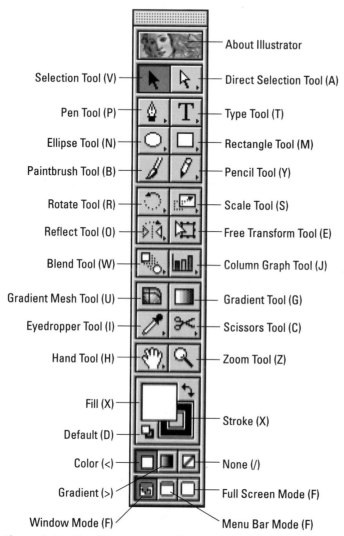

About Illustrator

Selection Tool (V) — — Direct Selection Tool (A)

Pen Tool (P) — — Type Tool (T)

Ellipse Tool (N) — — Rectangle Tool (M)

Paintbrush Tool (B) — — Pencil Tool (Y)

Rotate Tool (R) — — Scale Tool (S)

Reflect Tool (O) — — Free Transform Tool (E)

Blend Tool (W) — — Column Graph Tool (J)

Gradient Mesh Tool (U) — — Gradient Tool (G)

Eyedropper Tool (I) — — Scissors Tool (C)

Hand Tool (H) — — Zoom Tool (Z)

Fill (X) —

Stroke (X)

Default (D) —

Color (<) — — None (/)

Gradient (>) — — Full Screen Mode (F)

Window Mode (F) — Menu Bar Mode (F)

Figure 1-25: The Illustrator 8 toolbox

Figure 1-26: The tearoff option

Figure 1-27: The "torn off" tools become a palette

ASK TOULOUSE: Where's That Tool?

The Fonz: I can't find the Convert Direction Point tool.

Toulouse: It's to the right of the Pen tool.

The Fonz: I can't find the Pen tool either.

Toulouse: Are you sure you're using Illustrator?

The Fonz: Heeeeyyyyyy . . .

Toulouse: Just kidding. Someone might have been using another tool in that slot.

The Fonz: Is there any way to reset all the tools back to the original ones?

Toulouse: Sure. Just ⌘-Shift [Ctrl+Shift]-double-click on any tool to reset all of them.

Summary

✦ Illustrator seems difficult to learn at first, but with this book and a bit of dedication, it can be mastered.

✦ Illustrator works best with PostScript fonts.

✦ Illustrator can be interpreted as a good front-end for the PostScript page description language.

✦ There are four types of Anchor Points: Straight Corner Points, Smooth Points, Curved Corner Points, and Combination Corner Points.

✦ Curved paths in Illustrator are created with Bézier curves, named after the French mathematician Pierre Bézier.

✦ Curved segments are controlled by manipulating Control Handles, which extend from Anchor Points at either end of the segment.

✦ Illustrator has virtually unlimited available undos and redos.

✦   ✦   ✦

Creating and Painting Shapes

Technically, the name of this section should really be
"Placing, Sizing, and Colorizing Preformatted Open and
Closed Paths," but if it were, no one would read it — and this is
an important chapter because it introduces many concepts
that are built upon in later chapters.

Shapes

Drawing the most basic shapes — rectangles, ovals, polygons,
and stars — is precisely what a computer is for. Try drawing a
perfect oval by hand. Troublesome, isn't it? How about a
square that doesn't have ink bubbles or splotches at the
corners? How about a nine-point star? Yuck. Drawing these
objects and then coloring them in Illustrator is so easy and so
basic that after a few weeks of using Illustrator, you'll never be
able to draw a shape by hand again without wincing, maybe
even shuddering. Figure 2-1 compares shapes drawn by hand
with those drawn by a computer.

Getting rid of the shape you've drawn is even easier than
creating it (delete it by pressing the Delete or Backspace key).
And after the shape is created, it can be moved, rotated,
scaled, and manipulated in any way you like.

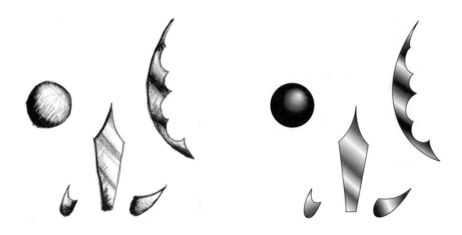

Shapes drawn by hand   Shapes drawn by computer

Figure 2-1: Hand-drawn shapes and their computer-drawn counterparts

Illustrator exemplifies the true power of object-oriented drawing programming.
No matter what you draw, you can adjust and move each piece of the drawing
independently until it's just right. Don't like the sun so high in your background?
Pull it down and tuck it in just a bit behind those mountains. Is the tree too small
for the house in your illustration? Scale it up a bit. This feature is great not only for
artists, but also for your pesky client (or boss) who demands that everything be
moved except that darned tree. Figure 2-2 shows an illustration drawn one way and
then modified in a matter of seconds by moving and transforming existing
elements.

Note   Traditional bitmap paint applications do not have the capability to move pieces of
a drawing (with the exception of the use of layers in software such as Photoshop
4 and Painter 5). After an image is moved in a bitmap program, a *hole* appears in
the place where the section used to be. And if there is anything under the section
where the image was moved to, that information is gone when the section is
replaced with the new image.

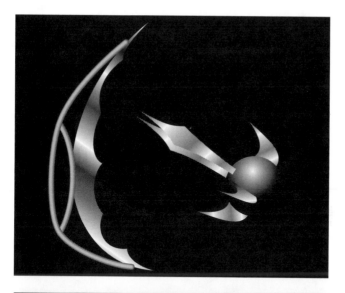

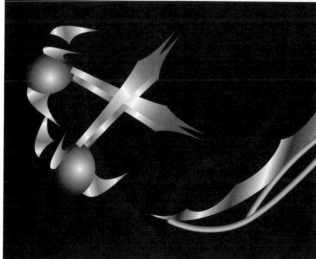

Figure 2-2: Illustrator objects moved from one drawing to the next

Drawing Rectangles

The most basic shape you can draw is a rectangle. The following steps, and the illustration of these steps in Figure 2-3, explain how to draw a simple rectangle.

1. Select the Rectangle tool (highlighted in the toolbox in Figure 2-3) by clicking it in the toolbox (or by pressing the letter M on the keyboard).

2. Click to set the origin and hold down the mouse button.

3. Drag diagonally (down and to the right) to the size you desire.

4. Release the mouse button. A rectangle is created. The farther the distance from the initial click until the point where you release the mouse button, the larger the rectangle.

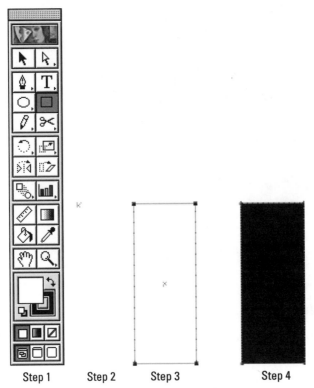

Step 1   Step 2   Step 3   Step 4

Figure 2-3: Steps for drawing a rectangle

After you release the mouse button, a white rectangle outlined in black (unless you have changed your default line and fill colors) appears with four blue points in the corners and one blue point in the center (if you are in Preview mode, the default viewing mode). The edge of the rectangle has thin blue lines surrounding it. The blue points in the corners are *Straight Corner Anchor Points*. The blue point in the center is the *Center Point*. The blue lines are *Straight Line Segments* that connect the Anchor Points of the rectangle. The blue points and blue lines together are considered a *path*. In Artwork mode, the rectangle has no Fill or Stroke, and the points and path appear black.

Tip

If you aren't sure what View mode you're in, display the View menu by clicking View and keeping the mouse button down. If the top item of the menu reads Artwork, you're in Preview mode. If it reads Preview, you're in Artwork mode. If this seems a little backward, choosing that menu item will change the viewing mode to the one you choose. So when you're in Preview mode, and you see and choose Artwork, you're switched to Artwork mode.

The initial click you make with the Rectangle tool is called the *origin point*. While you drag a figure, the origin point never moves; however, the rest of the rectangle is fluid, changing shape as you drag in different directions and to different distances with your mouse. Dragging horizontally with almost no vertical movement results in a long, flat rectangle. Dragging vertically with very little horizontal movement creates a rectangle that is tall and thin. Dragging at a 45° angle (diagonally) results in a squared rectangle.

Rectangles can be drawn from any corner by clicking and dragging in the direction opposite of where you want that corner to be. For instance, to draw a rectangle from the lower-right corner, click and drag up and to the left. As long as you have the Rectangle tool, dragging with it in the document window produces a new rectangle.

If you need to draw a rectangle that is an exact size, instead of dragging with the Rectangle tool, just click it once and release where you want the upper-left corner to be. The Rectangle dialog box shown in Figure 2-4 appears. Type in the width and height, click OK, and the rectangle draws itself, becoming precisely the size that you specified.

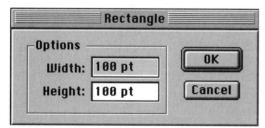

Figure 2-4: The Rectangle dialog box is used for specifying exact dimensions of a rectangle

If you click with the Rounded Rectangle tool, you get a third text field. The third text field in the Rounded Rectangle dialog box is for the size of the corner radius. This option makes the corners of the rectangle curved, although leaving the setting at a value of 0 keeps the corners straight. Rectangles whose sizes are specified in the Rectangle dialog box are always drawn from the upper-left corner unless you press the Option [Alt] key while drawing (see the next section, "Drawing Rectangles from Their Centers"). The largest rectangle you can draw is 10 feet by 10 feet. It's a wonder you can get anything done at all with these limitations!

When the Rectangle dialog box appears, values are usually already inside the text fields. Those numbers correspond to the size of the rectangle you last drew. To create another rectangle the same size, just click OK (or press Return or Enter). To make the rectangle a different size, replace the values with your own measurements. If a text field is highlighted, typing replaces the text in the text field and deletes what had been highlighted. To highlight the next field in a dialog box, press the Tab key. You can also highlight the preceding field in a dialog box by pressing Shift-Tab. If you'd like to highlight any text field instantly, double-click the value, or click the label next to that value. To accept the options in the dialog box, click OK or press Return or Enter.

When you first run Illustrator, all measurements are set to points. This means that the values inside the Rectangle dialog box appear in so many points (12 points in a pica). You can work in inches in three ways. The first way, before you bring up the Rectangle dialog box, is to choose File ⇨ Preferences ⇨ Units & Undo and choose inches as the measurement system. All dialog boxes in all new documents will then express their measurements in inches, not points. The second way is to choose File ⇨ Document Setup and choose inches in the Units pop-up menu, which will change the units to inches in that document *only*. The third way is to type either the inch symbol (") or **in** after the number, even though the text fields show points. Illustrator does conversions from points to inches and centimeters (and vice versa) on the fly, so after you enter a point value, the program converts the points into inches as soon as you press the Tab key. This little feature can be an excellent way for you to become more comfortable with points and picas.

To get out of the Rectangle dialog box without drawing a rectangle, click the Cancel button (or just press ⌘-Period [Esc]). Anything you have typed in that dialog box is then forgotten; the next time the dialog box is opened, it still has the size of the previously drawn rectangle inside it.

1. Using the Rectangle tool, draw a rectangle that is about 1 inch wide by 1 inch tall. Change the Fill color of the rectangle to 100% Black by clicking the Fill square in the toolbox, and then choosing Black in the Color palette. Change the Stroke to Black by clicking the Stroke icon in the toolbox and then choosing Black in the Color palette.

2. Choose the Selection tool and drag up and to the right just a little while holding down the Option [Alt] key. (The farther you drag, the greater the depth of the drop shadow.)

3. After you release the mouse button, you should have two overlapping rectangles. Change the fill color of the rectangle on top to 50% gray by clicking the Fill square in the toolbox, and then clicking on 50% Black in the Color palette. Change the Stroke to Black by clicking the Stroke icon in the toolbox and then choosing Black in the Color palette. Your illustration should now look like Figure 2-5.

Figure 2-5: A basic drop shadow box

Drawing Rectangles from Their Centers

Instead of drawing a rectangle from a corner, you can also draw one from its center. Rectangles are often placed on top of or under certain other objects, and there needs to be an even amount of space between the rectangle and the object it surrounds. Drawing from the corner forces you to "eyeball" the space around the object, while drawing from the center of the other object ensures that space surrounding the object is the same.

To draw a rectangle from its center, hold down the Option [Alt] key, click, and drag. The origin point is now the center of the rectangle. The farther you drag in one direction, the farther the edges of the rectangle go out in the opposite direction. Drawing from the center of a rectangle lets you draw a rectangle twice as big as the one you can draw if you drag from a corner. As long as the Option [Alt] key is pressed, the rectangle continues to be drawn from its center. If you release the Option [Alt] key before you release the mouse button, the origin of the rectangle changes back to a corner. You can press and release the Option [Alt] key at any time while drawing, toggling back and forth between drawing a corner rectangle and a centered rectangle.

Tip If you click without dragging when the Option [Alt] key is pressed, the Rectangle dialog box appears. The center of the rectangle is now where you clicked (normally, the corner of the rectangle is where you click). Unlike manually drawing (dragging) centered rectangles, the values you enter for the width and height are the actual width and height of the rectangle. The value is *not* doubled, as it is when you are dragging a centered rectangle.

You can also draw a rectangle from its center by pressing the Option [Alt] key while drawing with the Rectangle tool. The Option [Alt] key toggles from drawing from the middle to drawing from the corner. So if you keep the Option [Alt] key pressed until after you release the mouse button, the rectangle is drawn from the corner, not the center.

Drawing a Perfect Square

Few things in life really are perfect, but squares in Illustrator are pretty darn close.

When drawing, you can force Illustrator to create perfect squares by holding down the Shift key as you draw. When you press the Shift key while drawing a rectangle, it constrains to a square. (In review of your fourth-grade math class, the difference between a square and a rectangle is that a square is a rectangle with four sides of exactly the same length.) You can also use the Rectangle dialog box to draw a perfect square by entering equal values for the width and height.

To draw a square from its center, hold down the Option [Alt] and Shift keys while drawing. Make sure that *both* keys are still pressed when the mouse button is released.

Drawing Rounded Rectangles and Squares

Sometimes straight corners just aren't good enough. That's when it's time to create a rectangle with *rounded corners*. Why? Maybe you want your rectangles to look less "computery." A tiny bit of corner rounding (2 or 3 points) may be just what you need.

To draw a rectangle with rounded corners, choose the Rounded Rectangle tool, a pop-up tool that appears when you click on the Rectangle tool in the toolbox and drag to the right. Click and drag with this tool as if you were drawing a standard rectangle; the only difference is that this rectangle has rounded corners. The point at which you clicked is where the corner would be — if there were a corner. Of course, with rounded corners, there is no real corner, so the computer uses an imaginary point, called the *origin point,* as its onscreen corner reference.

The *corner radius* in Illustrator is the length from that imaginary corner (the origin point) to where the curve begins, as shown in Figure 2-6. The larger the value you enter in the Corner Radius field of the Rectangle dialog box, the farther the rectangle starts from the imaginary corner, and the bigger the curve is. For example, if you set the corner radius at 1 inch, the edge of the rectangle would start curving 1 inch from where a real corner would normally appear.

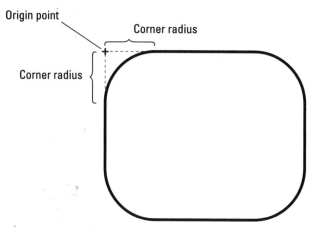

Figure 2-6: The corner radius

To draw a rounded rectangle from the center, press the Option [Alt] key and keep it pressed until you release the mouse button. To draw a rounded square, hold the Shift key while dragging and do not release it until after you release the mouse button. Drawing a rounded square from its center requires that you press and hold down both the Option [Alt] and Shift keys until you release the mouse button.

The *roundness* of the corners is determined by either the corner radius used by the most recent rounded-corner rectangle drawn or the radius set in the General Preferences dialog box (File ➪ Preferences ➪ General or ⌘-K [Ctrl+K]). The corner radius in the General Preferences dialog box changes each time you change the radius with the Rounded Rectangle tool. To change the radius of the next rounded rectangle to be drawn, go to the General Preferences dialog box and enter the new corner radius value. All rounded rectangles are now drawn with this new corner radius until this value is changed.

The corner radius can also be changed by clicking once with the Rounded Rectangle tool anywhere in the document to display the Rectangle dialog box. Changing the value in the Corner Radius field not only changes the current rounded rectangle's corner radius, but also changes the radius in the General Preferences box. This corner radius is used for all subsequently drawn rounded rectangles until the radius value is changed again.

Caution If the corner radius is more than one-half the length of either the length or width of the rectangle, the rectangle will appear to have perfectly round ends on at least two sides. If the corner radius is more than one-half the length of either the length or width of the rectangle, then the rectangle will be a circle!

How the Corner Radius *Really* Works

For all you geometry buffs, this is the real way that this whole corner radius business works: The width of any circle is called the *diameter* of that circle. Half the diameter is the *radius* of the circle, as shown in the following figure.

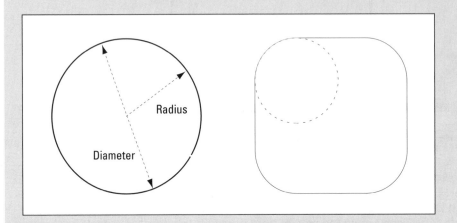

If you create a circle with a radius of 1 inch, the circle actually has a diameter of 2 inches. Put this 2-inch circle into the corner of the rectangle, as in the figure above, and the curve of the circle matches the curve of the rounded rectangle that has a corner radius of 1 inch. Huh?

To realistically determine the way a round corner will look, use the method that measures the distance from the imaginary corner to the place where the curve starts.

You are limited to a maximum of a 4,320-point corner radius, which works out to 5 feet. The largest rectangle you can create has a 10-foot length (the size of the Illustrator Pasteboard). So a 10-foot square with a 5-foot radius is another circle. (Those clever engineers. . . .)

Using the Round Corners Filter

If you have an existing rectangle with straight corners and you'd like to make the corners round, neither of the preceding methods will work. Instead, you must choose Filter ➪ Stylize ➪ Round Corners and enter the value of the corner radius you would like for the existing rectangle in the dialog box that appears. Using this filter allows you to change straight-corner rectangles to rounded-corner rectangles, but not rounded-corner rectangles to straight-corner rectangles. Using this filter on rectangles that already have rounded corners isn't recommended, as it will usually result in an unsightly (ugly) distortion.

Furthermore, this filter cannot change corners that have been rounded with either the Rounded Rectangle tool or by previous use of the Round Corners dialog box. Using this dialog box affects corners that are *not* round. Figure 2-7 shows the Round Corners filter applied to various rectangles and the results.

Figure 2-7: Rounded corners on rectangles

Rounding Corners Backward

What if you want your corners to round inward instead of out? Well, it would seem that you are initially out of luck, for Illustrator doesn't provide any way for you to enter a negative value for a corner radius. Instead, you need to manipulate the corners manually. The following steps, and the illustration of these steps in Figure 2-8, explain how to create a reverse rounded-corner rectangle.

1. Choose File ⇨ Preferences ⇨ General and set the Corner radius to 0.25". Draw a rounded rectangle that is about 3 inches wide by 1 inch tall.

2. Select the topmost point on the left side of the rounded rectangle with the Direct Selection tool (hollow arrow). One Control Handle appears, sticking out to the left.

3. Using the Rotate tool, click the Anchor Point once to set the origin. Click the Control Handle again and drag it down below the Anchor Point. Press the Shift key to ensure that the Control Handle Line is perfectly vertical and then release the mouse button.

4. Select the second point from the top on the left side with the Direct Selection tool. A Control Handle appears, sticking straight up out of this Anchor Point.

5. Using the Rotate tool, click the Anchor Point once to set the origin. Click the Control Handle again and drag it to the right of the Anchor Point. Press the Shift key to ensure that the Control Handle line is perfectly horizontal and then release the mouse button.

6. Repeat these steps for each of the corners. After you get the hang of it, the points start flying into position almost by themselves.

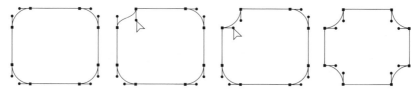

Figure 2-8: Steps for creating "backward" rounded corners on a rectangle

Drawing Ellipses and Circles

Drawing ellipses and circles is *almost* as easy as drawing rectangles and squares. You can create a variety of ellipses and circles in Illustrator.

To draw an ellipse (what Illustrator calls ovals), choose the Ellipse tool, click, and drag diagonally. The outline of an ellipse forms and when you release the mouse button, the ellipse itself appears onscreen. Ellipses, like rectangles, have four Anchor Points, but the Anchor Points on an ellipse are at the top, bottom, left, and right of the ellipse.

Drawing an ellipse is harder than drawing a rectangle because the point of origin on an ellipse is outside the ellipse. With a rectangle, the point of origin corresponds to either a corner of the rectangle, which also happens to be an Anchor Point, or the center of the rectangle. On an ellipse, there are no corners. This means that clicking and dragging does not align the top or bottom, or left or right, but one of the 45° curves to the origin point (an *arc*). Figure 2-9 shows that the top of the curve extends above the origin point, the bottom of the curve extends below the origin point, the right edge extends to the right of the origin point, and the left edge extends to the left of the origin point. (More detailed — and largely unnecessary — math is available at the end of this section.)

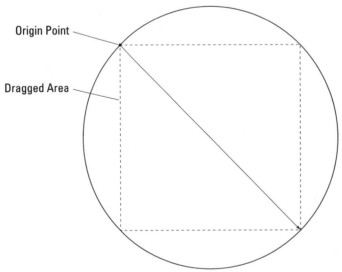

Origin Point

Dragged Area

Figure 2-9: The curves of an ellipse extend beyond the boundaries of the dragged area

Drawing an ellipse from its "corner" is a difficult task when the top, bottom, left, and right edges of the oval need to be at a specific location. On the other hand, tracing elliptical objects is easier because clicking and dragging on the edge of an existing elliptical object results in a close-to-perfect match, as shown in Figure 2-10.

Figure 2-10: Tracing a dimmed EPS image with the Rectangle and Ellipse tools

For easier tracing of circles, change the Constrain Angle value (File ⇨ General Preferences) to 45°. Now you can place the cursor on the top, bottom, or sides of the circle, and drag horizontally or vertically for a perfect fit. This technique doesn't work for ellipses because the ellipse will be angled at 45° if drawn this way.

1. Place the Snowman file from the Artwork folder on the *Illustrator 8 Bible* CD-ROM in Illustrator. Choose Window ⇨ Show Layers. In the Layers palette, double-click Layer 1 and check the Dim Placed Images option.

2. Use the Rectangle tool to trace the frame of the picture, the walls, and the pieces of the snowman's arms. Place the cursor in a corner of the object to be traced and drag toward the opposite corner. Use the Rotate tool to rotate the arms. For the hat, choose File ⇨ Preferences ⇨ General (⌘-K) [Ctrl+K] and change the Constrain Angle to 14°. Trace the hat and brim at this angle and then change the Constrain Angle back to 0°.

3. Use the Ellipse tool in the same way as the Rectangle tool to trace the snowman circles, eyes, nose, mouth, snowballs, and snowdrifts. If you can't see an entire circle, as is the case with most of the snowdrifts and the bottom section of the snowman, just estimate.

To draw from the center of an ellipse, press the Option [Alt] key and drag. As long as you are holding down the Option [Alt] key when you release the mouse button, the ellipse uses the initial click as the origin point and is drawn from the center.

Clicking without dragging with the Ellipse tool brings up the Ellipse dialog box, where you can enter any value for the width and height of your ellipse. The ellipse is drawn from the upper-left arc. Entering identical values results in a circle. Option[Alt]-clicking brings up the same dialog box, but the ellipse is now drawn from the center instead of the left arc.

To draw a perfect circle, hold down the Shift key as you drag. The oval now has equal width and height, making it a circle. Make sure that you keep pressing the Shift key until you release the mouse button; otherwise, the ellipse loses its equal proportions. To draw a circle from the center with the Ellipse tool, hold down both the Option [Alt] and Shift keys and drag diagonally.

Ellipses are drawn from the upper-left corner and extend about 20% of the total height above the origin point and about 20% of the total width to the left of the origin point. It's not just a coincidence that the right edge and bottom also extend 20% past the release point. The way this works out in mathematics (numerophobics should skip ahead to the next paragraph now) is that the height and width of the ellipse will be the square root of 2 (about 1.414) times the height and width of the box that is dragged from corner to corner.

Only rectangles and ellipses were used to create the illustration in Figure 2-11. Through a creative use of Fills, the illustration comes alive.

Figure 2-11: An illustration drawn with only rectangles and ellipses

Moving Rectangles and Ellipses While Drawing

While drawing a rectangle or ellipse, you may realize you want to move it. In Illustrator 8, you can move any rectangle or ellipse by holding down the Spacebar while your mouse button is depressed and dragging your shape to a new location. When you let up on the Spacebar, you can continue to draw your object. (This feature worked only for polygons, stars, and spirals in Version 7, but in Version 8, it is available for rectangles and ellipses as well.)

1. Change the Paint Style to a Fill of None and a Stroke of 1-point black.

2. Using the Ellipse tool, drag to create the juggler's body and then his head, as shown in Figure 2-12.

3. To tilt backward the juggler's head, select the head oval and double-click the Rotate tool. Then enter a value of 30°, which angles the head backward.

4. Next, create one of the rings by pressing the Shift key and dragging to create a perfect circle.

5. Duplicate the circles by pressing the Option[Alt] key and dragging one of the circles to a new location. As long as the Option[Alt] key is pressed when you release the mouse button, the circle is duplicated rather than moved.

6. Draw a much smaller circle for one of the balls the juggler is balancing on his head. Using Option[Alt] and drag, duplicate the balls in the same way you duplicated the rings.

7. Option[Alt] duplicate two more ball-sized circles to create hands, one for the white area of the eye, and one for the mouth.

8. Choose File ⇨ General Preferences (⌘-K) [Ctrl+K] and change the Constrain Angle to 45°.

9. Using the Rectangle tool, create first the top part of the hat and then the rim of the hat, as shown in Figure 2-13. The pieces will automatically be angled at 45°.

10. Change the Constrain Angle back to 0° and draw both arms. They may need to be rotated individually, depending on the location of the rings.

11. Draw the rectangular background and choose Object ⇨ Arrange ⇨ Send To Back (⌘-Shift-[) [Ctrl+Shift+[].

12. Select individual paths and Fill them with different colors and gradients.

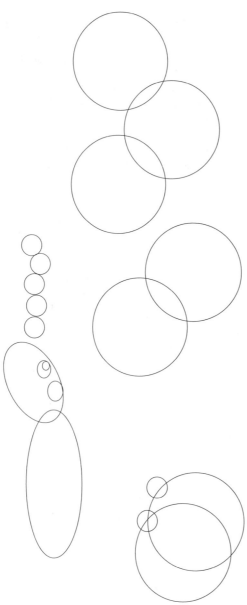

Figure 2-12: Ellipses and circles

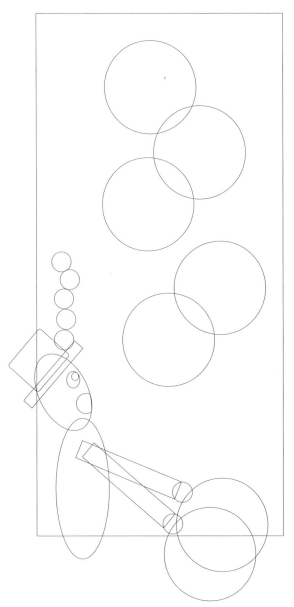

Figure 2-13: Rectangles are added to the illustration

Creating Cool Shapes

Although it's loads of fun to create more and more ovals, rectangles, and rounded rectangles, sooner or later you're going to get bored. There are other, dare I say, *more interesting* shapes that you can create automatically by using some of the additional shape tools that come with Illustrator. Most of them are located in the Oval tool slot in the toolbox (see Figure 2-14).

Figure 2-14: The Ellipse tool slot and its tools

Creating Polygons

To create a polygon, select the Polygon tool (to the right of the Ellipse tool in the Ellipse tool slot, and shown in Figure 2-15) and click and drag in a document. As you drag, the polygon will grow from its center and get larger and larger.

Figure 2-15: The Polygon tool

To specify the number of sides for your polygon *before* you draw the polygon, Option[Alt]-click with the Polygon tool. That will bring up the Polygon dialog box (shown in Figure 2-16), where you can specify both the number of sides and the size of the polygon.

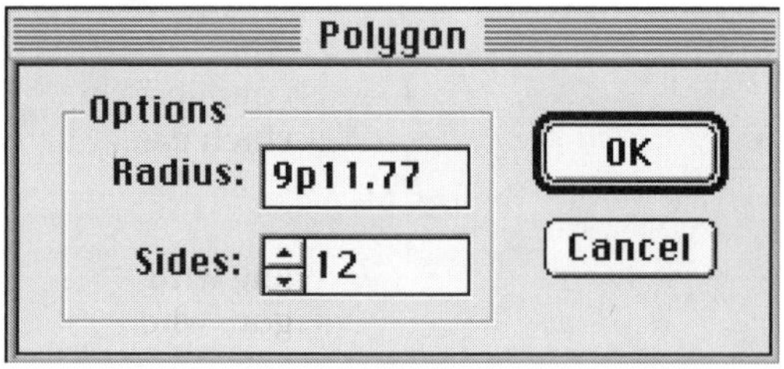

```
┌─────────────────── Polygon ───────────────────┐
│  ┌─Options ─────────────────┐                  │
│  │   Radius: │9p11.77│       │   ┌────OK────┐   │
│  │                           │   └──────────┘   │
│  │   Sides: │▲▼│12 │         │   ┌──Cancel──┐   │
│  │                           │   └──────────┘   │
│  └───────────────────────────┘                 │
└────────────────────────────────────────────────┘
```

Figure 2-16: The Polygon dialog box

The radius is the distance from the center of the polygon to the corners of the polygon. For even-sided shapes (4, 6, 8, 10 and so on sides), the radius is half the width of the object, from one corner to the opposite corner. For odd-sided shapes, the radius is *not* half the width of the object, but instead, can *only* be measured by going from one corner point to the center.

All polygons created with the Polygon tool are equilateral polygons. I looked up *equilateral,* just to make sure I wasn't spouting off multisyllabic words to sound impressive, and it means "sides of the same length." So every polygon you create has sides that are all the same. That's why every four-sided object you create is a square, and each six-sided object is a perfect hexagon. You may find the square capabilities of the Polygon tool useful (really); it can save you a step when you want to draw a square at an angle. That's something that can't be done with the Rectangle tool unless you change the Constrain Angle in General Preferences prior to drawing the square or use the Rotate tool on the square after it is drawn. I've found using the Polygon tool's square capabilities helpful on several occasions.

While drawing a polygon, you can change the number of sides on the fly. To increase the number of sides, press the up arrow. To decrease the number of sides, press the down arrow. Figure 2-17 shows different polygons drawn with the Polygon tool.

Figure 2-17: Polygons drawn with the Polygon tool

If you press the Shift key while dragging, the polygon you're creating is upright; it aligns to the current Constrain Angle (usually 0°). This means that if you're creating a triangle and you press Shift, the triangle has one side that is perfectly horizontal (the bottom) unless you have a different Constrain Angle, in which case that edge of the triangle aligns to that angle.

Press the Spacebar to move your polygon around when dragging with the Polygon tool. You can do this at any time during the creation of a Polygon; when you release the Spacebar, the tool functions as before.

Tip Possibly the niftiest function of the Polygon (and the Star and Spiral tools) is the wonderful Spaz function that comes from using the tilde (~) key. Press it when you're drawing and you'll see several shapes appear rapidly. As Figure 2-18 shows, Spazzing can create all sorts of questionable designs.

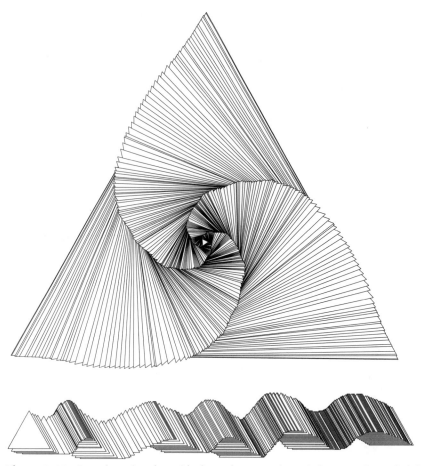

Figure 2-18: Spazzing triangles with the Polygon tool. Funky? Yes. Art? Doubtful.

Seeing Stars

To create stars, choose the Star tool from its hiding place next to the Polygon tool in the Ellipse tool slot and drag in the document. As you drag, a star is born. Several stars are shown in Figure 2-19.

Figure 2-19: Stars

Stars have several of the same controls as polygons when they're being drawn: Shift aligns the star to the constrain angle, the Spacebar moves the star around, and the tilde (~) key makes millions of duplicates. The up and down arrows work a bit differently, however. Instead of adding and removing sides, the arrows add and remove entire points. So, in a way, they're actually adding two sides. Stars have to have an even number of sides or they're not really stars, they're the pointy lumps you doodled during your Poly Sci classes as a sophomore.

The Star tool adds two additional keys for other functions. Pressing the Option [Alt] key makes every other side align with each other. It's hard to describe, but these stars look "perfect." Adobe refers to them as *fixed* stars, but I'm not aware of any neutering or spaying taking place when the Option [Alt] key is pressed. ("It's the responsible thing to do; press the Option [Alt] key when you draw stars.") These fixed stars are shown in Figure 2-20. In case it's keeping you up at night, the Option [Alt] key has no effect on stars with four points, and it turns three-pointed stars into triangles.

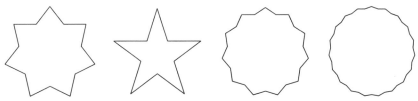

Figure 2-20: Fixed stars drawn while the Option [Alt] key is pressed

Stars can come in all shapes, not just the fixed and standard shapes. These shapes are created by pressing the ⌘ [Ctrl] key when you drag. When the ⌘ [Ctrl] key is held down, the outer points are extended only; the interior points remain fixed in place. Figure 2-21 shows the same star (points, rotation, size) with points extended differently.

Figure 2-21: These stars are the same except for the difference in the distance between the inner points and outer points

You can also specifically design a star by clicking with the Star tool to display the Star dialog box, where you can enter the number of points and both the first and second radius of the points.

Of course, all of these stars created with the star tool consist of regular-looking stars. For a more dramatic looking starburst, follow these steps.

1. Create a star with about 30 sides. Make it look something like the one shown in Figure 2-22.

2. Choose Filter ➪ Distort ➪ Roughen.

3. In the Roughen dialog box (Figure 2-23), change the Size to 5% and the Detail to 0 (keeping the Detail at 0 won't let Roughen add any anchor points). Check the Corner checkbox (so we don't have curves on our starburst) and click OK. You can also check the Preview checkbox; each time you check and uncheck it, a new random preview results; clicking OK uses the Roughen preview you see onscreen. My result appears in Figure 2-24.

4. Add any extras, like a drop shadow, text, and so on. My end result is shown in Figure 2-25.

Figure 2-22: A star about to become a starburst

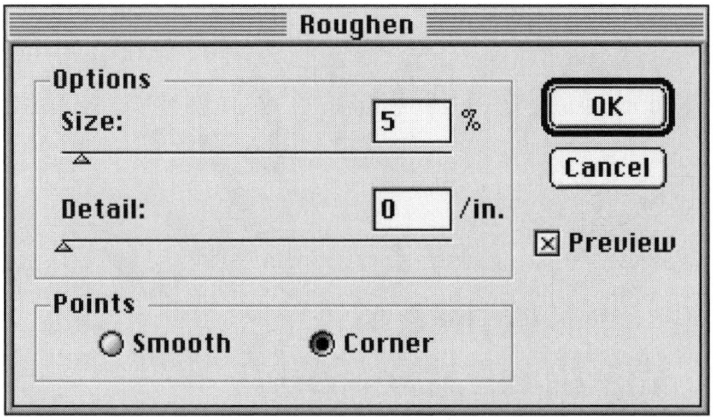

Figure 2-23: The Roughen dialog box set up to change a star into a starburst

Figure 2-24: The resulting starburst

Figure 2-25: The final, ready-for-stamping-on-the-front-of-the-book starburst

Spiral Madness

If there's one really good thing to say about being able to draw spirals with the Spiral tool in Illustrator, it's that it was hellish to create spirals before a Spiral tool (or filter) existed. If there's another good thing to say, I haven't quite figured it out yet.

The Spiral tool (located at the far right end of the Ellipse slot tools) makes spirals — all sorts of spirals. What would you use a spiral for? Well, I used the Spiral tool to create a simulated Lucy and the Rugrats' "Live Dinner LP," which included such classics as "Eat It Before It Dies," "Watch Out, Tomcat," and the Top Ten hit "No Control (I'm in Heat)." Of course, the path was exceedingly long and refused to print on most imagesetters. Other than that, I've created lots of art for this and other Illustrator books using spirals. I'm still waiting for a practical use to rear its twisted, spun head. Figure 2-26 shows several useless spirals I've manufactured with the Spiral tool.

Figure 2-26: Spirals

Caution   Spirals beg to be stroked, not filled. Putting just a fill on a spiral makes it look like the circle you drew in that Poly Sci class—lumpy and not quite round.

Here's a rundown of keys you can press while spiraling out of control with the Spiral tool:

✦ **Tilde (~):** It duplicates here as well, but *don't* do it with spirals. The mess is usually disastrous on all but the most windless spirals.

✦ **Shift:** This keeps the spiral aligned to the Constrain Angle. Actually, it keeps the protruding line segment of the spiral aligned to a 45° variant of the Constrain Angle.

✦ **Option [Alt]:** Pressing this key makes the spiral grow by adding or removing line segments (winds) to the spiral's outermost edge. Dragging away from the origin (where you initially clicked) adds segments; dragging toward the origin removes segments.

✦ **⌘ [Ctrl]:** Pressing the ⌘ [Ctrl] key while dragging changes the decay of the spiral. Dragging away from the origin decreases the decay %, making the space between winds larger toward the outer edge of the spiral. Dragging toward the origin increases the decay %, making the space between winds similar from inside to outside. A decay of 100% results in a perfect circle. The decay can never be less than 5%.

✦ **Spacebar:** Pressing the Spacebar lets you move the spiral around the screen.

If you click in your document with the Spiral tool, the Spiral dialog box (see Figure 2-27) appears, and you can enter specific values for a spiral. Handy for all those times your client or boss wants that 82.5% decay spiral.

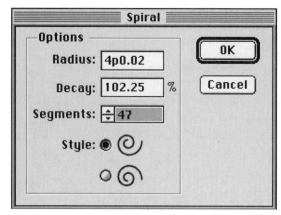

Figure 2-27: The Spiral dialog box

Drawing Shapes at an Angle

Normally, when you draw a shape with a tool, it appears to be oriented with the document and the document window. For instance, the bottom of a rectangle is parallel to the bottom of the document window.

But what if you want to draw shapes that are all angled at 45° on the page? Well, one possibility is to rotate them after they are drawn using the Transform Each command or the Rotate tool. Better than this alternative, however, is to set up your document so that every new shape is automatically angled.

The angle of the shapes is dependent on the *constrain angle.* Normally, the Constrain Angle is 0°, where all shapes appear to align evenly with the borders of the document. To change the Constrain Angle, choose File ➪ Preferences ➪ General and enter a new value in the Constrain Angle text field inside the General Preferences dialog box.

When you are done drawing these angled shapes, make sure that you change the Constrain Angle setting back to 0°, or all new shapes will be created at the altered Constrain Angle.

Tip   The Constrain Angle affects shapes and other objects created in Illustrator, such as type. In addition, dragging objects with the Shift key pressed will constrain them to the current Constrain Angle or to a 45° or 90° variation of it. The Constrain Angle is much easier to see if you have Grids turned on (choose View ➪ Show Grids, or press ⌘- " [Ctrl+ "]). The grid shown on the page is always aligned to the Constrain Angle.

ASK TOULOUSE: Preference Practical Jokes, Part 27

Apollo: I want to play a practical joke on my buddy, Boomer.

Toulouse: Good man. I've got a great Illustrator one for you. Change the General Preference setting called Constrain Angle to 180°.

Apollo: What'll that do?

Toulouse: At first, everything will seem perfectly normal. But then . . .

Apollo: His computer'll explode, right?

Toulouse: Not quite. Actually, everything will work normally except type, which will appear upside down. All the time!

Apollo: Ha! That's great.

Toulouse: There's a worse one, you know.

Apollo: Would Boomer get really mad at this one?

Toulouse: Depends. For a really good joke that he probably won't discover until he prints, set the Constrain Angle to 0.2°.

Apollo: And that'll do. . . .

Toulouse: It'll make everything off by just a fraction. Could wreck his day, however . . . and thus, yours.

Apollo: Noted.

Filling and Stroking Shapes

One of the most powerful capabilities of Illustrator is its capability to color objects. In Adobe Illustrator, you can color both the Fill and the Stroke of the paths you have created.

Fills

The *Fill* of an object is the color inside the shape. If a path is closed, the Fill exists only on the inside of the path. If the path is open (meaning that it has two End Points), the Fill exists between an imaginary line drawn from End Point to End Point and the path itself. Fills in open paths can provide some very interesting results when the path crosses itself, or the imaginary line crosses the path. Figure 2-28 shows an example of Fills in open and closed paths and how the paths appear in Artwork mode. For text, the Fill is the color of the text. Fills do not appear in Artwork mode, only in Preview mode. Depending on the complexity of the path and the type of Fill, Illustrator may refuse to preview the Fill and will automatically switch to Artwork mode.

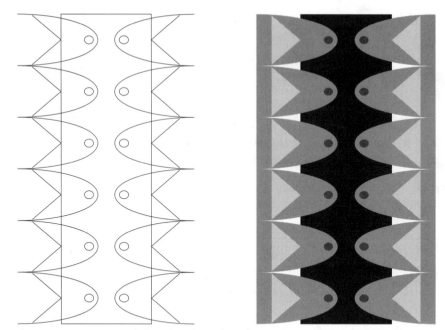

Figure 2-28: Open and closed paths in both Artwork mode (left) and Preview mode (right)

The Fill color options include White, Black, Tints, Process Colors, Spot Colors, Patterns, and Gradients. The Fill option for an object can also be set to None, where the Fill is transparent. This lets you see behind a path to what is underneath it when the Stroke of an object is the visible part.

Strokes

The *Stroke* of an object is made up of three parts: color, weight, and style. Strokes appear where there are paths or around the edges of type. Like Fills, any one path or object may have only one type of Stroke on it; the color, weight, and style of the Stroke are consistent throughout the length of the path or the entire text object. (Individual characters in a text object can have different Strokes if they are selected with the Type tool when the Stroke attributes are applied.)

The Stroke color options are White, Black, Tints, Process Colors, Spot Colors, Patterns, and None (the Stroke is off). When the Stroke color option is set to None, then the object is said to have no Stroke. Strokes cannot display patterns in Preview mode, nor can they have gradients applied to them.

The weight of a Stroke is how thick it is. On a path, the Stroke is centered on that path, with half the thickness of the Stroke on one side of the path and half the thickness on the other side of the path. Strokes can be anywhere from 0 to 1,000 points thick.

The style of a Stroke consists of several parts, including the cap style, join style, miter limit, and dash pattern. The *cap style* is the way that the ends of a Stroke look and can be either butt cap, rounded cap, or projected cap. The *join style* is the way that Corner Points on paths appear when stroked and can be either mitered join, rounded join, or beveled join. Figure 2-29 shows examples of the cap styles and join styles.

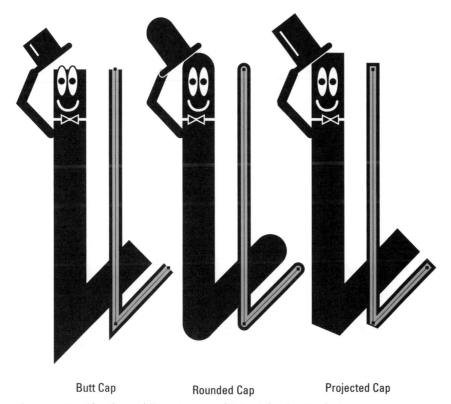

Butt Cap   Rounded Cap   Projected Cap

Figure 2-29: The three different cap and join styles for Strokes

The *miter limit* is the length at which miter joins are cropped. If a path has a thick stroke and there is a tight angle (like those that appear on some stars with a tiny inner radius and a large outer one), the point at which the outside edges of the stroke would meet might be ridiculously far from where the points are set. Using a miter limit tells Illustrator that if the meeting point of the outside edges is more than so many times the thickness of the stroke, to crop it off at the point.

Normally, the *dash pattern* for a Stroke is solid, but various dash patterns can be created for different effects. Figure 2-30 shows different miter limits on different corners.

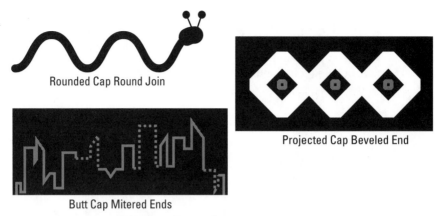

Rounded Cap Round Join

Projected Cap Beveled End

Butt Cap Mitered Ends

Figure 2-30: "Whatcha talkin' about Willis?" A sampling of all the different cap styles, join styles, miter limits, and dash patterns for Strokes

Combining Strokes with Fills

Many times, paths in Illustrator require both Fills and Strokes. When you give both a Fill and a Stroke to a single path, the Stroke knocks out the Fill at the edges of the path by one-half the weight of the Stroke. Figure 2-31 demonstrates this.

Original object with a
6-point Stroke
and a Black Fill

How the Stroke knocks
out the Fill by half of the
weight of the Stroke

Figure 2-31: A Stroke knocks out a Fill by one-half the weight of the Stroke

Tip If knocking out the fill of a path presents a problem for your design, you can correct this problem by copying the path and pasting it in front, removing the frontmost path's Stroke. The Filled path, on top of the Stroked path, will knock out the "inner" half of the Stroke. This technique is discussed in detail in Chapter 17.

Applying Fills and Strokes

The toolbox contains two icons, one for Fill and one for Stroke, located in the Paint Style section of the toolbox (see Figure 2-32).

Figure 2-32: The Paint Style section of the toolbox

By default, the Fill is set to White and the Stroke is set to 1-point Black. In fact, at any time you can reset to the default Fill and Stroke by clicking the Default Fill and Stroke icon in the lower-left corner of the Paint Style section.

 Tip You can quickly reset the fill and stroke colors to their default by pressing the D key.

You can quickly swap between the colors in the Fill and Stroke icons by clicking the Swap Fill and Stroke icon located in the upper-right of the Paint Style section.

When you first start Illustrator, the Fill icon is in front of the Stroke icon. This means that any changes made in the Color or Swatch palettes affect the Fill. When the Fill icon is in front of the Stroke icon, the Fill is said to be in *focus*. You can change the focus to the Stroke by either clicking the Stroke icon or by pressing the X key. Figure 2-33 shows the focus on the Stroke and the focus on the Fill. When the focus is on the Stroke, changes made in the Color or Swatch palettes affect the Stroke, not the Fill.

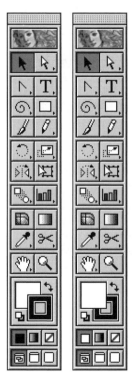

Figure 2-33: Focus on the Stroke (left) and focus on the Fill (right)

Tip   Use the X key. It's by the modifier keys (where your left hand should be anyway), and it's extremely handy, not to mention easier and faster than clicking on the Stroke or Fill icons to change focus.

The Fill and Stroke icons change in appearance to match the current Fill and Stroke. For instance, if you have a green Fill and an orange Stroke, the Fill icon is green and the Stroke icon is orange, and you obviously slept through the color lectures in your design classes. The Fill icon displays a gradient or pattern if that is the current Fill.

The three icons at the bottom of the Paint Style section are used to determine the type of Fill or Stroke:

✦ **Color:** This icon is used when the Fill or Stroke is a solid color or a pattern. Press the comma key (, or <) on the keyboard to quickly push the color icon.

✦ **Gradient:** This icon is used when the Fill contains a gradient. Strokes cannot be colored with gradients; clicking this icon when the Stroke icon is in focus changes the Fill to gradient and changes the focus to Fill as well. Press the period key (. or >) to quickly push the gradient icon.

✦ **None:** This creates an empty Fill or no Stroke. Fills of None are entirely transparent. Strokes of None are neither colored nor have any Stroke weight. Press the forward slash key (/) to quickly push the None icon.

Oddly enough, you don't need to determine the type of Fill when switching between color and gradient by using the color and gradient icons; you can simply click the appropriate swatch in the Swatches palette to change the Fill type. There is, however, no swatch for None, so to change the Fill or Stroke to None you must either click the icon or press the forward slash (/) key. Get used to the forward slash key; it will save you loads of time when changing colors for objects. I'll often do a quick combination of X and / keys to change focus and apply None to the Stroke or Fill.

Using the Swatches Palette

View the Swatches palette (see Figure 2-34) by choosing Window ➪ Show Swatches or by pressing F5. The Swatches palette has gained a buddy in Illustrator 8. The Brushes palette has joined up with the Swatches palette. You can access either palette by clicking its respective tab.

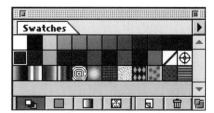

Figure 2-34: The Swatches palette

By default, the Swatches palette contains and displays several commonly used colors, patterns, and gradients. Change the display by clicking on the icons along the bottom of the palette:

✦ **Show All Swatches:** This displays all color, gradient, and pattern swatches.

✦ **Show Color Swatches:** This displays only the color swatches.

✦ **Show Gradient Swatches:** This displays only the gradient swatches.

✦ **Show Pattern Swatches:** This displays only the pattern swatches.

You can also view the swatches in either small or large squares, or view all the swatches in a list, with names if they have them (see Figure 2-35). Change the view mode by selecting the appropriate option from the Swatches pop-up menu.

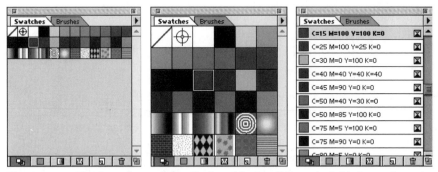

Figure 2-35: The Swatches palette displayed in Small Swatch (left), Large Swatch (middle), and Name views (right)

Create a new swatch based on the current paint style (shown in the Paint Style section of the toolbox) by clicking the New Swatch icon along the bottom of the Swatches palette. If you press Option [Alt] when creating a new swatch, the New Swatch dialog box appears, enabling you to initially name the swatch and set its color mode to either process (CMYK) or spot. You can also create a new swatch by choosing New Swatch from the Swatches palette pop-up menu.

Double-clicking a swatch displays the Swatch Options (shown in Figure 2-36) for that swatch. The Swatch Options dialog box lets you change the name of the swatch (primarily for use in Name view mode), set the color type of the swatch to either process or spot, and the color mode of CMYK, RGB, HSB, or Grayscale.

In addition, you can select one or more swatches to edit, duplicate, or remove them from the Swatches palette. Click on a swatch to select it; a frame appears on the selected swatch. When a swatch is selected, choosing Swatch Options from the Swatch menu also displays the Swatch Options for the selected swatch.

Tip Regardless of the view mode (Small, Large, or Name), ⌘-Option-clicking [Ctrl+Alt+clicking] the Swatches palette makes the palette respond to keyboard entry for selecting swatches. For instance, if you wanted to use the swatch called PrenatalGoo you would ⌘-Option-click [Ctrl+Alt+click] in the Swatches palette and then type the first few letters of the swatch name; in this case the letters *P-R-E* should do it. When you stop typing, the swatch whose name is closest to the one you typed is highlighted, and pressing the Enter key makes that the active (selected) swatch in the Swatches palette. This is extremely useful for selecting Pantone colors in the huge Pantone Swatches palettes.

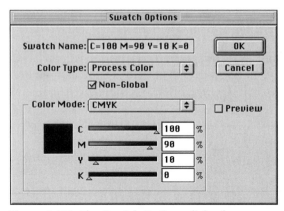

Figure 2-36: The Swatch Options dialog box

Choosing Duplicate from the pop-up menu duplicates the selected swatches. You can also drag a selected swatch to the New Swatch icon (the little piece of paper) to duplicate the swatch. If you press Option [Alt] while duplicating a swatch, the New Swatch dialog box appears; this is really the same as the Swatch Options dialog box (but the swatch is new, so the box has a different name).

To delete a swatch, select the swatch and click the Trash icon or choose Delete from the Swatches palette pop-up menu. A warning dialog box (see Figure 2-37) appears, asking if you want to delete the swatch selection. Click Yes to delete the swatch.

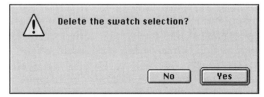

Figure 2-37: The Warning dialog box that appears when you attempt to delete a swatch

New Feature   New to Illustrator 8 is the capability to undo a swatch deletion. The unlimited undo's now apply to the Swatch palette deletions.

You can select more than one swatch by pressing the ⌘ [Ctrl] key and clicking additional swatches. If you press the Shift key and click additional swatches, a contiguous (connected) set of the swatches is selected, from where you initially clicked to where you Shift-clicked. Deselect individual swatches by ⌘[Ctrl]-clicking selected swatches. Deselect all the swatches by clicking an empty area of the Swatches palette. By selecting multiple swatches, you can duplicate and delete several swatches at once.

The Swatches pop-up menu (shown in Figure 2-38) has other functions as well. Choosing Select All Unused selects the swatches in the Swatches palette that aren't being used in the current document. You can then delete those swatches if necessary. Sort By Name organizes the swatches (regardless of which viewing mode the swatch palette is in) alphabetically. Sort By Kind sorts the swatches to appear starting with color, then gradients, then patterns.

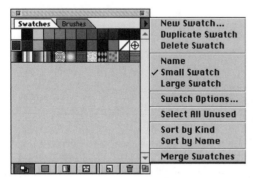

Figure 2-38: The Swatches palette pop-up menu

If you want to sort the swatches manually, you can do so by selecting any number of swatches and dragging them to a new location within the Swatches palette.

Spot/Process Swatches and Color Space Indicators

You can tell the difference between spot colors and process colors in Small Swatch and Large Swatch viewing modes by looking at the lower-right corner of the swatch. A white triangle with a dot in it indicates that the color is a spot color.

In Name viewing mode, both the color space (grayscale, RGB, or CMYK) and Process/Spot status are indicated to the right of the color chip and name.

The Other Swatch Libraries

In addition to the standard Swatch Library palette, several other default Swatch Library palettes are accessible from the Swatch Libraries submenu of the Window menu (see Figure 2-39). You can also create a new Swatch Library palette from any Illustrator document.

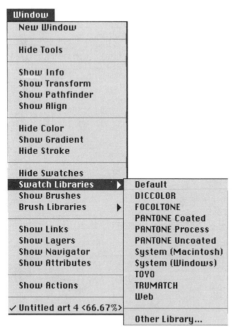

Figure 2-39: The Window menu and
Swatch Libraries submenu

To view one of the other default Swatches palettes, choose it from the Swatch
Libraries submenu. You cannot edit these Swatch libraries; you can only add
swatches from these libraries to your main Swatches palette.

To add a swatch (or several selected swatches) to your main Swatches palette,
select the swatches to be added and choose Add To Swatches from the library's
pop-up menu, or drag the swatches to the main Swatches palette. Fortunately, the
main Swatches palette is saved with your document; this way you can customize a
palette for a specific document, or edit the Adobe Illustrator Startup document's
Swatches palette to use a certain set of colors in each new document you create.
(Using and abusing the startup document is covered in Chapter 6.)

Otherwise, these swatch libraries work the same way as your main Swatches
palette; you can choose colors for Fill and Stroke, sort the swatches by Kind or
Name, and view the swatches by Name, Small Swatch, or Large Swatch. Figure 2-40
shows three swatch libraries in different views.

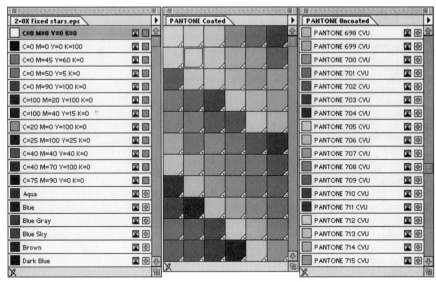

Figure 2-40: Three swatch libraries

Choosing and Mixing Colors

You can create any color to be used in an illustration by defining it in the Color palette (shown in Figure 2-41). The Color palette provides basic color selection via the Color Ramp along the bottom of the palette, and more precise control via sliders and percentage entries in grayscale, RGB, CYMK, HSB, and spot color spaces.

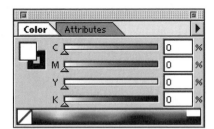

Figure 2-41: The Color palette

New Feature

New to Illustrator 8 is the improved Color palette. Along the Color Ramp the choices for None, Black, and White have been added. When creating or mixing a color, you now have the choice to have it applied to the Fill or Stroke swatch. When you apply None to either the Fill or Stroke, a new Last Color option pops up in the Color palette (see Figure 2-42), which is a really cool function. This means you can apply the last color mixed by clicking the mouse to set the color.

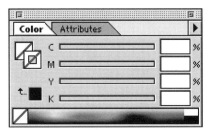

Figure 2-42: The Last Color option
in the Color palette

The Color palette has a pop-up menu that enables you to display options and to choose from the available color spaces. The "options" are really the color mixing sliders; I've never found a reason to hide them. In fact, the sliders take up such a small amount of space that once they're in view, you'll probably never hide them either.

The color space options let you switch between

✦ **Grayscale:** White to black with all shades of gray in between (see Figure 2-43).

✦ **RGB:** Red, green, and blue. This is the color space used by computer monitors, and it's perfect for multimedia and Web-page graphics (see Figure 2-44). You can enter RGB values as percentages or as values from 0 to 255. Double-click to the right of the text fields to change the RGB measurement system from percentages to the numeric 0 to 255 system and back.

✦ **HSB:** Hue, Saturation, Brightness. This RGB-derived color space is best for adjusting RGB colors in brightness and saturation (see Figure 2-45).

✦ **CMYK:** Cyan, magenta, yellow, and black. These are considered typical printing process colors, although Illustrator calls any colors *process* that aren't spot (see Figure 2-46).

✦ **Tint:** This isn't really an option in the pop-up menu, but if you select a spot color swatch (or choose a spot color with the Eyedropper tool), the color palette goes into a sort of tint color space, where you can tint the color from 100% to 0% of that color (see Figure 2-47).

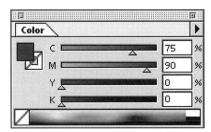

Figure 2-43: The Color palette
displaying grayscale color space

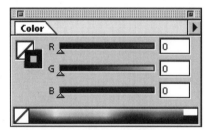

Figure 2-44: The Color palette displaying RGB color space

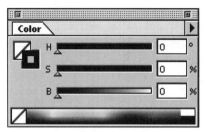

Figure 2-45: The Color palette displaying HSB color space

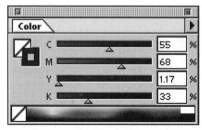

Figure 2-46: The Color palette displaying CMYK color space

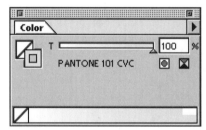

Figure 2-47: The Color palette displaying tint color space for the color Pantone 101 CVC

When you change color spaces, the Color Ramp along the bottom of the palette changes as well to show the colors in that color space.

Tip Shift-click the Color Ramp to cycle through the color spaces; this is much faster than choosing a color space from the pop-up menu.

As you drag a slider, the other sliders also change in color. This gives you a sort of preview for what would happen if you were to drag along the sliders. The icon to the left of the sliders shows the current color and whether you're adjusting the Fill (solid box) or Stroke (box with a hole). Instead of dragging, you can also just simply click a different location along the slider to change its value.

Tip Press the Shift key to adjust RGB and CMYK sliders proportionately. This is a great way to tint process colors. Shift-drag the slider with the largest value for the most control. When you release the mouse button, the new color will be a tint of the original.

You can also change the slider values by typing in values for each of the individual color channels (Cyan is a color channel in CMYK, for instance). Press the Tab key to highlight the next text field, or Shift-Tab to highlight the previous text field.

Tip Quickly highlight the text fields by clicking to the right of the text field, or by clicking the name of the text field on the other side of the slider.

ASK TOULOUSE: The Color Purple

Cassiopeia: How can I make a purple color with the CMYK sliders?

Toulouse: Try 50% Cyan and 100% Magenta.

Cassiopeia: Wow, that was easy. How'd you know that?

Toulouse: Well, I sorta cheated. All the sliders in the Color palette are interactive.

Cassiopeia: They provide a real-to-life multimedia experience?

Toulouse: Not exactly. But the sliders change color relative to what the current color is. For instance, when I set Magenta to 100%, I looked at the other sliders, and saw there was purple in the middle of the Cyan slider bar. So I dragged the Cyan slider to 50% and voilà!

Cassiopeia: Voilà, indeed. You know, someone should stick that in a book somewhere. . . .

Toulouse: Good idea . . .

Tip Most of Illustrator's palette's text fields are mathematically adept. You can add, subtract, multiply, and divide in them. This is useful when entering color percentages in the text fields of the Color palette. To add 5% to the current value, type +5 after the current value. To subtract 5%, type -5 after the current value. To divide the current value by 2, type /2 after the current value. To multiple the current value by 2, type *2 after the current value.

Tip Press Shift-Return/Enter after entering values to rehighlight the current text field. In this way you can type in different values without ever having to reselect the text field.

The Color Ramp

The Color Ramp enables you to quickly pick a color from the current color space. When you rest your cursor above the Color Ramp area, the cursor changes into an eyedropper. Figure 2-48 shows the Color Ramps for grayscale, RGB (which is the same as HSB), CMYK, and Spot colors.

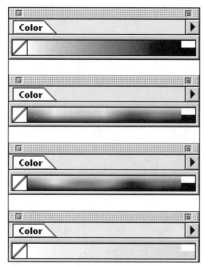

Figure 2-48: Color Ramps from top to bottom: grayscale, RGB, CMYK, and Spot colors

New Feature New to Illustrator 8 is the addition of the None swatch to the Color palette. This is available in all Color Ramps. Click the None swatch to apply no color to the Fill or Stroke swatch. When you click the None swatch, you'll get the option to apply the last color that was previously in the swatch before you applied None.

ASK TOULOUSE: Tinting Process Colors

Starbuck: Why isn't there a tint control for process colors?

Toulouse: That would be too confusing: you'd have a 50% tint of 20% cyan, 50% magenta, and 10% black, which would really be 10% Cyan, 25% Magenta, and 5% Black.

Starbuck: Do I have to do all that math each time I want to change a process tint?

Toulouse: You can, but there's a shortcut. . . .

Starbuck: I thought all the letters on the keyboard were used up, but go ahead, tell me.

Toulouse: All you do is press Shift before you drag a slider, and all the sliders with values move along with the one you're dragging.

Starbuck: Wow! Great! Wait, it goes too fast, much too hard to control . . .

Toulouse: When adjusting the tint this way, be sure to move the slider with the largest percentage, as it gives you more control. The other sliders will move proportionately with that one.

Click any portion of the Color Ramp to select that color. In Illustrator 8, the RGB, HSB, and CMYK Color Ramps have even larger rectangles of black and white than in previous Illustrator versions to make choosing them easier. The grayscale and Spot Color Ramps have large areas for both 0% and 100% to make selecting those percentages easier. You can also drag over the Color Ramp, watching the large square in the top of the Color palette (if Options are showing) to see the color you're dragging over. If Options aren't shown, look at the active Fill/Stroke icon in the toolbox to see the color you're currently positioned over (this *only* works when the mouse button is pressed as you pass across the Color Ramp).

 New Feature New in Illustrator 8, Fill and Stroke swatches are now available in the Color Palette.

 Tip You can press the X key while dragging around the Color Ramp to switch between the Fill and Stroke focus. This way you can quickly select colors for both Fill and Stroke with *one* mouse click! If the Fill is in focus, click and drag through the Color Ramp to the appropriate color. Then, with the mouse button still pressed, press the X key; you'll now be picking a color for the Stroke. Want to change the Fill again? Just press X, keeping the mouse button down.

 Tip Here's a supercool power tip: Option[Alt]-clicking anywhere on a Color Ramp affects the opposite attribute! For instance, if Stroke is in focus on the toolbox, Option[Alt]-clicking on a Color Ramp changes the Fill color, not the stroke. Be aware, however, that Option[Alt]-clicking on a swatch in the Swatches palette does *not* affect the opposite attribute; this only works on a Color Ramp (and the color box in the Color palette).

Gamut Trouble

If you choose certain colors in the RGB or HSB color spaces, a little icon will appear in the lower left of the Color palette (see Figure 2-49). This icon is indicating that the current color is out of gamut with CMYK color space. This issue is only important if you'll be printing the document using CMYK process colors. If you'll be using the image onscreen, such as in Web or multimedia publishing, it doesn't matter if the color is in gamut or not.

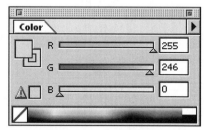

Figure 2-49: The Out of Gamut indicator appears when the current color cannot be accurately converted into CMYK values

The best way to reset the current color to CMYK color space is to click the Out of Gamut icon. The RGB or HSB values change so that the resulting color is well within CMYK color space. Another way to change the current color to CMYK color space is to choose CMYK from the Color palette pop-up menu.

Tip

If you want to change the color space of several objects — or perhaps your entire document — to CMYK, select the objects to be changed and choose Filter ➪ Colors ➪ Convert to CMYK. There are also filters for changing the color space to grayscale and RGB.

Spot Colors

Spot colors are colors in Illustrator that aren't separated into process colors (Cyan, Magenta, Yellow, and Black) when printed. Instead, they are printed on a different separation. A commercial printer uses special ink (commonly Pantone) for this spot color.

You can use as many spot colors in an illustration as you would like, though it isn't usually practical or desirable to have more than four in one document (because CMYK printing can duplicate most colors, process colors are often a better choice than four spot colors). Illustrator's default Swatch libraries (choose Window ➪ Swatch Libraries ➪ Your Library) contain mostly spot colors that you can choose among, or you can create your own. To create your own Spot color, create a new swatch with the appearance (using the color sliders) you want. Then change the Swatch type from Process to Spot in the Swatch Options dialog box (access Swatch Options by double-clicking the swatch). When you use that swatch as a Fill or Stroke, it will be considered a spot color when it comes time to print.

Spot colors are indicated in the Swatches palette in Small Swatch and Large Swatch views by a white triangle containing a black dot in the lower right of the spot color swatch. Name view shows a square with a circle inside of it (a "spot") on the right edge of the swatch listing.

Tip You can convert any spot color to a standard CMYK color (the color, not the swatch) by selecting the spot color and then changing the color space in the Color palette to CMYK. You can even change the color space to grayscale, RGB, or HSB in this way. This only works on the selected paths; the swatch itself is not affected.

Putting All the Color Palettes to Use

Now you know how the palettes work, but how do you change the color of paths to what's in the palettes? The easiest thing to do is to select the path you want to change the Fill or Stroke (or both) of, change the focus (if necessary) of the Fill/Stroke icons, and select a color from either the Color or Swatches palette. Press X to change the color for the other (Fill or Stroke).

The key here is *selecting*. If you have the paths selected, any changes you make will affect those selected paths.

When you create a new path, it will be the Fill and Stroke that are currently displayed in the Paint Style section of the toolbox.

To apply colors to text, you can either select an entire text area with a Selection tool, or select individual characters with a Type tool.

Caution Selecting Type with a Selection tool can cause type paths and type areas to be Filled and Stroked as well as the type. You can use the Group Selection tool to deselect the associated paths, or, better yet, just use the Type tool and drag across the characters you want to select.

Dif'rent Strokes for Dif'rent Folks

The Stroke palette (shown in Figure 2-50) contains everything you need to control the way your stroke looks — except its color. To change the color of a stroke, the Stroke icon must be active (in front of the Fill icon, in focus). Then you can select a swatch from the Swatches palette or choose a color from the Color palette.

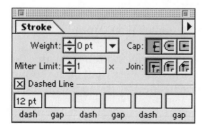

Figure 2-50: The Stroke palette

Instead of changing the color of the Stroke, the Stroke palette lets you change the thickness of the Stroke, the caps and joins, and the dash pattern of the Stroke.

Stroke Weight

The thickness of the Stroke is called the Stroke Weight, which you can change by either selecting a preset weight from the Weight pop-up menu, or by typing in a value in the Weight text field. The Weight of a stroke is always evenly divided between each side of the path to which it is applied. So a 1-point Stroke has ½ point on each side of the path.

Tip   Use mathematical operations in the Stroke Weight palette! You can mathe-matically change the current Stroke Weight by adding, subtracting, multiplying, or dividing. Just place the appropriate symbol (+ for add, - for subtract, * for multiply, and / for divide) after the current value, and then the number you want to perform the operation by.

Strokes can never be wider than 1,000 points. A Stroke with a weight of 0 can exist in Illustrator, though I wouldn't recommend that you choose such a value. Instead, set the Stroke to None. If you do set a weight to 0, the path will have a stroke as thick as 1 device pixel of the output device. For a 300-dpi laser printer, that would be a healthy quarter-point thick. For a typical 1270-dpi imagesetter, that would be about ¹⁄₁₇th point, or a fourth of a quarter point; much too small to use for most purposes. Because a stroke of 0 will change to match the output device (it will appear 1 pixel thick onscreen, appearing to be a 1-point stroke), the potential changes in thickness can drastically change the way an image looks. Be very careful if you choose to venture into this area of Illustrator.

Caps

There are three different Cap styles that can be applied to strokes:

✦ **Butt Caps** chop the stroke off perpendicularly at the end of the path, in addition to being good ammo for Illustrator bathroom humor.

✦ **Rounded Caps** are smooth, rounded ends that resemble a half-circle. These caps protrude from the End Point ½ the Stroke Weight.

✦ **Projected Caps** project from the endpoint ½ the Stroke Weight and appear perpendicular to the direction of the path at its End Point.

Caps apply only to End Points on open paths. You can choose a Cap style for a closed path (with no End Points), but nothing will happen; if the path is cut into an open path, that Cap style goes into effect.

The Cap styles are shown in Figure 2-51.

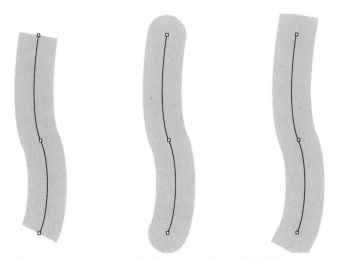

Figure 2-51: Butt Caps (left), Round Caps (middle), and Projected Caps (right)

Joins

Three different Join types can be applied to paths:

✦ **Mitered Joins** cause the outer edges of the stroke to meet at a point. This Join type is the only one affected by the miter limit.

    ✦ **Rounded Joins** round off the outside edge of corners.

    ✦ **Beveled Joins** are cropped off before the angle can reach a corner.

The three Join styles are shown in Figure 2-52.

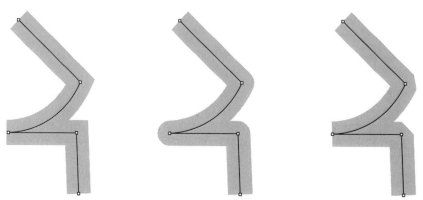

Figure 2-52: Mitered Joins (left), Rounded Joins (middle), and Beveled Joins (right)

Joins only affect Corner points, including Straight Corner points, Curved Corner points, and Combination Corner points. In all cases, Join types only affect outside corners. Inside corners always appear mitered.

The Miter Limit option controls how far a corner can extend past the edge of the path. This is important for tight corners of paths with large Weights, as the place where the outside edges would meet in a corner could be really far away from the original edges of the paths. The number in the Miter Limit controls how many times the width of the stroke the Miter can extend beyond the point. The default is 4, which is good for the majority of applications.

Dashes

The bottom of the Stroke palette controls if and how dashed strokes should appear. Checking the Dashed Line box allows you to enter different values for up to three dash and gap lengths. Figure 2-53 shows different Stroked paths with their Dashed Line settings.

Chapter 17 provides Stroke dash charts and several projects for utilizing Strokes to their fullest.

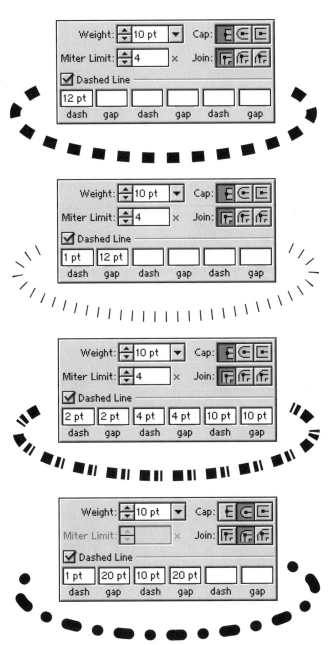

Figure 2-53: Dashed lines and their settings

The Eyedropper and Paintbucket Tools

The Eyedropper and Paintbucket tools are lifesavers for those of us who are constantly using up notes to jot down what the percentages of CMYK (Cyan, Magenta, Yellow, and Black) are in one path so that we can apply those same amounts to another path. Double-clicking either tool brings up the Paintbucket/ Eyedropper dialog box (shown in Figure 2-54), where you can select or deselect multiple options regarding paint style information.

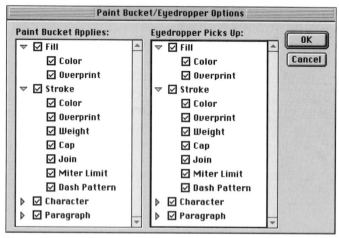

Figure 2-54: The Paintbucket/Eyedropper dialog box

 New Feature   New to Illustrator 8 is the capability to use the Eyedropper and Paintbucket tools with Type. This makes it speedy to absorb and apply colors to type. For more on this new feature see Chapter 8.

The Eyedropper Tool

The Eyedropper tool, shown with the Paintbucket tool in Figure 2-55, samples paint style information from a path or a placed image and stores it in the Paint Style fill and stroke boxes (on the toolbox), without selecting that path. The information stays there until you change the information in the color palette, select another path with different paint style information, or click any other path or placed image with a different paint style. Pressing the Shift key when the Eyedropper tool is active allows it to do *Direct Sucking*. Direct Sucking is used to pull colors from anywhere, including such areas as palettes, window edges, and from within gradients.

 Figure 2-55: The Paintbucket and Eyedropper tools

Tip If you have paths selected when you click with the Eyedropper tool, all selected objects in the document are changed to the paint style of the path that you clicked on. If you hold down the Option [Alt] key and click the Eyedropper tool, it toggles to the Paintbucket tool.

The Paintbucket Tool

The Paintbucket tool is used for applying the current paint style to both paths and 1-bit TIFF images.

Holding down the Shift key when clicking a path fills the Paintbucket tool with the current paint style and also selects that path. If the path was already selected, a Shift-click deselects it. Pressing the Option [Alt] key toggles from the Paintbucket tool to the Eyedropper tool.

ASK TOULOUSE: Why Use the Eyedropper and Paintbucket Tools?

Baltazar: Why should I use the Paintbucket and Eyedropper tools? It seems like a lot of work.

Toulouse: One reason is that you can be assured that your colors are consistent throughout the illustration. So, for example, if you used a custom color somewhere that you want to use again somewhere else, you don't try to duplicate it with a CMYK mix that may not be an exact match. And you don't have to select the objects you're clicking with the Paintbucket tool.

Baltazar: What's all this nonsense about sampling colors from pixel-based images?

Toulouse: You can sample colors from any placed image. And that's not all.

Baltazar: It's not?

Toulouse: You can sample colors right on your desktop or from within a Photoshop document that's open in the background.

Baltazar: Wow. Does the Eyedropper sample an average color, like that "other" illustration program?

Toulouse: No, it samples the exact pixel you click on.

Baltazar: Thanks for the info. I won't tell the Cylons, honest.

Toulouse: Oh, sure, rat out your race but keep quiet about graphics applications. . . . I believe you.

Summary

✦ Illustrator provides basic drawing capabilities by allowing you to quickly draw basic objects with specialized tools, such as the Rectangle, Ellipse, Star, Polygon, and Spiral tools.

✦ The toolbox contains Fill and Stroke icons; choose one to change its color attributes.

✦ The Swatches palette is used to store and apply commonly used colors.

✦ Pantone colors can be accessed by choosing Window ➪ Swatch Libraries ➪ Pantone.

✦ The Color palette enables you to choose colors from a Color Ramp and to mix colors using interactive sliders.

✦ Change the color space from grayscale to CMYK to RGB to HSB by selecting one from the Color pop-up menu.

✦ The Stroke palette is used to change the Stroke weight, cap and join style, and Dash pattern.

✦ Paths and type can be colored quickly by using the Eyedropper tool (to sample colors from paths or placed images) and the Paintbucket tool (to apply those sampled colors).

✦ You can apply the most recently selected color to an object by using the Last Color option in the Color palette.

✦   ✦   ✦

Drawing and Manipulating Paths

The most effective (and challenging) way to create paths is to draw them with one of the drawing tools. The Paintbrush and Pencil tools have been enhanced in Version 8. Adobe has added a Brushes palette as well as three new brushes: the Art Brush, the Scatter Brush, and the Pattern Brush. Illustrators looking for the Calligraphic option will find it as a brush option to choose from in the Brush palette. The Pencil tool has added the Smooth tool and the Erase tool to its pop-up menu which cuts editing time drastically.

Drawing Paths in Illustrator

Using the Paintbrush tool is the easiest way to create paths. It is even more amazing when you use it with a pressure-sensitive tablet. The Pencil tool is simple to use to create paths and with its new editing capabilities, it can be quite indispensable. The Pen tool is the most difficult to use, but the results from it can be better than the Paintbrush or the Pencil tool.

Each drawing tool does something better than any of the others, as well as having its own limitations. However tempting it may be, don't ignore any one of these tools because you think that another tool can perform the same function.

If I were a gambling man, I'd bet that the one tool that you want to avoid is the Pen tool. Unfortunately, mastering Illustrator becomes impossible if you avoid learning how to use this tool. Hey, I won't kid you — mastering the Pen tool is like mastering calculus: It makes no sense at first and even less sense when people explain it to you. But, as with calculus, the more you use the Pen tool, the more you like it, and the more technically amazing things you can do with it. (Personally, I think the Pen tool is easier to learn than calculus, and, fortunately, this shaky analogy ends here.)

Note   Understanding how the Pen tool works helps you understand not only how Illustrator works but also how PostScript and many other tools in other programs work. Adobe Photoshop also has a Pen tool that is virtually identical to Illustrator's Pen tool; so by understanding and using the Pen tool in Illustrator, you've already learned one of the most difficult tools to use in Photoshop.

Figure 3-1 was drawn with a combination of all three drawing tools. Throughout this chapter, I explain how the various parts of this illustration were drawn and how they were manipulated to produce the final drawing.

Figure 3-1: This illustration was drawn using the Paintbrush, Pencil, and Pen tools

About the Paintbrush Tool

The Paintbrush tool has changed in version 8. Now instead of drawing only a closed path that is difficult to edit, it draws a stroked path. This makes life so much easier when it comes to editing.

The Paintbrush tool is similar to paintbrush-type tools in painting programs; the Paintbrush has a certain width and you can paint with this Paintbrush at this width anywhere in your document. The big difference between paint programs' paintbrushes and Illustrator's paintbrush is that when you finish drawing with Illustrator's Paintbrush tool, a stroked path has been created.

To use the Paintbrush tool, choose the tool, then choose the brush from the Brush palette, and start drawing. A freeform path appears wherever you drag. That's all there is to it. Kinda. Figure 3-2 shows a drawing that was created with the Paintbrush tool set to a variable width with a pressure-sensitive stylus.

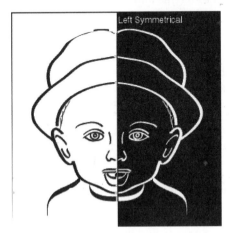

Figure 3-2: A drawing created with the Paintbrush tool using a Wacom tablet with a pressure-sensitive stylus

Drawing with the Paintbrush tool is a bit more complicated than I just explained. The most important consideration is the width of the paintbrush stroke. The paintbrush stroke can be as narrow as 0 points and as wide as 1,296 points (that's 18 inches to you and me).

Although 0 is the smallest width, a paintbrush stroke drawn with a width of 0 points actually has a width bigger than 0 points. To change the paintbrush stroke width (the default is 9 points), double-click the brush in the Brush palette (*not* the toolbox) and enter a number in the Diameter text field. Remember that you are actually changing that default brush. If you want to create a totally new brush, choose New Brush from the Brushes palette pop-up menu and select the type of new brush you want to make.

Results achieved with the Paintbrush tool vary depending on two very important characteristics: your artistic ability and your ability to control the mouse. If you can't draw with a pencil or other forms of traditional media, there is very little likelihood that using a mouse will turn you into a Michelangelo (the artist, not the turtle). If Michelangelo had to use a mouse to draw, he probably would have become a philosopher or sunk so low as to be an editor for a Mac magazine, constantly complaining about the inefficient means by which cursors are controlled.

A mouse is *not* an intuitive drawing tool, and not being able to draw in the first place makes it even more difficult to draw with the Paintbrush tool. So, if artists have trouble with the mouse, what's the point of having the Paintbrush tool at all? Well, instead of a mouse, you can use several types of alternative drawing devices. The best of these is a pressure-sensitive tablet. Trackballs with locking buttons are also good for drawing with the Paintbrush tool (this allows more control over the direction and speed of the paintbrush).

Note   When you're drawing with any of the tools in Illustrator, dragging off the edge of the window causes the window to scroll, which creates a frightening effect for the uninitiated. If you don't want the window to remain where it scrolled to, don't let go of the mouse button; instead, drag in the opposite direction until the window returns to the original position. To scroll the other way while still using a tool, drag off the other side of the window.

To help you draw more precisely, you have the option of changing the cursor shape from the cute little brush into cross hairs. Press the Caps Lock key (to engage it), and the cursor changes into cross hairs with a dot in the center. Press the Caps Lock key again (to release it), and the cursor returns to the brush shape. The dot at the center of the cross hairs is the center of any paintbrush stroke drawn with the Paintbrush tool. Normally, when the cursor is in the shape of a paintbrush, the tip is the center of the paintbrush stroke. Some people find it easier to draw when the paintbrush cursor is replaced with the precise cross hairs.

Drawing with the Paintbrush Tool

In this section, you create the grass and the horse outlines previously shown in Figure 3-1. Both can be drawn with or without a pressure-sensitive tablet (which is discussed in detail in "Variable Widths and Pressure-Sensitive Tablets," later in this chapter), although you can achieve better effects if you use a tablet.

1. Choose the Paintbrush tool from the toolbar, then choose a brush size from the Brushes palette. If the palette is not visible, then choose Window ➪ Show Brushes. Choose New Brush from the Brushes palette pop-up menu and choose the New Calligraphic Brush. In the Calligraphic Brush Options dialog box, set the Roundness to 50%, the Angle to 45°, the Diameter to 3 points, and the Variation to 0.5 point.

2. Using the Paintbrush tool, draw each piece of the basic shape of the horses, as shown in Figure 3-3. The more individual pieces you draw, the easier it is to use the Paintbrush tool. Long strokes are difficult to produce and aren't as appealing as shorter strokes. Don't worry about filling in the horses with color at this point. You are using the Paintbrush tool only to create the smoothly flowing outlines of the horses. If you make a mistake while drawing, choose Edit ➪ Undo (⌘-Z) [Ctrl+Z].

3. To draw the tall blades of grass, just draw a few select blade outlines to create a clump of grass. For the best effects, drag the Anchor Points from the base of the clump up and outward with the Scale tool and the Option [Alt] key pressed.

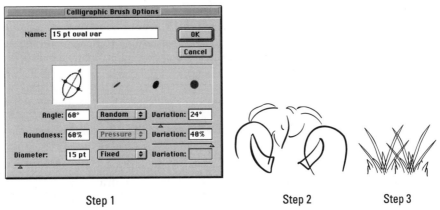

Step 1   Step 2   Step 3

Figure 3-3: Horse and grass outlines created with the Paintbrush tool

Creating a Brush

There are two ways to create a brush. If you like another brush, but not all aspects of it, duplicate that brush and edit its options to make it as you like. To edit a brush, double-click on the brush, or choose Brush Options from the pop-up menu or icon at the bottom of the Brushes palette. The other way to create a brush is to choose New Brush from the pop-up menu or to click on the New Brush icon at the bottom of the Brushes palette. This brings up a dialog box asking you to choose the type of brush you want to create (see Figure 3-4). You can create a Calligraphic Brush by filling in the text fields of the Calligraphic Brush dialog box. To create any of the other brushes, you have to have your art drawn first, then choose New Brush.

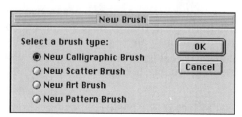

Figure 3-4: The New Brush dialog box

Brush Options

With each brush you have brush options to choose from. The Calligraphic, Scatter, Art, and Pattern brushes are your brush choices and each brush has different options to choose from.

The Calligraphic Brush

A Calligraphic Brush was made to simulate the actual calligraphic pen tip. You set the angle and size and draw to your heart's content. You can also create a perfectly round brush in the Calligraphic Brush dialog box by not entering an angle and by keeping the Roundness at 100%.

The Calligraphic Brush Options (shown in Figure 3-5) are as follows:

✦ **Name**: This option lets you give your new brush a name or rename an existing brush (maximum of 30 characters).

✦ **Angle**: You can set the angle of the Calligraphic paintbrush. The angle you should choose depends on what is going to be drawn. To mimic hand-drawn lettering in a calligraphic style, the angle should be set to 45° (or if you're left-handed, it should be set to –45°).

✦ **Roundness**: This does what you'd think it does. It sets the roundness of the brush. The higher the value the rounder the brush.

✦ **Diameter**: The diameter option will set the maximum diameter of the brush.

✦ **Variation**: If you choose the Random option from the Angle or Roundness pop-up menu, you then enter a value for Variation. The Variation for the Angle value is in a degree that you want to vary from the original setting. The Variation for the Roundness is set in percentages. A slider sets the Variation for the Diameter or you can enter a number. The Diameter Variation goes from your original value up to the Variation value.

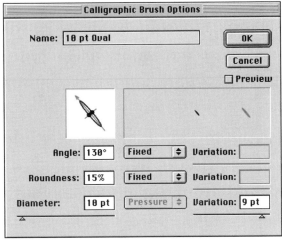

Figure 3-5: The Calligraphic Brush Options

Defining a Calligraphic Brush

There are many ways to use the Calligraphic Brush. You can choose an existing brush and get started. If you load additional brush libraries, you'll find quite a variety of brushes to choose from. You can also create your own brush from an existing one or from scratch. To create a new brush, I use an existing style that I like, but that I want to alter. To create a brush like this, choose Duplicate Brush from the Brush palette pop-up menu. You first have to select the brush you want to duplicate. To edit that duplicated brush, double-click on the duplicate brush, or select Brush Options from the pop-up menu. In the Brush Options dialog box, change the brush to your specifications.

Variable Widths and Pressure-Sensitive Tablets

If you have a pressure-sensitive tablet — some call them a Wacom (pronounced "walk 'em") tablet because a large majority tend to be made by Wacom — you can select the Pressure option beside the Diameter field in the Brush Options dialog box (accessed by double-clicking on a brush in the Brushes palette). If you don't have a pressure-sensitive tablet, the Pressure option is grayed out (unselectable).

Note   A *pressure-sensitive tablet* is a flat, rectangular device over which you pass a special stylus. The more pressure exerted by the stylus on the tablet, the wider a paintbrush stroke will be, providing the Pressure option in the Calligraphic dialog box is checked. When using the Pressure option, try to set the Variation different from the original specified diameter to see the difference when you press harder or lighter.

The Scatter Brush

The Scatter Brush copies and scatters a predefined object along a path. You have some default Scatter Brushes to choose from such as dog tracks, fall leaf, ladybug, pushpin, strawberry, and twinkling star. Figure 3-6 shows an example of each default Scatter Brush.

Figure 3-6: The Scatter Brush defaults applied to a path

The Scatter Brush Options (see Figure 3-7) are:

✦ **Name**: You can name your brush with up to 30 characters.

✦ **Size**: In the size area, you have two pop-up options: Fixed and Random. If you choose Fixed, then the size slider will only display the left options. The fixed size lets you enter a percentage so that all of the scattered images will be the exact same size. If you choose Random, the pop-up will display two sliders. With the Random option you can set up large and small scattered-images by changing the sliders for each. If you want really big images and small images that vary in size, then drag the sliders in opposite directions.

✦ **Spacing**: This option adjusts the space between each object.

✦ **Scatter**: The Scatter option adjusts how the objects follow the original path on each side of the path. If you set a high amount, the objects are farther away from the original path.

✦ **Rotation**: This option adjusts how much the object will rotate from its original position.

✦ **Rotation relative to**: This option gives you two choices from a pop-up menu: Page and Path. The Page option rotates objects according to the page setup. The Path option rotates objects tangent to the path.

✦ **Colorization**: There are four Colorization choices: None, Tints, Tints and Shades, and Hue Shift. For more on colorization and colorization tips, see "Colorization Tips," later in this chapter.

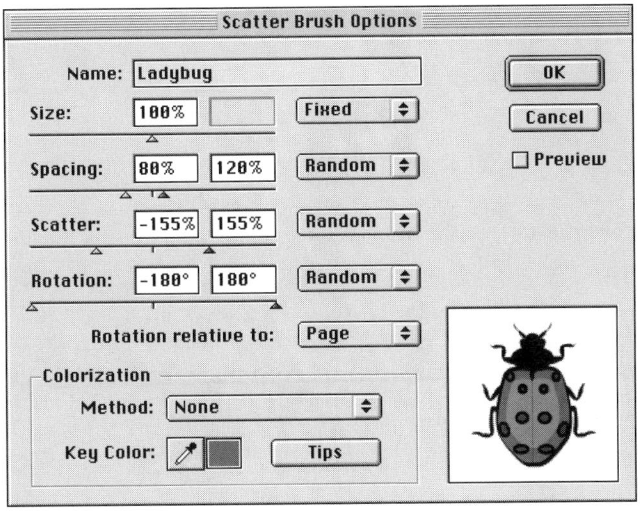

Figure 3-7: The Scatter Brush Options

The Art Brush

The Art Brush, like the Scatter Brush, uses an object along a path. The difference is that the Art Brush will stretch the object to the length of the path rather than repeat and scatter the object. The object is centered evenly over the path and then stretched. You can choose from the default Art Brushes or create an object of your own to use. Figure 3-8 shows the five default Art Brushes: Marker, Tapered Stroke, Arrow, Paintbrush, and Type.

Figure 3-8: The Art Brush default brushes

The Art Brush Options (see Figure 3-9) are:

✦ **Name**: You can name your new Art Brush or rename an existing Art Brush with up to 30 characters.

✦ **Direction**: This option lets you choose from four directions. The directions are relative to how you drag the paintbrush.

✦ **Size**: This option scales the art when it is stretched. You can choose Proportional to keep the object in proportion.

✦ **Flip**: The Flip option lets you flip your object along or across the path.

✦ **Colorization**: There are four Colorization choices: None, Tints, Tints and Shades, and Hue Shift. For more on colorization and colorization tips, see "Colorization Tips," later in this chapter.

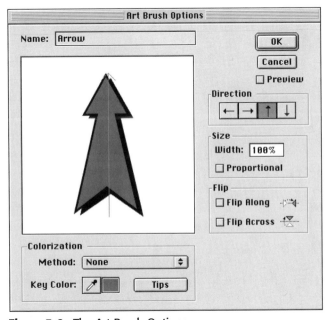

Figure 3-9: The Art Brush Options

The Pattern Brush

The Pattern Brush repeats a tiled object along a path. The Pattern Brush can have tiles to display the sides, inner corner, outer corner, beginning, and end. If you think of a Pattern Brush as you would a regular Pattern tile, but keep in mind the corners, you'll have no problem creating your own interesting Pattern Brushes. I like to take apart an existing pattern to see how it was created. To do this, select the Pattern Brush in the Brushes palette and drag it to an open area on your document. You'll see the individual tiles. Figure 3-10 shows all of the default Pattern Brushes.

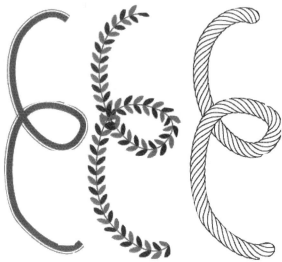

Figure 3-10: The default Pattern Brushes

The Pattern Brush Options (see Figure 3-11) are:

✦ **Name**: Enter a new name or change an existing name (up to 30 characters).

✦ **Tile button**: This is where you choose which of the five tiles you want to create.

✦ **Size**: This option lets you enter the size in proportion and the space between the tiles.

✦ **Flip**: This option lets you flip the pattern along or across the path.

✦ **Fit**: In this option, you can choose Stretch to Fit, Add Space to Fit, or Approximate Path. Stretch will lengthen or shorten a tile to fit your object. Add Space will add a blank space between the tiles to fit the path proportionately. Approximate Path will make the tile fit as close to the original path without altering the tiles.

✦ **Colorization**: There are four Colorization choices: None, Tints, Tints and Shades, and Hue Shift. For more on colorization and colorization tips, see "Colorization Tips," later in this chapter.

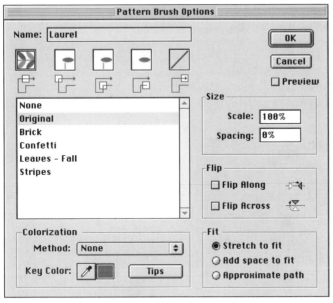

Figure 3-11: The Pattern Brush Options

Creating a Scatter, Art, or Pattern Brush

To create your own Scatter Brush design, first create the object that you want to use. Next, select all of the parts of the object that you want as a brush and choose New Brush from the Brushes palette pop-up menu. Then choose the type of brush you want to create. The Brush Options dialog box will display and you will see your new design there. Now all you have to do is set the rest of the options and you are ready to use this new brush. The following steps give an example of how to create a new Art Brush; the steps are illustrated in Figure 3-12.

1. Starting with your ellipse tool create an oval for the outside of the eye. Make that oval with no Fill and a Black 1-point Stroke.

2. Create a circle inside your oval by holding down the Shift key. Give that circle a color.

3. Create another circle inside the colored one and give it a Black Fill.

4. Create another circle a little offset from the Black one and give it a White Fill.

5. Select the whole eye and choose New Brush from the Brushes palette pop-up menu.

6. Choose the Art Brush for your brush type. (You could choose Scatter, Art, or Pattern.)

7. Change the options as you'd like, then click OK.

8. Drag a path with the Brush tool to see the results.

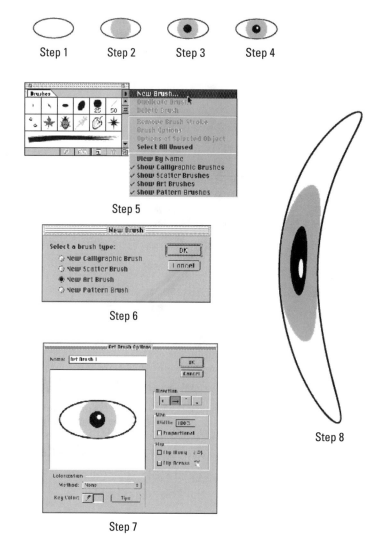

Figure 3-12: The steps to create an eyeball Art Brush

Colorization Tips

The Colorization Tips displays a dialog box that explains the different colorization options. Figure 3-13 shows the Colorization Tips dialog box. There are four areas of Colorization: None, Tints, Tints and Shades, and Hue Shift.

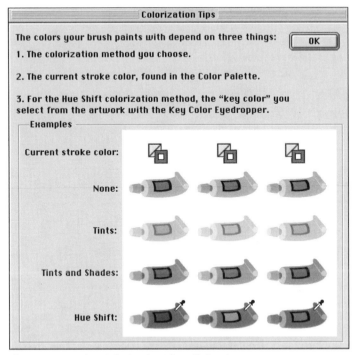

Figure 3-13: The Colorization Tips dialog box

To see how the Colorization options work, first create four copies of a brush. For example, use the red arrow brush. Then draw four red arrows. The first arrow uses the default of None. For the next three arrows change the Stroke color (you won't see anything happen yet). On the second arrow, double-click one of the copy arrow brushes you made and select Tint. Apply to Stroke when asked in the dialog box. The color should change at this point. Select the third arrow and double-click a different copy of the arrow brush and select Tints and Shades. Select the last arrow and double-click the last copy and select Hue Shift. All of the arrows should look different.

Brush Libraries

The Brush Library that displays when you choose the Brush palette is the default Library. You have seven additional Libraries to choose from. Adobe has really come up with some cool brushes for our creative pleasure. The Brush Libraries are found under the Window menu, as shown in Figure 3-14. Figure 3-15 shows all of the Brush Libraries you have to choose from.

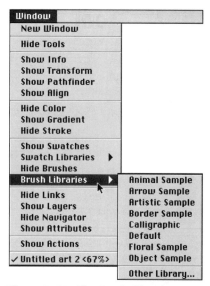

Figure 3-14: The Brush Libraries pop-up menu under the Window menu

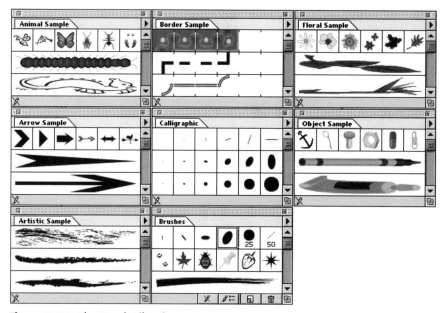

Figure 3-15: The Brush Libraries

Drawing Loosely with the Pencil Tool

The Pencil tool initially seems to be a primitive version of the Paintbrush tool. Like the Paintbrush tool, the Pencil tool draws a freeform Stroked path wherever the cursor is dragged, but instead of creating a closed path that is a certain width, the result is a single path that approximately follows the route you've taken with the cursor. You can get the resulting path to follow your cursor-drawn line exactly by lowering the curve-fitting tolerance.

When you need to draw rough edges or realistic illustrations that don't look "computery," the Pencil tool is the tool to use. It draws a path wherever you drag the tool with the mouse, creating Smooth Points and corner Anchor Points relative to how you draw. Although the Pen tool is the tool to use to get precise, super-straight lines, it is difficult to use. The Pencil tool is much easier to use, but it draws lines that are far from perfect.

The Pencil tool has the unique capability to make the lines you draw with the cursor look . . . well . . . good. A swooping, uneven, jagged line that looks terrible as it is being drawn can be instantly transformed into a beautifully curved piece of artwork reminiscent of lines drawn traditionally with a French curve.

Still, the Pencil tool has some limitations. The main limitation is that, unlike the Pen tool, it is an *imprecise* path-drawing tool. It is difficult to draw a straight line with the Pencil tool. It is even more difficult to draw a shape with precise curves. The location of a path drawn with the Pencil tool is directly relevant to the direction and speed that the cursor is moving. Despite these limitations, and because of these limitations, Adobe has added two new tools to the Pencil tool's pop-up options: the Smooth tool, which smooths out lines of a selected path, and the Erase tool, which erases sections out of a selected path.

Using the Pencil Tool

Before you use the Pencil tool for the first time, it's a good idea to change the Paint Style attributes to a Fill of None and a Stroke of Black, 1 point. Having a Fill other than None while drawing with the Pencil tool often results in bizarre-looking shapes.

To use the Pencil tool, select it from the toolbox, click in the document window, and begin dragging the mouse. As you drag, a series of dots follows the cursor. These dots show the approximate location of the path you have drawn. After you release the mouse button, the path of dots is transformed into a path with Anchor Points, all with Control Handle Lines and Control Handles shooting off from them. The faster you draw with the Pencil tool, the fewer points that are created. The slower you draw, the more points that are used to define the path.

1. Choose File ➪ Preferences ➪ Type & Auto Tracing and set the Auto Trace tolerance setting to 2, which allows for detail in the paths without making all the segments straight lines. Using the Color and Stroke palettes, set the Fill to C100 Y70 and a Stroke of Black, 1 point.

2. You can create the short grass by drawing three different clumps of grass (see the top of Figure 3-16) and then duplicating the clumps to create the appearance of random blades. To do this, select the Pencil tool and drag up and down to create the blades; then drag across under the blades to connect the bottom to form a closed path. Repeat this procedure to create three or four clumps of different sizes. Be sure to change the Fill color to a slightly different greenish color each time.

3. Using the Selection tool, click the clumps of grass and Option[Alt]-drag them side by side, overlapping them slightly. (Pressing the Option [Alt] key duplicates the dragged clumps.) Repeat this process until there are enough clumps to resemble a grassy area.

4. To create the tree, first change the Auto Trace tolerance setting to 7 in the Type & Auto Tracing preferences dialog box. Drag with the Pencil tool to create the outline of the tree branch, trunk, and roots. Connect the ends of the path to close it and change the Fill to a dark brown (C75 M100 Y100 K25), keeping the Stroke set to Black.

5. To create the textured areas of the bark on the tree, change the Fill to None and the Stroke to a dark shade of Gray. Drag along the contours of the tree, which creates circles and wavy patterns.

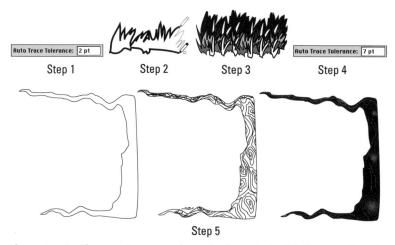

Figure 3-16: Clumps of grass and tree bark created with the Pencil tool

Every Anchor Point created with the Pencil tool has two Control Handles shooting out of it; this means that Straight Corner Points cannot be drawn with the Pencil tool. This lack of Straight Corner Points makes constructing precise objects not only difficult, but also nearly impossible. Also, although they may appear to exist at first glance, smooth Anchor Points are not created with the Pencil tool, which can be especially deceiving when the Auto Trace option is set to a high number and all the Anchor Points look like they are Smooth Points. This is *not* the case. In fact, most Anchor Points created with the Pencil tool—except for its End Points— are *Curved Corner Points,* which are Anchor Points with two independent Control Handles shooting out. If the Auto Trace setting is high enough, you'll get Smooth Points as well. (See "Jagged Paths versus Smooth Paths," later in this chapter for more information.)

Normally, the Pencil tool resembles a little pencil when you are drawing, which is far better than having to draw with the little squiggle that appears in the toolbox. The line of dots that is drawn comes directly from the point (tip) of the pencil cursor. Pressing the Caps Lock key (engaging it) changes the cursor from the pencil shape to cross hairs, which looks suspiciously like the cross hairs from the Paintbrush tool. The line of points comes from the dot in the center of the cross hairs.

Note
If you like using the cross hairs cursors all the time, but get really mad that every time you start typing you forget to take off the Caps Lock key, you've got short-term memory problems. Fortunately, you can set your cursors to *always* be cross hairs style just by going to General Preferences (⌘-K) [Ctrl+K] and checking the Use Precise Cursors checkbox. When this option is checked, the Caps Lock key changes the cursor back to the regular tool.

Drawing Open Paths and Closed Paths

You can draw both open and closed paths with the Pencil tool. An *open path* has two separate, distinct End Points. A *closed path* has no End Points. To change an open path into a closed path, the End Points must be joined together. (Joining is discussed in Chapter 7.)

Paths in Illustrator may cross themselves. When these paths cross, the Fills may look a little unusual. Strokes look normal; they just overlap where paths cross.

To create an open path, draw a path with the Pencil tool, but make sure that the beginning and end of the path are two separate points at different locations. Open paths with Fills may look a little bizarre because Illustrator automatically fills-in between the End Points on the path, even if the imaginary line between the End Points crosses the path itself. Figure 3-17 shows both open and closed paths drawn with the Pencil tool.

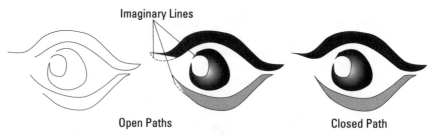

Imaginary Lines

Open Paths

Closed Path

Figure 3-17: Paths drawn with the Pencil tool

To create a closed path, end your path at the same place that you started the path. When the pencil cursor is directly over the location where the line begins, the eraser end of the pencil (at the opposite end from the tip) turns black and a little circle appears to the lower right of the pencil. This change means that the path is a closed path if you release the mouse button when that particular cursor is showing.

Drawing Semistraight Segments

You can draw semistraight segments — that is, segments that look straight but, on closer inspection, are really just a teeny bit curved — with the Pencil tool. To draw these segments, start drawing with the Pencil tool and press the ⌘ [Ctrl] key at the point where you want the semistraight segment to begin. The cursor changes to an eraser (see the next section for details on erasing). Keep dragging to where you want the semistraight segment to end and release the ⌘ [Ctrl] key to continue drawing with the Pencil tool.

Notice that the dots that normally appear along the path that the Pencil tool takes do not appear between the area where you first pressed the ⌘ [Ctrl] key and where you released the ⌘ [Ctrl] key; this is normal. After you are done drawing, release the mouse button and a semistraight line segment appears between the locations where you pressed and then released the ⌘ [Ctrl] key. On further inspection with the Direct Selection tool, you will see that Control Handles extend out from the Anchor Points on either side of the semistraight segment.

One of the important things to remember in this process is that you should never release the mouse button while pressing the ⌘ [Ctrl] key. You can create as many semistraight segments in a path drawn with the Pencil tool as you like by pressing and holding the ⌘ [Ctrl] key for each of them. Keep in mind, however, that when drawing multiple semistraight segments, there must be some movement of the mouse between drawing the semistraight segments. After you press the ⌘ [Ctrl] key, move the mouse, and then release the ⌘ [Ctrl] key, you *must* move the mouse before you press the ⌘ [Ctrl] key again to create a new segment. If the mouse is not moved between ⌘ [Ctrl]-key presses, only one segment is drawn, from the location where the ⌘ [Ctrl] key is initially pressed to the location where it is ultimately released.

A problem with drawing semistraight segments is that it is difficult to see exactly where to place the End Point of the segment because the cursor looks like a huge eraser. If you press the Caps Lock key before the ⌘ [Ctrl] key, the big fat eraser cursor becomes the suave dotted cross hairs cursor.

Of course, it is my belief that the ⌘ [Ctrl] key was never intended to be used with the Pencil tool to draw these semistraight lines. In fact, the only real reason the ⌘ [Ctrl] key does anything like this at all is because it is used for erasing.

Jagged Paths versus Smooth Paths

Because drawing nice-looking paths with the Pencil tool and a mouse is just a tad difficult and frustrating ("Really?" you ask sarcastically), Illustrator provides a way to determine how rough or smooth your path will be *before* you draw it.

Normally, paths that appear from the dotted lines created with the Pencil tool are fairly similar to those dotted lines in direction and curves and such. When lines are being drawn, though, human error can cause all sorts of little bumps and *skiddles* (a skiddle is a little round misdrawn section resembling a small fruit-flavored candy) to appear, making the path look lumpy. In some cases, lumpy is good. More often than not, though, lumpy is an undesirable state for your illustrations.

The smoothness of the resulting paths drawn with the Pencil tool relies on the Auto Trace option in the Preferences dialog box, which determines how jagged or smooth each section will appear from the dotted line to the path.

The Auto Trace option is a value between 0 and 10 that determines the smoothness of the paths drawn, with 0 being rough, and 10 being really smooth. To change the Auto Trace options, choose File ➪ Preferences ➪ Type & Auto Tracing and enter a number between 0 and 10 in the Auto Trace text field. Figure 3-18 shows the same clump of grass created with different Auto Trace settings. After the number is changed, the new setting affects all paths drawn *after* the new value has been entered. Previously drawn curve-fitting paths are not affected by a change in the Auto Trace setting. The default value is 2, which is a good all-around value that supplies partially smooth curves and some detail.

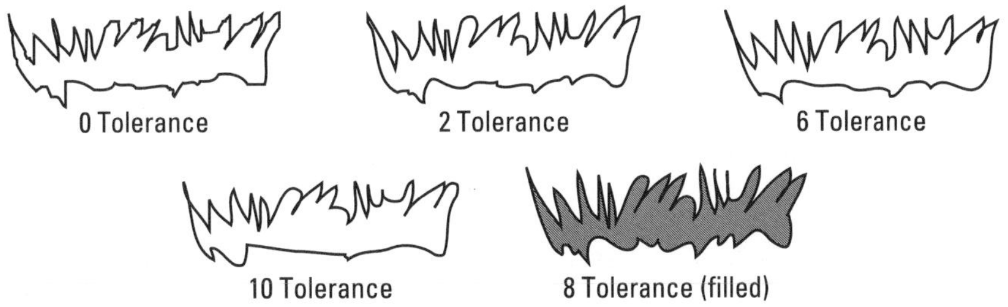

0 Tolerance 2 Tolerance 6 Tolerance

10 Tolerance 8 Tolerance (filled)

Figure 3-18: The result of different Auto Trace values

At an Auto Trace setting of 0, paths appear jagged and rough. Also, many more Anchor Points are present, although there are still no Straight Corner Points. A setting of 0 is great for creating some photorealistic illustrations of complex, detailed objects, such as tree leaves and textures. When the setting is this low, the resulting path follows the dotted line as closely as possible.

When the Auto Trace option is set to 10, paths created with the Pencil tool appear extremely smooth. The smallest number of Anchor Points is used, and the curve of the line appears to be very graceful. Because so few Anchor Points are used, much detail is lost, and the path wavers from the original dotted line of the Pencil tool by a significant amount. Even though it appears that all the Anchor Points are Smooth Points, they are actually Curved Corner Points with two independent Control Handles.

Because the Auto Trace setting is changed in the General Preferences dialog box, it retains its current value until it is changed, even if you quit Illustrator or restart the entire system.

Note   Auto Trace affects the way the Auto Trace tool (discussed in more detail in the next chapter) works in the same way as it affects the Pencil tool (higher numbers for smooth paths with few Anchor Points and lower numbers for jagged paths with many Anchor Points).

Adding to an Existing Open Path

To continue drawing on an existing path (which could have been drawn with the Pen tool or the Pencil tool), the existing path must first be an open path with two distinct End Points. After you pass your drawing tool over one end of the path with the Pencil tool, the pencil cursor changes into a pencil with a black eraser. This action means that if you click and drag, you can now extend the path with the Pencil tool. If the Caps Lock key is engaged, the cursor looks like cross hairs with a hollow box in the center.

Although you are continuing with the same path, you may not erase that part of the path that was in place before you added to it. You may, however, press the ⌘ [Ctrl] key and erase any part of the dotted line that appears from the new segment that you are drawing.

So far, all the points in paths drawn with the Pencil tool have been Curved Corner Points. This changes when you add to an existing path with the Pencil tool. The point that connects the existing path to the newly drawn path is a Smooth Point. No matter which way you drag, the point always is a Smooth Point. However, you can force a Curved Corner Point in place of the Smooth Point by pressing the Option [Alt] key while clicking the end of the existing path.

If you drag to the other open end of the existing path, you have the opportunity to make the path into a closed path. This point will also be a Smooth Point—unless you press the Option [Alt] key, at which time it changes into a Curved Corner Point.

You can add on only to End Points on an existing path. Anchor Points that are within paths cannot be connected to new (or existing, for that matter) segments. If you attempt to draw from an Anchor Point that is not an End Point, you create an End Point for the path you are drawing that is overlapping but not connected to the Anchor Point you clicked above.

Caution   Illustrator's pencil cursor changes the eraser to black whenever the pencil tip passes over any Anchor Point, not just End Points on open paths. This change can be a little confusing at first, so remember that you *absolutely cannot* add a new path to an existing path on an Anchor Point that is not an End Point.

Using the Smooth Tool

The Smooth tool is new to Illustrator 8. This extremely cool editing tool makes changing any path a breeze. The Smooth tool is found in the Pencil tool's pop-up tools. The Smooth tool works on any path regardless of what tool created it. To use the Smooth tool, you drag over a selected path to smooth out the line. In the Type and Auto Trace preferences, you set the sensitivity of the Pencil and Smooth tools. A lower setting results in more mouse movement being recorded and more anchor points. At a higher setting, fewer anchor points are used and the path is smoother. Figure 3-19 shows a path before and after using the Smooth tool. As you can see, the top path has more anchor points than the smoothed bottom path.

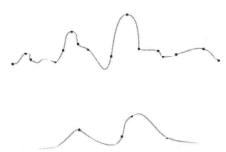

Figure 3-19: The path on the top is the original path. The path on the bottom is the same path after using the Smooth tool on it.

Using the Erase Tool

The Erase tool is another new feature of Illustrator 8. The Erase tool is found in the Pencil tool's pop-up menu. Like the Smooth tool, the Erase tool works on any path, no matter how it was created. The Erase tool does what you'd think, it erases a path at the point where you have dragged the Erase tool over the path. You can use the Erase tool to cut a path by dragging across a section. The section you dragged over will be removed. You can use the Erase tool to cut a line like you would the Scissor tool. If you just click one time on the path, the path would be cut exactly in that spot. Unlike Photoshop's clunky eraser-looking tool, this is much more refined and easier to use.

Precision Drawing with the Pen Tool

The Pen tool is the most powerful tool in Illustrator's arsenal because you are dealing more directly with Bézier curves than with any other tool. It's one thing to adjust paths, Anchor Points, and Control Handles with the Direct Selection tool, but using the Pen tool to create paths out of nothing is dumbfounding.

During the first several months of my using Illustrator, I avoided the Pen tool like it was the plague. Then I slowly worked up to where I could draw straight lines with it comfortably and, finally, curved segments. Even after I had been drawing curved segments for a while, I really didn't understand how the tool worked, and I was missing out on a lot of its capabilities because of that lack of knowledge. The manuals for Illustrator really aren't very clear on how to use the Pen tool, and no one I knew could do any better. To learn how to use it, I forced myself to use the Pen tool to draw objects that I could have just traced with the Auto Trace tool.

While practicing with the Pen tool, I necessarily learned about the four types of Anchor Points — Smooth Points, Straight Corner Points, Curved Corner Points, and Combination Corner Points — because the key to using the Pen tool is understanding how Anchor Points work.

The Pen tool draws points one at a time. The first click of the Pen tool produces one Anchor Point. The second click (usually in a different location) creates a second Anchor Point that is joined to the first Anchor Point by a line segment. Clicking without dragging produces a Straight Corner Point.

After you get the hang of it, the Pen tool isn't so bad — ask anyone who has been using Illustrator for, say, two years or longer. They like the Pen tool. I use the Pen tool more than the Paintbrush, Auto Trace, and Pencil tools combined.

I have approached this tool delicately because, although it is a little frustrating and confusing to use well, it is the most important tool to learn, and this is the one section of this book that you should really read carefully. (On the enclosed CD-ROM, there are several examples that should help to clarify the Pen tool's use.)

In our sample illustration (Figure 3-1), the weeds in the upper-right corner were created with the Pen tool. The weeds are composed entirely of straight lines that were duplicated in clumps, just as the long and short grasses were. Figure 3-20 shows the process used for creating the mass of weeds in the illustration.

1. Change the Paint Style to a Fill of Black and a Stroke of None. Using the Pen tool, click (don't drag!) at the top of the first weed (1). Then click lower at the bottom right of the first weed (2). Click to the left (3) and click back at the start point (4) to complete the weed. When the last weed in the clump has been finished, click the first Anchor Point to close the path.

2. Repeat Step 1 to create additional weeds, making clumps of them similar to the one in Figure 3-20.

3. With the Selection tool, Option[Alt]-drag the clumps a few times to create a mass of weeds.

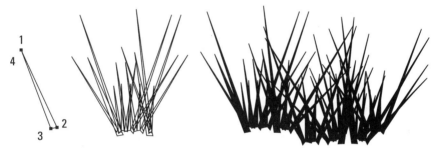

Figure 3-20: A clump of weeds drawn with the Pen tool

Caution

When drawing straight lines with the Pen tool, never drag with the mouse while pressing the button. Doing so results in at least one curved segment.

The Pen tool draws both curved and straight precise lines. With a little practice and by using the tips given in these pages, you can master the tool. In the process, you will understand Illustrator much better than is possible otherwise.

It would be really simple if the Pen tool did *all* the work, but you do have to do some of the labor involved in creating curves and straight lines yourself. Actually, using the Pen tool is easier than I have been letting on. All you have to do is place Anchor Points where you want the path to go.

Okay, I've oversimplified it just a bit. Drawing with the Pen tool isn't *just* placing Anchor Points. The first obstacle is to figure out where the heck those Anchor Points are going to go. Two drawings with the same number of Anchor Points can look totally different depending on where they're placed. You have to think ahead to determine what the path will look like before you draw it.

Points should always be located where there is a change in the path. That change can be a different curve or a corner. The three changes to look for are:

> ✦ A corner of any type.
>
> ✦ The point where a curve changes from clockwise to counterclockwise or vice versa.
>
> ✦ The point where a curve changes *intensity:* from tight to loose or loose to tight (by far, the hardest change to judge).

The second obstacle is to decide what type of Anchor Point you want to use. Remember, there are four different Anchor Points to choose from when drawing with the Pen tool:

> ✦ **Smooth Points** are Anchor Points with two connected Control Handles sticking out, resulting in a path that moves smoothly through the Anchor Point. Changing the angle of one Control Handle changes the angle of the other Control Handle. Changing the length of the Control Handle Line does not affect the other Control Handle. A Smooth Point guides the path along its journey but doesn't severely or suddenly alter that path's direction.
>
> ✦ **Straight Corner Points** are Anchor Points where two line segments meet in a corner. The line segments are not curved where they reach the Anchor Point, and there are no Control Handles. Straight Corner Points usually, but not always, distinctly change the direction of the path at the location where it passes through the Anchor Point.
>
> ✦ **Curved Corner Points** are Anchor Points where two different curved segments meet in a corner. There are two Control Handles coming out of a Curved Corner Point, but the Control Handles are independent of each other. Moving one Control Handle does not affect the other.
>
> ✦ **Combination Corner Points** are Anchor Points where two segments meet, one curved and one straight. There is one Control Handle on a Combination Corner Point. That Control Handle affects only the curved segment, not the straight segment.

If the path is smoothly curving, you use a Smooth Point. If there is a corner, use one of the Corner Points.

ASK TOULOUSE: Why Use the Pen Tool?

Vinnie: Why should I use the Pen tool instead of the other drawing tools?

Toulouse: The Pen draws paths *exactly* where you want them.

Vinnie: Yeah . . . that's it?

Toulouse: The Pen tool also draws curves.

Vinnie: I thought that's what the Pencil tool was for.

Toulouse: Yes, but the Pen draws *precise, perfect* curves.

Vinnie: Like the Ellipse tool.

Toulouse: Ah, there's a difference: The Pen draws curves one line segment at a time.

Vinnie: It sounds like a lot of work.

Toulouse: No, you just click and drag for each point. Once you get the hang of it, you'll be amazed that you ever used Illustrator without it.

Figure 3-21 shows each of the Anchor Point types.

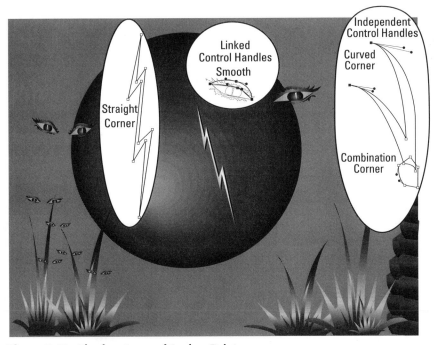

Figure 3-21: The four types of Anchor Points

The third obstacle arises when you decide that the Anchor Point should be anything but a Straight Corner Point because all the other Anchor Points have Control Handles. The obstacle is figuring out how to drag the Control Handles, how far to drag them, and in which direction to drag them.

Drawing Straight Lines

The easiest way to start learning to use the Pen tool is by drawing straight lines. The lightning bolt in Figure 3-22 was created entirely with straight lines. The great thing about straight lines drawn with the Pen tool is that there are no Control Handles to worry about or fuss over.

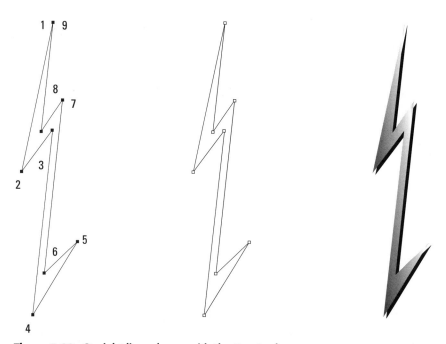

Figure 3-22: Straight lines drawn with the Pen tool

To draw the lightning bolt in Figure 3-22, click at each number with the Pen tool in order. Before you click at number 9, the Pen tool changes to a pen cursor with a little circle in the lower-right corner. This change signifies that the path is going to close when you click this point.

The simplest straight line is a line drawn with only two Anchor Points. To draw a line like this, select the Pen tool and click and release where you want the first End Point (the beginning of the line) to appear. Then click and release where you want the second End Point (the end of the line) to appear. A line appears between the two points. Too easy, isn't it?

Tip   Hold down the Shift key to keep the line constrained to a 45° angle (0, 45, 90, and zoom).

To draw another separate line, first click the Pen tool in the toolbox or hold down the ⌘ [Ctrl] key and click. Either action tells Illustrator that you are done drawing the first line. Clicking and releasing again in one spot and then another draws a second line with two End Points. Be careful not to drag when clicking the Pen tool to form straight lines.

Paths drawn with the Pen tool, like the Pencil tool, may cross themselves. The only strange result you may see involves the Fills for objects whose paths cross. In open paths created with the Pen tool, Fills may look unusual because of the imaginary line between the two End Points and any paths that the imaginary line crosses.

Closing Paths

If you want to create a closed path (one with no End Points), return to the first Anchor Point in that segment and click. As the Pen tool crosses over the beginning Anchor Point, the cursor changes to a pen with a circle in the lower-right corner. After you have created a closed path, there is no need to click the Pen tool again. Instead, the next click of the Pen tool in the document automatically begins a new path.

You must have at least three Anchor Points to create a closed path with straight lines. You can change the identity of one of these points to a different type of Anchor Point by curving one of the segments and giving the closed path some substance.

Drawing Curves

Initially, the worst thing about drawing curves with the Pen tool is that the whole process is rather disorienting. You actually have to think differently to grasp what the Pen tool is doing. The difference that you notice right away between drawing straight lines and drawing curves is that to draw a curve, you need to drag with the Pen tool; whereas, when drawing straight lines, you click and release.

The most basic of curves is the bump (a curved segment between just two points). A bump was used to create a path to fill the horses' rears (previously shown in Figure 3-1). Use the following steps to create the bump that is illustrated in Figure 3-23.

1. Click with the Pen tool and drag up about ½ inch. You'll see an Anchor Point and a Control Handle Line extending from it as you drag.

2. When you release the mouse button, you will see the Anchor Point and a line extending to where you dragged with a Control Handle at its end.

3. Position the cursor about 1 inch to the right of the place you first clicked.

4. Click with the mouse and drag down about ½ inch. As you drag, you see a curve forming that resembles a bump. When you release the mouse, the curve is Filled with the current Fill color. You also see the Control Handle you just dragged.

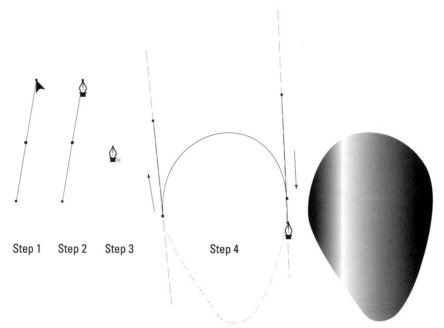

Step 1   Step 2   Step 3   Step 4

Figure 3-23: The four steps for creating a basic bump curve

Before you try to draw another curve, remember that the Pen tool is still in a mode that continues the current path; it does not start a new one. To start a new path, choose Deselect All (⌘-Shift-A) [Ctrl+Shift+A] or hold down ⌘ [Ctrl] and click an empty area onscreen. The next time you use the Pen tool, you will draw a separate path.

To create an S shape, one more set of steps is needed. The steps for creating the S shape are described below and illustrated in Figure 3-24.

1. Click and drag with the Pen tool about ½ inch to the left.

2. Release the mouse button. You should see the Anchor Point and the Control Handle that you just drew with a Control Handle Line between them.

3. Position the cursor about 1 inch below where you first clicked.

4. Click and drag to the right about ½ inch.

5. Release the mouse button.

6. Position the cursor about ½ inch below the last point you clicked.

7. Click and drag to the left, about ½ inch. Now you have an S shape. To make the S look more like a real S, change the Fill to None and the Stroke to Black, 1 point.

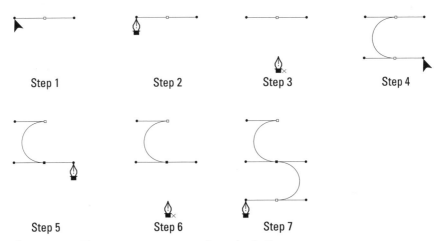

Figure 3-24: The seven steps to creating a basic S curve

All the Anchor Points we have created in these two examples are Smooth Points. The Control Handles were dragged in the direction of the next curve to be drawn, and the lengths of the Control Handle Lines on either side of the Anchor Point were equal.

The lengths of the Control Handle Lines on either side of the Smooth Point do not have to be the same. Instead, a Smooth Point may have both long and short Control Handle Lines coming out of it. The length of the Control Handle Line affects the curve, as shown on the S curve in Figure 3-25.

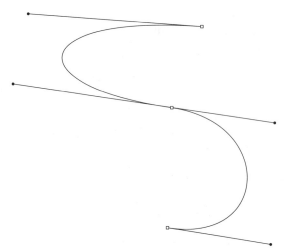

Figure 3-25: The length of the Control Handle
Lines controls the shape of the curve

ASK TOULOUSE: Making Bad Waves with the Pen

Boom-Boom Washington: I'm having loads of trouble with my paths and the Pen tool.

Toulouse: What sort of trouble? Lines not connecting? Lumps everywhere? Pen running out of ink?

Boom-Boom Washington: Actually, I'm getting the "wave" thing happening, except my waves have . . .

Toulouse: Curved tips. I've been there. It isn't pretty.

Boom-Boom Washington: Wow, it's like you're in my head, looking out. . . .

Toulouse: The wave effect you're describing usually happens when you click and drag with the Pen tool. . . .

Boom-Boom Washington: Uh-huh . . .

Toulouse: And then let go, and the next click is right on top of the Control Handle you've dragged out. You drag out again, the next click is on the handle you've dragged out…and so on.

Boom-Boom Washington: So, how do I prevent it?

Toulouse: Just remember that each time you drag, you're setting the location of the Control Handle, not the path itself. Don't click the Control Handle, click far away from it.

Boom-Boom Washington: Like, if the first click is right in the middle of the page, the next click should be in, what, Jersey?

Toulouse: Not quite that far away. Now I know why you were 28 and still in 11th grade.

To create a Smooth Point with two Control Handle Lines of different lengths, first create a Smooth Point along a path. Go back to this point after it has been created and click and drag it again using the Direct Selection tool. You can adjust the angle for both Control Handle Lines and the length for the new Control Handle Line that you are dragging. Note that as you are dragging out this Control Handle Line, the other Control Handle Line wobbles to the angle that you are dragging. This happens because on any Smooth Point the Control Handle Lines *must* be at the same angle, and as you drag out the new Control Handle Line, you are changing the angle for both Control Handle Lines simultaneously.

Knowing the Pen Commandments

The Pen Commandments are laws to live by — or, at least, to draw by — as shown dramatically in Figure 3-26 and described in detail following the figure.

Figure 3-26: The Pen Commandments

The commandments are:

✦ **Thou shalt drag approximately one-third of the length of the next curved segment.** What this means, as shown at the bottom of Figure 3-27, is that the Control Handle you drag from the Anchor Point should be about one-third of the distance between this Anchor Point and the next one you click. (This technique takes some planning ahead.) In fact, you have to be aware of where the next Anchor Point is going to be located before you can determine the length of the Control Handle Line you are dragging. Dragging by one-third is always an approximation — a little more or a little less doesn't hurt and, in fact, is sometimes quite necessary. You might run into trouble when the Control Handle Line is more than half or less than one-quarter of the next segment. If your Control Handle Line is too long or too short, chances are the line will curve erratically. Remember not to drag where the next point will be placed, just one-third of that distance.

✦ **Thou shalt remember that Control Handle Lines are always tangent to the curved segment they are guiding.** Tangent? Well, a simpler way of putting this commandment may be that Control Handle Lines go in the same direction as the curve and that they are always outside of the curve, as previously shown in Step 4 of Figure 3-24. Don't get the outside of the curve and the outside of the shape you are drawing confused — they may well be two different things. If your Control Handle lies inside the curve you are drawing, it will be too short and overpowered by the next Anchor Point. Control Handles *pull* the curve toward themselves; this makes them naturally curve out toward the Control Handle Lines. If you fight this natural pull, your illustrations can look loopy and silly.

✦ **Thou shalt always drag the Control Handle in the direction that you want the curve to travel at that Anchor Point.** Once again, the Control Handle pulls the curve toward itself by its very nature; doing otherwise will certainly cause some trouble. If you drag backward toward the preceding segment, you will create a little curved spike that sticks out from the Anchor Point. This commandment applies *only* to Smooth Points, as previously shown in Step 4 of Figure 3-24. If the Anchor Point is to be a Curved Corner Point, then the initial drag should be in the direction the curve was traveling, and the next drag (an Option[Alt]-drag) should go in the direction that the curve is going to travel. If the Anchor Point is a Combination Curve Point and the next segment is straight, then the dragging motion should be in the direction that the curve was traveling; then the Anchor Point should be clicked and released. If the Combination Curve Point's next segment is curved, the first click should be clicked and released, and the second click should be dragged in the direction of the next curve.

✦ **Thou shalt use as few Anchor Points as possible.** If your illustration calls for smooth, flowing curves, use very few Anchor Points. If, on the other hand, your illustration should be rough and gritty, use more Anchor Points. The fewer Anchor Points there are, the smoother the final result, as demonstrated in Figure 3-27. When there are only a few Anchor Points on a path, changing its shape is easier and faster. More Anchor Points mean a bigger file and longer printing times, as well. If you're not sure if you need more Anchor Points, don't add them. You can always add them later with the Add Anchor Point tool.

✦ **Thou shalt place Anchor Points at the beginning of each "different" curve.** Anchor Points should be used as *transitional* points, where the curve either changes direction or increases or decreases in size dramatically. If it looks as though the curve will change from one type of curve to another, then the location to place an Anchor Point is in the middle of that transitional section. The top drawing in Figure 3-28 shows good locations to place Anchor Points on a curved path.

✦ **Thou shalt not overcompensate for a previously misdrawn curve.** If you really screw up on the last Anchor Point you've drawn, don't panic and try to undo the mistake by dragging in the wrong direction or by dragging the Control Handle out to some ridiculous length. Doing either of these two things may temporarily fix the preceding curve but usually wrecks the next curve, causing you to have to overcompensate yet again. The results of just minor overcompensation are shown in the bottom drawing in Figure 3-29.

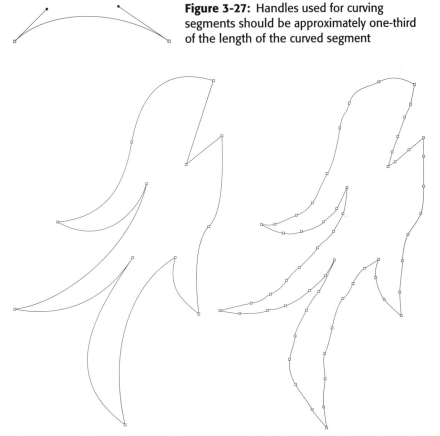

Figure 3-27: Handles used for curving segments should be approximately one-third of the length of the curved segment

Figure 3-28: The path on the left was created with 12 Anchor Points; the path on the right was created with 60

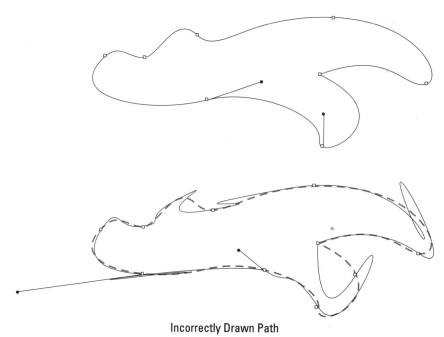

Incorrectly Drawn Path

Figure 3-29: The Anchor Points on the top path are placed where the curve changes. The path at the top was drawn correctly; the path on the bottom was drawn by overcompensating for previously misdrawn curves.

Closing Curved Paths with the Pen Tool

The majority of the paths you draw with the Pen tool will be closed paths, not the open ones we've drawn so far. Like open curved paths, any closed curved path must have at least two Anchor Points, just as paths with Straight Corner Points need three distinct points to create a closed path.

When the Pen tool is placed over the starting point of the path you've drawn, a little circle appears to the right of the pen shape. This is an indicator that the path will become a closed path if you click this Anchor Point.

Of course, to ensure that the initial Anchor Point remains a Smooth Point, you need to click and drag on the initial Anchor Point. Simply clicking produces a Combination Corner Point, which only has one Control Handle associated with it.

Curved Corner Points

Curved Corner Points are points where two different, usually distinct, curved segments meet at an Anchor Point. Because the two curves meet this way, a Smooth Point does not provide the means for their joining correctly. Instead, a Smooth Point would make the two different curves blend into each other smoothly.

Points on a Path to Make a Figure 8

How few points does it take to create a basic curved shape? This is a good test of your abilities. The following infinity shape was drawn with the least number of Anchor Points possible.

The number of points used to draw this shape was a number something less than infinity.

After you've tried to do this a few times, look ahead a couple of pages to see some of the different ways it can be done.

The main difference between a Curved Corner Point and a Smooth Point is that a Smooth Point has two linked Control Handles on their ends; a Curved Corner Point has two *independent* Control Handles. As the name indicates, Control Handles and their associated Control Handle Lines move independently of each other, enabling two different, distinct types of curves to come from the same Anchor Point.

To create a Curved Corner Point, create a Smooth Point in a path and then Option[Alt]-drag the Control Handle you just drew. As you Option[Alt]-drag the Control Handle, you are breaking the Control Handles independently. The next segment will curve as controlled by this Control Handle, not by the original one.

The clumps of grass in Figure 3-1 were created using Curved Corner Points. The process is explained in the following steps.

1. As shown in Figure 3-30, click the first point (1) and drag up and to the left. Try to duplicate the locations of all the points for the best results.

2. Click at (2) and drag left and down just a little bit, which creates the curved segment between (1) and (2). You won't see the Control Handle you are dragging on the figure on the right because Step 3 replaces it.

3. To create the first Curved Corner Point, Option[Alt]-click on (2) and drag up and to the right.

4. Click at (3) and drag to the lower right.

5. Continue to Option[Alt]-drag Control Handles when drawing a new segment, effectively creating independent Control Handles until you have created a clump of grass.

6. Option[Alt]-copy and transform the clumps to create several clumps of grass.

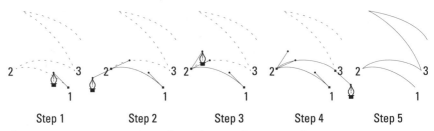

Figure 3-30: How to create paths with Curved Corner Points

 Tip When creating Curved Corner Points, you can press the Option [Alt] key (to create independent points) all the time, not just when starting a new segment.

Combination Corner Points

A Combination Corner Point is a point where a curved segment and a straight segment meet each other. At this Corner Point, there is one Control Handle coming from the Anchor Point from the side where the curved segment is located and, on the other side, there is no Control Handle, indicating a straight segment.

To create a Combination Corner Point with the Pen tool, draw a few curved segments and then go back to the last Anchor Point. There should be two linked Control Handles displayed at this point. Simply click once on the Anchor Point and one of the two Control Handles will disappear. The next segment then starts out straight.

 Tip You can change existing Smooth and Curved Corner Points into Combination Corner Points simply by dragging one of the Control Handles into the Anchor Points.

Using the Pen Tool

In the sample illustration that was shown in Figure 3-1, the Pen tool was used not only to draw the spiky weeds, but also to draw the horses on the hill and the Fill shapes for the hill. The horse outlines and the blade outlines were created with the Paintbrush tool.

Points on a Path to Make a Figure 8: The Answers

There are several ways to make a figure 8, as shown below.

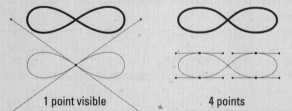

1 point visible   4 points   8 points

Compare these figures to the one you've drawn.

Your score is as follows:

1 visible point (really 2 overlapping): PenMaster

2 points, both visible: Lots of Pentential

3–4 points: ApPentice

6 or more points: The sword is still mightier

To Fill the hillside, click where the left edge of the hill should begin and drag down and to the right about ½ inch. Next, click at the top of the hill and drag just a tiny bit (less than ¼ inch) to the right. Click again at about halfway down the hill and drag at about the same angle as the hill. Click again at the base of the hill and drag to the right 1 inch. Click without dragging on the far side of the illustration. To finish off the hillside Fill, click the lower-right and lower-left corners and then click the starting point. Fill the path with a gradient that complements a hillside and change the Stroke to None.

To create the horse Fill shape, create a path with the Pen tool by using mostly Smooth Points that go right through the center of the horse outlines. Make separate shapes for the head area, manes, body area, and the tails. Fill the paths with gradients or solid colors and choose a Stroke of None.

To create the long grass blade Fills, use the Pen tool to draw paths that go right through the center of the blades of grass. Create separate paths for each blade, and Fill the blades with a green linear gradient.

Selection Tools

If there is one group of tools in Illustrator you absolutely *must* have, it is the set of three selection tools. As in most applications, to alter something (move, transform, and so on), you must first select it. When you draw a new path or when you paste in Illustrator, the program automatically selects the object you're working on; however, as soon as you draw another path, the preceding object is deselected and Illustrator automatically selects the object with the new path. The selection tools allow you to select paths and perform additional manipulations on them. Illustrator has three selection tools: the Selection tool, the Direct Selection tool, and the Group Selection tool, as shown in Figure 3-31.

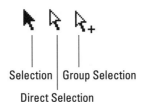

Selection | Group Selection

Direct Selection

Figure 3-31: The Selection tools. The Group Selection tool is accessed by clicking and holding on the Direct Selection tool slot in the toolbox.

There are several different ways to make selections in Illustrator, depending on what you wish to change:

✦ **InterPath selecting:** *InterPath selecting* means that at least one point or segment within a path is selected, usually with the Direct Selection tool. InterPath selecting is used to adjust individual points, segments, and series of points.

- Even though just a portion of the path is selected, many changes will affect the entire path — not just the selected points. For example, most of the attributes available in the Object menu (including Pathfinder, Masking, and Compound Paths) affect the entire path even when only a point or segment is selected.

- InterPath selecting also allows you to use most of the functions in the Arrange menu, such as hiding, locking, or grouping. But these options lock, hide, or group the entire path.

- Selected Anchor Points on InterPath-selected paths are solid squares; unselected points are hollow squares. Visible Control Handles and Control Handle Lines on either side of the segment indicate selected segments if the selected segment is curved. If the selected segment is not curved, no indication that the segment is selected appears onscreen. If you delete a segment or point, the entire remaining path becomes selected at the second level.

- Figure 3-32 shows InterPath selection.

✦ **Path selecting:** *Path selecting* means that all points and segments on a path are selected. When a path is clicked by using the Group Selection tool or the Selection tool, the entire path is automatically selected. (Drawing a marquee entirely around a path with the Direct Selection tool also selects the entire path.)

- All the capabilities from InterPath selecting are available, such as the entire Object menu and the Arrange menu and most of the functions in the Filter menu.

- After you select a path, the entire path is affected by moving, transforming, cutting, copying and pasting, and deleting. An example of Path selecting is shown in Figure 3-33.

✦ **Group selecting:** You can select and affect a series of grouped paths as if it were a single object by using *Group selecting*. All paths in the group are affected in the same way as paths that you select with Path selecting. The Selection tool selects entire grouped paths at once. If you use the Group Selection tool instead, you need a series of clicks to select a group of paths. Figure 3-34 shows what you can accomplish with Group selecting.

✦ **InterGroup selecting:** You can select and affect groups of paths within other groups by using *InterGroup selecting*. All paths in the group are affected in the same way as paths that you select with Path selection. Use the Group Selection tool to select a group of paths at once. Each successive click on the same path selects another set of grouped paths that the initial path is within. InterGroup selecting is demonstrated in Figure 3-35.

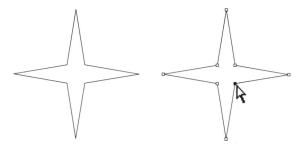

Figure 3-32: InterPath selection on paths

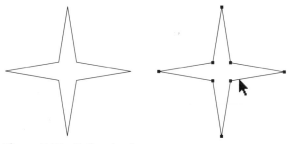

Figure 3-33: Path selection

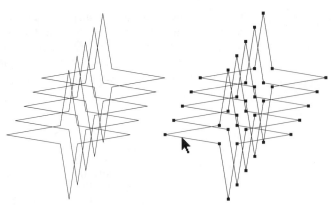

Figure 3-34: Group selection

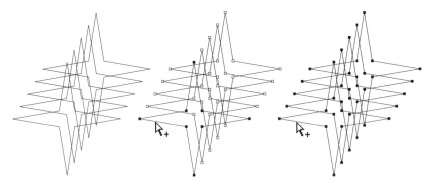

Figure 3-35: InterGroup selection

To select everything in your document that hasn't been hidden or locked, choose Edit ➪ Select All (⌘-A) [Ctrl+A], which selects all the points and segments on every path in the document. You can also select everything in the document by drawing a marquee around all the paths with any selection tool.

Normally, after you select something new, everything that you have previously selected becomes *deselected*. To continue to select additional points, paths, or segments, you must hold down the Shift key while clicking.

The Shift key normally works as a toggle when used with a selection tool, selecting anything that is not selected and deselecting anything that is currently selected. Each selection tool works with the Shift key a little differently, as described in the following sections.

Tip   To deselect everything that is selected, click a part of the document that is empty (where you can see the Pasteboard or Artboard) without using the Shift key. You also can deselect everything by choosing Edit ➪ Deselect All (⌘-Shift-A) [Ctrl+Shift+A].

You can use the selection tools for manually moving selected points, segments, and paths. Personally, the thought of manual labor terrifies me, but when I do something *manually* in Illustrator, I am usually referring to the process of dragging or clicking with the mouse. You use *automatic* or *computer-assisted manipulations* when you type in specific values in Transform palette, for example. The next few sections cover the selection tools and their functions.

Using the Selection Tool

The Selection tool selects entire paths or complete groups at one time. You can't select just one point or a few points on a path with the Selection tool. Instead, the entire path on which that point lies is selected (all the Anchor Points turn black). Drawing a marquee (clicking and dragging as a box forms behind the cursor) around parts of paths or entire paths also selects entire paths.

Bounding Box and the Selection Tool

New to Illustrator 8 is the addition of a Bounding Box when using the Selection tool. This Bounding Box enables you to move or scale the selected objects by simply dragging. When an object is selected, a Bounding Box appears around the whole object. This Bounding Box has points on the 4 corners as well as points on the midline of each side of the box. These points enable you to scale the object any way you like. By holding down the Shift key and dragging one of the corner points, you can easily scale the selected object proportionately. You can enable or disable the Bounding Box feature in the General Preferences (⌘-K [Ctrl+K]).

Using the Direct Selection Tool

To select individual points, line segments, or a series of specific points within a path, you need to use the Direct Selection tool. It is the *only* tool that enables you to select something less than an entire path. You can also draw a marquee over a portion of a path to select only those points and segments within the area of the marquee. If the marquee surrounds an entire path, the entire path is selected. Individual points or a series of points on different paths can also be selected by drawing a marquee around just those points. You can permanently switch to the Direct Selection tool by pressing A on the keyboard. Press A again to choose the Group Selection tool. Another press of the A key takes you back to the Direct Selection tool.

The Shift key is used with the Direct Selection tool to select additional points or segments or to deselect previously selected points. If only one segment or point on a path is selected and you Shift-click on that segment or point with the Direct Selection tool, the entire path is deselected.

If you press the Shift key, the Selection tool works as a toggle between selecting and deselecting paths. While you hold down the Shift key and click on paths that are not selected, they become selected. When paths that are selected are Shift-clicked, they become deselected. The Shift key can be used in this way to add to or subtract from a series of selected paths.

Selecting items with the Direct Selection tool can be a little intimidating because Anchor Points show up as *solid* when selected and *hollow* when deselected. Furthermore, a selected segment does not have any Anchor Points selected; instead, any Control Handles and Control Handle Lines associated with that segment become selected. If there are no Control Handles associated with a segment, such as a segment that is in between two Straight Corner Points, then it is difficult to tell which segment is selected.

After you select a point or series of points, those selected points can be manipulated in a number of ways, including being moved and transformed (via the transformation tools) and having certain filters applied to them. Individual segments and series of segments can be selected and modified in the same way points are transformed.

The Group Selection Tool

The Group Selection tool is driven by a very cool concept: It first selects a path, then the group that the path is in, then the group that the other group with the path is in, and so on.

For the Group Selection tool to work properly, choose the first path or paths by either clicking them or drawing a marquee around them. To select the group that a particular path is in, however, requires you to click one of the initially selected paths. To select the next group also requires a click; if you drag at any point, only the paths you drag over are selected.

This process may seem a little fuzzy at first, but it will get easier the more you use the Group Selection tool. Remember, the first time that you select something with the Group Selection tool, you are selecting only the paths that you click or drag over. The next time you click an already-selected path, all the paths in its group will be selected.

Caution   Still confused about how the Shift key selects and deselects paths? I can make it worse. The Shift key is an odd duck when used with the Group Selection tool. What happens when you click an unselected path with this tool while holding down the Shift key? The path is selected. But what happens when you click a selected path? The process deselects *just one path.* What makes more sense to me is if you would click again with the Shift key, and it then would deselect the entire group. Nope. Ain't gonna happen. The Shift key works as a toggle on the one path you are clicking—selecting it, deselecting it, and so on.

Dragging a marquee around paths with the Group Selection tool works only for the first series of clicks; dragging another marquee, even over the already-selected paths, just reselects those paths.

ASK TOULOUSE: Too Many Selection Tools?

Marcia: I'm getting mouse wrist because of all these different selection tools.

Toulouse: How so?

Marcia: It's such a pain to keep going up to the toolbox to select different selection tools. And then there are the other tools as well. . . .

Toulouse: You use the toolbox to access the selection tools?

Marcia: No, I have them flown in from Hackensack when I wanna use them. Of *course* I use the toolbox.

Toulouse: Actually, you can use the keyboard to jump around each of the selection tools.

Marcia: I have a keyboard. Tell me more.

Toulouse: No matter what tool is selected in the toolbox, pressing ⌘ [Ctrl] will toggle to the Selection tool.

Marcia: Wow! This is great!

Toulouse: You can toggle between the regular Selection tool and the Direct Selection tool by pressing ⌘-Tab [Ctrl+Tab].

Marcia: No kidding.

Toulouse: When you have the Direct Selection tool, press Option [Alt] and you'll access the Group Selection tool!

Marcia: You should really write a book on this stuff.

If you have selected several paths at once, clicking a selected path selects only the group that the selected path is in. If other selected paths are in different groups, those groups are not selected until you click those paths with the Group Selection tool. However, clicking multiple times on any of the paths in the selected group continues to select "up" in the group that the selected path is part of.

The Group Selection tool is the most useful when dealing with graphs and blends, but it can be used in a number of other situations to greatly enhance your control of what is and is not selected. People who are always ungrouping and regrouping paths (groupies) can greatly benefit from using the Group Selection tool. In fact, proper use of this tool prevents you from ever having to ungroup and regroup objects for workflow reasons.

Tip   You can access the Group Selection tool when the Direct Selection tool is selected by holding down the Option [Alt] key. If the Direct Selection tool is not chosen, then select it by holding down the ⌘ [Ctrl] key (you may have to press ⌘-Tab [Ctrl+Tab] to toggle from the Selection tool to the Direct Selection tool) and pressing the Option [Alt] key at the same time.

Selecting, Moving, and Deleting Entire Paths

Usually, the best way to select a path that is not currently selected is by clicking it with the regular Selection tool, which highlights all the points on the path and enables you to move, transform, or delete that entire path.

To select more than one path, you can use a number of different methods. The most basic method is to hold down the Shift key and click the successive paths with the Selection tool, selecting one more path with each Shift-click. Shift-clicking a selected path with the Selection tool deselects that particular path. Drawing a marquee around paths with the Selection tool selects all paths that at least partially fall into the area drawn by the marquee. When drawing a marquee, be sure to place the cursor in an area where there is nothing. Finding an empty spot may be difficult to do in Preview mode because Fills from various paths may cover any white space available. Drawing a marquee with the Selection tool when the Shift key is depressed selects nonselected paths and deselects currently selected paths.

If paths are part of either a compound path or a group, all other paths in that compound path or group are also selected.

To move a path, click the path and drag (in one motion) with the Selection tool. To move several paths, select the paths and then click an already-selected path with the regular Selection tool or the Direct Selection tool and drag.

 Caution If you have been selecting multiple paths by using the Shift key, be sure to release it before clicking and dragging on the selection. If the Shift key is still pressed, the clicked path becomes deselected and no paths move. If this does happen, just Shift-click the paths that were deselected and drag.

To delete an entire path, select it with the Selection tool and press the Delete key. To delete multiple paths, select them and press the Delete key.

Often, many objects need to be moved and duplicated at the same time. To duplicate paths when moving them, hold down the Option [Alt] key while the mouse button is released.

The short grass, long grass, and silhouetted horses can be duplicated the same way, by choosing one and dragging it to the left or right and pressing Option [Alt] while the mouse button is released.

Choosing Select All (⌘-A [Ctrl+A] or ⌘-period [Ctrl+period] when the screen is not redrawing) from the Edit menu selects all paths in the active document. If a type tool is selected and there is an insertion point in the text, all the type in that story will be selected.

Choosing Select None (⌘-Shift-A) [Ctrl+Shift+A] from the Edit menu deselects all selected objects. Select None does *not* work with type selected with a Type tool.

Selecting, Moving, and Deleting Portions of Paths

To select just a portion of a path, you *must* use the Direct Selection tool. To select an Anchor Point or a line segment, simply click it. To select several individual points or paths, click the points or paths to be selected while holding down the Shift key. Series of points and paths can be selected by dragging a marquee across the paths that are to be selected.

Individual points that are selected become solid squares. If these points are Smooth, Curved Corner, or Combination Corner Points, Control Handles appear from the selected Anchor Point.

Line segments that have at least one Anchor Point that is either a Smooth, Curved Corner, or Combination Corner Point may display a Control Handle Line and Control Handle coming out from that Anchor Point. Samples of each of these selected types of Anchor Points are shown in Figure 3-36.

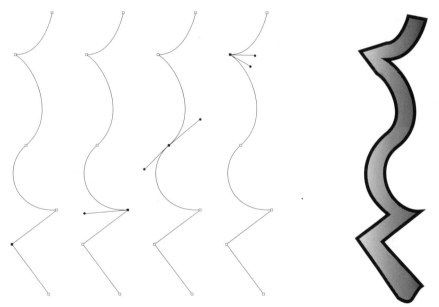

Figure 3-36: The four different types of Anchor Points when selected

To move these selected points or paths, release the Shift key and click a selected path or point and drag.

Illustrator doesn't tell you when a straight-line segment is selected or which one is selected. The first time you click a straight-line segment, all the Anchor Points on the path appear as hollow squares, which is just telling you that something on that path is selected. Selected points turn black, and curved line segments have one or more Control Handles and Control Handle Lines sticking out from the ending Anchor Points, but straight-line segments don't do anything when selected. The inventive side of you may think that you can get around this problem by dragging the selected segments to a new location or by copying and pasting them and then undoing, but this solution doesn't work because of Illustrator's habit of selecting all points on paths when undoing operations on those paths.

Tip   When you run into this problem of not knowing whether a straight-line segment is selected, do the following: Instead of moving, copying, or pasting, simply whack the good ol' Delete key and whatever disappears is what you had selected. Now when you undo, just the segments that were selected before the deletion are still selected, not the entire path.

To delete points and segments, select them as described previously and press Delete. Remember that line segments exist only when there is one point on either side of the segment. Even if the line segment is not selected, if one of its Anchor Points is deleted, the line segment is deleted as well. A path is made up of points, and those points are connected via segments. If the points are gone, the paths disappear along with them. But if you delete all the segments, all the points can still remain.

Portions of paths can be duplicated when pressing the Option [Alt] key while the mouse button is being released. Duplicating segments also duplicates the Anchor Points on either side of that segment.

Locking and Hiding Objects

All objects in Illustrator can be locked or hidden—including guides. Locking and hiding work about the same, and the results are only marginally different. In a way, Hiding is an "invisible lock."

Locking

To lock an object, select it and choose Object ⇨ Lock (⌘-2) [Ctrl+2]. The selected object is not only locked but also deselected. In fact, an object is unselectable when locked. Locked objects cannot be moved or changed, but they are always visible and will always print (locked objects cannot be hidden). Because a locked object can't be selected, it can't be changed, and in Illustrator, as in most Macintosh applications, objects are modifiable only when selected.

A locked object remains locked when the document is saved and closed. As a result, locked objects are still locked the next time the document is opened. Locked objects print with no indication as to whether they are locked or not.

To change a locked object, choose Object ➪ Unlock (⌘-Option-2) [Ctrl+Alt+2], unlocking (and selecting) all objects. There is no way to unlock just a few objects locked with the Lock command.

Tip A tricky way to invisibly "copyright" your illustration is to create a small text box in a far corner of the pasteboard with your copyright information in it, color the text white, and lock the text box. No one will know it is there, and it can't be easily selected. In fact, it'll even print if it is placed on top of a background in another program.

I like to lock objects under these circumstances:

✦ When the document is full of complex artwork, so I can do a Select All and not have to wait forever for the selection to finish.

✦ When I don't want to accidentally move or change certain artwork.

✦ When I can't easily select paths that are under other paths (in which case, I lock the ones on top).

✦ When I have to fit an illustration into a certain area (in which case, I'll create a box of that size and lock it so I have an instant boundary to work with).

Hiding

Sometimes you don't want to see certain objects on your document page — perhaps because they obstruct your view of other objects or they take a long time to redraw. In these cases, it's a good idea to hide the objects in question. To do so, select them and choose Object ➪ Hide Selection (⌘-3) [Ctrl+3].

Hidden objects are invisible and unselectable; they still exist in the document, but they do not print. When a document is reopened, hidden objects reappear.

Tip Holding down Option [Alt] and choosing Object ➪ Hide Selection or typing ⌘-Option-U [Ctrl+Alt+U] hides all the objects that are *not* selected.

To show (and select) all hidden objects, choose Object ➪ Show All (⌘-Shift-3) [Ctrl+Shift+3]. Think of it as "unhide." There is no way to show just a few of the hidden objects when using the Show All command.

Object Information

Choosing Window Show ➪ Attributes (F11) brings up the Attributes palette. In this palette, notes can be added to any selected object, the path direction can be reversed (if the object is part of a compound path), the center point of the object can be made to display or hide, and the flatness characteristics (output dpi) can be changed. At least one object must be selected in order to choose Attributes.

Tip

Another useful way to "copyright" your artwork is to select all the objects and then go to the Attributes palette and enter your copyright information within the palette.

Note

The Attributes palette also allows you to set a URL (Uniform Resource Locator) for a selected object or objects. This feature is discussed in more detail in Chapter 16.

Stacking Order

Stacking order is a crucial concept that you need to understand in the world of Adobe Illustrator. This concept is not the same as the layer concept that is discussed in Chapter 7; rather it is the forward/backward relationship between objects within each layer.

After you create the first object in Illustrator, the next object is created *above* the first object, or on top of it. The third object is created above both the first and second objects. This cycle continues indefinitely, with objects being stacked one on top of another.

A great deal of planning goes into creating an illustration so that the object you draw first is on the bottom of the pile and the last thing you draw ends up on the top. To make your life much more pleasant, Illustrator has the capability to move objects up and down (forward or backward) through the stack of objects. In fact, Illustrator's method of moving objects up and down is so simple and basic that it is also quite limiting.

You can change the stacking order of objects in Illustrator relative to foreground and background either all the way to the bottom or all the way to the top, or you can move objects up or down through the stacking order. Figure 3-37 shows the same illustration after various objects were moved in the stacking order.

To move an object to the front, choose Object ➪ Arrange ➪ Bring to Front (⌘-Shift-]) [Ctrl+Shift+]]. The selected object is brought forward so that it is in front of every other object (but only in that layer; Chapter 7 explains how layers work). If more than one object is selected, the topmost object of the selected group will be at the very top and the bottom-most object of the selected group will be beneath all the other selected objects — but all the selected objects will be on top of all the nonselected objects. Bring to Front is not available when no objects are selected. Multiple-selected paths and grouped paths still retain their front/back position relative to each other.

To move an object to the back, choose Object ➪ Arrange ➪ Send to Back (⌘-Shift-[) [Ctrl+Shift+[]. The selected object is sent to the back so that it is behind every other object. Send to Back is not available when there are no objects selected. Multiple selected paths and grouped paths still retain their front/back position relative to each other.

Figure 3-37: The original art (left) and after the stacking order of various pieces has changed (right)

Illustrator enables you to move selected objects through the stacking order one object at a time, forward or backward. To move selected objects forward one object at a time, choose Object ⇨ Arrange ⇨ Bring Forward (⌘-]) [Ctrl+]]. To move selected objects backward one object at a time, choose Object ⇨ Arrange ⇨ Send Backward (⌘-[) [Ctrl+[].

Individual characters in a string of text work in a similar manner to their object cousins when it comes to front/back placement. The first character typed is placed at the bottom of the text block, and the last character typed is placed at the top, as shown in Figure 3-38. To move individual characters forward or backward, you must first choose Type ⇨ Create Outlines (⌘-Shift-O) [Ctrl+Shift+O] and select the outline of the character you wish to arrange.

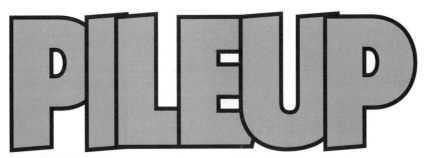

Figure 3-38: Text characters that overlap each other

Try as you might, you cannot change the forward/backward relationship of Strokes and Fills. Strokes are always in front of Fills for the same path. To get the Fill to cover or overlap the Stroke, you must copy the path, use the Paste in Front command (choose Edit ⇨ Paste in Front or press ⌘-F [Ctrl+F]), and then remove the Stroke from the path you just pasted.

Pasting Objects in Front of and Behind Selected Objects

Choosing Paste in Front (⌘-F) [Ctrl+F] from the Edit menu pastes any objects on the Clipboard on top of any selected objects or on the top of the current layer if no objects are selected.

Choosing Paste in Back (⌘-B) [Ctrl+B] from the Edit menu pastes any objects on the Clipboard behind any selected objects or on the bottom of the current layer if no objects are selected.

In addition, both Paste in Front and Paste in Back paste objects *in the same* location as the copied object, even from document to document. If the documents are different sizes, Illustrator pastes them in the same location relative to the center of each document. If the Clipboard is empty, or if type selected with a Type tool is on the Clipboard, these options are not available.

Note

Copied items in Illustrator always retain their layer name and related layer information. When you copy an item that is on layer "X-Flies" and paste that item in another document that contains an X-Flies layer, the item will appear on the X-Flies layer. If the document doesn't contain that layer, a new layer will be created with that name and the item will appear on that layer. This only works if the Paste Remembers Layers option is checked in the Layers palette. Chapter 7 contains more information on layers.

Grouping and Ungrouping

Grouping is the process of putting together a series of objects that need to remain spatially constant in relationship to each other. Groups can be made up of as little as one path, and they may contain an unlimited number of objects.

To group objects together, they should first be selected with any of the selection tools. After you select the objects, choose Object ⇨ Group (⌘-G) [Ctrl+G] to make the separate objects stay together when selected.

Selecting any object in a group with the regular Selection tool selects all the objects in that group and makes all the points in a path solid (selected). To see how the Group Selection tool works with selecting groups, see "Using the Group Selection Tool" at the end of this chapter.

Not only can several objects be grouped together, but groups can also be grouped together to form a group of groups in which there is a hierarchical series of grouped groups. In addition, groups can be grouped to individual objects or to several other objects.

After a set of objects or groups is grouped together, grouping it again produces no effect. The computer does not beep at you, display a dialog box, or otherwise indicate that the objects or groups you are attempting to group together are already grouped. Of course, it never hurts to choose Object ⇨ Group (⌘-G) [Ctrl+G] again if you are not sure if they are grouped. If they weren't grouped before, they now are, and if they were grouped before, nothing unusual or unexpected happens. If you choose Group again after the selected objects have already been grouped, nothing happens.

In our example illustration shown in Figure 3-1, the objects will be much easier to manipulate if they are grouped. Group the short grass together as one group, the long grass as one group, the horse outlines and Fills as one group, and the hillside outline and Fills as one group. The tree outline and bark detail should be one group as well.

Tip   If you are having trouble selecting all the objects for each type in a group, choose Object ⇨ Select ⇨ Same Paint Style after one object is selected. This process usually (but not always) selects all the objects of one type.

Grouping similar areas is helpful for moving entire areas forward or backward as well as for doing any type of horizontal or vertical movement or transformation upon a set of objects.

Grouping is also helpful for controlling blends.

Ungrouping

To ungroup groups (separate them into standalone paths and objects), choose Object ⇨ Ungroup (⌘-Shift-G) [Ctrl+Shift+G], and any selected groups become ungrouped. Ungrouping, like grouping, works on one set of groups at a time. For example, if you have two groups that are grouped together, ungrouping that group results in the two original groups. (Don't worry, I'm just as confused as you are in this area.) If Ungroup is chosen again, those two groups will also become ungrouped.

Tip   When you absolutely do not want anything in a group grouped with anything else — and you suspect that there may be several minigroups within the group you have selected — simply press ⌘-Shift-G [Ctrl+Shift+G] several times. You do not need to select the subgroups individually to ungroup them. To get rid of all the groups in your illustration, choose Edit ⇨ Select All (⌘-A) [Ctrl+A] and then proceed to ungroup (⌘-Shift-G) [Ctrl+Shift+G] several times. To remove certain objects from a group or compound path, select just these objects, cut, and Paste in Front (or Paste in Back).

When you're ungrouping, groups must be selected with either the Group Selection tool or the regular Selection tool.

Using the Group Selection Tool

The Group Selection tool is used primarily to select groups within other groups or individual paths within groups. To access the Group Selection tool, click the Direct Selection tool in the toolbox and drag to the right to the Group Selection tool. Clicking once with the Group Selection tool on any path selects that particular path. Clicking again with the Group Selection tool on the same path selects the group that path is in. Clicking yet again selects the group that the previously selected group is in.

To move a path that is part of a group, do not ungroup the path; instead, select the path with the Group Selection tool and move it.

Tip   If you select a path in a group with the Group Selection tool and then click the same path again to move it, the group that path is in will be selected instead. To avoid this problem, either select and move the group at one time or use the Direct Selection tool to select and move the path.

If several different paths are selected with the Group Selection tool either by dragging a marquee or Shift-clicking, clicking again on a selected path or object selects the group that object is in. If that object's group is already selected, then the group that the selected group is in will be selected.

The Group Selection tool also selects compound paths. One click selects an individual path within the compound path, and the second click selects the entire compound path.

Using the Shift key with the Group Selection tool on selected paths or objects deselects just one path at a time. Shift-clicking a path that has just been deselected reselects that path; it does not deselect the group that path is in.

Tip   For quick access to the Group Selection tool, press the Option [Alt] key when the Direct Selection Tool is the active tool. But release the Option [Alt] key before the mouse button is released or you'll have a duplicated path or object. The Direct Selection tool can be selected by pressing the ⌘ [Ctrl] key (⌘-Tab [Ctrl+Tab] toggles between the Direct Selection and regular Selection tools). Pressing the ⌘ [Ctrl] and Option [Alt] keys together can be used to access the Group Selection tool, no matter which tool is selected in the toolbox!

Summary

✦ Use a pressure-sensitive tablet with the Paintbrush tool for the best results.

✦ The Scatter Brush can create repeating objects with various sizes and rotation along a path.

✦ The Art Brush stretches an object over a path.

✦ The Pattern Brush repeats a tile pattern on a path.

✦ The Paintbrush tool creates open paths that are stroked.

✦ The Pencil tool creates single paths that are open or closed.

✦ The Smooth tool smooths any path by dragging a new path over a selected path.

✦ The Erase tool easily cuts or erases sections of an open or closed path.

✦ Control the roughness of Pencil tool-generated paths by setting the Auto Trace tolerance *before* you draw with the Pencil tool.

✦ The Pen tool is the most powerful tool in Illustrator because it enables you to create perfectly formed curves and straight paths.

✦ Clicking with the Pen tool creates straight-line segments; dragging with the Pen tool creates curved segments.

✦ Keep the distance of Control Handle Lines to about one-third the length of the affected curved line segment for the best results.

✦ The Selection tool selects entire paths or groups with one click.

✦ The Direct Selection tool selects individual points, segments, or portions of paths that are surrounded with a drag marquee.

✦ Quickly duplicate objects in Illustrator by dragging them and then releasing the mouse button while pressing the Option [Alt] key.

✦ Locking objects prevents paths from being selected or altered in any way.

✦ Lock selected objects by pressing ⌘-2 [Ctrl+2] or lock unselected objects by pressing ⌘-Option-2 [Ctrl+Alt+2]; unlock all locked objects by pressing ⌘-Shift-2 [Ctrl+Shift+2].

✦ Group paths together by selecting more than one path and pressing ⌘-G [Ctrl+G]; ungroup selected groups by pressing ⌘-Shift-G [Ctrl+Shift+G].

✦ Use the Group Selection tool to select paths and groups within other groups.

✦   ✦   ✦

Tracing, Grids, and Guides

CHAPTER

4

It's often much easier to create artwork in Illustrator by
starting with something to trace, whether it's a logo, a floor
plan, or your cousin Fred's disproportionate profile. Even the
best artists use some form of template when they draw to keep
proportions consistent, to get angles just right, and for other
reasons that help them to achieve the best possible result.

This chapter discusses different methods and techniques for
tracing different types of artwork within Illustrator (and even
outside of Illustrator). Don't think of this as cheating, but
instead, as a way to do better, faster, and more accurate
artwork.

Okay, it's cheating just a little bit. . . .

Templates (a.k.a Placed Images)

Templates went out with Version 6 of Illustrator. Instead, to
do tracing, either manually or automatically (using the Auto
Trace tool), you can use any image just by placing it into
Illustrator.

Templates from older versions of Illustrator consisted of 1-bit
PICT or PAINT images (black and white only) that were limited
to certain sizes. They looked ghastly onscreen, and getting the
right pixels to appear black (gray, actually) was always a
tedious process in Photoshop.

Now that placed images are considered templates by
Illustrator, a few things are different:

> ✦ **There is no Hide/Show Template option.** Instead,
> templates are placed image objects that can be selected
> and hidden (⌘-3) [Ctrl+3]. However, I recommend setting
> up a special layer just for your placed image if you'll be
> using it as a template.

✦ **Templates will print.** This is usually a bad thing. If your image is on its own, separate layer, however, you can turn layer printing off for that layer in the Layer Options dialog box.

✦ **Images must be dimmed manually.** Templates of the past were always gray, which made it easy to spot your paths, points, and handles. Placed images can be any color. However, you can dim them by choosing the Dim Images option in that layer's Layer Options dialog box. You also can choose the amount of dimming to be applied to the Placed image.

✦ **Templates can move.** Using a placed image as a template gives you both the freedom and the problem of being able to move it. The plus side to this is that you can position the image in the best place to trace it; the minus side is that it can be easy to bump accidentally. Lock the image or, even better, lock the image layer.

The best Illustrator templates were never really templates; they were placed files that you locked into place. You can dim any placed image, as described in the following steps and illustrated in Figure 4-1.

1. Place an image into the document by choosing File ➪ Place and selecting the image. You can also rasterize any vector artwork by selecting it and choosing Object ➪ Rasterize.

2. Move the image into the proper position and transform it if necessary.

3. Open the Layers palette by choosing Window ➪ Show Layers (F7). In the Layers palette, double-click Layer 1. In the Layer Options dialog box, select the Dim Images checkbox and then click OK.

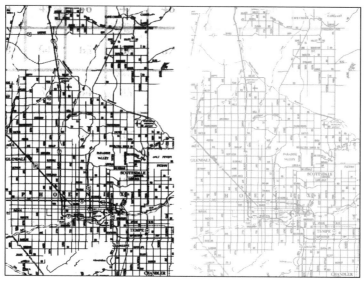

Figure 4-1: The original image (left) and after dimming (right)

Placed images work well as templates because their resolution is independent of the Illustrator document. You can scale placed images up or down, *changing their onscreen resolution* as you change their size. For instance, if you scale a 72-dpi (dots-per-inch) image down to one-fourth of its imported size (making the dpi of the placed image 4 x 72-dpi, or 288-dpi), you may zoom in on the image in Illustrator at 400%. At 400%, the placed EPS (Encapsulated PostScript) image still has a 72-dpi resolution because one-fourth of 288-dpi is 72-dpi. The more the placed image's dpi is increased by scaling it down, the more you may zoom in to see the details of the image. If the placed image's dpi is already higher than 72, you'll be able to zoom in to a certain amount and retain quite a bit of detail automatically.

Another plus: A placed image "template" is a full-color template that keeps all the shading and colors and enables you to see all the fine details easily.

Tracing

Now that you've got your template (placed image) all set up, you're ready to trace it — or so you would think. There are lots of different ways to go about tracing, and I've included the "best of the best" techniques in this section to help you muddle through this mess.

You can trace templates in two ways: manually and automatically. Manually tracing consists of using the Pencil and Pen tools to tediously trace the edges of a template — often a very time-consuming task. Using the Auto Trace tool, though, speeds up the process.

Automatically Tracing Placed Images

The Auto Trace tool (hidden in the same slot as the Blend tool) can be used for basic tracing of placed images, both black and white and full color. However, the results obtained by using this tool are usually less than satisfactory, requiring a great deal of time-consuming cleanup.

To use the Auto Trace tool, click the edge of a colored area of a placed image; the Auto Trace tool attempts to trace the edge of a solid area and applies the current Paint Style to it.

Tip   Always use the Auto Trace tool from the outside in. This ensures that bigger paths around the outside don't overlap the inside paths.

The Curve Fitting Tolerance setting in the Type & Auto Tracing preferences dialog box (⌘-K) [Ctrl+K] directly affects the Auto Trace tool in much the same way that it affects the Pencil tool — the higher the number, the less precise the tracing. A Curve Fitting Tolerance setting of 2 or 3 works pretty well for automatically tracing templates, but neither setting enables the Auto Trace tool to follow the ridges created from the template's diagonal and curved edges.

Manual Tracing

Most designers prefer manually tracing templates. Using the Pen and Pencil tools provides illustrators with a level of precision not found with the Auto Trace tool. Furthermore, illustrators may add detail, remove oddities, and change curves, angles, and the like to their satisfaction (as opposed to an image that has been automatically traced, which gives it a more final appearance with less editability).

I've found that a combination of manual and automatic tracing works quite nicely for drawing fairly basic illustrations, especially those illustrations with type and straight lines. Automatically trace the basic shapes first and then use the path editing tools to add or remove Anchor Points and move paths so that the image has a consistent look. After fixing the traced section, use the Pen and Pencil tools to draw in the intricate shapes.

About Adobe Streamline 4

Adobe Streamline is the Auto Trace tool on a natural high (actually, it's more like a coke rush, I'm told, but I hate to equate software to drugs . . . though both can be addicting and expensive). Anyway, Streamline can automatically trace full-color images, *retaining their color* automatically.

Adobe Streamline is extremely cool. It takes tracing images to a whole 'nother plane. Streamline's tools, features, and interface are found on the CD in an Acrobat PDF file for easy reference.

Using Layers for Tracing

You can use layers for more than just dimming images for tracing.

One of the unsung features of Illustrator's layers (more features are sung in Chapter 7) is the capability to show some layers in Preview mode and others in Artwork mode.

This is great for tracing because now you can take any placed image, put it on a layer that is shown in Preview mode, lock that layer (so the "template" isn't moved), and then create a new layer *above* the existing one and set it to Artwork view. Not only will you be able to see the placed image in color, but also the paths you draw will be outlines with the placed image visible below them.

You can also use layers to turn off the printing for placed images used as templates. Lock the template layer so you don't move it accidentally, and then use the Hide Layer function (in the Layers palette) to hide the artwork when you don't want to view it. Finally, when you're done with the template, remove it quickly by deleting the layer it is on.

Measuring

You can measure distances in Illustrator in four ways:

✦ Using the Measure tool

✦ Using the rulers along the side of the document window

✦ Placing objects whose dimensions are known against the edges

✦ Eyeballing it (popular since the first artist painted his recollections of the preceding day's battle with the saber-toothed animals of his time)

The Measure Tool

The fastest way to obtain a precise, exact measurement in Illustrator is to use the Measure tool (shown in Figure 4-2). The Measure tool has moved in Illustrator 8. The Measure tool is a pop-up tool found with the Hand tool and the Page tool. As soon as you click an object with the Measure tool, the Info palette appears, showing the distance between the location first clicked and the next location clicked or the distance between where the tool was first clicked and where the mouse was released after dragging. Double-clicking the Measure Tool pulls up the Guides and Grid Preferences dialog box (which is discussed and illustrated later in this chapter).

 Figure 4-2: The Measure tool

If the Snap To Point option in the General Preferences dialog box (⌘-K) is checked, the Measure tool automatically snaps to nearby paths and points.

As soon as the Measure tool measures a distance, it routes that information to the Move dialog box, shown in Figure 4-3. The next time you open the Move dialog box (by choosing Object ⇨ Transform ⇨ Move, or by double-clicking the Selection tool), it will hold the values sent by the Measure tool.

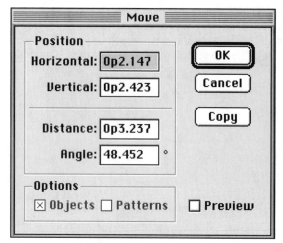

Figure 4-3: The Move dialog box

Tip

Know anything about PostScript? Well, one thing you absolutely have to know is that pages in PostScript are always measured from the lower-left corner of the page. That means moving something along the *Y* axis with a positive number will move it up, not down. It's a math thing. Your geometry teacher would've thought that's the way to measure things, while the rest of the world thinks it's stupid.

If you hold down the Shift key, you can constrain the movement of the measuring line to the following:

✦ In Preview mode, the measuring line defines a 45° or 90° angle if no paths or Filled parts of paths are under the cursor.

✦ In Artwork mode, your cursor snaps to the paths.

✦ In Preview mode, the cursor snaps to any Filled part of any path.

Sizing Objects with the Transform Palette

The Transform palette (choose Window ➪ Show Transform) shows the height, width, and location of any selected path or paths, as illustrated in Figure 4-4.

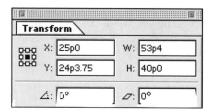

Figure 4-4: The Transform palette

X and *Y* show the location of the object on the page, measured (as always) from the lower-left corner.

W is the width of the selected object (or the total width of the selected objects when more than one is selected), while *H* is the height or total height of the selected object or objects.

All these measurements are in points — unless, of course, you know how to change the measurement units, which, coincidentally, is the topic of my next section.

Changing the Measurement Units

When you first use Illustrator, you are faced with points. That's great for type and numbering star tips, but when was the last time your art director said, "I'd like you to design a 360 x 288-point ad and make the logo at least 144 points high." (Or your grandmother said to you, "Gosh, you must be at least 5,600 points tall, maybe taller. You've grown at least 100 points since I last saw you. Does your mother let you wear *that* to school?!")

Points don't work for everything, so Adobe lets us change the measurement units to picas, inches, centimeters, or millimeters. The way to choose this is to temporarily indicate a different unit of measurement each time you enter a value, by appending a character or two to the end of your numerical value. For instance, to enter 2 inches you'd type **2 inch, 2 in,** or **2"**. To enter 2 millimeters, you'd enter **2 mm.** To enter 2 points you'd enter **2 pt** or **p 2.** You can enter picas by putting a *p* after the number, such as **2p** for 2 picas. You can also combine picas and points by sticking a *p* between them, as in **2p6** for 2 picas, 6 points. For centimeters, type **2 cm.**

Centimeters and Points/Picas units of measure have been available since Version 7 of Illustrator. In the centimeter system, there are 100 centimeters in a meter and 10 millimeters in a centimeter (if you live in the U.S. and have not yet been metricized). The other system, which is much more significant to Illustrator users, is the pica/point system. When the pica measurement system is selected in the Units and Undo Preferences, measurements are displayed using the common (common to typesetters and designers, anyway) system of picas followed by points. So a distance of 3 picas and 6 points is displayed as 3p6. Such a measurement would be displayed as 42 points using the point system.

A quick refresher on measurement units and their relations:

1"	=	6p	=	72 pt	=	25.4 mm	=	2.54 cm
.17"	=	1p	=	12 pt	=	4.2 mm	=	.42 cm
.01"	=	p1	=	1 pt	=	.35 mm	=	.035 cm
.04"	=	p2.83	=	2.83 pt	=	1 mm	=	.1 cm
.39"	=	2p4.35	=	28.35 pt	=	10 mm	=	1 cm

ASK TOULOUSE: Picas Picas

Chrissy: I'm about to get fired.

Toulouse: I thought you had a stake in the Thighmaster thing. . . .

Chrissy: No, things I print don't measure correctly.

Toulouse: How so?

Chrissy: Well, picas don't equal picas.

Toulouse: Actually, that's a common occurrence. But you're not doing anything wrong.

Chrissy: Pardon me for asking, but why the hell does it happen?

Toulouse: Well, when you measure, you're probably using one of those pica sticks, right?

Chrissy: Sure. It's *the* weapon of the graphic artist.

Toulouse: Okay. The problem is that until just recently, most pica sticks were *traditional picas*, which aren't the same as *new picas*, which are sometimes called *Adobe picas*.

Chrissy: And traditional picas are different from Adobe picas?

Toulouse: Um, yeah . . . See, there are 72.27 points in an inch using traditional points and picas, and there are 72 points in an inch using Adobe points and picas. So picas, which are 12 points, are different sizes in each system.

Chrissy: So, which programs use Adobe picas and which ones use traditional picas?

Toulouse: Actually, by default, most software uses Adobe picas and points. Some programs, such as QuarkXPress, let you switch between them.

Chrissy: How confusing.

Toulouse: It is. You know, step by step . . .

To permanently alter your measurement units, choose File ➪ Preferences ➪ Units and Undo and change the General pop-up menu in the Units section to the measurement system you want.

Using Rulers

You can toggle rulers on and off by choosing View ➪ Show/Hide Rulers (⌘-R) [Ctrl+R]. Normally, the rulers measure up and across from the document's lower-left corner; however, you can alter this orientation by dragging the ruler origin (where the zeros are) from its position in the upper-left corner, between where the two rulers meet. Because rulers take up valuable onscreen real estate, it's usually a good idea to leave them turned off unless you are constantly measuring things or you want to display your illustration at a higher magnification. Rulers are easy to show and hide—just press ⌘-R [Ctrl+R] when you want to see them and press ⌘-R [Ctrl+R] again to lose them. To reset the rulers to their original location, double-click in the origin box of the rulers.

Tip   If you change the ruler origin to the middle of the document page, try to move it back to a corner when you are finished. When you zoom in, rulers may be the only indicator of your location within the document.

One of the rulers' nicest features is the display of dotted lines that correspond to the cursor's position. And yet, at times, measuring with rulers works no better than eyeballing; although the process requires precision, you are limited by the rulers' hash marks in pinpointing the cursor's exact position. The rulers are best suited for measuring when the document is at a very high zoom level.

ASK TOULOUSE: Measuring Trouble

Jack: You know, my measurements never seem accurate.

Toulouse: Really? How far are they off?

Jack: It varies. Sometimes they'll be right on, and at other times they'll be half the size, twice as big. . . . Once they were $1/16$ the actual size!

Toulouse: I hate to ask this, but what are you using to measure the onscreen objects?

Jack: The rulers on the monitor, of course.

Toulouse: Well, that's very weird. I've always found those rulers to be quite accurate.

Jack: You've used my computer?

Toulouse: No, but I have rulers on my system, too.

Jack: But how do you know they're the same as mine?

Toulouse: You know, I'm thinking there's a lack of communication somewhere here. . . .

Jack: The real problem was getting them to stay in place.

Toulouse: Huh?

Jack: Yeah, I ended up hot-gluing each ruler to the edges of the monitor. Duct tape would've been my next choice.

Toulouse: You know, there are rulers *within* Illustrator.

Jack: You're kidding me.

Toulouse: ⌘-R [Ctrl-R]. Check it out.

ASK TOULOUSE: More Measuring Woes

Furley: This isn't working. I'm no mathematician.

Toulouse: Trouble with rulers?

Furley: Yeah. I want to place objects at certain distances from the edges of different pieces of artwork.

Toulouse: Why's that a problem?

Furley: Well, my object is at about 2.3" across the page, and 6.7" from the bottom. I can't work this way.

Toulouse: You can reset the way the rulers measure, so you can measure from the top left of any artwork on the page.

Furley: Without doing the math?

Toulouse: No math. Just drag the origin (that's where the rulers meet at the top left of the page) to the point you want to measure from.

Furley: Wow! This is great! I haven't been this excited since Stanley took off for his own show! Which then bombed, of course, leaving me on a top 10 show.

Toulouse: If I recall, wasn't the ratings high point *before* you came on the show?

Furley: I've never really done the math. . . .

Measuring with Objects

Using objects to compare distances can be more effective than using either the Measure tool or the rulers, especially when you need to place objects precisely — for example, when you want several objects to be the same distance from one another.

If you place a circle adjacent to an object (so that the objects' edges touch), you know that the second object is placed correctly when it's aligned to the circle's other side. (A circle is the object most commonly used because the diameter is constant.)

You can use other objects for measuring, including these:

 ✦ Squares — when you need to measure horizontal and vertical distances

 ✦ Rectangles — when the horizontal and vertical distances are different

 ✦ Lines — when the distance applies to only one direction

To enable better precision, turn the measuring object into a guide. (Guides are discussed in more detail later in this chapter.)

Using Offset Path (for Equidistant Measuring)

There may be times when you may want to place several objects the same distance from a central object. Using any of the previously mentioned measuring techniques can be time-consuming and even inaccurate, especially when you deal with complex images. Illustrator's Offset Path (see Figure 4-5), however, enables you to automatically align objects equidistantly from a central object.

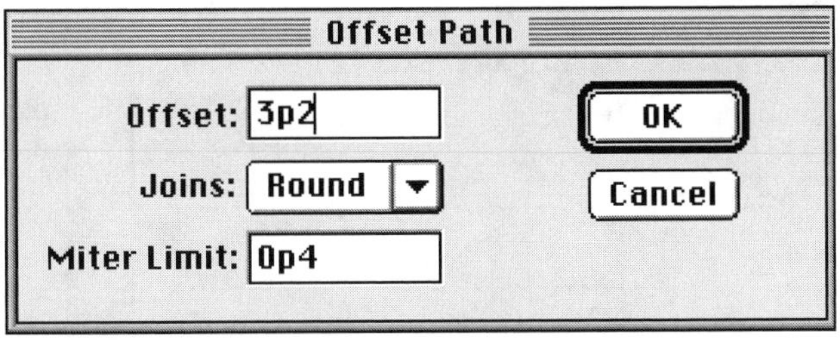

Figure 4-5: The Offset Path dialog box

First, select the central object. Then choose Object ➪ Path ➪ Offset Path and enter the desired distance (in points, millimeters, or inches) in the Offset text field. After the new path is created, check the corner areas to see whether there are any overlapping areas that appear as loops. If so, use Unite to eliminate these unsightly aberrations by choosing Unite from the Pathfinder palette. Change the new path into a guide and align your objects to this guide.

Grids

There is nothing I've found more useful on a day-to-day basis than the Grid feature. Grids act as a framework for your artwork, providing an easy method for aligning and positioning images. Figure 4-6 shows an Illustrator document that has grids turned on.

Display grids by choosing View ➪ Show Grid (⌘-") [Ctrl+"]. Once grids are displayed, you can automatically snap to the grid points by turning on the Snap To feature: choose View ➪ Snap to Grid (⌘-Shift-") [Ctrl+Shift+"]. Turn off grids by choosing View ➪ Hide Grid (⌘-") [Ctrl+"].

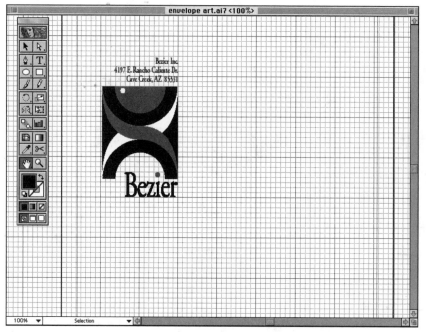

Figure 4-6: A document with Illustrator's Grid function turned on

Grids start from the origin of your document (usually the lower-left corner). If you want to change the position of the grid, you can do so by dragging the origin point (at the Origin Marker where the rulers meet) to the new starting position for the grid. Reset the grid position (and the ruler origin) by double-clicking the Origin Marker.

Tip   If you would like grids to be displayed in each new document, open your Adobe Illustrator Startup file in your Illustrator Plug-Ins folder and turn on grids in that document. Then save the Startup file. All new documents will have grids displayed when you first create them.

Grid Color, Style, and Spacing

You can customize the way grids look by changing the Grid preferences. Choose File ⇨ Preferences ⇨ Guides & Grid, and the Guides & Grid Preferences dialog box (Figure 4-7) appears. Here you can change the grid color and spacing. Pick a new color from the list of colors or choose Other to use the color picker to pick a new color for your grids. Because I'm just too darn picky, I pick cyan, and then go to the color picker and lighten it substantially. The result is nonrepro-blue-looking lines that make my grid resemble graph paper (which I've always thought should be called grid paper).

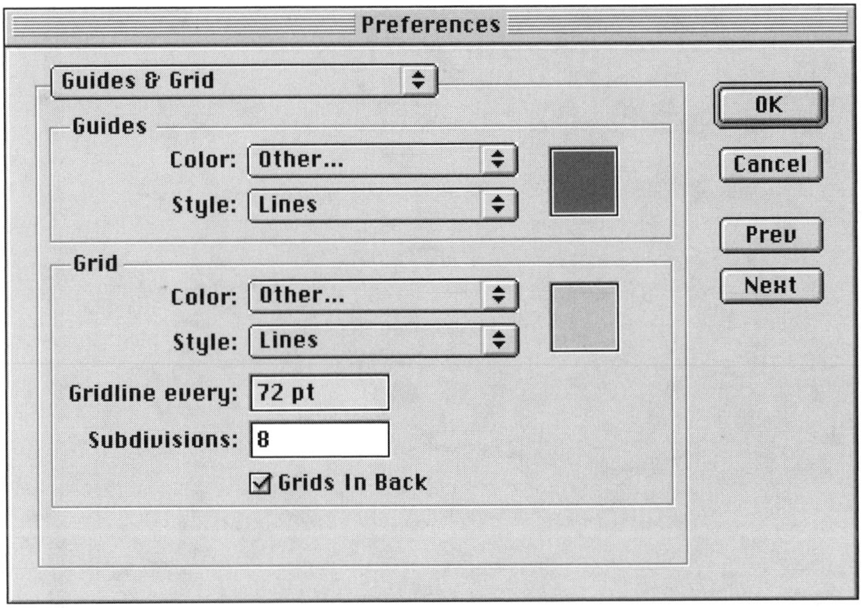

Figure 4-7: The Guides & Grid Preferences dialog box

You can also choose between lines and dots as the grid style. I prefer to use lines for my grid, as dots can turn an already busy-looking page into one with all sorts of, well, dots all over the place.

New Feature New to Illustrator 8 is the Grids in Back checkbox in the Guides & Grid preferences. The box is checked by default so that the gridlines aren't running on top of your artwork.

To change the space between the major (darker) gridlines, enter a value in the Gridline Every text field. To create subdivisions (minor) between the dark values, enter a number for how many sections should be created between the main lines. If you enter 1 as the value, no subdivisions are created. Because you're defining the number of divisions, not the number of lines, entering 2 will create one line between the two main lines. The standard 1-inch gridline with eight subdivisions creates ⅛-inch squares.

The Magically Spinning Grid

Your grid doesn't have to consist of just vertical and horizontal lines. You can rotate the grid to any angle you like by changing the Constrain Angle in General Preferences (⌘-K) [Ctrl+K]. Figure 4-8 shows a grid set at an angle of 6.275°. This is perfect for working with angled artwork; even if only a portion of the artwork is at an angle, the Constrain Angle can be set temporarily to the angle of the artwork.

Figure 4-8: A grid rotated to 6.275°

The Secret Power of Grids

If what I listed above were all that grids could do, I'd be way happy. After all, this is a feature that makes Illustrator closer to CAD programs without losing any of its wonderful design capabilities. But the one secret feature of grids that Adobe doesn't want you to know about (actually, I'm sure they don't really care either way) is this: Grids are the perfect transparency indicator layer.

What the heck am I talking about? Well, because Illustrator's paper color (the document and the Artboard) is always white, it can be hard to tell whether paths are Filled with white, Filled with None, or are the hole part of a compound path. Displaying the grid ends the confusion instantly. Objects with a white Fill don't display the grid behind them; objects with a Fill of None or that are simply a hole in a compound path show the grid through their openings. Even if you aren't going to use the grid for alignment or snap-to, the transparency indicator feature is a great way to know *exactly* what's going on with questionably filled paths. Figure 4-9 shows objects with Fills of white and None on a grid background.

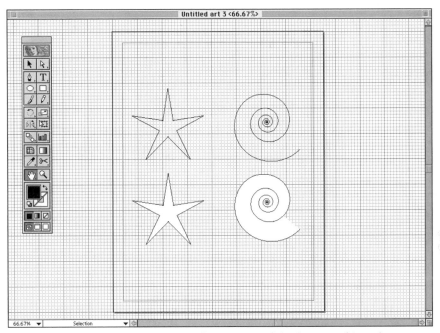

Figure 4-9: The top objects have a Fill of None and the bottom objects have a Fill of white

Guides

Guides are teeny, tiny little people who show you around Illustrator. The more of them you make, the easier it is to use the program. (Uh huh . . . I know, let you know when the shuttle lands. . . . Sigh.)

Okay, actually, *guides* are dotted or solid lines that help you align artwork. Guides do not print, and they are saved with documents. In Illustrator and most desktop-publishing software, guides are straight lines extending from one edge of a document to the other. But in Illustrator, you can also turn *any* path into a guide (see the following section).

Creating Guides

You can create guides in two ways: by pulling them out from the rulers and by transforming paths into guides.

To pull a guide from a ruler, first make the vertical and horizontal rulers visible by choosing View ➪ Show Rulers (⌘-R) [Ctrl+R]. To create guides that span the entire Pasteboard, click the vertical or horizontal ruler and drag out.

To transform an existing path into a guide, select the path and choose View ➪ Make Guides (⌘-5) [Ctrl+5].

Tip   And now a word about the Magic Rotating Guide (possibly the coolest tip you'll ever learn): When you drag a guide out from the vertical ruler, hold down Option [Alt] and the vertical guide becomes a horizontal guide. And vice versa.

Moving Guides

Moving an unlocked guide is simple — click it and drag. If guides are locked, unlock them by choosing View ➪ Lock.

If you aren't sure whether the guides in your document are locked or unlocked, click and hold on the View menu. If you see a check mark next to Lock Guides, the guides are locked (and all new guides will also be locked). To unlock all the document's guides, choose View ➪ Lock Guide; to lock guides again, choose View ➪ Lock Guide (yes, it's a toggle).

All guides in a document have a special status of "lockedness," where all guides are either locked or unlocked. Weirdly enough, however, guides can be locked and unlocked individually as well by selecting them and choosing Object ➪ Lock (⌘-2) [Ctrl+2] and Object ➪ Unlock All (⌘-Option-2) [Ctrl+Alt+2].

Releasing Guides

To release a guide, or change it into a path, select the guide and choose View ➪ Release Guides (⌘-Option-5) [Ctrl+Alt+5].

To release multiple guides first, make sure that the guides are unlocked; in other words, make sure that there's no check mark next to Lock Guides in the View menu. Then select the guides (in the same way you select multiple paths: either drag a marquee around the guides or Shift-click each guide) and choose View ➪ Release Guides (⌘-5) [Ctrl+5].

Tip   Selecting *all* guides — even those that are currently paths — by dragging a marquee or Shift-clicking can be a chore. Here's another way: Make sure that the guides are not locked and choose Edit ➪ Select All (⌘-A) [Ctrl+Alt]. Then select View ➪ Release (⌘-Option-6) [Ctrl+Alt+6]. This releases all guides and, more importantly, selects all paths that were formerly guides (all other paths and objects are deselected). Then choose View ➪ Make Guides (⌘-5) [Ctrl+5] and all guides become guides again and are selected.

For the most part, guides behave exactly like their path counterparts. As long as guides are unlocked, you may select them, hide them, group them, and even paint them (although paint attributes will not be visible onscreen or on a printout until the guides are converted back into paths).

Clear Guides

Let's say you have just finished a fantastic drawing that you created with the help of many guides. Now that the image is complete you want to delete those guides. Sure, you can unlock them and select them holding down the Shift key. Or, if you were really thinking, you could put those guides on a layer and simply Select All then Delete. Well, Illustrator 8 has just made your life even easier. By choosing the Clear Guides option under the View menu, all guides are miraculously deleted.

Smart Guides

New to Illustrator 8 is the welcome addition of Smart Guides. These guides pop-up to help you create a shape with precision, align objects with accuracy, and move and transform objects with ease.

Some of the Smart Guide display options are:

✦ **Text Label Hints**: These hints pop-up when you drag over your object. They tell you what each area is. For example, if you drag over a line, the hint will pop-up with the word "path." If you drag over an anchor point, the hint will say "anchor point."

✦ **Transform Tools**: When you are rotating, scaling, or shearing an object with this option checked, Smart Guides will show up to help you out.

✦ **Construction Guides**: These let you view guidelines when using Smart Guides.

✦ **Object Highlighting**: This option will highlight the object you are pointing to.

Checkboxes enable you to turn these options on and off.

Angles

The Smart Guides dialog box lets you pick what angles will display guides when you drag an object. You can choose from seven presets or create a Custom Angle of your own.

Snapping Tolerance

Snapping Tolerance isn't how much patience you have with a spouse before you explode. Rather, it lets you choose how close you have to have an object to another object before the first object automatically "snaps" to the second object. You set the Snapping Tolerance in points, the lower the number the closer you have to move the objects to each other. If the number is pretty high, then an object will snap to another object if it's merely passing by.

Guide Preferences

In the Guide Preferences dialog box (choose File ➪ Preferences ➪ Guides & Grid), you can change the style and the color of the guides. Choose a color from the pop-up menu or select Other to choose a color from the color picker. Unlike with grids, I like to use a darker, more vibrant color than a watered-down cyan. No matter which color you choose, keep it different from the Grid color and a contrasting color to colors you're using in your document.

Guide Style can be set to either dots or lines; which you choose is a matter of preference. However, you may want to pick the opposite of what you've chosen for grids, to further differentiate the two.

Measuring for Printing

Thinking ahead to the time your job will be printed is always a good thing, and two of the most important areas of printing are the placement and the sizing of your artwork within the Illustrator document. This section deals with production-oriented issues you might face while using Illustrator to create printable pieces.

Stepping

Oftentimes, you'll create something that's quite small and you'll need to have several copies of the artwork on the page at once. Setting up your artwork for optimal spacing and printing is referred to as *stepping*.

Illustrator doesn't do stepping automatically, but it does provide the tools you need to step your artwork.

1. Make sure the Control palette is open. Then select the finished artwork and open the Move dialog box (double-click the Selection tool).

2. Enter the width of the art in the Horizontal field. Enter **0** (zero) in the Vertical field. Click the Copy button (or press Option-Return).

3. Choose Object ➪ Transform ➪ Transform Again (⌘-D) [Ctrl+D] to create another duplicate of the artwork. Press ⌘-D [Ctrl+D] until there is the right number of pieces across the page.

4. Select the entire row of artwork, and open the Move dialog box again.

5. Enter **0** (zero) in the Horizontal field, and enter the height of the art in the Vertical field. Click the Copy button (or press Option-Return).

6. Choose Object ⇨ Transform ⇨ Transform Again (⌘-D) [Ctrl+D] to create another duplicate of the row of artwork. Press ⌘-D [Ctrl+D] until there is the right number of pieces down the page, as shown in Figure 4-10.

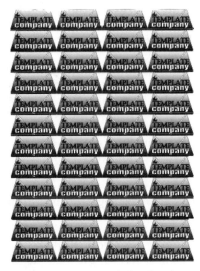

Figure 4-10: Artwork that has been stepped and repeated on a page

Creating Crop Marks

Crop marks are little lines that are designed to help you cut (or crop) along the edges of your illustration after the document has been printed (see Figure 4-11). Crops (that's the slang term; if you're even half cool you won't say "crop marks") don't intrude on the edges of the artwork, but instead are offset a bit from the corners of where the edges are.

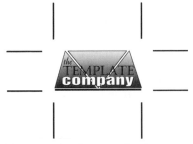

Figure 4-11: Crop marks show where the edges of the artwork are

Unfortunately, you can only create one set of crop marks per document. Making multiple crop marks by drawing them yourself or using the Trim Marks filter (Filter ➪ Create ➪ Trim Marks) isn't enough for color separations. Black crop marks that you create by drawing may be 100% of process colors but will not contain any other spot color that you may have in your illustration. (This problem is the result of a serious limitation in Illustrator: The program does not allow you to choose "registration" as a color, which would print on every color plate.) Trim marks created with the Trim Marks filter are 100% black.

Here's a workaround: Choose the crop marks and/or trim marks you created and Stroke them with 100% of all four process colors when you are printing out four-color separations. If you are printing out spot-color separations, you must copy the cropmarks, choose Edit ➪ Paste in Front (⌘-F) [Ctrl+F] or Edit ➪ Paste in Back (⌘-B) [Ctrl+B], and then color the Stroke of the crops with the spot color you are using, choosing the Overprint Strokes option in the Paint Style palette. Additional crop marks need to be pasted in front or pasted in back for every additional color separation in your document.

To transform a selected rectangle drawn with the rectangle tool into crop marks, choose Object ➪ Crop Marks ➪ Make.

Caution   The rectangle can only be modified prior to becoming crop marks by moving it or resizing it via the Scale tool. If any transformation is done to the rectangle, a message appears saying that you can only make crop marks out of a single rectangle. If a rectangle is drawn with a Constrain Angle set to an angle other than 0°, 90°, 180°, or 270° (–90°), you will not be able to make crop marks out of that rectangle.

If you choose Object ➪ Crop Marks ➪ Make when nothing is selected, crop marks will appear around the edge of the single full page. If Tile Imageable Areas is enabled in Document Setup, the cropmarks will appear only around the first page. If crops are set to the size of the page and the page is moved with the Page tool, or if the document has been resized with the Document Setup dialog box, the crop marks *will not move*.

To release selected crop marks, choose Object ➪ Crop Marks ➪ Release. If the crop marks were created from a rectangle, then that rectangle is an editable path that can be resized and changed back into crop marks, deleted, or modified. Any rectangle that has been changed back from being a set of crop marks will have a Fill and Stroke of None.

Note   You cannot choose Object ➪ Crop Marks ➪ Release when no crop marks are in your document. In addition, Object ➪ Crop Marks ➪ Release does not release trim marks made with the Filter ➪ Create ➪ Trim Marks command.

Japanese Crop Marks and Trim Marks

Instead of using standard crop marks, you can choose to use Japanese Crop Marks, which are different looking, yet seemingly no more functional than regular crop marks. If you check the General Preference setting Japanese Crop Marks, both crop marks and trim marks will take on the characteristics of Japanese Crop Marks (shown in Figure 4-12).

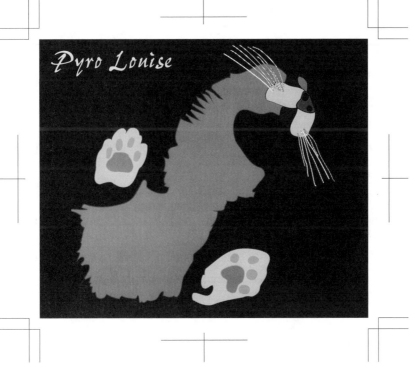

Figure 4-12: Japanese Crop Marks

You can create a document that has both traditional and Japanese trim marks. To do so, select the object you would like traditional trim marks on and apply the Create Trim Marks filter (Filter ➪ Create ➪ Trim Marks). Then check the Japanese Crop Marks checkbox in General Preferences (File ➪ Preferences ➪ General, ⌘-K) [Ctrl+K], select the next object, and reapply the filter (just press ⌘-Shift-E [Ctrl+E]). The second set of trim marks will be Japanese.

I checked with several local printers and designers (in the United States) and most of them said that they would be able to use the Japanese Crop Marks as well as traditional ones. Each, however, expressed concern that there is a greater chance of trimming or measuring incorrectly with Japanese Crop Marks because of their unfamiliarity with them.

Summary

✦ Templates are used in Illustrator to make your drawing easier and more precise.

✦ The Auto Trace tool works with any placed bitmap image.

✦ Manual tracing will usually generate better results than using the Auto Trace tool.

✦ The Measure tool provides a quick way to measure distances in your Illustrator documents.

✦ Measurements generated by the Measure tool will appear in the Move dialog box the next time you open it.

✦ Guides can be created from any object by selecting the object and pressing ⌘-5 [Ctrl+5].

✦ You can quickly create document high/wide guides by dragging out from the rulers.

✦ Use the Copy button within the Move dialog box to step and repeat artwork.

✦ Use the new Smart Guides feature to make editing much easier.

✦   ✦   ✦

Working with Illustrator Files

Illustrator has a way of working that is unique, at least in the world of desktop publishing and graphics. As soon as you run the program, an empty document window appears, ready for you to begin drawing. No hassles, just an instant drawing area. A new document window that is ready to use is shown in Figure 5-1.

Setting Up a New Document

Choosing New (⌘-N) [Ctrl+N] from the File menu when you're already *in* Illustrator creates a brand new document and makes that new document the *active* document. In previous versions of Illustrator, users were hit with an evil dialog box, where they had to indicate which template they wanted to use. Because most users did not normally use templates, this command was altered to instantly create a new document with no questions asked.

Many other graphics and desktop-publishing programs, including PageMaker, Photoshop, and QuarkXPress, ask you to set up your document size before the document is created. When you create a new Illustrator document, it defaults to the size of the startup document that is located in the Plug-Ins folder (see Chapter 6 for more information on altering the startup document). By default, this document is 8.5 x 11 inches, and it is in the *portrait* orientation (meaning that the width is less than the height). The document window initially shows up at Fit in Window size. In the title bar at the top of the window, you see Untitled Art 1 <100%> (or whatever percent the document is displayed at). As soon as you save the document, the title bar contains the name of the document.

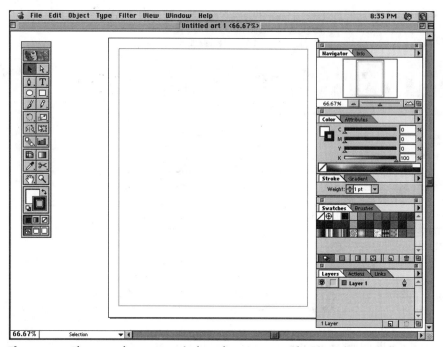

Figure 5-1: The new document window that appears when you first run Illustrator

You cannot change the way that some things appear when you first start Illustrator. For example, the Selection tool is always selected in the toolbox. Another unchangeable item is the initial Paint Style that you begin drawing with: a Fill of white and a Stroke of 1-point Black. The character attributes are always the same: 12-point Helvetica, Auto Leading, Flush Left alignment. In addition, the initial layer color is always light blue (a color that is just dark enough so that it doesn't conflict with cyan).

Changing the Document Setup

To change almost anything about the document structure and how you work with that document, you need to go to the Document Setup dialog box (see Figure 5-2) by choosing File ⇨ Document Setup or pressing Option-⌘-P [Alt+Ctrl+ P]. In this dialog box, you can change the size of the Artboard, define how and when paths are split, change the ruler units, and change the way that printable page edges, patterns, and placed images are viewed.

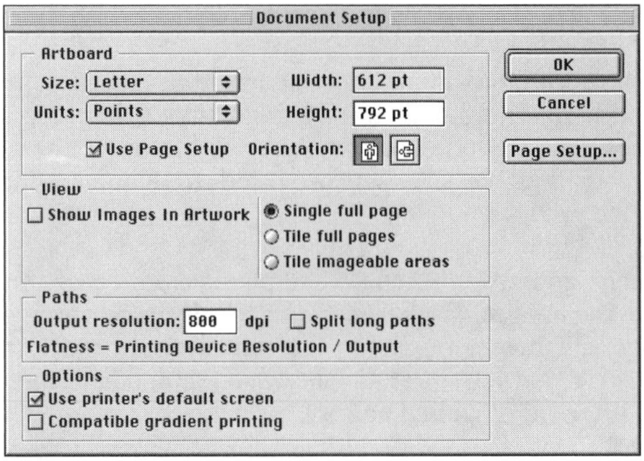

Figure 5-2: The Document Setup dialog box

The following sections describe the various options that are available in the Document Setup dialog box. Any changes that you make to these options are saved with the document.

The Dark Ages

Creating a new document hasn't always been easy. Back in the days of Illustrator 88, and even Illustrator 3 to some extent, creating new illustrations was rather annoying. Choosing New Document brought up a dialog box that politely, yet sternly, asked you to choose a template to trace in Illustrator. Most of the time, though, you didn't want a template, so you had to click the little None button in the dialog box. If you pressed Return, Illustrator would attempt to open a template.

Illustrator 3 was a little more flexible. It let you create a new document without having to deal with the dialog box that asked you to choose a template. You could either press ⌘-Option-N [Ctrl+Alt+N] or hold down the Option [Alt] key when you chose File ➪ New. If you forgot about the Option [Alt] key, you had another chance. Pressing ⌘-N [Ctrl+N] when you were in the dialog box would send the box away and create a new document with no template — as long as you didn't have Directory Assistance, Super Boomerang, or any other utilities that created a new open folder when you pressed ⌘-N [Ctrl+N].

Adobe slowly realized that you didn't want nor need a template to do everything, and now, fortunately, template-forcing is a thing of the past.

In fact, opening templates has been removed entirely, leaving you the one option of placing an image on the background layer. A layer can act as a template. Select Template in the Layers Options dialog box.

Artboard Options

In Illustrator, the *Artboard* defines the maximum drawing area that can be printed. The Artboard is useful as a guide to where objects on a page belong. In older versions of Illustrator, the maximum printable size was 11 x 17 inches; with version 6, it increased to 120 x 120 inches or 10 square feet (provided that you can find a printer that prints that big).

Note   Illustrator's separation setup ignores the Artboard and places crop marks around the entire imageable area. The imageable area, according to this dialog box, is only the area where artwork exists. It may be within the Artboard, but it also may extend onto the Pasteboard. When you export an illustration to another program, such as QuarkXPress, the Artboard is ignored entirely.

You can view a document in inches, points and picas, or centimeters. The measurement units affect the numbers on the rulers and the locations of the hash marks on those same rulers. The measurement system also changes the way measurements are displayed in the Info palette and in all dialog boxes where you enter a measurement (other than a percentage).

The measurement system is changed in either the Units + Undo Preferences dialog box (choose File ➪ Preferences ➪ Units + Undo) for all documents, or in the Document Setup dialog box (choose File ➪ Document Setup, or press Option-⌘-P [Alt+Ctrl+P]) for the currently active document.

Choose the size of the Artboard by selecting one of the following preset sizes in the Size pop-up menu:

✦ **Letter** is 8.5 x 11 inches.

✦ **Legal** is 8.5 x 14 inches.

✦ **Tabloid** is 11 x 17 inches.

✦ **A4** is 8.268 x 11.693 inches (21 x 29.7 centimeters).

✦ **A3** is 11.693 x 16.535 inches (29.7 x 42 centimeters).

✦ **B5** is 7.165 x 10 inches (18.2 x 25.4 centimeters).

✦ **B4** is 10.118 x 14.331 inches (55.7 x 36.4 centimeters).

✦ **Custom** is whatever size you type in the Dimensions text fields.

A4, A3, B5, and B4 are European paper sizes.

You define the orientation of your Artboard by choosing one of the two Orientation pages. On the left is Portrait orientation, where the lesser of the two dimensions goes across the page from left to right, and the greater of the two dimensions goes from top to bottom. On the right is Landscape orientation, where the greater of the two dimensions goes across the page from left to right, and the lesser of the two dimensions goes from top to bottom.

ASK TOULOUSE: Multiple Pages in Illustrator?

Kate: I think my Illustrator is broken.

Toulouse: I doubt it, but why do you think that's the case?

Kate: I can't put anything on page 2.

Toulouse: That might be because there is no page 2.

Kate: Ha, ha, ha. Okay, so how do I create page 2?

Toulouse: Look, this isn't Word or Xpress. There is no page 2.

Kate: Really?

Toulouse: Really. But you can kinda fudge it.

Kate: I'm trying to lose weight. . . . I put on some pounds after the Scarecrow gig ended.

Toulouse: Sorry to hear that. You can set up Illustrator to have either 1 or 9 pages.

Kate: One or 9? Oh, that makes sense.

Toulouse: Good. Now, to get 9 pages, go into Document Setup, and select the Tile Imageable Areas option.

Kate: And where are pages 2 through 9?

Toulouse: Zoom out a few times, and you'll see all 9 pages.

Kate: All I see is a big grid thing that divides my Artboard into 9 sections.

Toulouse: That's it!

Kate: You're kidding me.

Toulouse: Nope. And when you print, you can pick which pages to print. They're numbered 1, 2, and 3; then 4, 5, and 6; then 7, 8, and 9. So you normally start on page 5.

Kate: I think I'll wait for Illustrator 9.

If you check the Use Page Setup box, then the Artboard will default to the page size and orientation that is selected in the Page Setup dialog box.

View Options

You can control how certain things in Illustrator are viewed by checking the appropriate boxes:

✦ The **Show Images In Artwork** option displays placed EPS (Encapsulated PostScript) images. When the checkbox is not checked, placed artwork is represented as a box with an *X* inside it.

✦ The **Single full page** option creates one Page Setup size outline on the page.

✦ The **Tile full pages** option creates as many page outlines (from Page Setup) as will completely print. For example, if the Artboard is landscape, 11 x 17 inches, and the selected page size in Page Setup is portrait, 8.5 x 11 inches, then two page outlines appear side-by-side in the document.

✦ The **Tile imageable areas** option creates a grid on the document, with the size of each *block* equal to the page size that is chosen in the Page Setup dialog box. Little page numbers appear in the lower-left corner of each block, representing the pages you enter in the page *x* to page *x* fields in the Print dialog box.

To move the page outlines, select the Page tool and click and drag in the Artboard. The click-point of the page is always the lower-left corner.

Path-Splitting Options

Robot would be screaming his bubble-head off if Will Robinson ever thought about clicking the Split Long Paths checkbox. The checkbox looks friendly enough, but the results of checking it can be deadly. If you are quick enough, you can always undo the split paths function, but the actual splitting of paths doesn't always happen when and where you expect it to happen.

Instead, it happens only when you save or print a document. This feature presents some very interesting problems. First, if you save the document and close it right after you save it, the paths are split permanently, and you cannot undo the damage the next time you open the document. Second, after you print a document, saving and closing it is a very natural thing to do. But, once again, you return it to normal. Another problem arises when you are working in Preview mode: If you forget whether you checked the option, it's not always easy to determine whether paths have been split.

The Split Long Paths function tries to fix paths that are too long or too complex for your laser printer to handle. By entering the final output resolution for the Illustrator document, you can ensure that it will have a better chance of printing than if paths were not split. Every curve in Illustrator is made of tiny straight segments. The higher the resolution of the output device, the more straight segments that are needed to create the curve. The processing power of the laser printer limits how many little straight segments can be in one path. If you exceed that limit, Illustrator chops away at the paths, splitting them into several smaller sections. Because this problem occurs more frequently with low-resolution devices, the greater the number you enter in the Output resolution field, the more paths will be split. Figure 5-3 shows an original document and several examples of path splitting.

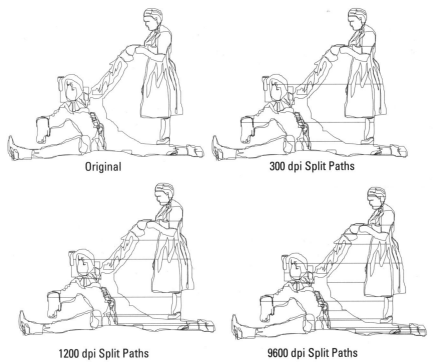

Original   300 dpi Split Paths

1200 dpi Split Paths   9600 dpi Split Paths

Figure 5-3: A document before and after path-splitting at different
output resolutions

The only reason to use the Split Long Paths function is if a document fails to print
because of a PostScript error (usually a limit check error). But instead of just
checking the Split Long Paths checkbox, first make a copy of the entire document
(doing a Save As or Save a Copy with another name will do this quickly) and then
split paths in the new document. The original file will not contain split paths. Split
paths are extremely difficult to reassemble, and the results from split paths can be
horrifying. Please use caution when you split paths.

Using the Printer's Default Screen

For gradients on low-resolution printers (600 dpi or less) when composite printing
only, Illustrator uses a dither pattern called Adobe Screens (not to be confused with
Adobe Accurate Screens) when Use Printer Default Screen is unchecked. This
increases the apparent levels of gray by fracturing the halftone cells.

You'll notice when you first open a document that the Use Printer Default Screens
checkbox is checked. But, the first time you Fill an object with a gradient, it

automatically unchecks itself. Illustrator assumes that when you use gradients that you want Adobe Screens turned on; if you don't want Adobe Screens on, you have to manually turn Use Printer Default Screen back on. When checking Use Printer Default Screens, you're just disabling Adobe Screens; you are *not* telling Illustrator to image the file at the printer's default line screen. Output software can still set the printer's line screen for the Illustrator file.

Compatible Gradient Printing

Checking this option allows gradients created with Illustrator to be printed on older PostScript Level 1 printers and PostScript-clone printers. However, checking this option when printing to a PostScript Level 2 printer can dramatically slow print processing time.

If you aren't sure if your printer can handle gradients properly, create a document with about 20 ellipses that are filled with gradients. If the document prints, you shouldn't have any trouble. If the document prints and there are empty or solid areas where there should be a gradient, you'll need to check this option when printing documents with gradients.

Navigating the Document

Being able to move through a document easily is a key skill in Illustrator. You rarely can fit the entire illustration in the document window at a magnification where you can see much of the detail of the image. Usually, you are zooming in, zooming out, or moving off to the side or above or below to focus in on certain areas of the document.

Who's Zoomin' Who?

The most basic of navigational concepts in Illustrator is the capability to zoom to different magnification levels. Illustrator's magnification levels work like a magnifying glass. In the real world, you use a magnifying glass to see details that aren't readily visible without it. In the Illustrator world, you use the different magnification levels to see details that aren't readily visible at 100% view. The magnification levels of Illustrator do not affect the illustration. If you zoom in to 200% and print, the illustration will be printed at the same size as it would if the view were 100%. It will *not* print twice as large.

The Zoom Tools

You use the two Zoom tools, Zoom In and Zoom Out, to magnify a certain area of artwork and then return to the standard view.

To use the Zoom In tool, select it in the toolbox, press Z, or press ⌘-Spacebar [Ctrl+Spacebar]. Whichever method you use, the Zoom In tool should appear. It looks like a magnifying glass with a plus sign in it. Clicking any spot in the illustration enlarges that part of the illustration to the next magnification level. The highest magnification level is 6400%. Of course, the Zoom In feature does have a pitfall: The more you zoom in on an illustration, the less of that illustration you see at one time. New to Illustrator 8, the Navigator palette helps you out of that pitfall. You can stay zoomed in and move easily to another section by dragging the red viewing rectangle within the Navigator window to another area.

New Feature New to Illustrator 8 is the capability to zoom in at any entered numerical amount. Adobe has given Illustrator users the capability to type in an amount to zoom in. This is quite an improvement over version 7, where you had only 17 different Zoom levels. To access the Zoom level, double-click the view area at the bottom left of Illustrator's window, type the new amount you wish to zoom in, and press Enter or Return.

Where you click with the Zoom In tool is very important. Clicking the center of the window enlarges the illustration to the next magnification level, but the edges (top, bottom, left, and right) are cropped off as the magnification increases. Clicking the upper-right corner crops off mostly the lower-left edges, and so forth. If you are interested in seeing a particular part of the illustration close up, click that part at each magnification level to ensure that it remains in the window.

New Feature New to Illustrator 8 is the automatic recentering of the object that you are zooming in on. In other words, when you click on a section of your illustration, it will zoom and center that section in the document window.

If you zoom in too far, you can use the Zoom Out tool to zoom out again. To access the Zoom Out tool, press Option while you click with the Zoom tool or press ⌘-Option-Spacebar [Ctrl+Alt+Spacebar]. Clicking with the Zoom Out tool reduces the magnification level to the next lowest level. You can zoom out to 6.25% ($\frac{1}{16}$ actual size).

When you use the Zoom tools, you change the size of everything in the document, not just the illustration. You change the size of all paths, objects, the Artboard, the Pasteboard, and the Page Setup boundaries relative to the current magnification level. However, the points and paths retain their shape and thickness at all times.

If you need to zoom in quite a bit, you can zoom in more easily by using the Zoom In tool to draw a marquee (by clicking and dragging diagonally) around the objects that you want to magnify. The area that is surrounded will magnify as much as possible so that everything inside the box just fits in the window that you have open, as shown in Figure 5-4. Dragging a box with the Zoom Out tool does nothing special; it works the same as if you had just clicked with the Zoom Out tool.

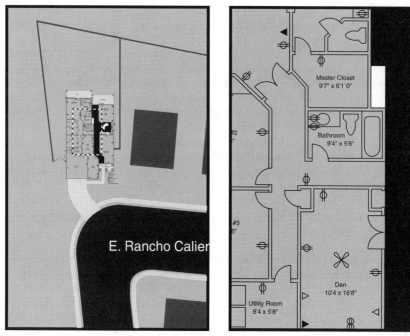

Figure 5-4: Zooming in to a certain area in the original image (left) results in the magnification and placement of the image shown on the right

Tip   You can move a zoom marquee around *while you're drawing it* by pressing the Spacebar after you've begun drawing the marquee but before you release the mouse button.

Other Zooming Techniques

You also can zoom in and zoom out by using commands in the View menu. Choose View ⇨ Zoom In (⌘-+) [Ctrl++] to zoom in one level at a time until the magnification level is 6400%. The Zoom In feature zooms from the center out. Choose View ⇨ Zoom Out (⌘--) [Ctrl+-] to zoom out one level at a time until the magnification level is 6.25%.

You can use two different methods to automatically zoom to 100%. The first method is to double-click the Zoom tool in the toolbox. This action changes the view to 100% instantly. A better way to zoom in to 100% is to choose View ⇨ Actual Size (⌘-1) [Ctrl+1], which not only changes the magnification level to 100% but also centers the page. At this view, an 8.5 x 11-inch piece of paper should fit squarely over an 8.5 x 11-inch document on your Illustrator screen. The accuracy of the fit depends on the pixels-per-inch of your monitor.

Choosing Actual Size also centers the document in your window (this is unlike double-clicking the Zoom tool, which resizes the page to 100% but brings the current center at the smaller or larger size to the center when resizing).

Tip You can choose from two different methods to change the document view to the Fit in Window size. Fit in Window instantly changes the magnification level of the document so that the entire Artboard (not necessarily the artwork, if it isn't located on the page) fits in the window and is centered in it. One way to automatically change to the Fit in Window view is to choose View ⇨ Fit in Window (⌘-0). Another way is to double-click the Hand tool.

To instantly zoom in to 6400%, draw a tiny marquee with the Zoom In tool. At actual size, the marquee must be smaller than ½ x ½ inches for the magnification level to go instantly to 6400%. It may be necessary to draw more than one marquee if the current magnification level is lower than 100%.

You can never undo any type of magnification level change. Choosing Edit ⇨ Undo after zooming will undo the last change you made to the document before you changed the magnification level.

ASK TOULOUSE: Zooming Out Wrong?

Charlie: You know, that marquee thing just isn't happening here.

Toulouse: I bet Joan Collins sabotaged your system.

Charlie: Uh, wrong show. Anyway, I drag and . . . nothing!

Toulouse: It doesn't zoom in? Maybe I should be calling you Blake?

Charlie: No, and no, it doesn't zoom out!

Toulouse: Well, it's supposed to zoom in, not out. I guess then it's only half broken.

Charlie: I thought the Zoom Out tool zoomed out. Hence the name.

Toulouse: You aren't trying to draw a marquee with the Zoom Out tool, are you?

Charlie: Sure. Is that a problem?

Toulouse: The Zoom Out tool doesn't work by drawing a marquee. You have to click with it. Drawing with a marquee is the same as clicking.

Charlie: But what if I want to zoom out really far, right away?

Toulouse: Double-click on the Hand tool to make the page fit in your window. Is that small enough?

Charlie: No . . . I want it smaller.

Toulouse: You can quickly go to 6.25% by Option[Ctrl+Alt]-clicking the Zoom tool.

Navigator Palette

New to Illustrator 8 is the addition of a Navigator palette (see Figure 5-5). The Navigator palette lets you move about your image without having to zoom in and zoom out or to set up custom views. Adobe took the Navigator palette idea from Photoshop and put it into Illustrator. You can zoom in and out a preset amount by pressing the Zoom In or Zoom Out button. Another way to navigate around is to drag the slider higher or lower. You can also type in an exact amount to zoom in or out. What is really nice about this feature is that you can type in any amount, even with decimal points. By dragging the rectangle in the Navigator palette, you can move about your illustration without having to scroll or to use the Hand tool over and over. The red rectangle can be changed to another color by choosing the Palette Options in the Navigator pop-up menu.

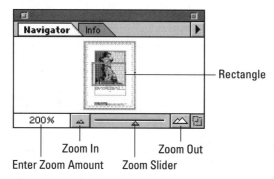

Figure 5-5: The Navigator palette

Using the Scroll Bars

Sometimes after you zoom in to a high magnification, part of the drawing that you want to see is outside the window area. Instead of zooming in and out, you can use one of two different scrolling techniques to move around inside the document.

The scroll bar on the right side of the document window controls where you are vertically in the document. Clicking the up arrow displays what is above the window's boundaries by pushing everything in the window *down* in little increments. Clicking the down arrow displays what is below the window's boundaries by pushing the document *up* in little increments. Dragging the thumbnail up displays what is above the window's boundaries proportionately by whatever distance that you drag. (Be careful not to drag too far or you will be previewing beyond the top of the Artboard.) Dragging the little elevator box down displays what is below the window's boundaries proportionately by whatever distance that you drag. Clicking on the gray bar above the little elevator box between the arrows displays what is above the window's boundaries in big chunks.

Clicking the gray bar below the little elevator box between the arrows displays what is below the window's boundaries in big chunks.

The gray area of the right scroll bar is proportionate to the size of the Pasteboard. If the little elevator box is at the top of the scroll bar, then you are viewing the top edge of the 120" x 120" Pasteboard. If it is centered, you are viewing the vertical center of the Pasteboard.

The scroll bar on the bottom of the document window controls where you are in the document horizontally. Clicking the left arrow displays what is to the left of the window's boundaries by pushing everything in the window *right* in little increments. Clicking the right arrow displays what is to the right of the window's boundaries by pushing the document *left* in little increments. Dragging the little elevator box left displays what is to the left of the window's boundaries by whatever distance proportionately that you drag. Dragging the little elevator box right displays what is to the right of the window boundaries by whatever distance proportionately that you drag. Clicking the gray bar between the arrows that is to the left of the little elevator box displays what is to the left of the window's boundaries in big chunks. Clicking the gray bar between the arrows that is to the right of the little elevator box displays what is to the right of the window's boundaries in big chunks.

Scrolling with the Hand Tool

The Hand tool improves upon the scroll bars. Instead of being limited to only horizontal and vertical movement, you can use the Hand tool to scroll in both directions simultaneously. It is especially useful for finding your way around a document when you are at a high magnification level. The higher the magnification level, the more you will use the Hand tool.

To use the Hand tool, either select it in the toolbox, press H, or press and hold the Spacebar. (If you are currently using the Type tool, press ⌘-Spacebar [Ctrl+Spacebar] and then release ⌘ [Ctrl] while keeping the Spacebar pressed.) Clicking and dragging the page will move the document around inside the document window.

Tip   When you click in the document, be sure to click the side that you want to see. Clicking at the top of the document and dragging down enables you to scroll down through almost an entire document at a height of one window. Clicking in the center and dragging enables you to scroll through only half a window size at a time. If the window of the document does not take up the entire screen space, you can continue to drag right off the window into the empty screen space. Just be sure that you first click within the document that you want to scroll.

The best thing about the Hand tool is that it works *live*. As you drag, the document moves under "your Hand." If you don't like where it is going, you can drag it back, still live. The second best thing is that to access it requires only one keystroke, a press of the Spacebar.

Caution You cannot use Undo (⌘-Z) [Ctrl+Z] to reverse scrolling that you have done with the scroll bars and the Hand tool.

Artwork Mode versus Preview Mode

In the old days, everyone worked in Artwork mode. You could occasionally check work in progress to see what the illustration would look like by switching to Preview mode. Usually the preview was not quite what you had in mind while you were in Artwork mode, so it was back to Artwork mode to fix everything, and then to Preview again to check, and so forth.

Illustrator enables you to work in both Artwork and Preview modes. The mode that you are in when documents are printing does not matter. Illustrator Fills and Strokes all paths and objects with the colors that are defined in the document, even if the document is in Artwork mode and those colors aren't visible. Saving the document while you are in Artwork mode does not affect anything in the document, but the next time you open it, it will be in Artwork mode. The same thing applies to Preview and Preview Selection modes: Whatever mode you are in is saved with the artwork.

You cannot undo a Preview or Artwork mode change (going from Preview Selection to Artwork, for example). If you make a Preview or Artwork mode change and then close your document, Illustrator asks you if you want to save changes, which in this case only refers to the view change.

Artwork (Only) Mode

To change the current document to Artwork mode, choose View ➪ Artwork (⌘-Y) [Ctrl+Y]. In Artwork mode, the illustration disappears and is replaced onscreen by outlines of all the Filled and Stroked paths. Text that has yet to be converted into outlines looks fine, although it is always black. Depending on your choice in the Document Setup dialog box (choose File ➪ Document Setup, or press Option-⌘-P [Alt+Ctrl+P]), a placed image is displayed as a box (if Show Images In Artwork is not checked) or as a black-and-white-only image surrounded by a box (if Show Placed Images is checked).

Working with a drawing in Artwork mode can be significantly faster than working with it in Preview mode. In more complex drawings, the difference between Artwork mode and Preview mode is significant; on very slow computers, working in Preview mode is next to impossible.

Artwork mode enables you to see every path that isn't directly overlapping another path; in Preview mode, many paths can be hidden. In addition, invisible masks are normally visible as paths in Artwork mode.

Placed artwork is displayed in black and white only, and templates are grayer than before. The main advantage to working in Artwork mode is the speed increase over Preview mode. The speed that you gain is even greater when the artwork contains gradients, patterns, placed artwork, and blends. In addition, you can select paths that were hidden by the Fills of other objects.

Tip If you have installed a plug-in called Artwork Speedup (originally located in the Utilities folder), your Anchor Points, Control Handle Points, and Control Handle Lines are black in Artwork mode.

Artwork mode can take some getting used to. To select paths in Artwork mode, you must click the paths or draw a marquee across them.

Artwork mode can be better than Preview because it's faster, and also because your brain can learn to know what the drawing looks like from seeing just the outlines, which show *all* of the paths, including masks (masking paths cannot be viewed in Preview).

ASK TOULOUSE: Artwork Schmartwork

Farrah: You know how you keep saying Artwork mode is so wonderful?

Toulouse: Well, it is.

Farrah: Then how come I still can't select certain paths?

Toulouse: Can you see the path you want to select?

Farrah: Sure, it's right next to the path that I keep selecting accidentally.

Toulouse: There's a couple things you can do.

Farrah: Great. And number one is . . . ?

Toulouse: First, you could zoom in really close, so the paths appear further apart. This allows for easier selecting.

Farrah: Makes sense. What if I don't feel like zooming in?

Toulouse: You could also select the path that keeps being selected and then press Shift and drag a marquee around both paths. That'll select the unselected path and deselect the selected path.

Farrah: That's it?

Toulouse: Since you asked — you could also lock the path you keep selecting; then the next click would select the other path.

Preview Mode

Choosing View ➪ Preview (⌘-Y) [Ctrl+Y] changes the view to Preview mode. In Preview mode, the document looks just the way it will look when you print it . . . except that you can't view overprinting.

New Feature

New to Illustrator 8 is the capability to view patterns in Strokes and in type. Previously, patterns in Strokes and type were displayed as gray areas, but printed fine.

In Preview mode, the color that you see on the screen represents only marginally what the actual output will be because of the differences between the way computer monitors work (red, green, and blue colors — the more of each color, the brighter each pixel appears) and the way printing works (Cyan, Magenta, Yellow, and Black colors — the more of each color, the darker each area appears). Monitor manufacturers make a number of calibration tools that decrease the difference between what you see on the monitor and the actual output. You can also use software solutions. One software solution, CIE calibration, is built into Adobe Illustrator (choose File ➪ Color Settings).

In Preview mode, you can see which objects overlap, which objects are in front and in back, where gradations begin and end, and how patterns are set up.

Note

Sometimes previewing complex drawings onscreen can take a long time. Usually this problem occurs when you are displaying paths with patterns or a great number of blends. To stop an illustration from being redrawn in Preview mode, press ⌘-period [Ctrl+period] to change the document to Artwork mode. If the redrawing has been completed before you press ⌘-period [Ctrl+period], everything is selected. Objects that were unselected are selected. This can be especially frustrating when you have spent a good deal of time selecting certain objects, but you didn't group these objects together. The selection or deselection of objects cannot be undone.

Preview Selection Mode

To change to Preview Selection mode, choose View ➪ Preview Selection (⌘-Shift-Y) [Ctrl+Shift+Y] to display all selected objects in Preview mode and all unselected objects in Artwork mode. Figure 5-6 shows an illustration in Preview Selection mode.

The Preview Selection mode can be useful in a complex illustration when you need to adjust a few object colors and want to see the results without waiting a long time. You can cancel redrawing in progress and return to Artwork mode by pressing ⌘-period [Ctrl+period]. You can even create new paths and adjust existing ones while in Preview Selection mode.

Figure 5-6: An image in Preview Selection mode

Combining Artwork and Preview Modes

Using the Layers palette, you can easily combine Artwork and Preview or Artwork and Preview Selection modes. You can force individual layers to display in Preview mode while other layers remain in Artwork mode. This feature can be useful when you have a layer with a placed image, gradients, or patterns (or all three) that would normally slow down the workflow. You can place those images on their own layer and set that layer to Artwork mode.

You also can view the same artwork in both Preview mode and Artwork mode at the same time by creating a new window for the current document. Choose Window ➪ New Window to create a window that is the same size as the original window. You can manipulate these two windows so that they are next to each other, and each window can have different viewing characteristics. One window can be in Preview mode, and the other one can be in Artwork mode. One window can be at Fit in Window size, and you can zoom the other to any percentage.

Tip

Using multiple windows to show Artwork and Preview modes of the same drawing simultaneously was used mainly when Illustrator did not enable artists to edit and create in Preview mode. This function is no longer as helpful as it once was, but you can still use it to preview an illustration when you want to select artwork that is hidden by Fills and Strokes of other artwork in Preview mode. In addition, two windows can be used for viewing the entire artwork at a small size, while editing a blown-up version in another.

Now You See It

Illustrator also provides options that enable you to show and hide various parts of an illustration:

✦ **Show Rulers** (choose View ➪ Show Rulers or press ⌘-R [Ctrl+R]) displays rulers (in the current measurement system) on the left side of the document and on the top of the document window. By default, all rulers measure up and to the right from the lower-left corner of the Artboard.

  • To change the measurement system that is displayed on the rulers, choose File ➪ Preferences ➪ Units & Undo and select the new measurement system for the General units. A quick way to instantly change ruler unit measurement systems is by pressing ⌘-Ctrl-U (Mac only), which cycles through the three measurement systems.

  • To change the origin of the rulers (0 across, 0 up), drag from the box where the rulers meet to the new intersection point. To return the rulers back to the default, double-click the white box in the upper left where the rulers meet.

  • Pressing ⌘-R [Ctrl+R] toggles between showing and hiding rulers. If rulers are showing, the menu item is Hide Rulers. If rulers are displayed when you save the document, they will be displayed the next time you open it. If rulers are not showing when you save the document, the rulers will be hidden the next time you open the document.

✦ **Show Page Tiling** (choose View ➪ Show Page Tiling) shows the outlines of the page guides from the Page Setup and Document Setup dialog boxes. When Page Tiling is visible, the menu item changes to Hide Page Tiling. The condition of Page Tiling is saved with the file.

✦ **Hide Edges** (choose View ➪ Hide Edges or press ⌘-H [Ctrl+H]) does not show paths, Anchor Points, Control Handles, or Control Handle Lines when it is selected in Preview mode and does not show Anchor Points, Control Handles, or Control Handle Lines in Artwork mode. When edges are hidden, the menu item reads Show Edges. Pressing ⌘-H [Ctrl+H] toggles between showing and hiding edges. Edges are always visible when you open a file, regardless of whether they were visible or hidden when you saved it.

Caution

Be careful to note when you have this feature enabled, as it can appear to the unwary that they are unable to select anything just because Hide Edges has been activated.

✦ **Show Guides** (choose View ➭ Show Guides or press ⌘-; [Ctrl+;]) shows all guides in your artwork, whether you created them by using rulers or by transforming paths into guides. Show Guides does not show guides that were hidden with the Hide (⌘-U) [Ctrl+U] command. The alternate, Hide Guides, hides all guides in the document. Whether you save a document with guides visible or hidden, they are always visible when you open a document.

Caution   Remember when this function is on so that you don't unwittingly pull guide after guide onto your document, wondering why they don't show up. Or you may choose Make Guides and wonder if you accidentally chose Hide instead because paths changed into guides simply disappear when Hide Guides is on.

Using Custom Views

Illustrator has a special feature called *custom views* that enables you to save special views of an illustration. Custom views contain view information, including magnification, location, and whether the illustration is in Artwork or Preview mode. If you have various layers in Preview mode and others in Artwork mode, custom views can also save that information. However, custom views do not record whether templates, rulers, page tiling, edges, or guides are shown or hidden.

To create a new view, set up the document in the way that you would like to save the view. Then choose View ➭ New View and name the view in the New View dialog box. Each of the first 10 views that you create is given a key command of ⌘-Option Shift-1 [Ctrl+Alt+Shift+1], ⌘-Option Shift-2 [Ctrl+Alt+Shift+2], and so on. You can create up to 25 custom views, but the last 15 will not have a key command. Custom views are saved with a document as long as you save it in Illustrator 8 format later.

Tip   If you find yourself continually going to a certain part of a document, zooming in or out, and changing back and forth between Preview and Artwork mode, that document is a prime candidate for creating custom views. Custom views are helpful to show clients artwork that you created in Illustrator. Instead of fumbling around in the client's presence, you can, for example, instantly show the detail in a logo, if you have preset the zoom factor and position, and saved the image in a custom view.

The Window Menu

The Window menu (see Figure 5-7) contains the various options for displaying the different palettes available in Illustrator, as well as any documents that are currently open:

✦ **New Window** creates a new window that displays the current document, usually at a different viewing percentage or in a different mode. This new window is initially the same size and has the same viewing options as the existing, front-most window, but the viewing options can be changed without affecting the other window.

✦ **Hide/Show Tools** hides the toolbox from view. If the toolbox is hidden, this command reads Show Tools.

✦ **Hide/Show Info** (F8) hides the Info palette from view. If the Info palette is hidden, this command reads Show Info. The Info palette appears automatically when the Measure tool is used.

✦ **Hide/Show Transform** hides the Transform palette.

✦ **Hide/Show Pathfinder** hides or shows the Pathfinder palette.

✦ **Hide/Show Align** hides the Align palette if it is displayed. If the Align palette is hidden, this command reads Show Align.

✦ **Hide/Show Color** (F6 or ⌘-I [Ctrl+I]) hides the Color palette from view. If the Color palette is hidden, this command reads Show Color.

✦ **Hide/Show Gradient** (F9) hides the Gradient palette from view. If the Gradient palette is hidden, this command reads Show Gradient. The Gradient palette also appears automatically when the Gradient tool is clicked or if the Gradient icon in the toolbox is clicked (in the paint style section of the toolbox).

✦ **Hide/Show Stroke** (F10) hides the Stroke palette. If the Stroke palette is hidden, this command reads Show Stroke.

✦ **Hide/Show Swatches** (F5) hides the Swatches palette. If the Swatches palette is hidden, this command reads Show Swatches.

✦ **Swatch Libraries** displays a submenu of swatch palettes that contain specialized color sets. Chapter 2 lists these palettes and their uses.

✦ **Hide/Show Brushes** hides the Brushes palette. If the Brushes palette is hidden, this command reads Show Brushes.

✦ **Brush Libraries** displays a submenu of the default brushes or the libraries that you have created.

✦ **Hide/Show Links** hides the palette that shows the embedded images that are linked in your file. If the Links palette is hidden, then this command reads Show Links.

✦ **Hide/Show Layers** (F7) hides the Layers palette from view. If the Layers palette is hidden, this command reads Show Layers.

✦ **Hide/Show Navigator** hides the Navigator palette from view. If the Navigator is hidden, this command reads Show Navigator.

✦ **Hide/Show Attributes** (F11) hides the Attributes palette. If the Attributes palette is hidden, this command reads Show Attributes.

✦ **Hide/Show Actions** hides the Actions palette from view. If the Actions palette is hidden, this command reads Show Actions.

✦ **Untitled Art 1** and all other titles below this dotted line are referencing the open Illustrator documents and duplicate document windows. A check mark appears in front of the title of the active document or window.

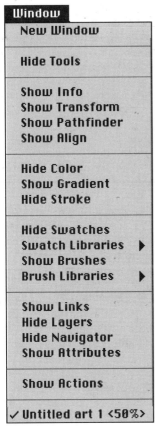

Figure 5-7: The Window menu

Managing Files

Controlling how files are saved in Illustrator can be a little daunting at first. Although you have many different options for saving file types, you need to follow one basic rule: Save as an EPS with a color preview if you are going to take the file into other applications. This type of file is not the smallest file type, but it is compatible with most software.

Opening files in Illustrator is fairly simple. Illustrator can open and manipulate only files that were created in Illustrator, Streamline, or Dimensions and files that were saved in an Illustrator format. It can open raster files, but they will be pixel-based.

Files placed in Illustrator can be almost any raster file format. PostScript files that are printed to disk usually can't be placed in Illustrator, although PostScript Level 1 files can be opened in Illustrator.

Other important file issues: Illustrator opens pixel files as a new Illustrator document with the pixels inside. Arbitrary PostScript Level 1 files can be opened with the built-in PostScript Interpreter. Illustrator files can be saved directly into pixel formats.

Saving Files

Saving Illustrator documents is the most important Illustrator activity you do. Saving often prevents damage to your computer — by keeping you from picking it up and sending it flying across the room. Saving often makes your life less stressful, and backing up your saved files helps you sleep better.

The amount of space that a saved Illustrator file takes up on a hard drive depends on two things: the complexity of the drawing and the Preview option (if any) that you've selected. Tiny Illustrator files take up the smallest amount, about 10K or so. The biggest illustrations are limited only by your storage space, but they can regularly exceed 2MB. As a practice, when you are working on a drawing, save it to the hard drive, not to a floppy disk or a removable cartridge. Hard drives are faster and much more reliable. If you need to place a file on a floppy disk, Zip, or Syquest cartridge, copy it there by dragging the icon of the file from the hard drive to the disk or cartridge. Because Illustrator uses *virtual memory* (the hard drive as RAM), you may want to keep additional hard drive space available, especially if you plan on working with lots of embedded images.

You should only save the file to another disk if you run out of room on the hard drive. To ensure that you never run out of room, always keep at least 10% of the hard drive space free. A hard drive that is too full can cause many problems that are more serious than being unable to save a file.

To save a file, choose File ⇨ Save (⌘-S) [Ctrl+S]. If you have previously saved the file, then updating the existing file with the changes that you have made takes just a fraction of a second. If you have not yet saved the file, the Save As dialog box shown in Figure 5-8 appears.

1. Decide how you are going to save the file. Choose the correct Preview and Compatibility options for the file. (See the descriptions in the "Illustrator EPS Preview Options" and "Compatibility Options" sections, later in this chapter.)

2. Decide where you are going to save the file and make sure that the name of the folder that you want to save it in is at the top of the file list window. Saving your working files in a location other than the Illustrator folder is a good habit. Otherwise, you can have trouble figuring out which files are yours, which files are tutorial files, and so on.

3. Name the file something distinctive so that if you look for it 6 months from now you will recognize it. Avoid using Untitled Art 1, Untitled Art 2, and so on. Such names are nondescriptive and, besides, you can too easily replace the file at a later date with a file of the same name. For the same reasons, do not

use Document 1, Document 2, and so on. Also avoid using Test1 (if I had a nickel for every Test1 or Test2 I've seen on people's hard drives, I'd have . . . well, I'd have a lot of nickels), stuff, #$*&!! (insert your favorite four-letter word here), picture, drawing, or your first name. A file name can have up to 31 characters, and you can use all the letters, numbers, and special characters (except a colon [:]) that are found on your keyboard, so make the most of them and describe the file.

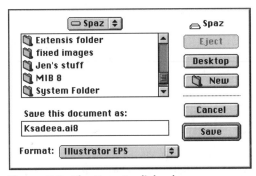

Figure 5-8: The Save As dialog box

When Should I Save?

You really can't save too often. Whenever I put off saving for "just a few minutes," that's when the system locks up, crashes, or gives me a Type 1 error. Depending on your work habits, you may need to save more frequently than other people do. Here are some golden rules about when to save:

✦ Save as soon as you create a new file. Get it out of the way. The toughest part of saving is deciding how and where you are going to save the file and naming it. If you get those things out of the way in the beginning, pressing ⌘-S [Ctrl+S] later is fairly painless.

✦ Save before you print. For some reason, PrintMonitor (on the Macintosh) and PostScript errors can crash a system faster than almost anything else.

✦ Save before you switch to another application. Jostling stuff around in a computer's RAM is an open invitation for the whole system to poop out.

✦ Save right after you do something that you never want to have to do again—such as getting the kerning "just right" on a logo or matching all of the colors in your gradients so that they meet seamlessly.

✦ Save after you use a filter that takes more than a few seconds to complete.

✦ Save before you create a new document or go to another document.

✦ Save at least every 15 minutes.

The Save As Command

The Save As command (⌘+Shift+S) [Ctrl+Shift+S] enables you to save multiple versions of the document at different stages of progress. If you choose Save As and do not rename the file or change the save location, you are prompted to replace the existing file. If you choose Replace, the file that you saved before is erased and replaced with the new file that you are saving. Most disk and trash recovery utilities cannot recover a file that you delete this way.

The Save As command is also useful for changing the Preview and Compatibility options (which are described in the "Illustrator EPS Preview Options" and "Compatibility Options" sections later in this chapter). If you have saved in Omit Header Preview and want to change to Color Preview, choose File ➪ Save As — don't change the file name or file location — and choose Color from the Preview pop-up menu.

Save a Copy

The Save a Copy command (⌘-Option-S) [Ctrl+Alt+S] saves a copy of your document at its current state without affecting your document or its name. Here's the scoop: Let's say you've designed a fairly nice logo — Whittles Logo — for Dr. Whittles, the plastic surgeon down the street. Dr. Whittles is pretty conservative, but his patients aren't. You need to show him both a basic logo and the same logo but spruced up. Once you've created the basic logo, you can Save a Copy as *Basic Logo* and continue working on *Whittles Logo*. The next time you press ⌘-S [Ctrl+S], your changes will be saved to *Whittles Logo,* and *Basic Logo* won't be affected at all.

Reverting to the Last Saved Version

Choosing File ➪ Revert is an option that automatically closes the document and opens the last saved version of it. This option is grayed out if the file has not yet been saved. When it is selected, a dialog box appears, asking you to confirm that you *do* want to revert to the last saved version of the document.

Caution   A Revert action cannot be undone, and you won't be able to redo anything you've done up to that point with the document.

File Types

You can save and export Illustrator 8 files in several ways. Actually, you can save in and export them to almost 30 different formats, although it makes no sense to save in or export to some formats.

Saving an Illustrator file with the wrong options can dramatically affect whether that file can be opened or placed in other software, as well as what features are included with the file when it is reopened in Illustrator. For example, saving the file as anything but EPS makes it virtually useless to every piece of software but Illustrator (although PageMaker, Photoshop, and a few other Adobe products can read Illustrator's native format). Saving a document as an older version of Illustrator may alter the document if the older version was missing features you used in your document.

As a rule, unless you're going to take your Illustrator document into another program, you can save it as an Illustrator file without any problems. This keeps the file size down and makes saving and opening the file much quicker.

Compatibility Options

Illustrator is one of the few software programs that is almost fully backward compatible. If you open a file in Illustrator 88 that you created in Illustrator 8, it looks almost exactly the same. Most software packages are forward compatible for one major version, but Illustrator is novel in that you can open an Illustrator 1.1 file in Version 8 of the software, even though more than 10 years have passed between those product versions.

ASK TOULOUSE: The Unopenable File

Bosley: Well, I did as you asked, saving and all. But now I'm screwed.

Toulouse: You forgot the name of the file?

Bosley: No, I'm getting an error, something about operators making illegal calls to Texas.

Toulouse: Ah, the old Illegal Operand "TZ" error.

Bosley: That's it. It won't let me open my document.

Toulouse: There's a way to fix that.

Bosley: Cool. What causes it?

Toulouse: If you use a certain symbol in the first font after the Symbol font, you'll get this error. Usually it's the degree sign that causes it.

Bosley: Yuck! But I can fix it, right?

Toulouse: Sure. Open the Illustrator document in a word processor.

Bosley: I can do that?

Toulouse: Yes, but you want to open it as a text file, not as a graphic.

Bosley: Done. What a mess!

Toulouse: Find the line: "/_Symbol_/Symbol 0 0 0 TZ" and add a "[" to the beginning of the line so it looks like this: "[/_Symbol_/Symbol 0 0 0 TZ." Save the document and open it in Illustrator. Voilà!

There are a number of reasons to save illustrations in older versions of Illustrator. The following list provides information about saving files in each version:

✦ **Illustrator 8** saves the file in a cross-platform (Mac and Windows) Illustrator 8 format. Illustrator 8 added support for EMF file format, and drag-and-drop to Microsoft Office products (Windows), Japanese format FreeHand files, and DXF file formats.

✦ **Illustrator 7** saves the file in a cross-platform (Mac and Windows) Illustrator 7 format. Illustrator 7 supports several bitmap file formats that Illustrator 6 could not. In addition, RGB color is not supported in previous versions of Illustrator.

✦ **Illustrator 6** saves the file in the Illustrator 6 format. The major file structure difference between Illustrator 6 and Illustrator 5.x is Illustrator 6's capability to import almost any type of raster image, while 5.x only supported EPS images. Other, not-so-obvious changes have to do with advanced object labels that plug-in developers use to achieve all sorts of effects.

✦ **Illustrator 5** saves the file in the Illustrator 5 format, which includes both Illustrator 5.0 and 5.5. The features that were added to Version 5.5 do not affect file content. Thus, files created in version 5.5 have the same structure as files created in version 5.0.

✦ **Illustrator 4** saves the file in the Illustrator 4 format, which is a version that is available only for Windows users. Saving a file in the Illustrator 4 format ensures that Illustrator 4 for Windows will open that Illustrator file. Gradients, views, layers, and custom Artboard sizes are not supported by the Illustrator 4 format. Technically, there is really no difference between the Illustrator 3 and 4 formats.

✦ **Illustrator 3** saves the file in the Illustrator 3 format. In fact, you can use the Illustrator 3 format for a lot of cheating — doing things that Illustrator normally doesn't enable you to do. For example, technically, you can't put gradients or masks into patterns. But if you save a gradient as an Illustrator 3 file and reopen it in Illustrator 7, the gradient becomes a blend, which you can use in a pattern (although Illustrator's Expand feature is quicker for this sort of thing).

✦ **Illustrator 88** saves the file in the Illustrator 88 format, which, for about 4 years (1988 to 1991), was the Illustrator standard. Much clipart was created and saved in the Illustrator 88 format. The main problem with saving in the Illustrator 88 format is that type changes occurred between Illustrator 88 and Illustrator 3. Illustrator 88 cannot handle type on a curve (called path type, which it turns into individual segments), and it doesn't deal correctly with compound paths (type converted to outlines are made up of several compound paths, one for each character).

✦ **Illustrator 1.1** saves the file in the oldest of Adobe Illustrator formats, version 1.1. Saving in the Illustrator 1.1 format is useful when you want to take files into older versions of FreeHand and many other older drawing programs. Illustrator 1.1 format doesn't support custom colors or masks.

Saving as Illustrator EPS

If you do have to place your Illustrator document in another program, such as QuarkXPress, you need to save the file as Illustrator EPS. After you select the Illustrator EPS option in the Save As box and name the file, clicking the Save button brings up yet another dialog box, which is shown in Figure 5-9.

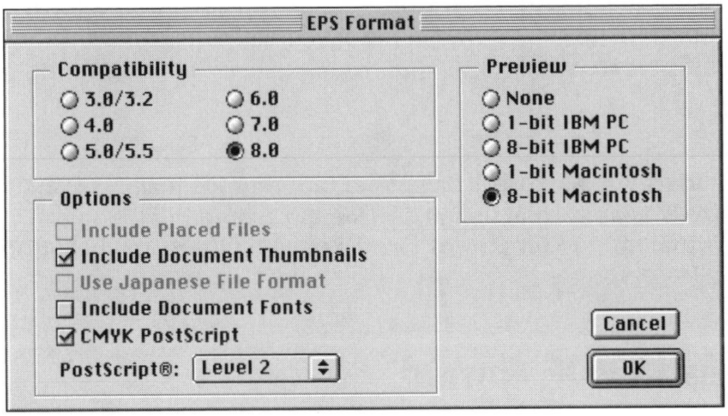

Figure 5-9: EPS Format dialog box

The options that are available when saving a file as an Illustrator EPS are discussed in the following section.

Illustrator EPS Preview Options

The following Preview options in Illustrator 8 affect the way that other software programs see Illustrator files when they are saved as Illustrator EPS files:

✦ **None** lets most software programs recognize the Illustrator document as an EPS file, but instead of viewing it in their software, you see a box with an *X* in it. Usually, this box is the same size as the illustration and includes any stray Anchor Points or Control Handles. The file will print fine from other software.

✦ **1-bit Macintosh** saves the EPS file with a PICT file preview as part of the EPS file. A PICT image is embedded within the EPS file (technically, a PICT resource); you do not have two separate files. Page-layout and other software programs display this illustration in a black-and-white preview with no shades of gray in it. This file may take up substantially more space than the Include EPSF Header file requires because of the PICT file. The larger the illustration measures, the more storage space the PICT file uses.

✦ **1-bit IBM PC** saves the file with a preview for IBM systems. Page-layout or other software for PCs that can import EPS files can preview illustrations that you save with this option.

✦ **8-bit Macintosh** saves the file with a color preview that is an embedded PICT image. Page-layout and other software programs display this file in 8-bit color (256 colors) when you place it in a document. An Illustrator file that you save with a color preview takes up more file space than a file saved with any other option.

✦ **8-bit IBM PC** saves the file with a color preview for IBM systems Page-layout and other software programs display this file in 8-bit color (256 colors) when you place it in a document. An Illustrator file that you save with a color preview takes up more file space than a file saved with any other option.

Exporting

Adobe Illustrator 8 allows you to export to several different file formats. Most of the export formats are bitmap formats such as TIFF, JPEG, and PICT. You can also export in PDF format so that Illustrator documents can be read with Adobe Acrobat Reader.

Exporting Files in PDF Format

The PDF format option saves files in Adobe Acrobat-compatible Portable Document Format (PDF). An Illustrator document saved as a PDF file will become a page when opened in Acrobat. Saving your Illustrator file this way removes several Illustrator attributes, such as layers, gradients, patterns, and path type.

Acrobat Reader is free on most online services and is provided on the CD-ROM that comes with this book.

Opening and Closing Illustrator Files

You can open any Illustrator file from any version of Illustrator in Illustrator 8. Regardless of which Preview options you select, Illustrator 8 can still open the file. When you choose File ➪ Open or press ⌘-O [Ctrl+O], the Open dialog box appears and asks you to find an Illustrator file. Find the file and double-click it to have it open into a document window on the screen.

To close the active Illustrator file, choose File ➪ Close (⌘-W) [Ctrl+W]. The active document is the one that is in front of all other documents and has a title bar with lines on it and text in black. Nonactive documents don't display any lines in their title bar, and the text in the title bar is gray. Closing an Illustrator document does not close Illustrator; it continues running until you choose Quit.

If you saved the file prior to closing it, it just disappears. If you have modified the file since the last time you saved it, a box appears, asking whether you want to save changes before closing. If you press Return or Enter to save the file, it is updated. If you have not saved the file at all, the Save As dialog box appears so that you can name the file, choose a location for it, and choose Preview and Compatibility options for the file. If you click the Don't Save button (D while the dialog box is showing), then any changes that you made to the document since you last saved it (or if you have never saved it, all the changes you made since you created it) are lost. Clicking Cancel (⌘-period [Ctrl+period] or Esc) takes you back to the drawing, where you can continue to work on it.

Placing Art

Files that you can place or import into Illustrator are EPS (Encapsulated PostScript), TIFF (Tagged Image File Format), and most other bitmap file formats. To place files, choose File ⇨ Place. A standard Open dialog box appears. Only files that can be placed appear in the file window. Because text files are also placed, be sure the file you've chosen is indeed an image document.

After you place art into Illustrator, you can transform it (move, scale, rotate, reflect, and shear it) in any way.

The quality of placed art is as good as the original; if the original file was bitmapped (created or saved in a paint program such as Photoshop), then the quality will lessen as the file is scaled up, and the quality will increase as the file is scaled down. If the file was in PostScript outline format (created in Illustrator or FreeHand, EPS only), then the quality will stay consistent as the file changes in size.

You can use placed raster images for tracing, but the Auto Trace tool does not recognize EPS and does not automatically surround it.

Illustrator shows placed art differently in Artwork mode and in Preview mode. In Artwork mode, placed art is in black and white, or just shows up as a box with an X inside of it.

When you save a document with placed art in it with a preview, you can link the placed art to Illustrator or include it in the Illustrator file. Normally, including the placed art within the Illustrator file is the better choice. This method prevents the two files from being separated; if you have one and not the other, you are out of luck. But you may want to link the file instead of including it for two reasons. First, placed art can be huge and may make your Illustrator file too large. Second, if you need to make changes to a placed art file that you have included in an Illustrator file that you have saved with a preview, you have to replace the placed art in the preview file with the new version. If you have linked the placed art instead of including it, the art is automatically updated when you make changes.

You may want to replace placed art with new versions or completely different artwork. Illustrator has made this process painless. If placed artwork is selected, a dialog box appears asking if you would like to replace current artwork or place new artwork, not changing the selected artwork.

Tip

The really cool part about changing placed art this way is that if you have placed artwork that has been transformed, the artwork you exchange with it via the Place Art command will have the exact same transformation attributes! For example, if you scale down placed artwork to 50% and rotate it 45°, artwork that is exchanged with that artwork is also scaled down 50% and rotated 45°.

You can dim placed art by checking the Dim Images To checkbox in the Layer Options dialog box on the Layers palette and entering a Dim value. (By a Dim value I mean a percentage you want your image dimmed, not a half-witted value.) If you dim placed art, then a ghost of the image appears instead of the solid image. This feature makes manually tracing placed art easy. Dimming placed art does not affect its printed output.

Placed Art Size Issues

Be careful when importing artwork other than EPS images into Illustrator, as TIFF and most other bitmap formats increase the size of your document dramatically. The reason for this is that the image information for TIFFs and other formats is stored within the Illustrator document, and is not linked to the document in the way Placed EPS images are. Making the issue even stickier, duplicating TIFFs within Illustrator increases the document size by the size of that TIFF once again.

Publish and Subscribe (Mac Only)

Publish and Subscribe is a convenient way to keep various elements in different documents current by updating affected documents when other related documents are changed.

The Edit menu contains the following Publish and Subscribe options:

✦ The **Publishing** option displays a category with four submenu items, all related to System 7's Publish and Subscribe feature. Publish and Subscribe allows certain users to publish documents that are subscribed to by others. As the Publisher changes its edition, the Subscriber receives updated information about that edition. You may neither publish nor subscribe text only, but you may publish and subscribe to entire type objects (such as an Area type or Path type).

✦ The **Create Publisher** option creates an edition file that other users can subscribe to (by choosing Subscribe in their application). The edition includes any selected objects at the time Create Publisher is chosen. After the edition is created, a light gray border appears around the edition's objects when one or more of those objects is selected. After you have created an edition using the Create Publisher command, it is updated every time you save the file that contains the edition. An edition border is a fixed size and cannot be changed.

✦ The **Subscribe To** option lets your document subscribe to an edition. A dark gray border appears around editions that you have subscribed to if that edition is selected. Your document is updated instantly whenever the edition is updated, even if your document is open.

✦ The **Publisher Options** give you the ability to manually update the edition, even without saving your file. You can also choose to Unpublish your edition at this point.

✦ The **Show Borders** option always shows the borders of both the edition files you have published (light gray) and the edition files to which you have subscribed (darker gray).

✦ The **Hide Borders** option reverses the Show Borders option.

Document Info

You can use the Document Info feature in any document by choosing File ➪ Document Info. A dialog box (shown in Figure 5-10) appears with a pop-up menu at the top.

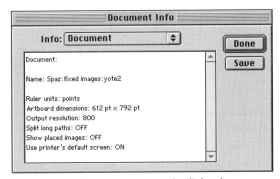

Figure 5-10: The Document Info dialog box

The pop-up menu has seven different ways to view information about the active document:

✦ The first option, **Document,** shows the document setup of the active document. All the relevant options from the Document Setup dialog box are shown, along with the name of the file.

✦ The second option is **Objects,** which lists how many paths, masks, compound paths, custom colors, patterns, gradients, fonts, and placed EPS artwork are used in the document. This can be used as a rudimentary guide to how long a file may take to print.

✦ The remaining options show the names of any enclosed custom colors, patterns, gradients, and fonts. The final option, **Embedded Images,** lists the name of the placed art and the disk path that tells Illustrator where to find it.

If you have anything selected, the Selection Info dialog box will contain only information about these selected objects.

Note Along the right side of the Document Info dialog box are two buttons: The Save button creates a TeachText format file with all eight categories of information about the document, while the Done button closes the dialog box.

Note TeachText format cannot be read in Illustrator. To view the saved Document Info file, you must double-click the file name or open it within a word processor.

Summary

✦ When you launch Illustrator, a new document automatically appears.

✦ New documents are based on the startup file size and attributes, and are created as soon as you choose New Document from the File menu.

✦ The current document setup can be modified in the Document Setup dialog box, accessed by pressing ⌘-Option-P [Ctrl+Alt+P] or by choosing File ➯ Document Setup.

✦ You can automatically use the current Page Setup as your artwork size by selecting the "Use Page Setup" checkbox in the Document Setup dialog box, or you can access Page Setup by pressing ⌘-Shift-P [Ctrl-Shift P].

✦ Path splitting is useful if you have several long paths and are getting PostScript limit check errors when printing.

✦ You can quickly change ruler measurement systems by pressing ⌘-Ctrl-U (Mac only) to cycle through the Inches, Points, Picas, Millimeters, and Centimeters options.

✦ Zoom in by pressing ⌘-Spacebar [Ctrl+spacebar] to access the Zoom In tool, and then drag a marquee around the area you wish to zoom into.

✦ You can zoom out rapidly by pressing ⌘-Option-Spacebar [Ctrl+Alt+Spacebar] and clicking.

✦ Pan around your document by pressing the Spacebar to access the Hand tool and then dragging the document around within its window.

✦ Artwork mode can be useful when drawing a complex piece of artwork. It allows Illustrator to operate quicker than in Preview mode and lets you select points and paths that might have been otherwise obscured.

✦ Preview Selection mode is handy for when you'd like to see just a portion of your illustration without having to wait for the entire document to redraw.

✦ Using various options in the View menu, you can specify which elements you'd like to view and which ones you'd like to hide.

✦ The Window menu allows you to show and hide all the different palettes in Illustrator and lets you arrange document windows.

✦ Unless you'll be importing the files into another application, you should save them as Illustrator 8 files.

✦ If you'll be importing files into another application, you probably want to save them as EPS, with an 8-bit preview.

✦ You can place any EPS image, bitmap, text, or vector file, by using the Place command, which is located in the File menu.

✦   ✦   ✦

Customizing Illustrator

Under the Apple menu (⌘) on a Macintosh and under the Help menu in Windows, you'll find some useful information.

About Illustrator displays a dialog box with the user information and scrolling credits for everyone, absolutely everyone, who had any teeny tiny, little thing to do with Illustrator. If nothing else, you'll become aware of the large number of people who are involved in creating the software.

About Plug-Ins displays a submenu that lists all the installed plug-ins. Choosing one of the items in the Plug-Ins submenu displays who made the plug-in, and, occasionally, some useful or interesting information about that plug-in.

On a Macintosh, About This Computer (in the Finder, while Illustrator is running under Mac OS 8) displays how much memory is allocated to Illustrator, and how much Illustrator is actually using of that allocated amount.

Tip

You can also determine how much memory is used and is currently available by clicking on the Status bar at the lower left of the Document window and selecting the Free Memory option from the pop-up menu. This displays how much memory is free both in megabytes and as a percentage of the total amount of memory.

Preferences

No two illustrators work the same. To accommodate the vast differences in styles, techniques, and habits, Illustrator provides many settings that each user can change to personalize the software.

Illustrator provides four major ways to change preferences. The most dramatic and difficult changes are to a small file called Adobe Illustrator Startup. The startup file changes how new documents appear and which custom colors, patterns, and gradients are available.

You can also control how Illustrator works by accessing the Preferences submenu (choose File ➪ Preferences). You make most of these changes in the General Preferences dialog box, which you access by choosing File ➪ Preferences ➪ General (⌘-K) [Ctrl+K]. Within the Preferences dialog box, a number of different preference panels can be selected from the pop-up menu at the top of the dialog box. You can go through each of the preference panels one by one by clicking the Next and Previous buttons, or simply by choosing a preference panel from the Preferences submenu. The preference panels are General, Type & Auto Tracing, Units & Undo, Guides & Grid, Smart Guides, Hyphenation Options, and Plug-Ins & Scratch Disk.

A third way to make changes is by changing preferences relative to each document. You usually make these changes in the Document Setup dialog box, but a few other options are available. There is more information on document-specific preferences later in this chapter.

The fourth way to customize preferences happens pretty much automatically. When you quit Illustrator, it remembers many of the current settings for the next time you run it. These settings include palette placements and values in toolbox settings.

Illustrator has a few settings that you cannot customize. These features can really get under your skin because most of them seem like things that you should be able to customize. See the "Things You Can't Customize" section later in this chapter for a list of these settings.

Modifying the Startup File

When you first run Illustrator, the program looks to the Illustrator startup file to check a number of preferences. Those preferences include window size and placement, as well as custom colors, gradients, patterns, zoom levels, tiling options, and graph designs.

New documents (such as the one created automatically when you first run the program) have all the attributes of the startup file. Opened documents have all the gradients, custom colors, patterns, and graph designs of the startup file.

1. Open the startup file. The startup file, which is called Adobe Illustrator Startup, is located in the Plug-Ins folder in the Adobe Illustrator folder. The file is an Adobe Illustrator 8 document, so double-clicking the file opens Illustrator, as well.

2. Figure 6-1 shows what the file looks like. Each square in the document contains a pattern, gradient, named color, or color-swatch square. Remove any square that contains patterns, gradients, or custom colors that you don't use. Then go to the Swatches palette and delete those same patterns,

gradients, and colors. (If you delete a pattern, custom color, or gradient from the startup file, it is gone. Kaput! The only way to get it back is to replace the startup file from the original disks or CD-ROM.)

3. To add something to the startup file, add the color, pattern, or gradient to the Swatches palette. (To add a graph design, create the graph design and apply it to a graph. Then place the graph in the startup file.)

4. To change the window size, just save the startup file with the window size that you want new documents to have.

5. To change the color swatches on the Swatches palette, add, replace, or delete color swatches while the startup file is open and then save the startup file.

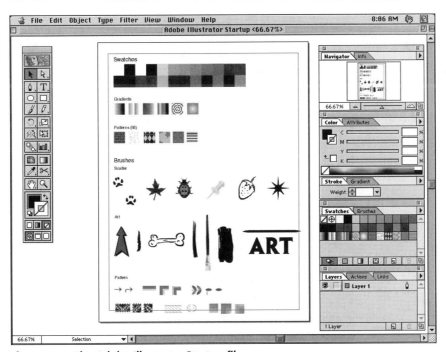

Figure 6-1: The Adobe Illustrator Startup file

If you delete the Adobe Illustrator Startup file, most patterns, gradients, and custom colors will not be available until you create a new startup file or place the original startup file from the disks or CD-ROM in the Plug-Ins folder.

To check whether changes that you made in the startup file will work, quit Illustrator and run the program again. You cannot tell whether the changes are in place until you quit and reopen Illustrator.

You can change both the window size of new documents and the viewing percentage. Most people like documents to fit in the window when it is created. For a 13-inch screen, use 50%; for a 16- or 17-inch screen, use 66%.

Changing General Preferences

The General portion of the Preferences dialog box (choose File ⇨ Preferences ⇨ General or press ⌘-K [Ctrl+K]) contains most of the *personalized* customizing options for Illustrator. The options in this box affect keyboard increments, measuring units, and the way that objects are drawn. These options are considered personalized options because they are specific to the way that each person uses the program. Few people have the same preference settings as others have (unless they never change the defaults). The General Preferences dialog box is shown in Figure 6-2.

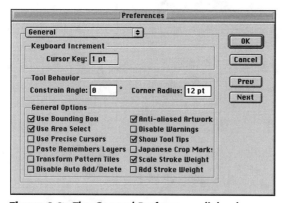

Figure 6-2: The General Preferences dialog box

Note   In most programs, "Preferences" is logically located on the Edit menu, not on the File menu. General Preferences, unlike everything else on the File menu, deals with the entire program rather than with a specific document.

The Keyboard Increment Option

The Cursor Key increment that you specify in this option controls how far an object moves when you select it and press the keyboard arrows.

I have this increment set to 0.5 point because this is the smallest amount that I usually need to move things. The default for this setting is 1 point, which many people feel is small enough. I make my increment smaller when I am working in 800% or 1600% views.

Tool Behavior

The Tool Behavior options control how most of Illustrator's tools work. Some tools have their own options, accessed by double-clicking that tool.

The Constrain Angle Option

The Constrain Angle option controls the angle at which all objects are aligned. Rectangles are always drawn "flat," aligning themselves to the bottom, top, and sides of the document window. When you press the Shift key, lines that you draw with the Pen tool and objects that you move will align to the Constrain Angle, or 45°, 90°, 135°, or 180°, plus or minus the constraining angle.

The Constrain Angle also affects how the four transformation tools transform objects. The Scale tool can be very hard to use when the Constrain Angle is not 0°, and the Shear tool becomes even more difficult to use than normal at different Constrain Angles. Pressing Shift when you are using the Rotate tool constrains the rotational angle to 45° increments added to the Constrain Angle. Chapter 7 discusses the Rotate tool and other transformational tools.

In Illustrator, 0° is a horizontal line and 90° is a vertical line. Figure 6-3 shows Illustrator angles.

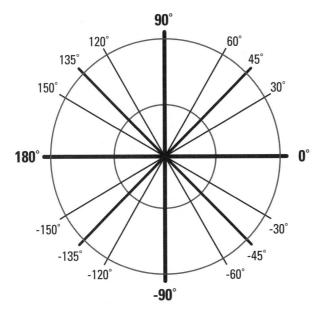

Figure 6-3: Angles in Illustrator

If you set the Constrain Angle at 20°, objects are constrained to movements of 20°, 65°, 110°, 155°, and 200°. Constrain Angles of 90°, 180°, and –90° (270°) affect only type, patterns, gradients, and graphs; everything else works normally.

When Option[Alt]-copying objects, you can use the Shift key in conjunction with a Constrain Angle to duplicate objects at a specific angle. Option[Alt]-copy means to press the Option [Alt] key while dragging an object and then to release the mouse button before releasing the Option [Alt] key to produce a duplicate of the object at the new location.

The Corner Radius Option

The Corner Radius option affects the size of the curved corners on a rounded rectangle. For a complete explanation of the corner radius and rounded rectangles, see Chapter 2.

The corner radius value changes each time you enter a new value in the Rectangle dialog box. This dialog box appears when you click the Rectangle or Rounded Rectangle tools without dragging in a document. If, for example, you create one rounded rectangle with a rounded-corner radius of 24 points, all rounded rectangles that you create from that point forward will have a radius of 24 points. The only ways to change the corner radius are to click a Rectangle tool without dragging in a document and then enter a new value in the Rectangle dialog box or to enter a new value in the Corner Radius text field in the General Preferences dialog box.

The real advantage to changing the corner radius in the General Preferences dialog box is that the corner radius will affect manually created (dragged with the Rounded Rectangle tool) rounded rectangles immediately. Changing the corner radius in the Rectangle dialog box requires that you know the exact dimensions of the rectangle or that you draw a rectangle by entering information in the Rectangle dialog box (clicking with the Rectangle tool without dragging) and specify the corner radius. You must then delete the original rectangle in order to draw a rounded rectangle with the correct corner radius manually.

Caution   Because you can change the Corner Radius setting easily, be sure to check it before you draw a series of rounded rectangles manually. There is no easy or automatic way to change the corner radius on existing rounded rectangles.

If you use 0 point as the Corner radius setting, the corners are not rounded at all. If you click with the Rounded Rectangle tool and enter 0 point as the corner radius, the Corner Radius setting in the General Preferences dialog box changes to 0 point.

General Options

The 12 checkboxes in the General Options section of General Preferences are Illustrator's version of the *Battlestar Galactica* ragtag fleet of unwieldy spacefaring craft. Some are quite powerful, others seem like they aren't capable of transferring millions of people across the galaxy, much less defending themselves against the evil menace of the Cylon empire. Okay, that wasn't the best analogy. The fact is, there is no other place in Illustrator where so many totally unrelated options share the same dialog box, and I had to come up with a snazzy introduction.

The Use Bounding Box Option

New to Illustrator 8 is the Bounding Box. The Bounding Box was added for new users who want to learn to edit easily. When the Use Bounding Box option is checked, you can manipulate a selected object just like you would if you used Microsoft Word or PowerPoint. The selected object has a box with 8 handles on it. When any of the handles are clicked and dragged, the object is automatically resized. The Bounding Box also enables you to reflect and rotate your object without selecting the Reflect, Rotate, or Scale tools from the toolbar. The Transform Again option, found under the Transform submenu of the Object menu, will also work with the Bounding Box feature. The Transform Again option will repeat the original transformation on another selected object. All in all, the Bounding Box levels the playing field for new users to Illustrator.

The Use Area Select Option

When the Use Area Select option is on, you can select an object in Preview mode by clicking the object's Fill. If the Use Area Select option is off, you select an object the same way that you select it in Artwork and Preview Selection mode — by clicking paths or Anchor Points of objects. The Use Area Select option has no effect on selecting objects in Preview Selection mode, but after you select them, you can move them by clicking and dragging a Filled area.

I have yet to have a good reason to turn this option off. The only reason that I can imagine for turning off this feature is if, for a particular illustration, I need to select specific paths from several overlapping, Filled objects. To be honest, I think that selecting individual paths in Preview would still be difficult because you can't see most of them.

Caution   The Use Area Select option does not allow you to select paths by clicking Strokes, unless you click the center of the Stroke where the path is (in which case you would be clicking the path anyway). In addition, you can't select "through" a compound path; instead, clicking in the empty areas of a compound path will result in selecting the compound path itself.

The Use Precise Cursors Option

Precise cursors are cursors that appear as a variation of a cross hair instead of in the shape of a tool. Figure 6-4 shows cursors that are different when the Use Precise Cursors option is on.

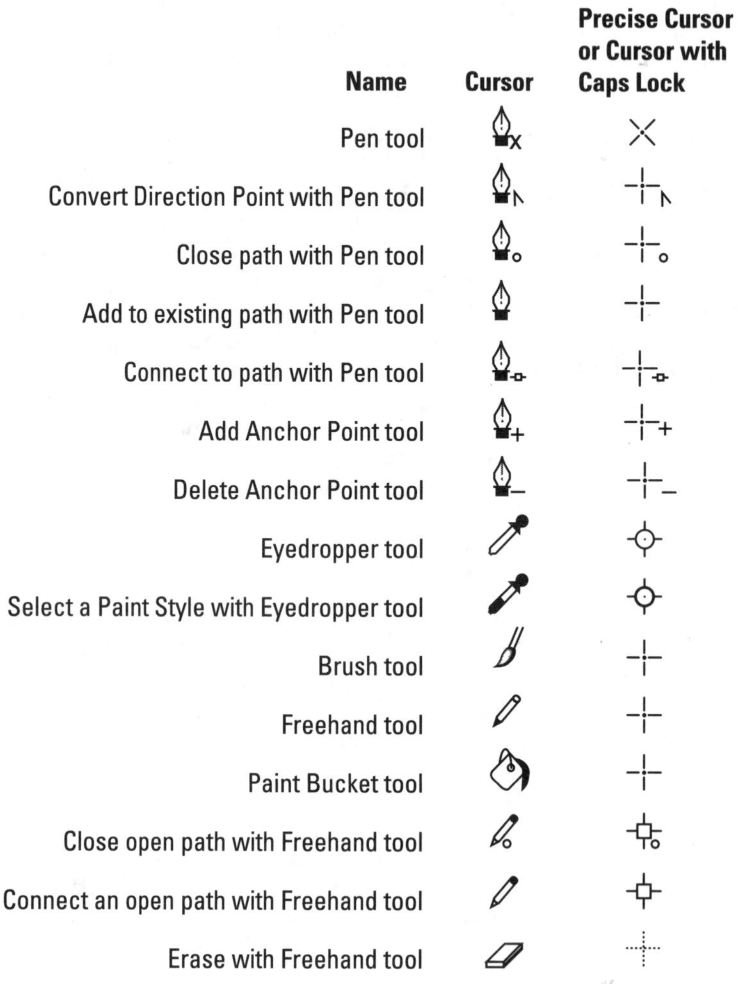

Name	Cursor	Precise Cursor or Cursor with Caps Lock
Pen tool		
Convert Direction Point with Pen tool		
Close path with Pen tool		
Add to existing path with Pen tool		
Connect to path with Pen tool		
Add Anchor Point tool		
Delete Anchor Point tool		
Eyedropper tool		
Select a Paint Style with Eyedropper tool		
Brush tool		
Freehand tool		
Paint Bucket tool		
Close open path with Freehand tool		
Connect an open path with Freehand tool		
Erase with Freehand tool		

Figure 6-4: The regular cursors are on the left, the precise cursors are on the right

Tip

The Caps Lock key toggles between standard cursors and precise cursors. When the Use Precise Cursors option is checked, the Caps Lock key makes the cursors standard. When the Use Precise Cursors option is not checked, the Caps Lock key activates the precise cursors.

I usually keep this option on and rarely engage the Caps Lock key to change the cursors back to normal. In particular, I've found the precise cursor for the Brush tool to be quite useful, seeing as how the standard Brush cursor is one giant amorphous blob.

The Paste Remembers Layers Option

Checking the Paste Remembers Layers checkbox causes all objects to be pasted on the layer that they were copied from, regardless of which layer is currently active. Unchecking this box causes objects on the Clipboard to be pasted in the current layer.

This option is available in the Layers palette as well, and if it is on, a check mark appears next to Paste Remembers Layers in the pop-up menu. When you turn the Paste Remembers Layers menu item on or off, the preference setting changes in the General Preferences dialog box.

Caution

One of the unheralded super features of the Paste Remembers Layers option is what happens when you paste in another document that doesn't contain that particular layer. A new layer with the same name as the one you copied the items from is created automatically. This is also a good way to quickly copy layers to another document — just delete the items after you've pasted them, and the new layers will remain.

The Transform Pattern Tiles Option

Check the Transform Pattern Tiles option if you want patterns in paths to be moved, scaled, rotated, sheared, and reflected when you use the transformation tools. When this option is checked, pulling up a transformation dialog box (Move, Rotate, Scale, Reflect, or Shear) automatically checks the Pattern checkbox. When the option is not checked, the Pattern checkbox is not checked in the transformation dialog box. This option controls whether selected patterns are transformed when the transform palette is used.

I usually check the Transform Pattern Tiles box, which sets all patterns to automatically transform and move with the objects that are being transformed and moved. This feature is especially useful when you want to create perspective in objects because the transformations of patterns can enhance the intended perspective.

Disable Auto Add/Delete

This option refers to the Pen tool's automatic add/delete feature, which is new in Illustrator 8. The default is unchecked. When the box is not checked, you can add or delete points while drawing with the Pen tool. As you are drawing a path with the Pen tool, you can click on the path to add more Anchor Points. You can also click an Anchor Point to delete it and continue to draw your path without having to switch tools. When you check this option, this new feature is turned off.

The Anti-Aliased Artwork Option

The Anti-Aliased Artwork option turns on anti-aliasing for onscreen representation of vector objects. Curved and diagonal edges appear smooth instead of jagged (or "stair-stepped"). The resulting effect is for *onscreen* viewing only, and won't affect output or rasterization of your artwork.

The Disable Warnings Option

This tiny little checkbox has the graphics community sending letters of thanks to Adobe. Version 6.0.1 of Illustrator allowed you to turn off some of the warnings, but it had to be done by editing the preference file, a task that most users found daunting at best. The warnings I'm referring to are those handy little messages that appear when you've clicked in the wrong spot with the wrong tool. For instance, clicking with the Scissors tool off a path would result in an ugly, overly long essay on the evils of clicking in empty space. Clicking with the Convert Direction Point tool brought up a dialog box condemning you for trying to convert something that wasn't a suitable Anchor Point. The first few times, the messages were helpful reminders. Years later, they became an annoying thorn in the side of experienced Illustrator users. Checking this box turns off the messages; instead of a nagging dialog box, a simple system beep noise is produced. This noise is still a bit annoying, but it does let you know you've clicked in an unacceptable portion of the document.

The Show Tool Tips Option

This option displays little pop-up names for each of the tools if you rest your cursor above them for one second. It's a great idea to keep this option on, as not only do you see the name of the tool, but also the key to press to access that tool.

The Japanese Crop Marks Option

When checked, the Japanese Crop Marks option will change the standard crop marks, usually created with Objects ➪ Crop Marks ➪ Make, to Japanese Crop Marks (see Figure 6-5).

Figure 6-5: Standard crop marks (top) and
Japanese crop marks (bottom)

The Scale Stroke Weight Option

When the Scale Stroke Weight feature is on, it automatically increases and reduces
line weights relative to an object when you uniformly scale that object manually.
For example, if a path has a Stroke weight of 1 point and you reduce the path
uniformly by 50%, the Stroke weight changes to 0.5 point.

Scaling objects nonuniformly (without the Shift key pressed) does not change the
Stroke weight on an object, regardless of whether the Scale Line Weight feature is
on or off.

The Add Stroke Weight Option

The Add Stroke Weight option refers to transformations. When you are applying a
transformation and you want the Stroke to be altered as well, you can check this
option in the General Preferences dialog box.

Type & Auto Tracing

The Type & Auto Tracing preferences enable you to affect your type options and your tracing options. There are six type options to choose from. The Auto Trace options affect how the Auto Trace and Pencil tools work. Figure 6-6 illustrates the Type & Auto Tracing dialog box.

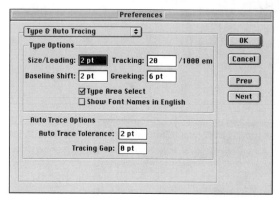

Figure 6-6: The Type & Auto Tracing dialog box

The Size/Leading Option

You can use the keyboard to increase and decrease type size by pressing ⌘-Shift- > [Ctrl+Shift+>] and ⌘-Shift- < [Ctrl+Shift+<], respectively. You can increase and decrease leading by pressing Option-↑ [Alt+↑] and Option-↓ [Alt+↓], respectively. In the Size/Leading text box, you specify the increment by which the size and leading change.

You can increase or decrease the type size and leading only until you reach the upper and lower limits of each. The upper limit for type size and leading is 1296 points, and the lower limit for each is 0.1 point.

Note   I keep my settings fairly high, at 10 points, because I have found that I require large point changes, usually quite a bit more than 10 points. If I need to do fine-tuning, I either type in the exact size that I want or use the Scale tool.

The Baseline Shift Option

The Baseline Shift feature moves selected type up and down on the baseline, independent of the leading. The increment specified in this box is how much the type is moved when you press the arrow keyboard commands. To move type up one increment, press Option-Shift-↑ [Alt+Shift+↑]. To move type down one increment, press Option-Shift-↓ [Alt+Shift+↓].

I keep the Baseline shift increment at 1 point so that I can adjust Path type better; specifically, I like to be able to adjust the baseline shift of type on a circle.

The Tracking Option

Tracking changes the amount of space between selected characters, and the setting in this text field represents the amount of space (measured in thousandths of an em space) that the keyboard command adds or removes. To increase tracking, you press ⌘-→ [Ctrl+→]; to decrease it, you press ⌘-← [Ctrl+←].

Tip　To increase the tracking by five times the increment in the General Preferences dialog box, press ⌘-Option-→ [Ctrl+Alt+→]. To decrease the tracking by five times the increment, press ⌘-Option-← [Ctrl+Alt+←].

The value in the Tracking text field also affects incremental changes in kerning. *Kerning* is the addition or removal of space between one pair of letters only. Kerning is done instead of tracking when a blinking insertion point is between two letters, as opposed to at least one selected character for tracking.

I set the Tracking increment to 10 because it produces a result that corresponds to twice the tracking generated by the QuarkXPress key command. (In QuarkXPress, pressing ⌘-Option-Shift-[[Ctrl+Alt+Shift+[] or ⌘-Option-Shift-] [Ctrl+Alt+Shift+]] increases or decreases, respectively, tracking by ¹⁄₂₀₀ em space.)

The Greeking Option

The number that you enter in this field defines the point at which Illustrator begins to greek text (see Figure 6-7). Illustrator *greeks* text — turns the letters into gray bars — when the text is so small that reading it on the screen would be hard or impossible. This change reduces screen redraw time dramatically, especially when the document contains a great deal of text.

Figure 6-7: Text on screen is so small that it is greeked

The size in this text field is relative to the viewing magnification of the document. At a limit of 6 points, 6-point type at 100%, 66%, 50%, 25%, or smaller will be greeked; but 6-point type at 150%, 200%, or larger will be readable. With the same limitations, 12-point type will be greeked at 50% and smaller, but it is readable at 66% and larger.

The Type Area Select Option

Turning this option on makes it possible to select text by clicking on the text itself instead of just the baseline of the text (as in Illustrator versions 1.0 to 6.0). Some people (especially long-time Illustrator users) find this option annoying, and are outraged at Adobe's audacity to have it turned on by default. I like it, and I know it makes selecting text much easier for Illustrator newcomers. Besides, that's why it's a preference — if you don't like Type Area Select, just turn it off.

The Show Font Names in English Option

If you have a font from another language installed on your system (like Kanji, the Japanese character set), this option will allow you to see these typefaces in the font/type menus as English words, rather than the seemingly indecipherable names that double-bit fonts turn into when they're displayed in Roman characters.

The Auto Trace Tolerance Option

The Auto Trace setting controls the accuracy of the paths that Illustrator creates when you compare them to the area dragged with the Pencil tool and to any templates being traced with the Auto Trace tool. Chapter 3 discusses Auto Trace settings and resulting paths.

The lower the Auto Trace setting, the more exact the resulting path. A higher setting results in smoother, less accurate paths. You can enter a value from 0 to 10, in increments of $\frac{1}{100}$ point (two decimal places).

The Auto Trace number is relative to the number of pixels on the screen that the resulting path may vary. A tolerance of 10 means that the resulting path may vary up to 10 pixels from the location of the actual dragged or traced area.

The Tracing Gap Option

When you use the Auto Trace tool to trace a placed image, the tool may encounter gaps, or white space, between solid areas. The Tracing Gap option enables you to specify that if the Auto Trace tool runs into a white-space gap of 1 or 2 pixels, it can jump over the gap and continue tracing on the other side of it.

A value of 0 prevents the Auto Trace tool from tracing over gaps. If you use a value of 1, the Auto Trace tool traces over gaps that are up to 1 pixel wide. If you use a value of 2 (the highest allowed), it traces over gaps that are 2 pixels wide. The Tracing Gap setting not only goes over gaps, it also adheres less closely to the original template.

I usually use a setting of 0 because when I trace any image in Illustrator, I examine it closely in Photoshop to make sure that it does not have any gaps. I can then be sure that the resulting paths will not be misshapen because of image-tracing inaccuracies.

Units & Undo

The Units & Undo preferences enable you to select the measurement system you want to use and set the number of times you can use the Undo key in a row. Figure 6-8 illustrates the Units & Undo dialog box.

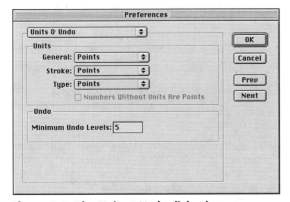

Figure 6-8: The Units & Undo dialog box

Units Settings

The General pop-up menu in the Units section changes the measurement system for the current document and all future new documents. The three areas the measurement can be specified for are: General (which includes the Rulers), Stroke, and Type. Illustrator contains five different measurement units: inches, picas, points, millimeters, and centimeters. The ⌘-Control-U command (Macintosh only) toggles between all five units for the Rulers.

Note   Changing the General units in the Units & Undo Preferences dialog box changes the Ruler units in the Document Setup dialog box (choose File ⇨ Document Setup or press ⌘-Option-P [Ctrl+Alt+P]).

Being aware of which measurement system you are working in is important. When you enter a measurement in a dialog box, any numbers that are not measurement-system-specific are applied to the current unit of measurement. For example, if you want to move something 1 inch and you open the Move dialog box (choose Object ⇨ Transform ⇨ Move or double-click the Selection tool), you need to add either the inch symbol (") or the abbreviation *in* after you type a 1 in the dialog box if the measurement system is not inches. If the measurement system is points and picas, entering just a 1 moves the object 1 point, not 1 inch. If the measurement system is inches already, entering just the number 1 is fine.

Usually a corresponding letter or letters indicates the measurement system: *in* for inch, *pt* for points, and *cm* for centimeters.

I use the points/picas system for several reasons. First, using points and picas is easier because you can specify smaller increments exactly (ever try to figure out what ½ inch is in decimals?). Second, type is measured in points, not inches. Third, points and picas are the standard in measuring systems for designers and printers.

Note   The default measurement is points and picas, so if you ever toss your preferences file or reinstall Illustrator, be aware that you may have to change the measurement system.

Undo Settings

Illustrator can set the minimum number of undos; the number that makes sure you always have a certain number of undos available. The higher you set the number, the more steps you'll always be able to undo. Of course, the higher the number, the more memory that Illustrator needs to be able to undo that far. If you can provide Illustrator with gobs of RAM (via the Gen Info box in the Finder), then set your undos to at least 10, maybe even 20. But if you're working with a complex document on your little sister's Mac LC or old 486, you may want to keep the number back to a more reasonable 1 or 2.

Guides & Grid

The Guides & Grid section of Preferences lets you control the color and style of your guides and grids, and the spacing of your grid. Figure 6-9 illustrates the Guides & Grid dialog box. Chapter 4 has the lowdown on getting the most out of grids and guides.

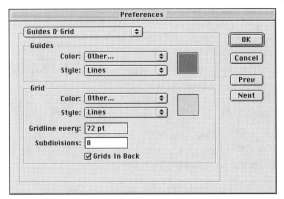

Figure 6-9: The Guides & Grid dialog box

 New Feature New to Illustrator 8 is the capability to have the grids in back of or in front of your image by checking or not checking the Grids In Back option in the Guides & Grid Preferences dialog box.

Smart Guides

Smart Guides are a new feature in Illustrator 8. You can check or uncheck four different Display Options as well as affect the angles and snapping tolerance. Figure 6-10 illustrates the Smart Guides dialog box.

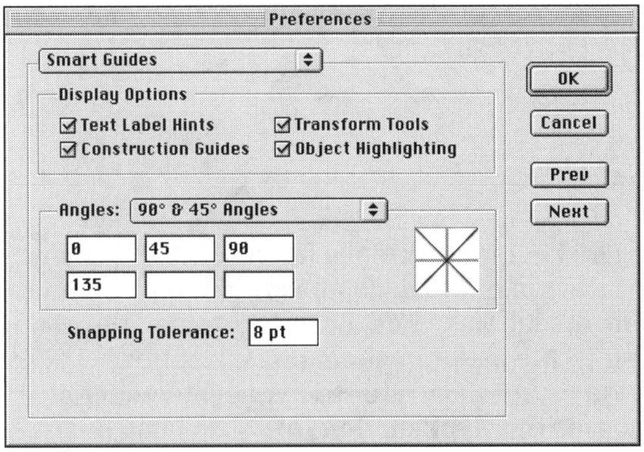

Figure 6-10: The Smart Guides dialog box

The Display Options

The four Display Options are:

✦ **Text Label Hints**: These hints pop-up when you drag your mouse cursor over your object. They tell you what each area is. For example, if you drag your mouse cursor over a line, the hint will pop-up with the word "path." If you drag your mouse cursor over an Anchor Point, the hint will say "anchor point."

✦ **Transform Tools**: When you are rotating, scaling, or shearing an object with this option checked, Smart Guides shows up to help you out.

✦ **Construction Guides**: This lets you view guidelines when using Smart Guides

✦ **Object Highlighting**: This option highlights the object that you are pointing to.

Angles

The Angles you can choose in the Smart Guides dialog box let you pick what angles will display guides when you drag an object. You can choose from seven presets or create Custom Angles of your own.

Snapping Tolerance

The Snapping Tolerance enables you to choose how close you have to have an object to another object before the first object automatically "snaps" to the second object. You set the Snapping Tolerance in points and the lower the number the closer you have to move the objects to each other.

Hyphenation Options

The Hyphenation Options dialog box contains options for customizing the way Illustrator hyphenates words. At the top of the dialog box is a pop-up menu that lists various languages. Select the default language. At the bottom of the dialog box is an area where you can add to the list of hyphenation exceptions. These exceptions are words that you don't want Illustrator to hyphenate under any circumstances. Figure 6-11 illustrates the Hyphenation Options dialog box.

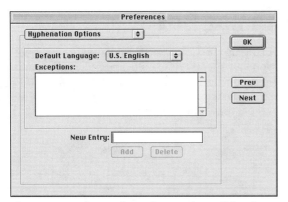

Figure 6-11: The Hyphenation Options dialog box

The Plug-ins & Scratch Disk Preferences

The last preference item in the Preference pop-up menu is a two-trick pony, the Plug-ins & Scratch Disk Preferences dialog box (see Figure 6-12). The first section in this dialog box enables you to specify a folder for plug-ins. The default is the Plug-Ins folder in the Adobe Illustrator folder.

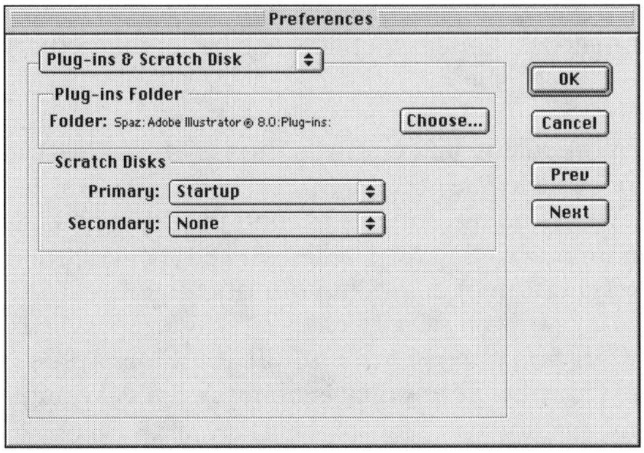

Figure 6-12: The Plug-ins & Scratch Disk dialog box

The second section in the Plug-in & Scratch Disk dialog box lets you define what drives to use as scratch disks — the place where Illustrator stores information when it runs out of RAM.

The Color Settings Dialog Box

Choose File ➪ Color Settings to bring up the Color Settings dialog box (shown in Figure 6-13). In this dialog box, you can specify how colors are to appear on the monitor. The way that colors appear on the monitor does not affect the output, but it may affect your perception of the colors on the screen. Changes that you make, based on what you see on the screen, may affect the output.

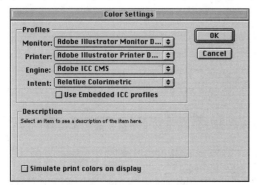

Figure 6-13: The Color Settings dialog box

Note   Because monitors and printed pieces are based on different display technologies, their colors are never exact matches. Certain monitors are better than others for color matching.

The Profiles section at the top of the dialog box controls the way that Illustrator displays color on your system relative to the color output device. The first pop-up menu lets you pick the monitor you're using, and the second pop-up menu allows you to pick the printer you plan on outputting to. These two settings combine to give an excellent onscreen representation of colors in your document.

The third pop-up menu, Engine, lets you choose from Adobe ICC CMS, Apple ColorSync, or Apple Default CMM for how your color is being derived. Windows has Adobe Reliable and Kodak Digital as choices.

The fourth pop-up menu, Intent, specifies, in general, what you'll be using the document for. The settings include Perceptual (Images), which is great for scanned material; Saturation, which is great for graphics; Relative Colorimetric, which attempts to show the color representation on the color's media white point; and Absolute Colormetric, which shows color based on the illuminate white point.

When checked, the Use Imbedded ICC Profiles box imbeds your PDF, Photoshop 5, TIFF, and JPEG files with the ICC color profiles.

Placement and Toolbox Value Preferences

Most Illustrator users take many preferences for granted. But if Illustrator didn't remember certain preferences, most Illustrator users would be quite annoyed.

Palettes (including the toolbox) remain where they were when you last used Illustrator. Illustrator remembers their size and whether they were open. Values in the toolbox are still whatever you set them to last. For example, the options in the Paintbrush/Eyedropper dialog box remain the same between Illustrator sessions.

The Simulate Print Colors on Display checkbox lets you see how your illustration will look on the printer. This option displays colors within the gamut.

For more information on color matching and about getting output to resemble what you see onscreen, see Chapter 20.

ASK TOULOUSE: Practical Preference Joke #436

Starsky: Uh, I'm trying to come up with a good practical joke for my buddy, Hutch.

Toulouse: Really? What'd he do to you?

Starsky: Nothing . . . well, a little thing with my type. Ticked me off pretty good.

Toulouse: Ah. You'll have to tell me about it.

Starsky: Yeah. I almost shot him. I carry a gun, you know.

Toulouse: I know. How about messing around with his colors?

Starsky: It's not like he's in a gang, but what the heck, I'll give it a shot.

Toulouse: All right. Go into the Color Matching dialog box, in the File Preferences submenu.

Starsky: Gotcha. Nice colors.

Toulouse: Change Black to White and White to Black. That's it.

Starsky: That's it? What'll it do?

Toulouse: It'll make everything on the screen look the opposite of what it is, at least for black and white. But it'll print fine. Of course, if your partner tries to compensate for the problem, it'll look fine onscreen, but print reversed.

Starsky: I'll try it. If it doesn't work, I can always shoot him.

Things You Can't Customize

There are a few things that you cannot customize in Illustrator, and they can be annoying:

✦ Type information always defaults to 12-point Helvetica, Auto Leading, 100% Horizontal Scale, 0 Tracking, Flush Left, Hyphenation Off. There is no easy way around this set of defaults.

✦ Layers for new documents are limited to one, which is colored light blue and called Layer 1.

✦ When you create new objects, they are always 0% Black Fill and a Black 1-point Stroke.

✦ The Selection tool is always the active tool.

If any of these things, or anything else, annoys you too much, call Adobe Tech Support at (206) 628-2757 and tell them about it. Usually (when you can get a human on the line), they are receptive to hearing your problem, and they may have an easy way for you to do something that you thought the program couldn't do. In addition, if enough users complain about adding certain features (real multiple pages, for instance), Adobe is likely to listen and implement those features in new versions of their software.

Summary

✦ Two different preference areas can be changed in Illustrator: Preferences and the startup file.

✦ By changing the Adobe Illustrator Startup file, you can change the default colors, patterns, gradients, and zoom level of each new document created in Illustrator.

✦ Many preferences in Illustrator can be changed in the General panel of the Preferences dialog box.

✦ The Constrain Angle option controls the angle at which objects are drawn and moved when the Shift key is pressed.

✦ The Auto Trace option controls the behavior of both the Pencil tool and the Auto Trace tool.

✦ The General Units option controls how all measurements are controlled in Illustrator.

✦   ✦   ✦

Putting Illustrator to Work

Now that you've learned the basics, it's time to start experimenting with some of the more interesting features in Illustrator. Part II guides you through the steps of adjusting your artwork just so, adding type to illustrations, and taking advantage of some of the more advanced features of Illustrator such as compound paths, masks, blends, live blends, gradient mesh, and patterns.

You'll have the most fun when you use Adobe Illustrator to create really incredible artwork. An illustration comes to life when you add all sorts of interesting special effects that give it a personality all its own.

Fine-Tuning Illustrator Artwork

Once you've created, traced, or even stolen someone else's artwork, there's always that period where you look at the artwork and you realize it's not quite right. That's where this chapter comes in. No, I won't do your finishing for you, but I'll show you how to take advantage of Illustrator's many tools to get the best end result, from slight Control Handle manipulations to massive scalings and rotations, to dramatic effects created with the Pathfinder palette.

The focus of this chapter is on modifying individual paths and the points on those paths by cutting them, combining them, and adjusting them. Think of this chapter as the Portions of Paths chapter, while Chapter 3 covers working with entire paths and multiple paths.

This is the chapter that separates the adult from the child, but even so, I didn't think it quite appropriate to name it "Chapter 7: Path Puberty. . ."

Path Editing

The path-editing tools are the Scissors tool; the Knife tool; the Add Anchor Point, Delete Anchor Point, and Convert Direction Point pop-up tools in the Pen tool slot; and the Smooth and the Erase pop-up tools in the Pencil tool slot. Clicking and holding down the Pen tool displays the Pen tool, Add Anchor Point, Delete Anchor Point, and Convert Direction Point. Dragging out to a path-editing tool replaces the default Pen tool with the newly selected pop-up tool. If you press the Caps Lock key at the same time that you choose a path-editing tool, the tool cursor resembles a cross hair. The cross-hair cursors enable precision positioning of cursors.

The purpose of each path-editing tool is:

✦ The **Scissors** tool is used for splitting paths. Clicking with the Scissors tool on a closed path makes that path an open path with the End Points directly overlapping each other where the click occurred. Using the Scissors tool on an open path splits that open path into two separate open paths, each with an End Point that overlaps the other open path's End Point.

✦ The **Knife** tool slices through *path areas*. The knife tool is the only path-editing tool that doesn't require that you have paths selected; it works on all unlocked paths that fall under the blade. You can slice very precisely with the Object ➪ Path ➪ Slice function, which turns a selected path into a Knife path.

✦ The **Add Anchor Point** tool is used for adding Anchor Points to an existing path. If an Anchor Point is added to a straight segment (one that has no Control Handles on either end), then the Anchor Point will be a Straight Corner Point. If the segment is curved — meaning that you have at least one Control Handle for that segment — then the new Anchor Point will be a Smooth Point.

✦ The **Delete Anchor Point** tool gets rid of the Anchor Point you click on. A new segment is created between the Anchor Points that were on either side of the Anchor Point you clicked. If the Anchor Point you clicked on is an End Point, no new segment is drawn; instead, the next Anchor Point on the path becomes the new End Point.

✦ The **Convert Direction Point** tool has two functions. The first is to simply change an Anchor Point from its current type of Anchor Point to a Straight Corner Point by clicking and releasing it. You can also change the current type to Smooth by clicking and dragging on the Anchor Point. The second function is to move Control Handles individually by changing Smooth Points to Curved Corner Points and by changing Combination Corner Points and Curved Corner Points to Smooth Points. (Straight Corner Points don't have any Control Handles, so using this method can't change them.)

✦ The **Smooth** tool does what it sounds like it should do. The Smooth tool enables you to smooth or redraw a selected path. When you drag the Smooth tool over a path to create a direction, a new path is created from where you started the path to where you ended the path. Figure 7-1 shows a path before and after smoothing.

✦ The **Erase** tool erases sections of a selected path. No matter how the path was drawn, you can erase sections of it with the Erase tool. In the case of an ellipse or rectangle, you have to ungroup the shape first. In many ways, I prefer to remove sections using this precise tool rather than the Knife tool.

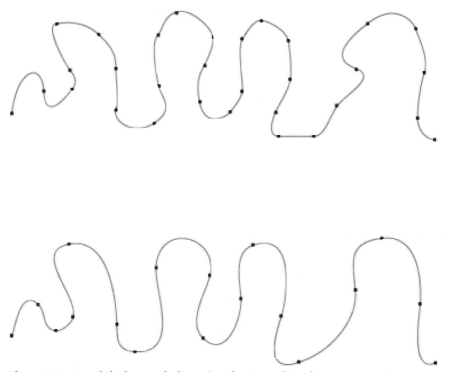

Figure 7-1: A path before and after using the Smooth tool

You can add and remove Anchor Points in two different ways. I mentioned one method in Chapter 3, where I demonstrated how to add Anchor Points with the drawing tools and remove them simply by selecting them and pressing the Delete key.

The techniques that I cover in this chapter are unlike the methods discussed previously. Instead of adding new points that create an extension to an existing path, you learn how to add points in the middle of existing paths. Instead of deleting points and the line segments connected to them, you learn how to remove points between two Anchor Points and watch as a new line segment connects those two Anchor Points.

In Figure 7-2, the top row shows a drawing with a point added, resulting in a new curved section. The second row shows a point being removed and then readded. Adding points, even to the same areas where they were removed, will not change the path back to the shape that it was before the points were removed. That path will have to be altered to resemble the original path. I discuss these and other issues throughout this chapter.

Note   Figure 7-2 shows a very simple example. The Delete Anchor Point tool is most
often used to remove unnecessary points from overly complicated drawings.

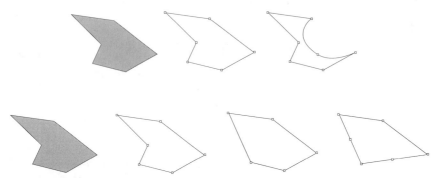

Figure 7-2: Adding Anchor Points after they've been removed will not return the
shape to its original shape

Adding Anchor Points

To add an Anchor Point to an existing path, select the Add Anchor Point tool and
click a line segment of a path. You may not place an Anchor Point directly on top of
another Anchor Point, but you can get pretty darn close. Figure 7-3 shows a path
before and after several Anchor Points are added to it.

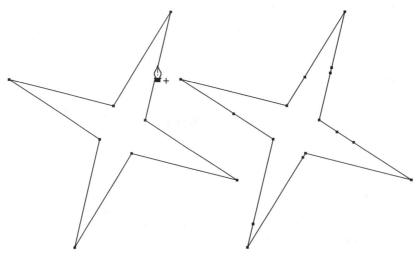

Figure 7-3: Adding Anchor Points to a path doesn't alter the shape of the path,
but it *does* allow the path to be modified more easily than if the points had
not been added

Caution I like to select the paths to which I am adding Anchor Points before I start actually adding the points. This technique ensures that I don't accidentally get the annoying message "Can't Add Anchor Point. Please use the Add Anchor Point tool on a segment of a path." It seems that if there is just one point in the middle of a path, that's where I end up clicking to add the point. After I add one point, the path becomes selected automatically.

Anchor Points added to paths via the Add Anchor Point tool are either Smooth Points or Straight Corner Points, depending on the segment where the new Anchor Point is added. If the segment has two Straight Corner Points on either side of it, then the new Anchor Point is a Straight Corner Point. If one of the Anchor Points is any type of Anchor Point other than a Straight Corner Point, the new Anchor Point is a Smooth Point.

See Chapter 14, which discusses the Roughen filter, for another way to add Anchor Points to a path without adding length to the path.

The Add Anchor Points Function

The Add Anchor Points function (choose Object ➪ Path ➪ Add Anchor Points) adds new Anchor Points between every pair of existing Anchor Points it can find. New Anchor Points are always added halfway between existing Anchor Points.

Tip Add Anchor Points is related to the Add Anchor Point tool. This function adds Anchor Points the same way as the tool does, only more efficiently. Points that are added to a smooth segment are automatically Smooth Points; points added to a straight segment are automatically Corner Points.

For example, if you have one line segment with an Anchor Point on each end, Add Anchor Points will add one Anchor Point to the segment, exactly in the middle of the two Anchor Points. If a rectangle is drawn and Add Anchor Points is applied, it will have four new Anchor Points: one at the top, one at the bottom, one on the left side, and one on the right side. Figure 7-4 shows an object that has had the Add Anchor Points function applied once, twice, and three times.

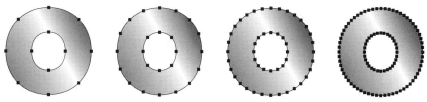

Figure 7-4: The Add Anchor Points function doubles the number of Anchor Points, adding new Anchor Points directly between existing points

Tip   Want to know how many points are being added to your path when Add Anchor Points is applied? Each time the function is reapplied, the number of Anchor Points doubles on a closed path and is one less than doubled on an open path.

Adding Anchor Points is useful before using the Punk & Bloat filter and the Scribble and Tweak filter, and before using any other filter that bases its results on the number and position of Anchor Points.

Tip   If you need to add a large number of anchor points quickly, use the Roughen filter with a size of 0% and the detail at how many Anchor Points you want per inch. The nice thing about Roughen is that the Anchor Points are equally distributed, regardless of where the original Anchor Points were in the selected path (as opposed to Add Anchor Points, which places new points between existing ones, resulting in "clumping" in detailed areas).

Removing Anchor Points

Removing Anchor Points is a little trickier than adding them. Depending on where you remove the Anchor Point, you may adversely change the flow of the line between the two Anchor Points on either side of it, as shown in Figure 7-5. If the point removed had any Control Handles, the removal usually results in a more drastic change than if the Anchor Point had been a Straight Corner Point. This situation occurs if Control Handles on the Anchor Point being removed controlled at least half the aspect of the curve. A Straight Corner Point affects only the location of the line, not the shape of its curve.

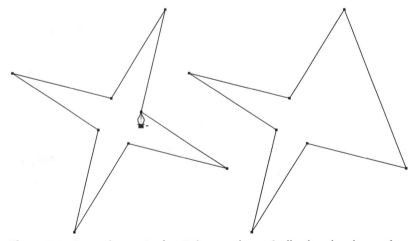

Figure 7-5: Removing an Anchor Point can dramatically alter the shape of a path

To remove an Anchor Point, click an existing Anchor Point with the Delete Anchor Point tool. Like the Add Anchor Point tool, you can remove points without first selecting the path, but, of course, if the path is not selected, you can't see it or the points that you want to remove. If you miss and don't click an Anchor Point, you will get a message informing you that to remove an Anchor Point, you must click one.

After you remove Anchor Points, you cannot usually just add them back with the Add Anchor Point tool. Considering that the flow of the path will change when you remove a point, adding a point — even the correct type of point — will not give the same result as just undoing the point deletion.

If there are only two points on an *open* path, the Anchor Point you click is deleted and so is the segment connecting it to the sole remaining Anchor Point. If there are only two points on a *closed* path, both line segments from the Anchor Point you click are deleted along with that point, leaving only one Anchor Point remaining.

Simplifying Paths by Removing Anchor Points

Some artwork can be unnecessarily complicated, with many more Anchor Points than are actually needed. These additional Anchor Points most often occur with artwork that has been traced either by Illustrator's Auto Trace tool or by Streamline. Unfortunately, Illustrator doesn't have a built-in method for cleaning up messy paths (the Cleanup function isn't it, unfortunately). To make matters worse, Streamline won't allow you to paste in Illustrator paths to clean them up (Streamline has built-in simplify functions). There are, however, a few solutions you might look into:

✦ Manually remove points via the Delete Anchor Point tool. This takes forever, but with patience you'll get good results. Unfortunately, the tool doesn't care what happens to the paths you're deleting from, and they'll change drastically in shape with each point removal.

✦ Pick up a copy of Logo Corrector from Illom Development. Logo Corrector is designed precisely to fix Streamlined artwork. It contains an amazing set of tools that can be used for that and also for other related types of work.

✦ If you have FreeHand, paste your paths into FreeHand and simplify using the Simplify function. Copy from there and paste back into Illustrator.

And when you're done with one of these three options, send e-mail to Adobe begging, pleading, and demanding that they include a spiffy simplify function in the next release of Illustrator.

Splitting Paths

To change a single path into two separate paths that together make up a path equal in length to the original, you must use the Scissors tool. You can also split paths by selecting and deleting Anchor Points or line segments, although this method shortens the overall length of the two paths.

To split a path with the Scissors tool, click anywhere on a path. Initially, it doesn't seem like much happens. If you clicked in the middle of a line segment, a new Anchor Point appears. (Actually, two will appear, but the second is directly on top of the first so you see only one.) If you click directly on top of an existing Anchor Point, nothing at all seems to happen, but Illustrator actually creates another Anchor Point on top of the one that you clicked.

After clicking with the Scissors tool, you have separated the path into two separate sections, but it appears that there is still only one path because the two sections are both selected. To see the individual paths, deselect them (⌘-Shift-A) [Ctrl+ Shift+A] and select just one side with the Selection tool. After a path has been split, one half may be moved independently of the other half, as shown in Figure 7-6.

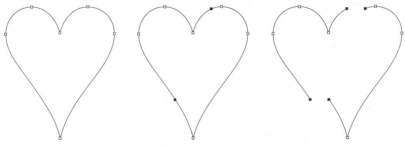

Figure 7-6: The original path (left), the path after splitting (center), and the path after the two pieces have been moved apart (right)

The Anchor Points created with the Scissors tool will be either Smooth Points or Straight Corner Points, depending on the type of Anchor Point that is next along the path. If the line segment to the next Anchor Point has a Control Handle coming out of that Anchor Point that affects the line segment, then the new End Point will be a Smooth Point. If there is no Control Handle for the line segment, the End Point will be a Straight Corner Point.

Caution   You cannot use the Scissors tool on a line's end point — only on segments and Anchor Points that are not End Points.

Tip   Tired of those annoying warning boxes when you click where you shouldn't with the Scissors tool (or the Add Anchor Points tool, or the Delete Anchor Points tool, or the Convert Direction Point tool)? You can turn those warnings off by clicking the Disable Warnings checkbox in the General Preferences dialog box.

Dividing and Duplicating Paths

Illustrator 8 provides several capabilities that allow for multiple types of dividing and duplicating of paths, even paths that aren't selected. This section discusses those different features, as well as the tool that makes this possible: the Knife tool.

The Knife Tool

The Knife tool is found to the right of the Scissors tool. Access it by clicking and holding on the Scissors tool in the toolbox, and then dragging over to the Knife tool. The Knife tool divides paths into smaller sections as it slices through them. Those sections are initially selected, but they're not grouped. Figure 7-7 shows a path before and after it crosses paths with the Knife.

Figure 7-7: The original path (left), the path of the Knife tool (center), and the resulting paths (right) after being dragged apart, all shown in Artwork mode

Pressing the Option [Alt] key when using the Knife tool doesn't cut paths beneath where you've cut; it makes a copy of those paths. Instead of tearing the paths into pieces, it duplicates the areas it has been dragged across. Figure 7-8 shows what happens with the same path from the previous example when the Option [Alt] key is pressed.

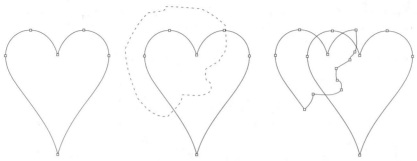

Figure 7-8: The original path (left), the path of the Knife tool (center), and the paths (right) that are the result of holding down the Option [Alt] key while using the Knife tool and after being dragged apart, all shown in Artwork mode

Caution   Remember that the Knife tool works on *all* paths that are under the existing path, selected or not.

Slicing with Other Paths

The Knife tool can be useful, but sometimes you might want to divide or duplicate a portion of existing paths without having to draw them with the mouse and your unsteady shouldn't-have-drunk-and-illustrated right hand (maybe you need perfectly sized cuts or duplicates in the shape of text). That's where Slicing comes in. The Slice function takes any selected path and turns it into a knife path, slicing through all paths beneath it. You can even press the Option [Alt] key when choosing Slice to duplicate the cut portion of the path without modifying the original path at all.

Cleanup

Cleanup removes three unwanted elements from Illustrator documents: stray points, unpainted objects, and empty text paths. Cleanup works on the entire document, regardless of what is selected. Use Cleanup by choosing Object ➪ Path ➪ Cleanup. The Cleanup dialog box is shown in Figure 7-9.

```
┌─────────────── Cleanup ───────────────┐
│  ┌─ Delete ──────────┐  ┌────────┐     │
│  │ ☑ Stray Points    │  │   OK   │     │
│  │ ☑ Unpainted Objects│ ├────────┤     │
│  │ ☑ Empty Text Paths │  │ Cancel │     │
│  └───────────────────┘  └────────┘     │
└────────────────────────────────────────┘
```

Figure 7-9: The Cleanup dialog box

ASK TOULOUSE: Point Removal

Murray: Cleanup doesn't really work.

Toulouse: Maybe you just don't have the things it cleans up in your document.

Murray: Oh, sure, it gets rid of *those* things, but the paths still have too many points.

Toulouse: Unfortunately, Cleanup doesn't get rid of excess points on paths.

Murray: What? Why not?

Toulouse: Hey, I only write *about* the program.

Murray: Well, Streamline has had a Simplify command since version 3.0, which was released in 1993.

Toulouse: You'd think they'd incorporate that into Illustrator, huh? Maybe in 9.0.

Cleanup doesn't work on locked or hidden paths, paths turned into guides, or paths on locked or hidden layers.

The Delete options in the Cleanup dialog box are:

✦ **Stray Points** selects and deletes any little points flying around. These points can cause all sorts of trouble, as a point can have paint attributes but can't print.

✦ **Unpainted Objects** gets rid of any paths that are Filled and Stroked with None, and that aren't masks (masks are always Filled and Stroked with None).

✦ **Empty Text Paths** finds any text paths with no characters and deletes them. This is *not* the same as the old Revert Text Paths from Illustrator 5/5.5, which changed empty text paths back into standard paths.

If you aren't sure if your document contains these three items, run Cleanup. If none of these items are found, a dialog box appears telling you so.

Offset Path

Offset Path (choose Object ➪ Path ➪ Offset Path) draws a new path around the outside or inside of an existing path. The distance from the existing path is the distance that you specify in the Offset Path dialog box, which is shown in Figure 7-10. In a sense, you are creating a Stroke, outlining it, and uniting it with the original all in one swoop. You can specify the distance the path is to be offset by entering a value in the Offset box.

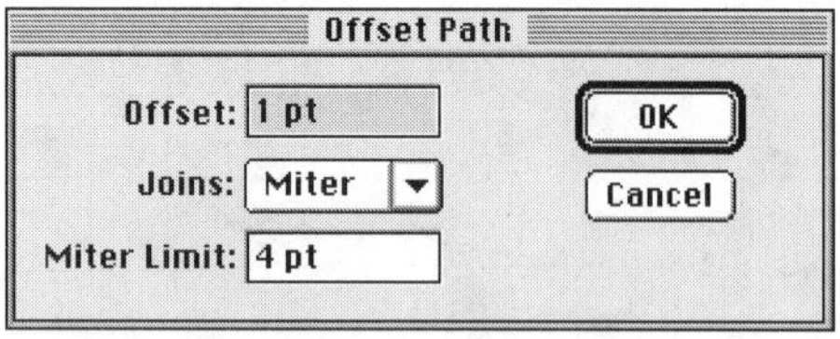

Figure 7-10: The Offset Path dialog box

A positive number in the Offset Path dialog box creates the new path *outside* the existing path, and a negative number creates the new path *inside* the existing path. When the path is closed, figuring out where the new path will be created is easy. For open paths, the outside is the left side of the path, as it runs from start to end, and the inside is the right side of the path, as it runs from start to end.

The Joins pop-up menu enables you to select from different types of joins at the corners of the new path. The choices are miter, round, and bevel, and the result is the same effect that you get if you choose those options as the stroke style for a Stroke.

The Miter Limit affects the miter size only when the Miter option is selected from the Joins pop-up menu, but the option is available when round and bevel joins are selected. Just ignore the Miter Limit when you are using round or bevel joins. (You cannot use a value that is less than 1.)

Often, when you are offsetting a path, the new, resulting path will overlap itself, creating *skiddles* (small, undesirable bumps in a path). If the skiddles are within a closed-path area, select the new path and choose Unite from the Pathfinder palette. If the skiddles are outside the closed-path area, choose Divide from the Pathfinder palette and then select and delete each of the skiddles.

ASK TOULOUSE: Scaling versus Offsetting

Ted: I don't know what the big deal is about Offset Path. I just use the Scale tool.

Toulouse: But the Scale tool does something totally different than Offset Path.

Ted: Not if you use Offset Path on a circle or a square.

Toulouse: Yes, in those few exceptions, it is exactly the same.

Ted: So why use it at all?

Toulouse: Well, let's say you wanted to make a rectangle bigger by 1 inch on each side.

Ted: I'd scale it up, pressing the Shift key.

Toulouse: That wouldn't work. The "shorter" dimension would be less than the larger one.

Ted: Then to hell with the Shift key. I'd eyeball it.

Toulouse: Oh, that would be exact. It would be easier to use Offset Path.

Ted: Okay, maybe in that isolated occurrence.

Toulouse: In almost every occurrence. Such as for text; try scaling versus offsetting and you'll see a huge difference.

Outline Path

Outline Path creates a path around an existing path's Stroke. The width of the new path is directly related to the width of the Stroke.

I use Outline Path for two reasons. The first reason is the most obvious: to Fill a Stroke with a gradient or to be able to view a pattern that is inside a Stroke. The second reason is that when you transform an outlined Stroke, the effect is often different from the effect that results from transforming a Stroked path. Scaling an outlined Stroke changes the width of the Stroke in the direction of the scale. The same is true when using the Free Distort filter, which also changes the width of the Stroke in the direction of the scale, sometimes resulting in a nonuniform Stroke. Figure 7-11 shows the difference between transforming/distorting a Stroked path and an Outlined Stroke.

Figure 7-11: The original Stroked path is to the left. The middle path has been transformed and distorted various ways. The path on the right was outlined via Outline Path and then transformed and distorted exactly the same way as the middle path.

The End and Join attributes of the Stroke's style determine how the ends and joins of the resulting Stroke look.

Outline Path creates problems for tight corners. It causes overlaps that are similar to those generated by Offset Path.

Use Unite to remove the skittles that result from overlapping paths. Not only will Unite make the drawing look better as artwork and prevent overlapping Strokes, but it also will reduce the number of points in the file, making the illustration smaller so that it can print faster.

Caution   Using a Dash pattern on the Stroke and using Outline Path changes the Stroke back to a solid line and then Outlines it.

Averaging Points and Joining

Averaging points is the process in which Illustrator determines the location of the points and figures out where the center of all the points will be on a mean basis. *Joining* is the process in which either a line segment is drawn between two End Points, or two End Points are merged into a single Anchor Point.

Averaging and joining are done together when two End Points need to change location to be one on top of the other and then merged into one point. You can perform these steps one at a time, or you can have Illustrator do both steps automatically by pressing ⌘-Option-Shift-J [Ctrl+Alt+Shift+J].

Averaging Points

To line up a series of points either horizontally or vertically, use the Average command. The Average command also works to place selected points one on top of the other. Figure 7-12 shows the different types of averaging.

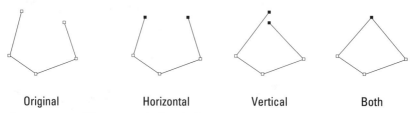

Original   Horizontal   Vertical   Both

Figure 7-12: Different types of averaging

To average points horizontally, select the points to be averaged with the Direct Selection tool and choose Object ➪ Path ➪ Average (⌘-Option-J) [Ctrl+Alt+J]. The Average dialog box appears, asking which type of averaging you would like to do. In this case, choose Horizontal, which will move selected points only up and down.

Caution Be sure to select the points to be averaged with the Direct Selection tool. If you select a path with either the Group Selection tool or the regular Selection tool, every point in the path will be averaged! This mistake can do quite a bit of damage when averaging both horizontally and vertically.

To average points vertically, choose the Vertical option in the Average dialog box. To average points both vertically and horizontally, choose Both. The Both option places all selected points on top of each other.

When averaging points, Illustrator uses the mean method to determine the center. No, Illustrator isn't nasty to the points that it averages; rather, Illustrator adds together the locations of the points and then divides by the number of points, which provides the mean location of the center of the points.

If you want to average entire paths, use the Align palette, which is covered later in this chapter, in the section "Aligning and Distributing Objects."

Joining

Joining is a tricky area to define. Illustrator's Join feature does two entirely different things: It joins two End Points at different locations with a line segment, and it also combines two Anchor Points into one when they are placed one on top of the other.

To join two End Points with a line segment, select just two End Points in different locations (not on top of each other) with the Direct Selection tool and choose Object ➪ Path ➪ Join (⌘-J) [Ctrl+J]. A line segment will be formed between the two points, as shown in Figure 7-13.

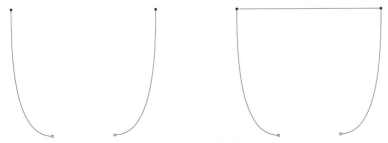

Figure 7-13: Joining two End Points with a line segment

To combine two End Points into a single Anchor Point, select the two points that are *directly* one over the other and choose Object ⇨ Path ⇨ Join (⌘-J) [Ctrl+J]. The Join dialog box appears, asking what type of point should be created when the two End Points become one Anchor Point. If you choose Smooth Point, then the point will become a Smooth Point with two linked Control Handles. If you choose Corner Point, the point will retain any Control Handle position that is part of it. And if no Control Handle is on the line, there will be no Control Handle on that side of the Anchor Point.

Not only can you join two separate paths, but you can also join together the End Points on the same open path (overlapping End Points) to create a closed path in the same way that two End Points from different paths are joined.

To make sure that End Points are overlapping, turn on the Snap to Point feature in General Preferences and drag one End Point to the other with a selection tool. When the two points are close enough, the arrowhead cursor (normally black) will become hollow. Release the mouse button when the arrowhead is hollow, and the two points will be directly one above the other.

Another way to ensure that the End Points are overlapping is to select them, choose Object ⇨ Path ⇨ Average (⌘-Option-J) [Ctrl+Alt+J], and select the Both option in the Average dialog box.

Caution   When creating an Anchor Point out of two overlapping End Points, make sure that the two points are precisely overlapping. If they are even the smallest distance apart, a line segment will be drawn between the two points instead of transforming the two End Points into a single Anchor Point. You can tell immediately whether the points are overlapping correctly when you select Join. If a dialog box appears, the points are overlapping. If no dialog box appears, the points were not overlapping, and it is best to undo the join.

Tip   To make the points overlap and join at once, press ⌘-Option-Shift-J [Ctrl+Alt+ Shift+J], which will both average and join the selected End Points. This method works only on End Points. The End Points are averaged both horizontally and vertically and are also joined into an Anchor Point that is a Corner Point, with Control Handle Lines and Control Handles unchanged.

Joining has these limitations:

✦ Joins may not take place when one path is part of a different group than the other path. If the two paths are in the same base group (that is, not in any other groups before being grouped to the other path, even grouped by themselves), the End Points can be joined.

✦ If one path is grouped to another object and the other object has not been previously grouped to the path, the End Points will not join.

✦ The End Points on text paths cannot be joined.

✦ The End Points of guides cannot be joined.

If all the points in an open path are selected (as if the path is selected with the regular Selection tool), then choosing Object ➪ Path ➪ Join (⌘-J) [Ctrl+J] automatically joins the End Points. If the two End Points are located directly one over the other, the Join dialog box appears, asking whether the new Anchor Point should be a Smooth Point or a Corner Point.

Joining is also useful for determining the location of End Points when the End Points are overlapping. Select the entire path, choose Object ➪ Path ➪ Join (⌘-J) [Ctrl+J], and choose Smooth Point. These steps will usually alter one of the two segments on either side of the new Anchor Point. Undo the join and you will know the location of the overlapping End Points.

ASK TOULOUSE: Join Trouble

Mary: I can't join my two paths.

Toulouse: They're both open paths?

Mary: Yep.

Toulouse: You've selected just the End Points you want to join?

Mary: Yep.

Toulouse: You're choosing Join from the Object ➪ Path submenu?

Mary: Yep.

Toulouse: Are both paths ungrouped?

Mary: Yep. Uh . . . I mean . . . I'm not sure.

Toulouse: Select them both and Ungroup. Then try.

Mary: That was it!

Toulouse: Remember that you can't join paths when they're part of different groups.

Aligning and Distributing Objects

The Align palette (see Figure 7-14) contains several buttons that are used for aligning and distributing objects with a simple click of a button. Align treats paths, type objects, and groups as single objects, allowing for quite a bit of flexibility when aligning and distributing.

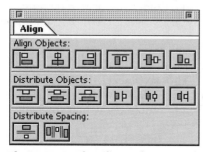

Figure 7-14: The Align palette

To use the Align palette, select the objects you wish to align and/or distribute, and click the appropriate button in the palette. Each click in the palette counts as a change in Illustrator, which means that if you click 20 times, you'll need to undo 20 times to get back to where you started.

New Feature New to Illustrator 8 are the Distribute Spacing options in the Align palette. You have two choices: Distribute Vertical Spacing or Distribute Horizontal Spacing.

Caution The Distribute functions distribute along the edges or the center only. There is no reset button on the palette (a most unfortunate oversight), so you'll have to undo if you click the wrong button.

Converting Anchor Points

The title of this section should probably have been "Converting Direction Points" because this section deals with the Convert Direction Point tool. However, because the Convert Direction Point tool only converts Anchor Points by adjusting Control Handles, the use of the term *direction points* is wrong.

The Convert Direction Point tool works differently with each type of Anchor Point. The different types of Anchor Points are shown in Figure 7-15. (See Chapter 3 for detailed definitions of the four different types of Anchor Points and how they're drawn with the Pen tool.)

Figure 7-15: The four types of Anchor Points

You can use the Convert Direction Point tool on either extended Control Handles or on Anchor Points. When there are two Control Handles on an Anchor Point, clicking either Control Handle with the Convert Direction Point tool "breaks" the linked Control Handles (so that when the angle of one is changed, the other is changed as well), and makes them independent (the Control Handle's length from the Anchor Point and the angle can be altered individually).

Press ⌘-Option [Ctrl+Alt] to access the Convert Direction Point tool.

Converting Smooth Points

Smooth Points can be changed into the other three types of Anchor Points by using both the Direct Selection tool and the Convert Direction Point tool as follows:

✦ To convert Smooth Points into Combination Corner Points, use the Direct Selection tool or the Convert Direction Point tool to drag one Control Handle into the Anchor Point.

✦ To convert Smooth Points into Curved Corner Points, use the Convert Direction Point tool to drag one of the Control Handles. After being dragged with the Convert Direction Point tool, the two Control Handles become independent of each other (the movement of one will not affect the other).

The following steps show you how you can use the Direct Selection tool and the Convert Direction Point tool to change shapes — in this case, from a circle to a diamond.

1. Draw a circle with the Ellipse tool. Remember to keep the Shift key pressed so you end up with a perfect circle.

2. Select the Convert Direction Point tool.

3. Click on each of the Anchor Points and release. The diamond should look like the illustration in Figure 7-16.

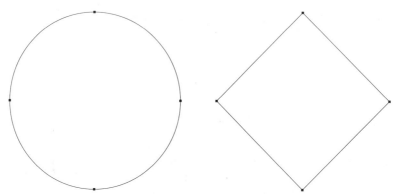

Figure 7-16: Convert the circle (left) to the diamond (right) by clicking on each anchor point with the Convert Direction Point tool

Converting Straight Corner Points

You can change Straight Corner Points into one of the other three types of Anchor Points by using both the Convert Direction Point tool and the Direct Selection tool as follows:

✦ To convert Straight Corner Points into Smooth Points, use the Convert Direction Point tool to click and drag on the Anchor Point. As you drag, linked Control Handles appear on both sides of the Anchor Point.

✦ To convert Straight Corner Points into Combination Corner Points, use the Convert Direction Point tool to click and drag on the Anchor Point. As you drag, linked Control Handles appear on both sides of the Anchor Point. Select one of the Control Handles with the Convert Direction Point tool or the Direct Selection tool and drag it toward the Anchor Point until it disappears.

✦ To convert Straight Corner Points into Curved Corner Points, use the Convert Direction Point tool to click and drag on the Anchor Point. As you drag, linked Control Handles appear on both sides of the Anchor Point. Then use the Convert Direction Point tool to drag one of the Control Handles. After being dragged with the Convert Direction Point tool, the two Control Handles become independent of each other.

Converting Combination Corner Points

You can change Combination Corner Points into one of the other three types of Anchor Points by using both the Convert Direction Point tool and the Direct Selection tool as follows:

✦ To convert Combination Corner Points into Smooth Points, use the Convert Direction Point tool to click and drag on the Anchor Point. As you drag, linked Control Handles appear on both sides of the Anchor Point.

✦ To convert Combination Corner Points into Straight Corner Points, use the Convert Direction Point tool to click once on the Anchor Point. The Control Handle disappears.

✦ To convert Combination Corner Points into Curved Corner Points, use the Convert Direction Point tool to click and drag on the Anchor Point. As you drag, linked Control Handles appear on both sides of the Anchor Point. Then use the Convert Direction Point tool to drag one of the Control Handles. After being dragged with the Convert Direction Point tool, the two Control Handles become independent of each other.

The following steps are another example of how you can change shapes using the Direct Selection tool and the Convert Direction Point tool—this time, a circle into a heart.

1. Draw a circle with the Ellipse tool. Remember to keep the Shift key pressed so that you end up with a perfect circle.

2. Click on the lowest point on the circle with the Direct Selection tool.

3. Click on the right Control Handle of that Anchor Point and drag it up, as shown in Figure 7-17.

4. With the Convert Direction Point tool, click on the left Control Handle of that point and drag it up.

5. Click on the Anchor Point at the top of the circle and drag it down a little.

6. With the Direct Selection tool, click on the left Control Handle of the topmost point and drag it up.

7. Click on the right Control Handle with the Convert Direction Point tool and drag it down. If you turn the Grid on (⌘-') [Ctrl+'], you'll find making adjustments such as this much easier and more precise.

8. Adjust the Anchor Points and Control Handles until the heart looks really . . . well . . . nice.

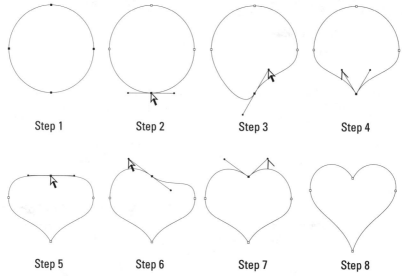

Step 1   Step 2   Step 3   Step 4

Step 5   Step 6   Step 7   Step 8

Figure 7-17: Steps for converting a circle into a heart

Converting Curved Corner Points

You can change Curved Corner Points into one of the other three types of Anchor Points by using both the Convert Direction Point tool and the Direct Selection tool as follows:

✦ To convert Curved Corner Points into Smooth Points, use the Convert Direction Point tool to click and drag on the Anchor Point. You can then use the Direct Selection tool to adjust the angle of both Control Handles at once.

✦ To convert Curved Corner Points into Straight Corner Points, use the Convert Direction Point tool to click once on the Anchor Point. The Control Handles disappear.

✦ To convert Curved Corner Points into Combination Corner Points, use the Direct Selection tool to drag one Control Handle into the Anchor Point.

Smoothing a Rough Line

The Smooth tool is found in the Pencil tool's pop-up tools in the toolbar. This fabulous new tool smooths lines drawn with any tool. Whether you used the Pencil, Pen, or Brush tool, the Smooth tool can smooth any line just by dragging over it. The Smooth tool really helps if you have a smooth-hand or a pressure-sensitive tablet. Figure 7-18 shows a path before and after using the Smooth tool to even out the kinks. The Smooth tool will try to keep close to the shape you started with when you edit.

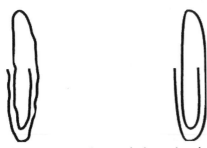

Figure 7-18: Before and after using the Smooth tool

Figure 7-19 shows the Smooth Tool Preferences dialog box, which you can access by double-clicking on the Smooth tool. Tolerances and Options are the settings you can choose from. Tolerances are determined by pixels. (Yes, I know this is a vector-based program, but bear with me.) The Tolerance setting follows the nuances of your hand moving the mouse or pressure-sensitive tablet pen. If you have a high setting of Fidelity and Smoothness, the lines will be smoother with fewer anchor points. If you choose a low setting for Fidelity and Smoothness, the lines will be bumpier with more anchor points. Figure 7-20 shows selected lines with a high Tolerance setting (left) and a low Tolerance setting (right), with the Bounding Box option turned off.

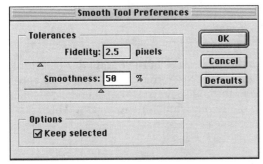

Figure 7-19: The Smooth Tool Preferences dialog box

In the Options area, you can check or uncheck the Keep Selected option. By default this box is checked, that way the line remains selected after you apply the Smooth tool to it. If you uncheck this box, it will deselect after you apply the Smooth tool to it.

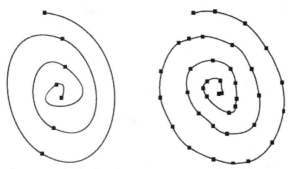

Figure 7-20: The left line shows the results of a high Tolerance setting and the right line shows the results of a low Tolerance setting in the Pencil/Smooth tools

Erasing a Section of a Path

Another newcomer to Illustrator 8 is the Erase tool found in the pop-up tools of the Pencil tool in the toolbox. The Erase tool enables you to remove sections of a path just as if you were using a real eraser on paper. You drag over the area you want removed and it is deleted. This is a pretty cool new tool. If you just click once over the path, it will cut the path, but not remove a section. You can drag the two pieces apart. The longer you drag the greater the number of parts of the path that will be erased. The Erase tool works on any path, but it doesn't work on text or a gradient mesh object.

The Pathfinder Palette

The most powerful path functions in Illustrator are in the Pathfinder palette. They do things that would take hours to do using Illustrator's traditional tools and methods. The only drawback to the Pathfinder palette is that there are so many options that it's pretty darn hard to figure out which one to use for which job. Figure 7-21 shows the new Pathfinder palette.

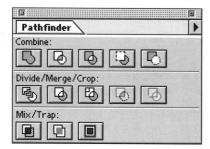

Figure 7-21: The Pathfinder palette

The Pathfinder options take over most of the mundane tasks of path editing that could otherwise take hours. Everything that the Pathfinder options do can be done manually with Illustrator tools, but the Pathfinder options do them much more quickly. Common activities such as joining two paths together correctly and breaking a path into two pieces are done in a snap.

The Pathfinder options change the way that two or more paths interact. The cute little symbols on each of the Pathfinder options are supposed to clue you in to what each option can do, but the pictures are small and most don't accurately depict exactly how each option works.

If you have the Hot Help feature active, the name of each of the Pathfinder options pops up when you hold your cursor over its option symbol. However, these names can be a little confusing. The names were undoubtedly chosen to signify what each of the Pathfinder options can do, but most of them can't be defined easily with just one word. The Pathfinder options fall into three categories. The Combine options for the most part combine two or more paths. The Divide/Merge/Crop options are what I call the "overlay" Pathfinders, because they generate results from two or more paths that overlap. The Mix/Trap options mix the colors of overlapping paths, or generate trapping automatically, according to your specifications.

Tip　Now that the Pathfinder options are no longer on a pull-down menu (as in version 7), to reapply a Pathfinder function you can use the Repeat Pathfinder function found in the Pathfinder palette's pop-up menu (see Figure 7-22) or press ⌘-4 [Ctrl+4].

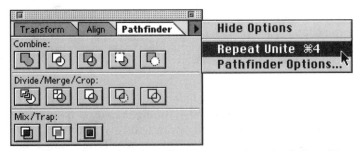

Figure 7-22: The Pathfinder palette's Repeat function is found in the pop-up menu

The Pathfinder Options Dialog Box

To access the Pathfinder options, choose Pathfinder Options in the pop-up menu of the Pathfinder palette, previously shown in Figure 7-22. This displays the Pathfinder Options dialog box, shown in Figure 7-23, which enables you to customize the way that the Pathfinders work.

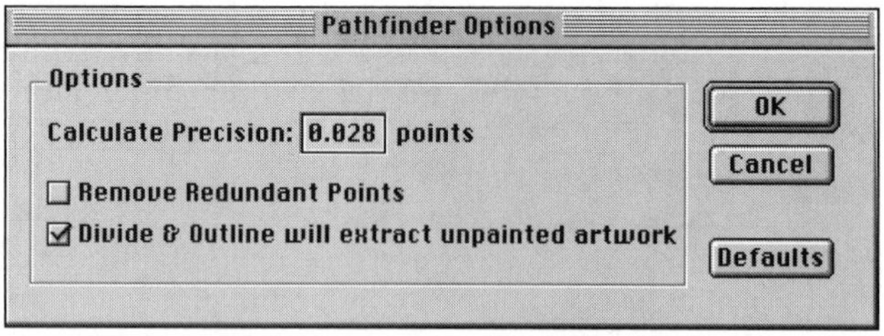

Figure 7-23: The Pathfinder palette options

The value in the Calculate Precision text field tells Illustrator how precisely Pathfinders should operate. The more precisely they operate, the better and more accurate the results are, but the longer the processing time is. This speed differential is most apparent when you apply Pathfinders — especially Trap — to very complex objects. The default value is 0.028 points, which seems to be accurate enough for most work.

The Remove Redundant Points option gets rid of overlapping points that are side-by-side on the same path. I can't think of why you would want overlapping points, so keeping this option checked (the default) is a good idea.

If the "Divide & Outline will extract unpainted artwork" option is checked, it automatically deletes unpainted artwork. This relieves you from having to remove all those paths that Divide always seems to produce that are Filled and Stroked with None.

Usually, the defaults in the Pathfinder Options dialog box are the best options for most situations. If you change the options, be aware that the Pathfinder Options dialog box will reset to the defaults when you quit Illustrator.

Unite

Unite unites the selected objects if they are overlapping. A new path outlines all the previously selected objects. There are no paths where the original paths intersected. The new object takes the Paint Style attributes of the topmost object. If any objects are within other objects, those objects will be assimilated. If there are "holes" in the object, the holes will become reversed out of a compound path.

You'll find that Unite is one Pathfinder option that you'll use often. Play with combining various paths for a while so you know what to expect, and you will develop a sense of when using Unite is a better option than doing the same tasks manually.

Unite combines two or more paths into one path, as described in the following steps.

1. Create and select the artwork that you want to apply Unite to. In the example in Figure 7-24, the artwork is type converted into outlines. (Pathfinders work only with paths — you have to convert type into outlined paths, and you cannot use EPS (Encapsulated PostScript) images.)

2. Choose the Unite option from the Pathfinder palette. Any overlapping artwork is united into one path. (The color of the united path is always the color of the path that was the topmost selected path before you used Unite.)

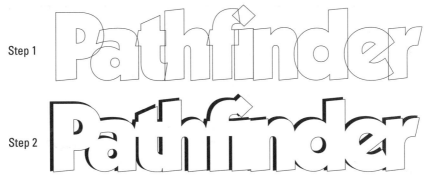

Figure 7-24: Using Unite

When you use Unite, paths that don't overlap but are outside of other paths become part of a group. Illustrator draws paths between End Points of open paths before it unites those paths with other paths. Compound paths remain compound paths.

ASK TOULOUSE: Style Sheets with Unite

Phyllis: So, is that all Unite is good for?

Toulouse: You mean joining abutting and overlapping paths?

Phyllis: Yeah. That's it?

Toulouse: Actually, no. You can use Unite to create compound paths.

Phyllis: That's interesting.

Toulouse: You can also use Unite to create pseudo style sheets.

Phyllis: How so?

(continued)

(continued)

Toulouse: If you want several paths to have the same paint style, and the paint style might change in the future, unite them. Make sure the topmost path is the color you want it to be.

Phyllis: And that works as a style sheet?

Toulouse: Sorta. By selecting any of those paths and changing the paint style, all the paths will change to that paint style. Of course, if you want real style sheets, you can use Alien Skin's full-featured Stylist plug-in, or VectorTools' Vector Object Style.

Intersect and Exclude

These two Pathfinders are opposites. Using one results in the opposite of what you get from using the other. Kind of the "Punk & Bloat" of the Pathfinder variety.

Intersect creates only the intersection of the selected paths. Any part of a selected path that does not intersect is deleted. If two paths are intersecting and selected, only the area that intersects between the two paths will remain. If three or more paths are selected, all must intersect at a common area for the function to produce results. If the paths selected do not intersect at all, nothing will happen. If one selected path is contained within all the other selected paths, the result will be that contained path. The resulting path will have the Paint Style attributes of the topmost path.

Exclude is pretty much the opposite of Intersect. Choosing Exclude deletes the intersecting areas, grouping together the outside pieces. If you are having trouble making a compound path, use Exclude; any path within another path will be reversed, creating a compound path automatically.

After you select two or more paths and click the Intersect button on the Pathfinder palette, only the overlapping portions of the paths remain. If you select three paths, the only area that remains will be the area where all three selected paths overlap each other.

If you use Exclude, only the areas that don't overlap will remain. Exclude follows the Winding Number rule, which is discussed in Chapter 9.

The color of the intersected or excluded path is always the color of the path that was the topmost selected path before you used Intersect or Exclude.

Minus Front and Minus Back

Each of these Pathfinders works on the principle that one path, either the frontmost or backmost of the paths selected, will have all the other overlapping paths subtracted from it.

Minus Front subtracts all the selected paths in front of the backmost selected path from the backmost selected path. With two objects, it is quite simple: The object in front is deleted, and the area where the object in front was located is also deleted. It gets a little more confusing when you have more objects, but the function performs the same operation on all of them, all at once to all the selected paths. If the area to be subtracted is totally within the path it will subtract *from,* then a compound path results.

Minus Back is the opposite of Minus Front: It subtracts all the selected paths behind the frontmost selected path from the frontmost selected path. With two objects, it is also quite simple: The object in the back is deleted and the area where the object in back was placed is also deleted. It gets a little more confusing when you have more objects, but it does the same thing, all at once to all the selected paths. If the area to be subtracted is totally within the path it will subtract *from,* then a compound path results.

When you apply Minus Front, the color of the remaining path is the color of the backmost path before you applied it. When you apply Minus Back, the color of the remaining path is the color of the frontmost path before you applied it.

Figure 7-25 shows the same paths with several different Combine Pathfinders applied to them.

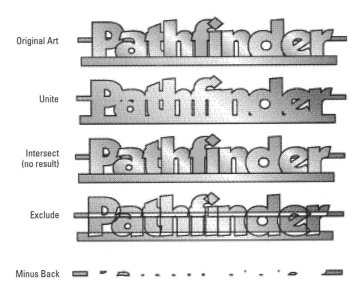

Figure 7-25: Selected paths with different Combine Pathfinder options applied to them

Divide

The Divide option in the Pathfinder palette checks to see where the selected paths overlap and then creates new paths at all intersections where the paths crossed, creating new paths if necessary. Fills are kept, but any Strokes are changed to None. In the process, Divide also groups the pieces of the Fill together. Divide also keeps sections their original colors; the illustration appears to look the same unless it previously had Strokes. To keep the Strokes, copy before using Divide, and then Paste in Back (⌘-B) [Ctrl+B].

Simply put, Divide divides overlaying paths into individual closed paths, as described in the following steps and illustrated in Figure 7-26.

1. Create the artwork that you want to divide into sections.

2. Create a path or paths where you want to divide the object. (If the division lines consist of more than one path, you do not need to make those paths into a compound path, although it doesn't hurt.)

3. Select all paths, both artwork and dividing paths, and choose the Divide option in the Pathfinder palette.

4. If you wish to move the pieces apart, you first have to ungroup them (Divide groups them automatically).

Figure 7-26: Using Divide

Outline

Outline creates small sections of paths wherever paths cross and color the Strokes, using the Fill of the path they were part of and giving the Strokes a weight of 1 point. Outline is useful for spot trapping as it will automatically create the sections needed that have to be chosen for overprinting, although many times the colors will be incorrect.

Outline creates smaller path pieces than Divide does; but instead of making each section a closed path, each path maintains its individuality, becoming separate from adjoining paths. The result of outlining is several small Stroke pieces. Instead of maintaining the Fill color of each piece, each piece is Filled with None and Stroked with the Fill color.

Note   Divide and Outline completely ignore the Stroke color.

Trim

Trim removes sections of paths that are overlapped by other paths. Frontmost paths are the only ones that will remain. This Pathfinder is very useful for cleaning up complex overlapping illustrations, although it can take a bit of time to complete.

Tip   I'll often use Trim if I want to use a piece of artwork for one portion of the Soft Pathfinder (described later). This removes overlapping paths, which would otherwise change in color when Soft is applied.

ASK TOULOUSE: Trim Your Blends

Garrett: What can Trim do for me?

Toulouse: First of all, you can trim your blends.

Garrett: Why? Are they overgrowing into the neighbor's yard?

Toulouse: Actually, it removes overlapping paths, allowing you to use Soft and Hard with a blend.

Garrett: And why would I want to do that?

Toulouse: I trim blends to use them for shadowing or to apply highlights to objects.

Merge

Merge combines overlapping paths that have the identical Fill applied to them. Even if the Fill is different by as little as 1%, Merge will create two separate paths. This Pathfinder is much more efficient than Unite for making areas of the same color into one object.

The following steps describe how to use Merge, and Figure 7-27 illustrates these steps.

1. Create the artwork that you want to use Merge for.

2. Select the artwork to be merged and choose the Merge option in the Pathfinder palette. All paths that were overlapped are removed, leaving only the paths that had nothing in front of them. All adjacent areas that contained identical colors are united.

Figure 7-27: Using Merge

Crop

Crop works in much the same way as masks work, except that anything outside the cropped area is deleted, not just masked. To use Crop, bring the object that you wish to use as a cropper to the front, select all the paths you wish to crop with it and the cropper itself, and choose the Crop option in the Pathfinder palette. Everything outside the cropper will be deleted. The objects that were cropped are grouped together in the shape of the crop.

Unlike masks, there is no outside shape after a crop is made. The cropper used to crop the image is deleted when Crop is chosen.

Hard and Soft

The first two Mix/Trap Pathfinder options, Hard and Soft, simulate transparency or shadows between two or more paths. Hard combines the colors at their full amount, while Soft enables you to specify the amount of color from each path that shows up in the intersecting paths.

Hard adds the values of overlapping path Fills. The more objects that are overlapping, the darker the Fill. Each section that overlaps is a new path, just like what happens when you choose Divide. Any Strokes are changed to none and ignored.

Soft adds colors together based on a percentage that you enter into the Mix Soft dialog box.

The following steps describe how to use Soft and Figure 7-28 illustrates these steps.

1. Create and select the overlapping paths that you want to use Soft for.

2. Choose the Soft option in the Pathfinder palette. The Pathfinder Soft Mix dialog box appears. Enter the amount that you want the colors to mix. (How the colors mix depends not only on the mixing rate percentage, but also on the drawing order of the objects.)

3. Click OK.

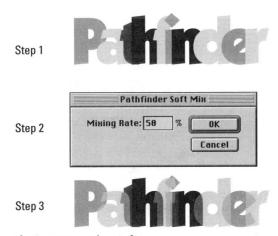

Figure 7-28: Using Soft

Soft can be a little difficult to understand at first. Soft determines how much of the background color will bleed through the foreground color. If each of the colors is at 100% and you use a setting of 50% for the function, the background color will be 33.3% and the foreground color will be 66.6% (50% of 66.6% = 33.3%, and 33.3% + 66.6% = 100%).

Note   Soft and Hard create the same path sections as Divide creates.

ASK TOULOUSE: Strokes Are Gone

Ida: My Strokes are gone!

Toulouse: Yikes! What happened?

Ida: I was just Pathfindering around, and suddenly . . . no more Strokes.

Toulouse: Almost all Pathfinders zap your Strokes into oblivion.

Ida: I'd rather they didn't. What if I want to use Strokes from the paths *before* they're chopped up into little pieces?

Toulouse: The best thing to do is to copy the paths before you apply Pathfinders, and then Paste in Front.

Ida: But they'll cover up the new Pathfindered paths!

Toulouse: To see the paths underneath, change the Fill of the Paste in Front paths to None. Keep the Strokes as they are.

Trap

Trap takes some of the drudgery away from trapping. The only limitation for Trap is that it doesn't work well on extremely complex illustrations because of time and memory constraints. The other concern with Trap is that it leaves your illustrations "pseudo-uneditable" because it creates extra paths around your original trap and makes it really difficult to edit. It doesn't affect the existing paths, but if you do much editing, you'll have to delete the trap paths and retrap.

Tip   Prior to trapping, I create a layer called *Traps*. Immediately after trapping, I move all the trap objects to the Traps layer. This keeps the traps together, in case I need to redo, adjust, or delete them.

Trap automatically creates a trap between abutting shapes of different colors. You set the amount (width) of trap in a dialog box that appears after choosing Trap.

1. Create and select the artwork that you want to trap. (If the artwork is overly complex, you may want to select only a small portion of the artwork before you continue.)

2. Choose the Trap option in the Pathfinder palette. In the Trap dialog box, enter the width of the trap in the Thickness text field (the default is 0.25 points). Enter the amount that you want the height of the trap to differ from the width, which allows for different paper-stretching errors. For example, entering the maximum, 400%, widens the horizontal thickness of the Stroke to four times the amount set in the Thickness text field and leaves the vertical thickness the same. Enter a Tint reduction value that specifies how much the lighter of the two colors should be tinted on that area. Check the Traps with Process Color checkbox to convert spot colors to process equivalents only in the

resulting trap path that is generated from Trap. Check the Reverse Traps checkbox to convert any traps along the object that are Filled with 100% Black but no other colors to be less black and more of the lighter abutting color.

3. Click OK. Figure 7-29 shows these three steps as well as the trap as a separate piece below the original object.

Figure 7-29: This figure shows the trap with a large point size and the trap darkened so you can see it

All traps generated by Trap result in Filled paths, not Strokes, and are automatically set to overprint in the Attributes palette.

The Reshape Tool

To use the Reshape tool (see Figure 7-30) on any path, just click where you want to bend the path and drag. To use the Reshape tool on several paths at once, use the Reshape tool to select the points you wish to move. At least one point (that's not a Straight Corner point) must be selected on each path. Then drag on a Reshape-selected point; all the curved points will be moved as well.

 Figure 7-30: The Reshape tool

ASK TOULOUSE: Trapping to Placed Images

Rhoda: Can I trap to placed images?

Toulouse: Oops. Uhh. Well, not really.

Rhoda: You're kidding me.

Toulouse: No, I wouldn't kid you about that.

Rhoda: Why can't I?

Toulouse: Think of it this way: When you bring in a placed image, it's this little self-contained image. It knocks out everything in its path (pun intended).

Rhoda: Anything I can do?

Toulouse: You might want to have your printer do it manually with the film separations.

The Twirl Tool

Have you ever wanted to twist your artwork around its middle, continuously until you can't make out what the original artwork was? Me neither. But to humor someone at Adobe, the Twirl tool was incorporated into Illustrator, hiding to the right of the Rotate tool.

To use the Twirl tool, click and drag either left or right. Any selected artwork will spin around the center of the combined objects. Figure 7-31 shows artwork before and after twirling.

Figure 7-31: Artwork before (left) and after (right) twirling with the Twirl tool

You can twirl around any origin simply by clicking to set an origin point and then dragging. The artwork will twirl around the origin point you set. I took the original artwork from Figure 7-31 and twirled it around a couple of different origins (not the center) to get the funhouse effect shown in Figure 7-32.

> **Tip**
>
> To twirl a specific amount, Option[Alt]-click at the origin point you wish to twirl around.

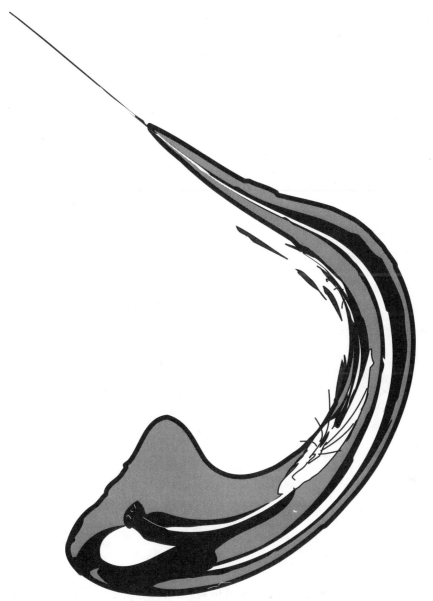

Figure 7-32: Funhouse effect achieved by twirling around different origin points

Transforming Objects

PostScript has the capability to transform any PostScript object by scaling it, rotating it, reflecting it, and shearing it. Illustrator takes this power and enhances it by providing you the flexibility of using certain tools, each of which does one of those transformations.

The following four tools in the Illustrator toolbox (shown in Figure 7-33) address four fundamental functions: the Rotate tool, the Scale tool, the Reflect tool, and the Free Transform tool. Before any of these tools can be used, however, one or more objects (including paths, points, and segments) must be selected. The selected paths are the paths that are transformed.

Figure 7-33: The Transformation tools

New Feature   New to Illustrator 8 is the Free Transform tool. This great tool provides the capability to scale, rotate, skew, and reflect at one time.

There are five ways to transform selected objects:

✦ Click with the Transformation tool to set an origin point and then drag from a different location. (This is called a *manual transformation*.)

✦ Click and drag in one motion to transform the object from its center point (or last origin point).

✦ Option[Alt]-click to set the origin and then enter exact information in the tool's transformation dialog box. (This method is more precise than manually transforming.)

✦ Double-click a Transformation tool to set the origin in the center of the selected object; then you can enter information in the tool's transformation dialog box.

✦ Use the Transform palette (where all four transformation functions are located).

All the Transformation tools work on a relative basis. For instance, if an object is scaled by 150% and then is scaled again by 150%, the object is now 225% of its original size ($150\% \times 150\% = 225\%$). If the object is initially scaled to 150% of its original size, and you want to return it to that original size, you must do the math and figure out what percentage is needed to resize it — in this case, 66.7% ($100\% \div 150\% = 66.7\%$). Entering 100% in the Scale dialog box leaves the selected objects unchanged.

Illustrator automatically creates a visible origin point (shown in Figure 7-34) when you are using a Transformation tool. Because the origin is in the center of the selection, if you just drag with the Transformation tool, the origin point is visible as soon as you select the Transformation tool. If you click without dragging to set the origin, it shows up at that location until the origin is reset. Having the origin point visible (as a blue cross hair) makes the transformation tools much more usable and functional.

 Figure 7-34: The origin point that appears when using any of the Transformation tools

When manually transforming objects, you can make a copy of the selected object (and thus leave the original untransformed) by holding down the Option [Alt] key before and after releasing the mouse button. In a transformation dialog box, you can make a copy by clicking the Copy button, pressing Option[Alt]-Return, or Option[Alt]-clicking OK.

If the Patterns checkbox is available (you must have a pattern in one of the selected paths for this option not to be grayed out) inside any of the transformation dialog boxes, you can check its option box to transform your pattern along with the object. You can also transform the pattern only, leaving the object untransformed, by unchecking the Objects box.

Tip   You can manually transform just patterns (and not the objects themselves) by pressing the tilde (~) key while using any of the Transformation tools (including the Selection tool for moving).

Manually transforming objects is fairly simple if you remember that the first place you click (the point of origin) and the second place should be a fair distance apart. The farther your second click is from the point of origin, the more control you have when dragging to transform. The Shear tool is an exception — although it does matter where you click — because you can lose control of your shape anywhere.

All the Transformation tools perform certain operations that rely on the Constrain Angle setting as a point of reference. Normally, this setting is set to 0°, which makes your Illustrator world act normally. You can change the setting by choosing File ⇨ Preferences ⇨ General (⌘-K) [Ctrl+K] and entering a new value.

You can access each of the Transformation dialog boxes from the Object ⇨ Transform submenu (see Figure 7-35).

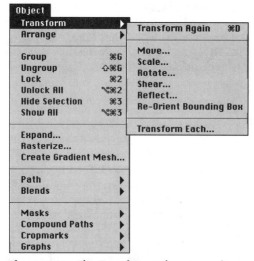

Figure 7-35: The Transform submenu as it appears in the Object menu

The Rotate Tool

The Rotate tool rotates selected objects within a document. Double-clicking the Rotate tool displays the Rotate dialog box, where the precise angle of the selected item's rotation can be entered in the Angle box. The object rotates around its origin, which by default is located at the center of the object's bounding box. A positive number between 0 and 180 rotates the object counterclockwise that many degrees. A negative number between 0 and –180 rotates the selected object clockwise. The Rotate tool works on a standard 360° circle of rotation, although it is usually easier to type in numbers between 0 and 180 or 0 and –180, than numbers such as 270, which is the same as –90°.

Holding down the Option [Alt] key and clicking somewhere in the document also brings up the Rotate dialog box (see Figure 7-36); however, the object now rotates around the point where the Rotate tool was clicked. This point can be on or off the selected object. Be careful because it is quite easy to rotate an object right out of your viewing area! Illustrator has many precautions, however, to prevent you from transforming or moving an object off the Pasteboard.

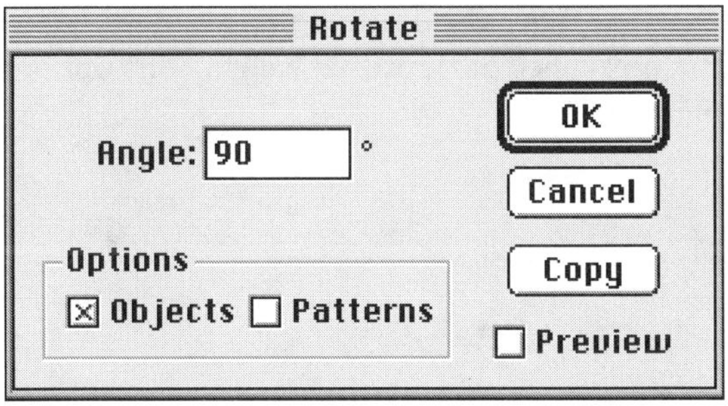

Figure 7-36: The Rotate dialog box

Click once to set the origin point from where the object's center of rotation should be and then click fairly far from the origin and drag in a circle. The selected object spins along with the cursor. To constrain the angle to 45° increments as you are dragging, hold down the Shift key. This angle is dependent on the Constrain Angle box (File ⇨ Preferences ⇨ General or ⌘-K [Ctrl+K]), and is in 45° increments plus the angle in this box. Figure 7-37 shows an illustration before and after rotation.

Figure 7-37: An illustration before (left) and after (right) rotation

The Scale Tool

The Scale tool resizes objects both uniformly and nonuniformly. You can also use the Scale tool to flip objects, but without the precision of the Reflect tool. (It is impossible to keep both the size and proportions of an object constant while flipping and scaling.)

Double-clicking the Scale tool brings up the Scale dialog box, shown in Figure 7-38. All selected objects are scaled from its origin, which by default is located at the center of the object's bounding box. If the Uniform option is chosen, numbers typed into the text field result in proportionately scaled objects (where the width and height of the object remain proportional to each other). Numbers less than 100% shrink the object; numbers greater than 100% enlarge it. When the Uniform option is chosen, you may also check the box called Scale Stroke Weight (this option is grayed out if nonuniform scaling is used).

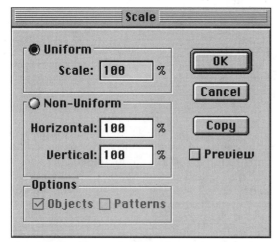

Figure 7-38: The Scale dialog box

Nonuniform scaling resizes the horizontal and vertical dimensions of the selected objects separately, distorting the image. The way nonuniform scaling works is related to the Constrain Angle box (File ➪ Preferences ➪ General or ⌘-K [Ctrl+K]), where the angle set there is the horizontal scaling, and the vertical scaling is 90° from that angle.

Tip   Pressing the Option [Alt] key and clicking in the document window also brings up the Scale dialog box, but now the objects are scaled from the location in the document that was Option[Alt]-clicked.

Manual resizing is achieved by clicking your point of origin and then clicking away and dragging to scale. If you cross the horizontal or vertical axis of the point of origin, the selected object flips over in that direction. Holding down the Shift key constrains the objects to equal proportions (if the cursor is dragged at approximately 45° from the point of origin) or constrains the scaling to either horizontal or vertical scaling only (providing the cursor is being dragged along at about a 90° angle from the point of origin relative to the constrain angle).

The Reflect Tool

The Reflect tool makes a mirror image of the selected objects, reflected across an axis of reflection. Double-clicking on the Reflect tool reflects selected objects across an axis of reflection that runs through the center of the selected objects. In the Reflect dialog box, you can enter the axis of rotation. If you want to rotate the object along either the horizontal or vertical axis, click the appropriate button.

Tip   Option[Alt]-clicking in the document window also brings up the Reflect dialog box, but the axis of reflection is now not in the center of the selected object, but in the location in the document where you Option[Alt]-clicked.

Manual reflecting is done by clicking once to set the origin point (the center of the axis of reflection) and again somewhere along the axis of reflection. If you click and drag after setting your origin point, you can rotate the axis of reflection and see what your objects look like reflected across various axes. The Shift key constrains the axis of reflection to 90° angles relative to the constrain angle (File ➪ Preferences ➪ General or ⌘-K [Ctrl+K]). Holding down the Option [Alt] key during the release of the click leaves a copy of the original object. Figure 7-39 shows an illustration before and after being reflected.

Figure 7-39: An illustration before (left) and after (right) being reflected across the vertical axis

The Shear Tool

This tool should actually be called the "Swear" tool because it causes more cursing (no, not cursoring; that's different) than any other tool (except perhaps for the mighty Pen tool). Another good name for the Shear tool (one that I have heard many people use) is the "Stupid" tool because that's usually how you feel when trying to get good results from its use. It's a terrifying feeling to see the artwork you spent an hour touching up until it's just right go zinging off the screen, seemingly all by itself.

The Shear tool is now found in the pop-up menu with the Reflect tool. The Shear tool is rightfully distrusted because using it manually is usually a quick lesson in futility. Double-clicking on the Shear tool brings up the Shear dialog box, shown in Figure 7-40, which is much more controllable. Double-clicking causes the origin to be in the center of the selected object. The Angle box is simple enough; in its text box, you enter the angle amount the object should shear. Any amount over 75° or less than –75° renders the object into an indecipherable mess, because at this angle or higher the art has been "flattened." The Shear tool reverses the positive-numbers-are-counterclockwise rule: To shear an object clockwise, enter a positive number; to shear counterclockwise, enter a negative number. The Axis Angle box is for shearing an object along a specified axis.

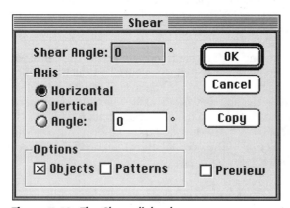

Figure 7-40: The Shear dialog box

Tip   Option[Alt]-clicking in the document window also brings up the Shear dialog box, with the origin of the shear being the location of the preceding Option[Alt]-click.

Manual shearing is something else again because you are doing two things at once: changing both the angle of shearing (the distance from the beginning of the second click until it is released) and the angle of the axis of shearing (the angle the mouse is dragged during the second click). Usually, it's best to start your second click fairly far away from the point of origin. Holding down the Shift key constrains the axis of shearing to a 45° angle relative to the constraining angle. Figure 7-41 shows an illustration before and after being sheared.

Figure 7-41: An illustration before (left) and after (right) being sheared

The Free Transform Tool

Illustrator 8 has added a new tool to its toolbox, the Free Transform tool. Free Transform enables you to rotate, scale, reflect, and shear all with one tool. This way you can create multiple transformations at one time.

What is unique about this tool is that you can select more than one object to change the size, shape, and placement in one step. The Free Transform tool replaces the Free Distort filter (if you check out the filter menu, you'll find that the Free Distort filter is gone). Using this cool tool to create distorted effects is easier than using the Free Distort filter.

Moving

The most common way to move an object is to use a Selection tool and drag the selected points, segments, and paths from one location to another.

The precise way to move an object is to use the Move dialog box (see Figure 7-42) or the Transform palette (see the following section). Select the object you want to move and then choose Object ➪ Transform ➪ Move. The Move dialog box appears, and you can enter the appropriate values in either the horizontal or vertical text fields. If you want to move an object diagonally, enter a number in the Distance text field and then enter the angle of movement direction in the Angle text field.

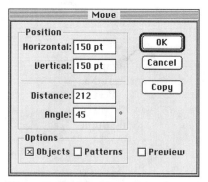

Figure 7-42: The Move dialog box

Any selected object (except for text selected with a Type tool) can be moved via the Move dialog box, including individual Anchor Points and line segments.

By default, the Move dialog box contains the distance and angle that you last moved an object, whether manually (with a Selection tool) or in the Move dialog box. If you used the Measure tool prior to using the Move dialog box, the numbers in the Move dialog box correspond to the numbers that appeared in the Info palette when you used the Measure tool.

Tip   Double-clicking on the Selection tool in the toolbox displays the Move dialog box.

In the Move dialog box, positive numbers in the Horizontal text field move an object from left to right, while negative numbers move an object from right to left. Positive numbers in the Vertical text field move an object from bottom to top, while negative numbers move an object from top to bottom. Negative numbers in the Distance text field move an object in the opposite direction of the Angle text field. The Angle text field works a bit differently. Negative numbers in the Angle text field move the angle in the opposite direction from 0° (so entering –45° is the same as entering 315° and entering –180° is the same as entering 180°).

The measurement system in the Move dialog box matches the system set in the General Preferences dialog box. To enter a measurement different from the current measurement system, use these indicators:

✦ **For inches:** 1" or 1in (1 inch)

✦ **For picas:** 1p or 1pica (1 pica)

✦ **For points:** 1pt or 0p1 (1 point)

✦ **For picas/points:** 1p1 (1 pica, 1 point)

✦ **For millimeters:** 1mm (1 millimeter)

✦ **For centimeters:** 1cm (1 centimeter)

The Horizontal and Vertical text fields are linked to the Distance and Angle text fields; when one of the fields is changed, the others are altered accordingly.

Pressing the Copy button duplicates selected objects in the direction and distance indicated, just as holding down Option [Alt] when dragging duplicates the selected objects.

Tip   The Move dialog box is a great place to enter everything via the keyboard. Press Tab to move from text field to text field, press Return to push the OK button, and press ⌘-Period [Esc] to push the Cancel button. Pressing Option[Alt]-Enter or pressing Option [Alt] while clicking OK pushes the Copy button. The same is true for all of the transformation dialog boxes.

The Transform Palette

Imagine, if you will, a palette that combines four of Illustrator's five transformation capabilities into one place. Then take a look at Figure 7-43, which shows Illustrator's Transform palette in all its glory.

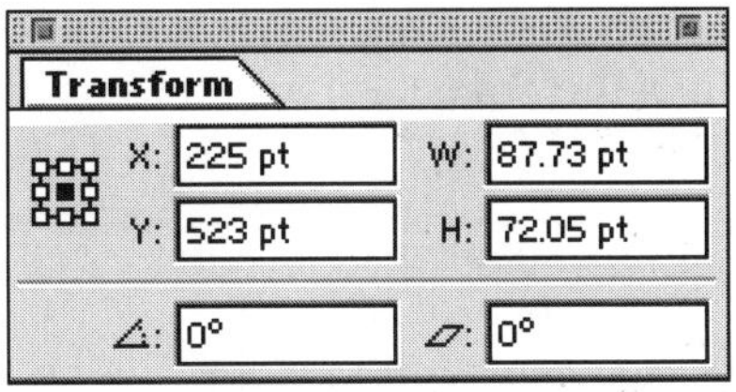

Transform		
X: 225 pt	W:	87.73 pt
Y: 523 pt	H:	72.05 pt
∠: 0°	⟋:	0°

Figure 7-43: The Transform palette

The Transform palette provides a way to Move, Scale, Rotate, and Shear selected artwork. There's no reflect option (you'll need to use the tool or the transform submenu option to reflect artwork). Instead of manually setting an origin point or transforming from the center by default, the Transform palette gives you nine "fixed" origin points based on the bounding box of the selected objects (the bounding box is the blue box that surrounds any selected objects). Choose an origin point before entering values in the palette, and the transformations will originate from the corner, center of a side, or the center of selected objects.

The text fields in the Transform palette are as follows:

✦ **X:** This is the horizontal location of the artwork, measured from the left edge of the document (or horizontal ruler origin if it has been moved from the left edge).

✦ **Y:** This is the vertical location of the artwork, measured from the bottom edge of the document (or vertical ruler origin if it has been moved from the bottom edge).

✦ **W:** This is the width of the artwork's bounding box.

✦ **H:** This is the height of the artwork's bounding box.

✦ **Rotation:** This field lets you apply a rotation to the selected artwork.

✦ **Shear:** This field lets you apply a shear to the selected artwork.

To use the palette, type the new value you'd like to use in any field and then press Enter. If you have another value to enter, press the Tab key to go to the next text field (or Shift-Tab to go back a field). Pressing Option [Alt] when you press Enter or Tab creates a duplicate of the selected artwork with the transformations you specified.

For Scaling, you can enter either absolute measurements (the size in inches, picas, and so on, that you want the artwork to be), or by percentage by adding the % symbol after your value. You can also force Illustrator to scale uniformly, regardless of whether you're using absolute measurements or percentages, by pressing ⌘ [Ctrl] when you press the Enter or Tab keys.

Okay, time for me to 'fess up. I'm not a big fan of the Transform palette, and here's why:

✦ **No Reflect option:** Couldn't we have a button enabling us to enter a negative scale value to reflect across the horizontal/vertical axis?

✦ **Each option:** Transform Each is hard to get to, and this would've provided an easy way to do these transformations.

✦ **No Random option:** Transformations are perfect for random values, as evidenced by Transform Each's Random check box.

✦ **No Keyboard commands to highlight the text fields:** Even the Transformation tools can be accessed by pressing the keyboard keys.

✦ **After rotating and shearing, the value reverts back to 0° instantly:** I'd like the values here to show how far the art has been transformed since it was created. There are a few technical issues to work out here (groups? compound paths? portions of paths? objects pasted?), but I'm sure Adobe can figure them out.

✦ **No keyboard command to show/hide the palette:** This is a chicken-and-egg dilemma.

✦ **No automated repeat function:** A text field for number of duplicates would be handy (I hate pressing ⌘-D [Ctrl+D] 34 times when I want to duplicate/rotate an object around a circle at 10° increments).

✦ **No Apply at Once feature like Transform Each has.**

✦ **No floating origin point:** I have to use one of the nine presets — and there's no way to change them automatically or revert to center using the keyboard.

Okay, sure, many of the things I don't like about the Transform palette are wish-list features, not missing functionality. But if I'm going to have this palette sucking up valuable screen real estate, I want something back for it. Most of Illustrator's other palettes are worthy of taking up chunks of pixels; the Transform palette isn't.

Note

The previous comments are here for two reasons. First, because I think you should know that while I love Illustrator (my program of choice were I to be stuck on a desert island with a computer), there are a few things I don't like, or that I feel could be improved. The second reason is to show a sample of the types of communication that Adobe and other software companies use to determine what features take priority for future implementation. If instead of listing what I don't like and would like to see in the next version of Illustrator I just said, "I don't like the transformation palette," Adobe would just shrug and ignore me. But their concern is to make the best software they can, and that means addressing their customers' needs. If you have suggestions or ideas for Adobe (or for third-party plug-in developers such as Extensis), make sure you're both as concise and descriptive as possible.

Transform Each

Transform Each provides a way to do several transformations in one shot, but that's only the beginning. The unique thing about Transform Each is that each selected object is transformed independently, as opposed to having all the selected objects transformed together. Figure 7-44 shows the difference between "normal" rotating and scaling, and the Rotate and Scale functions in Transform Each.

Figure 7-44: An illustration (left) after being rotated and scaled (right top), and then after using the same values with the Rotate and Scale functions within Transform Each (right bottom)

To access the Transform Each dialog box (see Figure 7-45), choose Object ⇨ Transform ⇨ Transform Each. In the dialog box, use the sliders/dial or type in values for each of the transformations. The Random checkbox on the right side of the dialog box gives each object selected a random value that falls within the default (100% for Scale; 0 for Move and Rotate) and the value set by the slider/dial.

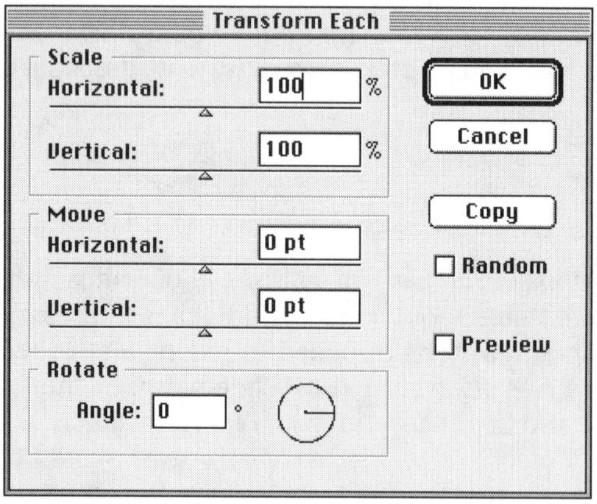

Figure 7-45: The Transform Each dialog box

But of all things, the randomize function of Transform Each is its most powerful asset. Checking the Random checkbox can turn a grid into a distinct random texture, as shown in Figure 7-46.

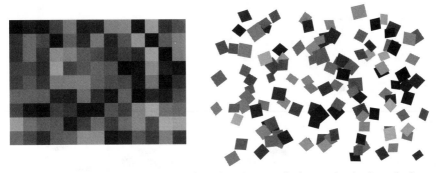

Figure 7-46: Transform Each's Random function applied to a checkerboard of colored squares

The following steps show you how to use the Transform Each function, and Figure 7-47 illustrates these steps.

1. Create a rectangle (like the one shown in Figure 7-47) and fill it with the Purple, Red, Yellow gradient.

2. Use the Direct Selection tool to move the upper-right point down and the lower-right point up.

3. Add a color stop to the gradient (in the Gradient palette) that's black.

4. Expand the Gradient (Choose Object ⇨ Expand) using 100 blend steps. Choose Object ⇨ Pathfinder ⇨ Crop. This will crop the blend along the angles you defined in Step 2.

5. In the Align palette, choose the Align Vertically button (second from the left, top row).

6. Horizontally scale the objects until they resemble those shown in Step 6 of Figure 7-47.

7. Choose Filter ⇨ Distort ⇨ Zig Zag, and enter 10%, 2 segments, and Smooth.

8. Choose Filter ⇨ Distort ⇨ Scribble and Tweak, and Scribble at 5% Horizontal, 5% Vertical, with all options checked.

9. Choose Object ➪ Transform ➪ Transform Each, enter a rotation of 180°, and check the Random box. This will rotate the objects anywhere between 0° and 180°.

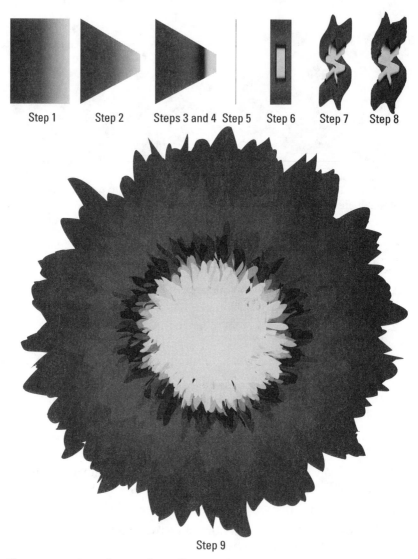

Figure 7-47: Steps for creating a flower using Transform Each

Transformation Effects

The transformation tools open a world of possibilities within Illustrator. The following tips and ideas should give you a head start in exploring the amazing power of transformations.

Choosing Transform Again (⌘-D) [Ctrl+D] from the Transform submenu of the Object menu redoes the last transformation that was done to a selected object. Transformations include Move, Rotate, Scale, Reflect, Shear, and Transform Each. Transform Again also makes a transformed copy if a copy was made either manually or by clicking the Copy button in the prior transformation dialog box.

Tip   Transform Again remembers the last transformation no matter what else you do, and it can apply that same transformation to other objects or reapply it to the existing transformed objects.

Creating Shadows

You can create all sorts of shadows by using the Scale, Reflect, and Shear tools, as shown in the illustrations in Figure 7-48.

Figure 7-48: Creating shadows with the Transformation tools

1. Select the path where you want to apply the shadow and click the bottom of the path once with the Reflect tool. This action sets the origin of reflection at the base of the image. Drag down while pressing the Shift key. The image flips over, creating a mirror image under the original. Press the Option [Alt] key (keeping the Shift key pressed) before and during the release of the mouse button.

2. Using the Shear tool, click the base of the reflected copy to set the origin. Click and drag left or right at the other side of the reflection to set the angle of the reflection.

3. Using the Scale tool, click once again on the base of the reflected copy to set the origin. Click and drag up or down at the other side of the reflection.

4. Color the shadow darker than its background.

To create a shadow for type, you must first vertically scale a copy of the type. Hold down the Option [Alt] key when you release the mouse button to make the copy, and hold down the Shift key to constrain the scaling to vertical as you drag the mouse up or down. Setting the origin of the scale to the baseline of the type helps, as does using all caps or type with no descenders.

Send the copy to the back (⌘-Shift-[) [Ctrl+Shift+[] and shear the shadow off to one side or the other, once again setting the origin at the baseline of the type. Holding down Shift as you shear prevents the baseline of the copy from angling up or down.

If you want the shadow in front of the type (making it appear as if the light source is coming from behind the type), use the Reflect tool to flip the copy of the type across the baseline of the type.

Transforming Gradients

You can transform gradients in the same way that you transform objects that are colored by gradients. All of the transformation tools affect gradients, but the best effects are achieved by scaling and shearing gradients, especially radial gradients, as shown in Figure 7-49.

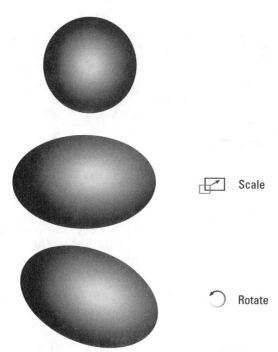

Scale

Rotate

Figure 7-49: Transforming a gradient

To create an effect similar to that of Figure 7-49, create a radial gradient inside a circle with no Stroke. (Use a circle so that no portions of it are cropped outside of the shape when it is distorted.) Scale and shear the circle with the radial gradient, and the radial gradient becomes scaled and sheared as well.

Rotating into a Path

Clever use of the Rotate tool can create a realistic, winding path by duplicating the same object at different rotational intervals, rotated from different origins.

Start by creating an object of some sort. (The illustration in Figure 7-50 uses paw prints.) Select the objects (I've found it best to group them together) and choose the Rotate tool. Click to set an origin a little distance from the side of the object. Click the other side of the object and drag. As you drag, you see the outline of the shape of the object that you are dragging. When the object is a good distance away, press the Option [Alt] key (to copy) and release the mouse button; then release the Option [Alt] key. A copy of the object appears. Press ⌘-D [Ctrl+D] (Transform Again) to create *another* object the same distance away.

Figure 7-50: Paw prints that have been rotated into a path the old-fashioned way

After using the Transform Again command (⌘-D) [Ctrl+D] a few times, click with the Rotate tool on the other side of the object to set another origin. Click and drag the outline of the object about the same distance; then press the Option [Alt] key and release the mouse button. Use the Transform Again command a few more times.

The farther you click from the objects to set the origin, the smaller the curve of the path of objects. Clicking right next to the objects causes them to turn sharply.

Making Tiles Using the Reflect Tool

You can make symmetrical tiles with the Reflect tool. You can use a set of four differently positioned, yet identical, objects to create artwork with a floor-tile look, as shown in Figure 7-51.

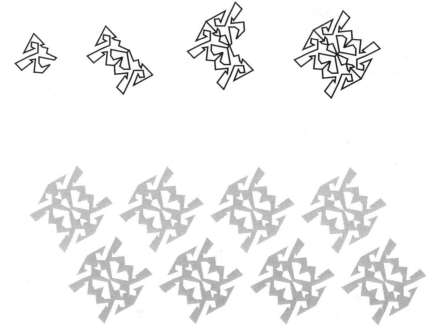

Figure 7-51: Creating tiles with the Reflect tool

1. Create the path (or paths) that you will make into the symmetrical tile. Group the artwork together.

2. Take the Reflect tool and click off to the right of it to set the origin. Click and drag on the left edge of the object and drag to the right while pressing the Shift and Option [Alt] keys. (Using the Shift key reflects the image at only 45° angles.) When the object has been reflected to the right side, let go of the mouse button, still pressing the Option [Alt] key. Release the Option [Alt] key. You now have two versions of the object.

3. Select the original and reflected object and reflect again, this time across the bottom of the objects. There are now four objects, each mirrored a little differently, that make up a tile. You can now use this tile to create symmetrical patterns.

Using Transformation Tools on Portions of Paths

When using the Transformation tools, you don't need to select an entire path. Instead, try experimenting with other effects by selecting single Anchor Points, line segments, and combinations of selected Anchor Points and segments. Another idea is to select portions of paths on different objects.

> **Tip**   When you're working with portions of paths, one of the most useful Transformation tool procedures is to select a Smooth Point with the Direct Selection tool and then choose a Transformation tool.

You can achieve precise control with the Rotate tool. Click the center of the Anchor Point and drag around the Anchor Point. Both Control Handles move, but the distance from the Control Handles to the Anchor Point remains the same. This task is very difficult to perform with just the Direct Selection tool, which you can also use to accomplish the same task.

You can accomplish the exact lengthening of Control Handle Lines by using the Scale tool. Click the Anchor Point to set the origin and then drag out from one of the Control Handles. Both Control Handles will grow from the Anchor Point in equal proportions.

When working on a Smooth Point, you can use the Reflect tool to switch lengths and angles between the two Control Handles.

Here are some more portion-of-path transformation ideas:

✦ Select all the points in an open path except for the End Points and use all the different Transformation tools on the selected areas.

✦ Select the bottom-most or top-most Anchor Point in text converted to outlines, and scale, rotate, and shear for interesting effects.

✦ Select two Anchor Points on a rectangle and scale and skew copies into a cube.

If you have ever wondered how to create a splendid spirograph, the following steps and Figure 7-52 will show you how.

1. Create a star with lots of points, and a fairly tight inner radius (see Figure 7-52).

2. Select just the middle points with the Direct Selection tool.

3. Use the Rotate tool to "twist" the inner points around.

4. Use the Scale tool to invert the inner points outside of the outer ones.

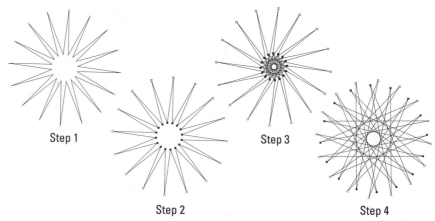

Figure 7-52: Steps for creating a spirograph

Rotating into Kaleidoscopes

By rotating and duplicating objects that have strokes, you can make kaleidoscopic illustrations, such as the one in Figure 7-53. You may have trouble working with the last two or three objects, but this section shows you how to work through any difficulties.

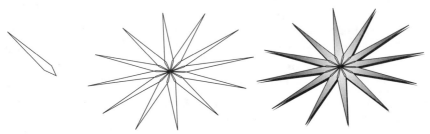

Figure 7-53: Objects that have been rotated into kaleidoscopes

First, select the object that you wish to rotate and duplicate. Choose the Rotate tool and Option[Alt]-click at one end or corner of the object. In the Rotate dialog box, enter an angle that goes into 360° evenly, such as 18° (20×18 = 360), and press the Copy button (Option[Alt]-Return). Choose Transform Again (⌘-D) [Ctrl+D] until the object circles around the origin back to the beginning.

The trouble that you may run into here is that if the objects have a Fill and they overlap at all, the last object looks as if it's on the top and the original object looks as if it's on the bottom, which destroys the perspective of the kaleidoscope. So either the original or the last object has to be fixed. It is generally easier to fix the original (bottom-most) object.

Start by selecting the bottom-most (original) object. Copy (⌘-C) [Ctrl+C] it and paste it in front (⌘-F) [Ctrl+F]. Then create two breaks in the path of the object with the Scissors tool, one on either side of the area where the two objects overlap. Remove that portion of the path by deselecting all (⌘-Shift-A) [Ctrl+Shift+A] and selecting it, and then delete just that portion. Many times this step alone fixes the path. If there is a Fill and a Stroke, however, your problems may not work out quite so easily. Copy the remaining piece of the copied object, choose Paste in Front (⌘-F) [Ctrl+F] again, and change the Fill to None. This procedure corrects any Stroke deficiencies from the first copy.

Transforming Patterns

The option in all transformation dialog boxes (and the Move dialog box) to apply transformations to patterns can produce some very interesting results, as shown in Figure 7-54.

Figure 7-54: A pattern that has been scaled up inside the text and rotated

One of the most interesting effects results from using patterns that have transparent Fills. Select an object that has a pattern Fill and double-click a Transformation tool. Enter a value, check the Pattern tiles box, uncheck the Objects box, and then click Copy. A new object (which is unchanged) will overlap the original object, but the pattern in the new object will have changed. If desired, use the Transform Again command (⌘-D) [Ctrl+D] to create additional copies with patterns that have been transformed even more.

Tip   You can transform patterns "live" by pressing the tilde (~) key while dragging with any Transformation tool (including the Selection tool for moving).

The Select Functions

Illustrator has several special select functions (they were filters in Illustrator 5/6). The Select functions are used for selecting paths with common or specific attributes. The Select functions make mundane, repetitive tasks easy to accomplish by doing all the nasty work for you.

To access the Select functions, choose Edit ⇨ Select and the appropriate selection function from that submenu (shown in Figure 7-55).

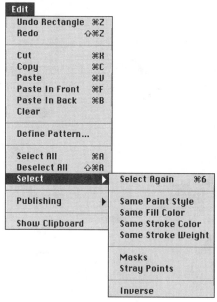

Figure 7-55: The Select submenu is found under the Edit menu

New Feature   New to Illustrator 8 is the capability to Select Again (⌘-6) [Ctrl+6]. This will reselect the last object or objects that you selected.

Four selection functions — Same Paint Style, Same Fill Color, Same Stroke Color, and Same Stroke Weight — use the Paint Style attributes of currently selected objects to select additional objects. Using these functions makes object selection quick and intuitive. The main limitation of these functions is that they are limited to four categories of comparison, each of which must be used independently of the others. This limitation causes problems in selecting objects that share more than one attribute, such as objects that have the same Stroke color and the same Stroke weight.

The Select Masks function makes the process of manipulating masks much easier by showing you where masks are in the document.

The Select Stray Points function selects all isolated Anchor Points. Individual Anchor Points don't print or preview, and you can see them in Preview mode only when they are selected. After you cut portions of line segments, stray points often appear. These individual points often interfere with connecting other segments. You can't use this selection function enough.

The Select Inverse function is perfect for selecting all paths that aren't selected. You can use this selection function to instantly select paths that are hidden, guides, and other objects that are hard to select.

Select Same Paint Style

Same Paint Style (Edit ➪ Select ➪ Same Paint Style) selects objects that have almost exactly the same paint style as the paint style of the selected object. The following information has to be the same:

✦ The Fill color (as defined in the next section, "Select Same Fill Color")

✦ The Stroke color

✦ The Stroke weight

Some things in the object's Paint Style that don't matter (that is, they don't prevent Same Paint Style from selecting an object) are any of the Stroke style attributes and the overprinting options.

Caution If you select more than one object, don't select objects with different paint styles. If you have different paint styles selected, no object will be selected by the selection function. The best thing to do with Same Paint Style, as with Same Fill Color, is to select only one object.

If you have a spot color selected, the Select functions will select all other occurrences of that spot color, regardless of the tint. This can be troublesome.

Note Extensis VectorTools has a VectorMagicWand, which works like the Select Same Paint Style function, except that you can select *similar* paths to the original clicked-on path. The tool appears in the middle of the toolbox and is invaluable.

Select Same Fill Color

Same Fill Color (Edit ➪ Select ➪ Same Fill Color) selects objects that have the same Fill color as the currently selected object. This function selects objects regardless of their Stroke color, Stroke weight, or Stroke pattern. You cannot select objects with different Fills for Same Fill Color to work, but you may select two objects that have the same Fill.

Same Fill Color considers different tints of spot colors to be the same color. This function works in two ways. First, if you select one object with any tint value of a spot color, then Same Fill Color will select all other objects with the same spot color, regardless of the tint. Second, you can select more than one object, no matter what tint each object contains, provided that the selected objects have the same spot color.

Note   To be selected with Same Fill Color, process color Fills have to have the same values as the original. Even single colors, such as yellow, have to be the same percentage. Same Fill Color considers 100% Yellow and 50% Yellow to be two separate colors.

If you use spot colors often, Select Same Fill Color is extremely useful. It enables you to instantly select all objects that are Filled with the spot color, regardless of the tint of the selected object or the tints of the objects to be selected.

Caution   Same Fill Color also selects objects that are Filled with the same gradient, regardless of the angle or the starting or ending point of the gradient. This function does not, however, select objects that have the same pattern Fill.

Select Same Stroke Color

Same Stroke Color (Edit ➪ Select ➪ Same Stroke Color) selects objects that have the same Stroke color, regardless of the Stroke weight or style and regardless of the type of Fill.

The color limitations that are defined in the "Select Same Fill Color" section, earlier in the chapter, also apply to Same Stroke Color.

Although you can choose a pattern for a Stroke that makes the Stroke look gray, Same Stroke Color does not select other objects that have the same Stroke pattern.

Select Same Stroke Weight

Illustrator's Same Stroke Weight function (Edit ➪ Select ➪ Same Stroke Weight) selects objects that have the same Stroke weight, regardless of the Stroke color, the style, or the Fill color.

Even if the Stroke is a pattern, other paths that have the same Stroke weight as the patterned Stroke will be selected when you use Same Stroke Weight.

Don't select more than one Stroke weight if you select more than one object. If you select different Stroke weights, no paths will be selected. The best thing to do with Same Stroke Weight, as with Same Fill Color and Same Paint Style, is to select only one object.

Custom Paint Style Selections

Unfortunately, you cannot do multiple-type selections with any of the special selection functions. You cannot, for example, select at one time all of the objects that have the same Stroke color and Fill color, but have different Stroke weights.

The Lock Unselected command (press Option [Alt] and Object ➪ Lock or ⌘-Option-2 [Ctrl+Alt+2]) is the key to specifying multiple selection criteria. The following instructions describe how to perform multiple-type selections in a few steps.

1. Select a representative object that has the Stroke and Fill color that you want.

2. Choose Edit ➪ Select ➪ Same Fill Color. All objects that have the same Fill color as the original object will be selected, regardless of their Stroke color.

3. This step is the key step. Press Option [Alt] and choose Arrange ➪ Lock (⌘-Option-2) [Ctrl+Alt+2] to lock any objects that are not selected. The only objects that you can modify or select now are the ones that have the same Fill color.

4. Deselect All (⌘-Shift-A) [Ctrl+Shift+A] and select the original object, which has both the Fill color and the Stroke color that you want to select.

5. Choose Edit ➪ Select ➪ Same Stroke Color. Only objects that have the same Stroke and Fill colors are selected.

ASK TOULOUSE: Selecting More than One Color

Archie: How can I select all occurrences of two different Fill colors?

Toulouse: You'll need to use Same Fill Color.

Archie: I tried that, but it doesn't work.

Toulouse: Do it this way: Select a representative of the first color, and then run the function.

Archie: Okay, but now I'm stuck.

Toulouse: Not really. Lock those objects with ⌘-2 [Ctrl+2], then select a representative of the second Fill color, and run Same Fill Color again.

Archie: I'm still stuck.

Toulouse: Ah . . . here's the tricky part. Lock those objects as well.

Archie: Excuse me for noticing, but now I *can't* select those objects. They're all locked.

Toulouse: Just Unlock All (⌘-Option-2) [Ctrl+Alt+2], and they'll all be selected!

Archie: You know, I really don't think these different colors should be mixed.

Select Masks

Select Masks (Edit ⇨ Select ⇨ Select Masks) selects all the objects that are currently being used as masks. The only masks in the document that are not selected are the masks that are locked or hidden and the masks that are on layers that are locked or hidden.

Select Stray Points

Select Stray Points (Edit ⇨ Select ⇨ Select Stray Points) selects Anchor Points in the document.

Individual Anchor Points are nasty beasts, because although they don't show in preview or printing, they contain Fills and Strokes that can cause separation software to print additional blank color separations that aren't needed.

Stray points can be created in various ways:

✦ Clicking once with the Pen tool creates a single Anchor Point.

✦ Deleting a line segment on a path that has two points by selecting the line segment with the Direct Selection tool and pressing Delete will leave behind the two Anchor Points.

✦ Using the Scissors tool to cut a path, and while deleting one side or another of the path, not selecting the points turns these points into stray points.

✦ Ungrouping an oval or rectangle in Illustrator 3.2 or older and then deleting just the frame of the shape leaves the center point in the document.

Bringing an Illustrator 4 or older document that has still-grouped rectangles or ovals into Version 8 automatically deletes the center point and turns on the Show Center Point option in the Attributes palette (choose Window ⇨ Show Attributes or press F11).

Be careful not to think that center points of objects are stray points — they aren't, and you cannot select them without selecting the object they belong to. Center points of objects are visible when the Show Center Point option is chosen in the Attributes palette. Selecting the center point of an object selects the entire object, and deleting the center point deletes the entire object.

Select Inverse

Select Inverse (Edit ⇨ Select ⇨ Select Inverse) quickly selects all objects that are not currently selected. For example, if 1 object is selected and the document contains 15 other objects, the 15 objects will become selected, and the 1 object that was selected originally will become deselected.

Caution   Select Inverse does not cause locked or hidden objects to be selected and does not select guides unless guides are not locked. Objects on layers that are locked or hidden are not selected either.

Select Inverse is useful because selecting a few objects is usually quicker than selecting most objects. After you select the few objects, Select Inverse does all the nasty work of selecting everything else.

When no objects are selected, Select Inverse selects all the objects, just as Edit ⇨ Select All (⌘-A) [Ctrl+A] would. When all objects are selected, Select Inverse deselects all the objects, just as Edit ⇨ Deselect All (⌘-Shift-A) [Ctrl+Shift+A] would.

Layers

The layering feature of Illustrator provides an easy and powerful way to separate artwork into individual sections. A layer is a separate section of the document that is on its own level, above, under, or in between other layers, but never on the same level as another layer. You can view these sections separately, locked, hidden, and rearranged around each other. Figure 7-56 shows objects that have been layered, along with a snazzy poem.

You create, control, and manipulate layers by using the Layers palette. Each layer can have its own color, and that color will show when all paths and points of objects are selected.

Note   You can create as many layers as you want, up to the limitations of application memory. To make sure that the Adobe people were on the up-and-up about this, I created 5000 layers in one document. It worked without ever questioning my need for 5000 layers. Why would you need 5000 layers? I hope you wouldn't, but you shouldn't have any fears that you will not be able to create enough layers for an illustration. Of course, having all those layers to work with slowed the operation of Illustrator to a crawl. I had to click the mouse button and hold on the menu bar for about 3 seconds before the menu appeared. Suffice it to say, the more layers you create after a certain point (several hundred), the slower Illustrator runs.

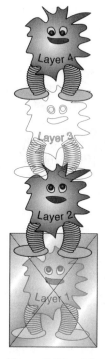

The Paths and Points and Handles
All of them wearing open-toed sandals
Had a dilemma, a confusing vector problem
That stumped even the most brightest of them
(Editors noted that this rhyming was sad
"It's unbalanced and ugly and just plain bad")

W'ever objects would meet, yet stay separated
They'd still be intermingled and some even dated
Groups were formed with a hierarchical slant
"We paths stick together" was their war cry and chant
Yet that wasn't enough, grouping groups was confusing
After keeping score for a while, the users were losing

Adobe Techs fielded support calls by the hundred zillions
So busy their Sega scores never made it to the millions
Suddenly the engineers assigned to make vectors better
Thought "We'll make layers, and make them to the letter"
Layers were magic and frosting and sugar and spice
The things of calories, tooth decay, and Disney mice

Vector objects rejoiced and cheered and screamed in glee,
"This is how life in a PostScript application should be"
Layers could be moved and previewed and printed
They could be colored and of course the fonts were still hinted
When the Paths and Points and Handles heard this great news
They ditched those open-toed sandals and bought leather dress shoes....

Figure 7-56: A layers' Seussian story

Getting Started with Layers

After you realize that you need to use layers, what do you do? The only way to manipulate, create, and delete layers is by using the Layers palette.

1. If the Layers palette is not showing, choose Window ➪ Show Layers (F7). When you open the Layers palette for the first time in a new document, you see only Layer 1 listed.

2. To create a new layer, Option[Alt]-click the New Layer icon at the bottom of the palette (it looks like a piece of paper with the corner folded over). You can also click the triangle in the upper-right of the palette to display a pop-up menu. Drag over to the first item, New Layer, to display the New Layer dialog box.

3. In the Layer Options dialog box, the name of the new layer, Layer 2, is highlighted. To change this name, type a new name, and it will replace the generic name.

4. The options below the name affect how the layer works and is viewed. The first option is the color of the paths and points when objects on that layer are selected. Choose one of the preset colors from the pop-up menu or select the Other option to use a Custom Color. Each time you create a new layer, a different color (going in order from the list) is applied to that layer.

5. Select any of the options that you want for this layer. Show makes the objects in the layer visible. Lock prevents objects on this layer from being selected and prevents any objects from being put on this layer. Print enables you to print objects that are on this layer. Preview makes the objects on this layer preview. Dim Placed Images dims any placed images on the layer, making them about 80% lighter than normal.

6. Click OK after you choose all the options you want. The new layer appears above the existing layer in the Layers palette. If you want the objects on the new layer to appear below the objects on the existing layer, click the name of the new layer and drag it under Layer 1.

7. To modify the existing layer, double-click it. You see the Layer Options dialog box again. Make the changes and choose the options that you want for this layer and then click OK.

Tip

The Layer Options dialog box can be easily bypassed when creating new layers. Clicking on the New Layer icon (without pressing Option [Alt]), or pressing Option [Alt] while choosing New Layer from the Layer palette pop-up menu, will create a new layer with the default naming scheme. You can always double-click on that layer to access the Layer Options for that layer.

Using the Layers Palette

The Layers palette (shown in Figure 7-57) is the control center where all layer-related activities take place. Most activities take place on the main section of the Layers palette, which is always visible when the Layers palette is onscreen. Other activities take place in the pop-up menu that appears when you press the triangle in the upper right of the palette.

New Feature

Illustrator 8 has added some enhancements and new features to the Layers palette. First, is the capability to thin the display of layers in the palette for those illustrations with tons of layers. Second, is version 6's capability to drag to a hidden layer has been put back in. Third, a layer that is not set to print will be displayed in italics so that you can see quickly what will print and what won't. Finally, the scrolling speed when moving between layers has been adjusted to make us all happy.

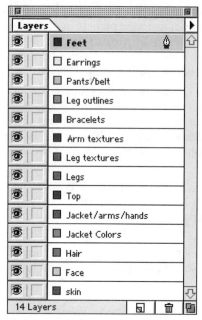

Figure 7-57: The Layers palette

The Main Section of the Layers Palette

Clicking the Close box in the upper-left corner closes the Layers palette. Another way to close the Layers palette is to choose Window ⇨ Hide Layers (F7). To bring the Layers palette back to the screen, choose Window ⇨ Show Layers (F7).

Clicking the Collapse box in the upper-right corner of the Layers palette resizes the palette to be collapsed, and then toggles to the previous height.

The left column controls how each layer is viewed. Solid eyes represent a layer that is in Preview mode. Hollow eyes mean that the layer is in Artwork mode. No eye means that the layer is hidden. Clicking a solid or hollow eye toggles it from showing to hidden. Clicking in the Show/Hide Column when no eye is present shows the layer. ⌘[Ctrl]-clicking the eye changes it from solid (Preview mode) to hollow (Artwork mode). Option[Alt]-clicking an eye shows or hides all other layers.

The right column is the Lock/Unlock column. The pencils with slashes through them in this column signify whether each layer is locked or unlocked. An empty column means that the layer is not locked. A pencil with a red slash means that the layer is locked from use. A pencil with a gray slash means that the layer is hidden, and that when the layer is shown it will be locked. You can move items to hidden layers as long as those layers are not locked, but you cannot change anything that is already on a hidden layer.

The column in the center of the palette lists the names of all the layers in the document. When no documents are open, no layers are listed. If one layer has a pen to the right of it, it is the active layer. All new objects are created on the active layer. Select more than one layer by Shift-clicking each layer to be selected. To deselect a layer, Shift-click it while it is selected. One layer must always be selected. If a pen with a slash through it is in that column, then that layer is active and it is locked.

The layer at the top of the column is the layer that is on top of all the other layers. The layer at the bottom of the column is the layer that is at the bottom of all the other layers. To move a layer, or layers, click it and drag it up or down. As you drag, a dark horizontal line indicates where the layer(s) will be placed when you release the mouse button.

You can undo all layer changes as they happen by choosing Edit ⇨ Undo (⌘-Z) [Ctrl+Z] right afterward.

To the right of the layer's name is the object status of the layer. If a square appears in that column, at least one object on that layer is selected.

1. Select the objects that you want to move from one layer to another. If the objects are on one layer, group them together so that you can reselect them easily. (Do not group objects from different layers together or all objects will be placed on the topmost layer.)

2. Open the Layers palette by choosing Window ⇨ Show Layers (F7). A square should appear next to one of the layers. The square represents the selected objects. (If you select objects on more than one layer, a square appears on each layer that has a selected object.)

3. Drag the square from its current layer to the target layer. The objects do not move left, right, up, or down, but now they may be in front of or behind other objects, depending on the layer that they are now on.

The Layers Palette Icons

There are two icons along the bottom of the Layers palette that make layer manipulation much easier than ever before. The first icon (a little piece of paper) is the New Layer icon. The second icon is the Trash icon.

Clicking the New Layer icon creates a new layer instantly, without the New Layer dialog box appearing. Option[Alt]-clicking the New Layer icon creates a new layer by way of the New Layer dialog box. Dragging a layer or layers to the New Layer icon duplicates those layers *and everything on them*.

Clicking the Trash icon deletes the selected layers. If there is art on a layer that is about to be deleted, a dialog box will appear to make sure that you really want to delete that layer. Option[Alt]-clicking the Trash icon deletes selected layers without a warning dialog box, whether or not art is on the selected layers. You can also drag a layer or layers to the Trash icon; the layers will be deleted without a warning dialog box.

The Layers Palette Pop-Up Menu

Clicking the triangle in the upper-right of the Layers palette displays a pop-up menu that shows the different options that are available relative to the selected layers (see Figure 7-58).

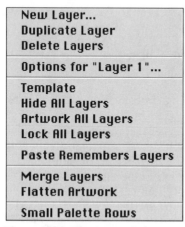

Figure 7-58: The Layers Palette
pop-up menu

The first option, New Layer, creates a new layer at the top of the list. When New Layer is selected, the New Layer dialog box appears, which is the same as the Layer Options dialog box, except for the title. When a new layer is created with Illustrator, it is automatically assigned the next color in the color list.

If you press the Option [Alt] key before you click the pop-up menu triangle, the first menu item will read New Layer Above First Layer, or New Layer Above whatever the name of the active layer is.

The second menu option is Duplicate Layer, which duplicates selected layers, along with any objects that are on those layers. You can also duplicate select layers by dragging them to the New Layer icon at the bottom of the Layers palette.

The next option is Delete Layers, which deletes the layer and any artwork on the layer. If the layer to be deleted contains artwork, a dialog box warns you that you are about to delete it. If several layers are selected, the entry reads Delete Layers, and all selected layers are deleted. You can undo layer deletions.

The fourth menu option is Options for Layer 1 (or Layer Options for whatever the name of the active layer is) — the menu item reads Layers Options if more than one layer is selected. Selecting Layer Options displays the Layer Options dialog box, in which you can choose a number of different options (see Figure 7-59). If more than one layer is selected, the layer options affect all selected layers.

Tip   Double-clicking a layer name also brings up the Layer Options dialog box.

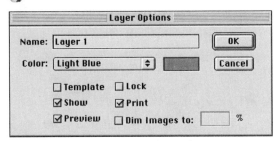

Figure 7-59: The Layer Options dialog box

The next four options are different ways of changing the locking and viewing templates. The first option, Template, is where you select the template. The next option reads either Show All Layers (if one or more is hidden) or Hide All Layers (if all are visible). Hide All Layers hides all the layers but the selected ones. This is like pressing the Option [Alt] key and clicking the column to the left of the selected layers. The next option is either Preview All Layers (if one or more is set to Artwork view) or Artwork All Layers, which changes all unselected layers to Artwork view. The final option in this group is either Unlock All Layers, if any layers are locked, or Lock All Layers, which locks all layers but the selected ones. This lock/unlock action can also be done in the Layers Palette (previously shown in Figure 7-57) by Option[Alt]-clicking the selected layers' Lock/Unlock column.

Checking the Paste Remembers Layers option causes all objects to be pasted on the layer they were copied from, regardless of which layer is currently active. Unchecking this menu item causes objects on the Clipboard to be pasted on the current layer.

The next option in the Layers Palette pop-up menu is Merge Layers, which combines selected layers into one. Merge Layers does two important things: First, it places art that you want on the same layer together in one step. Second, it eliminates all those empty layers automatically. When you've finished an illustration, if you know you won't need separate layers anymore, it's a great idea to go ahead and select all your layers and Merge them into one.

The Flatten Artwork option works just like Photoshop's Flatten Layers. This will take all of your layers and combine them as one layer.

The Small Palette Rows option allows you to see twice the number of layers in the Layers palette. This option crushes the viewable size of the layers in the Layers palette so that if you have a ton of layers, you can see them all easily.

ASK TOULOUSE: Inverse on Specific Layers

Miguel: I want to select the inverse of the objects I selected that are just on specific layers.

Toulouse: You've already selected the inverse objects of the ones you want?

Miguel: Yep. How do I select just the inverse on certain layers only?

Toulouse: Easy. Run the Select Inverse function.

Miguel: But there are lots of paths selected that *aren't* on those layers.

Toulouse: Then just lock all the layers you don't want paths selected on. Anything on a locked layer will deselect.

Layer Advice and Strategies

Layers take up RAM (Random Access Memory) and computer power, and the more layers you have, the slower your system will be.

Create layers when you believe that they will help you better organize an illustration. Even setting up one additional layer can dramatically ease selection and moving problems. One of the best uses for layers is to trace placed images. To learn exactly how to perform this procedure, see Chapter 4.

Use vivid, distinct colors for each layer. Using the same colors for all layers makes you miss out on half the power of layers. By choosing Select All (⌘-A) [Ctrl+A], you can quickly see which objects are on which layers, just by the color of the paths and points.

Summary

✦ Path editing is done in Illustrator by using the Direct Selection, Scissors, Smooth, Erase, and Convert Direction Point tools.

✦ Adding Anchor Points alone never changes the shape of a path.

✦ Adding Anchor Points doubles the number of points on selected paths.

✦ Use Add Anchor Points before using the Punk & Bloat filter or the Scribble and Tweak filter.

✦ Cleanup deletes unwanted path types from your entire document.

✦ Offset Path moves a path inward or outward by the number of points you specify.

✦ Outline Path creates a Filled path in the same location as a Stroke, at the size of the width of the Stroke.

✦ The Pathfinder palette options are path-specific.

✦ Unite joins together abutting and overlapping paths.

✦ Intersect creates paths where all the selected paths overlap, deleting the rest of the paths.

✦ Exclude creates paths only where there is no overlap.

✦ Back Minus and Front Minus subtract from the backmost or frontmost paths.

✦ Trap creates trapping in the amount you specify between abutting or overlapping paths.

✦ Removing Anchor Points can drastically change the shape of a path.

✦ Paths can be split one at a time with the Scissors tool.

✦ You can slice through paths with the Knife tool.

✦ You can erase through paths with the Erase tool.

✦ Quickly make duplicates of certain sections of paths by pressing Option [Alt] when using the Knife tool.

✦ Selected points can be aligned using the Average command.

✦ Use the Join command to join any two selected End Points.

✦ Use the Align palette to align entire objects.

✦ The Convert Direction Point tool changes the Anchor Point type.

✦ The five major types of PostScript transformations are represented by four tools, Rotate, Scale, Reflect, and Shear, and the Move dialog box.

✦ You can do many transformations at one time with the Free Transform tool.

✦ Transform Each incorporates the Move, Scale, and Rotate functions that work on selected objects independently.

✦ The Select functions aid in selecting objects.

✦ Same Fill Color selects objects with the same Fill color as the currently selected object.

✦ Same Paint Style selects objects with the same paint style as the currently selected object.

✦ Inverse selects everything that isn't selected, and deselects everything that is selected.

✦ Select Masks selects all paths used as masking paths.

✦ Layers can be used to effectively separate different sections of your artwork.

✦   ✦   ✦

Type

Type is a huge part of Illustrator. In previous versions of this book, I split type between several different chapters in different areas. But for the *Illustrator 8 Bible,* I've packed this one chapter full of everything I could about type, to the point where this version of the *Illustrator Bible* is a little type-heavy, and severely off balance.

But then, when I talk to Illustrator users, from veterans to those who are wet behind the ears, a lot of them tell me that the main thing they use Illustrator for is manipulating type. So here's what could be the most important chapter in the book.

The Type Menu

The Type menu, shown in Figure 8-1, contains all of Illustrator's type controls (with the exception of the Type tools). No longer is the Font menu a separate menu on the menu bar; it is now incorporated into a submenu in the Type menu.

Most of the Type options can be changed in either the Character palette (choose Type ➪ Character or press ⌘-T [Ctrl+T]) or the Paragraph palette (choose Type ➪ Paragraph or press ⌘-M [Ctrl+M]), which are discussed later in this chapter.

Type is set in Illustrator in *stories.* A story is a set of continuous, linked text. When the term *paragraph* is mentioned, it is usually referring to the characters that are between Returns. If there are no Returns in a story, then that story is said to have one paragraph. Returns end paragraphs and begin new ones. There is always exactly one more paragraph in a story than there are Returns.

The following sections describe each of the Type menu options.

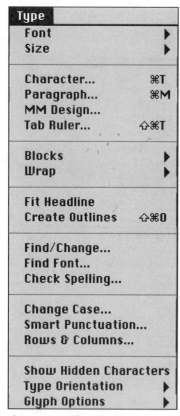

Figure 8-1: The Type menu

Font

Font displays a submenu with all the fonts that are currently installed on the computer you are using. Pressing ⌘-Option-Shift-F [Ctrl+Alt+Shift+F] or ⌘-Option-Shift-M [Ctrl+Alt+Shift+M] automatically highlights the Font field on the Character palette and shows or notes the palette as well. A check mark appears next to the font that is currently selected. If no check mark appears next to any of the fonts, more than one font is currently selected.

Note

If you are wondering why the folks at Adobe chose such an odd combination of keys and commands, you probably don't use QuarkXPress very much. Quark's key command for highlighting the font field in its measurement palette is ⌘-Option-Shift-M [Ctrl+Alt+Shift+M].

Size

Type Size displays a submenu with Other and various point sizes listed. When Other is chosen, the Character palette appears with the Size field highlighted. You can type any point size from 0.1 to 1296 in this field.

Tip Type created in Illustrator may be scaled to any size, but to go beyond the size limits, you must convert the type into outline paths by selecting the type and using the Create Outlines command (⌘-Shift-O) [Ctrl+Shift+O].

A check mark appears next to the point size that is currently selected. If the point size currently selected does not correspond to a point size in the Size submenu, a check mark appears next to the Other menu item. Point size for type is measured from the top of the ascenders (like the top of a capital letter *T*) to the bottom of the descenders (like the bottom of a lowercase *g*). If no check mark appears next to any of the sizes, more than one size is currently selected (even if the different sizes are all Other sizes).

You can also increase and decrease the point size of type by using the keyboard shortcuts ⌘-Shift-> [Ctrl+Shift+>], which increases the point size by the amount specified in Keyboard Increments Preferences, and ⌘-Shift-< [Ctrl+Shift+<], which decreases the point size by the amount specified in Keyboard Increments Preferences.

Yet another way to change point size is to use the Scale tool. Using the Scale tool to change point size lets you change to any size; that size is displayed in the Character palette as soon as you are done scaling. Once again, remember that the limit in scaling type is 1296 points, and that you cannot exceed that limit even with the Scale tool unless the type has been converted to outlined paths.

Character

Character (⌘-T) [Ctrl+T] brings up the Character palette with the Font field highlighted. In the Character palette, you can change fonts, styles, point size, leading, baseline shift, vertical scale, horizontal scale, and tracking/kerning values, all at one time!

When you choose the Show Options item from the Character palette's pop-up menu, the Horizontal and Vertical Scaling controls and the Baseline Shift control are available (see Figure 8-2). Choosing Multilingual Options displays the Multilingual Options area at the very bottom of the palette.

If the Character palette is currently open, choosing the Character option or pressing ⌘-T [Ctrl+T] will close (hide) it.

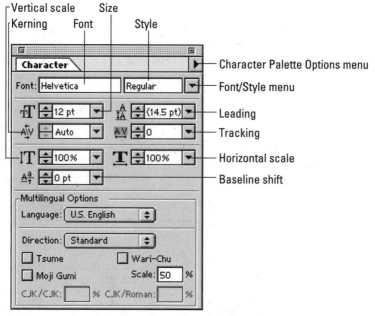

Figure 8-2: The Character palette, expanded to show both Options and Multilingual Options

Paragraph

Paragraph (⌘-M) [Ctrl+M] displays the Paragraph palette with the Left Indentation field highlighted (see Figure 8-3). You can use this palette to change the left, right, and first line indents, and to change the alignment by clicking the different alignment boxes. In addition, the Space Before Paragraph, Hang Punctuation, and Auto Hyphenate options are available for all fonts, as well as Repeated Character Processing and Line Breaking options for the Japanese fonts. In the bottom part of the palette (choose Show Options from the pop-up menu of the palette to see the bottom part), you can set spacing limitations and guidelines.

If the Paragraph palette is currently open, choosing the Paragraph command or pressing ⌘-M [Ctrl+M] will close (hide) it. ⌘-~ (tilde) will take you to the last entry field.

Choosing Hyphenation Options from the pop-up menu displays the Hyphenation Options dialog box (see Figure 8-4), where you can specify the number of letters before and after hyphens, and how many consecutive hyphens can appear in a paragraph.

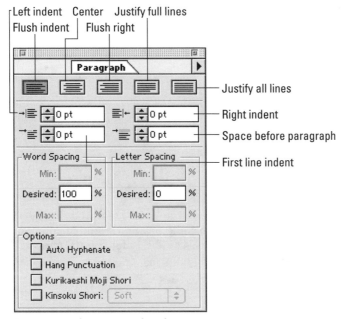

Figure 8-3: The Paragraph palette

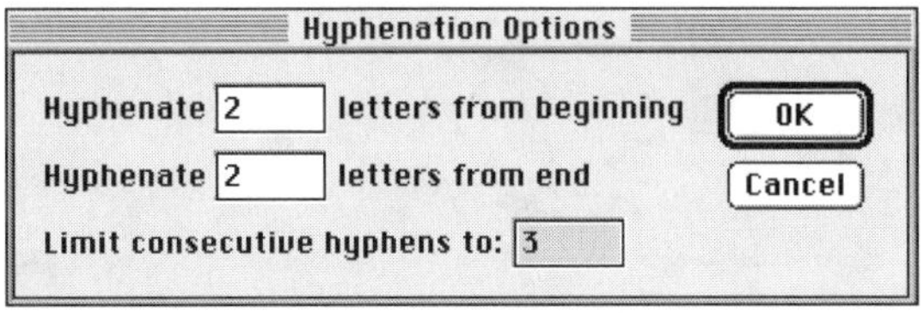

Figure 8-4: The Hyphenation Options dialog box

MM Design

Choosing Type ➪ MM Design displays the Multiple Master Design palette, where you can create variations of any installed Multiple Master fonts (see Figure 8-5). Multiple Master fonts are flexible fonts that can be modified in real time within Illustrator. These fonts are changed along several different "axes," such as weight, serif, italics, and width. The Multiple Master Design palette enables you to modify the axis available for each font.

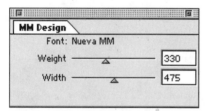

Figure 8-5: The Multiple Master Design
palette when Nueva MM is selected,
a Multiple Master font with two axes
(Weight and Width)

The Tab Ruler Palette

The Tab Ruler palette is used to set tabs the same way you would in your word-processing or page-layout software. To access the Tab Ruler palette, choose Type ➪ Tab Ruler. The Tab Ruler palette is shown in Figure 8-6.

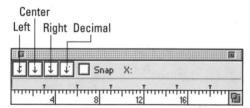

Figure 8-6: The Tab Ruler palette

To set tabs for type, select the type and choose Type ➪ Tab Ruler. The Tab Ruler palette appears above the type you have selected and automatically assumes the width of the type area.

To change the width of the Tab Ruler palette, click and drag on the Extend Tab Ruler button in the lower-right corner of the palette. The Tab Ruler palette can be made wider or thinner, but not taller. To reset the Tab Ruler palette back to the exact size of the type area, click on the Alignment box in the upper-right corner of the palette.

Tip   The Alignment box will move the Tab Ruler palette to make it flush left with the type and move it up or down so that it is right above the selected text area.

Illustrator automatically sets tabs at every half inch. These are called *Auto tab stops*. Once you set a tab, all the Auto tab stops to the left of the tab you have set disappear. The Auto tab stops work like left-justified tabs.

If the Snap option box is checked, tab stops correspond to ruler tick marks.

The measurement system shown on the ruler is the same system that is used by the rest of the document and can be changed in the Preferences dialog box.

To set a tab, select a tab from the four Tab Style buttons on the upper left of the Tab Ruler palette and click on the ruler below to set exactly where you would like the new tab. Once the tab has been set, you can move it by dragging it along the ruler, or remove it by dragging it off the top or bottom edge of the ruler.

There are four types of tabs you can set:

✦ **Left-justified tabs** make type align to the right side of the tab, with the leftmost character aligning with the tab stop.

✦ **Center-justified tabs** make type align to the center of the tab, with the center character aligning with the tab stop.

✦ **Right-justified tabs** make type align to the left side of the tab, with the rightmost character aligning with the tab stop.

✦ **Decimal-justified tabs** make type align to the left side of the tab, with a decimal or the rightmost character aligning with the tab stop.

To change a tab from one style to another, select a tab stop and click on the Tab style button that you wish to change to. To deselect all tabs, click in the area to the right of the Tab position box. (If you don't click far enough away from the Tab position box, you'll end up changing the units.) It is a good idea to get in the habit of deselecting tabs after they are set so that defining a new tab style for the next tab stop does not change the tab stop that was just set.

New Feature New to the Tab palette in Illustrator 8 are the first-line indent marker and the left indent marker.

Note There is no way to create dot leader tabs automatically by using the Tab Ruler palette. We may have to wait for version 9 of Illustrator for this feature to be incorporated (or you could use a page-layout program). As always, if you think this feature or any other feature that Illustrator lacks would be useful, send Adobe a note (a "feature request") at www.adobe.com and it *will* be considered.

Graphical Tabs

Graphical tabs are tabs that flow around objects (paths) in Illustrator automatically. The following steps show you how to use graphical tabs.

1. Create a rectangle type area and type in five words separated by tabs. (Yes, each word will be set at ½" apart — we'll fix that shortly.) Press Return after the last word entered.

2. Select All (⌘-A) [Ctrl+A] and Copy (⌘-C) [Ctrl+C]. Then click the last line of type (it should be blank) and paste it a few times (⌘-V, ⌘-V, ⌘-V, ⌘-V) [Ctrl+V, Ctrl+V, Ctrl+V, Ctrl+V].

3. Using the Pencil tool, draw a series of four straight or curved vertical lines that extend above the top and below the bottom of the type area. Select the lines and the type area and choose Type⌘Wrap⌘Make. The type should be tabbed to the lines that you drew.

Tabs will tab to the other side of text wrap objects. Play with this a little and you'll discover that this method is much more flexible than standard word processing tab stops.

The Link Blocks Option

The Link Blocks option (Type ⇨ Blocks ⇨ Link) links text from one area or rectangle to another, continuing a story from one area or rectangle to another (see Figure 8-7). Linked blocks act like groups, enabling you to use the regular Selection tool and click on just one area to select all areas. (Individual blocks can still be selected with the Direct Selection tool.) Whenever more text is available than can fit into a text area, a tiny little plus sign in a box appears, alerting you that there is more text in the box than you see.

To use Link Blocks, select a text area or rectangle and any other shapes, even text rectangles and areas, and choose Link Blocks. The text areas then act as if they are grouped. Text will flow from the back-most shape to the front-most in any group of linked blocks, so be careful to order your boxes correctly when setting up linked text. In fact, if you send a box to the back, that will be where the text starts from, going to the next box forward, and then the next, and so on. You cannot select Link Blocks if at least one text area and one other path or text area are not selected.

the trash can and grabbed the instructions out with the arm that hadn't been crushed beneath my body. Hours later, I was clawing my way around the apartment walls, one revolution at a time. There was no stopping me now. It was time to let go of the wall. Reading the instructions further I

makes sense, I thought. There is one problem with this method of riding. The faster I felt I was falling, the faster I pedalled, and soon I couldn't pedal fast enough to prevent myself from falling. To make a long story shorter, my face hit the floor at about sixty miles an hour, and as my nose was shoved through the back of my head, I watched the unicycle fly over my crumpled body, almost

discovered that to go forward a rider leans and pedals forward to prevent falling forward. If you feel you are falling forward, the instructions said, pedal faster. Sure, that

I looked at the instruction sheet, but after seeing that they wanted me to hold onto the wall for support to get started, like I was a little kid or something, I threw it out. Three seconds later, after the unicycle had, under its own power, flown out from under me towards the dog (he's still in therapy), I crawled over to

Figure 8-7: Text blocks linked together in the order of the arrows

The Unlink Blocks Option

The Unlink Blocks option (Type ➪ Blocks ➪ Unlink) destroys the links made with the Link Blocks command. Blocks can only be unlinked when all boxes linked together are chosen. This is done quite easily with the regular Selection tool. When blocks are unlinked, the text inside them is split into several stories, one for each block. If the boxes are later relinked with the Link Blocks command, they will be separated by paragraph returns.

The Make Wrap Option

The Make Wrap option wraps text around any paths, as shown in Figure 8-8. To use Make Wrap, select both the type and the paths you want the type to wrap around. The paths that the type wraps around must be in front of the type in order for the text to wrap around the paths. Choose Type ➪ Wrap ➪ Make. The objects then act like a grouped object; you can use the regular Selection tool to select all objects in a Make Wrap area.

Make Wrap only works with Area type and Rectangle type (the option is dimmed for Path type and Point type).

Make Wrap works in levels: You can Make Wrap with one type area or rectangle to a path and then Make Wrap again with the same type area or rectangle to another path, and the type will wrap around both paths.

Caution   Remember that Make Wrap only wraps around paths; regardless of how thick the Stroke on your path is, the wrap will not change. This can cause the wrapping object to run into the text if the object has a heavy Stroke.

Additional objects can be used to wrap. Just place them in front of the type area, select both the type area and the new wrapping object, and choose Type ➪ Make Wrap.

Tip   Text wrapping objects need no Fill or Stroke, but they do need to be closed. If you want to use an existing path and that path is not closed, simply copy the path, choose Edit ➪ Paste In Front (⌘-F) [Ctrl+F], and change the Fill and Stroke to None.

The Release Wrap Option

The Release Wrap (Choose Type ➪ Wrap ➪ Release) option releases any text wraps that are selected, all at one time. Release Wrap does *not* release wraps in the order that they were created. Because paths wrapped to type areas and rectangles do not lose or change attributes when they become wrapped paths, those paths retain their original Paint Style attributes when released.

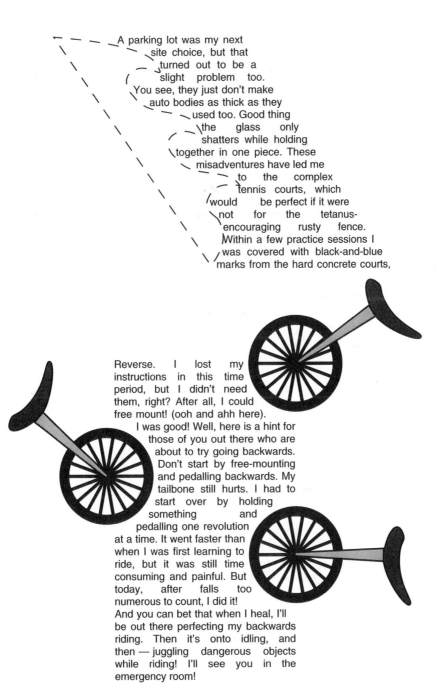

A parking lot was my next site choice, but that turned out to be a slight problem too. You see, they just don't make auto bodies as thick as they used too. Good thing the glass only shatters while holding together in one piece. These misadventures have led me to the complex tennis courts, which would be perfect if it were not for the tetanus-encouraging rusty fence. Within a few practice sessions I was covered with black-and-blue marks from the hard concrete courts,

Reverse. I lost my instructions in this time period, but I didn't need them, right? After all, I could free mount! (ooh and ahh here). I was good! Well, here is a hint for those of you out there who are about to try going backwards. Don't start by free-mounting and pedalling backwards. My tailbone still hurts. I had to start over by holding something and pedalling one revolution at a time. It went faster than when I was first learning to ride, but it was still time consuming and painful. But today, after falls too numerous to count, I did it! And you can bet that when I heal, I'll be out there perfecting my backwards riding. Then it's onto idling, and then — juggling dangerous objects while riding! I'll see you in the emergency room!

Figure 8-8: Text wrapped around different objects

The Fit Headline Option

The Fit Headline option is designed to automatically increase the weight and width of type using Multiple Master fonts in order to fit type perfectly from the left side of a type area or rectangle to the right side of that same type area or rectangle. Of course, for this to work, you must have Multiple Master typefaces. Personally, I think this feature would have been great if it just increased the point size of any type, Multiple Master or not, so that the type fit from left to right.

Tip   If you don't have Multiple Master typefaces, you can still use Fit Headline. Although the command only increases the tracking of the type until it is justified, it actually does a lot better job than the Justify All Lines command (in the Paragraph palette), which only puts space between words. Select the type using the Type tool and choose Type ➪ Fit Headline.

The Create Outlines Option

After your type is set (and spelled correctly), choose Type ➪ Create Outlines (⌘-Shift-O) [Ctrl+Shift+O] and the type selected is converted into *editable paths* (see Figure 8-9). To convert type to outlines, the type needs to be selected with a selection tool, not a type tool. Each letter is its own compound path, and each path can be edited with the Direct Selection tool.

Figure 8-9: Type converted into outlines with the Create Outlines command

Note Create Outlines only works with Type 1 PostScript and TrueType fonts, not bitmapped or Type 3 PostScript fonts. You must have both the screen and printer fonts for bitmapped and Type 3 fonts.

TrueType combines the screen and printer fonts into one file—if you can select a TrueType font in Illustrator, you can create outlines from it.

When type has been converted to outlines, you can apply gradients to its Fill, as well as apply patterns to its Fill that you can preview onscreen. Patterns can be applied to nonoutline type.

Caution While you can undo Create Outlines, be forewarned that there is no way to convert back to type in case you made a spelling error or wish to change the font or any other type attribute.

All forms of type, including Point type, Path type, Area type, and Rectangle type, may be converted to outlines.

Tip Creating outlines out of type is also very useful when you want to send the file to be outputted and the person doing the output does not have the font you are using. Simply use the Create Outlines option before you send the file, and it will print just fine. (This is not advised for 4-point type or smaller, as described in the "Hinting" section later in this chapter).

Type Outlines

The process of creating editable type outlines has many uses, including distorting mild-mannered characters into grotesque letters. More practical uses for editable type outlines include making type-based logos unique, arcing type (where one side is flat and the other is curved), special effects and masking, and avoiding font compatibility problems.

To change type from being editable text into an Illustrator path (for that is what an editable type outline really is), select the type with a selection tool, not a type tool. Choose Type ➪ Create Outlines or press ⌘-Shift-O [Ctrl+Shift+O], and the type changes into paths that you can edit. Figure 8-10 shows the "CHO" logo before and after being converted into outlines.

Caution After type has been changed into Illustrator paths using Create Outlines, the only way back is to use the Undo command (⌘-Z) [Ctrl+Z]. There is no "Convert from Paths to Type" function. Type cannot be edited in Outline mode. This means that if you misspell something, it will remain misspelled.

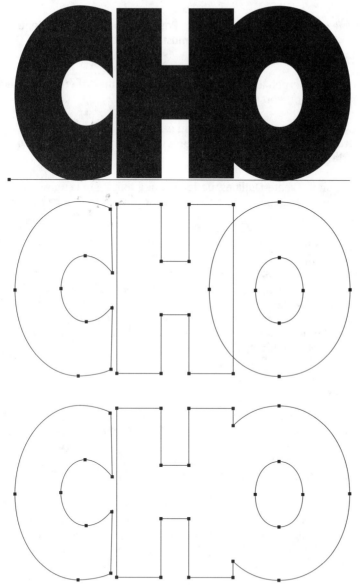

Figure 8-10: Type that has been converted to outlines and united via the Unite function

Initially, when type is converted into outlines, individual characters are turned into compound paths. This ensures that holes in letters, such as in a lowercase *a*, *b*, or *d,* are see-through, and not just white-filled paths placed on top of the original objects. (See Chapter 9 for an in-depth discussion of compound paths.)

Making Letters That Normally Appear in Your Worst Nightmares

After letters have been turned into outlines, there is nothing to stop you from distorting them into shapes that only resemble letters in the most simplistic sense of the word.

The results of letter distortion usually aren't all that eye pleasing, but they can be *fun*. Few things in life are as pleasing as taking a boring letter *Q* and twisting it into "the letter that time forgot." Or fiddling around with your boss's name until the letters look as evil as your boss does. Or adding pointed ears and whiskers to a random array of letters and numbers and printing out several sheets of them with the words "Mutant kittens for sale." Some samples are shown in Figure 8-11.

Figure 8-11: Fun with type outlines

When modifying existing letters, use the Direct Selection tool. Select the points or segments you wish to move, and drag them around to your heart's content. This can be great practice for adjusting paths, and you might accidentally stumble onto some really cool designs.

Creating Logos from Type Outlines

Type outlines provide you with the flexibility to manipulate letters to turn an ordinary, boring, letters-only logo into a distinct symbol embodying the company's image.

Outlines are flexible enough that there really are no limits to what can be done with something as simple as a word of type.

The examples in Figure 8-12 show some logos that have been "touched up" by changing them into outlines and moving around the paths that comprise them.

Figure 8-12: Type converted to outlines, edited, and ready to be used for logos

Distorting Words and Phrases

There is a difference between arced words and type on a circle. The letters in type on a circle are rotated individually, making each letter line up with one part of the circle. The letters in arced type are not rotated; instead, either the top or bottom of each letter is stretched to fit to a circular curve, as in the examples shown on the right side of Figure 8-12.

Tip Arcing type is easier and creates better results when the type is created as all capital letters, especially when the tops of the letters are being curved to fit a circle.

To arc type, first convert it into outlines, and then create an oval or circle above or below the outlines. As an example, the following steps arc type using the circle-below method.

1. Make sure that the tip of the top of the circle touches the center letters in the word so that these letters don't need to be changed. Always adjust the horizontal scaling prior to aligning the circle to the outlined type, as this prevents unnecessary adjustments.

2. Using the Scale tool, scale the first letter vertically only (hold down the Shift key) and drag until either the left or right side is even with the path of the circle. Do the same for the remaining letters.

3. After the letters are the correct approximate height, use the Direct Selection tool to adjust the bottoms of the letters to fit the curve well. This can take some time and a bit of practice to get the technique correct, but the results can be outstanding.

Tip The best way to arc type is by using a third-party filter, such as the KPT (Kai Power Tools) Warp Frame filter in the KPT Vector Effects set of filters.

Arcing curved letters is much more difficult than arcing straight ones, and arcing letters with serifs is slightly more difficult than arcing sans serif letters.

Arcing letters just on one side of a curve can be started easily by selecting just those letters on that half and using the Free Transform tool. Select the letter you want to distort and using the Free Transform tool, click and hold a point of the bounding box and ⌘-Shift [Ctrl-Shift] to adjust the perspective. This does the scaling even more accurately than using the Scale tool because the letters are scaled proportionately and angled automatically.

Masking and Other Effects

Standard type or type that has been converted into outlines can then be used as a mask or Filled with gradients or patterns, as shown in Figure 8-13.

Figure 8-13: Type that has been converted to outlines and is now Filled with a pattern (left) and used as a masking path (right)

For words to work as a single mask, they must first be changed into a compound path. Usually, individual letters of converted type are changed into individual compound paths, whether the letter has a hole in it or not. For masks to work properly, you must select the entire word or words you want to use as a mask and then choose Object ⇨ Compound Paths ⇨ Make (⌘-8) [Ctrl+8]. This changes all the selected letters into one compound path.

In some third-party (non-Adobe) and shareware typefaces, making a compound path out of a series of letters can produce results where the holes are not transparent. This issue is usually one of path direction, which can be corrected by selecting the inner shape (the hole) and changing the direction with the path direction buttons on the Attributes palette.

After the words are a compound path, place them in front of the objects to be masked, select both the words and the masked objects, and then choose Object ⇨ Masks ⇨ Make (⌘-7) [Ctrl+7].

ASK TOULOUSE: Masking Type Mishaps

Kim: I can't get masking with text to work right.

Toulouse: What's happening?

Kim: Only the last letter in the word I'm using as a mask is working like a mask. The other letters disappear.

Toulouse: Did you make a compound path out of all the letters in your word *before* you masked?

Kim: Uh, no. That's bad, huh?

Toulouse: Actually, yes. What's happening now is that the last letter in the word, which is in front of all the other objects that are selected, is trying to mask everything else that's selected.

Kim: Ah, including the other letters.

Toulouse: Exactly. Illustrator has to see the word as *one* path, which is what making a compound path out of the entire word does.

Kim: So to fix it?

Toulouse: First, release the mask, select just the letters, and make them a compound. Then select everything and click Make Mask.

Avoiding Font Conflicts by Creating Outlines

If you ever give your files to a service bureau or to clients, you've probably already run into some font compatibility problems. A font compatibility problem usually means that the place you gave your file to doesn't have a typeface that you used in your Illustrator document.

This is a problem that there is no great solution to, and the trouble seems to be worsening as more font manufacturers spring up — TrueType fonts being the Windows standard, and PostScript Type 1 fonts being the Mac standard. And then there are shareware typefaces, some of which resemble Adobe originals to an uncanny degree of accuracy. All this leads to a great deal of confusion and frustration for the average Illustrator user.

But there is a way around this problem, at least most of the time. Convert your typefaces into outlines *before* you send them to other people with other systems — they don't need your typefaces for the letters to print correctly. In fact, converted letters aren't really considered type anymore, just outlines.

Save your file before converting the text to outlines and then save it as a different file name after converting the text to outlines. This will allow you to do text editing later on the original file, if necessary.

Caution   Converting typefaces to outlines removes the hinting system that Adobe has implemented. This hinting system makes small letters on low-resolution (less than 600 dpi) devices print more accurately, controlling the placement and visibility of serifs and other small, thin strokes in characters. Type at small point sizes looks quite different on laser printers, although it retains its shape and consistency when it is output to an imagesetter or an output scanner system.

Hinting

Most Type 1 fonts have *hinting* built into them. Hinting is a method for adjusting type at small point sizes, especially at low resolutions. Although hinting is built into the fonts, when those fonts are converted into paths via the Create Outlines command, the hinting functionality is gone. This is part of the reason that type converted to outlines can look heavier than it does otherwise.

Creating outlines shouldn't cause that much of a problem when the type is to be output to an imagesetter, because the high resolution of the imagesetter makes up for the loss of hinting. However, very small type — 4 points or less — could be adversely affected.

Find

The Find/Change feature (Type ➪ Find/Change) uses the Find/Change dialog box that is shown in Figure 8-14 to search for and, if necessary, replace certain letters, words, or character combinations.

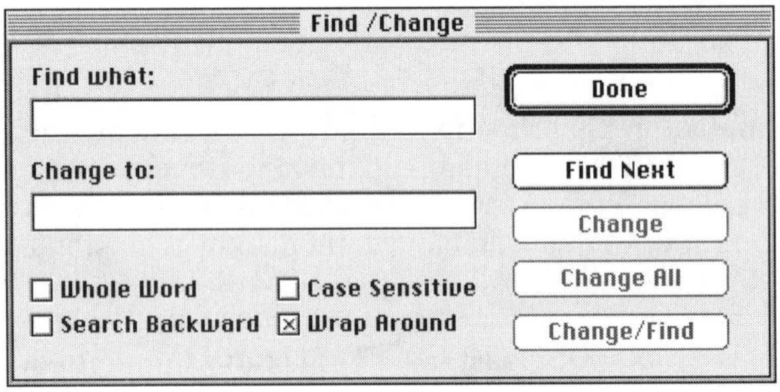

```
┌───────────────────── Find /Change ─────────────────────┐
│                                                         │
│  Find what:                   ┌─────────────────────┐   │
│                               │        Done         │   │
│  ┌───────────────────────┐    └─────────────────────┘   │
│  └───────────────────────┘                              │
│                               ┌─────────────────────┐   │
│  Change to:                   │      Find Next      │   │
│                               └─────────────────────┘   │
│  ┌───────────────────────┐    ┌─────────────────────┐   │
│  └───────────────────────┘    │       Change        │   │
│                               └─────────────────────┘   │
│                               ┌─────────────────────┐   │
│  ☐ Whole Word   ☐ Case Sensitive │    Change All    │   │
│                               └─────────────────────┘   │
│  ☐ Search Backward ☒ Wrap Around ┌────────────────────┐ │
│                               │    Change/Find      │   │
│                               └─────────────────────┘   │
└─────────────────────────────────────────────────────────┘
```

Figure 8-14: The Find/Change dialog box

The options available in the Find/Change dialog box are:

✦ **Whole Word**: Tells Illustrator that the characters you type in the Find What box are an entire word, not part of a word.

✦ **Case Sensitive**: Selects the characters only if they have the same uppercase and lowercase attributes as the characters you type in the Find What text field.

✦ **Search Backward**: Tells Illustrator to look before the current word for the next instance of the characters, instead of using the default, which is to look after the current word.

✦ **Wrap Around**: Keeps Illustrator going through all the text blocks and makes Illustrator continue looking and finding the next occurrence throughout each text block. When it reaches the last text block, it starts where it originally began and continues finding the word or characters that you specified in the Find What box.

The following steps describe how to use these options to find and replace text.

1. Choose Type ➪ Find/Change. The Find/Change dialog box appears.

2. Type the word, phrase, or characters that you want to find in the Find What text field. (You do not need to select areas of type with the Selection or Type tools — all that is necessary is that the document that you want to search be the open and active document.)

3. Check the appropriate options (described in the bulleted list that preceded these steps).

4. Click the Find Next button to find the first occurrence of the word or characters.

5. In the Change To box, type the word or characters that you want to use to replace the text that Illustrator found.

6. Click the Change button to replace the selected text. Click the Change/Find button and then the Find button to replace the selected text and automatically highlight the next matching word or characters. Click the Change All button to replace all occurrences of the word or characters throughout the document.

Caution   Illustrator cannot find words or characters that you have converted to outlines.

Find Font

Find Font looks for certain fonts in a document and replaces them with fonts you specify.

Select type with either a selection tool or with a type tool. Then choose Type ➪ Find Font. The Find Font dialog box appears, as shown in Figure 8-15.

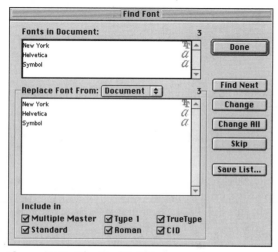

Figure 8-15: The Find Font box

To change all occurrences of a certain font to another font, select the font to be changed in the top window, titled Fonts in Document. Then select a font in the Replacement Font From Document or System pop-up menu window and click the Change All button. To change one particular instance, click the Change button. To find the next occurrence of that font, select Find Next. The Skip button skips over the currently selected text and finds the next occurrence of that font.

Pressing the Save List button enables you to save your font list as a text file. After the fonts are found, you have to select type with the Type tool, no matter how it was selected before Find Font was used.

Check Spelling

Check Spelling checks all text in a document to see if it is spelled (and capitalized) correctly. To use this feature, choose Type ➪ Check Spelling. The Check Spelling dialog box shown in Figure 8-16 appears.

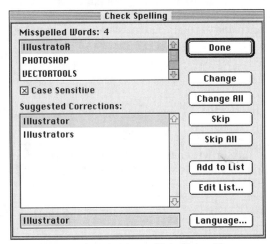

Figure 8-16: The Check Spelling dialog box

Note   Check Spelling uses a standard user dictionary as well as all foreign language and hyphenation dictionaries that are available.

If all words are spelled correctly, a congratulatory message appears telling you that your spelling is "excellent."

If you have any misspelled words or words that are not in the spelling dictionaries, those words are listed at the top of the Check Spelling dialog box in the Misspelled Words window. Selecting a word in this list displays similar words below in the Suggested Corrections window.

If the Case Sensitive option is checked, the capitalization of words must match the words in the spell checker's dictionary, or they will appear as misspelled words.

The Add to List button is used when you would like to add the selected "misspelled" word to your custom dictionary. Clicking the Edit List button displays the Learned Words dialog box, showing you which words are currently in the user dictionary. The Learned Words dialog box enables you to add, remove, or change entries in the user dictionary.

1. To add a new entry to the user dictionary, select the Edit List button in the Check Spelling dialog box, which displays the Learned Words dialog box.

2. Type in the word that you would like to add to the user dictionary. Click the Add button, and the word is added to the list of words in the user dictionary. (Capitalization is very important when adding words, so be sure to place initial caps on proper nouns and to use correct capitalization on all words that require it.) If the word you are trying to add exists in the user dictionary or the main dictionary, a dialog box appears telling you that it is already a dictionary entry.

3. Repeat Step 2 until all the words have been added.

4. If at any time you make a mistake, you may change the spelling of an entered word by selecting it in the window above, typing in the correct spelling, and then clicking the Change button. If you wish to delete an entry that exists in the Learned Words window, select that word and click the Remove button.

5. When you are finished, click the Done button.

The user dictionary words are saved in a file called AI User Dictionary, which is stored in the Plug-Ins folder. The file is in text-compatible format, but the character that separates the words is indistinguishable (it appears as an open rectangle, the symbol for a symbol that is not available in that typeface), so there is no way to add words to the dictionary by using a word processor.

Caution
Be careful not to delete or remove the AI User Dictionary file when reinstalling the software or moving the files in the Plug-Ins folder. Doing so causes Illustrator to create a new user dictionary file with no words in it. There is no way to combine two different user dictionary files. You can drag the AI User Dictionary from the Plug-ins folder of the old version of Illustrator to the Plug-ins folder of the new version.

While you're checking your spelling in the Check Spelling dialog box, clicking the Change button replaces the misspelled word with the highlighted word in the Suggested Corrections list. Clicking the Change All button replaces all misspelled occurrences of that word throughout the entire document with the correctly spelled word.

Clicking the Skip button ignores that occurrence of the misspelled word. Clicking Skip All skips all occurrences of that word in the document.

Clicking the Language button uses a dictionary for the language you specify. Illustrator supplies dictionaries for the United States and the United Kingdom, both located in the Plug-In filters files.

Clicking the Done button closes the Check Spelling dialog box.

Change Case

Change Case converts selected text to one of a variety of case options. To use this filter, select type with a Type tool and then choose Type ➪ Change Case. The Change Case dialog box appears, as shown in Figure 8-17.

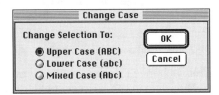

Figure 8-17: The Change Case dialog box

Type *must* be selected with a Type tool (characters must be highlighted) to use the Change Case feature. If type is selected with a Selection tool, then the filter will not work and a dialog box stating this displays.

The three Change Case options affect only letters, not numbers, symbols, or punctuation. The options are as follows:

✦ **UPPER CASE** converts all selected letters into uppercase, regardless of whether any letters were uppercase or lowercase.

✦ **lower case** converts all selected letters into lowercase, regardless of whether any letters were uppercase or lowercase. It also doesn't matter if the letters were originally uppercase because they were typed with the Caps Lock key engaged, or if the uppercase letters were uppercase because of a style format.

✦ **Mixed Case** converts all selected words into lowercase, with the first letter of each word becoming uppercase, regardless of whether any letters were originally uppercase or lowercase. It also doesn't matter if the letters were originally uppercase because they were typed with the Caps Lock key engaged, or if the uppercase letters were uppercase because of a style format. The Mixed Case option separates words by making *any* character that is between letters end one word and begin another. At the time of this writing, even apostrophes in contractions caused words like "don't" and "can't" to display as "Don'T" and "Can'T."

Smart Punctuation

The Smart Punctuation filter looks for certain fonts in a document and replaces them with fonts you specify. To use this filter, select type with either a Selection tool or with a Type tool. Then choose Type ➪ Smart Punctuation. The Smart Punctuation dialog box shown in Figure 8-18 appears.

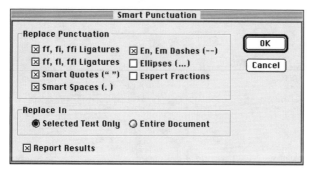

Figure 8-18: The Smart Punctuation dialog box

The Smart Punctuation filter works after the fact, making changes to text already in the Illustrator document. There are no settings, for instance, to convert quotes to curved quotes as you are typing them. The types of punctuation to be changed are determined by a set of checkboxes in the Smart Punctuation dialog box. A checked box means that Illustrator will look for these certain instances and, if it finds them, correct them with the proper punctuation.

The first two options are used for replacing ff, fi (or fl), and ffi (or ffl) with *ligatures*. Ligatures are characters that represent several characters with one character that is designed to let those characters appear nicer when placed next to each other. Most fonts have fi and fl ligatures, which look like fi and fl, respectively.

The remaining Smart Punctuation options work as follows:

✦ **Smart Quotes** replaces straight quotes (" " and ' ') with curly quotes, known as typesetter's quotes or printer's quotes (" " and ' ').

✦ **Smart Spaces** replaces multiple spaces after a period with one space. (In typesetting, there should only be one space following a period.)

✦ **En, Em Dashes** replaces hyphens (-) with en dashes (–) and double hyphens (--) with em dashes (—).

✦ **Ellipses** replaces three periods (...) with an ellipsis (…).

✦ **Expert Fractions** replaces fractions with expert fractions if you have the expert fractions for the font family you are using. Adobe sells "Expert Collection" fonts that contain these fractions. If you do *not* have expert fractions, your fractions remain unchanged.

Checking the Report Results box displays a dialog box when the filter is finished, telling you how many of the punctuation changes were made.

**ASK TOULOUSE: But My Insertion Point
Is Waaayyy Over There**

Hawkeye: My insertion point is possessed.

Toulouse: Possessed, eh?

Hawkeye: When I enter text using the Text tool, my cursor floats 2 to 6 spaces to the right of its actual position in the line of text.

Toulouse: This usually happens when you have both TrueType and Type 1 versions of the same fonts installed.

Hawkeye: How can I fix it?

Toulouse: Just remove one or the other. I'd recommend keeping the PostScript Type 1 version.

Rows & Columns

Rows & Columns divides rectangular paths (text or standard Illustrator rectangles) into even sections.

To use Rows & Columns, select a path and choose Type ➪ Rows & Columns. The Rows & Columns dialog box shown in Figure 8-19 appears.

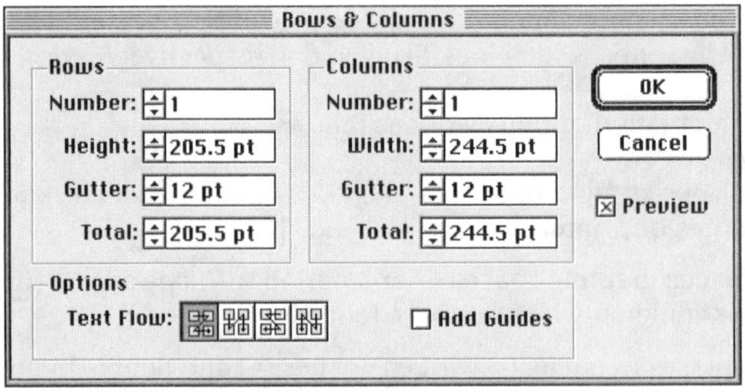

Figure 8-19: The Rows & Columns dialog box

Any text path, open or closed, can be selected and divided into rows and columns, with one catch: the object will become a rectangular shape, the size of the original path's *bounding box* (the smallest box that could completely contain the path).

There is no way to divide a nonrectangular path automatically. See the steps later in this section for a way to do this without Illustrator knowing about it.

The left side of the Rows & Columns dialog box determines the width of the columns. The right side determines the height of the rows. At the bottom of the dialog box is a Preview checkbox; checking this displays changes as you make them in the Rows & Columns dialog box.

Note   All measurements in the Rows & Columns dialog box are displayed in the current measurement system.

The first text field is the Number of Rows that the original path will be divided into. The second text field, Height, is the height of each of the rows. The Height must be less than the Total (the fourth field) divided by the number of rows. The third text field on the left is Gutter, which is the space between rows. The Total is how high the entire rectangle is.

As the Row Height is increased, the Gutter decreases. When Row Height is decreased, the Gutter increases. Likewise, as the Gutter is increased, the Height decreases. When the Gutter is decreased, the Height increases.

In the Column section, Number determines how many columns the selected path will be cut into. Below that, the Width text field determines the width of the columns. The Width must be less than the Total (fourth field) divided by the number of columns. The third text field is Gutter, which is the space between columns. The Total value is how wide the entire rectangle is.

As the Column Width is increased, the Gutter will decrease. When Column Width is decreased, the Gutter increases. Likewise, as the Gutter is increased, the Column Width decreases. When the Gutter is decreased, the Column Width increases.

Remember that using the Rows & Columns feature actually divides the selected rectangle into several pieces.

The Text Flow options determine the direction of text as it flows from one section to the next. You may choose between text that starts along the top row and flows from left to right, and then goes to the next lowest row, flowing from left to right, and so on. The second option is to have text start in the left column, flowing from top to bottom, and then to the next column to the right, flowing from top to bottom. The third option causes text to flow from the upper-right to the upper-left to the lower-right to the lower-left. The fourth (rightmost) option flows the text from the upper-right to the lower-right to the upper-left to the lower-left.

The Add Guides checkbox creates guides that extend off each edge of the page. These guides align with the edges of each of the boxes created from the Rows & Columns feature.

The following steps describe how to create rows and columns in a nonrectangular object, and Figure 8-20 illustrates these steps.

1. Create the object that you wish to divide into rows and columns. (In Figure 8-20, I used type converted to outlines and made the entire word one compound path.)

2. Copy the object to the Clipboard (choose Edit ➪ Copy or press ⌘-C [Ctrl+C]).

3. Choose Type ➪ Rows & Columns and divide the object into the number of rows and columns desired. Click OK. The object becomes rectangular.

4. Paste In Front. The original object appears in front of the rectangle that is divided into rows and columns.

5. Select all objects and choose Object ➪ Pathfinder ➪ Crop. The result is a nonrectangular shape that has been divided into rows and columns.

Figure 8-20: Steps for creating nonrectangular columns and rows

The following steps describe how to create angled rows and columns, and Figure 8-21 illustrates these steps.

1. Create an oversized object that will become the rows and columns.

2. Choose Type ➪ Rows & Columns and divide the object into the rows and columns, but this time specify the size of the rows and columns, not how many you want. Click OK.

3. Rotate the columns and rows you have just created.

4. Create the object that will contain the angled rows and columns, and place it in front of the rows and columns. (In Figure 8-21, I used a plain rectangle.)

5. Select all objects and choose Object ⇨ Pathfinder ⇨ Crop. The result is an object with angled rows and columns within it.

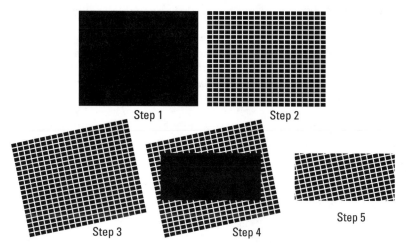

Figure 8-21: Steps for creating angled rows and columns (with outlined sections for easier viewing)

Show Hidden Characters

When you are typing, nonviewing characters such as spaces, returns, and tabs are included. Typically, you don't see these characters. You can choose to view the hidden characters by choosing Show Hidden Characters from the type menu.

Type Orientation

You can easily change the orientation of your type by choosing Type Orientation from the Type menu. That way if you wanted vertical type and did it as horizontal, you can change it easily without retyping it.

Glyph Options

The Glyph Options under the Type menu refers to Japanese fonts. That way you can replace certain characters depending on the variant you need.

Type Areas

For type to exist in Illustrator there must first be a *type area* defined. Type can never be outside these areas because type is treated very differently from any other object in Illustrator.

There are four different kinds of type areas: Point type, Rectangle type, Area type, and Path type. Point type exists around a single point clicked with the standard Type tool. Area type is type that flows within a specific open or closed path. Path type is type whose baseline is attached to a specific open or closed path.

Figure 8-22 shows the same sentence as Point type, Rectangle type, Area type, and Path type.

These are the days you'll remember. Never before and never since, I promise, will the whole world be warm as this.

These   are
the   days
y o u ' l l
remember.
N e v e r
before and
never since,
I   promise,
will   the
whole world
be warm as
this.

T h e s e
are the days
you'll   remember.
Never   before   and
never since, I promise,
will the whole world
be   warm   as
this.

Figure 8-22: The same sentence as it appears (top to bottom) in Point type, Rectangle type, Area type, and Path type

Using the Type Tools

Initially, the six Type tools are used to create type, and then later they can be used to edit that very same type. The default tool is the standard Type tool, which creates both Point type and Area type. The pop-up tools on the tear-away Type palette (shown in Figure 8-23) are the Area Type tool, the Path Type tool, the Vertical Type tool, the Vertical Area Type tool, and the Vertical Path Type tool. (All of these tools are explained in detail in the following sections.) Each of the type tools displays a different cursor.

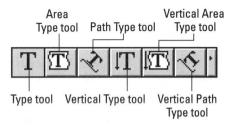

Figure 8-23: The Type tools

You can select type in Illustrator with the Selection tool, in which case *all* the type in the story is modified (a *story* is a contiguous set of type in Point type, Rectangle type, Area type, or Path type).

You select type with a Type tool by dragging across either characters or lines — every character from the initial click until the release of the mouse button is selected. Double-clicking with a Type tool selects the entire word you clicked, including the space after it. Triple-clicking (clicking three times in the same place) selects an entire paragraph.

You can enter new type into an existing story by clicking with a Type tool where you want the new type to begin and then typing. If type is highlighted when you begin typing, the highlighted type is replaced with the new type.

The original reason for the inclusion of a vertical type capability in Illustrator was for Japanese type (commonly referred to as Kanji) compatibility. Vertical type can have a number of specialized uses as well. The following sections that discuss the different types of type blocks (Point, Rectangle, Area, and Path) address both normal (horizontal) type and vertical type capabilities.

The Type Tool

With the Type tool, you can do everything you need to do with type. Clicking in any empty part of your document creates Point type, an Anchor Point to which the type aligns. Type created as Point type does not wrap automatically; instead, you must manually press the Return key and start typing the next line. Point type is usually used for creating smaller portions of type, like labels and headlines.

Clicking and dragging with the Type tool creates Area type—type that is bordered by a box, which you create when you click and drag the Type tool.

As the Type tool passes over a closed path, it changes automatically into the Area Type tool. Clicking a closed path results in type that fills the shape of the area you clicked. Holding down the Option [Alt] key as you pass over a closed path changes the tool into the Path Type tool. This intelligent switching of Type tools by Illustrator keeps you from having to choose different Type tools when you want a different kind of type.

If the Type tool crosses over an open path, it becomes the Path Type tool. Clicking an open path places type *on the path,* with the baseline of the type aligning along the curves and angles of the path. Holding down the Option [Alt] key when the Type tool is over an open path changes it into the Area Type tool.

The Type tool can be toggled to the Vertical Type tool by pressing the Shift key. In fact, pressing the Shift key with the Area Type and Path Type tools automatically toggles those tools to their Vertical Type counterparts. This holds true even if you press Shift along with the Option [Alt] key (when toggling between Area Type and Path Type tools).

The Area Type Tool

The Area Type tool is used for Filling closed or open paths with type. Even compound paths can be Filled in Illustrator.

Tip   You can toggle between the Area Type tool and the Path Type tool by pressing the Option [Alt] key.

The Path Type Tool

The Path Type tool is used for running type along any path in Illustrator. This is a great tool for putting type on the edges of a circle.

Tip   You can toggle between the Path Type tool and the Area Type tool by pressing the Option [Alt] key.

The Vertical Type Tools

Vertical type? I was a little confused when I first saw this tool in Version 7 (and its Area and Path counterparts). The easiest way to understand how the Vertical Type tools work is by example. Figure 8-24 shows the same line of type created with the regular Type tool and the Vertical Type tool. For the most part, the Vertical Type tool works like the regular Type tool, but instead of placing characters side by side, characters are placed from top to bottom. Because this area of Illustrator can be a little unusual, I've added a section later in this chapter that directly addresses vertical type and related issues.

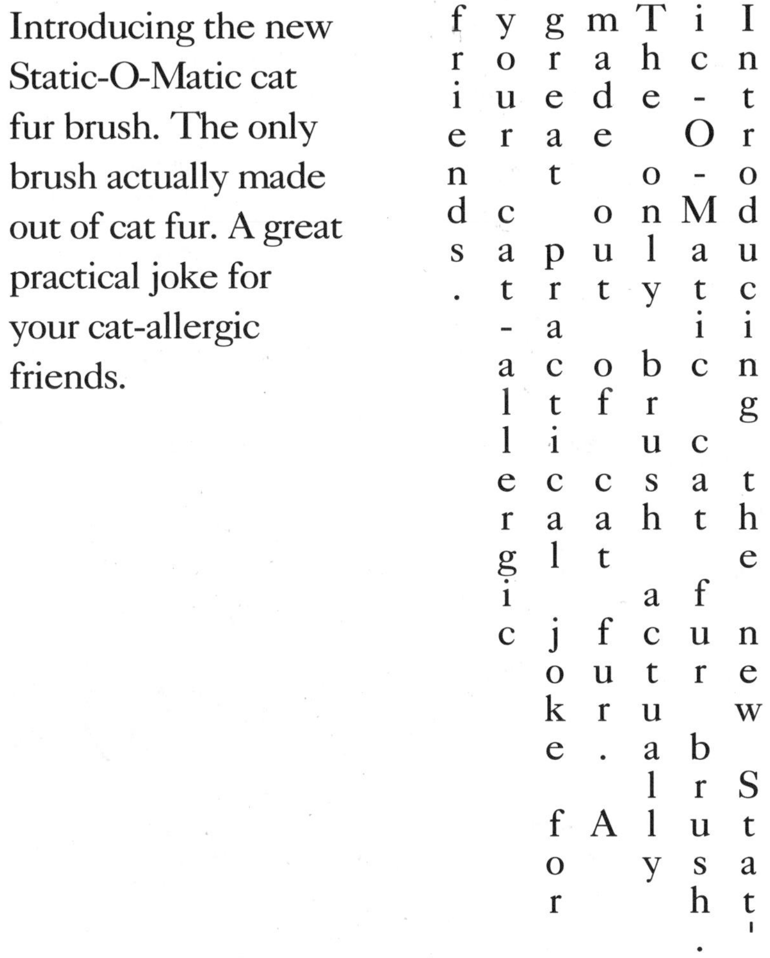

Introducing the new Static-O-Matic cat fur brush. The only brush actually made out of cat fur. A great practical joke for your cat-allergic friends.

```
f  y  g  m  T  i  I
r  o  r  a  h  c  n
i  u  e  d  e  -  t
e  r  a  e     O  r
n     t        o  -  o
d  c        o  n  M  d
s  a  p  u  l  a  u
.  t  r  t  y  t  c
   -  a        i  i
a  c  o  b  c  n
l  t  f  r     g
l  i        u  c
e  c  c  s  a  t
r  a  a  h  t  h
g  l  t        e
i        a  f
c  j  f  c  u  n
   o  u  t  r  e
   k  r  u     w
   e  .  a  b
         l  r  S
   f  A  l  u  t
   o     y  s  a
   r        h  t
         .        ı
```

Figure 8-24: Horizontal and vertical type

Point Type

To create type with a single point defining its location, use the Type tool and click a single location within the document window where there are no paths. A blinking *insertion point* appears, which signifies that type will appear where that point is located (see Figure 8-25). When you type on the keyboard, text appears in the document at that insertion point. Type cannot be entered when a Selection tool is being used. Type selected with a Selection tool appears at the bottom of Figure 8-25.

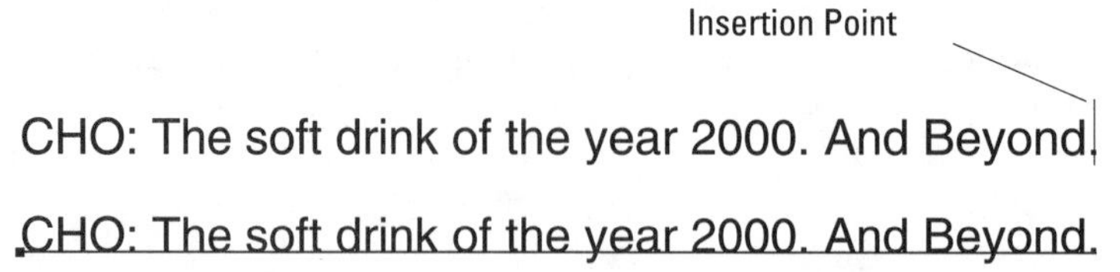

Insertion Point

CHO: The soft drink of the year 2000. And Beyond.

CHO: The soft drink of the year 2000. And Beyond.

Figure 8-25: Point type with an insertion point at the end of the line, and the same line of type selected with a Selection tool

Type the Right Way

Although at first it seems quite simple to outline characters of type using a 1-point Stroke in the Stroke palette, just slapping on a Stroke of a weight that seems to look good on the screen and changing the Fill to None or white is technically incorrect.

The right way to outline type is only a little bit more involved. First, select the type that you want outlined and give the type a Stroke that is twice the weight you want on the printed piece. Then Copy, Paste In Front, and give the new type a Stroke of None and a Fill of white. The white Fill knocks out the inside half of the Stroke, leaving the Stroke one-half the width you specified, which is what you really want.

The following figure shows both the right way and the wrong way to outline type. The top line is the original type. The middle line is outlined the wrong way with a 1-point Stroke and a Fill of white. The bottom part of the figure shows "100% Natural" outlined correctly, first with a white Fill and no Stroke, and then with a 2-point Stroke.

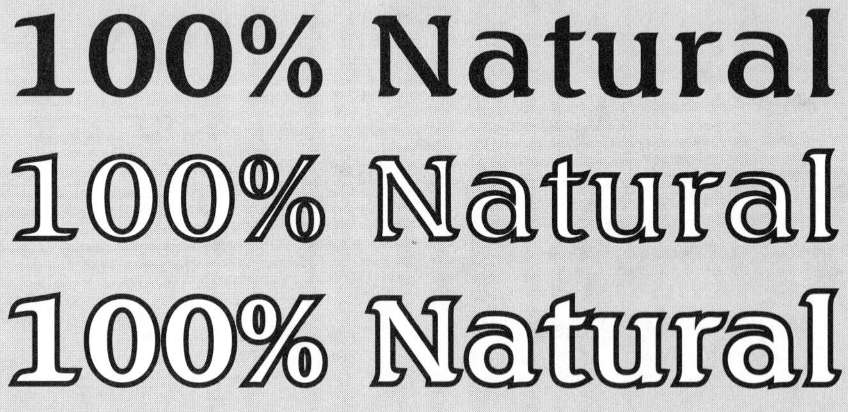

100% Natural
100% Natural
100% Natural

"Serif preservation," as it's known to a select few, requires a teeny bit of math, but it's worth the effort. The white area inside the Stroke is exactly the size of the character when done this way, as opposed to being smaller by half the width of the Stroke when done normally.

Note When the Illustrator program is first launched, text defaults to these values: 12-point Helvetica, Flush left, Auto Leading On, Spacing 0, Baseline Shift 0, Tracking/Kerning 0, Horizontal Scale 100%, Auto Kerning On, and no indentation or paragraph spacing. There is no method within Illustrator to automatically change this default at startup of the program.

Point type that is flush left has its left side flush against the vertical location of the point initially clicked. Centered type is centered left to right on the vertical location of the point. Flush right type has its right edge flush with the vertical location of the point. Point type cannot be justified with either of the two methods available.

Caution When creating Point type, remember that only a hard Return forces a new line of text to be created. If no Returns are used, text eventually runs right off the document. When importing text used as Point type, be sure that the text contains these hard Returns, or the text will run into oblivion. Hard Returns can be added after importing, but it may be difficult to do so.

Area Type As a Rectangle

There are two ways to create Rectangle type (see Figure 8-26). The easiest way is by clicking and dragging the Type tool diagonally, which creates a rectangle as you drag. The blinking insertion point appears in the top row of text, with its horizontal location dependent on the text alignment choice. Choosing flush right forces the insertion point to appear in the upper-right corner; centered puts the insertion point in the center of the row; and flush left, or one of the justification methods, makes the insertion point appear in the upper-left corner.

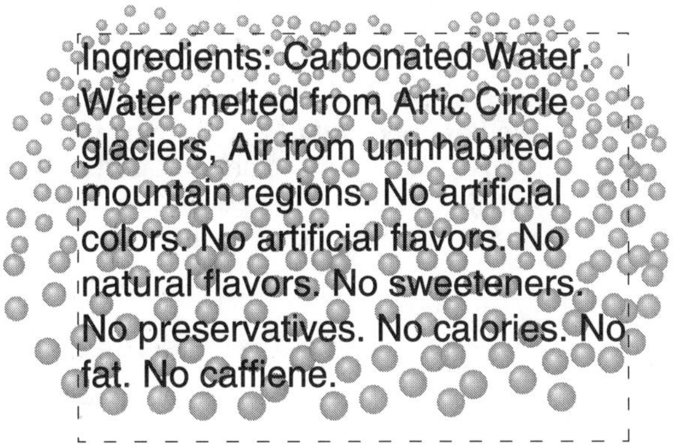

Ingredients: Carbonated Water. Water melted from Artic Circle glaciers, Air from uninhabited mountain regions. No artificial colors. No artificial flavors. No natural flavors. No sweeteners. No preservatives. No calories. No fat. No caffiene.

Figure 8-26: Area type (the dotted line is the border of the rectangle)

If you press the Shift key while drawing the rectangle, the rectangle is constrained to a perfect square. There is no need to drag from upper left to lower right — you can drag from any corner to its opposite — whichever way is most convenient.

To create type in a rectangle of specific proportions, draw a rectangle with the Rectangle tool by clicking once in the document window. The Rectangle Size dialog box appears, and you can enter the information needed. Then choose the Area Type tool and click the edge of the rectangle. The type will fill the rectangle as you type.

1. Using the Rectangle tool, click without dragging to get the Rectangle dialog box. Enter the exact dimensions of the type area.

2. Choose the Type tool and click the Type cursor on the edge of the rectangle. Any type entered into this box will be constrained to that particular rectangle.

Caution   Once a rectangle has been used as a type rectangle, it is always a type rectangle, even if the text is removed.

If you need to create a Rectangle type area that is a precise size but don't want to draw a rectangle first, open the Info palette by choosing Window ⇨ Show Info (F8) and as you drag the type cursor, watch the information in the Info palette, which will display the dimensions of the type area. When the W field is the width you want, and the H field is the height you want, release the mouse button.

Area Type

The capability of placing type within any area is one of the cooler features of Illustrator, right up there with the fact that the program comes in a hip, 1990s-looking box.

To create type within an area, first create the path that will be the area that confines the type. The path can be closed or open and any size. Remember that the area of the path should be close to the size needed for the amount of text (at the point size that it needs to fit). After the path has been created, choose the Area Type tool and position the type cursor over the edge of the path and click.

The type in Figure 8-27 was flowed into the outline of the CHO logo. Using text wraps, the type exists only inside the letters yet reads across all of them.

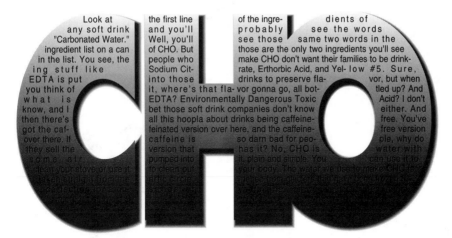

Figure 8-27: Area type created so that the text flows inside the outlines of "CHO"

Choosing the Good Shapes for Area Type

What exactly constitutes a "good" shape to be used for Area type? As a rule of thumb, gently curved shapes are better than harsh, jagged ones. Type tends to flow better into the larger lumps created by smoothly curving paths.

Try to avoid creating paths with wild or tight curves. Other designs that can cause problems are "hourglass" shapes or any closed path that has an area where the sides are almost touching. Figure 8-28 shows how type flows into a smoothly curved area and how it has trouble flowing into a sharp, spiky shape.

Try to make the top and bottom boundaries of the path have less "bumpiness" than the sides. This reduces the number of times that type jumps from one area to another.

For the best results with Area type, make the type small and Force Justify it (⌘-Shift-J) [Ctrl+Shift+J]. This will ensure that the type flows up against the edges of the path.

Figure 8-28: Type flows much better into a smoothly curved area (left) than a sharp, spiky one

Outlining Areas of Area Type

Placing a Stroke on the path surrounding Area type can be a great visual effect, but doing so and getting good results can be a bit tricky.

If the Stroke is thicker than 1 or 2 points, and you don't want the type to run into the edges of the Stroke, there are a few things you can do.

The fastest way to do this (although it requires a bit of math) is to copy the Stroked path that contains the type and paste it in front. Fill the shape with the background color and a Stroke equal to twice the amount of white space you would like between the Stroke and the text. Then hide the path and the type, and select the original path. Delete the text from this path and use the following formula to calculate the correct Stroke width:

(Desired Width + White Space Size) × 2 = Bottom Layer Stroke Weight

For example, if you want a Stroke that is 6 points wide on a shape and has 3 points of white space between the Stroke and the text, the bottom shape will have a Stroke of (6 + 3) × 2 = 18. The top layer will have a "white" Stroke of 6, with a Fill the same color as the Stroke.

The second way to do this is by using the Offset Path filter. This is better for two reasons: First, it requires much less math, and second, you don't have to worry about background color (especially if the background is a bunch of other objects or a placed raster image). Of course, there is a catch: The path cannot be turned into a text area boundary before Offset Path is applied to it.

1. Create a path for your Area type with any drawing tool. Close the path for the best results when using Offset Path.

2. Do not make the path into a type area by clicking the path with a Type tool at this point. Select the path you wish to use for Area type with the Selection tool and then choose Object ⇨ Path ⇨ Offset Path.

3. Determine the distance that you wish your text to be from the edge of the real path. If there is a Stroke on the edge of the real path, add half the width of the Stroke to your distance. In the Offset field, enter this distance in negative form. For example, if you want the distance from the edge of the path to be 6 points and the width of the Stroke is 10 points, you would enter **−11** points in the Offset field (6+(10/2)).

4. After you click OK, a new path is created inside the original. Click on this path with the Area Type tool; the text appears "inside" the edge, with a buffer (see Figure 8-29).

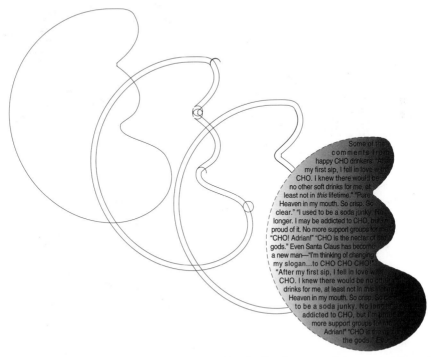

Figure 8-29: Steps to create Area type with a buffer between the type and the edge

Doing Bizarre Things with Area Type

Probably the most overlooked rule when it comes to manipulating Area type and the paths that create the type boundaries is the simple fact that the path and the type are treated equally, unless the path is chosen with the Direct Selection (or Group Selection) tool. Area type is selected when there is an underline under all the characters in the area.

When using the transformation tools, be sure that if you don't want to change any of the characteristics of the type, you select just the path. Use the Group Selection tool to click once on the deselected path, and only the path is selected, not the type.

If the type is selected as well as the path, then the transformations will affect both the type and the path. Figure 8-30 shows transformations taking place to both type and the surrounding path as opposed to transformations taking place to just the surrounding path.

Figure 8-30: The original (left) after both the type and the path have been transformed (top right) and after only the path has been transformed (bottom right)

Coloring Type That Is Anchored to a Path

When type is anchored to a path, either as Area type or Path type, there are some important considerations to think of before Filling and Stroking the type.

First, if just the type or just the path is selected with the regular Selection tool, the other (path or type) is selected as well. Do you want to put a Stroke along that path that surrounds your type? If you select the path with the regular Selection tool, then the type is selected as well, and each character in the type area will have the same Stroke you meant to apply to the path.

For changing just the path's Paint Style attributes, be sure to use the Direct Selection tool to select the path. If an underline doesn't appear under the text, then the text is *not* selected. To change all of the text, you must choose a Type tool, click within the text area, and then use the Select All command (⌘-A) [Ctrl+A]. Only then will just the text be affected.

Changing the Area, Not the Type

Many times, you'll need to adjust the path that makes up the area of the Area type, like scaling that path up or down so that the text flows better. The trick here is to make sure that the entire path is selected without selecting any of the characters. To do this, deselect the type and select the path with the Group Selection tool (the hollow arrow with the + sign).

Now any changes you make will only affect the path, so you can scale it, rotate it, or change its Paint Style attributes without directly affecting the text within it. Figure 8-31 shows a path that has been transformed, allowing the text inside to flow differently.

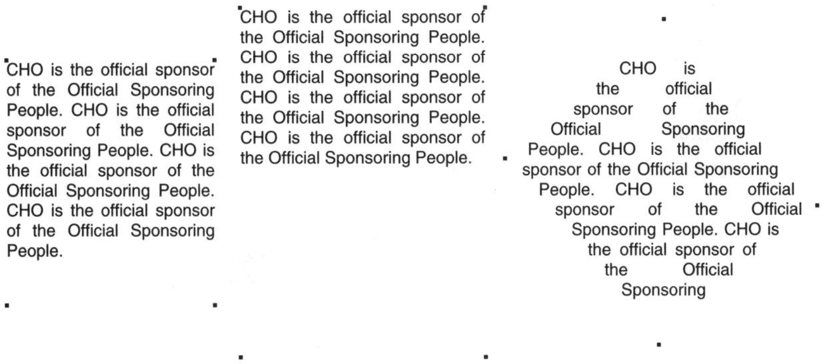

CHO is the official sponsor of the Official Sponsoring People. CHO is the official sponsor of the Official Sponsoring People. CHO is the official sponsor of the Official Sponsoring People. CHO is the official sponsor of the Official Sponsoring People.

CHO is the official sponsor of the Official Sponsoring People. CHO is the official sponsor of the Official Sponsoring People. CHO is the official sponsor of the Official Sponsoring People. CHO is the official sponsor of the Official Sponsoring People. CHO is the official sponsor of the Official Sponsoring People. CHO is the official sponsor of the Official Sponsoring People.

CHO is the official sponsor of the Official Sponsoring People. CHO is the official sponsor of the Official Sponsoring People. CHO is the official sponsor of the Official Sponsoring People. CHO is the official sponsor of the Official Sponsoring

Figure 8-31: Changing the size (middle) and rotation (right) of the original path (left) only affects the text flow, not the text itself

Type Color and the Color of Type

There is a difference between the *color of type* and *type color*. Type can be painted in Illustrator to be any one of millions of different shades, which determines the color we normally think of.

The color of type, on the other hand, is the way the type appears in the document and is more indicative of the light or dark attributes of the text. The actual red-green-blue colors of the type do work into this appearance, but many times the weight of the type and the tracking and kerning have a much more profound effect on color.

To easily see the color of type, unfocus your eyes as you look at your document, or turn the page upside down. This works better on a printed area than onscreen, but you can still get the gist of the way it will appear when viewing it on your monitor. Dark and light areas become much more apparent when you can't read the actual words on the path. This method of unfocusing your eyes to look at a page also works well when trying to see the "look" of a page and how it was designed. Many times, unfocusing or turning the page upside down will emphasize the fact that you don't have enough white space or that all the copy seems to blend together.

Heavy type weights such as boldface, heavy, and black, make type appear darker on a page. Type kerned and tracked very tightly also seems to give the type a darker feel.

The x-height of type (the height to which the lowercase letters, such as an *x*, rise) is another factor that determines the color of type. Certain italic versions of typefaces can make the text seem lighter, although a few make text look darker because of the additional area that the thin strokes of the italic type covers.

Combined with red-green-blue colors, type can be made to stand out by appearing darker, or blend into the page when lighter. When you add smartly placed images near the type, your page can come alive with color.

Area Type Flowing into Shapes

All sorts of nifty things can be done with type that has been flowed into areas — from unusual column designs to fascinating shapes.

Using nonrectangular columns can liven up a publication quite easily. *Mondo 2000* magazine uses curved columns that are easy to read and lend a futuristic, hip look to the publication. Angled and curved columns are simple to create in Illustrator by creating the shape of the column and flowing Area type from one shape to the next.

Traditionally, forcing type into an irregular (nonrectangular) area was quite a task. The typesetter had to set several individual lines of type, each specced by the art director or client to be a certain specific length so that when all the text was put together, the text formed the shape (see Figure 8-32). This is probably the main reason the world has not seen too much of this, except in overly zealous art students' portfolios.

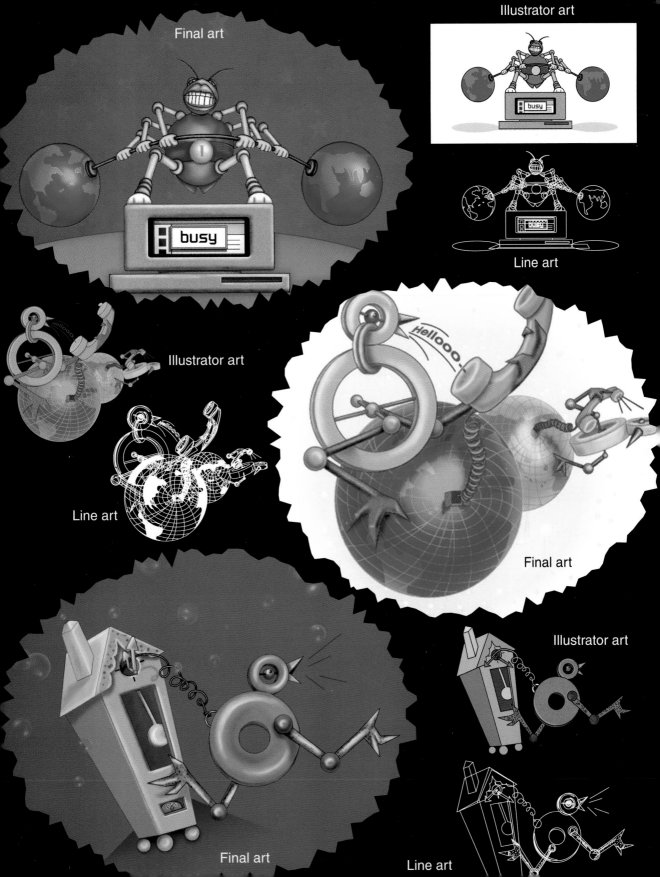

Final art

Illustrator art

Line art

Illustrator art

Line art

Final art

Final art

Illustrator art

Line art

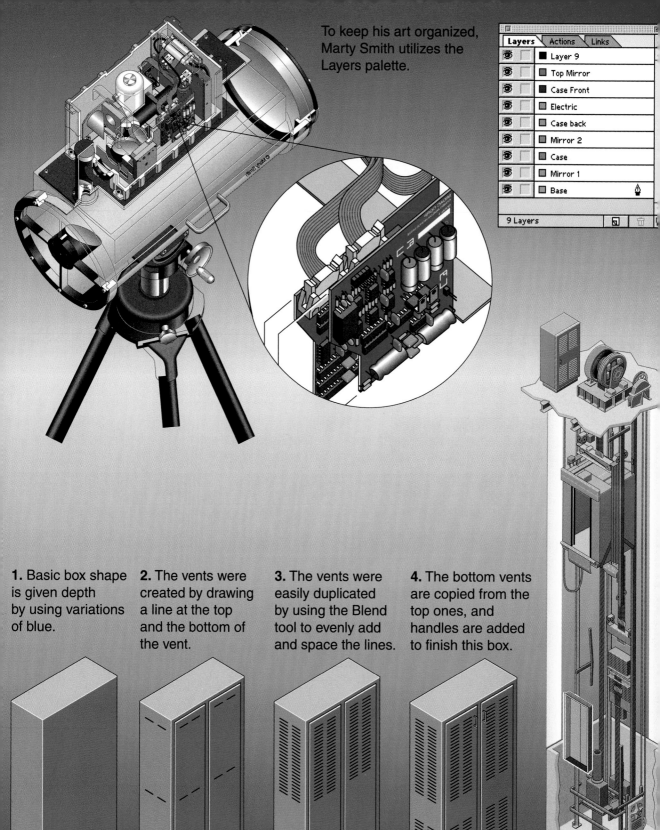

To keep his art organized, Marty Smith utilizes the Layers palette.

Layers | Actions | Links

Layer 9
Top Mirror
Case Front
Electric
Case back
Mirror 2
Case
Mirror 1
Base

9 Layers

1. Basic box shape is given depth by using variations of blue.

2. The vents were created by drawing a line at the top and the bottom of the vent.

3. The vents were easily duplicated by using the Blend tool to evenly add and space the lines.

4. The bottom vents are copied from the top ones, and handles are added to finish this box.

©1998 ART WORKS STUDIO

HOW
MACS WORK

BESTSELLER EDITION

- Understanding the **inner workings** of your Mac
- Learn how the **Mac ROM chip** gives the Mac its unique look and feel
- Part of the best-selling *How It Works* series

JOHN RIZZO AND K. DANIEL CLARK

In the cover image above, K. Daniel Clark talks about how he approached creating this illustration. "The publisher provided me with a Mac which I took apart and visualized into this whole piece. Visualizing how something will look with the roof torn off is the toughest part of my job. I can see all the parts on my desk, but to then reassemble them in my head-where they actually are in the machine-is very challenging and the task I enjoy the most."

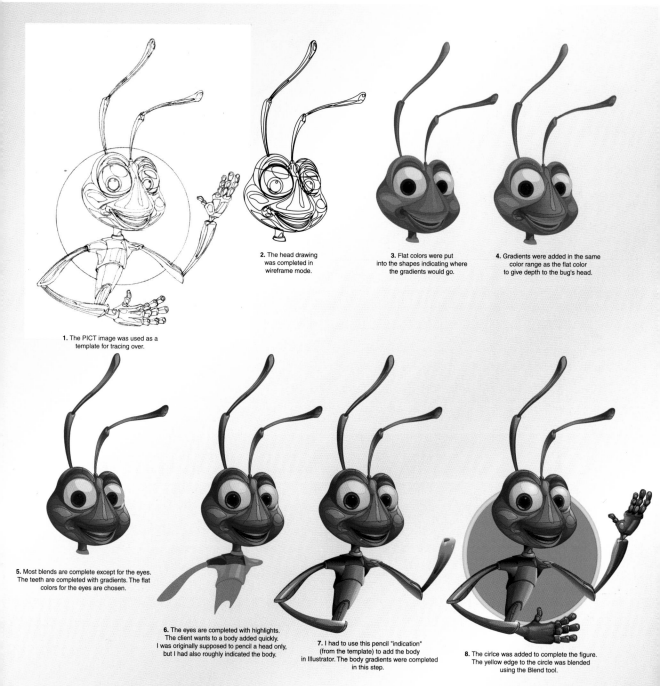

1. The PICT image was used as a template for tracing over.

2. The head drawing was completed in wireframe mode.

3. Flat colors were put into the shapes indicating where the gradients would go.

4. Gradients were added in the same color range as the flat color to give depth to the bug's head.

5. Most blends are complete except for the eyes. The teeth are completed with gradients. The flat colors for the eyes are chosen.

6. The eyes are completed with highlights. The client wants to a body added quickly. I was originally supposed to pencil a head only, but I had also roughly indicated the body.

7. I had to use this pencil "indication" (from the template) to add the body in Illustrator. The body gradients were completed in this step.

8. The cirlce was added to complete the figure. The yellow edge to the circle was blended using the Blend tool.

Line art

lid color is filled
in the shapes

adients are added
to create depth

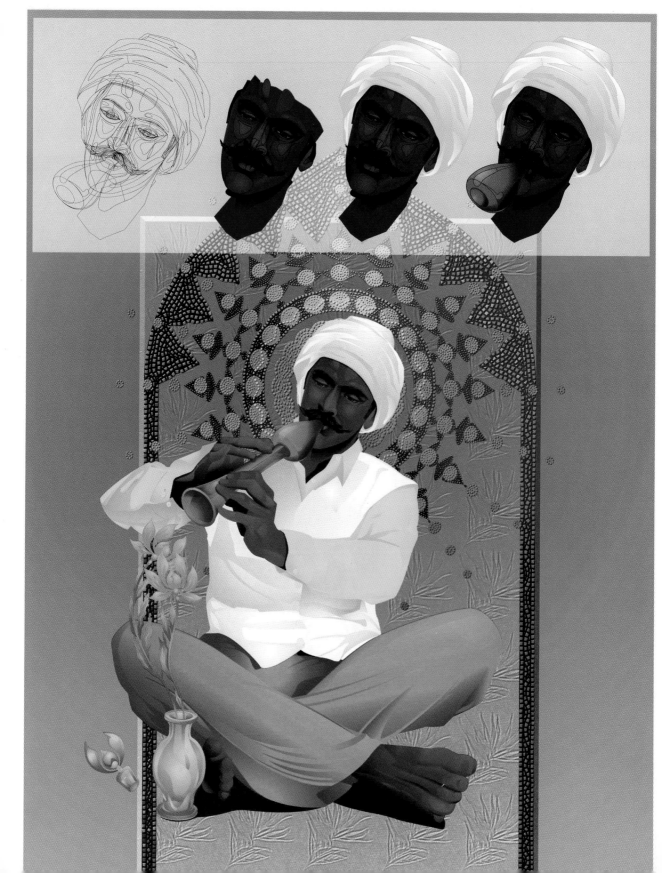

Robert Burger takes full advantage of patterns in his illustrations. After creating a new pattern, you can drop the pattern into the Swatches palette.

PARADIGM DIGITAL PARADIGM DIGITAL

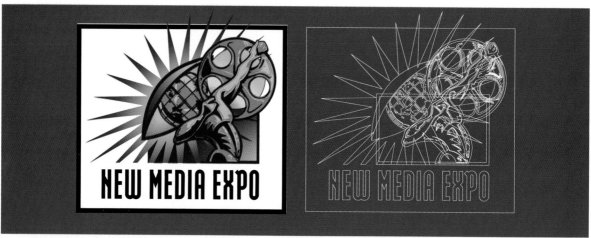

NEW MEDIA EXPO NEW MEDIA EXPO

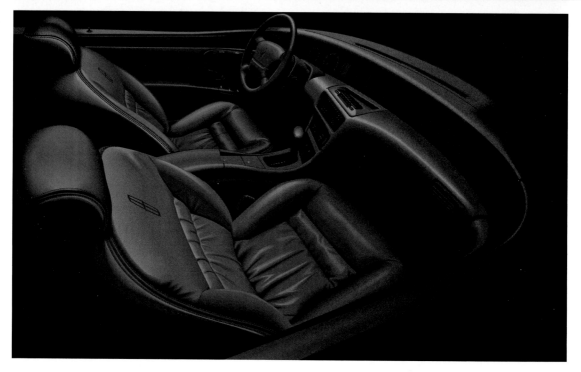

This amazing realistic car interior was totally
done in Illustrator using blends to the fullest

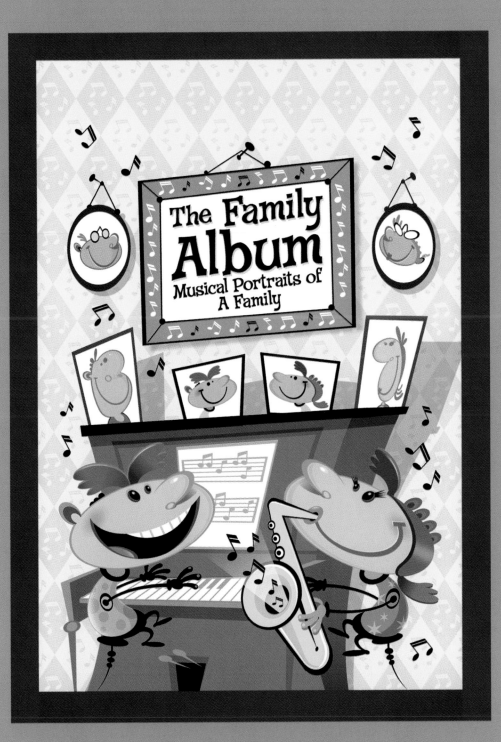

APRIL 1998 • $5.00

Presentations

TECHNOLOGY AND TECHNIQUES FOR EFFECTIVE COMMUNICATION

Engineers gave him a flat top view of the 8-sided robot-arm assembly which he used as the starting place. From that, Dan added the parts that connect outward, all this while still just a top view. Then he rotated and skewed it into a perspective type view. Then, he built the shapes vertically based on photographs. Dan used the outline paths filter to quickly create the many wires from single strokes. Once all the parts were correct, and he received approval from the client, the parts were fully rendered with all the subtle shadows and highlights. The front control panel was separated from the robot-arm assembly and the two were saved individually. The two files were then opened in Photoshop. The control panel was on the top layer and blended with the background using an anti-aliased eraser to clearly show the wafer being loaded into the processor.

Artist: K. Daniel Clark

Getting the Picture

TV Stations Develop New Enthusiasm for Digital Future

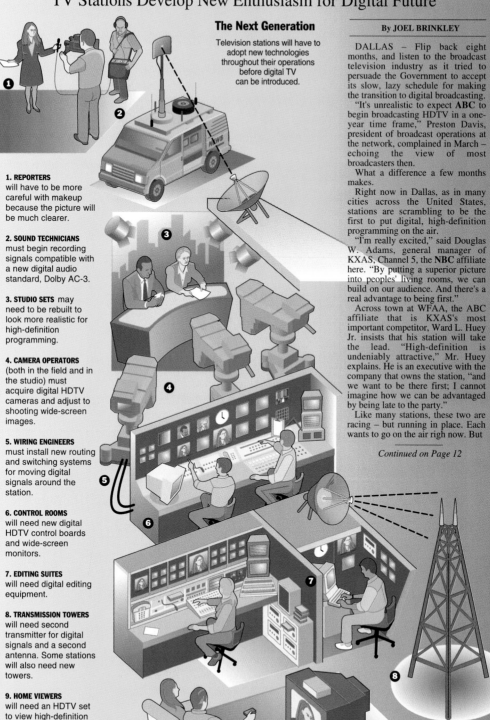

The Next Generation

Television stations will have to adopt new technologies throughout their operations before digital TV can be introduced.

1. REPORTERS
will have to be more careful with makeup because the picture will be much clearer.

2. SOUND TECHNICIANS
must begin recording signals compatible with a new digital audio standard, Dolby AC-3.

3. STUDIO SETS may need to be rebuilt to look more realistic for high-definition programming.

4. CAMERA OPERATORS
(both in the field and in the studio) must acquire digital HDTV cameras and adjust to shooting wide-screen images.

5. WIRING ENGINEERS
must install new routing and switching systems for moving digital signals around the station.

6. CONTROL ROOMS
will need new digital HDTV control boards and wide-screen monitors.

7. EDITING SUITES
will need digital editing equipment.

8. TRANSMISSION TOWERS
will need second transmitter for digital signals and a second antenna. Some stations will also need new towers.

9. HOME VIEWERS
will need an HDTV set to view high-definition programs, or a converter box to see shows in standard definition on older sets.

By JOEL BRINKLEY

DALLAS – Flip back eight months, and listen to the broadcast television industry as it tried to persuade the Government to accept its slow, lazy schedule for making the transition to digital broadcasting.

"It's unrealistic to expect **ABC** to begin broadcasting HDTV in a one-year time frame," Preston Davis, president of broadcast operations at the network, complained in March – echoing the view of most broadcasters then.

What a difference a few months makes.

Right now in Dallas, as in many cities across the United States, stations are scrambling to be the first to put digital, high-definition programming on the air.

"I'm really excited," said Douglas W. Adams, general manager of KXAS, Channel 5, the **NBC** affiliate here. "By putting a superior picture into peoples' living rooms, we can build on our audience. And there's a real advantage to being first."

Across town at WFAA, the ABC affiliate that is KXAS's most important competitor, Ward L. Huey Jr. insists that his station will take the lead. "High-definition is undeniably attractive," Mr. Huey explains. He is an executive with the company that owns the station, "and we want to be there first; I cannot imagine how we can be advantaged by being late to the party."

Like many stations, these two are racing – but running in place. Each wants to go on the air right now. But

Continued on Page 12

Illustration by Joe Shoulak for The New York Times

1. Joe Shoulak starts out with colored shapes that he'll blend to create the contours of the dinosaur's body.

2. Joe combines the use of blends with overlaying stripes to add the shadows and depth to the dinosaur

3. This illustration was done for The Weekly Reader It was created to accompany a story about "Supersonic Dinosaurs." It's theorized that the Diplodocus would whip its tail at the speed of sound and cause a sonic boom to keep predators away.

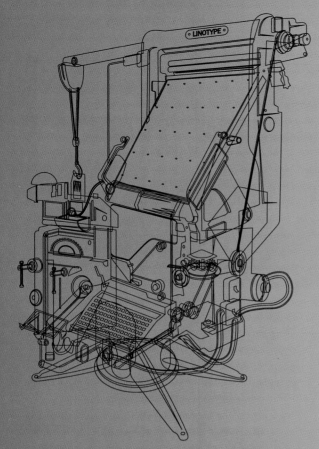

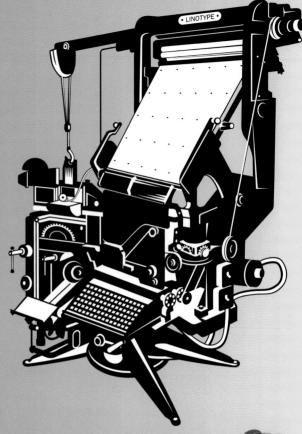

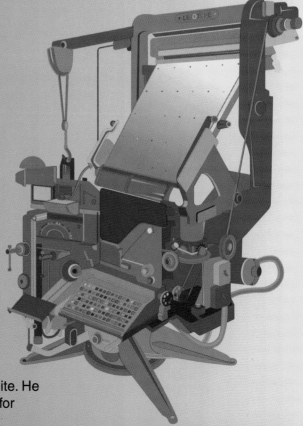

Joe Shoulak initially created this image in Black and White. He used the Extensis Vector Tools' "Random" fill color filter for coloring in the Linotype Machine.

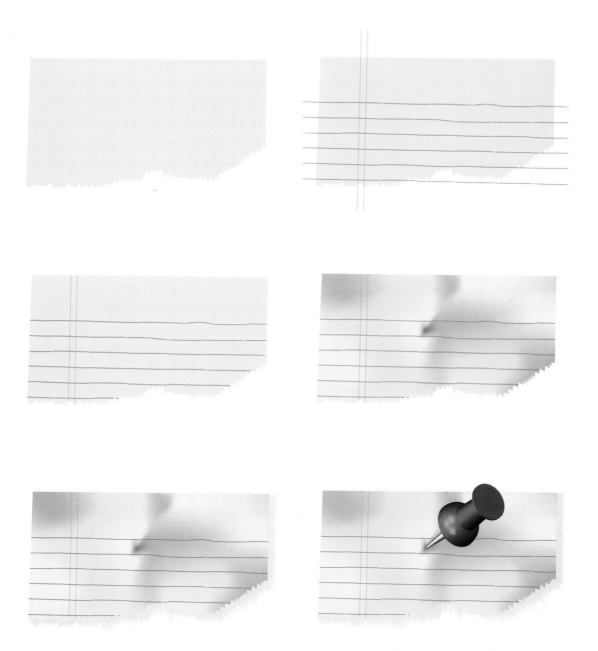

The initial paper was given a base color and a ragged edge. The lines were added on top and trimmed to fit the paper. The Gradient Mesh tool was used to create the folds and crinkle of the paper as well as the dimple of the push pin. A shadow was created under the paper using blends. The final push pin (done in Dimensions) was added. The artist for this image is Sandee Cohen.

Step 1: Inking and lines

Step 2: Add shading and blends

Step 3: Add dramatic background

Jennifer Alspach

City Three was created by Joe Jones of Artworks Studio. This is a prime example of how Illustrator is used to create the line art and color blocks before taking it into Photoshop for enhancing.

This illustration by Joe Jones was done using Illustrator for most of the drawing and color application. He then uses Photoshop to add some cool effects and photographic images.

Joe Jones of Artworks Studio

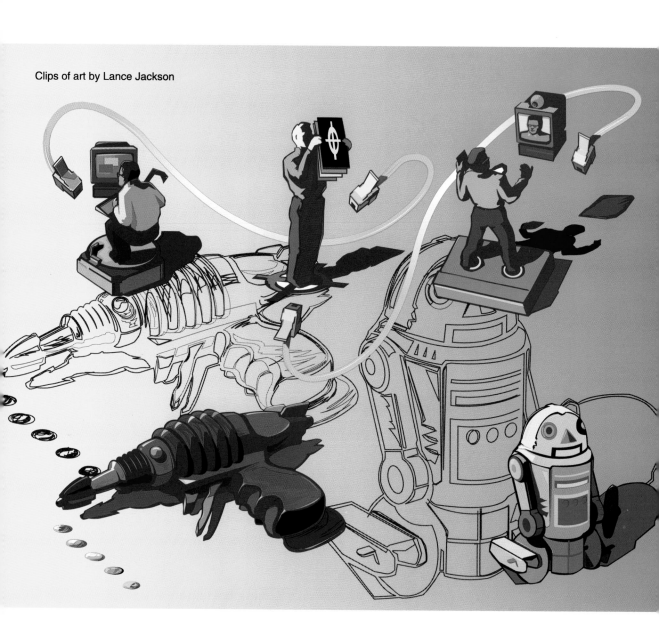

Clips of art by Lance Jackson

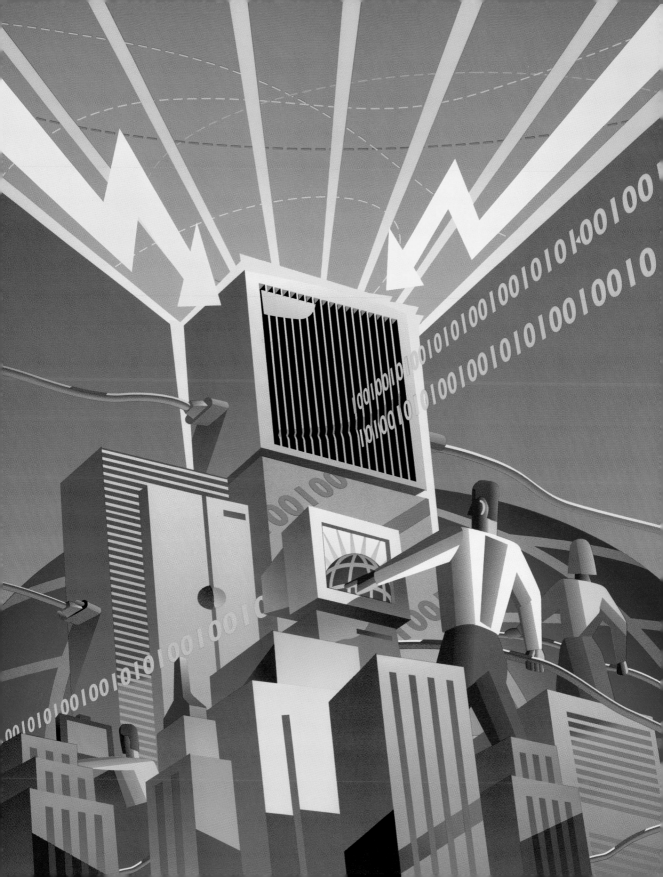

These unusual pet portraits were created using Adobe Streamline, Adobe Illustrator, and Extensis VectorTools. The images were Streamlined from a photograph, then brought into Illustrator to add text, borders, and alter color. The color was altered with VectorColor.

1998

January
```
          1  2
 3  4  5  6  7  8  9
10 11 12 13 14 15 16
17 18 19 20 21 22 23
24 25 26 27 28 29 30
31
```

February
```
 1  2  3  4  5  6
 7  8  9 10 11 12 13
14 15 16 17 18 19 20
21 22 23 24 25 26 27
28
```

March
```
 1  2  3  4  5  6
 7  8  9 10 11 12 13
14 15 16 17 18 19 20
21 22 23 24 25 26 27
28 29 30 31
```

April
```
          1  2  3
 4  5  6  7  8  9 10
11 12 13 14 15 16 17
18 19 20 21 22 23 24
25 26 27 28 29 30
```

May
```
                   1
 2  3  4  5  6  7  8
 9 10 11 12 13 14 15
16 17 18 19 20 21 22
23 24 25 26 27 28 29
30 31
```

June
```
       1  2  3  4  5
 6  7  8  9 10 11 12
13 14 15 16 17 18 19
20 21 22 23 24 25 26
27 28 29 30
```

July
```
             1  2  3
 4  5  6  7  8  9 10
11 12 13 14 15 16 17
18 19 20 21 22 23 24
25 26 27 28 29 30 31
```

Robert Forsbach

August
```
 1  2  3  4  5  6  7
 8  9 10 11 12 13 14
15 16 17 18 19 20 21
22 23 24 25 26 27 28
29 30 31
```

September
```
          1  2  3  4
 5  6  7  8  9 10 11
12 13 14 15 16 17 18
19 20 21 22 23 24 25
26 27 28 29 30
```

October
```
             1  2
 3  4  5  6  7  8  9
10 11 12 13 14 15 16
17 18 19 20 21 22 23
24 25 26 27 28 29 30
31
```

November
```
 1  2  3  4  5  6
 7  8  9 10 11 12 13
14 15 16 17 18 19 20
21 22 23 24 25 26 27
28 29 30
```

December
```
          1  2  3  4
 5  6  7  8  9 10 11
12 13 14 15 16 17 18
19 20 21 22 23 24 25
26 27 28 29 30 31
```

Art by Robert Farabach

	100%	90%	80%	70%	60%	50%	40%	30%	20%	10%	5%
Cyan											
Magenta											
Yellow											
Black											
Cyan/Magenta											
Cyan/Yellow											
Cyan/Black											
Magenta/Yellow											
Magenta/Black											
Yellow/Black											

Coated Pantone Colors in Illustrator Chart

The chart on this and the next three pages shows the actual printing colors of the entire Pantone' process color library. Refer to this chart to see the actual printing color of any of the Pantone colors when they are being printed using process colors. These pages are included on the *Illustrator 8 Bible* CD-ROM in case you would like to directly compare them within Illustrator to the printed versions. Doing so may allow for more accurate calibration of your monitor. However, be advised that the colors represented here may vary from your end printing result due to variances in paper, ink quality, the press used for printing, and also the experience and skill of your commercial printer.

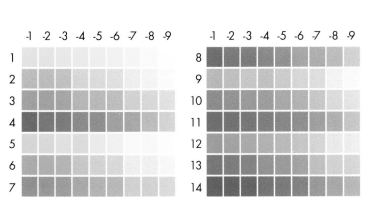

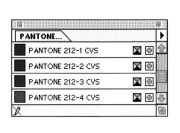

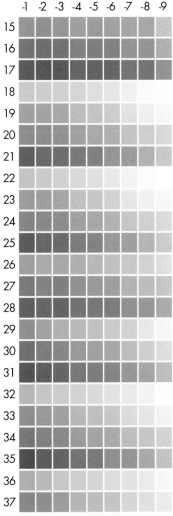

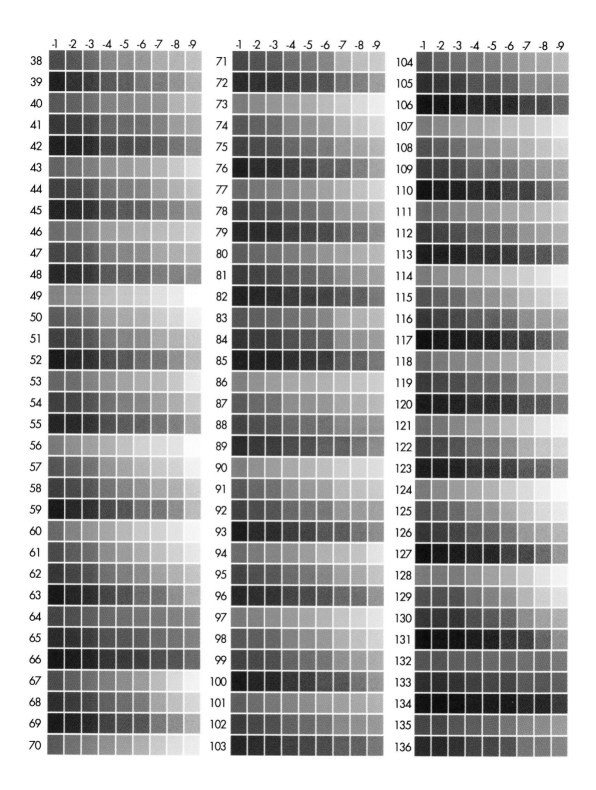

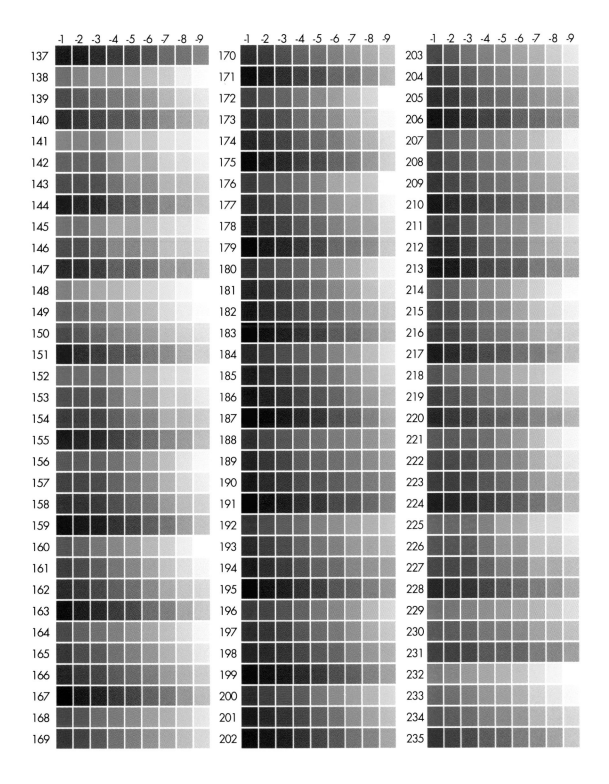

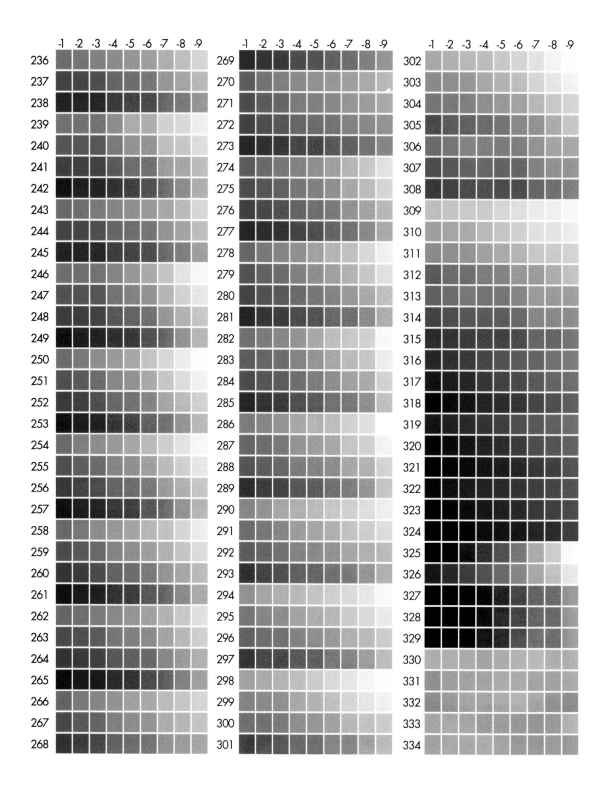

Figure 8-32: The subject matter fit into a related shape

For example, you can give a report on toxic waste in New Jersey more impact by shaping the text into the form of a hypodermic needle. Or you can make a seasonal ad in the shape of a Christmas tree. Look at some of the Absolut Vodka ads to see what they've done to flow text into that all-too-familiar bottle.

Path Type

The unique thing about type on a path is that when the path is not visible, the type *becomes* the path, as shown in Figure 8-33. This can produce some really fascinating results, especially when combined with various fonts of different weights, styles, colors, and special characters.

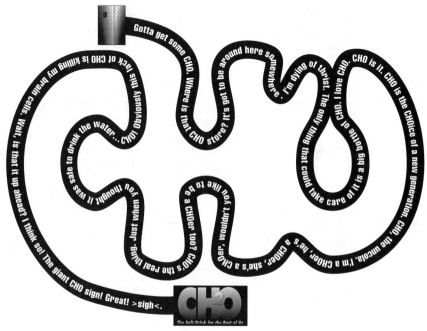

Figure 8-33: Type, when set on a path, can actually *become* the path

To create Path type, first create a path in your document. Then click the path with the Path Type tool to create an insertion point along the path. This works whether the path is a closed path or an open path.

Type aligns to the insertion point; if the type is set to flush left, the left edge of the type aligns to the location where the Path Type tool was first clicked. Unlike Point type, where a hard Return sent the type to the next line, hard Returns work just like spaces in Path type.

You can flow Path type along the path to which it is aligned by clicking the Insertion bar (which resembles a little I-beam) with any Selection tool and dragging along the path. If the I-bar is dragged to the other side of the path, then the type flips over in the direction of the bar. For this reason, it is a good idea to click the topmost part of the Insertion bar before dragging.

Tip As with other objects in Illustrator that can be moved by dragging, pressing the Option [Alt] key before releasing the mouse causes the object being dragged to duplicate instead of just move. This works with the Type I-bar, as well.

If you would like the type you are dragging to appear below the path but to not get flipped upside down and change direction, use baseline shift (found in the Character palette) to raise and lower the type to your liking. The key commands for baseline shift are Option-Shift-↑ [Alt+Shift+↑] and Option-Shift-↓ [Alt+Shift+↓] to move up and down by increments set in the Keyboard Increments Preferences dialog box. These commands are particularly useful when adjusting Path type.

Tip Even though there are six different Type tools, you only need to choose one. If you have the standard Type tool, it changes into the Area Type tool when you pass over a closed path and it changes into a Path Type tool when the cursor passes over an open path. You can access the Vertical types versions of these tools by pressing Shift.

Type on the Top and Bottom of a Circle

Everyone's doing it. Peer pressure is going to make you succumb as well. If you can put type on the top and the bottom of a circle so that it runs along the same path, you are quite the designer, or so thinks the average guy on the street. The simple "Type on a Circle" shown in Figure 8-34 can be created quite easily.

Figure 8-34: Type on the top and bottom of a circle

Follow these steps (which are also illustrated in Figure 8-35 at the end of this procedure), and with a little practice, you can create type on a circle in less than 15 seconds. Pretty impressive, even to those who understand how it's done.

1. Draw a circle with the Ellipse tool (hold down the Shift key to make sure it is a perfect circle). Then choose the Path Type tool and click the top center of the circle. The blinking insertion point appears at that point on the circle.

2. Type the text that is to appear at the top of the circle and press ⌘-Shift-C [Ctrl+Shift+C], which centers the type at the top of the circle.

3. Choose the Selection tool and click the top of the I-bar marker, dragging it down to the bottom center of the circle. Before letting go of the mouse button, center the type, making sure that it is readable from left to right, and press the Option [Alt] key. When you do release the mouse button, there will be type along the top and the bottom of the circle, but the type on the bottom will be inside the circle. (The Option [Alt] key duplicates the text and circle, moving them both to a new location in the process. If the Option [Alt] key were not pressed, the type would have just moved to the bottom of the circle.)

4. Select the bottom text with the Type tool and slowly scoot the type down below the baseline by pressing Option-Shift-↓ [Alt+Shift+↓]. This pushes the type down the baseline in the increments set in the General Preferences dialog box (the default is 2). Keep pressing the key combination until the type is vertically positioned to mimic the type on the top of the circle.

5. Select the text along the bottom of the circle with the Type tool. Type in the text that is to appear at the bottom of the circle. It replaces the selected text. You're finished. Amazing, isn't it? Just remember that you now have *two* circles with type on them, not one circle with two type paths (that can't happen).

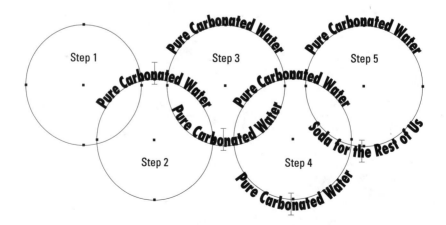

Figure 8-35: Steps for creating type on the top and bottom of a circle

Avoiding Path Type Trouble

The most common trouble with Path type usually occurs when the path has either corner Anchor Points or very sharp curves. Letters will often *crash* (run into one another) when this occurs.

Besides the most obvious way to avoid this problem, which is to not use paths with corner Anchor Points and sharp curves, the areas where the letters crash can sometimes be kerned apart until they aren't touching anymore.

When kerning Path type, be sure to kern from the flush side first. For instance, if the type is flush left, start your kerning from the left side and work to the right. If you start on the wrong end, the letters you kern apart will move along the path until they aren't in an area that needs kerning, but other letters instead will appear there.

Another method of fixing crashed letters is to tweak the path with the Direct Selection tool. Careful adjusting of both Anchor Points and Control Handles can easily fix crashes and letters that have huge amounts of space between them.

Tip
If the path that is the base of the letters doesn't need to be directly under the letters, use the baseline shift keyboard commands (Option-Shift-↓ [Alt+Shift+↓] and Option-Shift-↑ [Alt+Shift+↑]) to move the type until the path runs through the center of the text. This can automatically fix the spacing problems encountered by text that crashes over sharp turns and corners.

Path Type

One of the most desirable effects with Path type (and, in my opinion, much cooler than type on a circle) is Path type that is reversed, as described in the following steps and shown in Figure 8-36.

1. Create the path you want to use for the Path type. In my example, I used a rounded rectangle. Your path can be open or closed.

2. Click the path with the Path Type tool and type in the text for the path. Type with no descenders works better than type with descenders.

3. Vertically center the type on the path by adjusting the baseline shift (Option-Shift-↑ or -↓ [Alt+Shift+↑ or +↓]). If there are descenders, make sure the type is centered from ascender to descender.

4. Select the type with a Type tool and change the Fill to white. Select the path with the Direct Selection tool and change the Fill to None and the Stroke of the path to black. Make the weight of the Stroke just greater than the point size of the type.

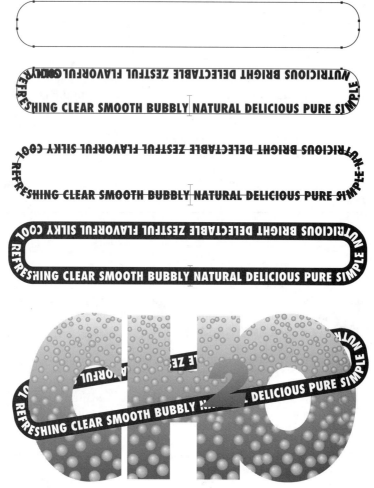

Figure 8-36: Steps for creating type reversed on a path

ASK TOULOUSE: Trouble with Path Type

Trisha: I'm having all sorts of trouble with Path type.

Toulouse: Aren't we all. Anything in particular?

Trisha: Well, for starters, I'm having a dickens of a time trying to move the little I-bar marker along the path.

Toulouse: The key to moving the I-bar marker is to click right at the top of it.

Trisha: Thanks. Also, it seems to flip over all the time.

Toulouse: Actually, grabbing the I-bar at the top will fix this as well.

Trisha: How come my type is sometimes below the path and sometimes above, but it reads the right way?

Toulouse: This usually happens after you've done something such as type on a circle, where you last changed the baseline shift to something less than 0. Change the baseline shift back to 0 and all will be well.

Selecting Type

Before you can make changes to text, you must first select it. There are two ways of selecting type: You can select type areas with a Selection tool, which selects every character in the type area, or you can select characters individually or in groups with any of the Type tools.

To select the entire type area or multiple type areas, click the baseline of a line of type within the type area you want to select. Any changes made in the Type menu, Font menu, Character palette, or Paragraph palette affect every character in the selected type areas.

Note If there are blank fields in any of the palettes or no check marks next to some of the menu items (for instance, no font is checked) when type areas are selected, that means that there are different options for each of those fields or menu items within the type area (for instance, Helvetica for some characters, Times for others). Changing a blank field or unchecked menu item after a type area is selected affects all characters in that area.

To select characters within a type area, you must use a type tool. As you near text that has been typed in the document, the dotted lines surrounding the cursor disappear. The *hot point* of the type cursor is the place where the short horizontal bar crosses the vertical bar (see Figure 8-37). It is this hot point that you should use when clicking with the type cursor.

To select an individual character, drag across the character to be selected. As a character is selected, it is reversed. To select more than one character, drag left or right across multiple characters; all characters from the location you originally clicked to the current location of the cursor are highlighted. If you drag up with the cursor over straight text, you select all the characters to the left and all the characters to the right of the cursor's current location. Dragging down does the reverse. The more lines you drag up or down, the more lines that are selected.

Hot point

Figure 8-37: The type cursor's hot point

To select one word at a time (and the space that follows it), double-click the word to be selected. The word and the space after it are reversed. The reason that the space following the word is selected is mainly due to the times you copy, cut, and paste words from within sentences. For example, to remove the word *Lazy* in the phrase "The Lazy Boy," you double-click the word *Lazy* and press Delete. The phrase is then "The Boy," which only has one space where the word *Lazy* used to be. To select several words, double-click and drag the type cursor across the words you want to select. Each word you touch with the cursor is selected, from the location initially double-clicked to the current location. Dragging to the previous or next line selects additional lines, with at least a word on the first line double-clicked and one word on the dragged-to line.

For the nimble-fingered clickers, you may also click three times to select a paragraph. Triple-click anywhere inside the paragraph and the entire paragraph is selected, including the hard Return at the end of the paragraph (if there is one). Triple-clicking and dragging selects successive paragraphs if the cursor is moved up or down while the mouse button is still pressed following the third click.

To select all the text within a type area with a Type tool, click once in the type area and choose Edit ➪ Select All (⌘-A) [Ctrl+A]. All the text in the type area is reversed. As in most programs, text can only be selected in contiguous blocks. There is no way to select two words in two different locations of the same type area without selecting all the text between them.

Type can also be selected through the use of the Shift key. Click one spot (we'll call it the beginning) and then Shift-click another spot. The characters between the beginning and the Shift-click are selected. Successive Shift-clicks select characters from the beginning to the current location of the most recent Shift-click.

ASK TOULOUSE: I Can't Select My Type!

Winchester: This is really annoying. Every time I select my type, nothing happens.

Toulouse: Nothing's supposed to happen. Selecting doesn't "do" anything.

Winchester: I know that, but my type isn't being selected.

Toulouse: Have you talked to Frank?

Winchester: Yes, but I don't have any other text areas in the document. It can't be that.

Toulouse: Well, it might be . . .

Winchester: And the really spooky thing is, that sometimes, when the type isn't selected, I can change the font and other type attributes.

Toulouse: Actually, the type is selected. . . . You just can't see it.

Winchester: I've been meaning to update my eyeglass prescription.

Toulouse: Actually, you probably have the Hide Edges option selected in the View menu.

Winchester: Whaddaya know, it *is* selected. But what does that have to do with my type?

Toulouse: Hide Edges doesn't just hide path edges and points, it hides the selection area when text is selected.

Winchester: That's silly.

Toulouse: Maybe, but it's a good way to change attributes of a few characters in a text story without having to see them in reverse.

Editing Type

There are limited text-editing features in Illustrator. By clicking once within a type area, a blinking insertion point appears. If you begin typing, characters appear where the blinking insertion point is. If you press Delete, you will delete the previous character (if there is one).

The arrow keys on your keyboard move the blinking insertion point around in the direction of the arrow. The right arrow moves the insertion point one character to the right, and the left arrow moves the insertion point one character to the left. The up arrow moves the insertion point to the previous line; the down arrow moves the insertion point to the next line.

Pressing the ⌘ [Ctrl] key speeds up the movement of the insertion point. ⌘-← [Ctrl+←] or —→ [Ctrl+→] moves the insertion point to the preceding or next word, and ⌘-↑ [Ctrl+↑]or ⌘ -↓ [Ctrl+↓] moves the insertion point to the preceding or next paragraph.

Tip

Pressing the Shift key while moving the insertion point around with the arrows selects all the characters that the insertion point passes over. This works for the ⌘-arrow [Ctrl+arrow] movements as well.

When you select characters with a Type tool, typing anything deletes the selected characters and replaces them with what is currently being typed. Pressing the Delete key when characters are selected deletes all the selected characters. If you paste type (⌘-V) [Ctrl+V] when characters are selected, the selected characters are replaced with the pasted characters.

Anti-Aliased Type/Artwork

Pixel-based software has always had the capability to display anti-aliased type onscreen, but Illustrator 8 is the first vector program to provide this capability. The main difference between anti-aliased type in Photoshop (or another pixel-based program) and Illustrator is that when you choose anti-alias in Photoshop, the text itself is anti-aliased. It both appears onscreen and when printed as anti-aliased type. In Illustrator, however, the anti-aliasing only takes place onscreen; printed text will appear sharp as ever.

So the obvious question is "Why bother?" Well, think back to the late 1980s, before Adobe Type Manager. All type shown on screens had to be at the installed point sizes (usually 10, 12, 14, 18, and 24 points) or it looked terrible. Bigger and smaller type looked especially atrocious. Of course, this type printed wondrously, which was what was really important. Anyway, along came Adobe Type Manager, which made Type 1 PostScript fonts (at that time there was no TrueType) render perfectly onscreen. That was a huge jump forward in display capabilities. Now, however, the next huge jump is here.

Anti-aliased type (for onscreen display purposes only) looks amazingly better than standard type that has either black or white pixels. Part of the problem is that the resolution of a computer monitor is quite low; an average of 72 pixels per inch results in small type that is inherently ugly, regardless of the font. Anti-aliasing makes type edges look softer and enhances readability — at least it does at larger and very small point sizes. At onscreen sizes between 9 and 14 points, the effect is negligible.

You can turn on anti-aliasing within Illustrator by checking the Anti-Aliased Artwork option in File ➪ Preferences ➪ General.

Character Attributes

The easiest way to change the attributes of characters is by using the Character palette, shown in Figure 8-38. Many of the changes in the Character palette are available as options in the Type menu. As a rule, if you have more than one change to make, it is better to do it in the Character palette than the menu, if just so that everything you need is in one place.

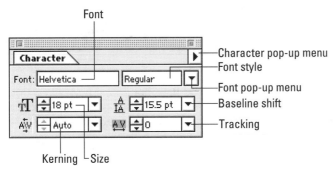

Figure 8-38: The Character palette

Character attribute changes affect only the letters that are selected, with the exception of leading (explained later), which should really be in the Paragraph palette.

Note   You can change several character attributes by increments. The increments are set in the Keyboard Increments Preferences dialog box (choose File ➪ Preferences ➪ Keyboard Increments). Increments can be changed for point size, leading, baseline shift, and tracking/kerning values. Where appropriate, the key commands for each attribute change are listed in the following sections.

The Character Palette

The Character palette can be displayed in three different modes: Standard, With Options, or Multinational. Choose Show Options from the Character palette pop-up menu to display the Options section (which includes Horizontal Scaling, Vertical Scaling, and Baseline Shift). Choose Show Multinational to display the Multinational options: the language, character direction, and several different Kanji options. You can display both Options and the Multinational options at the same time (which some consider four total modes, but that's getting a bit picky, don't you think?). The Character palette remembers which mode the palette was in the last time it was displayed and shows that view the next time you display it.

The Tab key can be used to tab across the different text fields. When in partial display palette mode, the Tab key works only in the partial palette; when the last field (Tracking/Kerning) is selected, the Tab key then goes back to the Font field. If a field in the lower part of the palette is highlighted when the palette is closed, the Font field will be highlighted. When the palette is in full view, tabbing past the last field (Baseline Shift) highlights the Font field as well. In addition to the Tab key tabbing forward through the text fields, pressing Shift-Tab tabs backward through the text fields.

Choosing Edit ⇨ Undo (⌘-Z) [Ctrl+Z] does *not* undo items typed in the Character palette while you are still in the text field. To undo something, you must first move along (tab) to the next field and then undo, and then Shift-Tab back. Canceling (Esc) does not cancel what you have typed but instead highlights the text (if a Type tool is selected).

Tip All of the text fields in the Character palette have both pop-up menus with common values in them for quick access and cute little up and down arrows to the left of each field. These arrows increase (up) and decrease (down) the values of each of the currently selected text fields. Pressing the Shift key while clicking on the little arrow buttons makes the change with each press even greater.

Tip You can use the keyboard to press these buttons. When the field is highlighted, press the Up arrow on your keyboard to press the up arrow button; press the down arrow on your keyboard to press the down arrow button. Press Shift at the same time to jump the value to a greater amount.

Font and Style Changes

The first field on the Character palette (in the upper-left corner) is the Font family field. When you type the first couple of letters of the font you want to use, Illustrator fills in the rest of the name for you. What happens if you type in a font that you don't have? Illustrator just ignores you, for the most part. In a nice touch, you don't get silly dialog boxes appearing telling you that there is no such typeface, but, instead, the blinking insertion point remains in the same location until a letter that works is typed.

Let's say you wanted to use the font TypoCity, but it isn't installed. You've highlighted the font field, and you start typing the name of the font. As you type the letter *T* the first font that starts with *T* is displayed, maybe Times. You type a *y* and discover to your horror that nothing happens. The blinking cursor remains between the *T* and the *i* in Times. You can verify that the font is indeed not installed by clicking on the pop-up font menu on the Character palette. The Font field can be automatically highlighted (and the Character palette displayed if it is not) by pressing either ⌘-Option-Shift-F [Ctrl+Alt+Shift+F], or ⌘-Option-Shift-M [Ctrl+Alt+Shift+F].

Measuring Type

So, you've finally mastered this whole silly point/pica concept—you know that there are 72 points in an inch, and you think that you're ready to conquer the world. And you are, as long as no one asks you to spec type.

At 72 points, the letter I is about 50 points tall. In inches that would be just under ³/₄". To get better results for specially sized capital letters, a good rule of thumb is that every 100 points is about a 1-inch capital letter. This works for most typefaces, and only for the first several inches, but it is a good start to getting capital letters that are sized pretty accurately.

Curves in capital letters are yet another wrench thrown into the equation. In many typefaces, the bottom and top of the letter O go beneath the baseline and above the ascender height of most squared letters (see the following figure). Serifs on certain typefaces may also cross these lines.

Type is measured from the top of the ascenders (like the top of a capital *T*) to the bottom of the descender (like the bottom of a lowercase *p*) as shown in the figure. So when people tell you they want a capital *I* that is 1-inch high, you can't just say, "Oh, there are 72 points in an inch, so I will create a 72-point *I* for them."

The field in the upper right, next to the Font field, is the Style field of the font family. The same rules for entering text in the Font field apply here. Type in the first couple of letters of the style, and Illustrator fills in the rest for you. Only if you have the font style installed on your system will you be able to type it in. Illustrator is very strict when it comes to bold and italic versions of typefaces. If there is not a specific type style for what you want, you will *not* be able to type it in, unlike most software programs, which have "bold" and "italic" checkboxes.

Tip   For every text field, the information entered may be applied by either tabbing to the next or preceding text field, or by pressing Enter or Return.

To the right of the font and style text fields is a little pop-up menu triangle that, when pressed, displays a list of all the typefaces installed on your system. The families are displayed in the main list, and arrows show which families have different styles. To select a font, drag the cursor over it until it is highlighted.

To select a specific style of a font family, drag the cursor to the font family name and then drag to the right to select the style name. The fields to the pop-up menu's left are updated instantly.

Size Changes

The field directly below the Font field is the Size field. Type in the desired point size (from 0.1 point to 1296 points in increments of ¹⁄₁₀,₀₀₀ point) and any selected characters increase or decrease to that particular point size. Next to the Size field is a pop-up menu triangle, which lists the standard point sizes available. Point size for type is always measured from the top of the ascenders to the bottom of the descenders. Type point size can be increased and decreased from the keyboard by typing ⌘-Shift-> [Ctrl+Shift+>] to increase and ⌘-Shift-< [Ctrl+Shift+<]to decrease the point size by the increment specified in the General Preferences dialog box.

Tip   The keyboard commands for increasing and decreasing typographic attributes, such as point size, leading, baseline shift, and tracking, are more than just other ways to change those attributes. Instead, they are invaluable for making changes when the selected type has more than one different value of that attribute within it. For example, if some of the characters have a point size of 10 and some of them have a point size of 20, using the keyboard command (with an increment set to 2 points) changes the type to 12 and 22 points. This would be tedious to do separately, especially if there are multiple sizes or just a few sizes scattered widely about.

Leading

Next to the Size field is the Leading text field. Enter the desired leading value (between 0.1 point and 1296 points, in increments of ¹⁄₁₀₀₀ point). To the right of the leading field is a pop-up menu triangle, from which common leading values can be chosen. In Illustrator, leading is measured from the baseline of the current line up to the baseline of the preceding line, as shown in Figure 8-39. The distance between these two baselines is the amount of leading.

Introducing CHO Light!

The world's best soft drink has just gotten better.   ↕ 23-Point Leading
Less Calories, Less Color, Less Carbonation, &
Less Filling means More that you can Drink!   ↕ 14.5-Point Leading

Figure 8-39: Leading is measured from baseline to baseline. The 23-point leading was set by selecting the second line and changing the leading. The 14.5-point leading was set by selecting the third and fourth lines and changing the leading.

If the Leading field is changed from the number that displays there by default, the Auto Leading entry in the Leading menu becomes unchecked. The Auto Leading box, when checked, makes the leading exactly 120% of the point size. This is just great when the type is 10 points because the leading is 12 points, a common point size-to-leading relationship. But as point size goes up, leading should become proportionately less, until, at around 72 points, it is less than the point size. Instead, when Auto Leading is checked, 72-point type has 86.5-point leading. That's a lot of unsightly white space.

Leading increments can be set in the General Preferences dialog box (⌘-K) [Ctrl+K]. Press Option-↑ [Alt+↑] to increase the leading (which pushes lines farther apart) and Option-↓ [Alt+↓] to decrease the leading.

Kerning and Tracking

Kerning is the amount of space between any specific pair of letters. Kerning values can only be changed when there is a blinking insertion point between two characters.

Tracking is the amount of space between all the letters currently selected. If the type area is selected with a Selection tool, then it refers to all the space between all the characters in the entire type area. If characters are selected with a Type tool, tracking only affects the space between the specific letters selected.

Although they are related and appear to do basically the same thing, tracking and kerning actually work quite independently of each other. They only *look* like they are affecting each other; they never actually change the amount of one if the other is altered. The Kerning field appears directly below the point size of the type, while the Tracking field appears below the leading (see Figure 8-40).

The Kerning field often reads Auto instead of a value when several letters are selected. If Auto appears in that field, the kerning built into the font is used automatically. Choosing a different value (if several letters are selected, only 0 can be chosen, but any number can be entered if a blinking insertion point appears between the letters) overrides the Auto setting and uses the value you type in. Auto Kerning works by reading the kerning values of the typeface that were embedded by the type designer when the typeface was originally created. The typeface designer normally defines the space between letters; different typefaces look like they have different amounts of space between letters. There are usually a couple hundred preset kerning pairs for common Adobe typefaces, although the expert sets have quite a few more. When Auto Kerning is in effect, those preset kerning values can be seen by clicking between kerned letter pairs (capital *T* with most vowels is a good one to check) and reading the value in the Kerning field. If Auto

Kerning is being used, the value will be shown in parentheses. Different typefaces have different kerning pairs, and kerning pairs don't only change from typeface to typeface, but also from weight to weight and style to style.

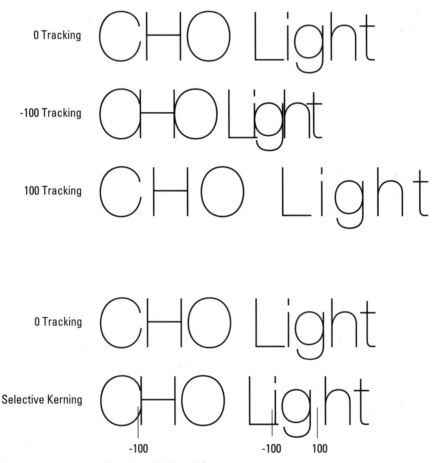

Figure 8-40: Examples of tracking and kerning

For example, a kerning pair of the letters *AV* in Adobe Garamond, when Auto Kerning is on, is set to (–80). If you type in a value of –150, that value will override the Auto Kerning, turning it off and using your new value of –50. Figure 8-41 shows the difference between a kerning of –80 and –150.

Figure 8-41: The left letters are using Auto Kerning (–80). The right letters are using –150 kerning.

To increase or decrease the kerning or tracking by the increments specified in the Keyboard Increments Preferences dialog box, insert the Type tool between two letters and press Option-← [Alt +←] or Option-→ [Alt +→]. To increase or decrease the tracking or kerning by a factor of five times the amount in the General Preferences dialog box, press ⌘-Option-← [Alt +←] or ⌘-Option-→ [Alt +→].

Tip
To quickly reset the tracking of selected characters to 0, press ⌘-Shift-Q [Ctrl+Shift+Q]. Sneaky, huh?

Kerning and tracking values are based on $1/1000$ *em space*. An em space is the width of two numbers (think of two zeros — they tend to be the widest-looking numbers) at that particular point size.

The values entered for tracking and kerning must be between –1000 and 10,000. A value of –1000 will result in stacked letters. A value of 10,000 will make enough space between letters for 10 em spaces, or 20 numbers. That's a *lot* of space.

Note
Different software works with kerning and tracking differently. In those programs that *do* offer numerical tracking, it is usually represented in some form of a fraction of an em space, but the denominator varies from software to software. In QuarkXPress, for example, tracking and kerning is measured in $1/200$ of an em space. Check the documentation that came with your software to determine the denominator in other software. This can get a little confusing when going from program to program, although the transformation from QuarkXPress to Illustrator is quite simple: To get the same tracking and kerning values in Quark that you used in Illustrator, divide the number you used in Illustrator by 5 (1000/200 = 5).

The bottom portion of the Character palette contains the Baseline Shift field, which, unlike leading, moves individual characters up and down relative to their baseline (from leading). Positive numbers move the selected characters up, and negative numbers move the characters down by the amount specified. The maximum amount of baseline shift is 1296 points in either direction. Baseline shift is especially useful for Path type. Baseline shift can be changed via the keyboard by selecting a letter with the Type tool and pressing Option-Shift-↑ [Alt+Shift+↑] to increase and Option-Shift-↓ [Alt+Shift+↓] to decrease the baseline shift in the increment specified in the General Preferences dialog box.

Vertical and Horizontal Scale

Also in the Options section of the Character palette is the Horizontal Scale field. Horizontal scale controls the width of the type, causing it to become expanded or condensed horizontally. Values from 1% to 10,000% can be entered in this field. Like most other fields in the Character palette, the values entered are absolute values, so whatever the horizontal scale is, changing it back to 100% returns the type to its original proportions.

Tip   You can quickly reset the Horizontal Scale field value to 100% by pressing ⌘-Shift-X [Ctrl+Shift+X].

The Language Barrier

If you're reading a translation of the *Illustrator 8 Bible* in a language other than English, I'd like to welcome you by saying hello in your native language: "Hello." Okay, I'm probably not fooling you here; through the magic of translators who speak several languages much more fluently than I speak "westernized east coast American English," my current language of choice, this book is translated into other languages without one iota of input from me.

If your language of choice is not English, you'll be interested in the Language option along the bottom of the Character palette. It allows you to change to your language of choice, so that functions such as the spelling dictionary and hyphenation dictionary work for words you'll be typing.

More Multinational Options

The other options along the bottom of the Character palette are specifically designed for Kanji character operations, with the exception of the Direction pop-up menu, which can be used with Roman characters to achieve various effects. The Direction pop-up menu is discussed later in this chapter in the vertical type section.

Paragraph Palette

Some changes that can be made to text affect entire paragraphs at the same time. Paragraph attributes include alignment, indentation, space before paragraphs, hanging punctuation, hyphenation, spacing, repeated character processing, and line breaking.

You can change paragraph attributes if you first select a type area using a Selection tool, in which case, the changes affect every paragraph within the entire type area. If you use the Type tool to select one or more characters, changes made to paragraph attributes affect the entire paragraphs of each of the selected characters.

To display the Paragraph palette (see Figure 8-42) using menu commands, choose Type ➪ Paragraph. To display the Paragraph palette with a key command, press ⌘-M [Ctrl+M].

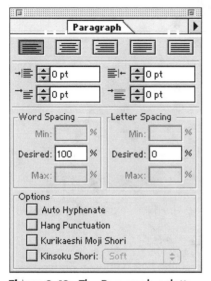

Figure 8-42: The Paragraph palette

Pressing Tab tabs forward through the text fields and Shift-Tab tabs backward through the same text fields. Press Enter or Return to apply the changes that were made.

The bottom part of the Paragraph palette contains information that doesn't get changed too often, so for the most part, it doesn't need to be displayed. If you wish to display it, choose Show Options from the Paragraph palette pop-up menu.

Alignment

There are five different types of paragraph alignment (see Figure 8-43). Each of them is represented by a graphical representation of what multiple lines of type look like when that particular alignment is applied.

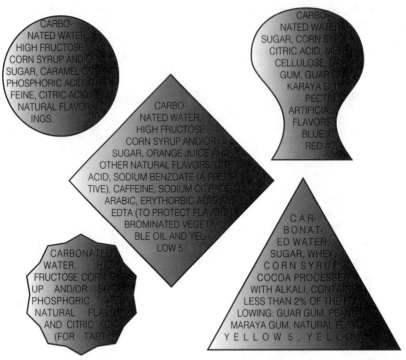

Figure 8-43: The five different types of alignment: Flush Left, Flush Right, Centered, Justify Full Lines, and Justify All Lines

The first alignment type is the most common: Flush Left, which experienced typesetters often refer to as *ragged right* due to the uneven right side of the text. You can also apply this type of alignment by pressing ⌘-Shift-L [Ctrl+Shift+L].

The next type of alignment is Centered, where all lines of type in the paragraph are centered relative to each other, to the point clicked, or to the location of the I-bar in Path type. You can also apply this type of alignment by pressing ⌘-Shift-C [Ctrl+Shift+C].

The middle alignment choice is Flush Right, in which type has a smooth, even right side and an uneven left side (no, ragged left isn't really a correct term). You can also apply this type of alignment by pressing ⌘-Shift-R [Ctrl+Shift+R].

The fourth type of alignment is Justified (Illustrator calls it Justify Full Lines), where both the left and right sides appear smooth and even. Extra space is added between letters and words, as defined in the "Spacing" section later in this chapter. The last line in a justified paragraph appears to be flush left. You can also apply this type of alignment by pressing ⌘-Shift-J [Ctrl+Shift+J].

The last alignment type is called Justify All Lines (commonly called Force Justify), which is the same as Justify except that the last line of every paragraph is justified along with the other lines of the paragraph. This can create some really *awful* looking paragraphs, and is done mainly for artistic emphasis, not as a proper way to justify type. Justify All Lines is particularly useful for stretching a single line of type across a certain width. You can also apply this type of alignment by pressing ⌘-Shift-B [Ctrl+Shift+B].

Note Justification only works on Area type. Illustrator will not allow you to select Justify or Justify All Lines for Path type or Point type.

Indentation

Paragraphs can be indented within the Paragraph palette by choosing different amounts of indentation for the left edge, right edge, and first line of each paragraph. The maximum indentation for all three fields is 1296 points and the minimum is –1296 points.

Using indents is a great way to offset type, such as quotes, that have smaller margins than the rest of the type surrounding the quote. Changing the indentation values is also useful for creating hanging indents, such as numbered or bulleted text.

To create hanging indents easily, make the Left Indent as large as the width of a bullet or a number and a space, and then make the First Line value the negative value of that. If the left indent is 2 picas, the first line would be –2 picas. This creates great hanging indents every time.

New Feature New to Illustrator 8 is the addition of the First Line Indent marker and a Left Indent marker.

Space Before Paragraphs

Illustrator lets you place additional space between paragraphs by entering a number in the Space Before Paragraphs text field. This measurement is added to the leading to determine the distance from baseline to baseline before the selected paragraphs. You can also enter a negative number to decrease space between paragraphs, if necessary. Values for Space Before Paragraphs can be between –1296 and 1296 points.

Spacing

Illustrator enables you to control the spacing of letters and words in text by editing the Spacing fields in the middle of the Paragraph palette (see Figure 8-44).

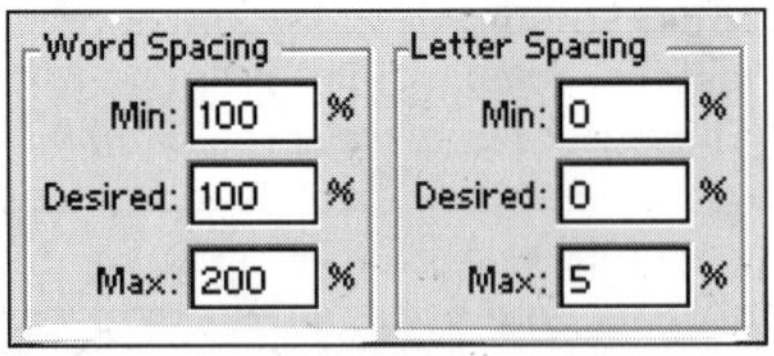

Figure 8-44: The Spacing section of the Paragraph palette

Spacing affects the space between letters and words regardless of the alignment, although Justified text has even more spacing control than Flush Left, Flush Right, or Centered text.

When Flush Left, Flush Right, or Centered alignment is chosen, the only text fields that can be changed are the Desired fields for Letter Spacing and Word Spacing.

You can enter values between 0% and 1000% for Word Spacing. The Minimum must be less than the amount in the Desired box and the Maximum must be more than the amount in the Desired box. At 100%, the word space is normal; at less than 100%, the word space is reduced; and at a number greater than 100%, the word space is increased.

The values for Letter Spacing must be between –50% and 500%. The Minimum must be less than the amount in the Desired box and the Maximum must be more than the amount in the Desired box. At 0%, the letter space is normal; at less than 0%, the letter space is reduced; and at a number greater than 0%, the letter space is increased.

The Minimum and Maximum boxes in the Word Spacing and Letter Spacing areas are mainly used to control where the extra space goes and where it is removed from when stretching out and compressing the lines of text.

Hyphenation

Hyphenation? In a drawing program? I couldn't believe it either, but there it was staring me in the face. A nice addition to Illustrator's text-handling capabilities, hyphenation works in the background, silently hyphenating when necessary.

To use Illustrator's hyphenation, you must check the Auto Hyphenate box in the lower-left of the Paragraph palette. After this is checked for selected text, that text hyphenates fairly well.

Hyphenation in Illustrator works from a set of hyphenation rules that you define in the Hyphenation Options dialog box (shown in Figure 8-45). View the Hyphenation dialog box by choosing Hyphenation from the Paragraph pop-up menu. Here you can specify how many letters must fall before the hyphen can appear and how many letters must fall after the hyphen. You can also limit the number of consecutive hyphens to avoid the "ladder look" of multiple hyphens.

Hyphenation Options

Hyphenate 2	letters from beginning	OK
Hyphenate 2	letters from end	Cancel
Limit consecutive hyphens to: 3		

Figure 8-45: The Hyphenation Options dialog box

Tip

When you need to hyphenate a word at a place where Illustrator doesn't seem to want to hyphenate it, you can create a discretionary hyphen. A discretionary hyphen is created by placing the blinking insertion point where the word should break and typing ⌘-Shift-Hyphen [Ctrl+Shift+Hyphen]. This causes the word to hyphenate at a certain part of the word only if that word has to be hyphenated. If the word doesn't have to be hyphenated, no hyphen appears. This is much better than just typing a normal hyphen, which works temporarily; but if the manually hyphenated word is moved from the edge of the line, the hyphen remains within it.

Hang Punctuation

If Hang Punctuation is checked, punctuation at the left edge of a Flush Left, Justified, or Justified Last Line paragraph appears outside the type area, as shown in Figure 8-46. Punctuation on the right edge of a Flush Right, Justified, or Justified Last Line paragraph also appears outside the type area. Strangely enough, Illustrator is one of the few programs that supports this very hip feature.

Those Unusual Options

Repeated Character Processing and Line Breaking % are two options that are only relevant to Kanji typefaces. They aren't available when a standard Roman typeface is being used. The Kurikaeshi Moji option lets you control the repeated Japanese text characters. By turning this option on, Illustrator inserts a repeat character rather than putting in two identical characters after each other. The other option, Kinsoku Shori, lets you control the character's line breaking.

"I watch it for the subtle nuances in plot, for the rich and dramatic characterizations of the title characters, and for a refreshingly accurate portrayal of pre-medieval times."

Jennifer Alspach, on why she's hooked on *Xena: Warrior Princess*

Figure 8-46: When the Hang Punctuation box is checked, quotes, periods, commas, and hyphens fall outside the boundary of the type area

Special Characters on a Mac

On a Macintosh, many special characters are available besides the standard letters, numbers, and symbols that appear on your keyboard. To show you these special characters, Apple's system software includes a desk accessory called KeyCaps, which displays the keyboard you are using and shows what each character will look like in the typeface you choose.

There are essentially four sets of characters in each font. The first set is reached by normal typing of the keyboard keys, which include numbers, lowercase letters, and a few symbols. The second set is reached by pressing the Shift key prior to pressing the keyboard key and includes capital letters and symbols that appear on the top half of the keyboard keys. The third set is reached by pressing the Option key before pressing a keyboard key. This set consists primarily of the common special symbols, such as a bullet (•), the cents symbol (¢), an ellipsis (…), and the pi symbol (π). The fourth set of characters can only be reached when both the Option and Shift keys are pressed before a keyboard key is pressed and includes less common symbols, like f ligatures (fi, fl), the double dagger (‡), and the Apple symbol (⌘).

While almost all typefaces have the first and second sets, many typefaces do not contain very many characters in the third and fourth sets. The list in Figure 8-47 shows the common symbols and their keyboard equivalents, but not all typefaces have all the symbols, and some of the symbols in some of the typefaces may have different keyboard commands.

1st set	2nd set + Shift	3rd set + Option	4th set +Option–Shift
`	~	`	`
1	!		⁄
2	@	™	º
3	#	£	‹
4	$	¢	›
5	%	∞	fi
6	^	§	fl
7	&	¶	‡
8	*	•	°
9	(	ª	·
0	)	º	‚
-	_	–	—
=	+	≠	±
q	Q	œ	Œ
w	W	∑	„
e	E	´	´
r	R	®	‰
t	T	†	ˇ
y	Y	¥	Á
u	U	¨	¨
i	I	ˆ	ˆ
o	O	ø	Ø
p	P	π	∏
[	{	"	"
]	}	'	'
\			«	»
a	A	å	Å
s	S	ß	Í
d	D	∂	Î
f	F	ƒ	Ï
g	G	©	˝
h	H	˙	Ó
j	J	Δ	Ô
k	K	˚	
l	L	¬	Ò
;	:	…	Ú
'	"	æ	Æ
z	Z	Ω	¸
x	X	≈	˛
c	C	ç	Ç
v	V	√	◊
b	B	∫	ı
n	N	˜	˜
m	M	µ	Â
,	<	≤	¯
.	>	≥	˘
/	?	÷	¿

Figure 8-47: The standard Mac keyboard set for most fonts

Symbol Typefaces on a Mac

There are several symbol typefaces available that contain symbols in place of letters and numbers. The most popular of these is the Symbol typeface, which has Greek letters and mathematical operands and symbols. The next most popular symbol font would have to be ZapfDingbats, which contains a wide variety of different symbols, as shown in Figure 8-48.

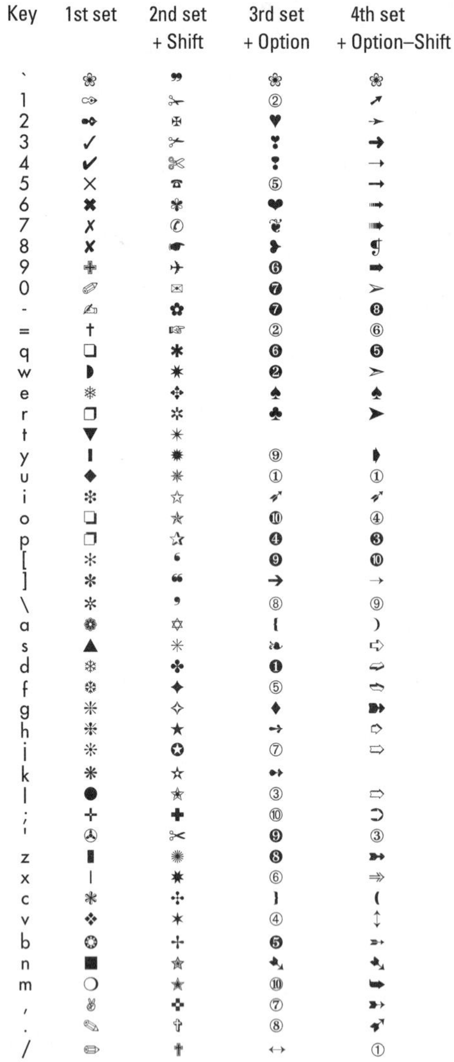

Key	1st set	2nd set + Shift	3rd set + Option	4th set + Option–Shift
`	❀	❞	❀	❀
1	➣	✃	②	↗
2	❥	✂	♥	➢
3	✓	✄	❣	➔
4	✔	✄	❣	→
5	✗	✆	⑤	→
6	✘	✇	♥	⇒
7	✗	✈	❦	⇒
8	✘	☛	❧	¶
9	✚	✌	⑥	➡
0	✒	☒	❼	➢
-	✑	✿	❼	➑
=	†	☞	②	➅
q	❑	✳	❻	➄
w	❒	✱	❷	➢
e	❉	✢	♠	♠
r	❐	✣	♣	➤
t	▼	✤		
y	❘	❋	⑨	♦
u	◆	✴	①	①
i	❊	☆	✐	✐
o	❑	★	⑩	④
p	❐	☆	❹	❸
[	❋	'	❾	⑩
]	✻	"	→	→
\	✽	'	⑧	⑨
a	❂	☼	❨	❩
s	▲	✵	❧	⇨
d	❈	✧	❶	⇌
f	❅	◆	⑤	⇐
g	✺	◇	◆	▶▶
h	❇	★	→	⇨
i	✼	✪	⑦	⇨
k	✶	☆	❧	
l	●	☆	③	⇨
;	✢	✜	⑩	⟲
'	☮	✂	❾	③
z	■	✷	❽	▶▶
x	❘	❋	⑥	⇒
c	✳	✛	❩	❨
v	❖	✶	④	↕
b	◉	✚	❺	➢➢
n	■	✭	❧	❧
m	○	★	⑩	➡
,	✄	✿	⑦	➢➢
.	✎	✿	⑧	➚
/	✏	†	↔	①

Figure 8-48: The character set of ZapfDingbats

Some other typefaces that contain primarily symbols are Carta, the map symbol typeface; Bill's Dingbats, a shareware set of symbols that nicely complements ZapfDingbats; and Mathematical Pi, a math font containing math symbols.

One of the great things about Symbol typefaces is that individual characters can be turned into outline characters and edited to create different illustrations.

Special Characters in Windows

To access special characters on a Windows system, you usually have to enter a code where you want the special character to be. Codes can be entered in Illustrator by pressing and holding Alt, and then typing in the four-digit code for that character. Figure 8-49 shows all the hidden special characters (ones that aren't shown on the keyboard) and the code needed to type them.

Char	Code	Char	Code	Char	Code
ƒ	0131	-	0173	×	0215
„	0132	®	0174	Ø	0216
…	0133	¯	0175	Ù	0217
†	0134	°	0176	Ú	0218
‡	0135	±	0177	Û	0219
ˆ	0136	²	0178	Ü	0220
‰	0137	³	0179	Ý	0221
Š	0138	´	0180	ß	0222
‹	0139	µ	0181	à	0223
Œ	0140	¶	0182	à	0224
	0141	·	0183	á	0225
	0142	¸	0184	â	0226
	0143	¹	0185	ã	0227
	0144	º	0186	ä	0228
'	0145	»	0187	å	0229
'	0146	¼	0188	æ	0230
"	0147	½	0189	ç	0231
"	0148	¾	0190	è	0232
•	0149	¿	0191	é	0233
–	0150	À	0192	ê	0234
—	0151	Á	0193	ë	0235
˜	0152	Â	0194	ì	0236
™	0153	Ã	0195	í	0237
š	0154	Ä	0196	î	0238
›	0155	Å	0197	ï	0239
œ	0156	Æ	0198	ð	0240
	0157	Ç	0199	ñ	0241
	0158	È	0200	ò	0242
Ÿ	0159	É	0201	ó	0243
	0160	Ê	0202	ô	0244
¡	0161	Ë	0203	õ	0245
¢	0162	Ì	0204	ö	0246
£	0163	Í	0205	÷	0247
¤	0164	Î	0206	ø	0248
¥	0165	Ï	0207	ù	0249
¦	0166	Ð	0208	ú	0250
§	0167	Ñ	0209	û	0251
¨	0168	Ò	0210	ü	0252
©	0169	Ó	0211	ý	0253
ª	0170	Ô	0212	þ	0254
«	0171	Õ	0213	ÿ	0255
¬	0172	Ö	0214		

Figure 8-49: The hidden special characters and their corresponding four-digit ANSI codes

To access a bullet, for instance, you would press Alt, type **0149,** and then release the Alt key. A bullet appears where your text cursor last was.

Customizing Fonts

Typefaces can be created and modified right on your computer, using tools very similar to the ones in Adobe Illustrator. Creating fonts is, in a way, the reverse process of outlining existing fonts because you are taking outlines and turning them into characters in typefaces. Figure 8-50 shows two of the most popular shareware fonts created through a combination of Illustrator and Fontographer: Lefty Casual and Ransom Note.

Figure 8-50: Lefty Casual and Ransom Note

By taking existing typefaces, you can customize the characters, creating a unique typeface. In a typeface you create, all the special characters can be ones you've designed especially for that face.

Caution Check with the original typeface manufacturer before customizing, to ensure that you will not be violating that particular font vendor's copyright.

Macromedia Fontographer is the most popular font-creation software currently available, boasting Multiple Master capabilities and very precise Bézier control tools.

Export/Place

To export text, select the text you want to export and choose File ➪ Export. A Save dialog box appears, which asks in what format and to where you want to save the text.

You can save text in most of the common formats, and you can import it back into Illustrator with the Place command (choose File ➪ Place when a text area is active with a Type tool). Word-processing software, page-layout software, or any other software that can read text files can open and use text that you saved in Illustrator.

Vertical Type

Vertical type is a fascinating capability in Illustrator. If you use Kanji characters, you'll find it invaluable. But even if you don't, you may find some interesting uses for setting type vertically, instead of horizontally.

There are two ways to make your type appear vertical instead of horizontal. You can create type using any of the three Vertical Type tools, or you can convert horizontal type into vertical type with Type ➪ Type Orientation ➪ Vertical. Figure 8-51 shows Rectangle type both horizontally and vertically. Note that Vertical type takes up a great deal more space than Horizontal type.

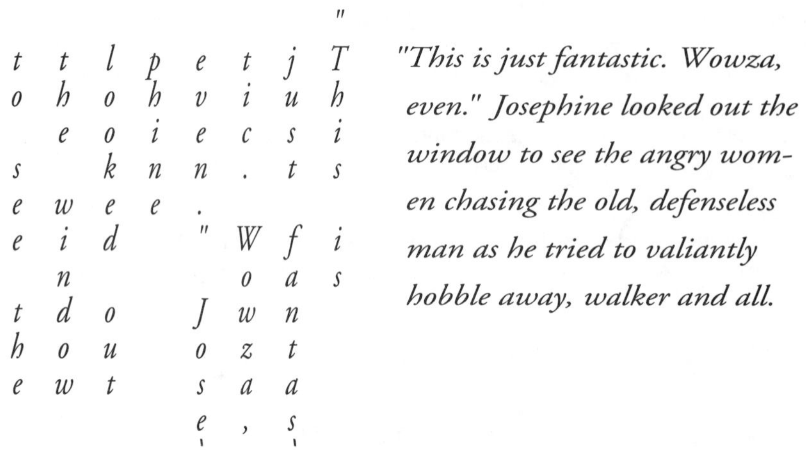

```
t    t    l    p    e    t    j    T        "This is just fantastic. Wowza,
o    h    o    h    v    i    u    h
     e    o    i    e    c    s    i        even." Josephine looked out the
s         k    n    n    .    t    s
e    w    e    e    .                       window to see the angry wom-
e    i    d         "    W    f    i
     n              o    a    s             en chasing the old, defenseless
t    d    o    J    w    n
h    o    u    o    z    t                  man as he tried to valiantly
e    w    t    s    a    a
                   e    ,    s              hobble away, walker and all.
```

Figure 8-51: Vertical type (left) and the same type reoriented to horizontal (right)

Most of Illustrator's standard character and paragraph palette changes work with vertical type, but not always in ways you would expect. For instance, type is set on a centerline, not a baseline. The centerline runs vertically through the center of each character. The following is a list of differences in the way each major function works:

✦ **Font:** Same

✦ **Size:** Same

✦ **Leading:** Changes the amount of space between the vertical "lines" of type, measured from centerline to centerline.

✦ **Kerning/Tracking:** Changes the amount of vertical space between each character. Because very few Roman characters have both ascenders and descenders, tracking and kerning substantially can really help get rid of the excess white space between characters that makes vertical type so hard to read.

✦ **Vertical Scale:** Changes the width (horizontal scale) of the characters.

✦ **Horizontal Scale:** Changes the height (vertical scale) of the characters.

✦ **Baseline Shift:** Moves the type left (negative values) and right (positive values) along the centerline.

✦ **Flush Left:** Words are flush top.

✦ **Center:** Words are vertically centered.

✦ **Flush Right:** Words are flush bottom.

✦ **Justify Full Lines:** Words on full (vertical) lines are justified from top to bottom.

✦ **Justify All Lines:** All lines are vertically justified.

✦ **Left Indent:** Top indent. Positive numbers move the text down and negative numbers move the text up.

✦ **Right Indent:** Bottom indent, with numbers working like Left Indent.

✦ **First Line Indent:** The rightmost line indent. Once again, positive numbers move the text down and negative numbers move the text up.

✦ **Space Before Paragraph:** Paragraphs go from right to left, so this control increases the space to the right of the selected paragraph(s).

✦ **Auto Hyphenate:** Hyphenates words the same way as horizontal type, but the hyphens appear at the bottom of each line.

✦ **Hang Punctuation:** Punctuation is hung above and below the text area.

✦ **Tab Ruler:** Appears to the right of text areas in vertical form.

✦ **Create Outlines:** Same.

Changing the Direction of Type

Direction and Orientation are two totally different things. The Orientation is a text area control; changing it affects the entire text area. The Direction control is a character-based control, which can affect all characters or one character. It is this one control that really makes vertical type worth using.

There are three options in the Direction pop-up menu (located in the Character palette):

✦ **Standard:** This keeps characters in the direction that is the default of the type area. This is usually displayed so that each character is "right side up."

✦ **Rotated:** This rotates characters –90°.

✦ **Tate Chu Yoko:** This "direction" affects selected characters and groups the selected characters onto one horizontal line. In Figure 8-52, I've selected each word separately and applied the Tate Chu Yoko direction to them. In addition, I increased the leading so that the columns of text would be easier to read.

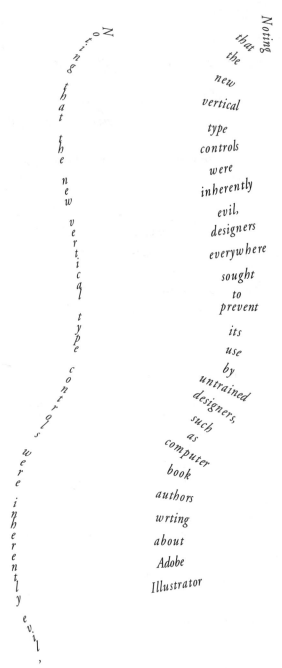

Figure 8-52: Vertical type on a curved path as it normally appears (left), and when each word has Tate Chu Yoko direction applied to it (right)

Path Type and Vertical Type

Type on a path takes on new life when you use vertical type. That, combined with the capability to group characters (words and so forth) together along the chain of text provides additional text capabilities that can't be found anywhere else.

Figure 8-53 shows type on a path with and without Tate Chu Yoko Character Direction adjustments.

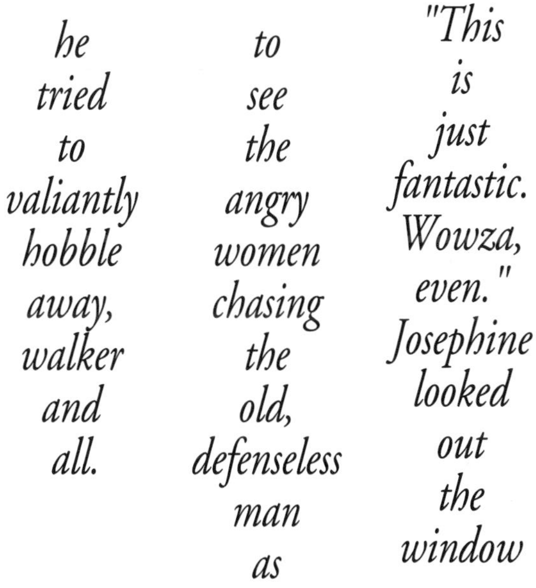

*he
tried
to
valiantly
hobble
away,
walker
and
all.*

*to
see
the
angry
women
chasing
the
old,
defenseless
man
as*

*"This
is
just
fantastic.
Wowza,
even."
Josephine
looked
out
the
window*

Figure 8-53: Vertical type with and without Tate Chu Yoko applied

Other Type Considerations

When you're using type in Illustrator, there are a number of things to remember to get good results:

✦ Make sure that the person you are sending the Illustrator file to has the same fonts you have. It isn't enough just to have the same name of a font; you'll need the exact font that was created by the same manufacturer.

✦ Try not to mix TrueType fonts with PostScript fonts. This usually ends up confusing everyone involved.

✦ If the person you are sending Illustrator files to does *not* have your typeface, select the type in that font and choose Type ➪ Create Outlines (⌘-Shift-O) [Ctrl+Shift+O].

✦ When you're printing an Illustrator file that has been placed in other software, missing type styles may go unnoticed until after the job has printed. Be doubly sure that the person outputting the file has all the fonts in the embedded Illustrator file.

✦ If you are saving your illustration as an EPS file to be placed into another program and you are not going to open the file, you can select Include Document Fonts in the EPS Save dialog box. This forces any fonts used in the illustration to be saved with the illustration and allows the illustration to print as a placed image from within another program or to print from Illustrator as a placed EPS.

Summary

✦ Most of the options used to control type can be found in the Type menu.

✦ There are four different ways to put type on a page: Point type, Rectangle type, Area type, and Path type.

✦ Point type has one point as its "anchor," and the type is aligned to that point.

✦ Rectangle type exists within a rectangle drawn with the Type tool.

✦ Area type is type that exists within the confines of any path.

✦ Path type is type that runs along the edge of a path.

✦ Type can be selected all at once by clicking the path (or point) of the type with the Selection tool.

✦ Individual characters, words, and paragraphs can be selected by using any of the Type tools.

✦ The Character palette (accessed by pressing ⌘-T [Ctrl+T]) contains all the character-specific information about selected type and can be used to change that information.

✦ Illustrator doesn't have type "styles"; instead, you must select the exact font you wish to use.

✦ Tracking and kerning remove or add space between groups or pairs of letters, respectively.

✦ The Paragraph palette (accessed by pressing ⌘-M) [Ctrl+M] contains all the paragraph-specific information about selected type and can be used to change that information.

✦ Type can be set to wrap around selected paths by using the Text Wrapping feature.

✦ Type can be set to jump from text block to text block by linking text blocks together.

✦ The Tab Ruler palette is used to set tabs for text areas.

✦ If you have both the screen font and the printer font of a Type 1 typeface, or if you have a TrueType font installed, you can convert the font into outlines via the Create Outlines command.

✦ Once type has been changed to outlines, you may use those outlines as a mask, or Fill those outlines with gradients or patterns.

✦ Many special characters can be accessed in each font on a Mac by pressing the Option key.

✦   ✦   ✦

Masks and Compound Paths

T wo of the most difficult areas of Illustrator to master are masks and compound paths. Of course, these are also two of the most powerful functions in Illustrator. A "mask" is used to hide portions of an image (mask them out), and compound paths are paths that consist of two or more separate paths that Illustrator treats as a single path.

Compound Paths

Compound paths are one of the least understood areas of Illustrator, but after you understand a few simple guidelines and rules, manipulating and using them correctly is simple.

Compound paths are paths made up of two or more open or closed paths. Where the paths cross or every other Fill area exists there is a transparent hole. You can specify which paths create the holes by changing the direction of the paths via the Reverse option in the Attributes palette. The general rule is that paths traveling in the opposite direction of any adjoining paths form holes. Compound paths can be fun or frustrating, depending on the location of Pluto relative to Saturn, Jupiter, and Mickey.

Creating Compound Paths

You can create compound paths of all sorts by following the steps described here (which are also illustrated in Figure 9-1). It's a good idea to make sure that none of the paths are currently compound paths or grouped paths before creating a new compound path.

1. Create all the paths that you need for the compound path, including the outside path and the holes.

2. Select all the paths and choose Object ➪ Compound Paths ➪ Make (⌘-8) [Ctrl+8]. Illustrator now treats the paths as one path. When you click one of the paths with the Selection tool, the other paths in the compound path are selected as well. Fill the object with any Fill. (I used a custom radial gradient for the illustration in Figure 9-2.)

3. Place the compound path over any other object. (I used a placed EPS image for this example.) The inner paths act like holes that enable you to see the object underneath.

Figure 9-1: The frame of this window is a compound path with several holes in it

Step 1   Step 2   Step 3

Figure 9-2: The steps in creating a compound path

You can select individual paths by clicking them once with the Group Selection tool. As always, you can select points and segments within each path by using the Direct Selection tool.

Clicking only once with the Group Selection tool on paths that you wish to select is important. Clicking those paths more than once with the Group Selection tool will select all the other paths in the compound path. To click (for moving or copying purposes) the selected individual paths after the Group Selection tool has clicked them once, click them with the Direct Selection tool.

Caution   Paths belonging to different groups cannot be made into a compound path unless all paths in all the groups are selected.

When you create a compound path, it takes on the Paint Style attributes of the bottom-most path of all the paths that were selected and have become part of that compound path.

You can create a compound path that is only one path, though there are few reasons to do so. If the singular compound path is selected as part of a larger compound path (with either the Direct Selection tool or Group Selection tool), the path directions may be altered. If you aren't sure whether an individual path is a compound path, select the path and choose Object ➪ Compound Path. If the Release option is available, the path is a compound path; if it is not available, the path is not a compound path.

Compound paths do not work in a hierarchical process as groups do. If a path is part of a compound path, it is part of that compound path only. If a compound path becomes part of another compound path, the paths in the original compound path are compounded only with the new compound path.

New Feature   You can blend between multiple-path compound paths. Select the Blend tool and click from one compound shape to the other shape. While the initial blend between the two objects is still selected, double-click on the Blend tool in the tool box to open the Blend Options dialog box. Select the Spacing pop-up menu and choose Specified Step and enter a number. Select Preview to see the results before you close the dialog box. The larger the number the smoother the blend. For really cool results make sure the two objects are different colors. For smoothest blends make sure you don't have a stroke color applied to your shapes.

Releasing Compound Paths

When you want to release a compound path, select the path and choose Object ➪ Compound Path ➪ Release (⌘-Option-8) [Ctrl+Alt+8]. The path changes into regular paths.

If any of the paths appeared as holes, they are, instead, filled with the Fill of the rest of the compound path. The results may be a little confusing because these holes then seem to blend right into the outer shape of the compound paths, as shown in Figure 9-3.

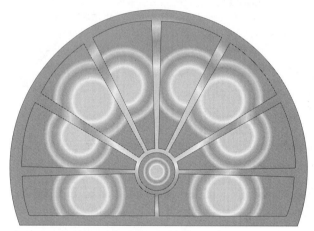

Figure 9-3: The compound path from Figure 9-2, after you release the path. The circles are the radial gradients that the compound path uses.

If the compound path that you are releasing contains other compound paths, they are released as well because Illustrator doesn't recognize compound paths that are within other compound paths.

Understanding Holes

Holes for donuts, Life Savers, and rings are quite simple to create. Just select two circles, one smaller than, and totally within, a larger circle, and choose Compound Path ⇨ Make (⌘-8) [Ctrl+8]. The inside circle is then a hole.

A compound path considers every path within it to lie along the borders of the compound path. Path edges within an object appear to you to be on the inside of an object, but they appear to Illustrator to be just another edge of the path.

With this concept in mind, you can create a compound path that has several holes, such as a slice of Swiss cheese or a snowflake. Just create the outermost paths and the paths that will be holes, select all the paths, and then select Object ⇨ Compound Path ⇨ Make.

ASK TOULOUSE: Blending Compounds

Mindy: I can't blend my compound paths right.

Toulouse: Actually, the Blend tool only works with a single path at a time.

Mindy: So I'm out of luck?

Toulouse: Not really. There are two different options available.

Mindy: And they are . . . ?

Toulouse: Well, what are you trying to do with the blend?

Mindy: I'm trying to make zooming text.

Toulouse: Ah. Well, instead of blending, you could use KPT (Kai Power Tools) Vector Effects. Some of the filters, ShadowLand specifically, do some amazing things with compound blends.

Mindy: Okay. The other way?

Toulouse: Change your compounds to "fake compounds," making them consist of truly one path.

Mindy: How do I do that?

Toulouse: It involves quite a bit of splitting paths and joining. But there's a catch.

Mindy: As long as it doesn't involve stalking. . . .

Toulouse: No . . . Actually, you just can't use Strokes, which would appear in the seams.

Mindy: Sounds fair. I'll try it.

Note   You aren't limited to one set of holes. You can create a compound path with a hole that has an object inside it with a hole. In that hole can be an object with a hole, and so on.

Overlapping Holes

Holes, if they really are paths that are supposed to be empty areas of an object, should not overlap. If anything, you can combine multiple holes that are overlapping into one larger hole, possibly by using Unite.

If holes within a compound path do overlap, the result is a solid area with the same Fill color as the rest of the object. If multiple holes overlap, the results can be quite unusual, as shown in Figure 9-4. (See "Reversing Path Directions," later in this chapter, to learn more about multiple overlapping holes.)

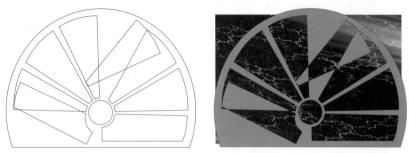

Figure 9-4: Overlapping holes in compound paths, in Artwork mode (left) and Preview mode (right)

Tip

In most cases, you will get the desired results with holes only if the outermost path contains all the holes. As a rule, Illustrator uses the topmost objects to "poke" holes out of the bottom-most objects. If you want holes to overlap, make sure that the holes are above the outside border.

Creating Compound Paths from Separate Sets of Paths

Compound paths are very flexible. You can choose two sets of paths, each with an outline and a hole, and make them into one compound path. This technique is especially useful for making masks, but you also can use it to alleviate the repetition of creating several compound paths and selecting one of them at a time.

For example, if you have two shapes, a square and a circle, and want a round hole in each of them, you draw two smaller circles and put them into place. After you position the two shapes in the correct locations, you select them and the round paths inside each of them, and then you choose Object ➪ Compound Path ➪ Make (⌘-8) [Ctrl+8]. Each of the objects now has a hole and they act as if they are grouped.

To move separate objects that are part of the same compound path, select each object with the Group Selection tool, which selects an entire path at a time, and then move them. Remember that once they're selected, you should use the Direct Selection tool to move the selected portions of a compound path.

Type and Compound Paths

You have been using compound paths as long as you have been using computer PostScript typefaces. All PostScript typefaces are made of characters that are compound paths. Letters that have holes, such as uppercase *B, D,* and *P* and lowercase *a, b,* and *d,* benefit from being compound paths. When you place them in front of other objects, you can see through the empty areas to objects behind them that are visible in those holes.

Each character in a PostScript typeface is a compound path. When you convert characters to editable outlines in Illustrator, each character is still a compound path. If you release the compound paths, the characters with empty areas appear to fill with the same color as the rest of the character, as shown in Figure 9-5, because the holes are no longer knocked out of the letters.

Tropical

Tropical

Figure 9-5: Type as it normally appears after you convert it to outlines (top) and after you release compound paths (bottom)

Tip   Many times, type is used as a mask, but all the letters used in the mask need to be one compound path. Simply select all the letters and choose Object ⇨ Compound Path ⇨ Make (⌘-8) [Ctrl+8]. This action creates a compound path in which all of the letters form the compound path. Usually, all the holes stay the same as they were as separate compound paths.

Any letters that overlap in a word that you make into a compound path can change path directions and thus affect the "emptiness" of some paths. If letters have to overlap, use Unite on them first and then select all the letters and choose Object ⇨ Compound Path ⇨ Make (⌘-8) [Ctrl+8].

Path Directions

Each path in Illustrator has a direction. For paths that you draw with the Pen or Pencil tool, the direction of the path is the direction in which you draw the path. When Illustrator creates an oval or a rectangle, the direction of the path is counterclockwise.

Tip

If you're curious about which way a path travels, click any spot of the path with the Scissors tool and then choose Filter ➪ Stylize ➪ Add Arrowheads. In the Add Arrowheads dialog box, make sure that the End button is selected and click OK. An arrowhead appears, going in the direction of the path. (Figure 9-6 shows several paths and arrowheads appearing for each path.) If the path is Filled and not Stroked, you see only half the arrowhead in Preview mode. Choose the Undo command twice (once for the arrowhead and once for the path splitting) to go back to where you started. You can also check the path direction in the Attributes palette. Show Attributes and select one path with the Group Selection tool and notice the Reverse Path Direction. Select the hole and notice it shows the path in the opposite direction.

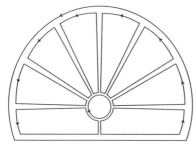 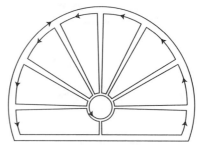

Figure 9-6: The paths on the left are individual paths. The paths on the right make up a compound path. The arrows represent the direction of the paths. Notice that the only difference in direction is on the outermost path.

Paths have directions for one purpose (one purpose that you need to know about, anyway), and that is to determine what the solid areas of a compound path will be and what the empty areas will be. The individual paths in a compound path that create holes from solid paths go in opposite directions.

Create a large circle and put a smaller circle within it. Both circles are traveling in the same direction—counterclockwise. Select both of them and choose Object ➪ Compound Path ➪ Make (⌘-8) [Ctrl+8]. The outside circle changes its direction to clockwise so that the two circles can work together to form a doughnut-like shape.

If two smaller circles are inside the larger circle, they still punch holes in the larger circle because both of them are traveling in the same direction. But what happens when the two inside circles overlap? The area where they overlap is inside the empty area, but both holes go in the same direction. The intersection of the two holes is solid because of the winding path rule.

The Winding Numbers Rule, or What Happened to My Fills?

Understanding the Winding Numbers Rule is helpful when you are dealing with compound paths. The Winding Numbers Rule counts surrounded areas, starting with 0 (outside the outermost edge) and working its way in. Any area with an odd number is Filled, and any area with an even number (such as 0, the outside of the path) is empty, or a hole.

You can apply this rule to most compound paths — although taking the time to diagram the paths you've drawn and place little numbers in them to figure out what is going to be Filled and what isn't is usually more time-consuming than doing it wrong, undoing it, and doing it right. I've done the work for you in Figure 9-7.

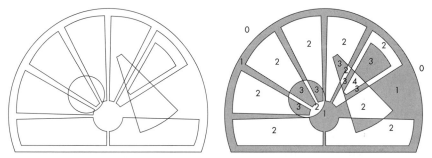

Figure 9-7: As the paths wind in from the outside, odd-numbered areas are Filled and even-numbered areas are empty

Reversing Path Directions

To change the direction of a path, select just the path using the Group Selection tool and choose Window ➪ Show Attributes (F11). In the Attributes palette box (see Figure 9-8), click the other (not darkened) direction button.

Figure 9-8: The Attributes palette

When paths are changed into compound paths, their direction may change. The strange thing about this is that the Reverse Path Direction button is usually on for objects that are traveling counterclockwise. The outermost path does not change direction from counterclockwise to clockwise until more than one overlapping path is made into a compound path. The paths that make up the holes don't change direction. They're still counterclockwise, but when you look at their Attributes, Reverse Path Direction is on.

One thing that is consistent when dealing with path directions is that holes must travel in the opposite direction from the outside path. As a result, if the Reverse Path Direction button is on for the holes, it is not on for the outside path. That scenario is the normal one when you create compound paths with holes. You can, if you so desire, check the Reverse Path Direction button for the outside path and uncheck it for the inside paths. The resulting image will have the same holes as produced by the reverse. Figure 9-9 shows a compound path and its path directions before and after four of the paths were reversed.

 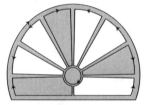

Figure 9-9: Reversing the direction of the four paths in the illustration on the left Fills those holes, as shown in the illustration on the right

Caution   Never, never, never attempt to change path direction when all paths of a compound path are selected. Clicking once on either button will make all the paths in the compound path go in the same direction at this point, which means that no holes will appear.

Using Unite to Create Compound Paths

Another way to make compound paths is by using Unite. Unite works a little differently from the Make Compound Path command. All the selected paths become a single compound path, but none of the path directions are reversed. This means that no holes are created when Unite is applied.

Unite is quite useful for creating compound paths when there are overlapping pieces of paths that you don't want to create holes between accidentally, such as text converted to outlines.

In addition, Unite removes any overlapping path areas where Filled areas or holes are, so if you Stroke the object, you'll get a much better result than if the object were just a plain compound path.

Faking a Compound Path

At times, using a compound path just doesn't work. You may need to cheat a little. Except in the most extreme circumstances, you can fake compound paths, but you need to make quite an effort.

If the background is part of a gradient, select the hole and the object that is painted with the gradient, apply the gradient, and use the Gradient Vector tool to make the gradient spread across both objects in exactly the same way. This trick can fool even the experts.

ASK TOULOUSE: Can't Make a Compound

Mork: I can't make a compound out of my selected paths!

Toulouse: That often happens when one or more of the paths is already a compound path.

Mork: Huh? How would I find out if that's the case?

Toulouse: Well, you can check and fix it at the same time. First, select the paths you'd like to make into a compound path.

Mork: Got it.

Toulouse: Then, go under Object to Compound Path and hold.

Mork: Okay.

Toulouse: Is Release gray or black?

Mork: Black.

Toulouse: That means that at least one of the selected paths is already a compound. Drag over to Release.

Mork: Done.

Toulouse: Then choose Object ⇨ Compound Paths ⇨ Make.

Mork: It worked!

Toulouse: And what did you learn this week?

> **Tip** One way to fake a compound path is by selecting the background, making a copy of it, making the hole a mask of the background area, and grouping the mask to the copy of the background.

Masks

In Illustrator, you use masks to mask out parts of underlying objects that you don't want to see. The path that you draw in Illustrator defines the shape of the mask. Anything outside the mask is hidden from view in Preview mode and does not print.

Masks are objects that *mask* out everything but the paths made up by the mask (see Figure 9-10). Masks can be open, closed, or compound paths. The masking object is the object whose paths make up the mask, and this object must be in front of all the objects that are being masked.

Figure 9-10: An object, its mask, and the resulting masked object

You can make masks from any path, including compound paths and text. You can use masks to view portions of multiple objects, individual objects, and placed EPS (Encapsulated PostScript) images.

Creating Masks

To create a mask, the masking object (the path that is in the shape of the mask) has to be in front of the objects that you want it to mask. You select the masking object and the objects that you want to mask. Then you choose Object ⇨ Mask ⇨ Make (⌘-7) [Ctrl+7]. In Preview mode, any areas of the objects that were outside the mask vanish, but the parts of the objects that are inside the mask remain the same. Figure 9-11 shows an illustration with masks and without them.

Figure 9-11: The image on the left uses masks to hide portions of objects. The image on the right is the result of releasing those masks.

Masks are much easier to use and understand in Preview mode than in Artwork mode.

If you want to mask an object that is not currently being masked, you need to select the new object and all the objects in the mask, including the masking object. You then choose Object ➪ Mask ➪ Make (⌘-7) [Ctrl+7]. The mask then applies to the new object as well as to the objects that were previously masked. The new object, like all others being masked, must be behind the masking object.

Like compound paths, masking does not work in hierarchical levels. Each time you add an object to a mask, the old mask that didn't have that object is released, and a new mask is made that contains all of the original mask objects as well as the new object. Releasing a mask affects every object in the mask, as described in "Releasing Masks," later in this chapter.

Tip Usually, grouping all the objects in a mask is a good idea, but group them only after you have created the mask. Having the objects grouped facilitates moving the mask and its objects and selecting them when you want to add other objects to the mask.

Masking Raster Images

There are two different ways to mask raster images. The first method is done in Photoshop by creating a *clipping path* and saving it as an EPS image. The second method is to use a mask in Illustrator.

Each of the two methods has its strengths and weaknesses, with the best solution being a combination of both methods. The main advantage to creating a clipping path in Photoshop is that the path can be adjusted while viewing the image clearly at 16:1. (Viewing an image at 1600% in Illustrator displays chunky, unrecognizable blocks of color.) In this manner, the path can be precisely positioned over the correct pixels so that the right pixels are selected for masking. One disadvantage to using Photoshop's clipping path is that the Path tool and path-editing controls in Photoshop are a limited version of Illustrator's Pen tool and path-editing controls, which maks it more difficult to create and edit a path. The second disadvantage to using a clipping path is that compound paths in Photoshop adhere to one of two different Fill rules, which control the way holes appear for differing path directions. Illustrator is much more flexible in this respect because you are able to change the path direction of each individual path with the Reverse Path Direction checkbox in the Attributes palette.

The best solution is to create the clipping path in Photoshop, and then, when the clipping path is selected, choose File ➪ Export ➪ Paths to Illustrator, which saves an Illustrator-compatible file with the clipping path intact. Save the Photoshop image as an EPS file and place it in Illustrator (File ➪ Place). Then open the Illustrator file (that was created by Paths to Illustrator) and copy the path to the document with the raster image. The path is sized to fit directly onto the raster image.

Tip   Copying the selected path in Photoshop enables you to paste it directly in Illustrator, even if you can run only one of those programs at a time. Just copy, quit Photoshop, run Illustrator, and paste it into the Illustrator document. This works when going from Illustrator to Photoshop (paths only) as well.

Masking Blends and Other Masks

You can mask objects that are masking other objects. Just make sure that you select all the objects in each mask and that, as with other objects, they are behind the path that you want to use for a masking object. You also can mask blends, as described in Chapter 12.

Stroking and Filling Masking Objects

Creating a basic mask requires four steps.

1. Select the path that you want to use as a mask and bring it to the front.

2. Select the mask and any objects that you want to mask and then choose Object ➪ Masks ➪ Make (⌘-7) [Ctrl+7]. Group the masked objects with the mask for easier selecting in the future.

3. Using the Group Selection tool, select the mask. Then change the Stroke to 1-point Black. The mask now has a 1-point Black Stroke. The result should resemble Step 4 in Figure 9-12.

Step 1

Step 2

Step 3

Step 4

Figure 9-12: Steps for creating a Stroked mask

New
Feature

In Illustrator 8, you can apply a Stroke or Fill to a masking object. A Fill and Stroke of None replace any Paint Style attributes that you applied to the object prior to transforming it into a mask. But if you select the object after it is a mask, you can apply a Stroke or Fill to that mask. If you release the mask, the path that was the masking object continues to have a Fill and Stroke of None.

Releasing Masks

To release a mask, first select the masking object (you may select other objects as well). Then choose Object ➪ Mask ➪ Release (⌘-Option-7) [Ctrl+Alt+7], and the masking object no longer is a mask.

If you aren't sure which object is the masking object or if you are having trouble selecting the masking object, choose Edit ➪ Select All (⌘-A) [Ctrl+A] and choose Object ➪ Mask ➪ Release (⌘-Option-7) [Ctrl+Alt+7]. Of course, this action releases any other masks that are in the document — unless they were separate masks that were being masked by other masks — got that?

To release all the masks in the document, even those masks that are being masked by other masks, Select All (⌘-A) [Ctrl+A] and choose Release Mask repeatedly. Usually three Release Masks gets everything, unless you went mask-happy in that particular document. You can also use the Select ➪ Masks option to check if there are any remaining masks.

Masks and Printing

As a rule, PostScript printers don't care too much for masks. They care even less for masks that mask other masks. And they really don't like masks that are compound paths.

Unfortunately, because of the way that Illustrator works, every part of every object in a mask is sent to the printer, even if only a tiny piece of an object will be used. In addition, controlling where the masking object slices objects requires a great deal of computing power and memory. You can have a problem, for example, when you have more stuff to mask than the printer can handle.

More important than any other issue involved with masks and printing is the length and complexity of the masking path.

The more objects in a mask, the more complex it is. The more Anchor Points, the more complex it is. The more direction points coming off those Anchor Points, the more complex the mask is. In other words, your printer would enjoy a mask if the masking object was a rectangle and no objects were being masked.

Caution   Masks are usually incredibly complex. This complexity causes many problems for printers (especially ones equipped with PostScript Level 1 and PostScript clones) and quite often results in PostScript printing errors. In addition, be careful not to go mask-crazy (using hundreds of masks), or your document may never see toner.

Masks and Compound Paths

Creating masks from compound paths is especially useful when you are working with text and want several separate letters to mask a placed EPS image or a series of pictures that you created in Illustrator.

The reason that you need to transform separate objects into compound paths is that a masking object can only be one path. The topmost object of the selected objects becomes the masking object, and the others become objects within the mask. Creating a compound path from several paths makes the masking feature treat all the objects as one path and makes a masking object out of the entire compound path.

You can use compound paths for masking when you are working with objects that need to have holes as well as when you are working with text and other separate objects. Figure 9-13 was created by making one compound path from all of the parts of the window frame and using that compound path as a mask for the space scene.

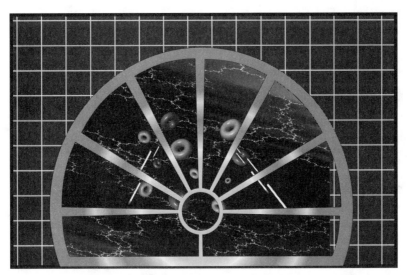

Figure 9-13: Creating a compound path out of all of the parts of the window frame made the window frame a mask for the space scene

Using Compound Paths and Masks in an Illustration

I used several compound paths and masks to achieve the effects in Figure 9-14. The compound paths are the word *Tropical* and the large strips of film across the lower half of the illustration. The masks are the word *Tropical,* the binocular shape, and the outside frame of the poster.

Figure 9-14: This poster was created by using several different compound paths and masks

ASK TOULOUSE: Masking vs. Cropping

Mearth: Should I mask or should I crop?

Toulouse: You mean with the Pathfinder Crop filter?

Mearth: No, I'm considering a career change in the direction of shucking corn.

Toulouse: I take it you're being sarcastic.

Mearth: Harumph.

Toulouse: It really depends. Cropping has two serious advantages over masking.

Mearth: And those are . . . ?

Toulouse: First, unnecessary paths are deleted, and second, potential printing problems that might occur when a mask is being used are eliminated.

Mearth: So I should crop.

Toulouse: Actually, there's more in favor of masking.

Mearth: Aha!

Toulouse: Yep. Masking allows you to edit the artwork in the future.

Mearth: That's a big one.

Toulouse: Real big. You can change the shape, size, whatever, of the mask and the masked objects.

Mearth: Good points.

Toulouse: And you can mask raster images and nonoutlined text.

Mearth: I'm sold.

In the first set of steps (described here and illustrated in Figure 9-15), you create the strip of film and place the island pictures into the film. You do not use masks in this process. I make this point so that you don't think that you always have to use masks, especially when another method is easier.

1. To create the film shape, draw a long, horizontal rectangle with the Rectangle tool and place five rounded-corner rectangles inside the long rectangle.

2. To create the sprocket holes in the film, place a right-side-up triangle next to an upside-down triangle and continue placing triangles until you have a row of triangles across the top of the film.

3. After you group all the triangles together, Option[Alt]-copy them (drag the triangles with the Option [Alt] key pressed, releasing the mouse button before releasing the Option [Alt] key) to create a second row of triangles along the bottom of the film.

4. Select all the pieces of the film and choose Object ⇨ Compound Paths ⇨ Make (⌘-8) [Ctrl+8]. Fill the compound path with a dark purple color that is not quite black.

5. This part looks as if you use a mask, but you don't need to do any masking here. Instead, place one image, size it so that it just covers the hole, and Option-copy it across the remaining holes. Select each image in turn, choose File ⇨ Place Art, and select a different image for each square. To complete the effect, simply bring the strip of film to the front.

6. Before you place the film into the poster, group the images and the film and rotate them slightly. Grouping them prevents the hassle of selecting each one later if you need to move or transform them.

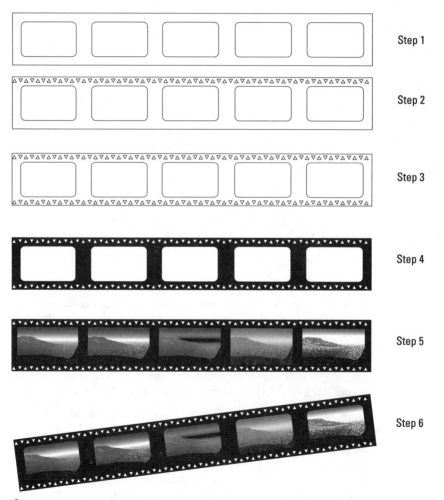

Figure 9-15: Steps for creating a complex compound path to achieve a masking effect

Instead of making the film a compound path, you could mask each of the photos and place each masked photo on top of the film. The method described in the preceding steps makes changing photos easier and takes less of a toll on the output device.

The next set of steps describes how to use the word *Tropical* to show the tropical island.

1. Place an image in the document and create a masking path for the top of it. Before you make the objects into a mask, select the image and choose Edit ➪ Copy (⌘-C) [Ctrl+C]. (You use this copy in Step 3.)

2. Select both the masking path and the image and choose Object ➪ Mask ➪ Make (⌘-7) [Ctrl+7].

   You can use the outline of the masking path as a shadow by Option-copying it before you perform Steps 1 and 2. Change the Fill in the copy to Black and place the copy below and to the right of the original.

3. Choose Edit ➪ Paste in Back (⌘-B) [Ctrl+B] to position the image directly underneath the original image. Choose File ➪ Place Art and substitute a slightly varied version of the original image. The letters stand out decisively, as Figure 9-16 shows. The image behind the word Tropical was changed in Photoshop using a Mosaic filter.

Figure 9-16: Using dissimilar raster images as masked objects makes the word *Tropical* stand out in the image

Summary

✦ Compound paths are one or more paths that Illustrator treats as a single path.

✦ Compound paths give you the ability to put holes in your paths.

✦ Changing the direction of a path via the Attributes palette can change the holes in the compound path.

✦ Each character of type converted to outlines consists of a compound path.

✦ Masks are paths that overlay other Illustrator objects, showing the objects only through the masking path.

✦ When using text outlines as a mask, make sure that all the paths that make up the text outlines are a single compound path.

✦   ✦   ✦

Blends and Gradients

In Illustrator, a blend is a series of paths that Illustrator creates based on two other paths. The series of paths transforms from the first path into the second path, changing Fill and Stroke attributes as it moves. Gradients are Fills that change from one color to another in either linear or radial form.

Understanding Blends and Gradients

At first glance, blends and gradients seem to do the same things but in different ways — so why have both? The Blend tool, moreover, seems to be much harder to use than the Gradient Vector tool. On the surface, it seems that more can be done with gradients than with blends. Blends are no longer limited to two colors; gradients can have tons of colors. Blends take a long time to redraw; gradients take a fraction of the time.

After all, if gradients are so much easier to use and produce so much better results, is it really necessary to have a Blend tool or a Blend function? Students, clients, and the occasional passerby have asked me this question quite often, and they seem to have a good point at first. Upon further study, however, it becomes apparent that blends are quite different from gradients, both in form and function.

Gradients are used only as Fills for paths. Gradients can be either linear or radial, meaning that color can change from side to side, top to bottom, or from the center to the outside. Every gradient can have as many distinct colors in it as you can create, limited only by RAM.

Blends, on the other hand, are series of transformed paths between two *end paths*. The paths between the end paths mutate from one end path into the other. All the attributes of the end paths change throughout the transformed paths, including shape, size, and all Paint Style attributes. The major benefit is that you can blend multiple colors at one time.

New Feature

With Illustrator 8 the blending got easier. There are two choices: You can blend either by using the Blend tool or by choosing Object ➪ Blend ➪ Make (⌘-Option-B) [Ctrl+Alt+B]. In Illustrator 8, you can create a blend with multiple shapes by pressing the right combination of keyboard commands.

To summarize, gradients are an easier way to create blends that change only in color, not in shape or size. Figure 10-1 shows how you can use blends and gradients to create a similar result.

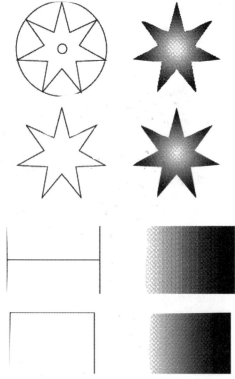

Figure 10-1: Each example was a blend or a gradient. The left side shows the image in Artwork mode; the right side shows the Preview mode.

If you remember that gradients work only with color, not with shapes, you should already have an idea of when to use which function. Linear and radial gradients usually look better than their blended counterparts because the quality is better and more colors can be added and manipulated. Changes to color are also more easily accomplished with gradients than with blends. In addition, changes to angles and the placements of the gradients are much easier to make than analogous position changes with blends.

One drawback to using gradients is their "computery" look. Gradients are exact blends that are even from start to finish. Of course, with a little practice, additional colors or tints can be added, and the midpoint balance between two adjacent colors can be offset, giving the blend a more natural look. In general, though, realistic effects aren't all that easy to achieve with gradients.

Blends, on the other hand, can be incredibly flexible when it comes to creating photorealistic changes in color, if you plan ahead. Changes to blends aren't really changes at all; instead, they are deletions of the transformed objects and changes in the attributes of the end paths. If you know what you want, blending colors can take on an incredibly realistic look by changing the shapes of the blend's end paths just slightly.

But even more useful than creating realistic changes in color is blending's capability to transform shapes from one shape to another, as shown in the examples in Figure 10-2. With a bit of practice (and the information in this chapter), you can transform any illustration into another illustration. There is a limit to the complexity of the illustrations that can be transformed, but the limit is due more to the time it takes to create the blends than to limitations inherent in Illustrator.

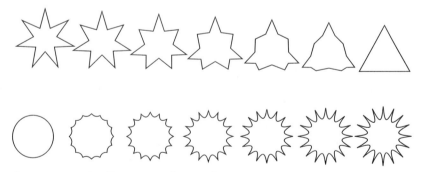

Figure 10-2: Blending to transform a shape

Because blends work on both Stroke and Fill attributes of objects, some really exciting effects can be created that aren't possible using any other technique, electronic or traditional.

Blends

In past versions of Illustrator, blends were used predominantly for what gradients are used for now: to blend between different colors, normally just two different colors. But some artists took it on themselves to stretch the capabilities of the Blend tool to create fantastic effects that amazed even the creators of the tool.

Originally, Adobe marketed the Blend tool (which was new to Version 88) as a tool whose primary purpose was to transform shapes, not blend colors. Yeah, that's cool, designers said, but instead they used the tool for blending colors to create what were known as vignettes, or what traditional artists called gradients.

The Blend tool creates in-between steps in the area between two paths, where the paint style and shape of one path transform themselves into the paint style and shape of the second path.

New Feature

Illustrator 8 has dramatically enhanced the Blending function. The big change is that blends are now live, or editable. This huge change enables users to change the color, shape, and location of the blend shapes and the blend will instantly reblend to the new changes. Another great change is the capability to blend along a path.

Although any blend takes into account both color and shape, I treat color and shape separately in this chapter because people using the Blend tool are often trying to obtain *either* a color effect *or* a shape effect, rather than both at once.

The Blend tool is the tool used to create blends, which are a group of paths (commonly referred to as *blend steps*) that change in shape and color as each path is created closer to the opposite *end path*.

1. Using the Rectangle tool, create a small (1-inch) vertical rectangle. With the Selection tool, Option[Alt]-copy the path a few inches to the side. Press Shift as you drag horizontally to constrain the movement of the path.

2. On the left rectangle, change the Fill to Black and the Stroke to None. Change the right rectangle to a Fill of White and a Stroke of None.

3. Choose the Blend tool (press the B key). Click the top-left point of the left path and then the top-left point of the right path. This step tells Illustrator to blend between these two paths and it uses the center points as reference. The Blend tool cursor changes from x to + in the lower right corner.

4. A spine is created between the two end paths (which are now transparent). Press ⌘-Shift-A [Ctrl+Shift+A] to deselect all selected paths. The blend is made up of 256 paths, including the two end paths. Each path is a slightly different tint of black. The default Blend Option is to create smooth color between the two shapes.

Note Adobe has changed the way you select blends. Gone is the annoying cross hair with the next to invisible ellipses. Replacing the cross hair is a small image of the Blend tool with an x in the lower right corner. The rectangle is white until you go over an Anchor Point. When the rectangle is black, then you are over a point to use in blending and a plus sign shows in the lower-right corner after you have clicked on the first shape and you are on top of the second shape.

You must use the Blend tool to click from one path to another path on each of two different paths. Paths can be open paths or closed paths.

Before you click any paths, the cursor looks like a small image of the Blend tool. When the cursor is over an object an x appears in the lower-right corner. After the first click of the Blend tool, the x is replaced by a + when the cursor is over an object. After the second point has been clicked, a spine is created between the two objects' center points, a blend is generated, and all the objects are grouped. The blend is dependent on the Blend Options. To change the Blend Options, select the objects with the selection tool, and double-click on the Blend tool in the toolbox to open the Blend Options dialog box.

Creating Linear Blends

Color blends are made by creating two end paths, usually identical in shape and size, giving each path different Paint Style attributes, and creating a series of steps between them with the Blend tool. The more end paths that are created, the more colors you can create.

The following steps describe how to create a basic linear blend and Figure 10-3 illustrates these steps.

Note The examples in this chapter are easier to understand when you are working in Preview mode.

1. Draw a vertical path with the Pen tool. Give it a Fill of None and a Stroke of 2 points Black.

2. Option[Alt]-copy the path to the right. Give the new path a Stroke of 2 points White.

3. With the Blend tool, click the path on the left and then the path on the right.

4. Deselect all (⌘-Shift-A)[Ctrl+Shift+A] to see the result.

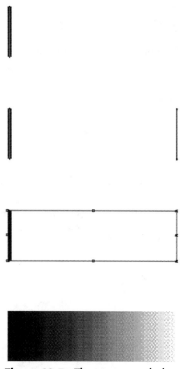

Figure 10-3: The steps needed to create a linear blend

Blend Options and Live Blending

Adobe has enhanced the Blending functions of Illustrator by making the Blend tool so much better and by adding a Blends option under the Object menu. The Blends options are Make, Release, Blend Options, Expand, Replace Spine, Reverse Spine, and Reverse Front to Back. You may wonder why you need a Blend tool at all? Well, the Blend tool enables you to blend between specific points. Now with Illustrator's Live Blend capability, it seems as if you may not need to release a blend to change it. You can use the Direct Selection tool to select the path and edit or change the color and the blend instantly updates. Live Blending is the capability to change the shape or color of a blend and update it automatically.

New Feature   New to Illustrator 8 is the option to blend multiple objects and paths at one time.

Using the Blend Options

After choosing the Blend function from the Object menu, or accessing it from the keyboard, you can access the Blend Option from the Object menu. Figure 10-4 shows the Blend Options dialog box. The three Spacing options are Smooth Color, Specified Steps, and Specified Distance. The Orientation options are Align to Page and Align to Path.

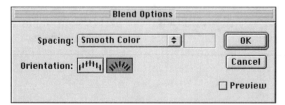

Figure 10-4: The Blend Options dialog box

The Blend Options work as follows:

✦ **Smooth Color:** This option automatically determines the best number of steps needed to make this blend look very smooth.

✦ **Specified Steps:** The Specified Distance option lets you choose how far apart each blend step will be from another blend step.

✦ **Specified Distance:** This option enables you to type in the distance between the steps.

✦ **Align to Page:** This option runs the blend vertically or horizontally depending on your page orientation.

✦ **Align to Path:** This option runs the blend perpendicular to the path.

Blending Multiple Objects

New to Illustrator 8 is the capability to blend multiple objects in one step. Gone are the days of blending, hiding, blending, hiding, and so on. Select all the objects you want to blend and choose Object ➪ Blends ➪ Make or click with the Blend tool on all the objects you want to blend.

Changing Blend Colors on the Fly

The Live Blend option lets you change the colors of a blend without having to redo the whole blend. With the Direct Selection tool select the path that you want to change the color of in the blended shape. Select a new Fill or Stroke color. The blend is updated instantly with the new color.

Moving a Blended Object

Another great aspect of Live Blends is the capability to edit the blend at any time and have it automatically update on the fly. A spine is created when a blend is made. With the Direct Selection tool you can select an Anchor Point on the spine and move it. This changes the location of that point and the blend updates accordingly.

Editing a Blended Object

Now you can edit lines by adding, deleting, or moving any part of your blend and it updates automatically. You can delete and add points or change the shape of a path with the Direct Selection tool. Figure 10-5 shows a figure before and after editing the blend.

Figure 10-5: Before and after editing a blend

Adjusting the Blend Options

The Blend Options dialog box lets you change the Spacing and Orientation aspects. Select the blend you want to adjust and either double-click the blend tool or choose Object ➪ Blends ➪ Blend Options to open the dialog box to change the settings.

Releasing a Blend

If you want to redo a blend, you have to release it first. By choosing Object ⇨ Blends ⇨ Expand the blend will expand into a mess of shapes.

Replacing the Spine

The Replace Spine option enables you to apply a blend to a selected path. To apply this effect, select the Stroked path and your blend and choose Replace Spine from the Blends submenu. Figure 10-6 shows the before and after of applying a blend to a path. Draw a path in the shape you want the spine of the blend to follow. Select the blend with the spine you want to change, and the new path that is to become the new spine. Choose Object ⇨ Blends ⇨ Replace Spine. The blend updates automatically.

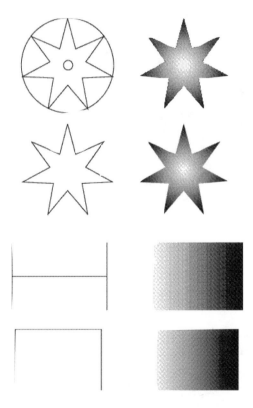

Figure 10-6: Before and after applying Replace Spine

Reversing the Spine

This option reverses the sequence of the objects you are blending. If you have a rectangle on the right blended to a circle on the left, choosing Reverse Spine will put the circle on the right and the rectangle on the left. Reversing the spine flips the position of the shapes on the spine.

Reversing Front to Back

The Reverse Front to Back option reverses the order in which your paths were drawn when you created your blend. If you drew a circle first and a star second, choosing Reverse Front to Back will display the star on top and the circle underneath (see Figure 10-7).

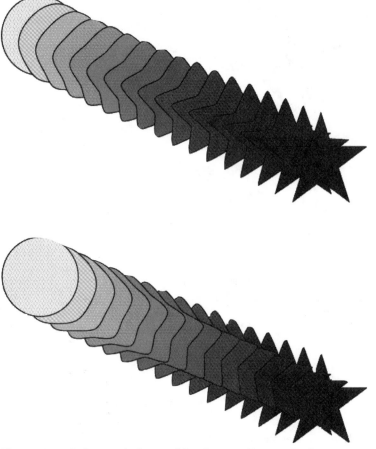

Figure 10-7: Before and after applying Reverse Front to Back

Expand

Choosing the Expand option lets you change any blend or gradient into Filled shapes.

Multiple Colors with Linear Blends

To create linear blends that have multiple colors, you must create intermediate end paths, one for each additional color within the blend.

1. Create two end paths at the edges of where you want the entire blend to begin and end. Don't worry about colors at this time.

2. Select the two paths and choose Object ⇨ Blends ⇨ Make (⌘-Option-B) [Ctrl+Alt+B]. Then choose Object ⇨ Blends ⇨ Blend Options. Change the Smooth Options to Specified Steps. Choose your orientation and enter a number for the steps. (I entered 3 to create three evenly spaced paths between the two end paths.)

3. Expand the newly created Strokes by choosing Object ⇨ Blends ⇨ Expand, then color each of the Strokes of the paths differently, and give them a weight of 2 points. Select all of the paths and choose Object ⇨ Blends ⇨ Make (⌘-Option-B) [Ctrl+Alt+B].

4. The result should look like the blend of colors at the bottom of Figure 10-8.

New Feature   In Illustrator 8, the blend automatically attaches itself to the original paths. The only way to select the original paths is to expand them first using the Expand feature of the Blends submenu.

Nonlinear Blends

End paths created with two End Points that make up blends don't have to be just horizontal or vertical. And when you create multiple color blends, the intermediate end paths don't have to be aligned the same way as the end paths are aligned.

Careful setup of intermediate blends can create many interesting effects, such as circular and wavy appearances, all created with straight paths.

Note   End paths that cross usually produce undesirable effects; if carefully constructed, however, the resulting blends can be quite intriguing. Blending crossed end paths creates the appearance of a three-dimensional blend, where one of the end paths blends "up" into the other.

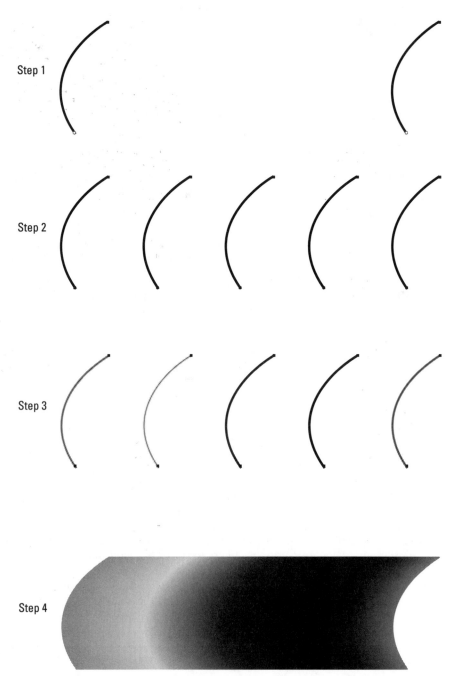

Figure 10-8: The steps to create a multiple-color linear blend

To create nonlinear blends, set up the end paths and either rotate them or change their orientation by using the Direct Selection tool on one of the End Points. Then blend from one end path to the intermediate end paths and then to the other end path. Figure 10-9 shows two examples of nonlinear blends.

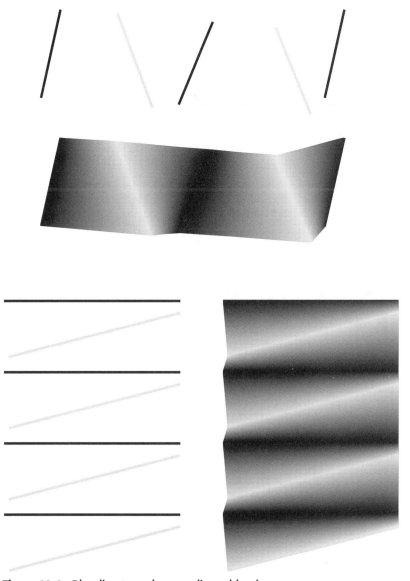

Figure 10-9: Blending to make a nonlinear blend

Masking Blends

Blends by themselves are great, but when masked by other paths, they can really take on a life of their own. To illustrate this concept, use the following steps to create a color wheel (see Figure 10-10).

1. Using the Pen tool, draw a straight segment and give it a 2-point Green (100% Cyan, 100% Yellow) Stroke and a Fill of None in the Color palette.

2. Choose the Rotate tool, press Option [Alt], and click one End Point of the path to set the origin. Type **60°** for the angle in the Rotate dialog box and press the Copy button (Option[Alt]-Return). This procedure creates a copy of the Stroke at a 60° angle, with one End Point directly on top of one of the existing ones.

3. Choose Object ➪ Transform ➪ Transform Again (⌘-D) [Ctrl+D]. Another Stroke is created at a 60° angle from the second. Continue to choose Transform Again until there are six Strokes. Each of these Strokes is used as an end path.

4. Color each Stroke as follows, moving clockwise: 1. Green (100% Cyan, 100% Yellow); 2. Yellow (100% Yellow); 3. Red (100% Magenta, 100% Yellow); 4. Magenta (100% Magenta); 5. Blue (100% Cyan, 100% Magenta); 6. Cyan (100% Cyan).

5. Blend each pair of end paths together either using the Blend tool on each end path, or by choosing (⌘-Option-B) [Ctrl+Alt+B]. The only catch in using the Blend function from the Object menu is that you still have to manually blend the last endpoints. When you are finished blending all the end paths together, the result is a beautifully colored hexagon. Because of the shape, the end paths really stand out as points on the hexagon.

6. To complete the illusion of a perfect color wheel, the blend needs to be in the shape of a circle. Using the Ellipse tool, draw a circle so that the edges are just inside the flat sides of the hexagon, with its center corresponding to the center of the hexagon. This process is easiest to do by Option[Alt]-clicking with the Ellipse tool at the center of the hexagon and pressing the Shift key as the oval is being drawn. Select the circle, the blend steps, and the end paths, and choose Object ➪ Masks ➪ Make (⌘-7) [Ctrl+7].

7. For a more realistic color wheel effect (one that resembles Apple's color wheel), create a Black Stroke on the mask and a small circle at the center that has a Fill of White and a Stroke of Black.

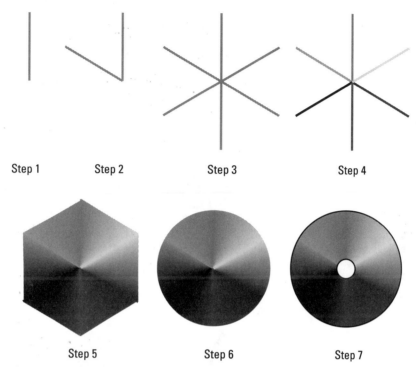

Figure 10-10: Creating a black-and-white color wheel

Tip Blends can be masked with any object. For some really great effects, mask your blends with text (converted to outlines).

Pseudolinear Blends

There is very little difference in the end product of straight-line linear blends and linear gradients. Both are very "computery" looking, but gradients are a little easier to manipulate. The important thing about blends is that the end paths of linear blends *don't have to be straight lines*. This blend capability makes all the difference in the world and is why using linear blends has a really cool aspect.

If you use a smoothly curving line, the blend takes on a fluidity and life of its own, gently caressing the objects it is behind, next to, or masked by. The curves (especially if the end paths are masked off) are not always visible to the eye, and this creates an effect that is both realistic and surreal, giving depth to your illustration in a way that flat linear blends can't.

Instead of smoothly curving lines, try broken, jagged paths, which can add fierce highlights to a blend. Once again, this type of blend is even more effective when the end paths are masked off. Figure 10-11 shows two examples of masked pseudolinear blends.

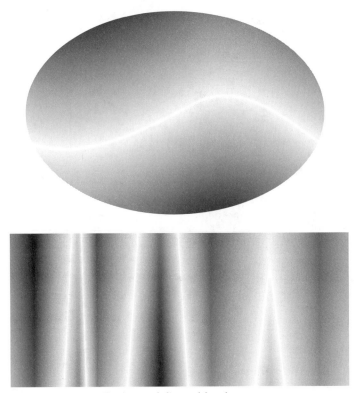

Figure 10-11: Masked pseudolinear blends

Guidelines for Creating Color Linear Blends

Although the preceding procedure should have gone smoothly with no problems, follow these guidelines when creating blends to get good results each time you print:

✦ For linear blends, use either rectangles with only four Anchor Points or a basic 2-point path. If you use a shape with any more Anchor Points or if you use a curved shape with any paths that aren't perfectly straight, you get extra information that isn't needed to create the blend, and printing takes much longer than usual.

✦ When creating linear blends, use one rectangle per end path and color the Fills of the paths, not the Strokes. Coloring the Strokes may appear to work, but it usually results in a moiré pattern when printed. Make sure that the Stroke is set to None, regardless of what the Fill is.

✦ Don't change the number that appears in the Specified Steps text field in the Blend dialog box if you want smooth color. Making the number higher creates additional paths that can't be printed; making the number lower can result in banding when printed (see the "Avoiding Banding" sidebar, later in this chapter).

End Paths for Linear Blends

In the previous linear blend example, I used lines with Stroke weights to create the blend. You can also use rectangles with Fills and no Strokes to achieve much the same printed result. Figure 10-12 shows both lines and rectangles used for end paths.

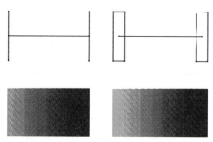

Figure 10-12: Lines (left) and rectangles (right) used for end paths in both artwork and final output

There is no good reason to use a rectangle as an end path instead of a single line with two End Points (at least, none that I can dig up). In fact, lines are better than rectangles for three reasons. First, lines use half as much information as rectangles because there are two Anchor Points on a line while there are four on a rectangle. Second, the width of a line (Stroke weight) is much easier to change after the blend has been created (just select the lines and enter a new weight in the Stroke palette) than it is to change the width of rectangles (you would have to use the Scale Each option). Third, creating a linear blend with lines (Strokes) creates a thick mess of paths, but creating a linear blend with rectangles creates a thicker mess, so much so that it is difficult to select specific rectangles.

New Feature

An open path can now be blended with a closed path and vice versa with Illustrator 8. Open or closed paths can be blended to any path by choosing Object ➪ Blends ➪ Make or using the Blend tool.

Calculating the Number of Steps

Whenever you create a blend, Illustrator provides a default value in the Specified Steps text field of the Blend Options dialog box that assumes that you will be printing your illustration to an Imagesetter or other high-resolution device capable of printing all 256 levels of gray that PostScript allows.

The formula Illustrator uses is quite simple. It takes the largest change that any one color goes through from end path to end path and multiplies that percentage by 256. The formula looks like this: $256 \times$ largest color change % = the number of steps to be created.

For instance, using our linear blend example, the difference in tint values is 100% (100% – 0% = 100%). Multiply 100% by 256, and you get 256. Because the total number of grays must be 256 or fewer, only 254 were created. When added to the two ends, there are 256 tints.

In the second example, where the first line was changed to a 10% Stroke, the difference in tint values is 10% (10% – 0% = 10%). 10% × 256 is 26, the number of steps Illustrator calculates.

In a process color example, if the first end path is 20% Cyan, 100% Magenta, and 40% Yellow, and the second end path is 60% Cyan, 50% Magenta, and 0% Yellow, the largest difference in any one color is Cyan (100% – 50% = 50%). The number of steps created is 128 or 50% × 256.

But, of course, not everything you create is output on an Imagesetter. Your laser printer, for example, cannot print 256 grays unless the line screen is set extremely low. To determine how many grays your laser printer can produce, you need to know both the dpi (dots-per-inch) and the line screen. In some software packages, you can specify the line screen, but unless the printer is a high-end model, it is usually difficult to specify or change the dpi. Use the following formula to find out how many grays your printer can produce:

```
(dpi/line screen)×(dpi/line screen) = number of grays
```

For a 300-dpi printer with a typical (for 300-dpi) line screen of 53, the formula looks like this:

```
(300/53)×(300/53) = 5.66×5.66 = 32
```

A 400-dpi printer at a line screen of 71 has the following formula:

```
(400/65)×(400/65) = 6.15×6.14 = 38
```

A 600-dpi printer at 75 lines per inch uses this formula:

```
(600/75)×(600/75) = 8×8 = 64
```

Sometimes you may want to reduce the number of blend steps in a blend from the default because either your printer can't display that many grays or the distance from one end path to another is extremely small (see "Airbrushing and the Magic of Stroke Blends," later in this chapter).

When reducing the number of blends, start by dividing the default by 2 and then continue dividing by 2 until you have a number of steps that you are comfortable with. If you aren't sure how many steps you need, do a quick test of just that blend with different numbers of steps specified and print it out. If you are going to an Imagesetter, don't divide by 2 more than twice or banding (oh no!) can occur.

Creating Radial Blends

To create a radial blend, make a circle about 2 inches in diameter, Filled with 100% Black. Make a smaller circle inside the larger circle and Fill it with White. Select both shapes and choose Objects ➪ Blends ➪ Make. To change the number of steps, choose Object ➪ Blends ➪ Blend Options. Illustrator will automatically choose the best amount.

Radial blends can be created with objects other than circles. In Figure 10-13, the radial blend was created with a star.

Tip   As with most other blends, when blending from two identically shaped end paths, always click the Anchor Point in the same position on each object. Figure 10-13 shows the difference between clicking the Anchor Points in the same position and clicking on those that are not in the same position.

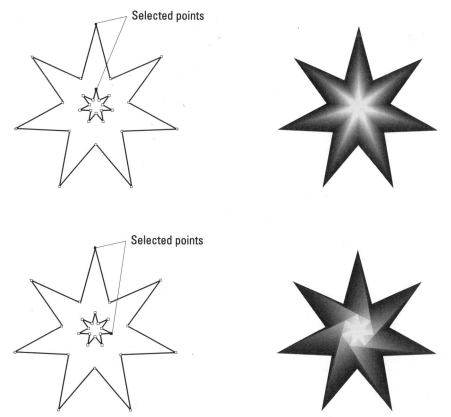

Figure 10-13: The top example was blended choosing the same position points in the images and the bottom example was blended choosing different position points in the images. The left side shows the image in Artwork mode; the right side shows the Preview mode.

Avoiding Banding

The graphic artist's worst nightmare: Smooth blends and gradations turn into large chunks of tints, as shown in the accompanying figure, and suddenly get darker or lighter instead of staying nice and smooth. *Banding*, as this nightmare is called, is an area of a blend where the difference from one tint to the next tint changes abruptly and displays a defining line showing the difference between the two tints. Individual tints appear as solid areas called *bands*.

Avoiding banding is easier when you know what is causing it. Usually one of three things in Illustrator is the cause: too few blend steps, too much of a distance between end paths, or too little variation in the colors of the end paths. Preventing banding due to any of these causes depends on the line screen setting and the capability of your printer to print it.

These causes pretty much make sense. Take the linear blend example earlier in this chapter. If there are only three intermediate steps between end paths, there will be only five colors in the blend, thus creating five bands. If the end paths are each on one side of a 17-inch span, each blend step created would take up the 5 points of width of the Stroke, making each shade of gray 5 points wide — a noticeable size. If the color on the left were 10% Black instead of 100% Black, there would be only 26 color steps between the two end paths.

So, to avoid banding use the recommended number of steps over a short area with a great variation of color.

If you find it hard to fix the banding problem and the blend is made of process colors, try adding a small amount of an unused color (Black, for instance) to cover up the banding breaks. A 5% to 30% change over distances may provide just enough dots to hide those bands. Keeping this in mind, there is more chance for banding if you use the same tints for different process colors. Alter the tint values for one of the colors at one of the end paths just a little, and this alteration will stagger the bands enough to remove them from sight.

See "Calculating the Number of Steps" earlier in this chapter for more information on banding.

One of the nice things about creating radial blends manually (not using the gradient feature) is that by changing the location and the size of the inner object, the gradient can be made to look vastly different. The larger the inner object, the smaller the blended area.

The Gradient feature enables you to change the highlight point on a radial Gradient without changing the source, or angle, of the highlight.

New Feature

The new Gradient Mesh tool in Illustrator 8 enables you to create easy highlights with the click of a mouse. See "The Gradient Mesh Tool" later in this chapter for more information on this new tool.

Creating Shape Blends

The difference between color blends and shape blends is in their emphasis. Color blends emphasize a color change; shape blends emphasize blending between different shapes.

There are a number of things to remember when creating the end paths that form a shape blend. Both paths must be either open or closed. If open, only End Points can be clicked to blend between the two paths. If the shapes also change color, be sure to follow the guidelines in the earlier section related to color blends.

For the best results, both paths should have the same number of Anchor Points selected before blending, and the selected points should be in a relatively similar location. Illustrator pairs up points on end paths and the segments between them so that when it creates the blend steps, the lines are in about the same position.

Shape Blend 1: Computer Vents

Look on the side of your monitor or on the side of a computer or hard drive case. You will undoubtedly see vents or simulated vents used for design purposes running back along these items. This type of blend (changing the angle of straight lines) is the most basic of shape blends and is rather easy to create, so I've added an extra tip at the end of this section to make these blends more realistic. The following steps describe the process for creating computer vents and Figure 10-14 illustrates this process.

1. Draw a rectangular shape that has been distorted to appear like the side of your monitor (use the Pen tool). Choose a Fill of 25% Black and a Stroke of 0.5-point, 50% Black.

2. Select the shape and double-click the Scale tool. Enter 90% in the Uniform field of the Scale dialog box and click Copy (Option[Alt]-Return).

3. With the Direct Selection tool, select and delete the two vertical segments of the shape. Select both of the horizontal segments and change the Fill to None.

4. Blend the two paths together. Then choose Object ⇨ Blend ⇨ Blend Options and change the Spacing to Specified Steps and the number to 15. One side of a monitor is now complete.

5. Select all the paths and copy them up 0.5-point by using the Copy button in the Move dialog box. Change the Stroke to 75% gray.

6. Draw a circle over the center of the group and select the group and the circle. Choose Object ⇨ Masks ⇨ Make and you have a "real" vent in the simulated one.

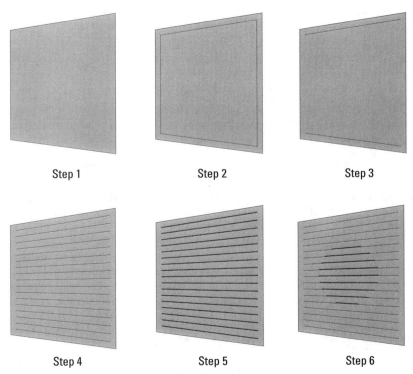

Step 1   Step 2   Step 3

Step 4   Step 5   Step 6

Figure 10-14: A computer vent blend

Shape Blend 2: Circle to Star

The preceding blend slowly transformed one path to another, but the paths were basically the same. The real power of the Blend tool is evident when it is used to generate intermediate paths between two totally different, distinct paths, as in the following example.

1. Create a 1-inch circle with the Ellipse tool. Create a 5-point star by clicking with the Star tool and entering **5** in the Points text field. Enter **0.19"** in the First Radius text field and **0.5"** in the Second Radius text field.

2. Fill both shapes with a color (I used light gray) and give each of them a 2-point Stroke of another color. Change the view to Fit In Window (⌘-0) [Ctrl+0] and place the two objects as far apart onscreen as possible.

3. Choose the Direct Selection tool and select the entire circle. Press the Shift key and click the four points on the star that closely match the four points on the circle. If you accidentally click a point that you decide should not be selected, just click it again with the Direct Selection tool. As long as the Shift key is pressed, the tool deselects only that point while all the other points remain selected.

4. After four points are selected on both the circle and the star, blend them together with the Blend tool. Click the corresponding points on each, such as the topmost points, and then choose Object ➪ Blends ➪ Blend Options. Change the Spacing to Specified Steps and the number to 7.

5. To see what happens if a different number of points are selected on each path, select both paths with the Selection tool. Click the topmost point of the circle with the Blend tool and then click the topmost point of the star. In the Blend dialog box, enter **7** in the Specified Steps text field and then click OK. The star appears to work its way out of a growth on the circle. Figure 10-15 shows the difference between blending without a corresponding number of Anchor Points selected and with a corresponding number of Anchor Points selected on each path.

Tip   Another way to get a smooth transformation between two paths with different numbers of Anchor Points is to add Anchor Points strategically to the path with fewer points. By selecting both of the paths with the Selection tool, you can get results that are similar to selecting similarly positioned points. The results can actually be better when Anchor Points are added because they can be added in positions that correspond to the Anchor Points on the other path.

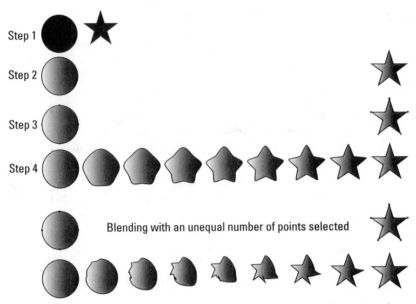

Figure 10-15: The difference between selecting the same number of Anchor Points on each path in a shape blend (top) and selecting a different number of Anchor Points on each path (bottom)

Complex-Shape Blending

Whenever a shape is complex (that is, it isn't a perfectly symmetrical shape, such as a circle or a star), a number of things may have to be done to create realistic and eye-pleasing effects. Figure 10-16 shows a complex-shape blend.

One thing you can do to make the blend better is to add or remove Anchor Points from the end paths. Even if the same number of points are selected and those points are in similar areas on each path, the results can be anything but acceptable.

The Add Anchor Point and Delete Anchor Point tools become quite useful here. By adding points in strategic locations, you can often fool Illustrator into creating an accurate blend; otherwise, the blend steps can resemble a total disaster.

Caution As a general rule, it is less disturbing to the composition of the graphic to add Anchor Points than to remove them. On most paths, removing any Anchor Points changes the shape of the path dramatically.

Figure 10-16: Complex-shape blending

Another method of getting the paths to blend more accurately is to shorten them by splitting a long, complex path into one or two smaller sections that aren't nearly as complex. Each path has to be blended, which can be done in one step by choosing Object ➪ Blends ➪ Make.

And then there is the third method of blending paths, cheating, which is described in the next section.

Shape Blend 3: Cheating

There are times when blending together two different shapes produces results that are grotesque no matter what you do with the Anchor Points. In these cases, a little fixing (which I call "cheating") is in order: The more blend steps you need, the more you benefit from this method.

To get more aesthetically pleasing results from shape blending, it is sometimes easier to create one or more intermediate (middle) end paths. Instead of blending from end to end, you blend from end to middle and then middle to end. Keep in mind that the middle should contain aspects of both end paths. Figure 10-17 shows how a blend would naturally appear (Steps 1 and 2) and how it appears after cheating (Steps 3 through 7).

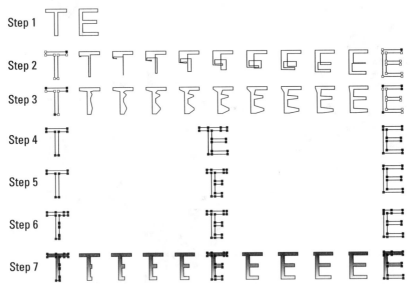

Figure 10-17: Blending a *T* to an *E* without cheating (Steps 1 and 2) and with cheating (Steps 3 through 7)

Remember that cheating is apparent only to you. The client or your boss will never know from seeing the final output that the results were forced. Surprisingly, many illustrators actually feel guilty about creating another end path using this method. If you can't live with yourself, by all means continue trying to select just the right points. However, I'll let you in on a secret: Adobe cheats, too. In one of the original ads for Illustrator 8 and in the accompanying videotape (watch it and check for the poor splicing!), you see an *S* transformed into a swan. Of course, in Adobe's case, it was misrepresenting the capabilities of the Blend tool by making it look as if the tool automatically made eye-pleasing middle paths when, in reality, the "blended" paths were only loosely based on the real blends.

1. In this example, create a text area with a 100-point T and E in any font (a sans serif font, such as Helvetica, is easier than a serif one, such as Times). Select the type with a Selection tool and choose Type ➪ Create Outlines (⌘-Shift-O) [Ctrl+Shift+O]. You are blending between these two letters. Change the Fill to None and the Stroke to 1-point Black.

2. Choose View ➪ Fit in Window (⌘-0) [Ctrl+0] and put each letter on either side of the document. Select both of them with the regular Selection tool and then blend them together with ten steps by choosing the upper-right point in each object and changing the Specified Steps in the Blend Options dialog box. The results are quite ugly. A common shape-blending problem called *blend arcing* occurs when you choose very few or no Anchor Points on either the top or bottom of end paths. In this case, you selected an Anchor Point along the top and no Anchor Points along the bottom, so the blend arc formed along the bottom of the letters.

3. Undo the blend. A better blending effect can be achieved by selecting the two upper-right points, the upper-left point, and the lower-left point of the *T* and the *E* (previously shown in Figure 10-17), but then the blend takes on an ugly, lumpy look.

4. Undo the blend again. The best thing to do in this case is to create an intermediate end path. Copy the *E* and *T* and place them so that one is over the top of the other and between the two original letters.

5. Select the overlapping letters and choose Unite from the Pathfinder palette. The two paths merge into one. Bring in the horizontal bars about halfway by using the Direct Selection tool.

6. Select both the *T* and the merged letters. Make sure that there are corresponding points for each path by adding Anchor Points to the *T* with the Add Anchor Point tool. Both paths should have the same number of Anchor Points. Add corresponding Anchor Points to the *E,* as well.

7. Blend the *T* to the merged path with the Blend tool by clicking the lower-right point of each and entering **4** in the Specified Steps field of the Blend Options dialog box. Blend the *E* to the merged path by clicking the lower-right point of each and entering **4** in the Specified Steps field of the Blend Options dialog box. The transformation should be almost perfect. If necessary, individual points can be touched up with the Direct Selection tool.

Tip   Some really interesting effects can be achieved by using the Rotate tool or the Rotate Portion of the Transform Each filter, which makes the paths appear to spin as they are transforming from one shape into another. Using these tools also serves to mask any anomalies in the blend steps.

Creating Realism with Shape Blends

To create a realistic effect with shape blends, the paths used to create the blends need to resemble objects you see in life. Take a look around you and try to find a solid-colored object — doesn't the color appear to change from one part of the object to another? Shadows and reflections are everywhere. Colors change gradually from light to dark, not in straight lines but in smooth, rounded curves.

Blends can be used to simulate reflections and shadows. Reflections are usually created with shape blends; shadows are usually created with Stroke blends.

In the following example, I show you how to simulate reflections with shape blends. This procedure is a little tricky for any artist because the environment determines a reflection. The artwork you create will be viewed in any number of environments, so the reflections have to compensate for these differences. Fortunately, unless you are creating a mirror angled directly at the viewer (impossible, even if you know who the viewer is in advance), you can get the person seeing the artwork to perceive reflection without really being aware of it.

The chromelike type in the word DON'T in Figure 10-18 was created by masking shape blends designed to look like a reflective surface.

1. Type the word or words you want to use for masking the reflective surface. The typeface and the word itself have an impact on how the finished artwork is perceived. I chose the word *DON'T* and the typeface Madrone. I also did a great deal of tracking and kerning so that all the letters touched, which makes the word look like one piece of material. In addition, I used baseline shift to move the apostrophe up several points.

2. Choose Type ⇨ Create Outlines (⌘-Shift-O) [Ctrl+Shift+O]. Choose a Fill of White for the text and a Stroke of Black. At this point, most of the serifs on the letters overlap.

3. Select all the letters and choose Unite from the Pathfinder palette. This command gets rid of any unsightly seams between the letters. Create a rectangle and place it behind the letters.

4. Set the Auto Trace Tolerance option to 2 in the General Preferences dialog box (File ⇨ Preferences ⇨ General or ⌘-K [Ctrl+K]). Using the Pencil tool, draw a horizontal line from left to right across the rectangle. With a low Auto Trace Tolerance setting, this step should result in a path with many points.

5. Option[Alt]-copy several paths from the original down to the bottom of the rectangle. An easy way to copy the paths is to Option[Alt]-drag down just a bit and then choose Object ⇨ Transform ⇨ Transform Again (⌘-D) [Ctrl+D] several times. In my example, I created five more paths. With the Direct Selection tool, randomly move around individual Anchor Points and direction points on each path, but try to avoid overlapping paths. I left the third and fourth paths virtually identical and kept them close together so that there would be a swift change in color that brings out a "shine." Color the Stroke of each path differently, going from dark to light to dark. In my example, I went from dark to light to dark to light and back to dark again.

6. Blend the Stroked paths together and mask them with the type outlines. In my example, I did this step twice. The first time, I created the front piece; the second time, I used lighter-color Strokes for a highlight, which I offset slightly up and to the left and placed behind the original type.

Figure 10-18: Steps for creating type with a reflective surface

In the preceding steps, I Option[Alt]-copied the path not only because it was easy, but also to ensure that the end paths in the blends would have the same points in the same locations. This technique is much more effective than adding or deleting points from a path.

Tip

With slight transformations, you can use the same reflection blend for other objects in the same illustration and no one will be the wiser. A method that I often use is to reflect the original, scale it to 200%, and then use only a portion of the blend in the next mask.

In the next example, I use shape blends to create the glowing surface of a light bulb (see Figure 10-19). The key to achieving this effect successfully is to draw the light bulb first and then use a copy of exactly the same path for the highlights. The relative locations of Anchor Points stay the same and the number of Anchor Points never changes.

1. Draw a light bulb. Take your time and get it exactly the way you want it, because this path is the basis for everything else in this example. Fill the light bulb with 30% Magenta, 80% Yellow, and a Stroke of None. The first four steps in Figure 10-19 show the light bulb in Artwork mode.

2. Option[Alt]-scale the light bulb down just a little bit, setting the origin on the base of the bulb. Option[Alt]-scale two more copies of the light bulb. Use the Direct Selection tool to change the shape of the paths until they resemble the paths in Step 2 of Figure 10-19. These paths are the basis for blends within the light bulb. Don't change the color of these paths.

3. Option[Alt]-scale down three copies of the path on the left and shape them to resemble the paths in Figure 10-19. While your paths do not have to be exactly like the ones in the picture, be sure that each smaller path does not overlap the larger path. Color the paths as follows, from inside to outside: Color the first (inside) path as 5% Magenta, 10% Yellow; the next path as 10% Magenta, 30% Yellow; and the last path as 15% Magenta, 40% Yellow. The outermost path should still be 30% Magenta, 80% Yellow.

4. Option[Alt]-scale one copy of each of the other two outermost paths and reshape them. Color the new paths 5% Magenta and 10% Yellow.

5. The paths should be in the correct top-to-bottom order, but if they are not, fix them. To see if they are in the correct order, go to Preview mode. If the smaller paths are not visible, then send the outer paths to the back.

6. Blend the paths together by selecting similar Anchor Point locations on each step.

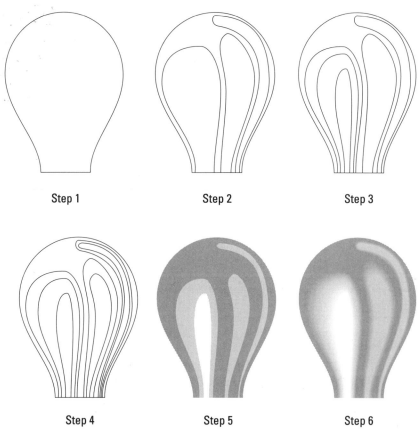

Figure 10-19: Steps for creating real surfaces of a light bulb

Airbrushing and the Magic of Stroke Blends

After wading through all the technical mumbo-jumbo about blending information, you are ready to enjoy your newfound blending powers. Blending can create effects that are usually reserved for bitmap graphics software, such as Fractal Design Painter and Adobe Photoshop, but without the limitation of pixels.

Blending identical overlapping paths together and varying their Stroke weights and colors creates most of the effects described in this section. This technique can provide some of the best effects that Illustrator has to offer.

ASK TOULOUSE: Complex Realistic Blends

Freddy: My blends aren't . . . well, they look fake.

Toulouse: So, they don't look like real blends?

Freddy: No, they don't look *real*.

Toulouse: An important key to getting shape blends to look really good is to blend from the background color of the shape to the first blend, or to make that first blend the background color.

Freddy: What'll that do?

Toulouse: That'll flow the blend smoothly into the background, so you can't tell exactly where the blend starts and stops.

Usually, the bottom-most Stroke has a heavier weight than the topmost Stroke, and as the color changes from bottom Stroke to top Stroke the colors appear to blend in from the outside.

Tubular Blends

Creating tubular blends with the Blend tool is quite often easier than creating any other type of Stroke blend for one simple reason: The two paths, while identical, are not placed *directly* one over the other, but instead are offset just slightly, giving the tube a three-dimensional appearance. If you prefer the exactly-over-the-top method, you can simply omit the moving part in Step 2 of the following procedure and blend the objects using Blends ⇨ Make Command (⌘+Option+B) [Ctrl-Alt-B].

1. Draw a path with the Pencil tool. Smooth curves work better than corners, so make the Auto Trace Tolerance high (7 to 10) in the Type and Auto Tracing dialog box before drawing the curves. Change the Fill to None and the Stroke to 50% Yellow, with a weight of 0.25 point in the Paint Style palette. The path may cross itself.

2. Copy the path and Paste in Back (⌘-B) [Ctrl+B]. Offset the copy about ½ point up and to the right by selecting Object ⇨ Transform ⇨ Move and entering the appropriate values in the text fields. Change the stroke on the copy to 50% Yellow and 100% Black and a weight of 4 points.

3. Blend the two paths together. Create a Black rectangle and send it to the back. The result should look similar to the tube in Figure 10-20.

Step 1

Step 2

Step 3

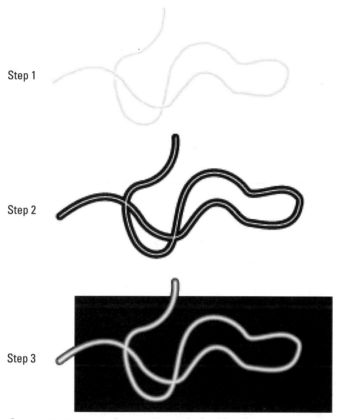

Figure 10-20: Steps for creating Tubular blends

Tip

When you're creating Stroke blends, the number of steps usually doesn't need to exceed 100. If the default is more than 100, divide it by 2 (as explained in the earlier section, "Calculating the number of steps") until the number is less than 100.

In order to see the End Points better on Stroke-blend end paths, draw a tiny marquee around one of the ends with the Zoom tool. If you still can't see the End Points, switch to Artwork mode while creating the blend. You can also choose Object ⇨ Blends ⇨ Make Command (⌘-Option-B) [Ctrl+Alt+B].

To create a Stroke blend that has more shine to it, make the Stroke lighter and thinner and do not offset it as far as in the preceding example.

To create a color Stroke blend that has more depth, make two end paths and color the bottom darker and wider and the top lighter and thinner. Then blend the paths together with one step between the end paths. Add a bit of Black (20% to 40%) to the bottom-most Stroke and then blend from the bottom to the middle and from the middle to the top. The extra Black usually creates a much more realistic appearance of depth than using just two colors, and it keeps Black from being in the upper-half of the tube.

Caution   Try not to use White as your topmost path when creating tubes, because White looks bad and can also cause problems when you print. The more subtle your color change, the more realistic your results. If necessary, you can always add highlights of much lighter colors after the Stroke has been blended.

There are many shapes besides free-flowing tubes that benefit from this type of Stroke effect, including stars, spirals, and line drawings. Objects that appear in everyday life that can be created with tubelike Stroke blends include wires, rods, paper clips, hangers, antennas, pins, and needles. The next section explains how to make one of the most confusing types of objects with blends — the spring tube.

Spring-Tube Blends

To create the curly section of a telephone cord (a spring tube), use the Spiral Tool to create a spiral with two winds and get rid of the inner spiral. Select the outer spiral and go through the steps to create a tube. Make this particular tube look like a section of a telephone cord, as shown in Figure 10-21.

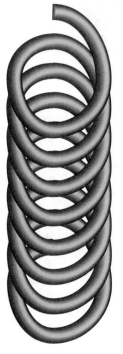

Figure 10-21: A telephone cord created with tubular blends

After the spring tube has been created, group the entire tube together and Option[Alt]-copy it until one side of the spiral lines up with the other side of the spiral. Choose Object ➪ Transform ➪ Transform Again (⌘-D) [Ctrl+D] until the telephone cord is the desired length. To curve the phone cord, draw a marquee around one of the ends with the Direct Selection tool and move it, if necessary. Then use the Rotate tool to change the direction of the curve. Option[Alt]-copy the next section and rotate that section into place.

For quicker but less effective changes in direction, select a small section of the telephone cord and just rotate that section.

Airbrushed Shadows

To create a realistic shadow effect, the edges of an object must be a little fuzzy. The amount of fuzziness on the edges of the path is relative to the distance of the object from its shadow and the strength of the light source. These two areas also affect how dark the shadow is.

To make really cool shadows, you can use either Soft Mix from the Pathfinder palette, which can be used to darken areas, or the Color Adjust filter, which can be used to change the types of color in a selected area. The Drop Shadow filter creates hard-edged shadows, which are usually good only for creating text shadows quickly.

A second way to create cool shadows is to use Stroke blends. Stroke blends can allow the shadows to fade smoothly into the background with a Gaussian Blur-like effect. You can combine Stroke blends with the Soft Mix option from the Pathfinder palette for even better effects. For information on using the Soft Mix option from the Pathfinder palette to create shadows, see Chapter 7.

1. Create a path (or copy it from an original object) for which you want to create a shadow. At this point, you may want to hide the object from which the shadow is being made so that it doesn't get in your way, especially if this object is right above where the shadow will be. Fill the shadowed path with the color you want the shadow to be and then make the Stroke the same color, with a 0.5-point Stroke weight.

2. Copy the shadow, choose Edit ➪ Paste in Back (⌘-B) [Ctrl+B], and then change the Stroke color to whatever the background color is (usually White, unless something else is under the shadow). Make the Stroke weight twice the distance you want the shadow to fade out to. In my example, I made the Stroke 12 points.

3. Now blend these two paths. This has been made easy with the new Blend tool. Watch for the cursor to change from an x to a +. The shadow slowly fades in from the background color to the shadow color. Show the hidden objects (you may have to bring them to the front), and your shadow effect has been created (see Figure 10-22).

Figure 10-22: Airbrushed shadows with linear blends

Creating Glows

Glows are very similar to soft-edged shadows, but instead of a dark area fading into the background, a lighter area fades into the background. Using the light bulb from Figure 10-19, you now can create a glow for that light bulb by using Stroke blending.

1. Select the edge of the object on which you want to create the glow. In my example, I use the light bulb shown in Figure 10-19. Copy the edge, Paste in Back (⌘-B) [Ctrl+B], and press ⌘-Option-Shift-2 [Ctrl+Alt+Shift+2]. These steps lock everything that is not selected. Give the copied edge a Stroke of 6% Magenta and 62% Yellow, and a Weight of 1 point.

2. Draw a Black rectangle around the outside edge of the object and send it to the back. Copy the edge of the light bulb and Paste in Back (⌘-B) [Ctrl+B] again. Change the Stroke to 6% Magenta, 60% Yellow, and 100% Black and make the Stroke about 40 points wide. Move this path about ½ point to the right and up.

3. Blend the two edge paths together to create the glow of the light bulb (see Figure 10-23). The larger the Weight of the second copied path from Step 2, the bigger the glow.

  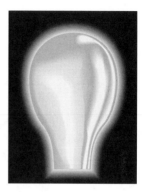

Figure 10-23: Creating a glow around the light bulb

Tip   When creating glows, make the initial glow area (around the edge of the object) *lighter* than the object edges if there are bright highlights in the object. Make the initial glow *darker* than the edges if the edges of the object are the brightest part of the object.

Softening Edges

Edges of objects can be softened in a manner very similar to that of creating shadows. The reason that edges are softened is to remove the hard, computerlike edges from objects in your illustration. Softening edges can be done to an extreme measure so that the object appears out of focus, or just a tiny bit for an almost imperceptible change.

When determining how much of a distance should be softened, look at the whole illustration, not just that one piece. Usually, the softening area is no more than 1 or 2 points (unless the object is being blurred).

To soften edges on an object, select the object, copy it, and then hide the original object. Choose Edit ➪ Paste in Back (⌘-B) [Ctrl+B] and then make the Stroke on the object 0.1 point, the same color as the Fill. Copy again, Paste in Back, make the Stroke the color of the background, and make the Weight 2 points (which makes the softening edge 1-point thick).

When softening objects, rather than moving the entire path in the background, try moving one Anchor Point out just far enough to be able to click it. Blend the two paths together and then show the original object (it may have to be brought to the front).

To blur an object, just make the bottom layer Stroke extremely wide (12 to 20 points or more, depending on the size of the illustration) and blend as described in the preceding paragraphs.

Neon Effects

To create neon effects with Stroke blends, you need to create two distinct parts. Part one is the neon tubing, which by itself is nice, but it doesn't really have a neon effect. The second part is the tubing's reflection off the background, which usually appears as a glowing area. These two separate blends give the illusion of lit neon.

Tip

Neon effects work much better when the background is very dark, though some interesting effects can be achieved with light backgrounds.

1. To make the tubing, create a path that will be the neon. In Figure 10-24, I used two paths: a candle and a flame. Give the Stroke of the paths a Weight of 4 and color them 100% Yellow. Make sure that the Fill is set to None. Change the cap of the Stroke to round and the join of the Stroke to curved.

2. Create a rectangle that is larger than the area of the path. Send it to the back and set the Fill to Black.

3. Select the neon path, copy it, and choose Edit ⇨ Paste in Front (⌘-F) [Ctrl+F]. Offset the copy by 0.25 point and change the Weight of the copy to 0.25 point. Hold down the Shift key and change the color of the Stroke by dragging the sliders to the left to make the color lighter. Do not make the copy White, but make it noticeably lighter than the neon color.

4. Blend the two paths together. This is the neon tube part of the illustration. Hide this tube.

5. To create the reflected area of the background, choose Edit ⇨ Paste in Back (⌘-B) [Ctrl+B]. This step pastes a copy of the original path behind the bottom part of the existing neon tube. Give the path a Stroke of 4 and change the color to 100% Yellow and 75% Black.

6. Copy the Stroke and Paste in Back (⌘-B) [Ctrl+B] again, changing the color of the Stroke to the same as the background and then making the weight of the Stroke 24 points. Offset this copy by 0.25 point and blend the two together.

7. Choose View Object ⇨ Show All (⌘-Option-3) [Ctrl+Alt+3]. Your result should now look similar to Figure 10-24.

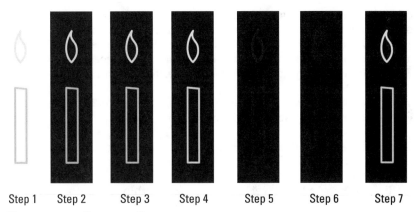

Step 1   Step 2   Step 3   Step 4   Step 5   Step 6   Step 7

Figure 10-24: Neon candles

 Tip   Try crossing paths with neon or, for an even more realistic look, create "unlit" portions of neon by using darker shading with no reflective glow.

Backlighting

Backlighting effects can be accomplished by simply creating a glow for an object and then placing that same object on top of the glow. By making the topmost object Filled with Black or another dark color, a backlit effect is produced, as shown in Figure 10-25.

Figure 10-25: Backlighting the word *DARK*

Gradients

The Gradient feature has no rivals. It is by far the most powerful gradient-creating mechanism available for PostScript drawing programs. Gradients in Adobe Illustrator can have 32 different colors, from end to end in a linear gradient, and from center to outside in a radial Gradient. Gradients can consist of custom colors, process colors, or just plain Black and White. The midpoint of two adjacent colors can be adjusted smoothly and easily toward either color. The Gradient palette can be made available at all times because it is a floating palette, and can be accessed or viewed by pressing F9. And, for what they do, gradients are easier to use than blends.

You can apply gradients only to the Fills of paths, not to Strokes or text objects. Gradients cannot be used in patterns, either.

Checking the Compatible Gradients checkbox in the Document Setup box prevents most gradient problems from occurring. When you're printing to PostScript Level 1 printers, checking this box speeds gradient printing dramatically. Compatible gradients bypass a high-level imaging system within Illustrator that older printers and printers without genuine Adobe PostScript (commonly referred to as "PostScript clones") cannot understand. Checking this box may cause documents to print slower on printers that would ordinarily be able to print those documents.

The Gradient Tool

You use the Gradient tool to change the angle and the starting and ending points for a linear gradient, as well as the location of the center and edges of a radial gradient. The tool is also used to offset the highlight on a radial gradient.

Unlike blends, which can be created only with the Blend tool, gradients can survive quite nicely without the Gradient tool. Gradients are created with the Gradient palette and applied from the Gradient or tool palette. Double-clicking the Gradient tool displays the Gradient palette.

To use the Gradient tool, you must select at least one path that is Filled with a Gradient. Dragging with the Gradient Vector tool on linear gradients changes the angle and the length of the gradient, as well as the start and end points. Dragging with the Gradient tool on radial gradients determines the start position and end position of the gradient. Clicking with the Gradient tool resets the highlight to a new location.

Using Preset Gradients

To choose a preset gradient, select a path and make sure the Fill box is active in the toolbox. In the Swatches palette, click the gradient swatch icon at the bottom of the palette. The four default Gradient presets appear alone in the Swatches. None of the options is selected until you click one of them.

Do you think it's strange that Illustrator doesn't have a preset radial fill that goes from White to Black? You're not alone. This is one of the great mysteries of modern times, right up there with "Why is the # symbol on a phone called the *pound* key?"

These preset gradients appear in Illustrator because they exist in the Illustrator startup file, which is discussed in Chapter 6.

Using the Gradient Palette

The Gradient palette, if nothing else, is really *neat* looking, with all sorts of nifty little controls at your disposal for creating and modifying gradients, as shown in Figure 10-26.

Figure 10-26: The Gradient palette

The bottom of the Gradient palette is where you control what colors are in the gradient and where the colors are in relation to one another.

To add a new color to the bar, click below the bar where you want the new color to appear. The new color will be a step between the left color slider and the right color slider. The percentage depends on how close you click to either end. In other words, the closer you click to the left end, the closer that color will be to the left slider. Then change the settings in the Color palette to create the color you want for that *color stop*. You can enter up to 32 color stops between the two end colors. When a color stop is selected, entering a different percentage in the text field on the right changes the color stop's position.

Tip   You can sample a color to the Gradient palette by Shift-clicking with the Eyedropper anywhere on the screen.

The diamonds above the color bar show where the midpoint between two color stops is. By moving the midpoint left or right, you alter the halfway color between two color stops. When a diamond is selected, entering a different percentage in the text field on the right changes the diamond's position.

1. Draw a series of vertical rectangles, some overlapping, with their bases horizontally even. In my example (Figure 10-27), I angled the top of one of the rectangles.

2. Fill the rectangles with the Black & White Gradient (by clicking it in the Swatches palette) and be sure that the Gradient angle in the Gradient palette is 0°.

3. In the Swatches palette, duplicate the Black & White Gradient and name the copy "Buildings." In the Gradient palette, enter a new color stop at 31% across and make the color 70% Black. Change the color of the leftmost color stop to 85% Black. Apply the Gradient "Buildings" to the rectangles.

4. Draw a rectangle and send it behind the buildings. Change the fill to the Black & White Gradient and change the Gradient angle to 90°.

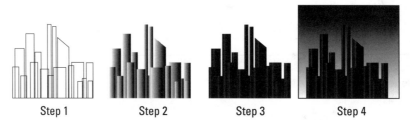

Step 1   Step 2   Step 3   Step 4

Figure 10-27: A cityscape created from rectangles and gradients

For added dramatic impact in a cityscape, copy the buildings one by one and Paste in Front (⌘-F) [Ctrl+F]. Fill the front copies with a Custom pattern of lights with a transparent background.

Shadows, Highlights, Ghosting, and Embossing

You can use gradients to simulate special effects by either duplicating and altering a gradient or by using the Gradient Vector tool on similar gradients.

You can simulate ghosting by using the Gradient Vector tool to slightly alter the starting and ending locations of the gradient.

1. Ghosting effects are easiest to see on text, so create a rectangle and then create large text on top of the rectangle.

2. Convert the type into outlines and position the type outline just to the right and below the center of the rectangle.

3. Select both the type and rectangle and apply a Gradient Fill to them. For Figure 10-28, I used the Red & Yellow Gradient at 90°.

4. Move the type to the center of the rectangle. The type appears to be ghosted there, as in Figure 10-28.

Step 1

Step 2

Step 3

Step 4

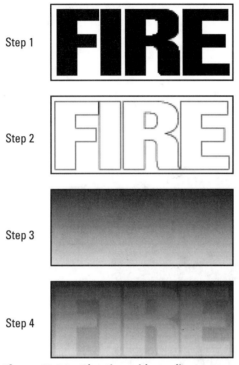

Figure 10-28: Ghosting with gradients

Offsetting two copies of the original graduated image creates embossed gradient images. In one offset image, the gradient is lightened; in the other, the gradient is darkened.

1. Create text and convert it to outlines.

2. Select the outlined type and choose Unite from the Pathfinder palette. Draw a rectangle around the type and send it to the back.

3. Select both the type outline and the rectangle and Fill them with a Gradient. Use a process gradient for this example. Drag the Gradient Vector tool across the rectangle (keeping both objects selected) to set the gradient length and angle.

4. In the Swatches palette, select the gradient used for both the rectangle and type outlines, and make two duplicates of it. Make one duplicate lighter by selecting each color stop and moving it to the left. Create one gradient darker than the original by moving each color stop to the right.

5. Using the Move dialog box, create a copy of the path that's offset a few points up and to the left. Create another copy offset a few points down and to the right.

6. Fill the upper-left path with the lighter gradient you created and the lower-right path with the darker one you made.

7. Select the middle type path and choose Object ⇨ Arrange ⇨ Bring to Front (⌘-Shift-]) [Ctrl+Shift+]]. The type appears embossed, as shown in Figure 10-29.

Step 1

Step 2

Step 3

Step 4

Step 5

Step 6

Figure 10-29: Steps for making embossed type

Tip To make embossed images seem sunken rather than raised, make the lighter image below and to the right and the darker image above and to the left. To make the image seem further raised or recessed, increase the distance between the original path and the offset images.

You can simulate shadows by creating darker gradients based on an existing Gradient. You create the new, darker Gradient in a path that is the same shape as the object causing the shadow.

1. For this example, use the cityscape created in Figure 10-27. Create a rectangle at the bottom of the city and give it a blend from light to dark. Send the rectangle behind the city. Duplicate the Gradient and add some Black to the color stops in the duplicate.

2. Select the city and choose the Reflect tool. Reflect a copy of the city across the base of the city.

3. Unite the reflected city buildings with Unite from the Pathfinder palette. Fill the united city with the darker gradient.

4. Select both the background and the city, and draw the Gradient tool across both paths. The shadow is automatically created.

5. Using the Scale and Rotate tools, adjust the shadow to more accurately resemble the light source. The result should resemble Figure 10-30.

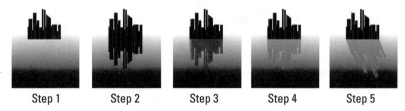

Step 1 Step 2 Step 3 Step 4 Step 5

Figure 10-30: Creating a shadow on a gradient

The Gradient Mesh Tool

New to Illustrator 8 is the Gradient Mesh tool. The Gradient Mesh tool changes a normal filled path into a multicolored object with the click of a button. You click and create a new color at the clicked point. The new color will blend smoothly into the object's original color. Use the Gradient Mesh tool to add highlights, shading, and three-dimensional effects. Figure 10-31 shows an object created with the Gradient Mesh tool.

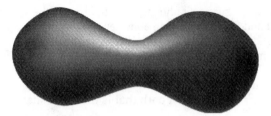

Figure 10-31: An object created with the Gradient Mesh tool

Drops of Color

Use the Gradient Mesh tool to add a highlight to an object or to add some shading. Always deselect the object you wish to add a point to, then pick the color of the point in the Color palette, then click to set the point.

Adding Highlights

Select a light color and click with the Gradient Mesh tool in the spot on the object where you want to add a highlight.

Taking Gradients Where Gradients Fear to Go

Many pieces of software accept Illustrator files but don't care for gradients very much. Dimensions 3, for example, ignores gradients. And even Illustrator says "uh-uh" when you try to use a gradient in a pattern.

The solution to this problem is to use the Expand feature (Object ➪ Expand), described in a later section. Expand converts gradients into blends automatically.

After expanding, select the blends and choose Merge from the Pathfinder palette, which gets rid of the overlapping areas always present with blends in Illustrator.

In addition, gradients cannot be used in Strokes of paths. To get around this limitation, select the path, make the Stroke the correct weight, and choose Object ➪ Path ➪ Outline Path. The Stroke is transformed into a closed path, which can then be Filled with a gradient.

Before using Outline Path, be sure that the weight of the Stroke on the path to be outlined is the correct weight; otherwise, there is no way, short of undoing the whole thing, to convert outlined Strokes back into a single path.

Changing Highlight Color

With the Direct Selection tool, select a point on the mesh and change its color values in the Color palette.

Adding Multiple Highlights

Clicking more than once on an object with the Gradient Mesh tool adds more blends to the object. The strange thing about this is that each click creates a new horizontal and vertical axis. This is the reason the tool is called a "mesh": The more clicks that are created, the more individual lines appear until the base object appears as a complex mesh of lines. Each intersection of lines is a point of color that can be changed. However, when you change a color, adjacent intersecting points aren't updated. The following steps give you an example of what happens when you add multiple highlights to an object.

1. Create a dark blue rectangle and deselect it.

2. Change the color in the Color palette to a bright yellow.

3. With the Gradient Mesh tool, click in the middle of the rectangle. A yellow point of light appears, creating a sort of radial gradient.

4. Deselect, change the fill color to bright green, and click another point. When you do this, two additional points that are somewhere between the blue background and the yellow and green highlights appear.

5. If you never manually change the color of the two new points, they'll continue to update to match the color of the surrounding points. But, if you change the color of one of those points, they're no longer "smart," and will remain that color regardless of the colors of the points around them.

You can create very complex gradient mesh objects with just a dozen or so clicks; these objects are editable, but you'll need to somehow keep track of which points were the originals, so that all the other ones will update automatically.

Tip   You can change the background color of the object you're editing after several highlights have been added by selecting *all* the points on the perimeter of the original object with the Direct Selection tool. Every click with the Gradient Mesh tool adds four points to the perimeter of the object.

Expand

In Illustrator, you can automatically change gradients into blends by selecting the Gradient you wish to change, and then choosing Expand (Object ➪ Expand). A dialog box appears like the one shown in Figure 10-32.

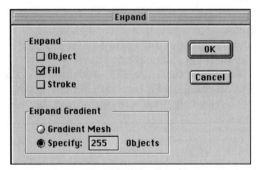

Figure 10-32: Expand dialog box

In the dialog box, you can specify whether to expand an Object, Fill, or Stroke. The Expand Gradient option lets you choose Gradient Mesh or the number of Objects that your selection will expand to.

Summary

✦ Blends and gradients may resemble each other on the surface, but their capabilities and functionality are quite different.

✦ Blends can be created between any open and/or closed paths.

✦ Blends can be masked so that a blend can be used as a Fill.

✦ Shape blends can be created to transform an object from one shape to another.

✦ Blends can be used to create smooth airbrushing effects.

✦ Blends are now as easy as Gradients to use.

✦ Blends are now Live so that they update automatically when you edit a path or change color.

✦ The Gradient Mesh tool makes adding shadows, highlights, and shaping a breeze.

✦ You can quickly turn gradients into blends by selecting the gradient and applying the Expand option.

✦   ✦   ✦

Patterns, Graphs, and Textures

No Illustrator book would be complete without discussing the how-to's of creating patterns, textures, and graphs. Sure you could create these three by the simple act of drawing them, but Illustrator has made their creation a breeze. Illustrator enables you to create a pattern and save that pattern for future use. You could create a line graph and painstakingly draw each line to show a progression of a product, but it is so much easier to do this with the Graph tool. And let us not leave out the desire to add some texture to make your flat images pop up. The Pen and Ink, and Photo Crosshatch options let you make those 2D images appear to have 3D qualities.

Patterns

"The Perfect Pattern is one in which you cannot determine the borders of its tiles," so says the Chinese *Book of Patterns*. If that is true, you can use Adobe Illustrator to create perfect patterns.

The Pattern function in Illustrator is twofold. First, you can Fill or Stroke any path with a pattern. Second, you can edit existing patterns or create new ones from Illustrator objects. The real strength of Illustrator's pattern features is that you can create patterns as well as apply them onscreen in almost any way imaginable.

A pattern in Illustrator is a series of objects within a rectangle that is commonly referred to as a pattern tile. When you choose a pattern in the Swatches palette, the selected pattern is repeated on each of the four sides of the rectangle as well as in the four corners, as shown in Figure 11-1.

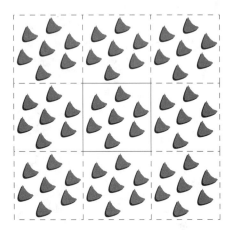

Figure 11-1: The area inside the solid rectangular outline in the center of the figure is the original pattern tile. The dotted-line rectangles represent additional pattern tiles that are aligned with the original to create the pattern and fill up the object.

Illustrator places the pattern tiles together for you. After you apply a pattern to an object, you can use any of the transformation tools to transform it, and you can move within the object by using the Move command. You can move and transform patterns with or without the objects they are within.

Note

Tile patterns can either have a background color or they can be transparent. Transparent patterns can overlay other objects, including objects Filled with patterns.

Using the Default Patterns

There are four patterns available at all times in Illustrator. You can open other libraries from the Swatch Libraries submenu of the Window menu. Under the Swatch Libraries submenu, there are 11 libraries to choose from. The last option (option 12) is the Other Library. Through Other Library, you can bring in saved libraries, as well as the sample libraries that ship with Illustrator.

Figure 11-2 shows the four Fill patterns and their names.

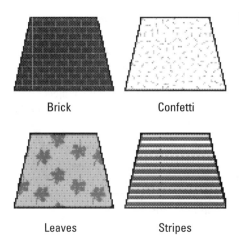

Figure 11-2: The default Fill patterns

Brick   Confetti

Leaves   Stripes

To Fill a path with a pattern, select that path, make sure the Fill icon is active, and click on the corresponding pattern swatch in the swatches palette. The path will be Filled with the pattern indicated.

While there are only four different default Fill patterns, each one can take on a whole new perspective if you use the various transformation functions — move, rotate, scale, reflect, and skew — on them. Figure 11-3 shows what appears to be several patterns; it's really only the same four patterns with various transformations applied.

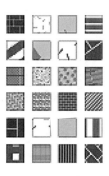

Figure 11-3: These patterns were created using the original four patterns by applying various transformations to them

Caution

Patterns used as Strokes can send your printer to a crashing halt. A pattern-Filled object has the object's path to figure out where to put the pattern when it is printed. The Stroke command in PostScript is a one-shot command that follows the path with thickness and a line join attribute. With a pattern in a Stroke, the PostScript interpreter must figure out where the Stroke should be and then Fill it with a pattern. A better solution is to apply the Outline Path filter, Object ⇨ Path ⇨ Outline Path. This converts the Stroke into a compound path that can be filled with a pattern.

In addition to the default patterns, you can choose from an incredible variety of patterns that are in the Adobe Illustrator Extras folder on the Illustrator CD-ROM. This folder contains Action Sets, Brush Libraries, Patterns and Textures, and Templates. Open the pattern file to see large blocks that contain the patterns as well as the art that was used to create the patterns.

The default patterns are stored in the Adobe Illustrator Startup file. To learn how to modify the startup file to have a specific set of patterns available every time you use Illustrator, see Chapter 6.

Patterns in Illustrator 8

With the removal of the Pattern dialog box from Illustrator versions earlier than 7, getting used to the Swatches palette is easy. Once you get the hang of it, you'll love this way of creating patterns. Until then, here are the changes to remember as you work with patterns in Illustrator 8:

✦ Patterns are now kept in the Swatches palette, which is used both to create and to apply patterns.

✦ Create patterns by dragging pattern elements to the Swatches palette. Select all the items to be in the pattern (including the boundary box if you have one), and drag them into the Swatches palette. A new swatch is created that contains that pattern.

✦ Apply patterns by clicking on the pattern swatch when a path is selected. Make sure the appropriate Fill/Stroke icon is active.

✦ Access existing patterns by dragging the swatch to your document. Instead of the old Paste button in the Patterns dialog box, you simply (and logically) drag the pattern swatch to your document.

✦ Duplicate patterns by dragging pattern swatches to the New Swatch icon.

✦ Delete patterns by dragging pattern swatches to the Delete icon.

✦ Name or Rename patterns by double-clicking on them.

Creating Custom Patterns

In addition to using the patterns provided with Illustrator, you can create custom patterns by following the steps described below and shown in Figure 11-4.

1. Create the artwork you would like to appear in the pattern tile. For this example, I created a bunch of different stars.

2. Select the artwork.

3. Drag it into the Swatches palette.

Step 1

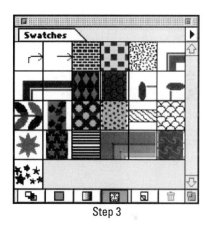

Step 3

Applied to the Fill of a path

Figure 11-4: Steps for creating a basic pattern tile

Figure 11-4 also shows the artwork applied as the fill of another shape; the pattern was scaled down dramatically when placed in the larger star shape.

Note

The old Pattern dialog box is gone. Don't look for it, as you won't be able to find anything that even resembles the classic Illustrator pattern definition box. Instead, as of Illustrator 7, Adobe opted for the much more clever method of using the Swatches palette as the home for all patterns.

ASK TOULOUSE: Changing Pattern Color

Julie: I can't change the color of the background of my pattern.

Toulouse: There are two ways you can do this.

Julie: Tell me the easiest way first.

Toulouse: Okay, the first way is to Duplicate the pattern and change the color.

Julie: Take me through it step by step.

Toulouse: First, drag the pattern swatch out of the Swatches palette and onto the document.

Julie: What does that do?

Toulouse: It puts a copy of the original pattern tile artwork in your document.

Julie: Cool.

Toulouse: Then select the background rectangle of the pattern and change its Fill color. Select the background and the rest of the pattern and drag them into the Swatches palette. You'll have another pattern with a different background color.

Julie: And the other way?

Toulouse: If you'll be changing colors all the time, or if you want to use a gradient or another pattern for your background . . .

Julie: I thought you couldn't do that with patterns.

Toulouse: That's why you need to know this workaround.

Julie: Gotcha.

Toulouse: Go ahead and drag the Pattern swatch like before, but this time make the background rectangle Filled with None.

Julie: Ahhhhh . . .

Toulouse: Yes. Now the new pattern won't have any background and you can paste a background behind the copy of the path that has the pattern.

Of course, creating patterns, although pretty easy initially, can actually be a little more time-consuming for specialty patterns. Patterns that need to appear symmetrical, random, or seamless require special steps. The following sections show different methods for creating these special pattern types.

Pattern Backgrounds and Boundaries

Any pattern tile you create can have the color background you specify, simply by making a rectangle to the size of the tile and placing it behind the objects in the pattern. When the pattern is created, just select the background with the pattern objects to color the pattern background automatically.

If you don't create a background rectangle, Illustrator uses the *bounding box* of the selected objects to determine the size of the pattern tile. The bounding box is a rectangle that is the exact size of all the selected paths in their current positions.

But what happens if you want the edge of the pattern tile to be somewhere inside the bounding box? Illustrator provides a way for you to define a boundary box to define pattern tiles that consist of objects that extend beyond the pattern edges. Create a boundary box by creating a Rectangle with the Rectangle tool, Fill it with None, and make it the back-most object in the pattern tile.

Tip

To quickly make a boundary box for a pattern tile that is to have a background, make the background rectangle the size of the tile (with any objects in front sticking out if necessary), copy and Paste in Back, and whack the Slash (/) key to set the Fill to None. Make sure you select both the background rectangle and the boundary box along with your other pattern elements when creating a pattern.

Making Seamless Patterns

To make patterns seamless, you need to remember that objects that lie across the edge of the pattern border will be cut into two sections, the outside section of which will be invisible. You also need to make sure that lines that stretch from one edge of a pattern border to the other side connect to another line on the opposite edge of the boundary. The second problem is more difficult to deal with than the first one. To make a line match well from one side to the other, you usually have to move one or both of the ends up or down slightly.

Use the following steps to fix objects that get sliced apart at the edges of the pattern tile boundary.

1. Create the boundary (always the back-most rectangle) and the pattern tile objects. The objects may overlap any of the edges, including the corners. In the example that I created (see Figure 11-5), the stones overlap all four sides as well as one of the corners. I created a background rectangle so that you can see the boundary clearly.

2. Select all of the objects, including the pattern boundary, and group them. Click the upper-left corner of the pattern and drag to the right until the arrow pointer is directly over the upper-right corner (it will turn hollow at this point indicating it is snapping into place). Press Option [Alt] and release the mouse button. A copy of the tile will be created to the right of the original.

3. Repeat the process in Step 2 until all four sides have copies of the pattern up against them.

4. Select all five sections and ungroup them. Select the boundary rectangles on the four copied sections and delete them.

5. Delete all the paths (stones, in the example) that don't cross the border of the rectangle.

6. Look at the corners of the rectangle. If an object overlaps any of the corners at all, it should overlap the other three corners. If it doesn't overlap the other three (as in the upper-right corner in the example), Option[Alt]-copy (drag the selected object, pressing the Option [Alt] key, and release the mouse button before the Option [Alt] key) that piece and the boundary to cover the empty corners. Move the boundary with a corner as before so that the piece lines up perfectly. Delete the rectangle after you finish.

7. Look for any overlapping pieces of art in the artwork, including areas of objects that are too close for your liking. Move any pieces of art that are not overlapping a boundary.

8. Make the boundary and objects into a pattern by dragging them into the Swatch palette. Apply it to a shape and check the seams to make sure that it is correct. (If I am even the least bit doubtful that a pattern may be showing seams, I zoom in to 1600% to examine the questionable area.)

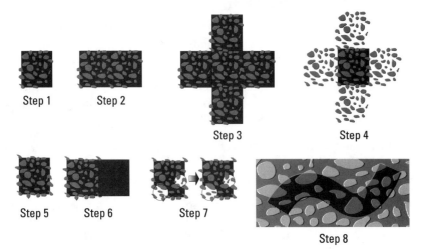

Figure 11-5: Steps for creating a seamless pattern

If you deleted the original pattern artwork, drag the pattern swatch to your document to place a copy of the original artwork on the screen.

To fix lines that cross the edges of the pattern tile boundary, you need to adjust both the lines and the boundary rectangle itself.

1. Create the artwork that you will use in the pattern.

2. Option[Alt]-copy all of the artwork to the right. At a few points inside the original tile boundary, use the Scissors tool to cut along each path in order to prevent any change to the location and angle of the lines as they meet the opposite edge. You must cut the paths inside the original boundary, not outside. Join the paths together, moving only the End Point of the path in the original tile boundary.

3. Option[Alt]-copy both the original and the copied artwork down. Use the Scissors tool to cut along the inside bottom edge of the tile boundary and join the pieces, moving only the End Point of the paths inside the original tile boundary.

4. Using the Scissors tool again, click about ½ inch down the outside right and bottom edges of the tile boundary. Select all paths that do not go into the tile boundary and delete them.

5. Select the tile boundary rectangle and move it ⅛ inch down and to the right. Make sure that no new paths are overlapped on the top and left edges; if they are, do not move the rectangle so far.

6. If you plan to use a blended line or a series of lines placed one on top of another, you may want to join the ends of the paths outside the rectangle to make the blends merge together and to keep layers of paths separate. I joined such ends in the example; if I hadn't, the pattern edges would not have lined up directly.

7. Add any other elements of the pattern and change the background color if necessary. In the example, I added meatballs and a sauce-color background. Select all the elements and make them into a pattern.

8. Fill a path with the pattern. Three variations on the pattern appear at the top of Figure 11-6.

Figure 11-6: Steps for creating seamless patterns with continuous paths

Why Patterns Aren't Always Seamless

For patterns to appear seamless, the edges of the pattern cannot be apparent. Avoiding this problem sounds rather easy: You just avoid creating any objects that touch the edges of a background rectangle. Well, that technique will do it, but when you use such a pattern, the pattern tiles become evident because of the lack of any objects along the borders.

So, then, you do want objects to cross the edges of the pattern rectangle. The catch is that those objects cannot appear to be broken. Doing an illustration the wrong way can help you understand this principle.

Start by drawing a background rectangle with a Fill of None. Draw a 1-point Black Stroked wavy path from left to right, overlapping both edges. Draw a circle that is Filled with 50% Gray and that overlaps the bottom of the rectangle. Select all the objects and define the pattern.

When you Fill an object with the new pattern, the edges of the pattern are very noticeable because the wavy path and the circle are both cut at the edges of the pattern boundary.

Symmetrical Patterns

You can easily create symmetrical patterns in Illustrator. The key to creating them is to draw the boundary box after you create the rest of the objects, drawing outward from the center point of one of the objects.

When you are creating symmetrical patterns, the main difficulty is judging the space between the objects in the pattern. Objects always seem too close together or too far apart, especially in patterns that have different amounts of space between the objects horizontally and vertically.

Tip To have an equal amount of space from the center of one object to the center of the next object both vertically and horizontally, use a square as the pattern tile boundary.

Using the method described in the following steps (and illustrated in Figure 11-7), you can visually adjust the amount of space between objects before you make the objects a pattern.

1. Create the artwork to use in the pattern.

2. Draw a rectangle from the center of the object so that the object is in the upper-left corner of the rectangle.

3. Option[Alt]-copy the object and the rectangle across and down. Delete the extra rectangles.

4. Using the Direct Selection tool, drag to select the objects on the right and Shift-drag (move the object with the Shift key pressed, releasing the mouse button before the Shift key) them left or right to change the horizontal spacing.

5. Drag the Direct Selection tool to select the objects on the bottom and Shift-drag up or down to adjust the vertical spacing.

6. Move the rectangle so that it surrounds only the initial object and delete the other three objects.

7. Make the objects into a pattern and fill a path with it. The pattern is the background for Figure 11-7.

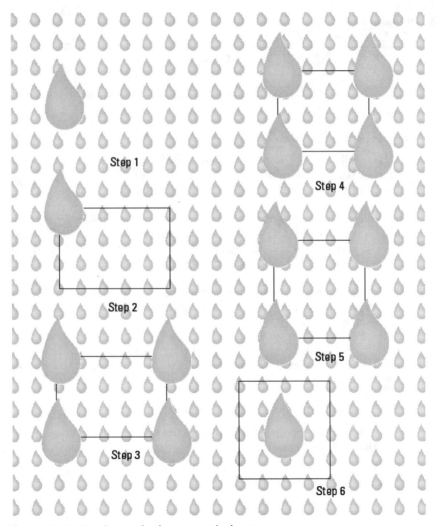

Figure 11-7: Creating perfectly symmetrical patterns

Line Patterns and Grids

Using lines and grids for patterns is ideal because they are so easy to create. The key in both types of patterns is the size of the bounding rectangle.

To create a line pattern with horizontal 1-point lines that are aligned on every ½ inch, do the following: Draw a rectangle that is exactly ½-inch tall, at any width, with a Fill and Stroke of None. Draw a horizontal line with a Fill of None and a Stroke of 1 point from outside the left edge of the rectangle to outside the right edge of the rectangle.

Tip

Creating grids is even easier than creating evenly spaced lines. Create a rectangle that is the size of the grid holes (for a ¼-inch grid, the rectangle would be ¼ inch x ¼ inch) and apply a Stroke to the object. Make the Stroke the weight that you want the grid lines to be. Make that rectangle into a pattern. That's it. You now have a pattern grid that is as precise as possible.

Make a pattern out of the two objects. The new pattern consists of 1-point horizontal Strokes that are spaced ½ inch apart.

You can use this technique with vertical lines, as well. Just make the bounding rectangle the width of the distance from line to line.

Tip

If you want the space between grid lines to be an exact measurement, make the rectangle bigger by the Stroke weight. A ¼-inch grid (18 points) with 1-point grid lines requires a rectangle that is 19 points x 19 points. Remember that four of these grids combined don't equal an inch; instead, they equal 4 points more than an inch.

Diagonal-Line and Grid Patterns

Creating diagonal-line and grid patterns can be difficult if you try to make a rectangle; draw a path at an angle, and then use the rectangle with the path in it as a pattern. Joining diagonal lines at the edges of the pattern is nearly impossible.

A better method is to create line and grid patterns in horizontal or vertical alignment, apply the pattern to a path, and then double-click the Rotate tool. In the Rotate dialog box, enter the angle to change the lines and uncheck the Object checkbox. The pattern will rotate to the desired angle inside the path.

Tip

Using this technique is also a great way to avoid making several patterns when you need line patterns that are set at different angles. Just make one horizontal line pattern and rotate the patterns within the paths.

ASK TOULOUSE: Patterns to Paths

Isaac: Is there an easy way to convert patterns to paths that really works?

Toulouse: Well, there are several options. The Expand option in the Object menu, KPT Gradients/Patterns to Paths (included on the *Illustrator 8 Bible* CD-ROM) and CSI Patterns to Paths.

Isaac: Which works the best?

Toulouse: Well, CSI gives you the option of keeping any transformations that were done to the patterns before they're converted.

Isaac: I sometimes get bad results with patterns to paths.

Toulouse: Actually, because of the way Illustrator patterns work, the patterns are always off-set a bit.

Isaac: Any way to fix this?

Toulouse: Just manually.

Transparency and Patterns

To make the background of a pattern transparent, don't use a background rectangle. Only the objects in the pattern will be opaque.

To make the objects in a pattern transparent, make the background rectangle and the other objects into a compound path. Select the compound path and make the objects into a pattern. You can achieve some fascinating effects by using the transformation tools to make transformed copies of patterns on top of themselves.

Caution When you make the bounding rectangle part of a compound path, it is no longer a rectangle and you cannot use it as the bounding rectangle. Always copy the rectangle before you make the objects and the rectangle into a compound path.

Another way to achieve interesting effects is by making a copy of the object behind the original. Select the object, choose Edit ➪ Copy (⌘-C) [Ctrl+C], and then choose Edit ➪ Paste in Back (⌘-B) [Ctrl+B]. Change the Fill in the copy of the object to a solid or a gradient or change it to another Pattern. Chapter 17 describes a technique for creating a hollow honeycomb effect.

Modifying Existing Patterns

To change an existing pattern, drag the pattern swatch to your document. A copy of the original artwork will be placed in the document.

Select individual parts with any of the selection tools and change Fill and Stroke attributes or change the shape of any of the objects with selection or transformation tools.

After modifying the artwork, select all the pattern-related objects and drag them to the Swatches palette on top of the original version to replace the old swatch.

Putting Patterns and Gradients into Patterns

Under normal circumstances, you cannot put gradients into patterns or patterns into other patterns. But if Illustrator doesn't think of the objects as patterns or gradients, you can put patterns and gradients into patterns.

To put a pattern into another pattern, drag the pattern that you want to put into the new pattern from the Swatches palette to your document. Group the pattern artwork and Option[Alt]-copy several squares. Draw a rectangle around the squares and add any additional artwork for the new pattern. Select the artwork and drag to the Swatches palette.

Including gradients in patterns is not quite so simple. First, create the object in the shape of the gradient and Fill it with the Gradient. Expand the gradient with the Object ➪ Expand command. You can then use the blended object in any pattern.

Caution When you transform gradients into blends via Expand for placement in a pattern, check for masked areas. You cannot use masks in patterns, so you need to release the mask before you incorporate the blend into the pattern. Also, try to keep the number of blend steps to a minimum.

Note Technical overkill: Patterns in Illustrator are actually saved as Type 3 fonts in your Illustrator file. Remember how long it takes some of those fancy Berthold fonts to print? Imagine stuffing hundreds of colored, tinted, twisted, turned objects into a font!

Transforming Patterns

After you create patterns and place them within paths, they may be too big or at the wrong angle, or they may start in an awkward location. You can use the transformation tools and the Move command to resolve these problems.

To transform a pattern inside a path, select the path and double-click the transformation tool that corresponds to the change that you want to make to the pattern. In the transformation tool's dialog box, uncheck the Object checkbox, which selects the Pattern checkbox, and check the Pattern checkbox. The Pattern and Objects checkboxes are grayed out if the selected object does not contain a pattern.

ASK TOULOUSE: Pattern Printing Problems

Stubing: Why does it take so long to print patterns?

Toulouse: Well, if you think of what patterns actually are, you'll know.

Stubing: If I knew, would I be asking?

Toulouse: It's just that patterns are really bunches of masked sections of — get this — Type 3 fonts. The masks are rectangles.

Stubing: Which means . . . ?

Toulouse: Masks can always cause printing problems, as can Type 3 fonts, but if you do complex transformations to complex patterns, you're asking for trouble.

Any changes that you make in the transformation tool's dialog box when only the Pattern checkbox is checked affect only the pattern, not the outside shape. The default (which cannot be changed) is for Objects to remain checked always.

If you are using any of the transformation tools manually, the pattern inside the selected object will transform with the object only if the Transform pattern tiles option in the General Preferences dialog box is checked.

To move a pattern within a path, choose Object ⇨ Transform ⇨ Move (or double-click the Selection tool). The Move dialog box also contains Pattern and Objects checkboxes. If you uncheck the Objects checkbox, which selects the Pattern checkbox, only the pattern will be moved.

Graphs

The Graphs feature seems to be one of the most underused features in Illustrator.

All the graph tools work in a manner similar to that of the shape creation tools: With the Graph tool selected, click and drag to set the size of the graph, or click to display the Graph Size dialog box and then enter the size information. If you press the Shift key while you drag, the graph is constrained to a perfect square (or to a circle, if it's a pie graph). If you press the Option [Alt] key while you drag, you drag from the center of the graph out. If you Option[Alt]-click, the graph you create is centered at the point you Option[Alt]-clicked. That's it. That's all you have to do to use the graph tools. Neat, huh?

Double-clicking the Graph tool brings up the Graph Data dialog box, shown in Figure 11-8. Choosing a different graph type at this point and clicking OK changes the tool to represent the type of graph you selected. You can choose from nine graph types; the column graph is the default.

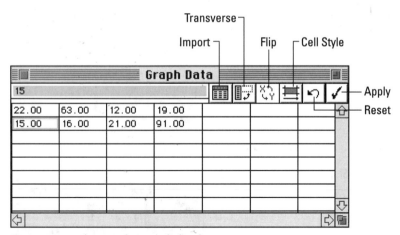

Figure 11-8: The Graph Data dialog box

One of the most exciting things about graphs in Illustrator is their fluidity. Not only can you create graphs easily, but after you create them, you can change them easily. In addition, if the data that you used to create a graph changes, you can enter the new data and have it show up in the graph instantaneously.

Figure 11-9 and the steps that follow describe the basics of creating and modifying a graph. The type of graph in this example is a grouped column graph, which is commonly used to compare quantities over time or between different categories.

1. Select the Graph tool and click and drag to form a rectangular area, in the same way that you use the Rectangle tool. The size of the rectangle that you create will be the size of the graph.

2. As soon as you release the mouse button, the Graph Data dialog box appears. Information that you enter in the Graph Data dialog box becomes formatted in graph form. The top row in the Graph Data dialog box worksheet area should contain the labels for comparison within the same set — in the example, I compare how many things I can juggle to what the current world records are for juggling those particular objects. The items in the top row appear as *legends* outside the graph area. In the leftmost column, you can enter labels that appear at the bottom of the grouped column graph as *categories* — I entered the types of objects that are to be compared in the graph. In the remaining *cells*, enter the pertinent information.

3. Close the window to have all the data that you entered used in the graph. The graph appears, and it should look something like the one in Step 3 of Figure 11-9.

4. After I created the graph, I edited it by changing the paint style of the bars and legends, adding a background, changing the point sizes and font of the type in the graph, and adding the lightened circles at the top of each bar and legend to make the elements in the graph look more three-dimensional.

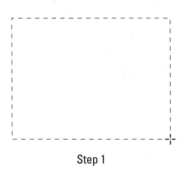

Step 1

	Me	World	Record
Balls	7	11	
Rings	6	12	
Plates	3	8	
Clubs	5	9	
Torches	4	7	
Bowling Balls	3	5	
Knives	4	7	

Step 2

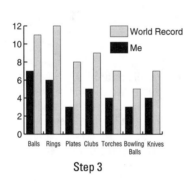

Step 3

Step 4

Figure 11-9: The basic steps for creating a graph in Illustrator

The Nine Types of Graphs

You can choose from nine different types of graphs in Illustrator. Each type gives a specific kind of information to the reader. Certain graphs are better for comparisons, others for growth, and so on. The following sections describe the graphs, explain how to create them, and tell how you can use them.

Grouped-Column Graphs

You primarily use grouped-column graphs to show how something changes over time. Often, they are referred to as bar graphs because the columns that make up the graphs resemble bars.

When to Use Graphs

Graphs are most useful when they show numerical information that would normally take several paragraphs to explain or that can't be expressed easily in words. Furthermore, you can express numerical information easily in graphs, and using graphs makes finding and understanding information easier than when the same information is in lines of text.

Numbers are fascinating concepts that most people have a good grasp of, but whose significance can be overlooked, especially when comparing different numbers. The numbers 2 and 9 are the same size when you type them; when used in a graph, however, they can represent a drastic difference.

Of course, although graphs are normally used to educate and inform, they are also well suited for misinforming. Stretching or crushing a graph can cause a great difference in the way the information appears. Even worse is the capability to stretch or compress information in just one part of the graph. The figure shows the same information in two radically different graphs.

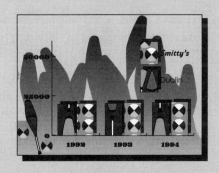

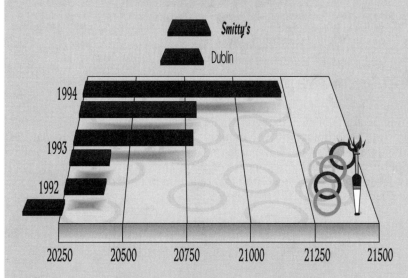

(continued)

(continued)

The information for the top graph, created by the Smitty's people, shows them to be even with their competitors. The text for the numbers, the column drop shadows, and the distracting images cause the data to make less impact on the reader than the data does in the bottom graph. Dublin's graph indicates that Dublin is doing substantially better than Smitty's. The vast difference in the length of the bars is one way to show the difference, as is the numbering scheme, which starts at 20250, making the first Smitty's bar appear to be a negative number.

Step 3 of Figure 11-9 shows a grouped-column graph as created in Illustrator. This graph contains seven categories, and each of the seven categories is represented by two different totals. The height of the bars represents the number in each case, with higher bars representing higher values.

The real strength of a grouped-column graph is that it provides for the direct comparison of different types of statistics in the same graph. In the sample graph, the number of rings that I can juggle is compared to the bowling ball juggling world record by the height of the bars.

Both column and cluster width are two customizable options for grouped-column graphs and stacked-column graphs. Column width refers to the width of individual columns, with 100% being wide enough to abut other columns in the cluster. Cluster width refers to how much of the available cluster space is taken up by the columns in the cluster. At 80% (the default), 20% of the available space is empty, leaving room between clusters.

You can widen columns and clusters to 1000% of their size and condense them to 1% of the width of the original column or cluster.

Stacked-Column Graphs

Stacked-column graphs are good graphs for presenting the total of a category and the contributing portions of each category. In Figure 11-10, I again used objects as categories and split each object into the number of those objects being juggled. The total of the time it takes (in weeks) to learn to juggle that number of objects is the height of the object's bar. The time for each number of objects juggled represents a certain portion of the entire time, reflected in each of the smaller sections of the bars.

	3	4	5	6	7	8	9
Balls	1	6	28	32	40	38	72
Rings	2	8	42	10	35	14	34
Clubs	4	38	50	75	140		

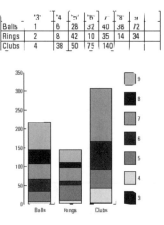

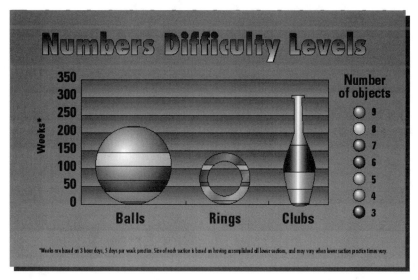

Figure 11-10: Data for a stacked-column graph; how the graph appears when it is first created in Illustrator; and the graph after it is altered

ASK TOULOUSE: Graph Trouble

Doc: Sometimes my data values change when I close a document and open it later.

Toulouse: Really?

Doc: Yeah, it's very annoying.

Toulouse: I'm just fooling with you. That's a problem within Illustrator.

Doc: What can I do to fix it?

Toulouse: The best thing to do is to change the graph into plain Illustrator artwork.

Doc: Done. Wait. How do I do that?

Toulouse: Select the graph and ungroup it.

Doc: But I get a message saying it won't work as a graph anymore.

Toulouse: That's the downfall, unfortunately.

Caution

To get the labels on the legends to read numbers only, I had to put quotation marks (" ") around each of the numbers. If I had not used quotation marks, the numbers would have been considered data, not labels.

This graph shows the same amount of information as the grouped-column graph, but the information is organized differently. The stacked-column graph is designed to display the total of all the legends, and the grouped-column graph is designed to aid comparison of all individual legends in each category.

Line Graphs

Line graphs (also known as line charts) show trends over time. They are especially useful for determining progress and identifying radical changes. For example, the line graph in Figure 11-11 shows the average income of three street performers on successive weeks throughout the summer.

The Mark Data Points option in the Line graphs area of the Graph Style dialog box (Object ➪ Graphs ➪ Style) forces data points to appear as squares. If this box is not checked, the data points are visible only as direction changes in lines between the data points.

If the Connect Data Points option is checked, lines are drawn between each pair of data points.

	Animated Suspension	The Flying Linguini	Disoriented Convolution
May	300	220	145
	240	190	120
	260	260	140
	320	300	200
June	380	360	150
	400	350	195
	395	320	230
	435	420	190
July	520	190	200
	600	290	195
	440	405	240
	380	340	150
August	300	210	200
	275	250	240
	360	280	230
	300	290	210
September	420	280	170
	220	140	110

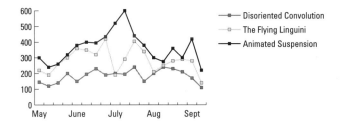

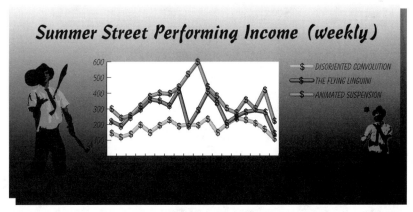

Figure 11-11: Line graph data (top); the graph as it first appears in Illustrator (center); and the graph after it is redesigned (bottom)

The Draw Filled Lines option and the corresponding text box for line width create a line that is Filled with the data point legend color and that is outlined with Black. The Fill Lines option changes the line from a single path with a Stroke weight into a Filled path with a Black Stroke.

The Edge to Edge lines option stretches the lines out to the left and right edges of the graph. Although the result is technically incorrect, you can achieve better visual impact by using this feature.

Area Graphs

On first glance, area graphs may appear to be just like Filled line graphs. Like line graphs, area graphs show data points that are connected, but area graphs are stacked one on top of the other to show the total area of the legend subject in the graph.

Pie Graphs

Pie graphs are great for comparing percentages of the portions of a whole. In Figure 11-12, pie graphs show how much of a juggling performance was spent doing particular activities. The higher the percentage for a certain activity, the larger its wedge.

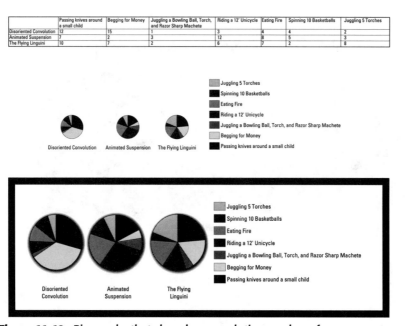

	Passing knives around a small child	Begging for Money	Juggling a Bowling Ball, Torch, and Razor Sharp Machete	Riding a 12' Unicycle	Eating Fire	Spinning 10 Basketballs	Juggling 5 Torches
Disoriented Convolution	12	15	1	3	4	4	2
Animated Suspension	7	2	3	12	8	5	3
The Flying Linguini	10	7	2	6	7	2	8

Figure 11-12: Pie graphs that show how much time each performer spent on certain activities were constructed from the data above

When you create pie graphs, you can remove the individual wedges from the central pie with the Group Selection tool to achieve an exploding pie effect.

The Legends in Wedges option is the only option in the Graph Style dialog box that is specifically for pie graphs. If Legends in Wedges is selected, the name of each wedge will be centered within that wedge. Illustrator doesn't do a very good job of placing the legend names, many times overlapping neighboring names. In addition, the letters in the legend names are black, which can make reading some of the names difficult or impossible.

Scatter Graphs and Radar Graphs

Scatter graphs, which are primarily used for scientific charting purposes, are quite different from all the other types of graphs. Each data point is given a location according to its *x-y* coordinates instead of by category and label. The points are connected, as are the points in line graphs, but the line created by the data point locations can cross itself and does not go in any specific direction. Scatter graphs have the same customization options as line graphs.

A Radar (or Web) graph compares values set at a certain point. This type of graph is viewed as a circle graph.

Customizing Graphs

When a graph is selected and the Graph Type dialog box is displayed, a number of options become available for most graphs:

✦ The Left or Right Axis options display the vertical values on either the left side (the default) or the right side. The Same Axis Both Sides option puts the same axis on both sides. Clicking the Left or Right button displays options for customizing axes.

✦ Checking the Drop Shadow option places a black shadow behind the graph objects. The shadow is offset up and to the right.

✦ The Legends Across Top option makes any existing legends appear across the top of the graph, instead of grouped together on the right side of the graph.

✦ The First Row in Front option places overlapping rows in order from left to right, wherever columns, clusters, or other objects overlap.

Each type of graph has its own customization options. The preceding sections that describe each type of graph explain those options.

Tip   To make visually striking graphs, use a combination of graph types. Simply use the Group Selection tool to select all the objects that are one legend type and then choose Object ⇨ Graphs ⇨ Graph Type and enter the new graph type for that legend.

Using the Graph Data Dialog Box

You can change the numbers and the text in the Graph Data dialog box (see Figure 11-13) at any time by selecting the graph and Object ⇨ Graphs ⇨ Data. Illustrator will recreate the graph to reflect the changes you make. If you have moved some of the graph objects around, they may revert to their original locations when Illustrator recreates the graph. If a number does not have quotation marks around it, Illustrator assumes that you want the number to be entered as a value in the graph.

	"3"	"4"	"5"	"6"	"7"	"8"
Balls	1.00	6.00	28.00	32.00	40.00	38.00
Rings	2.00	8.00	42.00	10.00	35.00	14.00
Clubs	4.00	38.00	50.00	75.00	140.00	

Figure 11-13: The Graph Data dialog box

Caution   Make sure that the graph is never ungrouped, at least not until you have finished making all graph data and graph style changes. If you ungroup the graph, you will not be able to use any of the graph options to change the ex-graph because Illustrator will view it as just a set of paths and text.

You can import graph data in tab-delimited word processing files. Tab-delimited files are text and numbers that are separated by tabs and returns. To import data from another file, click the Import button or click the Import button while you are in the Graph Data dialog box.

Illustrator is not really a graphing or spreadsheet program, so many of the usual controls for arranging data in such programs are not available, including inserting rows and columns and creating formulas.

The Cut, Copy, and Paste functions work within the Graph Data dialog box, so you can move and duplicate information on a very basic level.

One very useful feature in the Graph Data dialog box is the Transverse button. This function switches the x and y axes of the data, reversing everything that you have entered.

Using Marker and Column Designs

The most exciting part about the graphing functions in Illustrator is the capability to give column, line, and area graphs special icons to indicate values on the graphs.

On line and area graphs, marker designs are created, which you can use in place of the standard markers. For each value in the graph, the marker design is placed, adding visual impact to the graph.

Column designs are created for grouped-column graphs and stacked-column graphs. The strength of using column designs is most evident in grouped-column graphs, where images are placed side-by-side (see Figure 11-14).

1. Create the graphic object in Illustrator.

2. Draw a rectangle around the border of the object. Illustrator uses this border to determine the area of the object relative to the values entered for the graph.

3. Draw a horizontal line across the rectangle at a good place for the image to stretch. Make the horizontal line into a guide (View ➪ Make Guide or press ⌘-5 [Ctrl+5]). (This step is necessary only if you use the column design as a sliding design.)

4. Select the rectangle, object, and guide, and choose Object ➪ Graphs ➪ Design. Click the New button to make the selected object appear in the window. Name the design and click the OK button.

5. Select just one legend type by clicking twice on the legend graphic with the Group Selection tool. Choose Object ➪ Graphs ➪ Design and select the design from the list. Choose the column design type. Repeat this step for each legend.

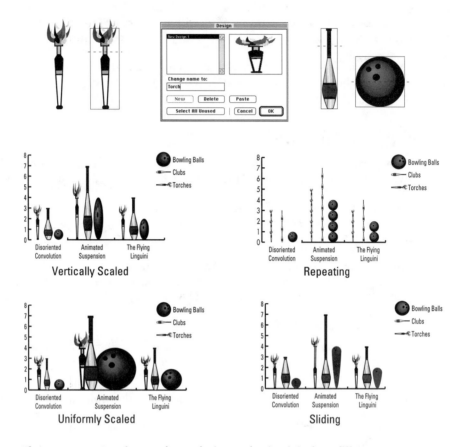

Figure 11-14: Creating a column design and using it in four different grouped-column graphs

You can combine column-design types by selecting a different type for each legend.

Texture Generation

One of the niftiest features in Illustrator is a filter called Pen and Ink. Pen and Ink takes basic Illustrator paths and turns them into random textures that you can control and manipulate through a variety of options.

To create a texture, select any path or paths and choose Filter ⇨ Pen and Ink ⇨ New Hatch. The New Hatch dialog box will appear, as shown in Figure 11-15.

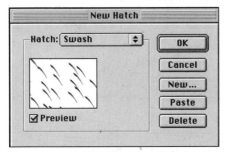

Figure 11-15: The New Hatch dialog box

Click the New button and name your hatch. Click OK and you can use that hatch as a Pen and Ink Fill.

After the hatch has been created, you're ready to apply it as a Fill for any selected path. To do so, select the path you wish to Fill and choose Filter ⇨ Pen and Ink ⇨ Hatch Effects. The Hatch Effects dialog box appears, as shown in Figure 11-16.

Inside the Hatch Effects dialog box, you have an infinite amount of combinations of various properties to apply to the hatch style. The effects are listed, with figures showing the effects of various property settings chosen from the pop-up menu.

The texture that is created is actually a grouped mask of several paths. This enables you to change the paint attributes of the texture after it has been applied. In addition, you can then modify the individual paths just as you would modify any other path in Illustrator.

Tip

Remember that the paths that you use in a hatch style can have both Fills and Strokes, but the thickness property only affects Stroke width.

Note

The Hatch Effect pop-up menu is a collection of presaved settings made from a specific hatch. You can select a setting from the Hatch Effects and select a different hatch from the Hatch pop-up menu to make a new texture. If you like the texture, save the settings.

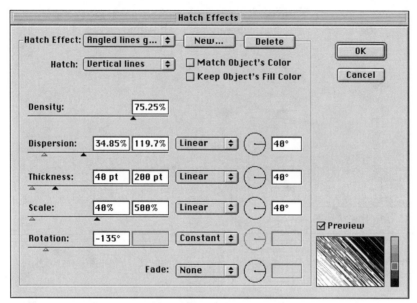

Figure 11-16: The Hatch Effects dialog box

Density

Density is how closely packed together the elements of the hatch style are. The closer together the pieces, the darker or thicker the texture will appear. You can adjust the density by dragging the Density slider to the left and right; left is less dense, right is denser. Figure 11-17 shows various amounts of density.

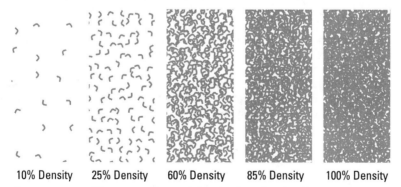

10% Density   25% Density   60% Density   85% Density   100% Density

Figure 11-17: Different amounts of density for a hatch effect

Dispersion

Dispersion controls how evenly the texture elements are spread within the Fill. Setting the dispersion to None results in a pattern-tile appearance that is very uniform, while increasing the dispersion randomizes the location and grouping of the pieces of the hatch style. Figure 11-18 shows various settings of the Dispersion slider.

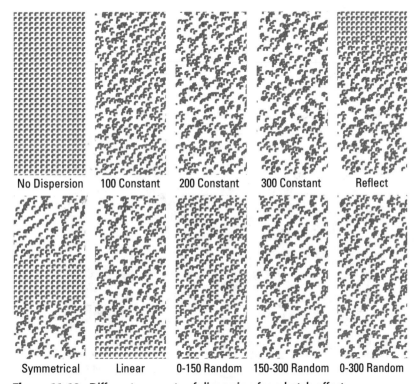

Figure 11-18: Different amounts of dispersion for a hatch effect

Each of the right-six pop-up settings in the Hatch Effects dialog box has different ways of creating each parameter. For instance, instead of a Constant dispersion, you can choose from None, Linear, Symmetrical, Reflected, or Random dispersion. Each of the other properties (with the exception of density) has these same controls.

The Hatch Effects options work as follows:

✦ **None** applies no effect to this setting.

✦ **Constant** keeps the setting the same throughout the entire Fill shape.

✦ **Linear** changes the amount of the effect across the Fill shape. The angle at which this is applied is changed in each effect section, either by moving the angle indicator or by entering a different angle in the Rotate field. There are two sliders to adjust, controlling the maximum and minimum amount of the effect.

✦ **Reflect** increases and decreases the amount of the effect (somewhat like a double-linear effect). The angle and minimum and maximum amounts are controlled in the same way as Linear.

✦ **Symmetric** creates a symmetric pattern of the effect. The angle and amounts are adjusted in the same way as they are in Linear and Reflect.

✦ **Random** generates random amounts of the effect, between the minimum and maximum amount that you specify.

Thickness

Thickness controls the Stroke thickness of the paths in the hatch style. Some of the variations of Stroke thickness are shown in Figure 11-19.

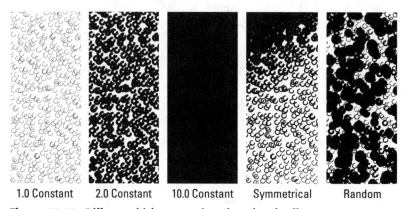

1.0 Constant   2.0 Constant   10.0 Constant   Symmetrical   Random

Figure 11-19: Different thickness settings for a hatch effect

Rotation

Rotation controls the angle of the pieces in the hatch style. A constant amount of rotation rotates each of the pieces in the hatch style the same amount. Other rotation options vary the amount of rotation, as shown in Figure 11-20.

1. Start by creating the path you wish to Fill with the symmetrical texture.

2. With the path selected, choose Filter ➪ Pen and Ink ➪ Hatch Effects, and select the hatch style to use.

3. Change the Rotation property setting to Linear, making the left and right sliders the same (for example 90, 90). Click the OK button to apply the texture to the path.

4. Select the path and rotate-copy the path 180° so that it overlaps itself. The texture will be symmetrical.

5. To finish, you may want to place a gradient behind the image, as I did in Figure 11-21.

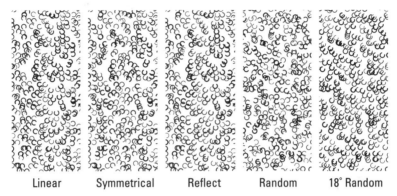

Linear   Symmetrical   Reflect   Random   18° Random

Figure 11-20: Different settings for the Rotation property

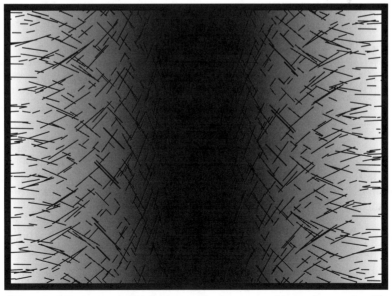

Figure 11-21: A symmetrical texture (don't stare at this too long or it will start to look really gross)

Scale

The Scale property changes the size of the hatch style pieces. It does *not* change the Stroke weight, however, just the size of the paths. Figure 11-22 shows sample scale settings.

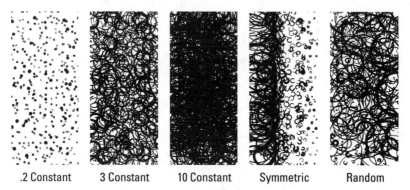

.2 Constant   3 Constant   10 Constant   Symmetric   Random

Figure 11-22: Different settings for the Scale property

Tip

If you are going to be using "lines" that you'd like to scale uniformly (instead of just the length changing, you'd like the width to change as well), then create thin rectangles instead of single paths. That way, the width of the rectangle increases with its length. However, the Thickness property will then not have an effect on the hatch style.

Other Ink Pen Fill Controls

Several other controls determine how your Fill interacts with the background. These controls are located next to the Hatch pop-up menu in the Hatch Effects dialog box.

Select the hatch style you'd like to use in the Hatch pop-up menu. The hatch color can Keep Object's Color (the color of the original paths when they were created as a hatch) or Match Object's Color of the Fill of the selected path. The Background color of the original object is changed to None or White. The Fade pop-up menu controls the fade of the hatch style. The Fade Angle option controls the angle of the fade.

Figure 11-23 shows two examples of the Fade to White option with the background (a gradient) and no background.

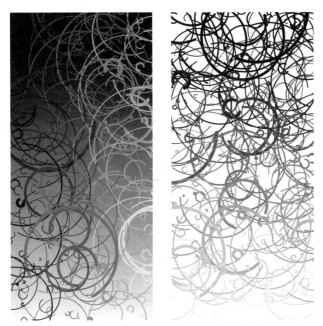

Figure 11-23: Fade to White with a gradient background and with no background

ASK TOULOUSE: Ink Pen Color Change

Gopher: I want to change the color of my hatch style.

Toulouse: After it's applied or before?

Gopher: Before, because I'm using the Fade to White option.

Toulouse: Okay. Open the Ink Pen Hatches dialog box.

Gopher: Done.

Toulouse: Then select the hatch style you wish to recolor.

Gopher: Done again.

Toulouse: Then click the Paste button.

Gopher: Paste does what?

Toulouse: Paste puts a copy of the hatch art in your document. Then change the color, go back to the Ink Pen Hatches, click New, and name your new hatch something else.

Photo Hatch Effects

New to Illustrator 8 is the capability to apply Hatch Effects to a photograph or any other rasterized image. The crosshatch effects are applied on top of the original image. The hatches are applied to the darkest areas of the image and feather out to the lightest areas.

Figure 11-24 shows the Photo Crosshatch dialog box.

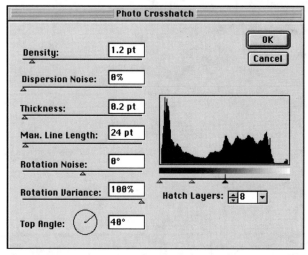

Figure 11-24: Photo Crosshatch dialog box

You use this dialog box to set these options:

✦ **Density**: Controls how close the hatches are to each other.

✦ **Dispersion Noise:** Affects how evenly the hatch lines cover the fill area.

✦ **Thickness:** Controls the line thickness of the hatch lines.

✦ **Max. Line Length**: Sets the maximum length of a hatch line.

✦ **Rotation Noise**: Controls the random rotation of the hatch lines in the Hatch Layers.

✦ **Rotation Variance**: Controls the rotation amount of the layers from each other.

✦ **Top Angle**: Controls the angle of the top layer of the Hatch Layers.

✦ **Hatch Layers**: The higher the Hatch Layer, the more layers of hatches that are applied to the image. The hatch color ranges from 0 to 256 tones of black.

Figure 11-25 shows a rasterized image before and after applying Photo Hatch to it. You can see that the crosshatch lines are on top of the photo. To see only the crosshatching, either hide (press ⌘-3 [Ctrl+3]) or delete the original photo (see Figure 11-26).

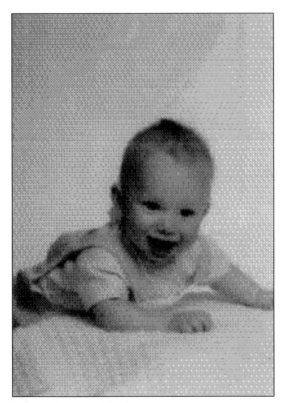

Figure 11-25: Original image

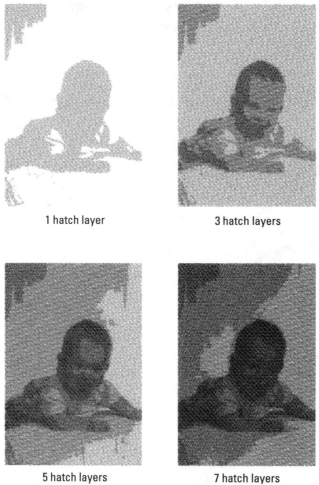

1 hatch layer

3 hatch layers

5 hatch layers

7 hatch layers

Figure 11-26: The Photo Crosshatch applied to Figure 11-25

Summary

✦ Patterns are a type of Fill that provides texture to any path.

✦ Several default patterns are supplied with Illustrator. These patterns can be transformed in the same ways that other Illustrator objects can be transformed.

✦ Almost anything in Illustrator can be used as a pattern, with the exception of masks, gradients, placed images, and other patterns.

✦ Diagonal-line patterns can be created by creating a horizontal-line pattern and rotating it with the Rotate tool while the pattern is filling a path.

✦ Graphs can be created in Illustrator just by entering the data.

✦ After a graph has been created, it can be adjusted and manipulated like any other path-based object.

✦ Textures can be created with the Pen and Ink Hatch Effects command.

✦ Cool effects can now be made to rasterized images with Photo Hatch Effects.

✦   ✦   ✦

Filters and Plug-Ins

P   A   R   T

✦   ✦   ✦   ✦

In This Part

Chapter 12
Illustrator's Built-In
Filters and Plug-Ins

Chapter 13
Using Photoshop
Filters and Raster
Images

Chapter 14
VectorTools

Chapter 15
Other Third-Party
Plug-Ins

✦   ✦   ✦   ✦

The Filter menu in Illustrator is unlike any menu in any other program. It can be remotely compared with the Filter menu in Photoshop, although Illustrator contains many of the Photoshop filters anyway. However, the comparison falls short because Illustrator is a *vector* program, and the filters and plug-ins do much more than modify colors and shapes.

Part III takes you on a journey of discovery into all the filters and plug-ins that exist for Illustrator, from the built-in filters to the fantastic third-party plug-ins from vendors such as Extensis (VectorTools), MetaCreations (Vector Effects), and hot door (CADtools).

Illustrator's Built-In Filters and Plug-Ins

Adobe introduced Illustrator filters in Version 5.0. Most users of Illustrator expected Photoshop-type filters and were disappointed with the Illustrator filters. Actually, the only filters that are like Photoshop filters are the Distort filters and a few of the Stylize filters.

The plug-ins and filters included with Illustrator are nice, but it's the third-party plug-ins and filters that really make the concept of filters and plug-ins exciting. Plug-ins such as Extensis's VectorTools and MetaCreations's VectorEffects give Illustrator capabilities that Illustrator users have wanted and dreamed about for years.

Filters in Illustrator

Instead of just changing the appearance of images, most of the filters in Illustrator perform tasks that took hours to do manually in previous versions of Illustrator. In a way, most of these filters work as intelligent macros, and they enable you to produce a variety of effects.

Some filters, such as the Zig Zag filter, seem to perform quite simple tasks. In reality, however, these filters are complex, math-based programs that accomplish certain tasks faster than the fastest illustrator could dream of performing without them.

So why are all these functions in the Filter menu, and not just functions within the software? Because none of them are really integrated into Illustrator; instead, each filter is an individual file called a *plug-in,* which resides in the Plug-Ins folder. For a filter to be available, the plug-in must be in the Plug-Ins folder.

Adobe, in its marketing wisdom, initially pushed two filters with grungelike names: Punk and Bloat. To be honest, I rarely use either of these filters, though I was quite intrigued the first time I saw them demonstrated. Cool names, little functionality. The same thing applies to the Twirl filter, which produces some really amazing effects.

Filter Organization

Illustrator 8 includes many of the Photoshop filters that ship with Photoshop 5. All the Photoshop (pixel-based) filters are set up to appear at the bottom of the Filter menu, while the vector-based filters appear at the top of the menu (see Figure 12-1).

Figure 12-1: The Filter menu

Illustrator and Photoshop Filters

The filters in Illustrator have to be different from the filters in Photoshop because Illustrator deals with vector-based images and Photoshop works with bitmapped graphics. Many electronic artists use Photoshop as a staple of their graphics work. For them, the word *filter* conjures up thoughts of blurring and sharpening, as well as some of the fantastic effects that they can achieve by using filters from third parties, such as Kai's Power Tools or Alien Skin Eye Candy.

The very term *filters* is based in photography terminology for special lenses that are attached to cameras to achieve special effects. Photoshop's filters are based on this concept, and they take it quite a bit further, creating controls for variety and exactness that a camera lens could never match.

For this reason, filter isn't really the best term for the manipulations that Illustrator performs when you choose a filter. The following list compares some of the Illustrator filters with their Photoshop counterparts:

✦ Illustrator: Filter ⇨ Create ⇨ Object Mosaic

  Photoshop: Filter ⇨ Stylize ⇨ Mosaic

  - The Mosaic filters take bitmap images and reduce the number of colored areas to large, single-colored squares.

  - These two filters produce results that are the most alike of any of the Illustrator and Photoshop filters. The dialog boxes are a little different, but the results are functionally the same. One big difference is that stylizing a mosaic in Photoshop is a fairly fast procedure, but creating an object mosaic in Illustrator is a complex task that eats up tons of RAM and can take up to ten minutes to complete.

✦ Illustrator: Filter ⇨ Distort ⇨ Twirl

  Photoshop: Filter ⇨ Distort ⇨ Twirl

  - Twirling spins an object or picture more in the center than around the edges.

Where Did All the Filters Go?

The Filter menu has been dramatically parsed down to only a few Illustrator-specific categories as well. It's not that any functions were taken away, but many of the functions were either combined or moved from the Filter menu to other menus in Illustrator.

To help make this clear, I need to give you a little background story. In 1993, when Illustrator 5.0 (the first version to support plug-ins) was introduced, Adobe thought that any add-on functionality created from plug-ins should be placed in the Filter menu (as was the practice in Photoshop 2.5). While most of the new plug-in-based enhancements really weren't filters in a Photoshop sense of the word, they thought that because Illustrator was such a different product from Photoshop, these new features really could be considered "vector filters."

By the time Illustrator 6.0 was released, that thought had changed substantially. The Illustrator engineers changed the API (Application Programming Interface) to let plug-ins be not just in the Filter menu, but also in any menu, or as a palette, or as a tool. Adobe started moving some things that were filters to tools (Spiral, Twirl, Polygon, Star), and others to palettes (align). With Illustrator 7, the only functions left in the Filter menu fell into the categories of Colors, Create (still not really filters), Distort, Ink Pen, and Stylize. The only change in Illustrator 8 was the addition of the Photo Crosshatch to the Pen and Ink filter (previously called Ink Pen), and the removal of some unnecessary filters.

Some features that you would expect to do the same thing in each program are not the same:

✦ Illustrator: Filter ⇨ Colors ⇨ Invert Colors

Photoshop: Image ⇨ Map ⇨ Invert

- Illustrator's Invert Colors filter is annoying because you expect a negative image but don't get it. Instead, you get Cyan, Magenta, and Yellow values that have been subtracted from 100, and a Black value that is untouched. Photoshop's Invert command creates a true negative, and it is a feature, not a filter.

✦ Illustrator: Filter ⇨ Colors ⇨ Saturate

Photoshop: Image ⇨ Adjust ⇨ Hue/Saturation

- The saturation filter in Illustrator increases/decreases the CMYK values for selected objects. In Photoshop, the color intensity is increased. Saturation in Illustrator is a misnomer, at least when compared to the functionality of Saturation in most other software packages.

The Plug-Ins Folder

All of the filters in Illustrator are in the Filter menu because a file with the same name as the filter is in the Plug-Ins folder. If the filter's file is not in the Plug-Ins folder, the filter will not appear in the Filter menu.

ASK TOULOUSE: What Are Filters?

Johnny: Now, how are filters in Illustrator different from the things I use to make sure all those little black things don't get in my coffee?

Toulouse: Filters in Illustrator do all sorts of amazing things that would be really difficult or time-consuming to normally do in Illustrator.

Johnny: That's nice, but then why have all the hard ways to do things in Illustrator if you've got these filters hanging around?

Toulouse: A good example is the Roughen filter. It adds points to paths and then randomly moves them around.

Johnny: Wouldn't the easy thing be to just draw the paths using the Pencil tool with a low Curve Fitting Tolerance? Seems like you could avoid the Roughen filter altogether that way.

Toulouse: Ah, but what if you want to roughen existing artwork? The Roughen filter does this in just a few seconds.

The Plug-Ins folder is put inside the first level of the Adobe Illustrator folder when Illustrator is installed. If you move the folder, you need to tell Illustrator where it is located.

1. In the Finder, with Illustrator not running, move or copy the Plug-Ins folder to the desired location.

2. Double-click the Illustrator icon.

3. Choose File ⇨ Preferences ⇨ Plug-Ins & Scratch Disk.

4. In the Plug-Ins dialog box, click the Choose button, find the Plug-Ins folder, and click the Select button at the bottom of the dialog box.

5. Quit Illustrator and double-click the Illustrator icon to restart Illustrator. The new Plug-Ins folder location is now used.

Third-Party Filters

Several companies are currently producing third-party filters for Illustrator. In fact, companies such as Extensis, Alien Skin, MetaCreations, and hotdoor are producing high-profile filter sets for Illustrator.

Because Illustrator filters are taking off like wildfire, Chapters 14 and 15 discuss third-party filter plug-ins. For additional information on Illustrator filters, pick up a copy of *Illustrator Filter Finesse,* which contains all sorts of Illustrator filter information that I couldn't squeeze into this book.

Why You Can Apply the Last Filter But Never Apply Last Filter

Whenever you start Illustrator, the top menu item in the Filter menu reads "Apply Last Filter," but it is grayed out. This causes some confusion initially. After you use a filter, its name appears where the menu once listed "Apply Last Filter." Thereafter, the name of the last filter that you used appears at the top of the menu. The key command for reapplying the last filter is ⌘-E [Ctrl+E].

Tip

To return to the last filter's dialog box, select Filter ⇨ *[Name of Last Filter],* located right below the Apply Last Filter option or press ⌘-Option-E [Ctrl+Alt+E].

The Color Filters

The color filters in the Color submenu of the Filter menu really take Illustrator's color capabilities to the next level in many ways. Unfortunately, they fall far short of Photoshop's color capabilities, but they're making good headway.

Note   Extensis VectorTools's VectorColor provides many of the color capabilities that Adobe left out. VectorColor contains Edit Curves (like Photoshop's Curves), Brightness/Contrast, Multitone (duotones, tritones, and so forth), and even a Randomize function. VectorColor is discussed in Chapter 14.

Adjust Colors

Adjust Colors increases and decreases process color Fills in each color component. The percentages entered in Adjust Colors are absolute changes, meaning that a 10% decrease of Cyan when Cyan is 100% results in 90%, and a 10% decrease of Cyan when Cyan is 50% results in 40%, not 45%. If the increase makes the tint of a color greater than 100%, it stays at 100%, but other colors may still increase if they are not yet at 100%. If the decrease makes the tint of a color less than 0%, that color remains at 0%, but other colors may still decrease, as long as they are not yet at 0%. For example, a 25% increase to both Yellow and Magenta to a path with 80% Yellow and 50% Magenta results in the colors being 100% Yellow and 75% Magenta. Reapplying this filter results in 100% Yellow and 100% Magenta. Reapplying this filter at this point results in no change at all.

The Adjust Colors filter is shown in Figure 12-2.

Figure 12-2: The Adjust Colors dialog box

At the bottom of the Adjust Colors dialog box are several options. The Preview checkbox lets you see the changes that have been applied so far. The checkbox automatically converts custom and Illustrator Black-based colors to process equivalents.

Tip   You can adjust colors using any color model, even if your selected paths are a different model. Click the Convert checkbox and choose a different model.

The Color Blend Filters

Blend Front to Back, Blend Horizontally, and Blend Vertically blend the colors of at least three objects whose ending objects are both process tints or both Black tints. The Blend filters do not work with custom colors, patterns, or gradients. Using the Blend filters is very similar to using the Blend tool, but instead of making different shape *and* color blends, the Blend filters create new colors inside the between objects automatically. If the ending paths' colors are different color *types,* the Blend filters will produce undesirable results.

The main difference between each of these filters is how each determines what the end paths are, and in what direction the blend flows.

The Convert to Filters

The three Convert to filters — Convert to CMYK, Convert to Grayscale, and Convert to RGB — allow you to change the color model of selected paths with a simple menu selection. In addition to switching between Grayscale, CMYK, and RGB, the Convert to filters change custom colors to those color models as well.

The Invert Colors Filter

Invert Colors works in strange and mysterious ways on selected paths. Whatever the color of the path, Invert Colors takes the first three colors in the Paint palette (Cyan, Magenta, and Yellow) and subtracts them from 100. If the original color was a shade of Red (for example, where Cyan = 0%, Magenta = 100%, and Yellow = 100%), then Invert Colors makes the new color Cyan = 100%, Magenta = 0%, and Yellow = 0%.

Caution   The percentage of Black is not affected by Invert colors. Therefore, this is *not* the same as getting a negative image.

Note   Although Invert works poorly with CMYK images, it works perfectly with both Grayscale and RGB images.

1. Select the art you wish to invert.

2. Choose Filter ➪ Color ➪ Convert to RGB.

3. Choose Filter ➪ Color ➪ Invert Colors.

4. Choose Filter ➪ Color ➪ Convert to CMYK.

Caution

When using the previous steps, be aware that slight differences may result from changing the color mode of your artwork.

The Overprint Black Plug-In

Choosing Filter ➪ Color ➪ Overprint Black displays the Overprint Black dialog box (shown in Figure 12-3), which enables you to apply overprinting of black to selected paths. A number of options can be selected, including whether to add or remove overprinting from the selected objects. Another option lets you specify the amount of black percentage that is the minimum that will be used to overprint.

Tip

A mistake I have made in the past is thinking that if I select an 85% Black to overprint that everything from 85% to 100% Black in my illustration will overprint. But that is not the case—you have to select each object and enter the specific value for that object.

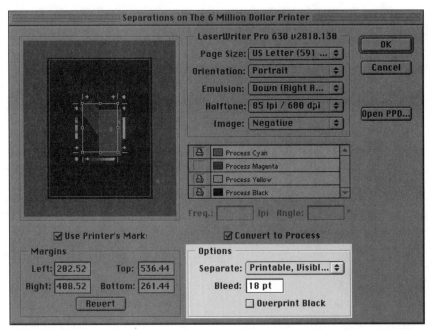

Figure 12-3: The Overprint options are found in the Separation setup dialog box

You can specify where the overprint affects Fills or Strokes or both. The other options determine whether black will overprint when combined with CMY or when part of a spot color.

The Overprint Black filter adds overprinting only to selected objects that are not currently overprinted when the Add button is selected, and it removes overprinting from objects that currently have overprinting when the Remove button is selected. In no circumstance does it remove overprinting when the Add button is selected, even if the overprinting object does not fall within the parameters of the settings of the Overprint dialog box.

Note In the Attributes palette, the appropriate checkboxes are selected when you use the filter on selected objects.

The Saturate Filter

Saturate adds or subtracts equal amounts of color to the selected objects. This filter does not correspond in any way to saturation changes made by Photoshop; instead, the color added is proportional to each color in a path. Using Saturate works in much the same way as pressing the Shift key and dragging a triangle to the right in the Color palette. Saturate does not work with patterns or gradients.

The Saturate dialog box (shown in Figure 12-4) enables you to saturate or desaturate, depending on the direction the slider is dragged. The Preview checkbox in this dialog box is quite helpful, letting you see what is happening to the paths in real time.

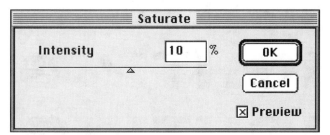

Figure 12-4: The Saturate dialog box

Manipulating Colors with the Color Filters

The color filters provide automated ways of changing colors for a variety of objects. Most of the filters work on paths that are Filled with black or a process color, and some of them work on the Strokes of the paths as well. The following sections describe various uses for the color filters.

Techniques for Creating Shadows and Highlights

You can easily use color filters to create shadows and highlights for black and process-color paths.

You create most shadows by simply creating a copy of the object and placing it under, and slightly offset from, the original. You can darken the copy in a number of ways, but the easiest way is to use the Adjust Colors filter. Figure 12-5 shows the four steps that you follow to create shadows and highlights.

You create highlights in the same way as you create shadows, but instead of darkening the copy, you lighten it.

1. Create an object that has several colors in it. Group the individual elements in the object.

2. Copy the object and choose Edit ⇨ Paste in Back (⌘-B) [Ctrl+B]. Offset the copy down and to the right.

3. Choose Filter ⇨ Colors ⇨ Adjust Colors. To darken the shadowed copy evenly, add 20% to Cyan, Magenta, and Yellow, and 40% to Black.

4. To create the highlight, choose Edit ⇨ Paste in Back (⌘-B) [Ctrl+B] and offset the copy up and to the left. Decrease all four process colors by 40% if the background is dark or 20% if the background is light. My background is dark, so I reduced the color in the highlight by 40% of each color.

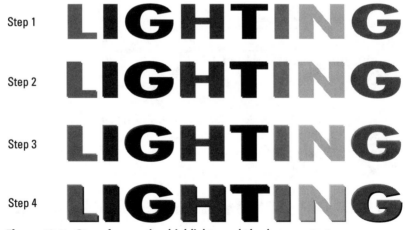

Figure 12-5: Steps for creating highlights and shadows on text

Creating Extruded Multiple Path Objects

Usually, you can make objects appear extruded by blending two objects together. If the objects contain multiple paths, however, you have to blend each of the paths separately. And if the objects contain compound paths, the blends that you create will not share the compound attributes of the original objects.

You can use the Blend Front to Back filter to make objects appear to be extruded, as described in the following steps.

1. Release any compound paths in the object and group all the paths in the object together.

2. In the Move dialog box (choose Object ⇨ Transform ⇨ Move), enter **0.25 pt** in the Horizontal text field and **0.1 pt** in the Vertical text field. Click the Copy button (or press Option-Return).

3. Choose Arrange ⇨ Transform Again (⌘-D) [Ctrl+D] until the object has been duplicated far enough to appear 3D. Copy the final duplicate object. (It should still be selected.)

4. Change the color of the final duplicate object to be the color of the front-most part of the blend. In my example, I made the final duplicate object black and left the rest of the objects red. (The color insert shows the result.)

5. Select all the objects and choose Filter ⇨ Colors ⇨ Blend Front to Back.

6. Choose Edit ⇨ Paste in Front (⌘-F) [Ctrl+F] and give a different color to the object just pasted. In the example, I used yellow. Choose Object ⇨ Compound Path ⇨ Make (⌘-8) [Ctrl+8] and then Object ⇨ Hide Selection (⌘-3) [Ctrl+3].

7. Continue to select each grouped object, making each group a compound path and then hiding it, until all the paths are hidden.

8. After you have hidden all the paths, choose Object ⇨ Show All (⌘-Option-3) [Ctrl+Alt+3] and then group all the paths together.

Caution

Do not make all of the paths one compound path or the color information for each path will be lost.

Tip

Actually, you can automate the whole process described in the preceding steps by using the VectorEffects' ShadowLand filter, which includes all sorts of shadowing effects, including a useful one for zooming.

Creating Negatives with the Color Filters

You can produce negative images in Illustrator almost automatically by using the Invert Colors filter. For a process color, the Invert Colors filter subtracts the tints of Cyan, Magenta, and Yellow from 100% and leaves Black as is. On an object that is Filled or Stroked with Black only, the filter subtracts the tint of Black from 100%.

To get around the way that this filter works when creating negatives, select all the objects that you want to reverse. Next, choose Filter ⇨ Colors ⇨ Invert Colors, select each path, and check whether the paths have a process color Fill that contains Black. If you find any Fills that contain Black, manually change black to the correct value.

Tip   After you check a path to see whether it is a process color that contains Black, hide that path. Using this method can help you be sure that you have checked every path, and you do not have to worry about wasting time by rechecking paths.

The Create Filters

There were bunches of create filters in version 5.5 of Illustrator. In Illustrator 8, the category is all but extinct, with only Create Object Mosaic and Trim Marks being the stragglers. The Star, Spiral, and Polygon filters have been replaced with tools.

As with most filters, you can manually perform the functions that the two create filters do, but using the filters is much easier.

Creating Object Mosaics

The Object Mosaic filter creates a series of tiles out of a placed bitmap image, as shown in Figure 12-6. Any size or color image may be used. When an image is converted through the Object Mosaic filter, it becomes a series of rectangles, each Filled with a different color.

Figure 12-6: An original TIFF image (left) and the image after Object Mosaic has been applied (right)

In the Object Mosaic dialog box (see Figure 12-7), you can specify the number of tiles that the image is made up of and the space between the tiles. You also can specify a different size for the entire object mosaic.

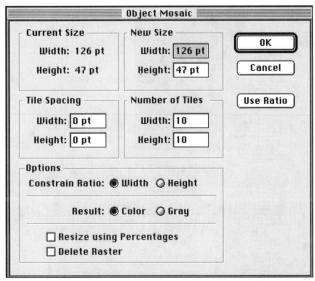

Figure 12-7: The Object Mosaic dialog box

Caution Be careful with Object Mosaic, for this filter, unlike almost any other, will run out of memory if the source image or number of tiles is too large. This is the one filter in Illustrator that does almost exactly what its counterpart in Photoshop does.

The more rectangles, the more detail in the mosaic. Bitmapped images are mosaics of a sort, with each pixel equal to 1 square.

Tip If you need to apply Object Mosaic to an illustration you've created in Illustrator, you can rasterize it using the Object ➪ Rasterize command. Do this at a low resolution (72-dpi works great for me), and then apply Object Mosaic to the rasterized image.

Use the following steps to create a fairly simple and basic mosaic in Illustrator.

1. Create a TIFF file and place it in Illustrator. You do not need to use a high-resolution TIFF file. The Illustrator object mosaic looks just as good when you convert a 72-dpi TIFF file as when you convert a 300-dpi TIFF file.

2. Choose Filters ➪ Create ➪ Object Mosaic. In the Object Mosaic dialog box, enter the size that you want the mosaic to be and also the number of tiles across and down. Click the Use Ratio button to keep the same proportions as in the original image.

3. Click OK when you are satisfied with the information that you have entered in the Object Mosaic dialog box. Figure 12-8 shows the results that are produced by entering three different tile widths and heights into the Number of Tiles boxes.

Step 1

333 × 419 PIXELS
(139,527)

Step 2

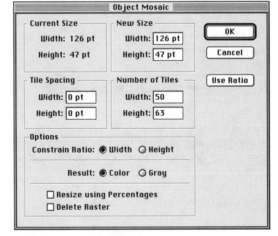

Step 3

15 × 19 TILES   30 × 38 TILES   80 × 101 TILES
(285)   (1,140)   (8,080)

Figure 12-8: Steps for creating object mosaics

Caution The number of tiles that Illustrator can produce is strictly limited and is directly related to the amount of RAM allocated to Illustrator. Exceeding the limit causes Illustrator to create only a portion of the tiles.

You can create some very exciting effects with the Object Mosaic filter when you use it in conjunction with other filters. The best ones to use with it are Round Corners, all of the Distort filters, and most of the color filters, as well as the Transform Each function. In the following example, I combined the Object Mosaic filter with the Round Corners filter and the Transform Each function.

1. Create an object mosaic with an average number of tiles (between 1,600 and 10,000 tiles, which would be from 40 × 40 to 100 × 100). In the example shown in Figure 12-9, I used an object mosaic with 50 × 63 tiles, or 3,150 tiles.

2. Select all the mosaic tiles and choose Filters ⇨ Stylize ⇨ Round Corners. In the Round Corners dialog box, enter a large number. I usually enter at least 10 points. As long as the tiles are not larger than 20 points wide, the Round Corners filter turns all the tiles into circles.

3. Copy all the tiles and choose Edit ⇨ Paste in Front (⌘-F) [Ctrl+F]. Select all the tiles (the image now has 6,300 tiles) and choose Object ⇨ Transform ⇨ Transform Each. In the Move section of the dialog box, enter **5** in both text fields and check the Random checkbox. Click OK. If you want less white space between all the circles, choose Edit ⇨ Paste in Front (⌘-F) [Ctrl+F] again and then choose Arrange ⇨ Transform Again (⌘-D) [Ctrl+D]. The results should look similar to Step 3 in Figure 12-9.

The tiles created with the Object Mosaic filter are placed on the page from top-left to bottom-right. The top-left tile is underneath all the other tiles (in the back), and the bottom-right tile is on top of all the other tiles (in the front). The tiles abut each other, so that none of them overlap.

Step 1

Step 2

Step 3

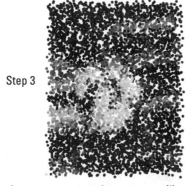

Figure 12-9: Creating a Seurat-like effect with the Object Mosaic filter

Because of the way that these tiles overlap, you can create a tiled or shingled roof quite easily, providing the original image is upside down. The following steps describe this process in detail.

1. Create a TIFF file to be used as the roof. In the example shown in Figure 12-10, I created the name of a restaurant. Then I rasterized it in Illustrator.

2. In Illustrator, rotate the image 135° clockwise. Choose Filter ⇨ Create ⇨ Object Mosaic. Make the number of tiles across about 50 or more, and click the Use Ratio button.

3. Rotate the entire mosaic by 135°. Using the Selection tool, draw a marquee around any white squares above, below, to the left, and to the right of the roof area to select them. Delete all white squares. Because the squares are white, you may need to switch to Artwork mode to see them all.

4. Select the remaining tiles and group them. Choose Object ⇨ Path ⇨ Add Anchor Points to add one Anchor Point to every side of every square in the mosaic. Choose Filter ⇨ Stylize ⇨ Punk and Bloat to make all the points on each square come out a little.

5. To round off the points and make the squares smoother, choose Filter ⇨ Stylize ⇨ Round Corners, and enter **10 pt** in the text field. Choose Object ⇨ Transform ⇨ Transform Each and enter **150** in both the Horizontal and Vertical fields of the Scale section of the Transform Each dialog box. Because the squares were scaled up, they now overlap.

6. Choose Object ⇨ Transform ⇨ Transform Each and enter **45°** in the Rotate section. In the Color and Stroke palettes, give each tile a Black Stroke of 0.25 point. Depending on the size of the tiles, the Stroke weight may vary.

7. Use the Free Transform tool to change the shape of the roof to be more . . . well . . . rooflike.

Step

Step 2

Step 3

Step 4

Step 5

Step 6

Step 7

Figure 12-10: Creating a tiled roof with the Object Mosaic filter

Note

It may seem strange that the mosaic gets rotated twice in the previous procedure, but there is a method to this seemingly mad busywork. By placing the upper-left tiles on the bottom and the lower-right tiles on the top, the image is rotated first so that the lower parts of the image are turned into squares. By the way, if I hadn't helped put shingles on a roof recently (you have to work from the bottom up), I would never have been able to figure this out. So I guess that this is one of those "real-life" examples!

The following steps describe how to make the tiles in a mosaic overlap with no white space between them. This technique can easily create a background image or a funky illustration, as shown in the steps and used in context in Figure 12-11.

1. Create an Object Mosaic from a raster image.

2. Choose Object ➪ Transform ➪ Transform Each, and enter the amount of movement for the tiles in the Move section. Check the Random checkbox. Measure one tile with the Measure tool. The tiles that I created for the example shown in Figure 12-11 are 3.3 points across, and the move distance that I used is 3.3 points. The most white space between any two tiles is 6.6 points.

3. Select Object ⇨ Transform ⇨ Transform Each. Enter the percentage that the tile must be scaled up to eliminate the white space in the Scale area. In this example, I entered 200%.

4. To see the edges of the tiles more easily, place a 0.25-point 100% Black Stroke on them.

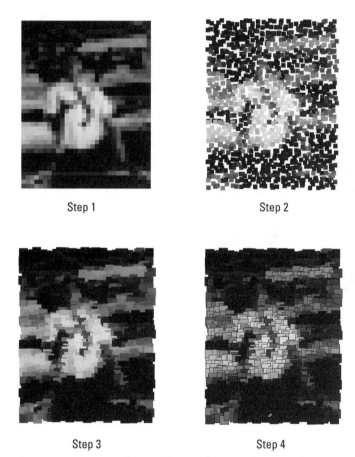

Step 1   Step 2

Step 3   Step 4

Figure 12-11: Steps for creating random overlapping tiles with no white space

By using the Object Mosaic filter in combination with the color blend filters, color sets can be created very easily. These color sets can be sampled for inclusion in the Swatch palette.

1. Create an Object Mosaic from any image, making the total number of tiles equal to the number of different tiles that you want in the color set.

2. Change the colors of the tiles that mark the beginning and end of each color set. In the example (Figure 12-12), I used the primary colors and white as the beginning and end of each color set.

3. Select one range of color and choose Filter ➪ Color ➪ Blend Front to Back to blend the colors from the upper-left tiles toward the lower-right tiles. Repeat this step for each range of colors.

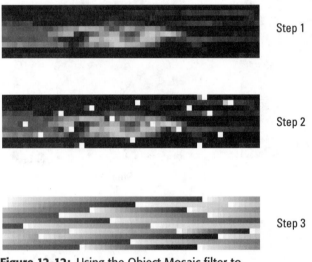

Step 1

Step 2

Step 3

Figure 12-12: Using the Object Mosaic filter to create color sets

The Distort and Stylize Filters

The following pages describe the Distort and Stylize filters (found in the Distort and Stylize submenus of the Filter menu). Tips and techniques for getting the most out of the filters are also provided.

New Feature If you're looking for the Free Distort filter, look in the Toolbar. In Illustrator 8, the Free Distort has turned into a tool. You can use this tool just like the filter, but quicker and slicker. For more about the Free Distort tool see Chapter 7.

The Punk and Bloat Filter

Although the Punk and Bloat filter undoubtedly has the coolest sounding name that Illustrator has to offer, this filter also is one of the least practical. But Illustrator is a fun program, right? And these filters make it lots of fun.

Punking makes objects appear to have pointy tips sticking out everywhere, and bloating creates lumps outside of objects. Punking and bloating are inverses of each other; a negative punk is a bloat, and a negative bloat is a punk. If you are bewildered by these functions, stop reading right here. The following information spoils everything.

Selecting Punk and Bloat opens the Punk and Bloat dialog box, where you may specify a percentage that you want the selected paths to be punked or bloated by either typing in the amount or dragging a slider.

Bloating causes the segments between Anchor Points to expand outwards. The higher the percentage, the more bloated the selection. You can bloat from –200% to +200%. Punk is the inverse of Bloat. While Bloat makes rounded, bubblelike extrusions appear on the surface of your object, Punk makes tall spikes appear on its path. When you drag toward Punk, you can enter how much you want to punk the drawing. Punk amounts can range from –200% to +200%. The number of spikes is based on the number of Anchor Points in your drawing. Figure 12-13 shows several punked and bloated objects.

Original   Punk   Bloat

Figure 12-13: Punked and bloated objects

The Punk and Bloat filter moves Anchor Points in one direction and creates two independent direction points on either side of each Anchor Point. The direction points are moved in the opposite direction of the Anchor Points, and the direction of movement is always toward or away from the center of the object.

The distance moved is the only thing that you control when you use the Punk and Bloat filter. Entering a percentage moves the points that percentage.

Tip   Nothing about the Punk and Bloat filter is random. Everything about it is 100% controllable and, to some extent, predictable.

1. Create and select the artwork that you want to punk, as shown in Figure 12-14.

2. Add Anchor Points or use the Roughen filter at 0% to create additional Anchor Points if necessary. I chose Object ➪ Add Anchor Points twice, increasing the number of Anchor Points from 4 to 16.

3. Choose Filter ➪ Stylize ➪ Punk and Bloat. In the dialog box, enter the amount that you want to punk or bloat the object, or drag the slider in the appropriate direction.

4. Check to see whether the result is what you intended.

5. Add other artwork to the punked or bloated object.

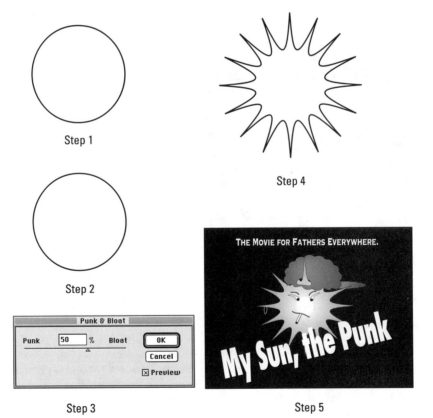

Figure 12-14: Steps for punking and bloating

ASK TOULOUSE: I Can't Get Punked Stuff Back to Normal

Squiggy: After I punk, I can never get the paths back to normal.

Toulouse: Undo doesn't work?

Squiggy: Sure, but I like changing things I've saved, closed, and reopened.

Toulouse: Undo won't work in that case.

Squiggy: So, I'm trying to bloat the paths I punked, since Bloat is the opposite of Punk.

Toulouse: It just doesn't work that way.

Squiggy: Why?

Toulouse: Punk and Bloat change each Anchor Point into a Curved Corner Point. Each point has two independent handles, and those handles are moved with Punk and Bloat.

Squiggy: Wouldn't bloating punked paths move the handles back to where they started?

Toulouse: No, because originally, many of those points didn't have handles at all.

Squiggy: Anything else that can be done?

Toulouse: Redraw or, if you have the patience, edit each of the points, unless you added Anchor Points before punking.

Twirl Filter

Like the Punk and Bloat filter, the Twirl filter reshapes objects in ways that would be time-consuming and tedious if you were using conventional Illustrator methods. The Twirl filter moves the innermost points a certain number of degrees around a circle. The farther away the points are from the center of the circle, the less they move; points at the outermost edges of the object hardly rotate at all.

Note   In Illustrator 8, there is both a Twirl filter and a Twirl tool, found in the Plug-in Tools palette. The Twirl filter is described here, while the Twirl tool is discussed in Chapter 7.

Selecting Twirl displays the Twirl dialog box, where you specify how much the selected objects will spin. You can set the twirl angle from –4000° up to +4000°. The very center of the selected objects rotates the degree specified, while the objects on the edges rotate around the center very little. Positive values rotate the selected paths clockwise; negative values rotate the selected paths counterclockwise. Figure 12-15 shows an object before and after being twirled.

Figure 12-15: The original paths (left) are twirled (right)

Tip   Until Illustrator 7's version of Twirl, adding more Anchor Points to your path didn't necessarily result in a better effect. I used to apply Add Anchor Points several times or add Anchor Points via the Roughen filter before applying the Twirl filter. Now, however, the Twirl filter is "smart" and curves paths automatically.

The Twirl filter can twirl single paths or multiple paths. When it twirls multiple paths, the twirling takes place from the center of the entire group of objects, not from within each object.

Note   The constraints on the Twirl filter are similar to the constraints on the Free Distort filter. You cannot twirl placed images, type that has not been converted to outlines, or patterns and gradients that are used as Fills.

1. Create the artwork that you want to use with the Twirl filter. In the example in Figure 12-16, I created a star with several points and a tiny first (inner) radius. Then I selected the center points with the Direct Selection tool and dragged them down and to the left.

2. Choose Filter ➪ Distort ➪ Twirl to see the Twirl dialog box. Enter the number of degrees that you want to twirl objects. In the example, I used 300°. Entering a positive number in the Angle text field twirls the object clockwise; entering a negative number twirls the object counterclockwise (which is opposite from how the degree setting for the Rotate tool works).

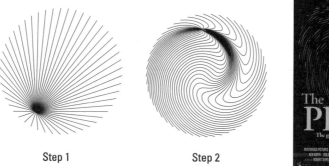

Step 1   Step 2

Figure 12-16: Steps for twirling artwork

I wanted the twirled artwork in the example to resemble a fingerprint, so I used the Scale and Rotate tools, and then the Scribble and Tweak filter (see the section "The Scribble and Tweak filter," later in this chapter) to achieve the desired effect. After scribbling the artwork just 0.5% horizontally and vertically, I added the background and the accompanying text. A larger version of the resulting poster is in the color section of this book. You can twirl paths up to 4000° in both directions (+4000 and –4000). The Twirl filter by itself enables you to create many different effects. By moving different objects to different positions, the Twirl filter can produce entirely different results. For example, you can use the following steps to create an arc in an illustration.

1. Create the type that you want to arc and convert it to outlines.

2. Make a copy of the type to the left of the original type and place an object between the two areas of type. Then place the same object at either end of the words. At this point, the illustration looks like Step 2 of Figure 12-17.

3. Select the objects and choose Filter ➪ Twirl. In the Twirl dialog box, enter **90°** and click OK.

4. Delete all the portions of the path except for the one shown.

5. Select the remaining portion and use the Free Transform tool. Use ⌘-Option-Shift [Ctrl-Alt-Shift] after you click on a corner of the bounding box.

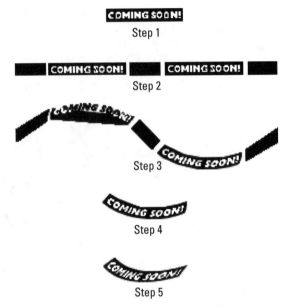

Figure 12-17: Steps for creating arced illustrations with the Twirl filter

The Zig Zag Filter

The Zig Zag filter changes normally straight paths into zigzagged versions of those paths. When you first select Zig Zag, the Zig Zag dialog box, shown in Figure 12-18, appears.

The dialog box allows you to specify various parameters of the zigzag effect, including the Amount, which is how large each zigzag is, and the number of Ridges, which is how many zigzags there are. In addition, you can specify whether you want the zigzags to be curved (choose Smooth) or pointed (choose Corner). Like most of the other Illustrator 8 filters, Zig Zag has a handy Preview checkbox. Figure 12-19 shows an example of zigzagged artwork.

Caution   Don't keep the Preview checkbox checked while you're changing values in the Zig Zag dialog box. Instead, change your settings first, and *then* click the Preview checkbox. This prevents massive slowdowns that can occur when the Preview checkbox is checked.

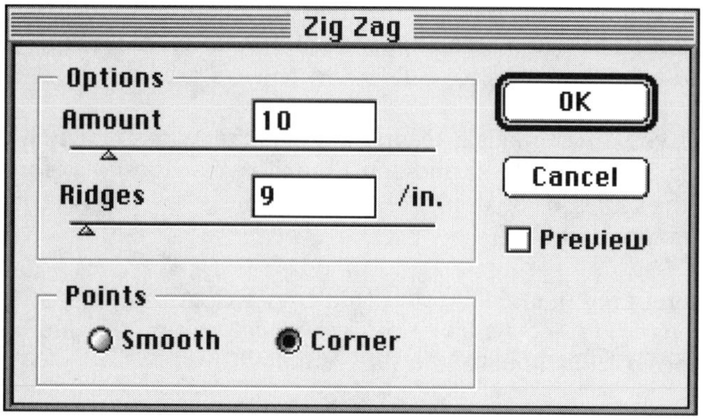

Figure 12-18: The Zig Zag dialog box

Original

Zigzagged

Figure 12-19: Zigzagged art

The Random Mangle Filters

The two Random Mangle filters — Roughen and Scribble and Tweak — both do similar things to paths. Roughen adds Anchor Points and then moves them randomly by a percentage that you define. Scribble and Tweak randomly moves existing Anchor Points and Control Handles by a percentage or by an absolute measurement that you define.

Because the mangle filters work randomly, you get different results when you apply the same settings of the same filter to two separate, identical objects. In fact, the results will probably never be duplicated. The mangle filters are a good reason for having the Undo command, so that you can apply the filter, undo, and reapply until you achieve the desired effect.

Tip   Using the keyboard, you can continually reapply any filter that works randomly and get different results. Select the object and apply the filter by choosing the menu item and entering the values. If you don't like the result, press ⌘-Z [Ctrl+Z] (Undo) and ⌘-E [Ctrl+E] (reapply last filter).

One important limitation of the mangle filters is that they work on entire paths, even if only part of the path is selected. The best way to get around this limitation is to use the Scissors tool to cut the path into different sections.

The Roughen Filter

The Roughen filter does two things at once. First, it adds Anchor Points until the selection has the number of points per inch that you defined. Second, it randomly moves all the points around, changing them into Straight Corner Points or Smooth Points, whichever you specified.

Selecting Roughen opens the Roughen dialog box (see Figure 12-20), where you can enter information to roughen up the illustration—literally.

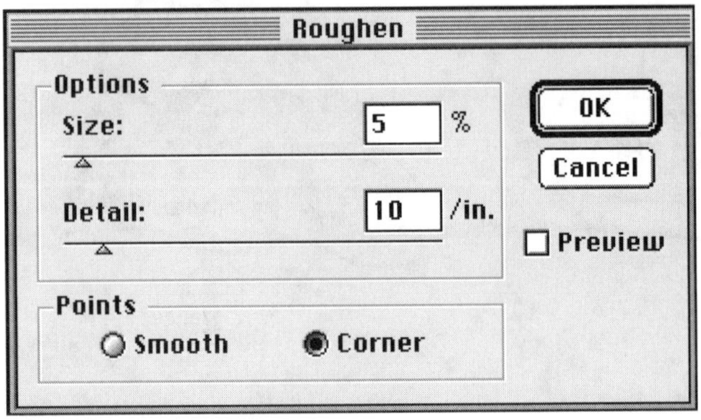

Figure 12-20: The Roughen dialog box

Three options are available:

✦ **Size:** How far points may move when roughed relative to the width or height (whichever is greater) of the selected path.

✦ **Detail:** How many points are moved. For example, if you have a 1-inch x 1-inch square, the number of points added is 36. (Four inches at the top, bottom, left, and right at 10 points per inch equals 40 points. There are already 4 points on a rectangle, so you only need 36 more points.)

✦ **Smooth or Corner:** If Smooth, all the Anchor Points added will be Smooth Points. If Corner, all the points added will be Straight Corner Points.

Roughen never takes away points when roughening a path.

Tip   The Roughen filter can be used as a very hip version of the Add Anchor Points filter. If the Size box is set at 0%, all points added will be added along the existing path all at once. Instead of going to Add Anchor Points again and again, just try entering a value of 25 in the Segments/Inch field of the Roughen filter. You have instant multiple Add Anchor Points. This is a great technique for Scribble and Tweak or anything else where you need a bunch of Anchor Points fast.

Tip   Using the Roughen filter on a path is fairly straightforward, but using it on a portion of artwork is not. Figure 12-21 and the following steps take you through setting up artwork so that only the Roughen filter affects a portion of the artwork.

1. Create the artwork that you want to tear.

2. Select the Pen tool and click from one edge of the artwork to another, crossing the path that you want to tear. If you don't want the tear to be straight, click additional points to change direction. If you want a curved tear, make the path curved. Connect the path by continuing around the outside of the artwork.

3. Select the artwork and the path. Choose Divide from the Pathfinder palette. Ungroup (⌘-Shift-G) [Ctrl+Shift+G] and choose Edit ➪ Deselect All (⌘-Shift-A) [Ctrl+Shift+A]. Select the paths on one side of the tear and drag them away from the remaining paths.

4. Using the Scissors tool, click the ends of the tear on one side of the split path. Drag the cut section away from the rest of the path. On the other half of the tear, cut that tear away and delete it as well.

5. Choose Filter ➪ Distort ➪ Roughen to see the Roughen dialog box. In the Size text field, enter the percentage that you want the Anchor Points to be moved. (In the example, I used 2% to move the points just slightly.) Next, determine how many points you want to add to the tear. (I chose 30 points per inch.) Then decide on the type of roughen: Rounded or Jagged. A Rounded roughen produces Smooth Points with Control Handles that stick out a very small amount from the Anchor Point, and a Jagged roughen has only Straight Corner Points.

6. Click OK and check the newly roughened path to ensure that it is roughened correctly. If it isn't, or if you don't like the random movement of the anchor Points, choose Edit ➪ Undo (⌘-Z) [Ctrl+Z] and select the Filter dialog box again (press Option [Alt] and choose Filter ➪ Distort ➪ Roughen). Continue undoing and roughening until the artwork is the way you want it or just adjust the Anchor Points with the Direct Selection tool.

7. Option[Alt]-copy the roughened path to the edge of the path that it was torn from. The best way to perform this task is to click on an End Point with the Selection tool and drag to the End Point of the existing path with the Option [Alt] key pressed. Average and join the points (⌘-Option-Shift-J)

[Ctrl+Alt+Shift+J]. Move the original roughened path to the other side of the path and average and join both points. (I usually zoom in, sometimes to 1600%, to make sure that the two points are one on top of the other and that only two points are selected.)

8. Add any other artwork to the torn paths. In the example, I rotated each of the sides a small amount.

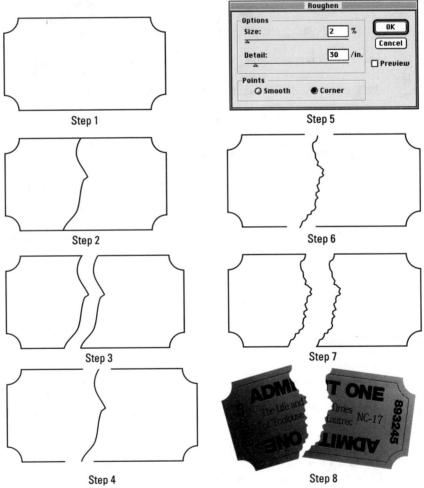

Figure 12-21: Steps for creating a tear in a path

Tip   The Roughen filter has a secret function that very few people know about: You can use it to add Anchor Points to paths. Simply enter **0%** in the first text field and the points that are added will not be moved at all. This method is especially useful as a substitute for Add Anchor Points when some of the paths in a compound path don't need as many additional Anchor Points as others. The Roughen filter evens out the number of points for each of the paths in a compound path.

If you want roughened edges to be *really* rounded, don't choose the Rounded option in the Roughen dialog box. Instead, choose the Jagged option and then choose Filter ⇨ Stylize ⇨ Round Corners. The Round Corners option changes only Straight Corner Points, so it will change all the points in the Jagged roughened object to smooth curves.

If you choose the Rounded option in the Roughen dialog box, the Round Corners filter has no effect on the roughened object.

The Scribble and Tweak Filter

Although it sounds like characters from *Animaniacs,* the Scribble and Tweak filter, as is true for most filters, creates effects that take an unrealistically long amount of time to do manually.

One important thing needs to be made clear right away: The Scribble and Tweak filter does one thing. The only difference between scribbling and tweaking is in the way that you enter the amount of random movement. When Scribble is selected, you enter percentages that are based on the size of the object's bounding box; when Tweak is selected, points are moved based on absolute measurements that you enter.

Tip   Because of the measuring system that Tweak uses, I have found that most of the time selecting the Tweak option is much easier than using the Scribble option. Having to enter percentages when Scribble is selected can be very confusing, especially because you have to be concerned with both horizontal and vertical proportions.

Selecting Scribble and Tweak displays the Scribble and Tweak dialog box. When the Scribble option is selected, you define the amount of scribble, including how much horizontal and vertical scribble and which points are moved (Anchor Points, In Control Points, or Out Control Points).

Note   No Anchor Points are added with the Scribble dialog box.

For Scribble, horizontal and vertical percentages correspond to the movement of the selected points. If 0% is entered in either field, no movement will occur in that direction. The percentage is based on the width or height of the shape, whichever is longer. If Anchor Points is checked, then all Anchor Points on the selected path are moved in a random distance corresponding to the amounts set in the Horizontal and Vertical text fields. If either In Control Points or Out Control Points is checked, then those points are moved the specified distance as well. The *In Control Points* are the points on one side of the Anchor Point; *Out Control Points* refers to the points on the other side of the Anchor Point.

Selecting Tweak displays the Tweak options. Instead of specifying a distance based on percentage, the Tweak option lets you enter the distance in real measurements (such as picas or inches) in whatever unit your measurement system is currently using. All Tweak options have the same effects as the Scribble options.

ASK TOULOUSE: Not the Same Effect

Carmine: You know, what I really hate about Illustrator is its inconsistency.

Toulouse: What's inconsistent?

Carmine: The Roughen filter, for one thing.

Toulouse: It's supposed to be inconsistent. After all, it does random stuff.

Carmine: But let's say I want to duplicate a roughen effect.

Toulouse: I think you're out of luck.

Carmine: How does Illustrator come up with the random values? Surely there's a chart somewhere.

Toulouse: Actually, most "random" numbers are generated based on the time and date. Because this always changes, you'll get a different "result" each time.

Carmine: So if I went back in time to when I applied the Roughen filter the first time, it would be the same.

Toulouse: Well, you'd have to do it at the exact moment when you applied it before. Which would be almost as hard as traveling back in time in the first place.

Carmine: I could change my system clock, couldn't I?

Toulouse: Yes, but still, we're talking fractions of a second. The odds are you won't be able to do it right, unfortunately.

Note I use the Scribble option when I am not sure of the size of the selected artwork, or when I can determine only that I want points moved a certain portion of the whole, but cannot determine an absolute measurement.

1. Create the artwork that you want to use with the filter. (The Scribble and Tweak filter does not work with type that has not been converted to outlines or with placed images; nor does it affect patterns or gradients that are being used as Fills.)

2. Choose Filter ⇨ Distort ⇨ Scribble and Tweak. In the Scribble and Tweak dialog box, enter the amount that you want points to be moved, both horizontally and vertically. (Moving the points a large amount usually results in overlapping, crisscrossing paths that aren't very attractive.) Check the options that correspond to the points that you want to move randomly (for example, checking the Anchor Points checkbox moves Anchor Points randomly). Check the In Control Points or Out Control Points checkbox to move the Control Handles. The In Control Points are the Control Handles that affect the segment that precedes the Anchor Point relative to the path direction; the Out Control Points are the Control Handles that affect the segment that appears after each Anchor Point relative to the path direction. (Path direction is explained in Chapter 9.)

3. Click OK. If the artwork isn't what you expected, choose Edit ⇨ Undo (⌘-Z) [Ctrl+Z] and then either reapply the filter (⌘-E) [Ctrl+E] or press Option and enter new values in the dialog box (choose Filter ⇨ Distort ⇨ Scribble and Tweak).

4. Add any further artwork to the completed object.

Figure 12-22 shows these four steps. At the bottom of the figure are eight different versions of the artwork. Each version has the same settings, but the points have been moved randomly eight different times.

The percentages that you enter in the Scribble dialog box move points relative to the size of the bounding box.

The bounding box is an invisible box that surrounds each object. If the bounding box is 5 inches wide and 2 inches tall and you enter a percentage of 10% for width and height in the Scribble dialog box, the filter moves the points randomly up to 0.5 inches horizontally and 0.2 inches vertically in either direction.

Caution When the Scribble option is checked, the most important thing to remember when entering horizontal and vertical percentages is that the height and width of any object are usually different. As a result, entering the same percentage in each box usually causes different amounts of movement for each dimension.

Step 1

Step 3

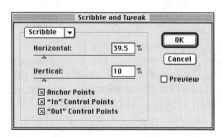

Step 2

Step 4

Figure 12-22: Steps for using the Scribble and Tweak filter

Pen and Ink Filter

New and improved, the Pen and Ink filter has undergone more than a name change. With Illustrator 8, the Pen and Ink filter has added the capability to apply a Photo Crosshatch to any rasterized image. Adobe has made the Pen and Ink filter much easier to understand from its first introduction. This filter adds a texture of lines on top of your selected image or photo. For more on the Pen and Ink filter, see Chapter 11.

The Stylize Filters

The Stylize filters are used for a variety of functions, kind of a catchall for filters that really couldn't go anywhere else. Add Arrowheads puts arrowheads (all sorts!)

onto the ends of open paths. Drop Shadow adds a darkened shadow to the selected path. Round Corners seems better suited to the Distort submenu, but Adobe has chosen to put it here.

The three Stylize filters fall into two different categories. The first category contains the Add Arrowheads and Drop Shadow filter. These two filters create additional objects that are based on existing objects.

The Stylize filters in the second category work in much the same way as the Distort filters. The Round Corners filter removes Corner Points and replaces them with Smooth Points.

Add Arrowheads

The Add Arrowheads filter is a boon to technical artists, sign makers, and anyone else in need of a quick arrow. The number one complaint about the Add Arrowheads filter is that Illustrator offers too many arrowheads to choose from. Some complaint!

Choosing Filter ➪ Stylize ➪ Add Arrowheads adds an arrowhead (or two) to any selected open path. If more than one path is selected, arrowheads are added to each open path. To use Add Arrowheads, select an open path and choose Add Arrowheads. The Add Arrowheads dialog box appears, as shown in Figure 12-23. In this box, you can pick which of the 27 different arrowheads you want to stick on the end of your path. Scale refers to the size of the arrowhead relative to the Stroke weight of the path; you may enter any number between 1% and 1000% in this box. Choosing Start places the arrowhead at the beginning of the path (where you first clicked to draw it); choosing End places the arrowhead on the ending of the path (where you last clicked to draw it); and choosing Start and End places the same arrowhead on both the beginning and ending of the path. Reapplying this filter to the same paths will continue to put arrowheads on top of arrowheads.

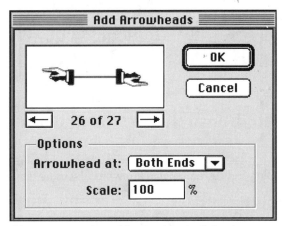

Figure 12-23: The Add Arrowheads dialog box

Caution   Add Arrowheads does *not* work on closed paths.

Arrowheads are grouped to the paths that were selected when they were created; it is sometimes necessary to rotate the arrowhead by either ungrouping it or choosing it with the Direct Selection tool.

The size of the arrowheads is based on the width of the Stroke, but you can alter each arrowhead's dimensions in the Scale text field in the Add Arrowheads dialog box. Figure 12-24 and the steps that follow show you how to create and customize arrowheads.

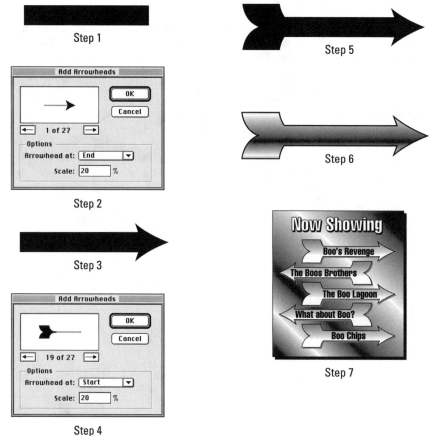

Figure 12-24: Steps for creating and customizing an arrowhead by using the Add Arrowheads filter

1. Use the Pen or Pencil tool to create an open path. Set the width of the path to the width that you want it to be with an arrowhead attached to it. (You have to use an open path — nothing happens when you select a closed path and apply the Add Arrowheads filter. Even if you want just the arrowhead, and not the path, you still have to create a path first — you can delete the path after the arrowhead appears.)

2. Choose Filter ➪ Stylize ➪ Add Arrowheads. The Add Arrowheads dialog box appears. Enter the size of the arrowhead (100% = normal size). Pick the end of the path where you want the arrowhead to appear. If you want the arrowhead on both ends of the path, click the Start and End option. (If you drew the path yourself with either the Pen or Freehand tool, the path direction is the direction that you drew the path — closed paths that were created with the Rectangle or Oval tools or the Create filters and were then cut usually go in a counterclockwise direction.) Pick an arrowhead from the 27 options. (Press down and hold on the directional arrows to flip through the arrowheads quickly — after arrowhead #27, you see arrowhead #1. Figure 12-25 shows all the arrowheads.)

3. Click OK. The path now has an arrowhead. Whenever arrowheads are created, they are grouped to the path. You have to use the Group Selection tool to select individual pieces of the arrow, or choose Arrange ➪ Ungroup (⌘-Shift-G) [Ctrl+Shift+G].

4. To add a different arrowhead to the other end of the path, select the path with the Direct Selection tool and then choose Filter ➪ Stylize ➪ Add Arrowheads. Change the buttons to indicate that the new arrowhead should go at the other end of the path and select the type of arrowhead.

5. Click OK. Make sure that the arrowhead is correct. If it isn't, choose Edit ➪ Undo (⌘-Z) [Ctrl+Z] and choose Filter ➪ Stylize ➪ Add Arrowheads. Then add a different arrowhead.

6. To make the arrowheads and path into one path, select the path and choose Object ➪ Path ➪ Outline Path. Then select both the new outlined path and the arrowheads and choose Unite from the Pathfinder palette. Now you can Fill the new arrow object with anything, including gradients, and Stroke the entire object at once.

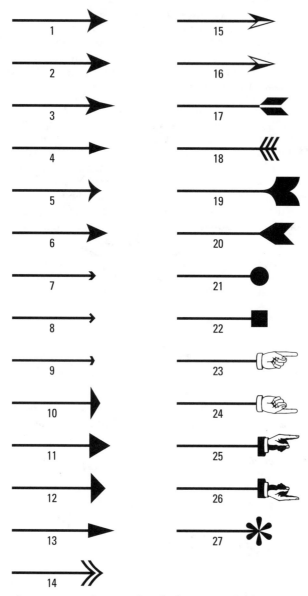

Figure 12-25: The arrowheads that are available in the
Add Arrowheads dialog box

Drop Shadow Filter

The Drop Shadow filter makes creating drop shadows for most paths a relatively
simple task.

Unlike most other filters, selecting Drop Shadow affects both Stroke *and* Fill. In the Drop Shadow dialog box (see Figure 12-26), you may specify the offset of the drop shadow by entering values for how far across the drop shadow should move (X) and how far up or down it should move (Y). Positive numbers move the shadow to the right and down; negative numbers move the shadow to the left and up.

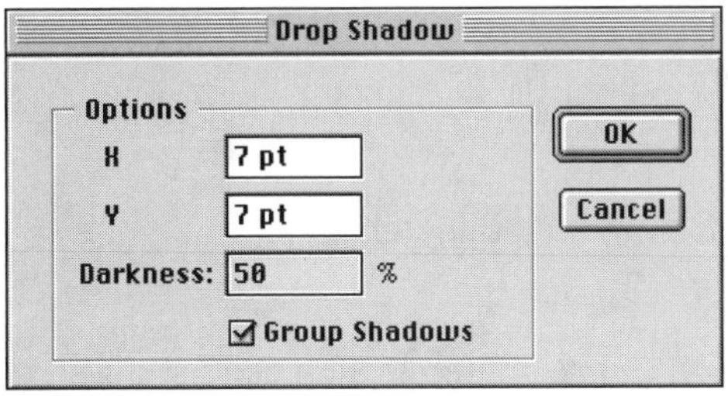

Figure 12-26: The Drop Shadow dialog box

The general rule in drop-shadowing is that the more offset the drop shadow is, the higher the original object looks. To make an object look as if it is floating far above the page, enter high offset values.

The percentage entered in Darkness is how much Black is added to the Fill and Stroke colors. Darkness does not affect any of the other custom or process colors. If you check Group Shadows, the drop shadow is grouped to the original object, which is a good idea, because you shouldn't just leave your shadow lying around.

1. Create and select the artwork that you want to give a drop shadow to.

2. Choose Filter ⇨ Stylize ⇨ Drop Shadow. The Drop Shadow dialog box appears, as shown in Figure 12-26.

3. Enter the amount that you want the drop shadow to be offset. A positive value in the X text field puts the shadow to the right of the object; a negative value in the X text field puts the shadow to the left of the object. A positive value in the Y text field puts the shadow below the object; a negative value in the Y text field puts the shadow above the object. (The larger the offset amounts, the higher up the object appears to float above the original object.)

4. The value that you enter in the Darkness field determines how much black will be added to the shadow to make it appear darker. If you check the Group Shadows box, the shadow is grouped to the original object.

5. Click OK. If the shadow isn't what you want, use the Undo command (⌘-Z) [Ctrl+Z], choose Filter ⇨ Stylize ⇨ Drop Shadow, and create a new drop shadow.

The Round Corners Filter

You can use the Round Corners filter to create round corners just like (snap your fingers) that. This filter works on any path that has corner points, but the best results seem to be on polygons and stars.

ASK TOULOUSE: Extra Points?

Laverne: I keep getting extra points after I apply Round Corners.

Toulouse: That's what Round Corners does. It replaces most corner points with two Smooth Points.

Laverne: But I only want one point there.

Toulouse: Well, you could change each point individually to a Smooth Point.

Laverne: How long would that take?

Toulouse: Let's see. If you had 20 paths, each with 15 Anchor Points. . . .

Laverne: I have a Cray handy to help you figure this out.

Toulouse: That would be 300 Anchor Points. If you take 3 seconds on each, and 3 seconds to find the next point . . .

Laverne: The Cray is smoking. Too tough.

Toulouse: . . . it would take you half an hour of constant clicking.

Laverne: Isn't that a kd lang tune?

Selecting Round Corners changes all types of corner points to Smooth Points. In the Round Corners dialog box, you specify what the radius of the Round Corners should be. The larger the number you enter for the radius, the bigger the curve.

Caution Don't apply the Round Corners filter to a rounded rectangle to make the corners more rounded. Instead of making the corners rounder, the flat sides of the rounded rectangle will curve slightly.

1. Select the artwork that will have its corners rounded. I used type converted to outlines in the example in Figure 12-27.

2. Choose Filter ⇨ Stylize ⇨ Round Corners. The Round Corners dialog box appears. Enter the amount that you want the corners to be rounded. Entering a large number usually ensures that all points will become as curved as possible. (I wanted my corners rounded as much as possible, so I entered 100 pt in the dialog box.)

3. Click OK.

4. Add other artwork to the final rounded artwork.

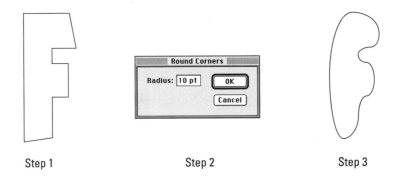

Figure 12-27: The Round Corners dialog box

You can use the Round Corners filter to smooth out overly bumpy edges. Using the Round Corners filter with Roughen can produce very smooth, flowing areas.

Summary

✦ Filters add extra functionality to Illustrator through commands in the Filter menu.

✦ Several filters from previous versions of Illustrator have been combined into other menus, or changed into tools or palettes.

✦ To use a filter, select the artwork you wish to "filterize" and select the filter from the Filter menu.

✦ The hardest thing about filters is knowing what they do, and when and how to use them; the filters themselves are pretty simple.

✦ Third-party companies have developed several filter sets for Illustrator and more are on the way.

✦ You can reapply the last filter quickly by pressing ⌘-E [Ctrl+E].

✦ Access the last filter's dialog box by pressing ⌘-Option-E [Ctrl+Alt+E].

✦ Adjust Colors adds and subtracts various amounts of process colors from multiple colored objects.

✦ The color blend filters look at two opposite paths and blend between the two colors.

✦ Saturate increases or decreases the amount of color in selected paths.

✦ The Object Mosaic filter takes rasterized files and square streamlines them into Illustrator paths.

✦ The Distort and Stylize filters work by moving points around selected paths.

✦ Punk and Bloat create spiked and bubbled effects, respectively.

✦ There are two ways to twirl artwork: with the Twirl filter or with the Twirl tool.

✦ Twirling adds Anchor Points as needed when twirling.

✦ Zig Zag creates even wavy or spiky paths.

✦ Roughen can be used to intelligently add Anchor Points.

✦ Scribble and Tweak are used to move existing points and Control Handles randomly.

✦ Add Arrowheads creates arrowheads at the ends of open paths.

✦ Drop Shadow creates instant drop shadows.

✦ Round Corners changes Straight Corner Points into Smooth Points.

✦   ✦   ✦

Using Photoshop Filters and Raster Images

CHAPTER

13

When I first learned that Illustrator would support Photoshop filters, all the wrong thoughts entered my brain. "Great, now I'll be able to Gaussian Blur my shadows without having to turn them into pixels first!" and "Wow, I wonder what'll happen with blends and some of the distort filters."

Of course, I was misled (those silly press releases again, I'm sure). Photoshop filters work only on *pixel-based* images, not vector-based images (paths and such). Fortunately, however, there is a command for making paths into pixel-based images (Rasterize). So, it's an extra step . . . but it works.

Vectors Versus Pixel-Based Images

I discussed this (sort of) in Chapter 1, but I'll go into a little more depth here. In its original version, Illustrator was a pure vector piece of software. There was nary a pixel to be found round these parts. But with Version 8, the border has been crossed, and Illustrator is just this side of the pixel border (which is nowhere near as smooth as the vector border).

When you think vectors, think Illustrator's paths. Illustrator's paths consist of outlines. Sure, they're outlines that can be filled with various colors and gradients, but they're still outlines. And it is the manipulation of these outlines that is the essence of Illustrator. Outlines can be resized and transformed in almost any way imaginable. Also, when you create a curve in Illustrator, it's really a curve—not a jagged mass of pixels. Vector-based images can be stretched bigger and look better for it (except blends and gradients if they're scaled up too large).

When you think pixels, think Photoshop's little teeny-tiny squares of color — squares that don't ever change position and that you don't add or delete. The only thing you change about pixels is their color. Pixels can only be square, and they take up space regardless of whether they're "empty" (filled with white or another background color) or "filled" (filled with a foreground color). Pixels exist on an immobile grid. Enlarging a pixel-based image results in giant, ugly squares of color.

Okay, I'm not a pixel person. If I were to be reincarnated as an electronic drawing tool, it wouldn't be as a Painter piece of chalk, but instead as Illustrator's Pen tool or Direct Selection tool. I'm a believer in vectors. Some say it's an obsession, but I'm too busy staring at control handles to pay attention to that nonsense.

Fortunately, my mind is not so closed that I ignore the importance of pixels or their place in our electronic graphics society. In fact, I wrote the best-selling *The Complete Idiot's Guide to Photoshop* just to prove that point.

So I'm glad there are pixels in Illustrator. After all, you can do things to pixels in Illustrator that you *can't* do in Photoshop. Ah, now I've got your attention.

Changing Illustrator Artwork into Pixels

There are several ways to turn Illustrator art into pixels, but the best way is to use the Rasterize command, which transforms any selected artwork into pixel-based artwork, at the resolution you specify. The following steps tell you how to do this, and Figure 13-1 illustrates the steps.

1. Create your artwork in Illustrator.

2. Select the artwork and choose Object ⇨ Rasterize. The Rasterize dialog box appears. Enter the ppi (pixels per inch) and click OK.

3. Your artwork has been rasterized.

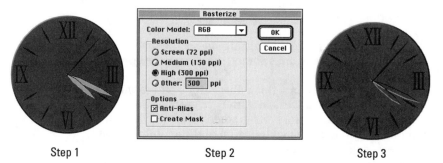

Step 1   Step 2   Step 3

Figure 13-1: Steps for rasterizing artwork

A funky little checkbox in the Rasterize dialog box asks if you'd like to make a mask of your artwork. This can be a good thing to do for items where sharp edges are important, such as text. Checking the Create Mask option creates an automatic mask around the edges of the artwork, and masks the image. In addition to keeping the edges nice and straight (because they're paths, not pixels), this masks off the areas of "white" or "empty" pixels, making those areas appear transparent. The Anti-Alias checkbox will soften the edges of the image you are rasterizing. It softens the edges by adding a pixel color between the image and the background so the edges aren't jagged.

As an Illustrator user, you may not be familiar with having to decide resolution as you do in Photoshop. The quick rule of thumb is that the resolution of pixel-based images should be 1½ to 2 times the line screen that the piece will be printed at. So if you'll be using a line screen of 133, your ppi should be between 199 and 266. It doesn't hurt to go higher than two times the line screen, but it is unnecessary. Because the math is easier, use double the line screen for the resolution.

Going to and from Photoshop with Pixels and Paths

Even with its pixel capabilities, Illustrator is no Photoshop. There are tools and features in Photoshop that are invaluable for adjusting pixel-based artwork. Adobe recognizes this, so it has provided several methods for moving pixels to Photoshop from Illustrator, and from Photoshop to Illustrator.

The most rudimentary way, which has existed for several versions of both software packages, is to save art in a format the other program can read and then to open or place the art in the other program. To place Illustrator art into Photoshop, save the art in Illustrator format and then open the art in Photoshop. To place Photoshop art into Illustrator, save in Photoshop as a format that Illustrator can read, such as TIFF, and then in Illustrator choose File ➪ Place and select the file.

The next way is through Adobe's wonderful PostScript on the Clipboard process, which allows for transferring artwork between Adobe software by simply copying in one program and pasting in another. To place Illustrator art in Photoshop, copy the art in Illustrator, switch to Photoshop, and paste the art in any open document. To place Photoshop art in Illustrator, copy the art in Photoshop, switch to Illustrator, and paste the art in any open document.

The easiest way to move art between these programs is to drag it from one program to the other. To drag art from Illustrator to Photoshop, select the art in Illustrator and drag it out of the Illustrator window onto a Photoshop window. To drag art from Photoshop to Illustrator, select the art in Photoshop and drag it out of the Photoshop window onto an Illustrator window.

You must have a window from the "to" application showing when you start dragging for drag-and-drop to work between programs.

You can also move just paths between the two programs. When opening or pasting
Illustrator art in Photoshop, a Paste dialog box appears. Click the Paste As Paths
option in this dialog box, as shown in Figure 13-2. Instead of Filled and Stroked
paths appearing in Photoshop, paths appear, which can be manipulated by the
Path tools on the Paths palette.

Figure 13-2: The Paste dialog box

To place paths from Photoshop into Illustrator, select the paths in Photoshop with
the Path Selection tool, copy the paths, and then paste them in Illustrator.

Colorizing One-Bit TIFF Images

One-bit TIFF images (black and white only) can be colored in Illustrator. This
effectively turns the black pixels into the color you specify. To color a 1-bit TIFF
image, select the imported image, and change the Fill color to the desired color.

  You can create an unlimited number of colors in a 1-bit image by creating additional copies and applying different masks to each one.

The following steps describe how to color portions of a 1-bit image and Figure 13-3
illustrates these steps.

1. Select the imported image you wish to color and apply a color to it by
   changing the Fill on the Color palette.

2. Copy the image and paint the copy with a different color.

3. Create a mask over the portion of the copied object that should be the
   different color. Group the mask with the copied image.

4. Realign the copied image or mask with the original image.

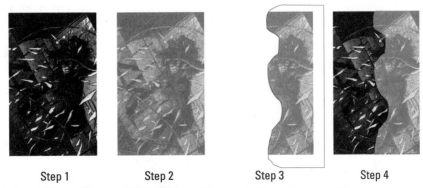

| Step 1 | Step 2 | Step 3 | Step 4 |

Figure 13-3: Steps for coloring a 1-bit image with multiple colors

Using Photoshop-Compatible Filters in Illustrator

By themselves, these Photoshop filters are really neat. However, because many Illustrator users also have Photoshop, are they necessary?

For starters, these filters make things a bit easier than before Illustrator could use Photoshop filters, especially for creating things such as drop shadows and other special effects. Instead of having to allocate memory to Photoshop, you can do filter operations right in Illustrator.

But here's the very cool thing, the one thing that Illustrator has over Photoshop when it comes to applying filters. It's so special that I've decided to offset it with one of those wonderful little "Power Tip" icons. . . .

Tip   Because Illustrator has multiple undos, you can apply several different filters to an imported image, and undo all of them in turn. Photoshop *can't* do that.

Photoshop filters work only on pixel-based images. If you'd like to apply a Photoshop filter to your Illustrator artwork, you have to first select it and choose Object ➪ Rasterize to turn it into a pixel-based image.

The following steps describe how to apply a Photoshop filter to an image and Figure 13-4 illustrates these steps.

1. Select the pixel-based image in Illustrator that you'd like to apply the Photoshop filter to.

2. Choose Filter ➪ *Name of Photoshop filter submenu* ➪ *Name of filter.* This could be, for instance, Filter ➪ Texture ➪ Mosaic Tiles.

3. In the Filter dialog box (if there is one), adjust the settings and values.

4. Click OK in the Filter dialog box to produce the effect.

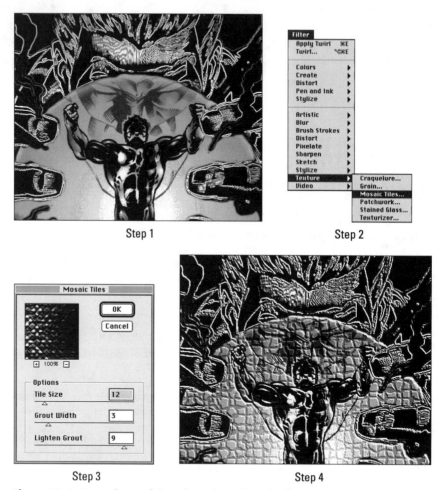

Figure 13-4: Steps for applying Photoshop filters in Illustrator

One big limitation of using Photoshop filters in Illustrator is that you can't make any selections *within* the pixel-based image. A way around this is to create a copy of the image, apply the filter, and then mask the area you'd like that effect applied to.

Illustrator's Photoshop Plug-Ins

Illustrator includes all the Photoshop plug-ins that were originally Aldus Gallery Effects (back in the days before Adobe bought Aldus). They're separated from the vector filters and appear below the vector filters (the logic being that you won't be using them as much as Illustrator filters, so why let them get in the way).

The plug-ins are primarily special-effect plug-ins, so I've included the following images to show the filter, the settings, and the result on the originally vector-based artwork, which is shown in Figure 13-5.

Figure 13-5: The original vector artwork

Other Third-Party Photoshop Filters

There are several Photoshop filter sets created by third parties, including Kai's Power Tools (KPT), KPT Convolver, and Alien Skin Eye Candy.

For Illustrator use, I've found KPT Convolver to be the most useful, as it has Gaussian Blur, Unsharp Mask, and other filter effects not otherwise available from Photoshop.

Figures 13-6 through 13-12 show examples of different types of filters.

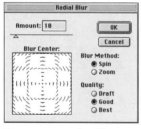

Figure 13-6: Art filters

Figure 13-7: Blur filter

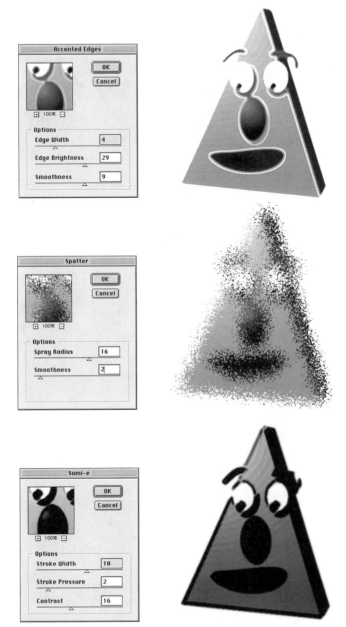

Figure 13-8: Brush Stroke filters

Figure 13-9: Distort filter

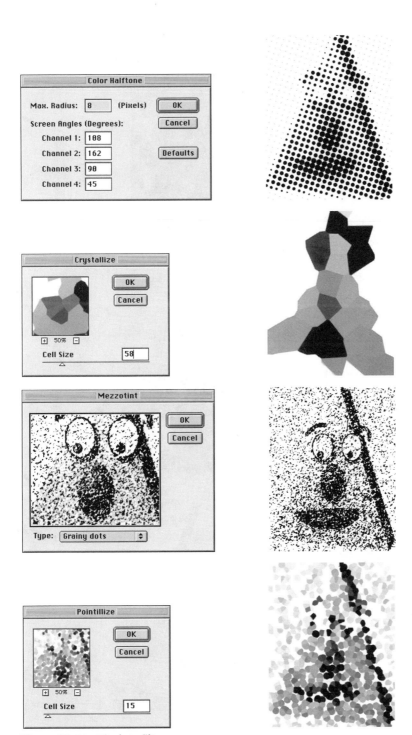

Figure 13-10: Pixelate filters

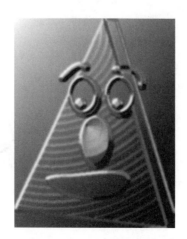

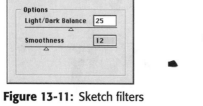

Figure 13-11: Sketch filters

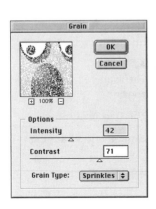

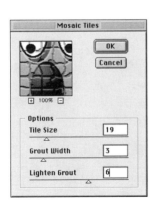

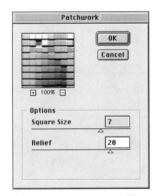

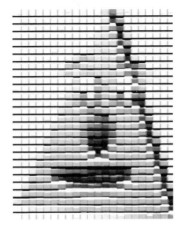

Figure 13-12: Texture filters

Summary

✦ Pixel-based artwork can be incorporated into Illustrator by importing it, by copying and pasting it, or by dragging it out of Photoshop and dropping it into Illustrator.

✦ The quickest way to move images between Illustrator and Photoshop is to drag-and-drop them between windows in each program.

✦ Paths can also be taken back and forth between the two programs.

✦ One-bit images can be colorized by selecting the image and changing the Fill color in the Color palette.

✦ Photoshop filters appear in the Filter menu underneath the Illustrator filters.

✦   ✦   ✦

VectorTools

When Extensis told me they would be updating their Illustrator plug-ins package DrawTools, I was thrilled. The package contained some amazingly powerful tools, but the interface was definitely substandard. I was hoping for a few new features in addition to increased ease of use — maybe palette-based color and shape controls and a few other goodies thrown in.

But when I finally learned what was going to be in VectorTools, I was blown away. The color and shape components *were* palletized and upgraded and are a dramatic improvement over the DrawTools versions. But they are no longer the core of the package. Instead, *seven* new, fully functional components were added, from the basic and handy VectorTips to the incredibly powerful VectorObjectStyles and VectorLibrary. And to top off all of this, it is available to both the Macintosh and Windows platforms. This package is every illustrator's dream come true.

Before you read more of my enthusiastic ramblings, be aware that I begged, pleaded, attempted to blackmail, and finally succeeded in coercing Extensis to let me do the Illustrator tips and tricks that appear in the product. So, in a way, I'm very proud of the one plug-in, Tips and Tricks. However, I consider it the least of the nine (count 'em, nine!) plug-in components.

Tip   As a purchaser of the *Illustrator 8 Bible,* you happen to be getting one of the plug-ins, fully functional, for free (Vector-Frame). You also are getting a 30-day fully functional trial set of VectorTools (see Figure 14-1). Both are located on the *Illustrator 8 Bible* CD-ROM. That's why I've taken the liberty of devoting an entire chapter to discussing how to use some of VectorTools' most useful and impressive features.

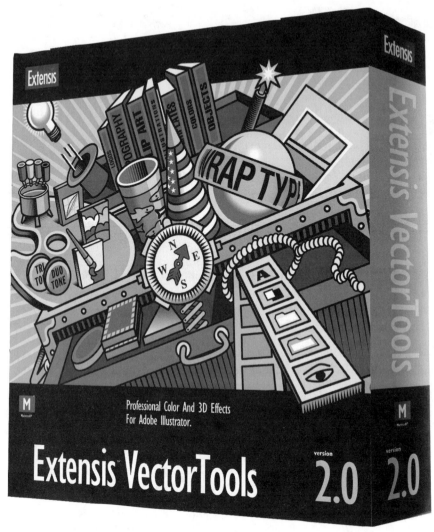

Figure 14-1: VectorTools

The VectorTools Components

There are a total of 11 components in VectorTools, but two of them are for FreeHand users only (don't worry; 2 of the remaining 9 are for Illustrator users only). Illustrator users don't need VectorCaps, which is similar to (though more powerful than) Illustrator's built-in Change Case function. FreeHand users also get a nifty plug-in called VectorTypeStyles, which is used for applying quick character-based formatting. Of course, those plug-ins pale in comparison to the two exclusive Illustrator plug-ins: VectorBars, which provides Extensis's toolbar technology to

Illustrator users, and VectorObjectStyles, which are fully functional Object Style Sheets in Illustrator. VectorTools version 2.0.3 (an upgrade that should be available by the end of 1998) is compatible with Illustrator 8. The new version has buttons that work correctly with the items in the menus and some of the functions have moved. When installing VectorTools version 2.0.3 you do not need to install VectorNavigator, because Illustrator 8 has its own navigator.

This section gives you a brief description of each of the VectorTools components.

VectorBars

VectorBars brings toolbars to Adobe Illustrator — full-color buttons, fully customizable floating palettes, or edge-of-the-screen bars. Buttons can be assigned a menu command, keyboard command, or even used to open a file or folder.

VectorLibrary

VectorLibrary is a floating palette that contains Illustrator artwork. You can add artwork to the library, drag it from the library to your document, and export the library to share with other Illustrator users.

VectorMagicWand

VectorMagicWand is a MagicWand tool that is used to select paths based on how much alike they are to the path you click. You can adjust the type and amount of similarity in such areas as Fill and Stroke color, Stroke weight, and object size.

VectorObjectStyles

VectorObjectsStyles bring object-based style sheets to Illustrator. By styling objects, you can make drastic changes to your entire document with one click, and also maintain consistency throughout your documents.

VectorColor

VectorColor offers Photoshop-quality color control in Adobe Illustrator. Instead of playing with the sliders on the Color palette, you can adjust path fills and strokes using the VectorColor palette, which features Curves, Brightness and Contrast, Multitone (duotones and so on), Grayscale, and Randomize.

VectorShape

The other lone holdover from DrawTools has been significantly upgraded as well, and is now based on a palette instead of a dialog box. Your 2D artwork can be wrapped around all sorts of 3D objects, including Spheres, Waves, Cylinders,

Cones, and Water. There's even a FreeDistort function that adds curving capabilities to Illustrator's Free Distort filter.

VectorFrame

Included free on the *Illustrator 8 Bible* CD-ROM, VectorFrame applies frames to selected objects. You can specify the frame style, the offset from the edges of the object, and whether it should frame individual objects, groups, or all at once.

VectorTips

VectorTips is a collection of hundreds of useful, indispensable tips for Adobe Illustrator. Written by Ted Alspach (Hey! That's me!), they can be set to appear at Illustrator's launch for a "tip of the day" or be used to search for a better, faster way to solve a problem you might have with Illustrator.

Installing and Using VectorFrame SE

While a fully functional trial version of VectorTools is included on the CD-ROM that accompanies this book, it will only work for 30 days before expiring. The VectorFrame SE plug-in we've included on the CD-ROM, on the other hand, is completely self-sufficient and won't expire. Ever!

If you're planning on buying VectorTools or already have it, then you can ignore the instructions in this section and use VectorFrame with the free trial or as a fully functional package. The only difference is that with the SE plug-in (on the CD-ROM included with this book), VectorFrame is chosen from the window menu.

 Tip   If you have both VectorFrame SE and VectorFrame installed, you now have a total of ten presets to work with. Preset 1 in SE is different from the regular preset 1, so you now have twice as many options.

To install VectorFrame SE, find it inside the VectorFrame SE folder on the *Illustrator 8 Bible* CD-ROM. Drag it into your Adobe Illustrator Plug-ins folder. Restart Illustrator and VectorFrame SE is accessible from the Window menu. To display the VectorFrame palette, select it from the Window menu.

Using VectorTools

The following sections contain the basics and several ideas and uses for various VectorTools components.

When VectorTools is installed, Illustrator gets an additional menu tacked on to the end of its menu bar, right after the Window menu. This menu is called

"VectorTools," and is shown in Figure 14-2. Even though keyboard commands don't appear in the menu, each component can be accessed using a keyboard command, which is also indicated in the figure.

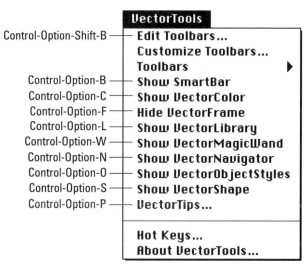

Figure 14-2: The VectorTools menu and the keyboard commands that correspond to each component (Mac only)

VectorFrame

VectorFrame is a floating palette (shown in Figure 14-3) that provides a quick and easy method for applying frames to selected paths and placed images.

Figure 14-3: The VectorFrame palette

1. Create a document with several placed images (see Figure 14-4).

2. In the VectorFrame palette, click the Apply button, set the Offset to 0, and choose the Each option.

3. Change the Paint Style to a fill of None and a stroke of 10-pt. Black.

4. Hold the Option [Alt] key and press the Apply button again. This creates a frame on the active frames.

5. Change the Frame options to All, and drag the slider to the right until the frame is away from the edge of the framed images (see Figure 14-5).

6. Change the background color to complement the placed images.

Figure 14-4: An Illustrator document with several placed images

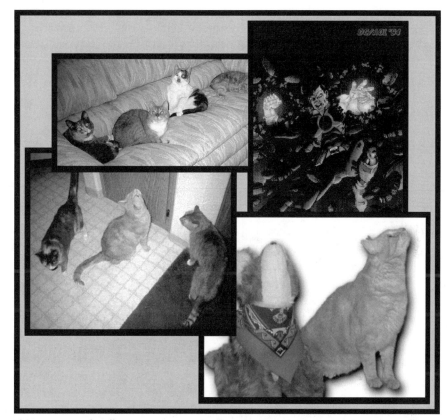

Figure 14-5: The Illustrator image after frames have been applied

There are five static presets available in VectorFrame. Each of these presets is for Fill and Stroke attributes. To set a preset, change the Paint Style of the Fill and Stroke to the desired settings. Then choose Set Preset # from the VectorFrame pop-up menu.

Tip Apply a frame to a frame by pressing Option-Apply [Alt+Apply].

VectorBars

I've never been a big fan of toolbars. But Extensis takes the concept several steps further; it allows me to create buttons for virtually every function within Illustrator. Any menu item or keyboard command can have a button applied to it. These buttons are placed on toolbars that can be floating palettes or embedded on any side of your screen. Extensis supplies several prefabricated bars ready for your use (see Figure 14-6). Fortunately, only a few appear by default, and you can choose to hide and show them by choosing an option from the VectorBars submenu (in the VectorTools menu).

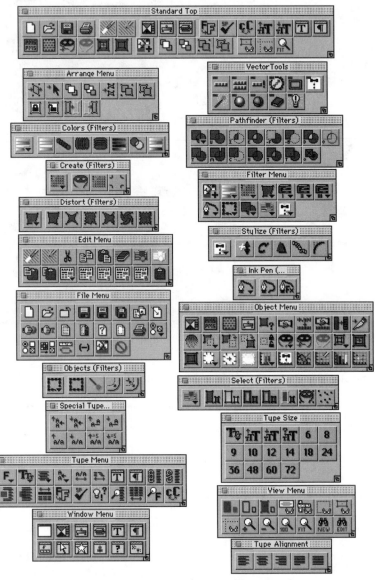

Figure 14-6: Every VectorBar Extensis has to offer—Wow!

Tip Move buttons from bar to bar by ⌘-dragging [Ctrl+dragging] them. Insert or remove space between buttons by ⌘-dragging [Ctrl+dragging] them along the bar. Remove buttons by ⌘-dragging [Ctrl+dragging] them off their current bar.

I've created a toolbar that contains the menu items I access the most. In my case, it's my job to know keyboard commands, so none of my buttons have corresponding keyboard commands. That doesn't mean that a button that can be accessed with a keyboard command is useless; rather, it can help free up your brain for additional, more important information (like your spouse's birthday, which can be significantly more important than ⌘-Option-Shift-M).

My toolbar, shown in Figure 14-7, contains the following buttons:

✦ **Invert Colors:** This command is indispensable for inverting the colors of selected objects. It doesn't work as well as swapping the curve in VectorColor, but it does the job for non-Black process fills and strokes.

✦ **Saturate Colors:** The poor man's version of real saturation/desaturation, but it does the job in a pinch.

✦ **Roughen:** Not only perfect for evenly adding anchor points (see Chapter 7), but also for converting the point type without dramatically altering the shape of the selected path or paths.

✦ **Ink Pen Effects:** Once you start filling with Ink Pen Effects, it's hard to stop. I'm at a point now where I'd like to have an Ink Pen swatch on the Swatches palette.

✦ **Trim Marks:** One click for trim marks is much better than Filter ➪ Create ➪ Trim Marks. And I use it for almost everything I get printed.

✦ **Round Corners:** For smoothing out computery-looking shapes, and for smoothing roughened paths.

✦ **Keyboard Increments Preferences:** This is the one Preference I'm in all the time, second only to General Preferences.

✦ **Divide, Unite, Crop, Merge, Intersect:** The Pathfinder functions I use all the time. Unite used to be the most common. Now it's Divide. Maybe I'm more mature now?

✦ **Show/Hide Transform:** This button makes it more usable (and allows me to have it tabbed with Info, which has a key command). Besides, Andrei says that the more I use it, the more I'll like it.

✦ **Show/Hide Tools:** There's no way to do this except via the menu command. Having a button right next to the toolbox is almost as good as a close box, or better, considering it shows as well as hides.

✦ **Show/Hide Tab Palette:** Hard to believe there's no key command for this, isn't it?

✦ **Show/Hide Page Tiling:** This is one of those "half the time I love it/half the time I hate it" options that I'm always fumbling around the View menu for.

✦ **Transform Each:** By far the dialog box I use the most that has no keyboard command.

✦ **Select Inverse:** Sure, I can Shift-drag around the entire document, but one click on a button is infinitely easier.

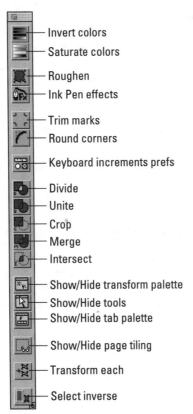

— Invert colors
— Saturate colors
— Roughen
— Ink Pen effects
— Trim marks
— Round corners
— Keyboard increments prefs
— Divide
— Unite
— Crop
— Merge
— Intersect
— Show/Hide transform palette
— Show/Hide tools
— Show/Hide tab palette
— Show/Hide page tiling
— Transform each
— Select inverse

Figure 14-7: The custom toolbar I use each and every day with Illustrator 8

VectorMagicWand

This amazing plug-in gives you Photoshop's Magic Wand tool with a few extra surprises. The Magic Wand is accessible from the Illustrator toolbox, right below the Selection and Direct Selection tools. Double-clicking the Magic Wand displays the VectorMagicWand palette (see Figure 14-8), where you can set the amount of tolerance for four different attributes. Yes, there are six sliders, but there are really only four attributes. I'll get to that in a moment.

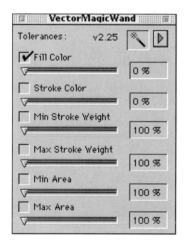

Figure 14-8: The VectorMagicWand palette

To use the VectorMagicWand, select the tool and click any path in the document. Other paths that fall within the tolerance settings will be selected along with the path you clicked.

Tip Shift-click to keep the selected paths selected when clicking. Option-click to subtract from the set of currently selected paths.

The tolerance settings are

✦ **Fill Color:** This is how different the fill color can be to be selected.

✦ **Stroke Color:** This is how different the stroke color can be to be selected.

✦ **Min Stroke Weight:** This is how much smaller the stroke weight can be to be selected.

✦ **Max Stroke Weight:** This is how much larger the stroke weight can be to be selected.

✦ **Min Area:** This is how much smaller the path can be to be selected.

✦ **Max Area:** This is how much larger the path can be to be selected.

At the settings of 0, 0, 100, 100, 100, 100, only paths that are filled and stroked with the same color, have the same stroke weight, and are exactly the same size are selected. Changing any of those values starts to increase the number of objects that can be selected.

VectorLibrary

VectorLibrary is a handy place to store often-used objects. You can place text, images, graphics, paths, and more into the library, give it a name for easy retrieval, and then sometime in the future pull the objects from the library. The VectorLibrary palette is shown in Figure 14-9.

Figure 14-9: The VectorLibrary palette

 Tip   You can change views from thumbnail (the default) to list view by clicking the view icon (the rightmost one) on the VectorLibrary palette.

Using the pop-up menu on the VectorLibrary palette, you can import and export library items to give to other users of VectorLibrary.

VectorColor

VectorColor provides Photoshop-style color control in Illustrator and FreeHand.

The VectorColor palette is displayed by choosing VectorColor from the VectorTools menu. The VectorColor palette (see Figure 14-10) appears.

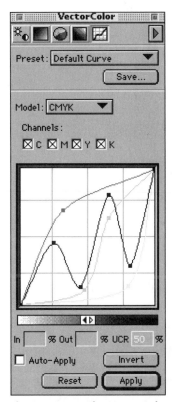

Figure 14-10: The VectorColor palette

Change the Color mode by clicking one of the five mode buttons along the top of the palette. The five modes are, in order, Brightness/Contrast, Grayscale, Randomize, Multitone, and Edit Curves.

Save presets in Multitone and Edit Curves by using the Save button in each of those panels. Apply presets in Multitone and Edit Curves by choosing a preset from the Preset pop-up menu.

Choose the Auto-Apply option to have Illustrator display each change as you make it. If Auto-Apply is not checked, then click the Apply button to make changes to selected artwork.

1. Open the document that contains the artwork you wish to recolor into one or two spot colors.

2. Select the artwork to be recolored.

3. Click the Multitone button in the VectorColor palette.

4. Add the color or colors you want to use in your illustration.

5. Remove Black if you don't want that as one of your colors.

6. With Auto-Apply engaged, use the ⌘[Ctrl] key to adjust the colors by steps, making an inverse step for the colors you don't want in that brightness level.

Using this technique, you can create an image that appears to have several colors in it, instead of the limited number that are available using Illustrator's standard tools.

1. Select the art you wish to randomize.

2. Fill and/or stroke the art with a named spot color.

3. In VectorColor Randomize, make sure the Use Existing Colorspace option is checked.

4. Click the Apply button on the Randomize panel.

5. In my example (see Figure 14-11), I used Curves to darken the midtones of the randomized stars so that the brighter ones would pop more.

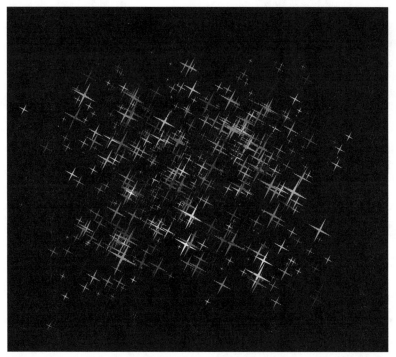

Figure 14-11: The stars in this background were randomized using the Use Existing Colorspace setting, which ensured that only the Brightness was randomized

Using Edit Curves in VectorColor

Click the Edit Curves button (far right) on the VectorColor palette and choose a color model (CMYK, RGB, and so on) from the Model pop-up menu.

Adjust the existing curve by dragging any visible points on that curve. Add a point to a curve by Shift-clicking the curve where you would like to add a point. Remove a point from a curve by Option[Alt]-clicking the point along a curve you'd like to remove.

Click the Invert button to swap curve positions along the *x-y* axes.

VectorShape

VectorShape lets you apply 3D effects to 2D artwork.

The VectorShape palette (see Figure 14-12) is displayed by choosing VectorShape from the VectorTools menu.

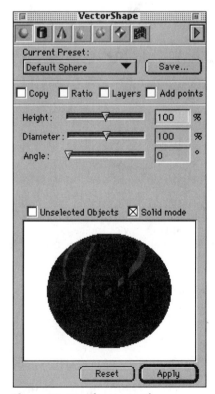

Figure 14-12: The VectorShape palette

Select the shape to wrap with by clicking one of the buttons along the top of the palette. The buttons, in order, are Sphere, Cylinder, Cone, Water, Wave, Diamond, and Free Projection.

Save a Preset by clicking the Save button. Apply a preset by choosing one from the Preset pop-up menu.

Tip After applying one VectorShape shape, reapply it or apply another shape. The results can be quite unusual. Figure 14-13 was created by applying the Sphere and Cone shapes to a grid.

Figure 14-13: The original art (left) and after VectorShaping (right)

Check the Solid Mode checkbox to see a full-color preview of the selected art in the preview window. Check the Unselected Objects checkbox to view unselected objects in the preview window.

Click the Apply button to apply the current settings to the selected artwork.

VectorObjectStyles

VectorObjectStyles provides object-based style sheets to Adobe Illustrator users. Although not as advanced as Alien Skin Stylist's approach, the palette (see Figure 14-14) is easy to use and takes up a tiny amount of screen real estate.

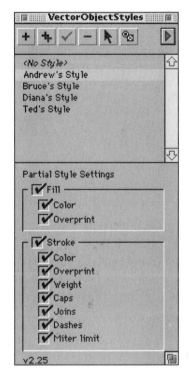

Figure 14-14: The VectorObjectStyles palette

The VectorObjectStyles palette is displayed by choosing VectorObjectStyles from the VectorTools menu.

Apply an existing style to selected objects by clicking the name of that style in the VectorObjectStyles palette. Create a new style by selecting an object with that style and clicking the New Style button in the VectorObjectStyles palette. Redefine an existing style by selecting a style, making Paint Style changes, and then clicking the Redefine button.

Import and export styles by choosing the appropriate menu item from the VectorObjectStyles palette's pop-up menu. Apply partial styles by clicking the Partial Style button and unchecking undesired attributes.

The color insert shows an illustration designed with the help of VectorObjectStyles.

VectorTips

VectorTips are the incredibly useful tips that, yes, I provided for VectorTools. Figure 14-15 shows just one of many pearls of wisdom.

Figure 14-15: A typical VectorTip

Summary

✦ VectorTools is a dramatic upgrade to Extensis DrawTools.

✦ VectorToolbars can provide you with one-click shortcuts for a number of common tasks.

✦ VectorColor brings Photoshop-style color controls to Adobe Illustrator.

✦ VectorFrame automatically creates frames on selected artwork by framing individual objects, groups, or all selected objects at once.

✦   ✦   ✦

Other Third-Party Plug-Ins

Yeah, I know, by the time you've gone to two parties, you're already pretty well sloshed, and usually it's not worth the effort to not pass out at that point. When we're talking software, though, "third-party" usually refers to a software publisher who produces an add-on for another package. All the companies that make filters and plug-ins for Illustrator are considered third-party publishers.

In 1994, three different filter packages were announced: Letraset Envelopes, BeInfinite FX (which has the distinction of being the first U.S. third-party filter set for Illustrator), and Sree's Cool Tools, which was later purchased from the developer Sreekant Kotay by MetaCreations, tweaked, and published as KPT Vector Effects. But none of these actually shipped in the United States until 1995.

The Year of the Adobe Plug-in was 1995. Sure, ever since Adobe Illustrator 5.0, which was released in 1993, Illustrator has had the capability to add plug-in filters from other manufacturers, but 1995 was when the third-party plug-ins started taking off big time. In addition, FreeHand 5.0 was released early that year and supported Illustrator-style plug-ins by making them usable from within FreeHand (as "Xtras," a slightly tacky moniker that Macromedia uses for all its products).

KPT Vector Effects and Extensis DrawTools were the big guns that shipped in 1995. In 1996, Alien Skin Stylist for creating styles in Illustrator appeared (a feature that is still missing from Version 8). Extensis came out with Extensis VectorTools in 1997, which is one of most innovative plug-ins for Illustrator. For more on VectorTools, see Chapter 14.

Other plug-in manufacturers, such as hotdoor, Vertigo, and Illom Development, have created plug-ins specifically for Illustrator 7 and 8.

These third-party plug-ins and filters are discussed in this chapter.

Third-Party Plug-In Roundup

The following summary of the third-party plug-in sets available at this writing makes this whole third-party business a little clearer:

✦ **Vector Effects:** This comprehensive filter set from MetaCreations, the maker of Kai's Power Tools (KPT), consists of several special-effects-oriented filters. Some of the highlights include KPT 3D Transform, which rotates and extrudes artwork in 3D; KPT ShatterBox, which fragments selected artwork into user-defined pieces; and KPT Warp Frame, an envelope-distortion filter.

✦ **Letraset Envelopes:** This one-shot filter is an envelope-distortion filter with several presets.

✦ **Extensis VectorTools:** These plug-ins (discussed in Chapter 14) contain color management, selection, 3D-effects, and more.

✦ **CADtools:** This is an amazing set of actual *tools* that turns Illustrator into high-powered drafting and CAD software. Many of the tools can be used for other things besides CAD drawing, making this one of the most exciting plug-in sets to appear for Illustrator.

✦ **Vertigo 3D Words:** This is a one-shot plug-in that makes 3D words. The amazing thing about this plug-in is that the words are set onto paths that curve in 3D space — something no other plug-in (or even Adobe's own Dimensions) can do.

✦ **Vertigo Pop-Art:** This plug-in lets you create 3D images out of 2D objects. You can add light and depth to your art with ease — all from within Illustrator.

✦ **MAPublisher 2.0:** This is a set of tools for mapmaking. Cartographers will have a field day with the 38 filters in this package.

✦ **Kara Fonts:** These aren't plug-ins, they're a unique set of fonts that are gradient-based. I wasn't sure where to put them, so for now, they're here.

✦ **Illom Development's plug-ins:** These weren't in finished form at the time of this writing, but the maker of LogoCorrector has some really snazzy tools for Illustrator users, including a Lasso for selecting and a point magnet.

✦ **Ted Alspach's Doodle Jr:** This is included on the *Illustrator 8 Bible* CD-ROM for free, courtesy of Cytopia. Doodle Jr. is an all-in-one distortion filter and color randomizer that can produce amazing effects and outstanding textures.

Contact information for the third-party publishers is provided in Appendix E, and most of the filter sets have demos provided on the *Illustrator 8 Bible* CD-ROM.

Installing and Using Third-Party Plug-Ins

Many of the big plug-in sets — such as VectorTools and VectorEffects — come with an installer that automatically places plug-ins in the Illustrator Plug-Ins folder. Other packages require that you copy the plug-ins to the Illustrator Plug-Ins folder manually. All come with a Read Me file with specific instructions.

So far, although I have installed all the plug-ins from most of the publishers listed in this chapter, I've not had any conflicts between plug-in sets. That doesn't mean there won't be any, but I haven't experienced any yet. If a conflict *would* arise, be aware that some serious problems can occur — from Illustrator not being able to start up to unexpected random crashes. If you start to experience problems after loading a set of plug-ins, check with the plug-in manufacturer about possible incompatibilities.

Third-party plug-ins can appear *anywhere* in Illustrator. Modal dialog box filters, such as VectorEffects and InfiniteFX, always appear at the bottom of the Filter menu.

MetaCreations KPT Vector Effects

Kai's Power Tools took the Photoshop world by storm a few years ago, and KPT Vector Effects have now had the same impact on Illustrator users. Sporting a scaled-down-from-the-typical-unusual-Kai-interface, Vector Effects (referred to as "Vex") is still different enough to get noticed, and friendly enough to be quite useful.

Vex filters, by themselves, are forces to be reckoned with; couple them with Illustrator's capabilities and suddenly there are oodles of options that never existed before. Because Vex is so big, the *Illustrator 8 Bible* CD-ROM can give you only a brief summary and a few examples of its incredible capabilities. For a more detailed overview of the amazing capabilities of Vex, pick up a copy of *Illustrator Filter Finesse* (Ted and Jennifer Alspach, Random House Electronic Publishing, 1995), which discusses filters from several manufacturers.

Note   Vector Effects plug-ins, while residing in the Filter menu, are not really filters. Of course, most of the plug-ins in Illustrator aren't filters, either, but MetaCreations is adamant about this. At MetaCreations, calling Vector Effects "filters" is a good way to lose a bit of job security, if you know what I mean. MetaCreations insists on calling them Plug-In Application Extensions, which is about as silly as Kai not quite understanding this craving we Illustrator users have for numeric input.

Most of the Vex filters are special effect oriented, making the creation of nifty stuff a no-brainer. A few others are more production oriented, but those select few filters help to round out the package. All of the filters are found in the Filters menu, in a submenu called KPT Vector Effects.

KPT has even included a special filter (included on the *Illustrator 8 Bible* CD-ROM) called KPT Gradients/Patterns to Paths, which converts both selected gradients and patterns to paths, allowing special effects and techniques to take place that otherwise wouldn't have been possible. This filter works better (and faster) than the Expand function of Illustrator.

VE Commonalities

Vector Effects have several different interfaces, but most of them share at least a half dozen features, including these:

✦ **The Options menu:** Many of the filters have an Options menu, accessible by clicking the umbrella with a triangle in it. In this menu, are options for preferences, a Reset command, and various other filter-specific options.

✦ **Zoom and Pan:** You can quickly Zoom and Pan using the keyboard shortcuts from Illustrator (⌘-Spacebar [Ctrl+Spacebar] to Zoom in, ⌘-Spacebar-Option [Ctrl+Spacebar+Alt] to Zoom out, and Spacebar to Pan). Or you can click the buttons at the top of the Preview window. You can also draw a Zoom marquee to Zoom into a precise location.

✦ **Balloon Help:** Clicking the ? at the lower left will toggle Balloon Help on and off, which is quite useful when you're initially fumbling around.

✦ **Sliders:** There are sliders all over the place in each dialog box (and there are others, undoubtedly just a bit different, on parallel worlds). Access them by clicking the black box with white letters and dragging left or right.

Tip

Pressing the Caps Lock key turns on interactive preview, where the preview changes while you are dragging the sliders, not just when you release them.

✦ **Presets:** You can use presets for certain filters by clicking the triangle at the bottom of the screen, and scrolling to the filter you want to use. Press Spacebar before clicking to view graphical presets, or just choose that option from the Preferences dialog box. When in Graphical Preview mode, you can also view the particular effect on the selected artwork by pressing ⌘ [Ctrl] when a preset is highlighted. If Caps Lock is pressed, all presets will display the effect on the artwork automatically.

✦ **Preset control:** If you create a particularly smashing effect in an extension dialog box such as ShatterBox that supports presets, you can store that preset for future use by clicking on the little + at the bottom of the dialog box. Delete the current preset by clicking –. At the bottom of the list of (nongraphical) presets, you can access the Presets Manager, which lets you import and export presets to and from each extension.

✦ **Cancel and OK:** The Cancel button is a circle with a slash through it. OK is a check mark.

✦ **Numeric control:** Each of the interfaces has an option to show exact measurements or percentages in numeric form. Check the option in the Preferences menu to see the numbers when you adjust a slider. The numbers shown below the sliders tell you what the value was originally (left) and what you're changing it to (right). You can also access the numbers and change them individually by ⌘-clicking [Ctrl+clicking] on the slider and typing in a new number or using the arrows (or arrow keys) to nudge the amount.

The remainder of this section discusses the filters briefly and shows some of the groovy things you can do with them (yes, groovy).

KPT 3D Transform

This is the most powerful of all the Vector Effects filters — it contains a fairly advanced 3D engine and produces truly astounding effects. It's quick, it's relatively easy to use, and the resulting paths it generates are impressive.

KPT 3D Transform takes selected paths and extrudes, bevels, and rotates them in 3D space. The 3D Transform dialog box is shown in Figure 15-1.

1. Type your text in a font that has lots of curves. (The Metallic setting in KPT 3D Transform works better with curves than with straight edges.) Convert the text to outlines using Type ⇨ Create Outlines (⌘-Shift-O) [Ctrl+Shift+O].

2. Fill the outlines with a slight cyan/magenta mix (no more than 20% of either).

3. With the outlines selected, choose Filters ⇨ KPT Vector Effects ⇨ KPT 3D Transform.

4. In the 3D Transform dialog box, select Full Preview from the Options menu (the little triangle in a half-circle at the upper-left of the Preview window). Engage the Caps Lock key; this shows all the changes you make immediately, even while you're dragging sliders. (If you don't have a Power Mac, you may want to stick with either the Rough or Wireframe Preview modes, both found in the Options menu. Experiment with the different settings to find what works best with your system.)

5. Adjust the Rotate sliders by dragging them left or right, watching the preview as you do so. Once the outlines have been rotated the way you want, drag the Metallic slider to the right about a quarter of its length.

6. Next, to give the outlines depth, drag the Extrude slider to the right.

7. If you want to give the outlines beveled edges, drag the Bevel Size slider to the right just a bit. Be careful not to drag too far as the bevels on nearby letters may intersect. To prevent this intersection in the future, increase the tracking of the text before you convert it to outlines.

8. Click the check mark at the lower right of the dialog box. This is the iconic version of the OK button. You can press Return or Enter as well.

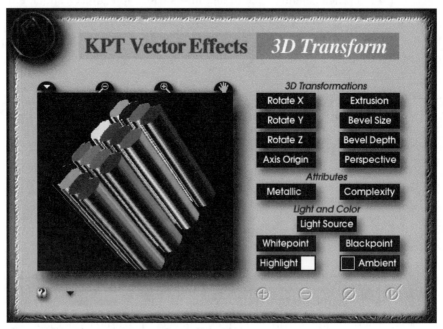

Figure 15-1: The KPT 3D Transform dialog box

After you've extruded the outlines, you may want to make the front of the letters metallic looking as well. To do this, select the front panels and change the Fill to a gradient. Figure 15-2 illustrates the final product.

KPT 3D Transform has all sorts of amazing capabilities deep within itself that you can play with, including perspective adjustments, the capability to change the source and color of lighting, and much more.

Figure 15-2: Metallic text created with KPT 3D Transform

KPT ColorTweak

The ColorTweak filter enables you to make changes to the color of the Fills and Strokes of selected artwork. Instead of the common ways of manipulating color through adjusting cyan, magenta, yellow, and black, KPT ColorTweak lets you change the hue, saturation, brightness, contrast, and grayscale levels, *and* play with the CMYK levels.

But what really sets ColorTweak apart from all the other color-adjustment filters (besides it being a *Plug-In Application Extension*) is the Randomize option in the Options menu. When the Randomize option is turned on, all the sliders being used generate random values and apply them to the selected paths.

1. Create a mishmash pattern of paths, similar to the one shown in Figure 15-3. I used the Roughen filters and PathFinder Divide to create the paths shown in Figure 15-3.

2. Select the paths and Fill them with a color (no Stroke) that represents the overall tone you'd like the texture to be.

3. With the paths still selected, choose Filters ⇨ KPT Vector Effects ⇨ KPT ColorTweak.

4. In the ColorTweak dialog box, shown in Figure 15-4, select the Randomize option from the Options menu (accessed by clicking and holding the little triangle in the upper-left of the previous window).

5. Adjust the Brightness slider to the right about 10%.

6. Click the check mark to exit the box.

7. Choose Filters ➪ KPT Vector Effects ➪ KPT ColorTweak again, pull the Brightness slider to the left about 10%, and click the check mark. The texture I created is shown in Figure 15-5.

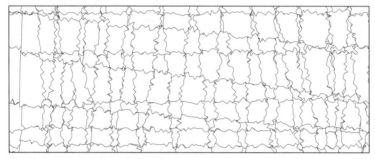

Figure 15-3: A mass of shapes

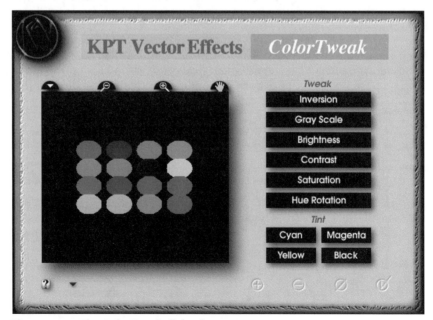

Figure 15-4: The ColorTweak dialog box

Figure 15-5: The final texture

 Tip ColorTweak works differently with process colors than it does with custom colors. For instance, you can't change the hue of a custom color. For the best results, change your custom colors to process colors *before* you use ColorTweak.

KPT Emboss

The Emboss filter is a one-shot filter that does what it does, and what it does it does quite well. Of course, I'm referring to embossing, which is making artwork look like it's indented or pushed out from the surface of the surrounding artwork. Figure 15-6 shows an example of embossed artwork created with KPT Emboss.

For Figure 15-6, I first changed the original artwork from color to grayscale to simulate various levels of depth.

There are all sorts of secret things hidden within Vector Effects. For instance, clicking on the Kai logo (when in Background mode) displays a preview as big as your monitor screen. Try pressing different keys when clicking there — of course, doing so may feel like a game, or as if you're being watched.

KPT Flare

This filter seems so basic and almost trivial when you first look at it that it may not receive a second glance. Well, look again and be amazed. Sure, the filter creates flares on artwork, but it doesn't stop there. The glow from the halo is actually blended into the background of the artwork. This makes the power of the filter and the complexity of the artwork go beyond anything similar to what you could do previously in Illustrator.

Figure 15-6: Embossed art

The KPT Flare dialog box, shown in Figure 15-7, has controls for adjusting the size, number of spikes, and halo size of a flare. In addition, you can add more than one flare to your artwork.

1. Select the artwork you wish to apply the flares to. Select as few paths as possible to reduce flare-generation time.

2. Choose Filters ➪ KPT Vector Effects ➪ KPT Flare.

3. Click the middle of the flare to move it; click a handle to resize it. Add spikes with the Amount slider. Change the size of the halo with the Halo slider. Change the inside radius with the Radius slider. (For some jazzy, multilength starburst effects, use a negative value in the Radius slider.)

4. Add additional sliders by selecting New Flare from the Options menu. You can also duplicate the current flare by selecting Duplicate Flare. To delete a flare, click it and press the Delete key.

5. After you've added as many flares as you'd like, click the check mark at the bottom-right of the dialog box.

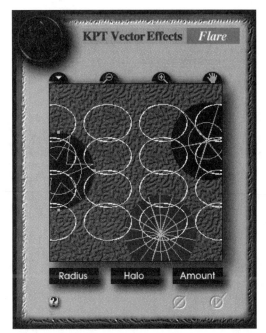

Figure 15-7: The KPT Flare dialog box

Figure 15-8 illustrates some of the effects you can create with this filter.

Figure 15-8: Three different flares that were applied to artwork at the same time

KPT Inset

KPT's Inset filter is a better way to inset or offset paths than is Adobe's Offset Path filter. The best part of this filter is its Preview option, which enables you to see just how far you're moving the path. Inset also has a Copy option, so you can make a duplicate of the selected paths.

Tip Use Inset to thicken or thin type characters that were converted to outlines, as in Figure 15-9.

Insettedness
Insettedness

Figure 15-9: The original type (top) and after having its weight increased with Inset (bottom)

KPT Neon

Chapter 10 has a set of steps for creating neon tubing . You'll also see that it's a lot of work to create neon tubes that way.

KPT Neon is easy, painless, and fun, with results that are nothing short of stunning. The KPT Neon dialog box is shown in Figure 15-10. There are only two sliders to move: Brightness and Amount.

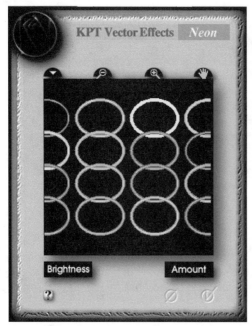

Figure 15-10: The Neon dialog box

Brightness controls the brightest point of the neon tubing. Amount controls the thickness of the tubes. Easy, huh? Well, you do have to remember one thing: The neon tubes only appear on paths. That means neon text you create will consist of tubes that surround the letters, not just a tube shaped in the form of the letter.

KPT Point Editor

This filter provides a way to position and move both points and their handles to exact locations. To use the filter, select a path whose points you wish to edit, and choose Filter ➪ KPT Vector Effects ➪ KPT Point Editor. The Point Editor dialog box, shown in Figure 15-11, then appears.

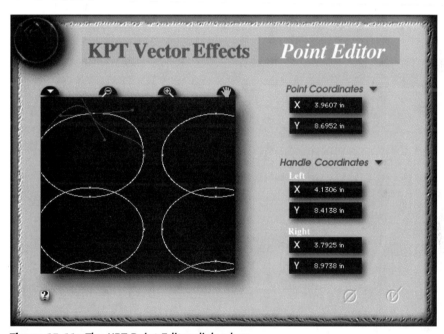

Figure 15-11: The KPT Point Editor dialog box

Select a point in the Preview window (zoom in if you can't see the point you wish to edit) and enter the new coordinates for it. If you wish to move the point by a certain amount, change the Point Coordinates menu (click the small triangle at the right) to Relative and enter the distance the point is to be moved.

You can also select and adjust any handles on the path the same way. While in the dialog box, you can adjust as many points and handles as you'd like; when you're all done, all of them will be affected.

KPT Resize and Reposition

This filter lets you move and scale selected artwork at the same time. In addition to entering a percentage for scaling, you can actually enter the new dimensions of the artwork, and KPT Resize and Reposition figures out the rest for you.

KPT ShadowLand

ShadowLand creates special-effect shadows for selected paths. It's also a place to play with shadows and shadow effects. Creating shadows in Illustrator has always been very difficult, but with ShadowLand, the process is quite enjoyable. To get started using ShadowLand, I suggest taking text and converting it to outlines, and then choosing Filter ➪ KPT Vector Effects ➪ KPT ShadowLand. The KPT ShadowLand dialog box is shown in Figure 15-12.

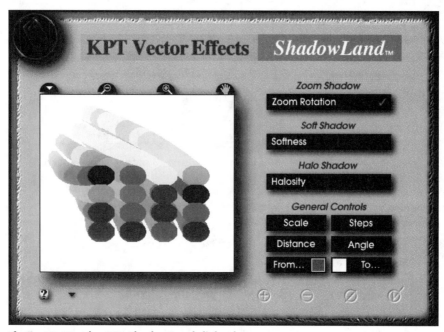

Figure 15-12: The KPT ShadowLand dialog box

There are three major types of shadow effects that can be created in ShadowLand:

✦ **Zoom Shadow** creates a zooming shadow from one color (the default is 50% of selected paths) to the background color (the default is white). You can control the scaling, rotation, and steps associated with the shadow.

✦ **Soft Shadow** gives Gaussian-blurred edges to the shadow, which makes the shadow smaller by the amount it's blurred.

✦ **Halosity** is the opposite of Soft Shadow; it, too, gives Gaussian-blurred edges to the shadow, but the blur expands the size of the shadow, rather than contracting it.

Figure 15-13 shows each of these effects applied to text.

Figure 15-13: Zoom Shadow, Soft Shadow, and Halosity

Zoom Shadow is the most powerful of the three shadow types, and with it you can create all sorts of un-shadowlike effects. For example, the logo in Figure 15-14 was created with Zoom Shadow, with the Connect setting steps turned off.

Figure 15-14: Zoom Shadow created the spinning curve behind the original logo

KPT ShatterBox

This is an amazing effect-generator that automatically splits your artwork into hundreds or thousands of little pieces.

Note   FreeHand Bashing Guideline #1824: KPT ShatterBox doesn't work in FreeHand. Create something funky with the extension and then show it to your green-with-envy FreeHand-user pals.

1. Select the path or paths you wish to shatter.

2. Choose Filter ➪ KPT Vector Effects ➪ KPT ShatterBox.

3. Drag one of the three main sliders (shown in Figure 15-15) to the right. Watch the preview and stop when you think enough lines are crossing the image.

4. Click the check mark in the lower right of the dialog box to make ShatterBox start shattering away.

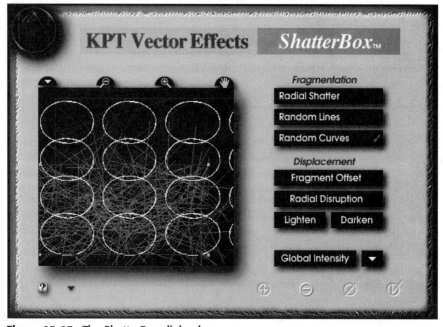

Figure 15-15: The ShatterBox dialog box

ShatterBox is a slow filter to use. Its speed depends on the number of Impacts and the complexity of each, as well as the number and complexity of selected paths.

1. Select the art you wish to use with ShatterBox.

2. Choose Filter ⇨ KPT Vector Effects ⇨ ShatterBox.

3. Click the Preset button and choose Preset Manager from the list. Click Import and find the "Shots Fired" preset on the *Illustrator 8 Bible* CD-ROM (in the Presets ƒ folder).

4. Click the check mark at the lower-right to use the effect. The effect should look something similar to that shown in Figure 15-16.

Figure 15-16: Bullet holes created with ShatterBox

KPT Sketch

The Sketch filter takes paths and gives them a (surprise!) sketchy look. It does this by moving the points and handles on the paths the amount you specify, and by adding another path on top of the original with a Stroke, not a Fill.

There are only two sliders in the dialog box: Stroke and Amount. Stroke controls the width of the duplicated path Stroke, while Amount determines how much the paths are moved. Figure 15-17 shows several applications of the Sketch filter on artwork.

Figure 15-17: The Sketch filter was applied to the original artwork several times with a low Stroke setting and a low Amount setting

The Sketch filter has three settings: Color Stroke, Pen Stroke, and Width Stroke. The Color Stroke option creates a darker stroke than the original color of the path. Pen Stroke creates a black Stroke. Width Stroke creates a Stroke the exact color of the original artwork.

One thing that KPT Sketch *doesn't* do is to add or subtract points during the sketching. To add points, you may want to apply the Roughen filter first, specifying between 5 and 10 points per inch and 0%. This dramatically changes the type of sketching that occurs, so experiment with different amounts of points added before finalizing your design.

KPT Vector Distort

Vector Distort applies distortion effects to artwork, but doesn't require that you add points first, or that you pronounce its unsightly acronym. Through some wizardry of mathematics, Vector Distort adds points only where necessary. This makes effects like "swirl" look much better than does Adobe's Twirl tool.

Figure 15-18 shows some of the different effects in KPT Vector Distort applied to the same artwork.

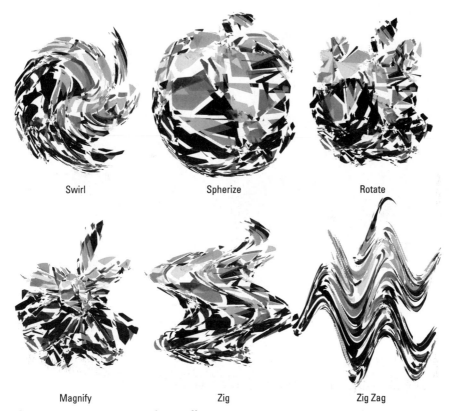

Swirl   Spherize   Rotate

Magnify   Zig   Zig Zag

Figure 15-18: KPT Vector Distort effects

The Vector Distort dialog box (shown in Figure 15-19) allows you to use one or more *influences*, which are the different types of effects listed on the sliders. To create a new influence, select the New Influence option from the Options menu. You can change the type of influence by clicking it and dragging a different slider. Each of the different types of influences has a different color, so you can quickly see what type of influence you're using.

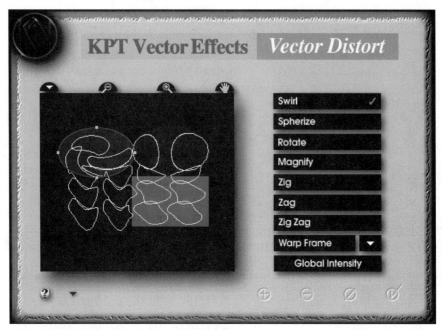

Figure 15-19: The Vector Distort dialog box

You can access many of the distortion effects by pressing a number key on the keyboard:

✦ 1 = Swirl

✦ 2 = Spherize

✦ 3 = Zig Zag

✦ 4 = Zig

✦ 5 = Zag

✦ 6 = Rotate

Tip   Using the keyboard you can access a double-secret distortion effect that almost no one knows about! (I had to tell the engineer, and he was really surprised, which may cause the average software user to lose a bit of sleep.) Pressing 7 activates the Scale function, which allows you to change the size of paths within the sphere of influence. To use this, the amount must be set in another influence first; then when 7 is pressed, scaling takes place there. Wow! The amazing thing about Scale is that it scales just the influenced portion of the path.

KPT Warp Frame

Warp Frame is a powerful distortion envelope for Illustrator, similar to Letraset Envelopes (which is described later). With it, selected paths are warped into a different shape from the basic bounding box rectangle they normally have.

The best way to get started with Warp Frame is to start applying some of the presets, which you access by pressing the little triangle at the bottom of the dialog box (shown in Figure 15-20).

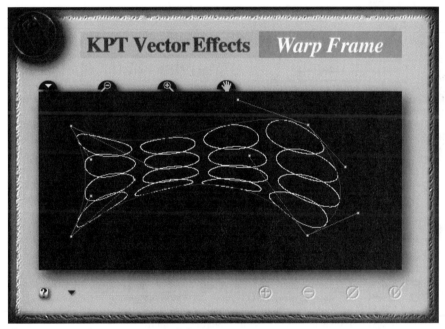

Figure 15-20: The Warp Frame dialog box

After a preset has been applied, you can click the points and handles around the edges of the envelope frame and drag them, changing the shape of the paths within. To start again from scratch (even if there's no itch), choose Reset All from the Options menu.

hotdoor CADtools 1.0

hotdoor CADtools has been shipping since Version 7 of Illustrator. Here are a few tidbits about it.

CADtools is an impressive set of tools that transforms Illustrator into CAD-capable software. The creation tools include wall, arc, fillet, chamfer, and trim. Measuring/dimensioning tools include angle, arc length, horizontal, vertical, radius, diameter, Bézier curvature, and more. Figure 15-21 shows the tools that CADtools adds to your Illustrator toolbox.

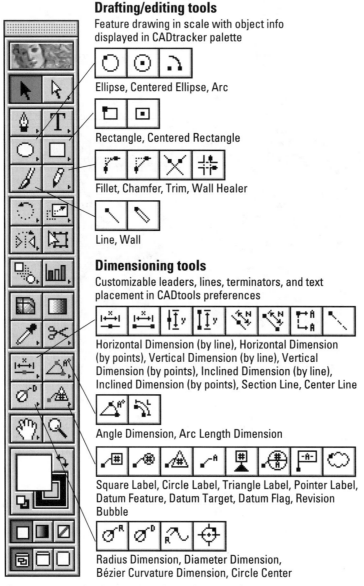

Drafting/editing tools

Feature drawing in scale with object info displayed in CADtracker palette

Ellipse, Centered Ellipse, Arc

Rectangle, Centered Rectangle

Fillet, Chamfer, Trim, Wall Healer

Line, Wall

Dimensioning tools

Customizable leaders, lines, terminators, and text placement in CADtools preferences

Horizontal Dimension (by line), Horizontal Dimension (by points), Vertical Dimension (by line), Vertical Dimension (by points), Inclined Dimension (by line), Inclined Dimension (by points), Section Line, Center Line

Angle Dimension, Arc Length Dimension

Square Label, Circle Label, Triangle Label, Pointer Label, Datum Feature, Datum Target, Datum Flag, Revision Bubble

Radius Dimension, Diameter Dimension, Bézier Curvature Dimension, Circle Center

Figure 15-21: The impressive slate of CADtools

In addition, one floating palette displays all the dimensioning information, and another floating palette displays tips on how to use each tool. Figure 15-22 shows a completed drawing with CADtools used throughout.

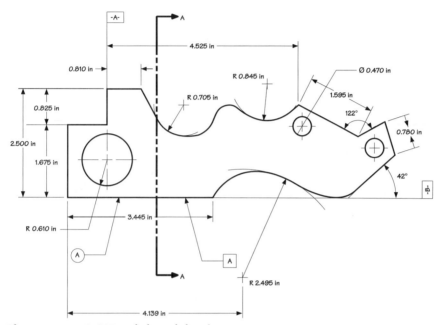

Figure 15-22: A CADtools-based drawing

I put a beta version of CADtools to use for a "real life" test and was pleasantly surprised to discover how useful the plug-ins are and the variety of options and preferences CADtools offers (so many preferences, in fact, that CADtools has its own multilevel dialog box just for those preferences). Figure 15-23 shows a CADtools-enhanced drawing that I used to help me as I designed a basketball court for my backyard patio (you can see the full color illustrations and a picture of the completed court in the color section of the *Illustrator 8 Bible*). Having printouts of this illustration handy as I was marking off the court to be painted was very helpful.

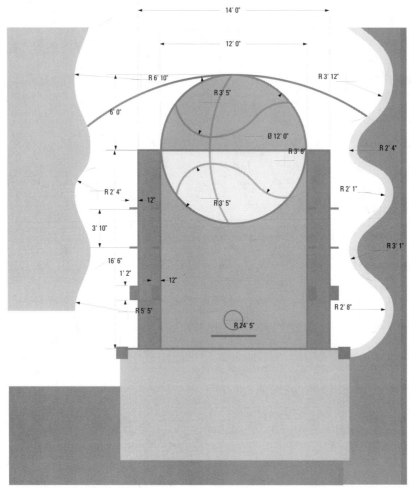

Figure 15-23: I used CADtools at ¹⁄₉₆ scale to produce one of many drawings used to create a basketball court on my backyard patio

One of the features I found exceedingly helpful was CADtools' automatic scaling feature. It allowed me to draw in "actual size," which would normally be quite difficult because the basic key of a basketball court is 12' wide, which is 2' wider than Illustrator's entire artboard. I set the scale to ⅟₉₆ (where ⅛" =1'), and from that point on I was able to draw real sizes. Using CADtools drawing tools, I could make the top of the key a circle that was exactly 12' in diameter.

If there's one feature that by itself is worth the price of the package, it is the Bézier Curvature Dimension tool. This handy tool gives you the radius of any portion of a curve, even drawing the curve radii at that point automatically. I used it to figure out the curves of the seams of the basketball image used at the top of the key.

One other thing worth mentioning (because you can't see this from a static image), is that most of CADtools' tools are 100% interactive. This means that as you're clicking and dragging, the information, labels, values, and so forth all appear on screen (with no flicker) and are modified as you move the mouse around. Try the Bézier Curvature Dimension tool and you'll see what I mean.

Vertigo 3D Words

Text effects are always fun to do, but with Vertigo 3D Words, text can take on a life of its own. The simple interface and straightforward options make using 3D Words pretty easy, but the results can be spectacular.

The interface of 3D Words consists of a floating palette, shown in Figure 15-24, which oddly enough isn't resizeable or actually interactive in the way most palettes are. Instead, it's like a dialog box that you can have up all of the time (although it is much too big for my taste and my monitors).

To use 3D Words, type some text in the text field and press Enter. The text appears on the path. Using the controls in the palette, you can modify the:

✦ **Font:** Just what you'd expect here. One font per text string.

✦ **Path:** This is a big pop-up menu full of true 3D paths for you to select from.

✦ **Color:** Sets the color that the string of text will be.

✦ **Move:** This moves the text along the path, sort of sliding it (similar to grabbing the I-bar of text-on-a-path in Illustrator).

✦ **Rotate:** This "twists" the text on the path. 0° text is upright and –90° is text lying on its back.

✦ **Depth:** The Depth control determines how extruded the text is.

✦ **Tracking:** Just like Illustrator's tracking, this option adds (or removes) space between letters.

✦ **Camera View:** This allows you to pick from one of several preset camera views.

Figure 15-24: Hey! I know him! The Vertigo 3D palette with some example text on a path

There are four buttons along the bottom of the palette that allow you to (in order) move, revolve, scale, and rotate the entire path in the viewing window.

After you have the settings just the way you like them, click the Place 3D Text button and the text appears in Illustrator. An example of placed text is shown in Figure 15-25 (after some finessing and duplication via the Scale tool and VectorColor).

Tip The Surprise me! setting in the Path pop-up menu is just that; a different 3D path every time you select it. To keep getting different paths, you'll have to select another option and then return to Surprise me!

Figure 15-26 shows additional VectorColor manipulation of the text generated by 3D Words. Of importance is that each "block" of color you see along the extruded sides is fairly large (there's no "complexity" setting as in KPT 3D Transform).

Figure 15-25: Shameless self-promotion via Vertigo 3D Words

Figure 15-26: A little randomizing never hurt anyone. Well, not too badly, at least.

Vertigo Pop-Art

This plug-in lets you do basic extrusions that remain "live" even after the document is saved and closed. That's right, you can open the document at a later time and make changes to the shape, and the 3D extrusion will move to match it! The biggest drawback to this plug-in is that the extrusions are created by way of blends, not gradients, which can make your file a bit larger than with gradients and not as easy to edit. The big benefit to this product is that it is much easier than Adobe Dimensions to use. You can export any object made by Pop-Art to another graphic program. Vertigo Pop-Art works with versions 7 and 8 of Illustrator.

Why Nobody Uses LetraSet Envelopes

Envelopes were one of the first plug-ins available for Illustrator 5. Unfortunately, they were plagued by bugs and limitations, which to my knowledge have never been addressed. LetraSet Envelopes are sort of a limited KPT WarpFrame, with a smaller preview window and less options. You may be able to see where I'm going with this: When you can get all of VectorEffects (12 other components in addition to WarpFrame), why would you want Envelopes? If you only need basic enveloping capabilities, you can achieve them in VectorTools' VectorShape as well.

Hopefully LetraSet will build a stronger product around Envelopes in the future.

MAPublisher 2.0

Here's an exciting product that does for the mapmaking industry what CADtools does for drafting. There are dozens of components, including a handy grid generator, which make mapmaking with Illustrator as easy as possible. Even if you're not a mapmaker, the variety of tools in MAPublisher can come in handy.

Kara Fonts

Kara Fonts aren't plug-ins and they're not really fonts, either. But they *seem* like plug-ins, so I've included a brief discussion of them here. One thing many people take for granted is that fonts are flat. Sure, you can extrude them with different software, but even then, the faces of those fonts are flat. Yuck.

Kara Fonts use Illustrator gradients to produce some heavily textured, 3D-looking fonts, such as the ones shown in Figure 15-27.

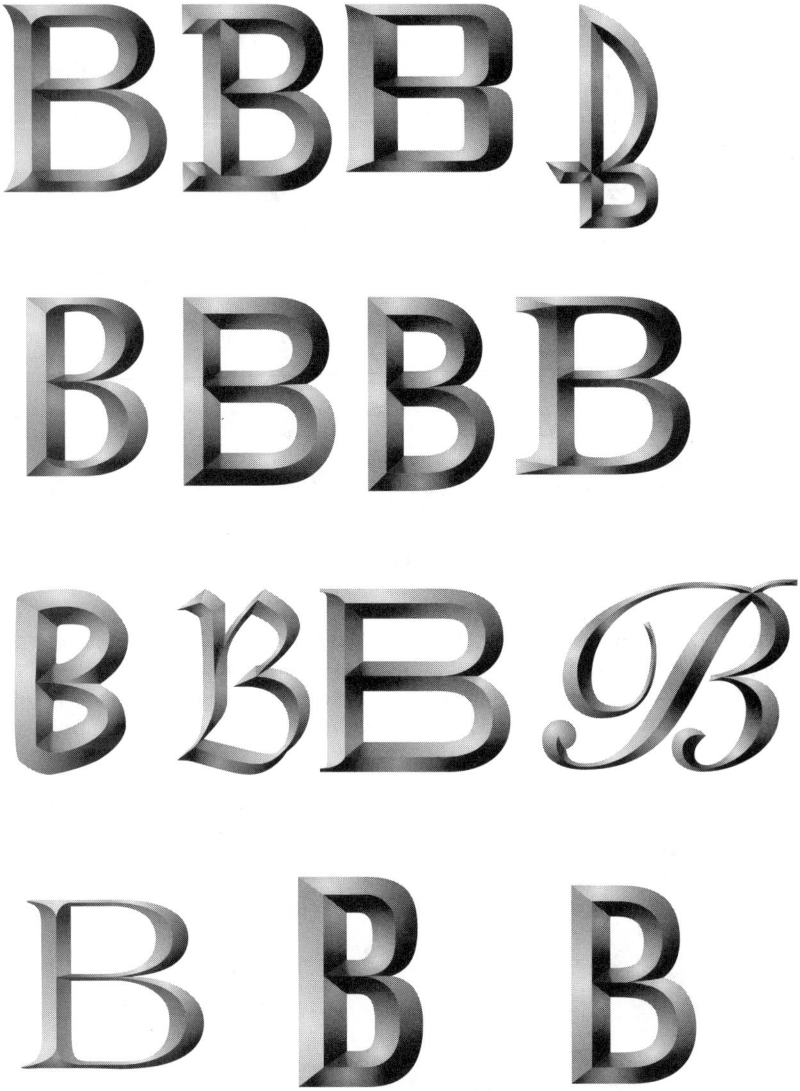

Figure 15-27: Some of the fonts that Kara Fonts can create

To use Kara Fonts, you actually run a little application (which *would* be more logical as a plug-in than an entire application) where you pick a font and enter text (see Figure 15-28). Then you copy the text to the clipboard and then paste the text into an Illustrator document.

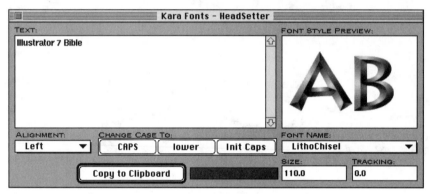

Figure 15-28: The Kara Fonts-Headsetter application window

Because the fonts consist of named gradients, you can quickly recolor an existing block of text just by Option[Alt]-dragging a new gradient on top of the one used in the font! Of course, what are generated are Illustrator paths, so they can be altered in any way. Figure 15-29 shows some text after some scaling has been applied to it.

Figure 15-29: After some tweaking and the addition of a drop shadow, I'm ready for even more shameless promotion

Creating Plug-Ins for Illustrator 8

While this section is aimed at potential plug-in developers, casual readers may find it interesting to discover what exactly can be done in Illustrator via an add-on plug-in. The little pieces of software are quite amazing.

The Illustrator API and SDK

Illustrator API is one of the most advanced APIs (Application Program Interface) for any software, allowing plug-in developers to add features by creating modal-based functions, floating palettes, and tools anywhere in Illustrator. The sad thing, in my opinion, is that no software developer (with the exception of Extensis VectorTools and hotdoor CADtools) has really taken advantage of all of these fantastic capabilities.

Maybe you're asking yourself, why bother with a plug-in when I can just create an application that does what I want? Why bother spending the time to learn the API? For starters, creating a plug-in within Illustrator allows you to take advantage of Illustrator's file importing/exporting options (Illustrator supports all of Photoshop's pixel formats, as well as Illustrator native, EPS (Encapsulated PostScript), and PDF (Portable Document Format) files), as well as printing issues. You don't need to worry about coding all of that boring stuff, but instead you get to dig into the meaty stuff that's really fun to create — and use. The Illustrator API makes it easy to perform almost all of Illustrator's functions and features through simple calls.

Even better, the SDK (Software Developer's Kit) can be found on the CD-ROM, with plenty of sample plug-ins and source code. A more recent (postshipping) version of the SDK is available from Adobe's Web site.

To create a plug-in for Illustrator you must have a basic knowledge of C programming, and you must own a compiler of some sort. For what little programming I've done, I wouldn't know where to start, but all my programmer/engineer buddies tell me that Metrowerks CodeWarrior is the only coding software that you'll ever need.

Plug-In Types

There are three major plug-in types in Illustrator: menu selectable modal dialogs, floating palettes, and tools.

✦ **Modal Dialogs** are the standard filter type of plug-ins common to Photoshop. The user selects a menu item, and a dialog box appears. MetaTools' Vector Effects, CSI Socket Sets, and BeInfinite's InfiniteFX use modal dialog boxes for their plug-ins. Versions 5.0 and 5.5 of Illustrator only supported modal dialog box-based plug-ins, and they were only accessible via a submenu of the Filter menu. Versions 6, 7, and 8 support putting menu items in *any* menu, not just the Filter menu.

✦ **Floating Palettes** are fully supported by Illustrator 8. If you use the API to create a palette in Illustrator, the palette is treated as a standard Illustrator palette and follows the behavior of other palettes in Illustrator, including snapping to the edges of other palettes, snapping to the document window, and snapping to the edges of the screen. Palettes you create via the API are also hidden and shown automatically when the user presses the Tab key.

✦ **Tools** are plug-ins that add tools to the Toolbox. Tools can interact with Illustrator objects in various ways. The Spiral, Polygon, Star, and Twirl tools were originally modal-based plug-ins (in Versions 5.0 and 5.5 of Illustrator), now transformed into tools with added functionality (double-clicking on the tools displays a dialog box that is eerily similar to the original filters).

Suites

One of the most useful API functions is that of suites. Illustrator 8 has several integrated suites that provide a lot of additional functionality. The two suites that you may find especially helpful are the Path Construction Suite and the Shape Construction Suite. These two suites assist in creating and adjusting paths, and are especially helpful with distortion filters.

How Extensis VectorTools Uses the Illustrator API

Extensis is shipping a collection of plug-ins for Illustrator, VectorTools 2.0 (see Chapter 14). With the exception of Extensis' trademark toolbars and tips, tricks, and techniques dialog box, the plug-ins for Illustrator were created using the Illustrator API. While VectorTools doesn't take full advantage of the Illustrator API, it does show some of its powerful capabilities, including palettes and tools. Some of the more interesting plug-ins (from a developer's point of view) are:

VectorLibrary, which is a floating palette that stores Illustrator objects. Using the Macintosh drag manager, the API allows objects to be dragged in and out of the palette without negatively affecting the artwork in the document.

VectorFrame, which is another floating palette that provides an interactive slider that places frames on selected objects. The slider adjusts the frame (an Illustrator path) in real-time.

VectorObjectStyles, which applies tagged styles to Illustrator paths. Each object in Illustrator can be tagged using the Illustrator API.

VectorMagicWand, which is clearly the most impressive plug-in (both technologically and otherwise) of the set. The plug-in creates a tool that is added to the Illustrator Toolbox. This tool is used for selecting paths that are similar to the path that is being clicked on with the tool. The amount of similarity is controlled by several sliders on a floating palette (which can be shown/hidden via a menu or by double-clicking on the tool). In addition, the palette contains a button that is used to select and deselect the MagicWand tool.

The most striking difference between the 5.0/5.5 distortion filter Twirl and its 6.0–8.0 counterpart (besides it also being a tool) is the way it works. Twirling a star in Versions 5.0/5.5 resulted in a twirling of points only; the path shape was only affected in that the line segments followed the path. The Illustrator 6.0–8.0 Twirl filter (and tool) uses the Shape Construction Suite to adjust the entire path, not just the selected points, resulting in a smooth twirling effect.

The capabilities of each suite are documented in the SDK.

Plug-Ins I'd Like to See

Now that Illustrator has such a powerful API, there are all sorts of plug-ins that could be created for it. Here are a few ideas of undeveloped plug-ins that Illustrator users have been clamoring for:

✦ **3D Transformation Tool, Find/Replace, Live Blends, Arc Tool:** FreeHand (that *other* Illustrator program) has these features and many others that could be included in Illustrator using the Illustrator API. Of course, FreeHand is a little feature-heavy, but the best place to start is the competition.

✦ **Levels Color Controls:** I use Levels in Photoshop as much as (or more than) curves. Levels is perfect for quick "watermarking" of images.

✦ **Layers Management:** Many layer-based functions could be automated or enhanced, such as automatic layer creation, layer sorting, and layer linking.

✦ **Enhanced Previewing:** A plug-in could create a viewing mode that shows anti-aliasing, overprinting, and individual separations.

✦ **Animation Plug-in:** Adobe Dimensions does basic key sequencing for animation, but Illustrator provides the tools that would allow a developer to create animation that could be viewed within Illustrator (like the SDK clock shown later in this chapter). The animated frames could be exported as QuickTime, GIF Animation, or sequential PICS.

✦ **Simulated Animation:** A plug-in that takes a selection and applies virtual animation to it by creating a series of more transparent copies along a path.

✦ **Spotlight/Lighting Effects Tool:** A tool that could shine a spotlight on the artwork, creating both a reflected light surface and a drop shadow.

✦ **Random Movement and Distortion:** A plug-in that scatters paths and points based on specific criteria.

✦ **Illustrator Document Viewer:** A plug-in that cycles through custom views, multiple documents, and more using a simple VCR-style palette; mouse clicks could be used to advance through images like a slide show.

✦ **Blur and Blur Tool:** Blurring can be done with vector objects, it just isn't that easy. A plug-in that automatically blurred would be a tremendous boon.

✦ **Real Transparency:** Objects in Illustrator can be set to overprint, but you never know what they'll look like until you print separations. And the Hard and Soft Pathfinder filters break paths into little pieces.

✦ **3D Path Splines:** VectorEffects extrudes and Dimensions both extrudes and revolves. However, there is no tool that allows paths to be constructed in three dimensions or to be displayed that way.

✦ **Stippling Tool:** A tool to create stippling effects in Illustrator, with varying intensity and color amounts.

✦ **Path Generator:** A plug-in that automatically generates random paths based on specific criteria. Perfect for backgrounds, random objects, and more.

✦ **Mosaic Creation:** A plug-in to create mosaic tiles from vector artwork; the current Object Mosaic is quite limited.

✦ **Area Tool:** Illustrator's Measure tool is fine for measuring distance. An Area tool would measure the area within several clicked points or selected paths.

Many of these plug-ins can be created using little more than the tools provided with the Illustrator API. Other plug-ins require a higher level of complexity, but most, if not all of them, are doable.

If you have plug-in ideas that you'd like to see developed, or if you've created a plug-in that you need marketed, contact the Adobe Developer's Association, which works with up-and-coming programmers to help them realize their plug-in goals. In addition, you may want to check with any of the existing plug-in developers, such as Adobe or Extensis. They may be interested in licensing your technology for inclusion in a future product.

Fun Plug-Ins on the Illustrator 8 Bible CD-ROM

The *Illustrator 8 Bible* CD-ROM contains a boatload of free, fully functional plug-ins for your use in Illustrator 8 (for Macintosh only). Some of these are freeware (like Matt Foster's Melt and Drip filters) and some are exclusive to the *Illustrator 8 Bible* (Ted Alspach's Doodle Jr., VectorFrame SE, and the Adobe plug-ins). The following sections describe the plug-ins and some uses for them.

KPT Gradients/Patterns to Paths

This handy filter takes paths filled with gradients or patterns, and converts the gradients to blends and the patterns to paths. This provides you with the capability to do some truly amazing effects that wouldn't be possible otherwise.

Matt Foster's Melt & Drip Filters

Matt Foster is one of the amazingly talented engineers at Adobe systems. He designed the Melt & Drip filters to show off some of the capabilities of the Illustrator Plug-in interface and to help programmers in writing their own filters for Illustrator. Little did he know I'd find all sorts of amazing uses for them. Melt & Drip filters affect selected paths. The dialog box for Melt is shown in Figure 15-30.

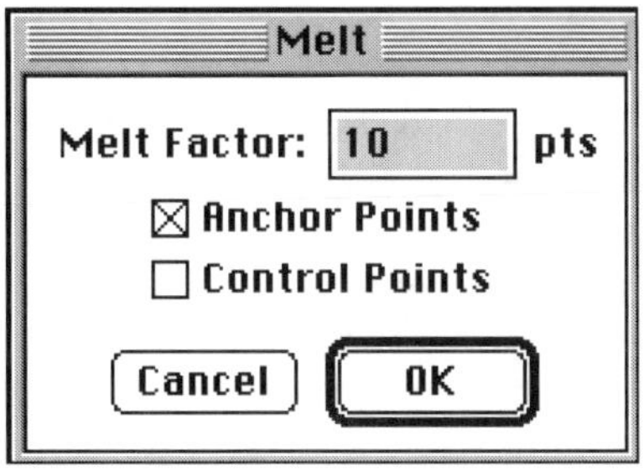

Figure 15-30: The Melt dialog box

The following images show how text can be manipulated with Melt & Drip to get various effects. Instead of the common Steps format, I've condensed the explanations to save space. For all the figures, first create type and then convert the type to outlines.

To achieve the effect in Figure 15-31, apply Add Anchor Points three times. Apply Drip at 20 points, with both the Anchor and Control points checkboxes checked. Apply Rounded Corners at 100 points. Apply Unite. Select the bottom-most points and scale them down with the Scale tool.

To achieve the effect in Figure 15-32, apply Add Anchor Points three times. Rotate the words 90°. Apply Melt at 10 points, with both the Anchor and Control points checkboxes checked. Rotate 180°. Reapply Melt (just press ⌘-E [Ctrl+E]) at the same settings. Apply Rounded Corners at 100 points. Rotate 90° (back to regular position). Apply Unite.

To achieve the effect in Figure 15-33, apply Add Anchor Points once. Apply Round Corners at 100 points. Apply Add Anchor Points twice. Apply Twirl at 90°. Apply Melt at 10 points, check the Control Points checkbox. Apply Twirl at –95°. Rotate with the Rotate Tool back to horizontal. Apply Drip at 20 points, with both the Anchor and Control points checkboxes checked. Apply Unite.

Figure 15-31: The original outlined path and after Dripping

Figure 15-32: The original outlined path after Melting

Figure 15-33: The original outlined path after Melting and Dripping

Ted Alspach's Doodle Jr

This filter (Figure 15-34) was designed to take advantage of some of the normally unseen path-manipulation capabilities of the Illustrator API. By playing with the various controls, you can distort and reshape artwork dramatically.

To use Doodle Jr., copy it to your Illustrator Plug-Ins folder and restart Illustrator. The filter appears in a new Filter submenu called Fun.

Tip   A hidden feature of Doodle Jr.: Click the Doodle Jr. logo and the selected objects are randomized.

Figure 15-34: Doodle Jr. is a distortion filter that lets you reshape your work

Adobe's Plug-Ins

I managed to twist Adobe's arm a little so that they would let me include three plug-ins that aren't quite ready for prime time. These plug-ins may or may not ever make it into Illustrator, so I'm giving you a pseudo sneak preview.

Caution   One of the reasons these otherwise useful plug-ins are not included with Illustrator is because they have not been properly tested by anyone other than the original engineer and a few red-eyed Illustrator users. There may very well be problems with the plug-ins (I haven't found any, but then again, I'm not a QA (quality assurance) person). That said, if you experience problems with Illustrator with these plug-ins installed, *take them out.* Neither Adobe nor I will provide any form of technical support for them. Boy, I'm getting harsh in my old age.

To install the plug-ins, drag them from the Adobe Exclusives folder on your *Illustrator 8 Bible* CD-ROM to your Plug-Ins folder. To remove them, take them out of the Plug-Ins folder. The two tools will appear in the toolbox (under the Blend tool and Graph tool), while the Clock functions will appear in the Object menu.

The Analog Clock

This is the amazing plug-in that manages to show some of the incredible power of Adobe Illustrator's API. Joe Holt of Adobe Systems, the chief engineer for Illustrator 6.0's suite-based API, developed the clock.

To install the plug-in, drag it out of the SDK folder on the *Illustrator 8 Bible* CD-ROM and place it in your Illustrator 8 application's Plug-Ins folder. Launch Illustrator. The Object menu (see Figure 15-35) will contain two new items: Create Clock and Pause Clock.

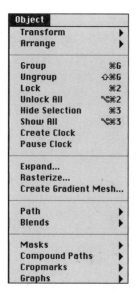

Figure 15-35: The Object menu when the Clock plug-in is installed

Choose Create Clock from the Object menu. A gray clock appears in the center of your document, with a ticking second hand (see Figure 15-36). When I first saw this, I thought, "Cool. Now I can see the time in Illustrator." I didn't grasp what was happening: The clock is made of Illustrator paths. The plug-in actually creates animated Illustrator paths, in this case a set of paths that keep time (based on your Mac's time setting).

Figure 15-36: The clock when you first create it (the time shown reflects the time on your system)

A few cool things you can do with the clock:

✦ Save the document and close it. Open it again a few hours, days, or months later, and you'll see that it's been keeping time correctly.

✦ Select the second hand and change the fill color . . . while the second hand ticks its way around the center of the clock.

✦ Pause the clock (using the command in the Object menu) and Option[Alt]-copy it several times. Change the position of the hour hands by rotating them around the center of each clock slightly. When you Resume the clock running, you'll have a virtual (and accurate) set of clocks displaying the time in multiple time zones (see Figure 15-37).

✦ Pause the clock and use any of Illustrator's tools to distort the paths, then Resume the clock (see Figure 15-38).

✦ Use the clock as a time stamp by shrinking it and placing it in the corner of an Illustrator document.

Figure 15-37: The time zones in the United States

Figure 15-38: It keeps on ticking!

These are just the possibilities from a user's standpoint. From a developer's point of view, this opens up a whole new area of plug-in development.

The Arrow Tool

This handy tool draws arrows. That's it. You don't even get to choose how the arrow looks. All you get to do is drag from the end of the arrow to the tip of the arrow. The Arrow tool is located in the toolbox under the Blend tool, as shown in Figure 15-39.

Figure 15-39: The Arrow tool in the toolbox

The arrow consists of a single closed path, so it doesn't look quite right with just a fill or just a stroke. Instead, give it a fill and stroke that are the same color, then change the stroke to match how thick you'd like the "tail" portion of the arrow to be. The tip of the arrow will increase in size as you do this, of course, so don't get carried away (see Figure 15-40).

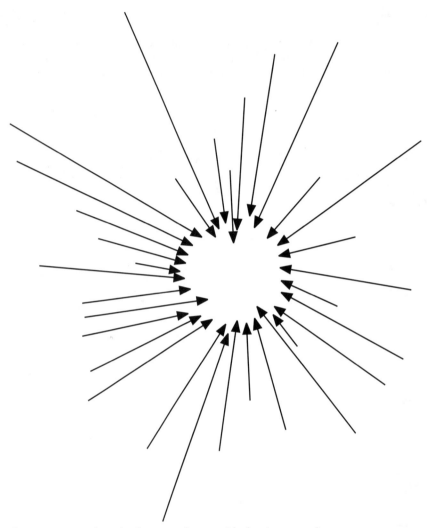

Figure 15-40: A bunch of arrows drawn with the Arrow tool

Point and Delete

The Point and Delete tool (see Figure 15-41) is rather simple, yet I've found it extremely powerful. To use it, simply click on any single path you wish to delete. The Point and Delete tool doesn't care if the object is part of a group or a compound path, it just deletes that single path.

    Figure 15-41: The Point and Delete tool

Summary

✦ Companies and individuals outside Adobe create third-party filters for Illustrator.

✦ KPT Vector Effects contains a baker's dozen of various filters, many for producing unique special effects with Illustrator.

✦ Extensis VectorTools are a plethora of plug-ins that let you create time-saving effects. For more on VectorTools, see Chapter 14.

✦ hotdoor CADtools gives Illustrator users precision drawing tools to use in Illustrator 8. You simply click and drag to add your dimension lines.

✦ Vertigo 3D Pop-Art lets you bring out the 3D in any Illustrator 2D object.

✦ Vertigo 3D Words allows you to create true 3D text in Illustrator.

✦ Several filters can be found on the CD-ROM included with this book; copy them to your Illustrator Plug-Ins folder and restart Illustrator to use them.

✦   ✦   ✦

Mastering Illustrator

There are many concepts in Illustrator that don't fall under one of the Illustrator menus, tools, or palettes. There are also several software packages (besides plug-ins) that work with Illustrator, adding features not found in the main program.

Part IV discusses a wide variety of Illustrator features that help round out your knowledge of Illustrator. The concepts presented in this part are unique and useful; in fact, even Illustrator experts will find information in here that they didn't know before.

Illustrator and the Web

As the century turns, the denizens of the Web don't appear to be overly concerned that the only real supported format for graphics is pixel-based. With the exception of the Acrobat PDF (Portable Document Format) format, graphics on the Web are limited to images consisting of pixels.

Before Illustrator 7, Illustrator had little to offer in the way of Web graphics. Sure, people would use it to set type because Photoshop 1 through 4 had such terrible type capabilities (unless you used the PhotoType component of Extensis's PhotoTools), but overall Illustrator was mostly left out in the cold.

Oddly enough, that didn't seem to stop Illustrator users from using Illustrator to create Web graphics.

But now, Illustrator is truly Web-ready and includes these Web-specific features:

+ RGB color support

+ GIF89A export capability

+ JPEG export capability

+ PNG export capability

+ URL assignment to objects

+ Image map creation

+ PDF 3.0 support

+ Web-specific Swatches palette

The one thing to remember if you're creating graphics for the Web is that the resulting image will be made of pixels, not vectors. This may or may not affect the way you design your image, but it's a good thing to remember.

The rest of this chapter provides guidelines for using Illustrator's Web features and some handy tips on Web page creation. If you're new to Web page design, get a copy of Adobe PageMill, which makes Web page creation a much simpler task than ever before.

Exporting to JPEG Format

The JPEG (Joint Photographic Experts Group) format has been the most popular lossy compression standard for pixel-based images by far. It allows images to be compressed to as little as one percent of their original size. Of course, this extreme compression comes at a price—loss of detail. Using the higher compression settings also can create blotches on images that look pretty terrible. Figure 16-1 shows an original image, and the same image after having the different JPEG settings applied to it.

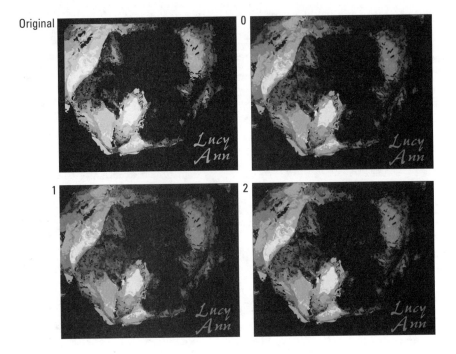

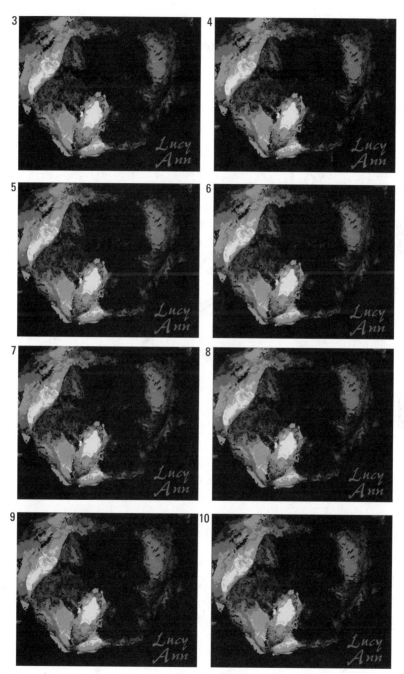

Figure 16-1: The original image and the resulting JPEG images, each saved at a different compression setting

As when exporting to any bitmapped format, make sure you don't give the file being exported the same name as the Illustrator file. If you give it the same name, the exported file overwrites the Illustrator file, which makes the Illustrator file uneditable.

Two benefits to using JPEG images are that you can use millions of colors (24-bit color) for Web pages and that all browsers support JPEG. The JPEG export dialog box is shown in Figure 16-2.

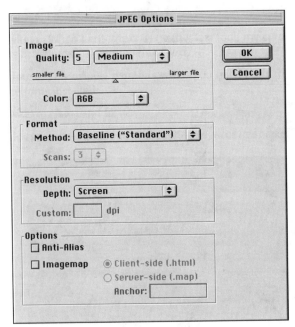

Figure 16-2: The JPEG export dialog box

Exporting to PNG Format

PNG (Portable Network Graphics) is the latest format and seems primed to take over from JPEG and many GIF (Graphics Interchange Format) uses, as it keeps file sizes small without losing any data. Files can be saved in up to 48-bit color for maximum quality. As of this writing, no currently shipping browsers support this technology without an additional plug-in.

Exporting to GIF Format

The GIF format is the closest to a standard that the World Wide Web has. One of the best things about GIF files is their flexibility. GIF files are used as plain images, images with transparency, image maps, and as animations. Their biggest drawback — the limited number of colors usable — is also a giant strength. The GIF89A export option is the one you'll probably use most when creating Web graphics with Illustrator.

The GIF export dialog box (see Figure 16-3) in Illustrator provides all the options you need to create the exact type of GIF file you want.

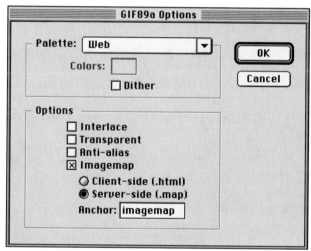

Figure 16-3: The GIF export dialog box

The Web-Ready Swatches Palette

Illustrator has a special Swatches palette that contains Web-specific colors. Using this palette, you can create illustrations that only use the 216 cross-platform colors commonly used for GIF images on the Web. You can access this palette (shown in Figure 16-4) by choosing Window ➪ Swatch Libraries ➪ Web.

If you'll be using the Web Swatches palette, be aware that using blends, gradients, color filters, and the Pathfinder function can dramatically change the colors in your document, creating potential dithering situations. If at all possible, stick to the solid colors found within the palette.

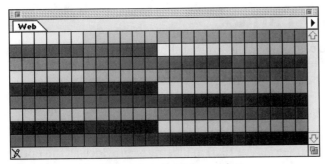

Figure 16-4: The Web colors Swatches palette

Assigning URLs to Objects

Objects in Illustrator can have URLs (Uniform Resource Locators such as `http://` and `ftp://` addresses) attached to them via the Attributes palette.

1. Select the path or group of objects you wish to attach the URL to.

2. Display the Attributes palette by choosing Window ➪ Show Attributes or by pressing F11.

3. If the URL field is not visible, choose Show All from the Attributes pop-up menu. The Attributes palette should look like the one in Figure 16-5.

4. Type the complete URL for the selected object, such as **http://www.bezier.com/vectorville**.

5. Press Return. The object now has that URL assigned to it.

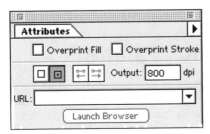

Figure 16-5: The Attributes palette

> **Tip**
>
> Each time you type in a new URL in the URL field, it is added to the URL pop-up menu (accessed by clicking to the right of the URL field). The Palette Options menu item (in the Attributes pop-up menu) lets you set the maximum number of URLs in the pop-up menu — up to 30 of them.

Creating Image Maps

The number one reason for assigning URLs to portions of an image is to generate GIF-based image maps from your Illustrator documents.

1. Assign pieces of artwork in your document to appropriate URLs.
2. Choose File ⇨ Export.
3. In the Export dialog box, choose GIF89A and name the file.
4. In the GIF89A dialog box, choose the Imagemap option. (Keep reading for an explanation of Client-side and Server-side image maps.)
5. Click OK.

Client-side creates an HTML file with the appropriate HTML code in it for use with the GIF image that is being created. By using the HTML code, you can use the image map easily.

Server-side creates a .map file that CGI (Common Gateway Interface) image map scripts use to determine the borders of your objects.

Illustrator 7 shipped with an image map exporter that only supported the RECT command (rectangles). Illustrator 8 is still limited to the rectangle shapes. Polygon support is planned, but several issues (interface, the image map limit of 100 sides per object, compound paths, and curves) have yet to be satisfactorily resolved.

Creating Web Page Headings with Illustrator

The number one strength of the GIF89A format is its capability to provide transparency. Illustrator is a perfect tool for creating partially transparent images — images without a rectangular background. In addition, the GIF89A format can be set up to use a minimum number of colors, which keeps file sizes amazingly small.

However, what the GIF89A format is ideal for is creating headlines for Web pages. To get a page to look really good, fonts are needed. Unfortunately, specifying a font via HTML only works in certain browsers and then only if the specified font is installed on the system that is viewing the Web page. Of course (as always), the best alternative is the PDF format; however, if you want a font on an HTML page, you'll probably end up creating a GIF file, which is something that Illustrator really excels at. And then, instead of just using a font, you can do all sorts of other things that HTML coders can only dream of.

Why use Illustrator instead of Photoshop for creating Web headings? The great thing about using Illustrator to create Web headings is that you can use the full power of Illustrator's type and distortion capabilities so that your headings look exactly the way you want. Many of Illustrator's type features — such as tracking, kerning, horizontal scaling, multiple fonts in one line, pattern and gradient fills, easy drop-shadows, type on a curve, and more — are either impossible in Photoshop or cause undue strain on Photoshop's limited type capabilities.

1. Type your heading in Illustrator.

2. Choose the Character attributes (font, tracking, and so forth) for the heading.

3. Change the size of the heading to the size you want the text to appear on your Web site. It's usually best to view the document at 100 percent.

4. Choose the Paint Style for the type. If you wish to use a gradient or pattern instead of a solid color fill, select the type and choose Type ➪ Create Outlines (⌘-Shift-O) [Ctrl+Shift+O] first. One of the advantages of using Illustrator for Web headings is that you can go back to the original Illustrator document, make changes, and then re-export the document for Web use.

5. To create a drop shadow (which can really make your text stand out), copy the text, Paste in Back (⌘-B) [Ctrl+B], and Fill the pasted copy with Black. Use the arrow keys to move the shadow down and to the right. If you've used text that is thin and you can see white space between the original text and the shadow, put a black stroke on the drop shadow that is thick enough to cover the gap.

6. Save the document as an Illustrator file (for example, `Heading.ai8`).

7. Export the document with a different name as a GIF89A file (`Heading.GIF`) in the same folder as your HTML page. In the GIF89A Options dialog box, choose Exact from the Palette pop-up menu (which uses *only* the colors in the heading), and select both the Interlace (which allows the heading to increase in resolution as it is downloaded to the browser) and Transparent options. Checking the Transparent option lets you place the heading on *any* background, even a tiled pattern.

Tips for Heading Design in Illustrator

Take advantage of Illustrator's powerful kerning and tracking capabilities. You can quickly kern between two letters by placing your cursor between the two letters and then press ⌘-Shift-[[Ctrl+Shift+[ ] to remove space or ⌘-Shift-] [Ctrl+Shift+]] to add space between the letters. For tracking, select the range of characters to track and use the same key commands.

If you have fonts in Adobe's Expert collection (such as Adobe Garamond), you can use small caps in your heading, which always look classy.

If you are using a gradient or a pattern as a fill, try to use a heavy sans serif font.

Only check the Anti-alias option in the GIF89A box if you'll be using the same background color on your Web page as the one in your document. Two things happen when this box is checked: The file size (due to the increased number of colors) increases dramatically, and the edges along the transparency border look "dissolved."

If horizontally scaling, try to avoid using fonts with big serifs, as they can often be stretched out of proportion.

Using the Heading in a Web Page (Text-Based Editors)

Here are the steps to follow to use your new Web heading:

1. Where you would like the Heading to be, type

   ```
   <IMG SRC="Heading.GIF">
   ```

2. Save your page and view it in your Web browser. If you rename or move the image, you'll need to type the correct path/file name into the IMG SRC code.

One of the benefits of creating a heading in Illustrator is that you can update it any time by opening the Illustrator file that contains the heading, editing the text (if it isn't outlines), and then doing an Export to replace the GIF file with an updated version.

The GIF file shown in Figure 16-6 is only 3,072 bytes, which means it should download to a 28.8 Kbps modem in 1 or 2 seconds. You can help make Web pages that contain GIF file headings load faster by specifying the image size in the source code. For instance, the image created in this example is 519 x 39 pixels, so I'll put this code in:

```
<IMG SRC="Heading.GIF" Width=519 Height=39>
```

Now the rest of the page loads first, and the heading will fill in afterward.

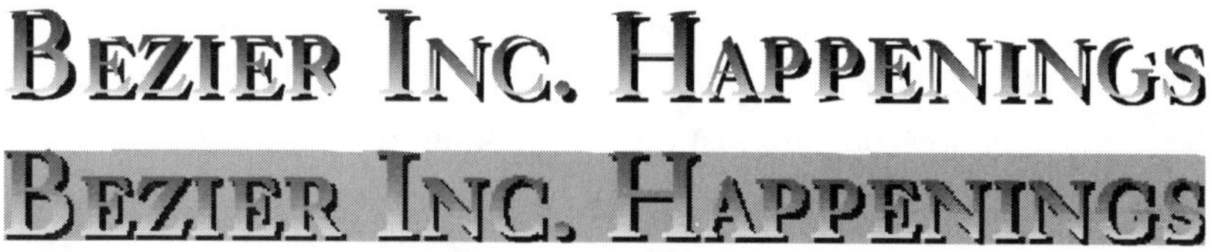

Figure 16-6: The original Illustrator image (top) and the GIF version of the image (bottom)

Heading Effects

Of course, using Illustrator to create such basic headings seems like a waste of all the great typographical power in Illustrator, so here are a few ideas to really spruce up those headings:

✦ **Path Type on Curved Paths.** Why use straight, boring type when you can use funky curved type? Why, indeed! Create a wavy line and click on it with the Path Type tool. Of course, path type is still completely editable.

✦ **Three-dimensional Type with VectorEffects.** Use MetaTools VectorEffects with Illustrator to create three-dimensional type for headings. You must turn text into outlines before doing this, which means you'll lose the capability to edit the text in the future.

✦ **Place an Image in the Text.** Use the type as a mask and mask a placed image. The image can be a photograph, a pattern, or anything else you want to mask with the text.

The PDF Situation

When Adobe Illustrator 7 shipped, it did not provide URL-embedding support for PDF documents. Adobe hopes to release a fix/update for this, but if you have Version 7, chances are that an exported PDF document from Illustrator will *not* retain assigned URLs. Once it does, however, Illustrator will be a valuable tool for creating PDF-based Web pages.

Summary

✦ The Web doesn't support vector-based graphics without specialized plug-ins, so Illustrator documents must be rasterized in order to be used on the Web.

✦ JPEG format is valuable because it supports an unlimited number of colors in any image.

✦ GIF89A images, while limited to 256 colors, provide transparency, image map capabilities, and interlacing.

✦ Assign URLs to objects (or several objects at once) by selecting them and using the Attributes palette.

✦ PDF exporting does *not* support URL embedding.

✦   ✦   ✦

Working with Strokes

The ability to Stroke a path in Illustrator is greatly underrated. Strokes can do more than just outline shapes and vary thicknesses and patterns.

In the first part of this chapter, I explain some of the greatest mysteries and unlock some of the deepest secrets that surround Strokes. If that sounds at all boring, take a look at the figures in this chapter. I created most of them by using Strokes, not Filled paths. Amazin', ain't it?

The Secret Magic of Strokes

You create most effects with Strokes by overlaying several Strokes on top of one another. By copying and choosing Edit ➪ Paste in Front (⌘-F) [Ctrl+F], you place an exact duplicate of the original path on top of itself.

Changing the weight and color of the top Stroke gives the appearance of a path that is a designer, or custom, Stroke. You can add Strokes on top of or under the original Stroke to make the pattern more complex or to add more colors or shapes.

The following steps describe how to create a specialty Stroke that looks like parallel Strokes, and Figure 17-1 illustrates these steps.

1. Use thePencil tool to draw a short line. I usually set the Auto Trace Tolerance (choose File ➪ Preferences ➪ Type and Auto Tracing) to 10-point for a very smooth path. Change the Fill to None and Stroke the path with 18-point Black.

2. Copy the Stroke and paste the copy in front (⌘-F) [Ctrl+F]. Change the copied (pasted in front) Stroke to 6-point white. Select both paths, copy them (⌘-C) [Ctrl+C], and lock them (⌘-L) [Ctrl+L]. The 6-point Stroke looks as if it has been subtracted from the 18-point Stroke. The result appears to be two separate 6-point black Strokes.

3. Choose Edit ➪ Paste in Back (⌘-B) [Ctrl+B]. Deselect All (⌘-Shift-A) [Ctrl+Shift+A] and click the top path. Change the weight of the Stroke to 30 points. Lock the path and select the remaining path. Change the Stroke on this path to 42. The 30-point Stroke is 12 points more than the 18 points of the black Stroke, or 6 points on each side. The 42-point Stroke is 12 points more than the white 30-point Stroke.

Step 1   Step 2   Step 3

Figure 17-1: Creating parallel Strokes

This example is just the tip of the iceberg in creating custom Strokes. Not only can you have paths that overlap, but you also can give the Stroke on each path different dash patterns, joins, and caps. You can even add Fills to certain paths to make the Stroke different on both sides of the path. And if all of that isn't enough, you can use Outline Path to outline Strokes.

Tip

When you are creating parallel Strokes, determine how thick each of the visible Strokes should be, multiply that number times the black *and* white visible Strokes that you want for the base Stroke, and work up from there. For example, if you want 10-point Strokes, and there are four white Strokes and five black strokes, the first Stroke would be 90-points thick and Black. The next Stroke would be 70-point White, and then 50-point Black, 30-point White, and 10-point Black.

Knowing the secrets doesn't let you in on the really good stuff, though. Read on to learn how to apply these to achieve truly amazing effects with Strokes.

Stroke Essentials

Strokes, which were introduced in Chapter 2, act and work differently than Fills. Remember these basics and rules (no pun intended) when using Strokes:

✦ The most important thing to remember when using Strokes is that Stroke-weight width is evenly distributed on both sides of a path. In other words, on a Stroke with a 6-point weight, there are 3 points of the Stroke on both sides of the Stroke's path.

✦ Patterns can be put into Strokes, and with Version 8 you can see the pattern on the Stroke.

✦ Gradients may *not* be used to color Strokes.

✦ Choosing Outline from the Pathfinder palette creates path outlines around the width of the Stroke. When a Stroke has been converted into an outline, it is really an outlined path object and can be Filled with patterns and gradients (both of which appear when previewing and printing).

✦ Stroke weight *never* varies on the same path.

✦ A Stroke with a color of None has no Stroke weight.

✦ Strokes are, for the most part, ignored when combining, splitting, or modifying paths with the Pathfinder functions. Strokes are never considered when the Pathfinder functions search for the locations of the paths.

Using the Stroke Charts

The stroke charts in Figures 17-2 through 17-5 show how some of the basic Stroke-dash patterns look with various options checked, at different weights, and in different combinations.

Color	Width	Dash	Cap	Join
Black 100%	3	0,1	Round	Round

Color	Width	Dash	Cap	Join
Black 100%	3	0,2	Round	Round

Color	Width	Dash	Cap	Join
Black 100%	3	0,3	Round	Round

Color	Width	Dash	Cap	Join
Black 100%	3	0,4	Round	Round

Color	Width	Dash	Cap	Join
Black 100%	3	0,5	Round	Round

Color	Width	Dash	Cap	Join
Black 100%	3	0,10	Round	Round

Color	Width	Dash	Cap	Join
Black 100%	3	0,1	Butt	Miter

Color	Width	Dash	Cap	Join
Black 100%	3	0,2	Butt	Miter

Color	Width	Dash	Cap	Join
Black 100%	3	0,3	Butt	Miter

Color	Width	Dash	Cap	Join
Black 100%	3	0,4	Butt	Miter

Color	Width	Dash	Cap	Join
Black 100%	3	0,5	Butt	Miter

Color	Width	Dash	Cap	Join
Black 100%	3	0,10	Butt	Miter

Color	Width	Dash	Cap	Join
Black 100%	3	0,2	Projected	Miter

Color	Width	Dash	Cap	Join
Black 100%	3	0,3	Projected	Miter

Color	Width	Dash	Cap	Join
Black 100%	3	0,5	Projected	Miter

Color	Width	Dash	Cap	Join
Black 100%	3	0,10	Projected	Miter

Color	Width	Dash	Cap	Join
Black 100%	3	0,10,0,5	Round	Round

Color	Width	Dash	Cap	Join
Black 100%	3	0,10,0,20	Round	Round

Color	Width	Dash	Cap	Join
Black 100%	3	2,2	Round	Round

Color	Width	Dash	Cap	Join
Black 100%	3	2,5	Round	Round

Color	Width	Dash	Cap	Join
Black 100%	3	2,10	Round	Round

Color	Width	Dash	Cap	Join
Black 100%	3	2,5,0,5	Round	Round

Color	Width	Dash	Cap	Join
Black 100%	3	2,10,0,10	Round	Round

Color	Width	Dash	Cap	Join
Black 100%	3	4,5,0,5	Round	Round

Color	Width	Dash	Cap	Join
Black 100%	3	4,10,0,10	Round	Round

Color	Width	Dash	Cap	Join
Black 100%	3	10,5	Round	Round

Color	Width	Dash	Cap	Join
Black 100%	3	10,10	Round	Round

Color	Width	Dash	Cap	Join
Black 100%	3	10,15,10,5	Round	Round

Color	Width	Dash	Cap	Join
Black 100%	3	20,10	Projected	Miter

Color	Width	Dash	Cap	Join
Black 100%	3	10,10,0,10	Projected	Miter

Color	Width	Dash	Cap	Join
Black 100%	3	20,10,0,10	Projected	Miter

Color	Width	Dash	Cap	Join
Black 100%	3	10,10,30,10	Projected	Miter

Figure 17-2: Thirty-two 3-point Stroke paths

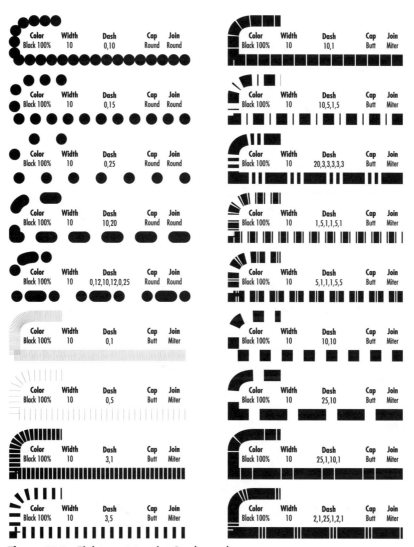

Figure 17-3: Eighteen 10-point Stroke paths

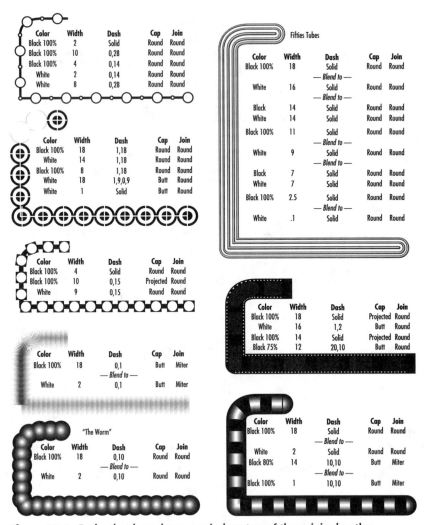

Figure 17-4: Paths that have been copied on top of the original paths

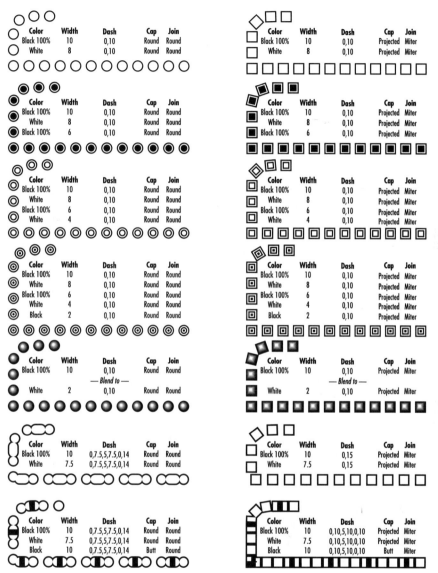

Figure 17-5: Another example of paths that have been copied on top of the original paths

All the paths in the charts were taken from an original shape that included a straight segment, a corner, and a curve. The charts should help you determine when to use certain types of Stroke patterns because, as you can see, some patterns work better than others with curves and corners.

The first chart (Figure 17-2) consists of thirty-two 3-point Stroke paths that have a variety of dash patterns and end and join attributes. The second chart (Figure 17-3) shows eighteen 10-point Stroke paths with similar attributes. These two charts show Stroke effects with only one path. The area in the middle of each path in the chart describes the path.

The third (Figure 17-4) and fourth charts (Figure 17-5) contain paths that have been copied on top of the original by using the Paste in Front command. The paths are listed in the order that they were created. The first path is described at the top of the list. The first path is copied, pasted in front (⌘-F) [Ctrl+F], and given the Paint Style attributes of the second item in the list. The changes progress from the top left of each chart to the bottom left and then from the top right to the bottom right.

Tip   In some cases, paths are blended from one to another. To be able to select an end point on each Stroke (usually they will overlap), offset one of the paths by 0.1 point. When blending, use a number that is less than 100 for the number of blend steps, dividing the suggested number by 2 until it is small enough.

When you create a Stroke pattern, frequently the original path is selected, copied, and then pasted in front or back (⌘-F [Ctrl+F] or ⌘-B [Ctrl+B]) several times. There is usually no need to recopy the original path after it has been copied. You can continue to paste it again and again on top of or under the original path.

In the middle of the right-hand column in the third stroke chart (Figure 17-4) is a Stroke that looks like a strip of film. The following steps describe how to create this film Stroke, which is a basic Stroke that produces a stunning effect.

1. Draw a wavy path with the Pencil tool.

2. Change the Stroke of the path to 18-point Black and the Fill to None.

3. Copy (⌘-C) [Ctrl+C] the path and choose Edit ⇨ Paste in Front (⌘-F) [Ctrl+F]. Change the Stroke to 16-point White, and use a Dash Pattern of Dash 1, Gap 2.

4. Choose Edit ⇨ Paste in Front (⌘-F) [Ctrl+F] again and change the Stroke to 14-point Black, Solid.

5. Choose Edit ⇨ Paste in Front (⌘-F) [Ctrl+F] once more and change the Stroke to 75% Black, 12 points, with a Dash Pattern of Dash 20, Gap 10.

Figure 17-6 shows these steps. You can use this procedure to create any of the Strokes in the third Stroke chart (Figure 17-4) by substituting the values that are listed in the chart for the Stroke that you want.

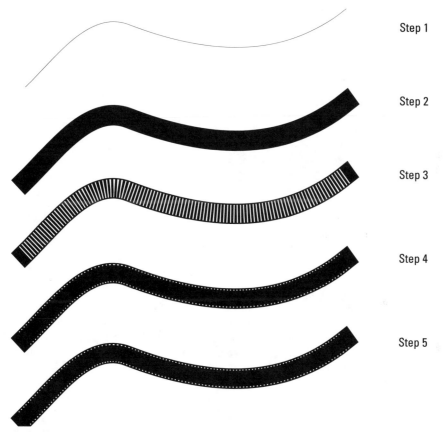

Figure 17-6: The steps for creating the film Stroke from Figure 17-4

Type

You can use Strokes to enhance type in a number of ways. The first example, described in the following steps and shown in Figure 17-7, is based on Stroke blends. For more information on Stroke blends, see Chapter 10; for more information on type, see Chapter 8.

1. Type a few words in a heavy-weighted font such as Helvetica Black, Futura Extra Bold, or Kabel Ultra.

2. Select the type with the Selection tool. Choose Type ➪ Create Outlines (⌘-Shift-O) [Ctrl+Shift+O] and change the Fill to None and the Stroke to Black or a light shade of gray. Change the weight of the Stroke to 0.1 point.

3. Copy (⌘-C) [Ctrl+C] the words and choose Edit ➪ Paste in Back (⌘-B) [Ctrl+B]. Move the copy a few points up and to the right. Change the Stroke on the copy to 4-point White and blend each set of paths together with the Blend tool.

4. Choose Edit ➪ Paste in Front (⌘-F) [Ctrl+F] and change the Fill to White and the Stroke to None.

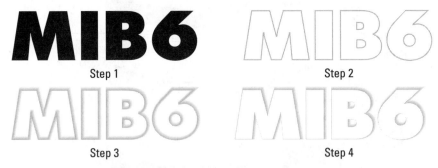

Figure 17-7: Steps for creating ghosted type

Another popular effect (okay, it was popular in the 1970s) for type is produced by creating several Strokes for each stroke of a letter, as described in the following steps and shown in Figure 17-8.

1. Create a word or words in a lightweight typeface.

2. Use the Pen tool to re-create the letters in the typeface. In Figure 17-8, I colored the letters in the original word light red and then locked those letters in place so that I could trace the letters more easily.

3. Group all the paths that you have drawn and give them a heavy Stroke. (I used 18 points.) Change the join and cap style in the Stroke palette to rounded.

4. Copy (⌘-C) [Ctrl+C] and paste in front (⌘-F) [Ctrl+F] in gradually decreasing Stroke weights. Change between white and a darker color as the weight decreases.

Figure 17-8: Making type that has multiple Strokes

Creating Rough Edges

You can create some of the most interesting Stroke effects by using the Roughen filter in combination with a heavy-weighted Stroke. Even with a Roughen filter setting of 1% or 2%, a heavy-weighted Stroke can have many sharp, long points, as described in the following steps.

1. Create an object to which you want to add jagged or explosive edges. I used text that was converted to outlines in the example (see Figure 17-9). Copy the object off to the side before continuing.

2. Use Offset Path to create a path that is offset by 20 points or more. Select all the paths and choose Unite from the Pathfinder palette.

3. Paste in front one last time and roughen as before, but give the Stroke a lesser weight and Fill the path with the same color as the Stroke. Place the original art (which you copied off to the side in Step 1) on top of the roughened paths.

Figure 17-9: Creating roughened paths with Strokes

Half-Stroked Paths

One technique that I don't think is used enough is hiding one side of the Stroke as the path layers are built up. To hide half of the Stroke at any level, paste in front as you normally do and then press ⌘-Option-2 [Ctrl+Alt+2]. This command locks everything that isn't selected; in other words, only the path that you just pasted (and which is currently selected) will not be locked.

Using the Pen tool, connect the ends of the just-pasted path and Fill it with the background color and a Stroke of None. This action obliterates one side of the Stroke because the file of the path covers the "inside" part of the Stroked path. Any Strokes that you place on top of this object will be visible on both sides of the path.

Workin' on the Railroad

Several effects that you can create with paths have a traveling theme, mainly because a path starts somewhere and finishes somewhere else. Railroad tracks, roads, highways, trails, and rivers all have a tendency to conform very nicely to Stroke effects with paths.

One of the trickiest traveling paths to create is a railroad track. To get the real railroad-track look, some advanced cheating is necessary, as described in the following steps.

1. Draw a path to represent the railroad. Create a background shape and Fill the background with a color. In the example (see Figure 17-10), I used dark green.

2. Copy the path. Give the path a Stroke weight of 30 points. Choose Edit ➪ Paste in Front (⌘-F) [Ctrl+F] and give this path a Stroke weight of 20 points.

3. Select both paths. Choose Outline from the Pathfinder palette to change the paths into outlined paths because Strokes cannot contain gradients. Fill the paths with a metallic gradient.

4. Select both paths and choose Exclude from the Pathfinder palette. This command subtracts the inner section of the track from the two outer sections.

5. Check the ends of the path and delete any excess paths that are not part of the tracks. In the example, I also joined the ends on each individual track.

6. Paste in back (⌘-B) [Ctrl+B] and give the new path a Stroke weight of 40 points. Choose Outline from the Pathfinder palette. Stroke and Fill this path with a gradient consisting of several woodlike browns. This path is the wood that underlies the tracks.

7. The last thing to do is to split the pieces of wood into individual railroad ties. Select the wood path and choose Edit ➪ Paste in Front (⌘-F) [Ctrl+F]. This command pastes a path right on top of the wooden area. Give this Stroke the same color as the background and give it a Dash Pattern of Dash 20, Gap 10. The gaps will be the see-through areas, showing the wood-filled path below them.

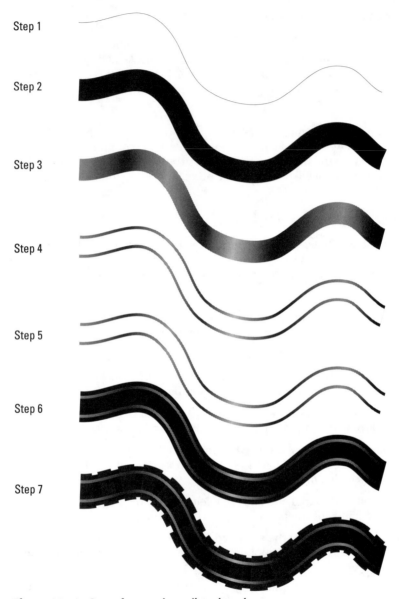

Figure 17-10: Steps for creating railroad tracks

Tip

To change the color of the new path in Step 7 easily, select the new path, choose the Eyedropper tool, and click the background.

Outline Path is often used on this type of Stroke design because Strokes can't have gradient Fills. The reason that the railroad ties were not given a dash pattern before Outline Path was applied is that Outline Path doesn't work with dash patterns.

The Wild River

A wild river is another path that you can create easily using Strokes. One problem in getting rivers to look good is that creating the rough, in-out texture of a river's bank is difficult. Also, because different parts of rivers are different weights, connecting the parts smoothly is difficult. The following steps describe how to create a river.

1. Draw the paths for the river. In the example (see Figure 17-11), I created a Y at one end of the river and an island. I used the Pen tool to draw additional paths next to the river.

2. Give the river a Stroke weight and color. In the example, I gave the main part of the river a Stroke of 18 points and the two additional parts 14-point Strokes. Copy all the paths, paste in front, and color the copy a little darker than the original river Stroke color. Make the Strokes on the copy a few points less wide than the Strokes on the original.

3. Blend the two Strokes together, using three blend steps.

4. Select all of the Strokes and choose Outline from the Pathfinder palette. Select one of the new paths and choose Edit ⇨ Select ⇨ Same Fill Color. Choose Unite from the Pathfinder palette. Repeat this process for each of the five different colors.

5. Select all of the paths and choose Filter ⇨ Distort ⇨ Roughen. In the Roughen dialog box, enter **0.3** and **40** segments per inch and then click OK. The edges of the river are now a little ragged, and they appear to have ripples, or waves, in them.

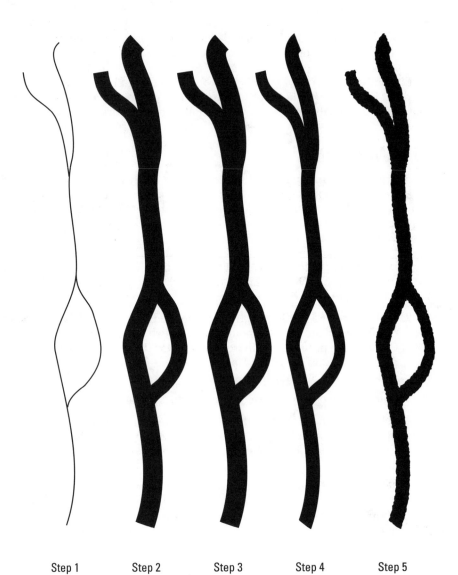

Step 1   Step 2   Step 3   Step 4   Step 5

Figure 17-11: Steps for making a river

The Highway

Figures 17-12 and 17-13 show a Stroke design that I discovered a few years back while I was playing with Illustrator. It has the makings of a cute parlor magic trick that you can use to impress your friends. Back when you had to work in Artwork mode, that is, before Illustrator 5.0, creating designs with Strokes was much more difficult. Artists couldn't see what they were drawing on-screen, so they had to envision it in their minds. Editing dashes and weights is almost a pleasure now that you can use the Stroke palette and undo multiple changes.

After creating the railroad tracks Stroke design, which I thought was pretty clever, I yearned for a similar effect — turning one path into some form of artwork. I especially liked the effect of doing several paths and several Stroke attributes in Artwork mode and then switching to Preview mode when I was finished.

Figures 17-12 and 17-13 show the steps to create a four-lane highway by drawing just one path. These steps are described here.

1. Use the Pencil tool to draw a slightly wavy path from the left side of the Artboard to the right side and then group the path.

2. Change the Path to a Fill of None and create a 400-point Stroke that is colored as follows: Cyan 100, Magenta 25, and Yellow 100. This path is the grass next to the highway.

3. Copy the path and paste in front. Change the paint style of the Stroke to Cyan 25, Yellow 25, and Black 85, with a weight of 240 points. This path is the shoulder of the highway.

4. Paste in front and change the paint style to Cyan 5 and Black 10, with a weight of 165 points. This path is the white line at the edge of the highway.

5. Paste in front and change the paint style to Cyan 15, Yellow 10, and Black 50, with a weight of 160 points. This path is the highway's road surface.

6. To create the dashed white lines for passing, paste in front, and change the paint style to Cyan 5 and Black 10, with a weight of 85 points, a dash of 20, and a gap of 20.

7. Paste in front and change the paint style to Cyan 15, Yellow 10, and Black 50, with a weight of 80 points. This path is the inner part of the highway's road surface.

8. To create the double yellow line, paste in front and change the paint style to Cyan 15, Magenta 20, and Yellow 100, with a weight of 8 points.

9. Paste in front and change the paint style to Cyan 15, Yellow 10, and Black 50, with a weight of 3 points. This path is the piece of highway that divides the double yellow line.

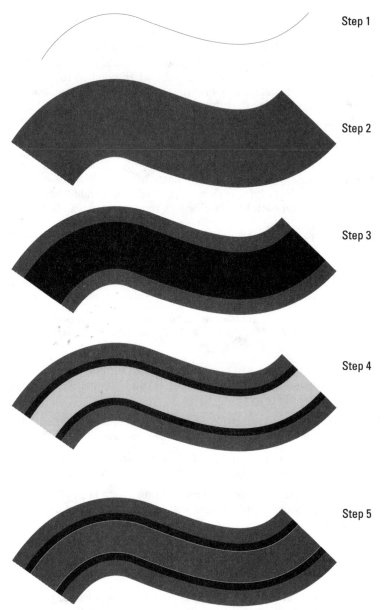

Figure 17-12: The first five steps in creating a highway

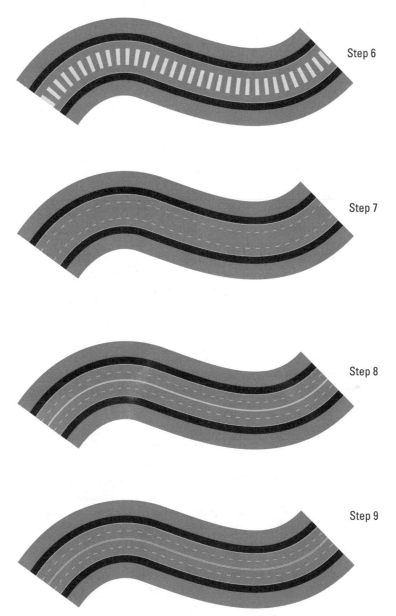

Figure 17-13: The last four steps in creating a highway

With Outline Path, I've taken the highway concept a step or two further by adding a passing zone to the highway. Use the following steps and the illustration in Figure 17-14 to create the passing zone.

1. Delete the top two paths of the original highway. Select all the paths and choose Object ⇨ Hide Selection (⌘-3) [Ctrl-3] to hide the base of the road temporarily. You don't need to change anything about these parts of the highway to create the passing zone effect.

2. Paste in front and change the paint style to Cyan 15, Magenta 20, and Yellow 100, with a weight of 8 points. This path is the same double yellow line as the one in Step 8 of the preceding instructions, but it is not yet split.

3. Copy and paste in front. Keep the paint style at Cyan 15, Magenta 20, and Yellow 100, but change the weight to 3 points. This line is the same width as the road from Step 9 in the preceding instructions, but the color is the double-yellow-line color.

4. Choose All (⌘-A) [Ctrl+A]. This command selects the last two paths that you placed on the illustration. Choose Outline Stroke from the Pathfinder palette. This command creates outlines around the edges of the Stroke so that it results in two Filled objects instead of two overlapping Stroked paths.

5. Choose Exclude from the Pathfinder palette. This command subtracts the top object (the 3-point path) from the bottom one, resulting in two Filled objects that are grouped together. Ungroup the two objects by choosing Object ⇨ Ungroup (⌘-Shift-G).

6. Deselect one of the two paths by Shift-clicking it once and deleting the selected object.

7. Paste in front to put the line with the double-yellow-line Stroke in front of the remaining Filled object. Change the paint style to Dash 20, Gap 20.

8. Paste in front and change the paint style to Cyan 15, Yellow 10, and Black 50, with a weight of 3 points. These settings create a gray line that divides the dashed section from the solid section of line. The dashed section is actually on both sides of the 3-point gray divider line, but you cannot see the part that overlays the solid line because it is the same color and size as the solid line.

9. Choose Object ⇨ Show All. The highway now has a dashed/solid yellow line.

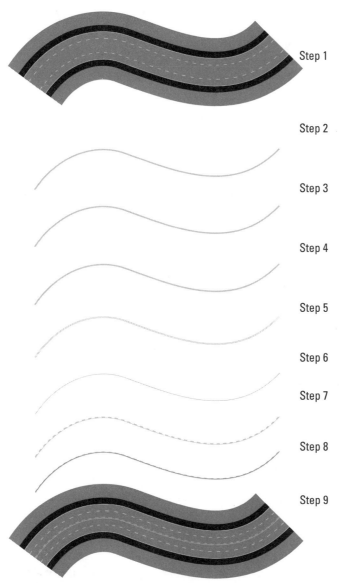

Figure 17-14: Steps for creating a passing zone for the highway

Type into Strokes

You can put type into Strokes by creating Path type and giving the path a heavy enough Stroke weight to surround the type, as described in the following steps. Using symbols and special typefaces, you can create almost any pattern when you put type inside Strokes. (For more information on creating Path type, see Chapter 8.)

1. Draw the path on which you want the type to appear.

2. Click the path with the Path Type tool. Type the letters, numbers, or symbols that will make up the pattern.

3. Select the characters, copy, and paste. Paste until the path is full of characters.

4. Using the Type tool, change the Fill on the characters. Using the Group Selection tool, change the Stroke of the path.

If you are blessed to own font-creation software, such as Macromedia's Fontographer, you can achieve even better results. Simply incorporate any artwork that you create in Illustrator into a font and then use that artwork as Path type by using that font when you type.

Incredibly Intricate Strokes

Unfortunately, what you can do with Strokes is limited to the Stroke palette's options. Sometimes you'll wish you could do just a little bit more with strokes. That's where Path Patterns come in. Path Patterns is a filter that enables you to place patterns on Strokes. These patterns increase in proportions as the Stroke changes shape. Path patterns are discussed in Chapter 11.

Summary

✦ The most attractive aspect of Strokes is that they can be used together, on top of one another.

✦ The Stroke charts provided in this chapter show some of what can be done with Strokes.

✦ When you Stroke type, be sure to put another copy of the Filled text on top of the Stroked type.

✦ Use Outline Path to create Filled paths out of Strokes.

✦ Use Fills to create half-Stroked paths.

✦   ✦   ✦

Printing, Separations, and Traps

You can print Illustrator documents in two ways: as a composite, which is a single printout that contains all the colors and tints used; and as a series of color separations, a printout for each color. Color separations are necessary for illustrations that will be printed on a printing press.

Prior to Printing

Before you start the printing process, there are a number of things that may need to be changed or adjusted. For instance, you may need to change the page size and orientation, or set how certain colors will separate. This section deals with the issues you should be aware of *before* you press ⌘-P [Ctrl+P] to send your file to the printer.

Document Setup

Choosing File ➪ Document Setup (⌘-Shift-P) [Ctrl+Alt+P] enables you to set the initial page size of an illustration via the Artboard. Bringing up the Document Setup dialog box (shown in Figure 18-1) displays a wealth of options that assist in printing. If the Use Page Setup box is checked, then the Artboard size is relative to the size of the page that is selected in the Page Setup dialog box. If the Artboard is smaller than the printable page, then anything entirely outside the edges of the Artboard will be cropped off when you print the illustration through Illustrator. Any objects that are partially on the Artboard will print. Anything outside the Artboard will print when you print the illustration through another application. The Page Setup command and dialog box are referred to as "Print Setup" in Illustrator 8 for Windows. Rather than resort to awkwardly repeated "Page Setup/Print Setup" throughout this chapter, I'm just sticking with "Page Setup."

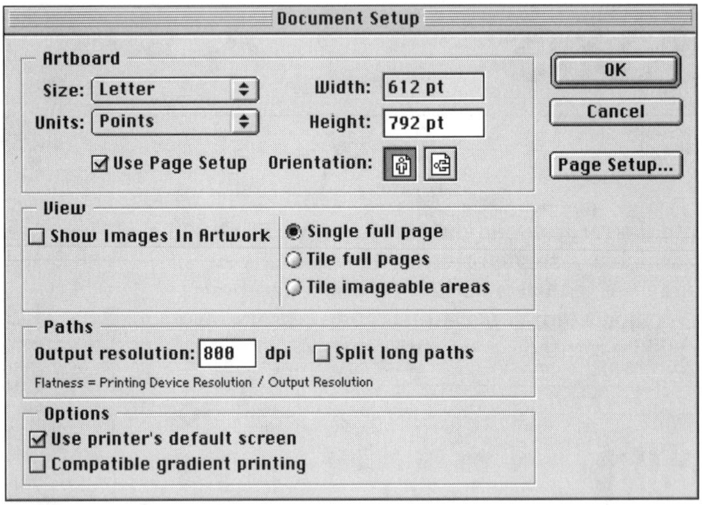

Figure 18-1: The Document Setup dialog box

Another option in the Document Setup dialog box is the Show Images in Artwork option, which enables you to choose whether patterns will preview and print. Unchecking this box prevents patterns from printing when you print the illustration from Illustrator.

The Page Tiling options also affect the way that pages appear when a document is printed from Illustrator:

✦ If you choose Single Full Page, only one page will print.

✦ If you choose Tile Full Pages, only full pages (as defined in the Page Setup dialog box) that appear on the Artboard will print. If no full pages can fit in the Artboard, everything in the Artboard will print.

✦ If you choose Tile Imageable Areas, a grid appears on the Artboard. Any block of the grid that has a piece of the illustration will print. When this option is chosen, you can specify in the Print dialog box that only certain pages should be printed.

Page Setup (Macintosh)

The Page Setup dialog box, shown in Figure 18-2, is used for specifying printing options when printing out a composite image.

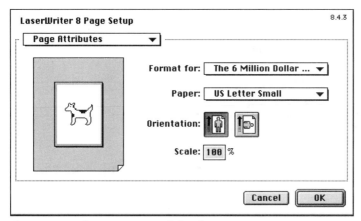

Figure 18-2: The Page Setup dialog box

The printing options on this dialog box are:

✦ **Page Attributes:** This pop-up menu lets you choose the Page Attributes or PostScript Options. The page attributes are listed below.

✦ **Format for:** In this pop-up you choose which printer you want to print to.

✦ **Paper:** You can choose any paper size, including one that your printer does not have the capacity to use. The Tabloid option is the first option in a set of choices in a pop-up menu that also lists envelope sizes and positions. The size that you choose shows up on the document as a dotted-line boundary when the Tile Full Pages or Single Full Pages option is selected in the Document Setup dialog box. Another dotted-line boundary, inside the page-size boundary, is the printable area. The printable area is also displayed when the Tile Imagable Areas option is selected in the Document Setup dialog box.

✦ **Orientation:** This option controls how the image is printed on the printed page — whether it is printed in portrait orientation (longest side vertical) or landscape orientation (longest side horizontal).

✦ **Scale:** This option affects how much the page that the illustration is on is scaled when it's printed. Reducing or enlarging affects the way that the dotted-line page boundaries and imageable-areas dotted lines appear in the document. A value above 100% makes the page smaller, while a value less than 100% makes the page and its boundaries larger. This feature is helpful when you want to print everything that's on a large Artboard. If you select a reduced size in the Page Setup dialog box, the dotted lines in the document reflect the reduced size.

If you choose the PostScript Options from the pop-up menu, the PostScript Options dialog box appears, as shown in Figure 18-3.

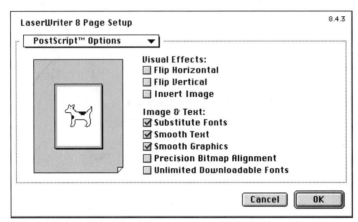

Figure 18-3: The PostScript Options dialog box

The options in the dialog box are as follows:

✦ **Flip Horizontal:** This option causes the document to print as a mirror image of itself, flipped horizontally. You can use it in combination with the Invert Image option to print negatives from Illustrator.

✦ **Flip Vertical:** This option causes the document to print as a mirror image of itself, flipped vertically. You can also use this option in combination with the Invert Image option to print negatives from Illustrator. Using the Flip Horizontal and Flip Vertical options together causes the document to rotate 180 degrees.

✦ **Invert Image:** This option prints a negative image of the illustration, where all white areas are black and all black areas are white.

✦ **Substitute Fonts:** Illustrator has built-in workarounds for font problems, and supposedly this checkbox is irrelevant to Illustrator users. For other programs, this option replaces any bitmapped fonts with corresponding fonts that are installed on the printer, which usually means that if you have Geneva, New York, and Monaco installed in bitmapped format only, Helvetica, Times, and Courier will take their places. Any other bitmapped font will usually be replaced with Courier. In general, if you don't have the PostScript printer font or the font in TrueType format, you shouldn't use that font with Adobe Illustrator, and you shouldn't check this box.

✦ **Smooth Text:** When Substitute Fonts is not checked and an illustration has a bitmapped font in it, Smooth Text will make the bitmapped font look slightly better. It will still look bad, but it will look better than just the plain bitmapped font.

✦ **Smooth Graphics:** Smooth Graphics does about the same thing that Smooth Text does, but it does it to graphics. Because this feature works only with PICT and Paint images, which you cannot print in Illustrator, you should not check this option.

✦ **Precision Bitmap Alignment:** This option resamples bitmapped graphics so that they print better at the resolution of your printer.

✦ **Unlimited Downloadable Fonts in a Document:** Checking this box interferes with Illustrator's own downloading mechanism. You shouldn't check it when printing from Illustrator. When printing from other programs, this option does more than enable you to use lots of fonts. Checking Unlimited Downloadable Fonts in programs *other* than Illustrator makes the RAM (Random Access Memory) in the laser printer adjustable. As part of the document comes in and is processed, the information that was used to process that part of the document and the fonts that were needed to print it are flushed out of memory. The next section and its needed fonts are then loaded. This method takes longer than loading all of the fonts in the entire document at one time and then processing the document, but it prevents out-of-memory printing errors when printing from programs such as QuarkXPress.

Print Setup

The Print Setup dialog box (accessed by clicking the Print Setup button in the Document Setup dialog box) contains Print Setup options that are specific to your printer. The Print Setup dialog box is shown in Figure 18-4. Clicking the Properties button displays a plethora of options for customizing page size and other print properties.

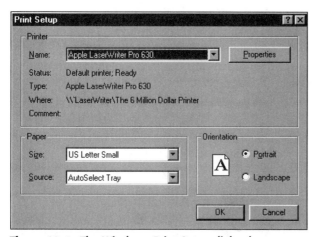

Figure 18-4: The Windows Print Setup dialog box

Printing Composites

A composite printout looks very much like the image that appears on the screen when you preview the document (choose View ⇨ Preview or press ⌘-Y [Ctrl+Y]). If you have a color printer, the image appears in color; otherwise, the colors are replaced by gray tints (see the next section, "Gray Colors").

Caution   Objects that are hidden or that exist on layers that are currently hidden will not print. Objects that exist on layers that have the printing option unchecked in the Layers Option dialog box also will not print.

The final printing step is to choose File ⇨ Print (⌘-P) [Ctrl+P]. This action opens the Print dialog box (the Mac version is shown in Figures 18-5 and 18-6; the Windows version is shown in Figure 18-7), in which you may choose which pages to print, how many of each to print, and several other options. If you click the Cancel button (⌘-period [Ctrl+period]), the dialog box disappears, and no pages are printed. To print, click the Print button or press Return or Enter.

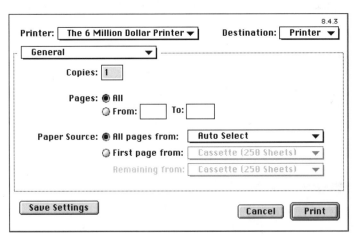

Figure 18-5: The Macintosh General Print dialog box

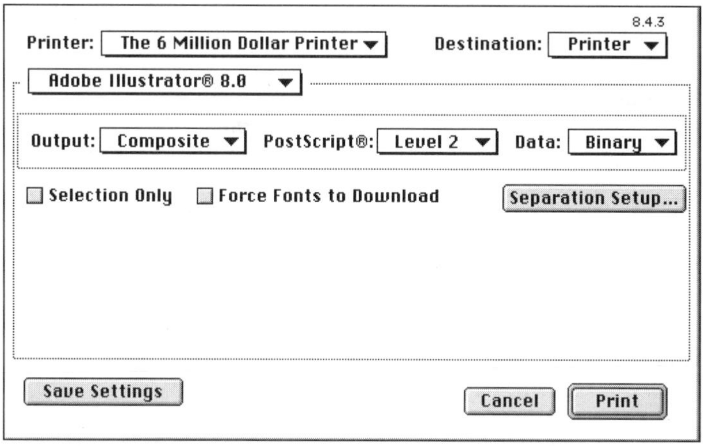

Figure 18-6: The Macintosh Illustrator Print dialog box

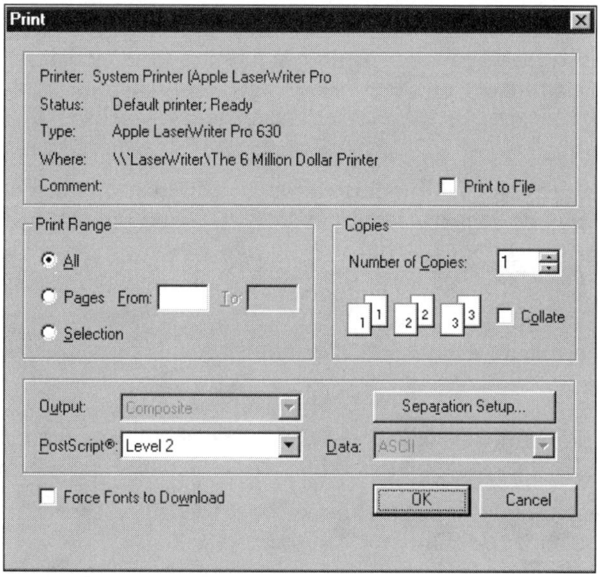

Figure 18-7: The Windows Print dialog box

The Macintosh General Print dialog box (shown in Figure 18-5) and the Windows Print dialog box (shown in Figure 18-7) contain these options:

✦ **Copies:** The number that you enter here determines how many copies of each page will print. All copies of a single page are printed at one time, so if you enter **4** when you are printing a four-page document, you get four copies of page 1, then four copies of page 2, and so on.

✦ **Pages:** If you check the All button, all the pages that have art on them will print. If you enter numbers in the From and To fields, only the pages that those numbers refer to will print. (Print Range in Windows)

✦ **Paper Source:** If Paper Cassette (the default) is selected, all pages will print on paper from the printer's cassette. If Manual Feed is selected, then the pages will print on paper from the manual feed tray. (Mac only)

The Macintosh Illustrator Print dialog box (shown in Figure 18-6) and the Windows Print dialog box (shown in Figure 18-7) contain these options:

✦ **Destination:** Choosing Printer prints the document to the laser printer as usual. Choosing File prints the document to a PostScript file on the hard disk drive that you can download to a laser printer at a future time by using a utility such as Font Downloader or LaserWriter Font Utility. A PostScript file can also be used with Acrobat Distiller (Windows or Mac) or Adobe ScreenReady. (Mac only)

✦ **Output:** This option determines if the illustration is printed as a composite or divided into individual color separations.

✦ **PostScript:** This pop-up menu enables you to specify the PostScript interpreter (Level 1 or Level 2) that is included in your Laser Printer.

Tip   Selecting Level 1 may eliminate various PostScript errors when printing to an older printer.

✦ **Data:** Keep this option on Binary, unless you have a very old printer that only understands PostScript data in ASCII format.

✦ **Selection Only:** This handy little option allows for printing just the selected objects instead of the entire document. (Mac only)

✦ **Force Fonts to Download:** When this option is checked, the document's fonts will download to the printer before printing.

✦ **Separation Setup:** This button opens the Separation Setup dialog box, discussed in detail later in this chapter.

If you click the Options button, the Print Options dialog box appears, as shown in Figure 18-8.

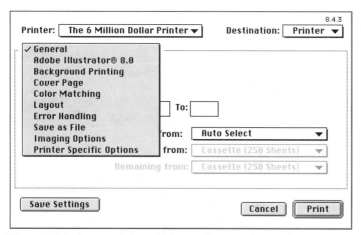

Figure 18-8: Some of the printing options to choose from

The options in this dialog box vary depending on your printer driver and printer choice. The basic options are:

✦ **Cover Page:** If you choose First Page or Last Page, a separate sheet, which contains information about the name of the computer, the name of the file, the number of pages, and the dates, will print. This feature is useful for making each print job easily identifiable when several people share a laser printer.

✦ **Error Handling:** This option allows for a detailed report to be printed when a PostScript error of some sort occurs.

Tip

Always select Print Detailed Report. When an illustration will not print, a sheet of paper will print with the error message on it.

✦ **Other Options:** The options in the lower section are specific to your printer. For instance, the printer information shown in the dialog box in Figure 18-8 is for an Apple LaserWriter Pro 630. Some of the other possible options are the resolution (300 or 600), and whether FinePrint and Photograde are turned on.

Caution

Always do a save before you print. Severe problems, when they happen, usually occur when you are printing. Don't let your unsaved document fall victim to one of those severe problems.

Gray Colors

When you are printing a full-color illustration to a black-and-white printer, Illustrator substitutes gray values for colors. In this way, the program creates the illusion that each color has a separate, distinct gray value.

Of course, each color can't have its own unique gray value, so the colors have to overlap at some point. Illustrator converts each of the process colors into specific gray values when it prints to a black-and-white printer.

Magenta is the darkest process color, ranging from 0% to 73% gray. Therefore, at 100% magenta, it prints at 73% gray. Cyan is second darkest, ranging from 0% to 57% gray. Yellow is extremely light, ranging from 0% to only 11% gray. Figure 18-9 shows a comparison of the four process colors at various settings and their printed results. The four bars show different values, indicated above the bars, for each process color. Within each bar is the percent of black that prints when you are printing that color at that percentage to a black-and-white printer.

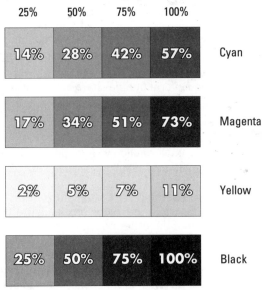

Figure 18-9: How colors appear when printed on a black-and-white laser printer

Different printers may produce different tints of gray. Lower-resolution printers, such as 300-dpi (dots-per-inch) laser printers, do not create an accurate gray tint because they use dots that are too large to create accurate tint patterns.

Color Separations

Color separations are necessary to print a color version of an illustration on most printing presses. Each separation creates a plate that is affixed to a round drum on a printing press. Ink that is the same color as that separation is applied to the plate, which is pressed against a sheet of paper. Because the ink adheres only to the printing areas of the plate, an image is produced on paper. Some printing presses have many different drums and can print a four-color job in one run. Other printing presses have only one or two drums, so the paper has to pass through the press four or two times, respectively, to print a four-color job.

The two types of color separation are process color separation and spot color separation. Each type has its own advantages and drawbacks, and you can use either type or a combination of both types for any print job.

Tip   You should always determine which type of separation you want *before* you begin to create a job electronically.

Spot Color Separation

Jobs that are printed with spot colors are often referred to as two-color or three-color jobs when two or three colors are used. Although you can use any number of colors, most spot color jobs contain only a few colors.

Spot color printing is most useful when you are using two or three distinct colors in a job. For example, if I needed only black and green to create a certain illustration, I would use only black and a green custom color for all of the objects in the illustration.

There are three main reasons for using spot color separation, rather than process color separation:

- ✦ It's cheaper. Spot color printing requires a smaller press with fewer drums. For process color separation, you usually need to use a press with four drums or run the job through a smaller press a number of times.

- ✦ Spot colors are cleaner, brighter, and smoother than the same colors that you create as process colors. To get a green process color, for example, you need to mix both cyan and yellow on paper. Using one spot color will result in a perfectly solid area of color.

- ✦ You cannot duplicate certain spot colors, especially fluorescent and metallic colors, with process colors.

Learning Printing from the Experts

If you have never visited a printing company, make a point to visit one and take a tour. Most printing companies have staff members who are more than willing to explain their equipment and various printing processes. In a 30-minute tour with a knowledgeable guide, you can learn enough to save yourself hours of work, money, and misunderstandings.

When you are talking to a printing rep, find out what type of media they want your work on. Printing companies commonly use imagesetters that can output the job for you, and some companies even perform this service at no charge or for a significant discount if you have the job printed there.

Imagesetters are similar to laser printers, except that they produce images with a very high dpi, from 1,273 to 3,600, and sometimes higher. Imagesetters can print directly to RC (resin-coated) paper or to film negatives (or positives). The paper or film runs through the imagesetter and then must run through a developing process for the images and text to appear.

Most printing company salespeople are fluent to a minor degree in desktop publishing–speak, although few will know the difference between TIFF and EPS. They can tell you when to give them negs (film negatives) and paper, and which service bureau to use if they don't have an imagesetter in-house. Many can tell you which software their clients prefer and which software packages create problems, and they can give you tips that can help you get your project through the process without problems.

A service bureau is a company that has on its premises an imagesetter, and whose function is to provide the general community of desktop publishers with imagesetter output at a cost between $7 and $40 per page. Service bureaus often have color output capabilities, and offer disk-conversion and other services that are sometimes needed by desktop publishers.

Better yet, do what I did: Work at a printing company for a short period of time. The first job I had out of college, working in the prepress department of a four-color commercial printer, taught me more than I learned in four years of school. The experience instilled in me some of the most important basic skills for graphics design that I still use and need every day. Ever wonder why your printer gets so grumpy when you say your negs won't be available until two days past the promised date? Working at a printing company can give you an understanding of job scheduling, an art of prophecy and voodoo that gives ulcers to printing company managers and supervisors.

The more you know about printing and your printer, the better your print job will turn out, and the fewer hassles you will have to deal with.

Illustrator creates spot colors whenever you specify a spot color in a swatch. If you use six different spot colors and Black, you could print out seven different spot color separations.

Spot colors do have their limitations and disadvantages. The primary limitation of using only spot colors is that the number of colors is restricted to the number of color separations that you want to produce. Remember that the cost of a print job is directly related to the number of different colored inks in the job.

The cutoff point for using spot colors is usually three colors. When you use four spot colors, you limit yourself to four distinct colors and use as many colors as a process color job that can have an almost infinite number of colors. Spot color jobs of six colors are not unusual, however. Sometimes people use more than three spot colors to keep colors distinct and clear. Each of the six colors will be bright, vibrant, and distinct from its neighbors, whereas different process colors seem to fade into one another.

Note   Spot colors are often incorrectly referred to as Pantone colors. Pantone is a brand name for a color matching system. You can select Pantone colors as custom colors and use them in Illustrator, and you can print them as either spot colors or as process colors.

Process Color Separation

Process color separation, also known as four-color separation, creates almost any color by combining cyan, magenta, yellow, and black inks. By using various combinations of different tints of each of these colors, you can reproduce many of the colors (more than 16 million of them) that the human eye can see.

Process printing uses a *subtractive* process. You start with bright white paper, and darken the paper with various inks. Cyan, magenta, and yellow are the subtractive primaries, and black is added to create true black printing, which the primaries together don't do very well.

The use of process color separation is advisable when:

✦ The illustration includes color photographs.

✦ The illustration contains more than three different colors.

How Many Colors?

Everyone always says that you can create as many colors as you could ever want when you are using process colors. Maybe.

In Illustrator, you can specify colors up to $\frac{1}{100}$ percent accuracy. As a result, 10,000 different shades are available for each of the four process colors. So, theoretically, $10,000^4$, or 10,000,000,000,000,000, different colors should be available, which is 10 quadrillion or 10 million billion. Any way you look at it, you have a heck of a lot of color possibilities.

Unfortunately, most imagesetters and laser printers can produce only 256 different shades for each color. This limitation of the equipment (not PostScript) drops the number of available colors to 256^4, or 4,294,967,296, which is about 4.3 billion colors — only 1 billionth of the colors that Illustrator can create.

This limitation is fortunate for us humans however, because the estimate is that we can detect a maximum of 100 different levels of gray, probably less. As a result, we can view only 100^4, or 100,000,000, different colors.

We can run into a problem when we preview illustrations, however. An RGB monitor (used on computers) can display up to 16.7 million colors, theoretically, if each Red, Green, and Blue pixel can be varied by 256 different intensities. Most low-end Macintoshes and Windows machines can create only 32,768 colors with their on-board video, and some are limited to 256 colors (or — gasp! — grayscale). You need to add special video cards or additional VRAM (Video RAM) to those computers to display the 16.7 million colors that monitors can produce.

Another problem is that about 30% of the colors that you can view on an RGB monitor can't be reproduced by using cyan, magenta, yellow, and black inks on white paper. You can't create these unprintable colors in Illustrator, but you can create them in most other drawing and graphics software packages. These colors are for on-screen viewing pleasure only.

The secret to process color separation is that the four colors that make up all the different colors are themselves not visible. Each color is printed as a pattern of tiny dots, angled differently from the other three colors. The angles of each color are very important. If the angles are off even slightly, a noticeable pattern that is commonly known as a *moiré* emerges.

The colors are printed in a specific order — usually cyan, magenta, yellow, and black. Although the debate continues about the best order in which to print the four colors, black is always printed last.

To see the dots for each color, use a magnifying device to look closely at something that is preprinted and in full color. Even easier, look at the Sunday comics, which have bigger dots than most other printed pieces. The different color dots in the Sunday comics are quite visible, and their only colors are magenta, cyan, yellow, and black.

The size of the dots that produce each of these separations is also important. The smaller the dots, the smoother the colors appear. Large dots (such as those in the Sunday comics) can actually take away from the illusion of a certain unified color because the different color dots are visible.

For more information on the common dot sizes and on the relation of dot size to the quality of the illustration, see the section "Setting Up the Halftone Screen," later in this chapter.

Figure 18-10 shows how process colors are combined to create new colors. In the figure, the first four rows show very large dots. The top three rows are cyan, magenta, and yellow. The fourth row is all four process colors combined, and the bottom row shows how the illustration looks when you print it.

Figure 18-10: The top three rows display cyan, magenta, and yellow; the fourth row displays their combination; and the fifth row displays the colors as they will print

Process color printing is best for photographs because photographs originate from a continuous tone that is made on photographic paper from film, instead of dots on a printing press.

In Illustrator, you can convert custom colors to process colors either before or during printing. To convert custom colors to process colors *before* printing, select any objects that have a specific custom color and tint and click the process color icon. The color will be converted to its process color counterpart, and all selected objects will be filled with the new process color combination.

After you click the Process Color icon, if the selected objects become filled with White and the triangles for each process color are at 0%, you have selected objects that contain different colors or tints. Undo the change immediately.

To make sure that you select only objects that have the same color, select one of the objects and choose Edit ⇨ Select ⇨ Same Paint Style. Objects that have different strokes or objects with different tints of the same color will not be selected.

You can convert custom colors to process colors in the Separation dialog box (see the "Working with Different Colors" section, later in this chapter) and in many page layout programs.

Combining Both Spot and Process Color Separations

You can couple spot colors with process colors in Illustrator simply by creating both process and named spot colors in a document.

Usually, you add spot colors to process colors for these reasons:

✦ You are using a company logo that has a specific color. By printing that color as a spot color, you make it stand out from the other coloring. In addition, color is more accurate when it comes from a specific ink rather than from a process color combination. Often, the logo is a Pantone color that doesn't reproduce true to form when you use process color separation.

✦ You need a color that you can't create by using process colors. Such colors are most often metallic or fluorescent, but they can be any number of Pantone colors or other colors that you can't match with process colors.

✦ You need a varnish for certain areas of an illustration. A varnish is a glazed type of ink that results in a shiny area wherever you use the varnish. You commonly use varnishes on titles and logos and over photographs.

✦ You need a light color over a large area. The dots that make up process colors are most noticeable in light colors, but by using a spot color to cover the area with a solid sheet of ink that has no dots, you can make the area smoother and enhance it visually.

In some circumstances, you need to use a spot color as a spot color and also use it as a process color. Normally, you can't do both, but the following steps describe one way to get around this problem:

1. If the color doesn't exist as a swatch, create a swatch for the color.

2. In the Swatch Options (double-click on the swatch), set the pop-up menu to Spot Color and click OK.

3. Duplicate the swatch by dragging it on top of the New Swatch icon (the little piece of paper).

4. In the Swatch Options for the duplicated swatch, set the pop-up menu to Process Color and click OK.

 Tip   You can tell which swatch is which by looking at the lower right corner of the swatches; the spot color swatch will have a white triangle with a "spot" in it, the process swatch will be solid.

The End of Adobe Separator

One of the biggest disappointments I ever experienced was seeing Adobe Separator in the Adobe Illustrator 5.0 and 5.5 folders on my hard drive after I installed those versions. You can imagine my joy when I heard whispers, rumors, and finally read the press release for Illustrator 6, which stated something grandiose like, "You can even print your separations directly from Illustrator 6!" I'll tell you, I'd like to meet the guy who writes those things and give him a piece of my mind. But that's old news, thank goodness.

Using Separation Setup

After you choose File ➪ Separation Setup, the Separation Setup dialog box appears (shown in Figure 18-11). The left side shows how the illustration is aligned on the page and which elements will print with the illustration. The right side contains all the options for how the illustration is to print on the page.

The picture on the left side initially shows the illustration on a portrait-oriented page, even if landscape was selected in Illustrator. The various marks shown on the page are the defaults. You can move or rearrange them by clicking and dragging.

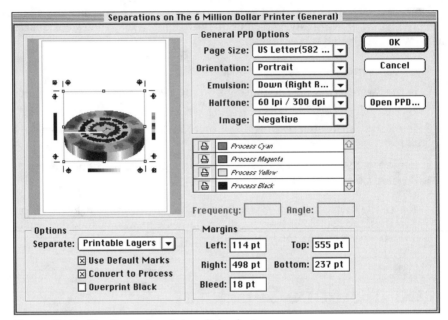

Figure 18-11: The Separation Setup dialog box

The Bounding Box and Bleed

A bounding box surrounds the illustration, and only the parts of the illustration that are within this bounding box will print. Anything outside of the bounding box will be cropped off. When you first open the Separation Setup dialog box, the bounding box is the size of the illustration. The bounding box is as wide and as tall as is necessary to include all the printable objects in the illustration.

When you resize the bounding box manually (by clicking on the edges or corners and dragging), the numbers in the bounding box text fields (at the very bottom of the dialog box) change because the four text fields correspond to the location of each edge of the bounding box. You also can resize the bounding box by typing new values in the bounding box text fields. The bounding box instantly reflects changes that you make in these text fields.

Tip   You can move the illustration within the bounding box by placing the cursor within the bounding box and clicking and dragging. As you move the illustration out of the bounding box, the illustration is cropped off at its edges.

The Bleed text field in the lower right of the Separation Setup dialog box defines how much of the illustration can be outside of the bounding box and still print. The default for bleed is 18 points, regardless of the size of the bounding box. To change the bleed, enter a distance in points in the Bleed text field. As you type the numbers, the bleed will change dynamically.

Bleed is useful when you want an illustration to go right up to the edge of the page. You need to account for bleed when you create an illustration in Illustrator so that the illustration is the correct size with *X* amount of bleed.

Changing Printer Information

To change the PPD, click the Open PPD button in the upper right of the dialog box. The Open a PostScript Printer Description (PPD) file window appears, as shown in Figure 18-12.

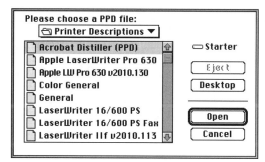

Figure 18-12: The Open a PostScript Printer Description file window

Select the PPD file that is compatible with your printer and click the Open button. Adobe Illustrator Installer places the PPD folder in the Utilities folder automatically.

Caution PPDs were created with specific printers in mind. Unpredictable and undesirable results can occur when you use a PPD for a different printer than it is intended for. If you don't have a PPD for your printer and must use a substitute, always test the substitute PPD before relying on it to perform correctly.

If your printer's PPD is not included with Illustrator, contact the dealer from whom you purchased the printer and ask for it. If you bought the printer by mail order or from a retail store, the dealer will probably not have a PPD for you and may not even know what a PPD is. In this case, contact the printer manufacturer directly. Another place to find PPDs from manufacturers is on online services such as America Online. Adobe does *not* have PPDs for printers other than the ones supplied with the software.

Tip If you have two or more printers in your workplace, chances are that from time to time you will change the PPD file in the Separation Setup dialog box. To make this task easier, open the PPD folder on the hard drive, select all the PPD files that you don't use, and drag them to the trash. Having a shorter list to choose from makes finding the right PPD much easier and frees up space on the hard drive. If you get a new printer at a later date and need a different PPD, you can get it from the Illustrator floppy disk or CD-ROM.

When you choose a different PPD file, the information in the main panel changes to reflect the new selection. Certain default settings in the pop-up menus are activated at this time. You can change the settings at any time, but most of them will revert to the defaults if you choose a new PPD.

Changing Page Size

The Page Size pop-up menu lists the available page sizes for the printer whose PPD is selected, *not* the printer selected in the Chooser or your default Windows printer. For laser printers, few page and envelope sizes are supported. For imagesetters, many sizes are supported, and an Other option enables you to specify the size of the page that you want to print on.

When you choose Other in the Page Size pop-up menu, you see the Other dialog box. The default measurements in the box are the smallest size area that the current illustration can fit within. Enter the width and height of the desired page in their respective boxes. You can use the Offset option to move the illustration a certain distance from the right edge of the page, and you can save media by using the Transverse option to turn the image sideways on the paper or film that it is printing on.

Imagesetters print on rolls of paper or film. Depending on the width of the roll, you may want to print the image sideways. For example, on a Linotronic 180 or 230 imagesetter, paper and film rolls are commonly 12 inches wide. For letter-size pages, you should check the Transverse option to print the letter-size page with the short end along the length of the roll. For a tabloid page (11 x 17 inches), do not check the Transverse option because you want the long edge (17 inches) of the page to be printed along the length of the roll. If you check Transverse for a tabloid-size document, 5 of the 17 inches will be cropped off because the roll is not wide enough. As always when trying something new with printing, run a test or two before sending a large job.

Note   The page size that you select in the Page Size pop-up menu determines the size of the page on the left side of the main panel. The measurements next to the name of the page size are not the page measurements; instead, they are the measurements of the imageable area for that page size. The imageable-area dimensions are always less than the dimensions of the page so that the margin marks can fit on the page with the illustration.

Changing the Orientation

The Orientation setting controls how the illustration is placed on the page. You have two choices from the pop-up menu: Portrait and Landscape.

Selecting Portrait causes the illustration to print with the sides of the illustration along the longest sides of the page. Selecting Landscape causes the illustration to print with the top and bottom of the illustration along the longest sides of the page.

Usually, the orientation reflects the general shape of the illustration. If the illustration is taller than it is wide, you usually choose Portrait orientation. If the illustration is wider than it is tall, you usually choose Landscape orientation.

Note

It doesn't matter to Illustrator whether the illustration fits on the page in one or both of these orientations. If you can't see all four edges of the bounding box, chances are the illustration will be cropped.

Orientation is quite different from Transverse in the Other Page Size dialog box. Orientation changes the orientation of the illustration on the page, but Transverse changes the way that the page is put on the paper. A seemingly small difference, but a distinct and important one to understand.

Figure 18-13 shows an illustration that is placed on a page in both Portrait and Landscape orientations, with and without the Transverse option selected.

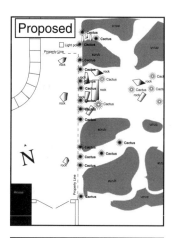
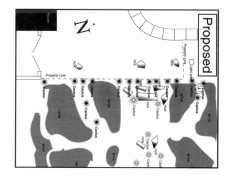
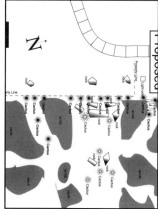
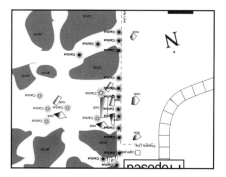

Figure 18-13: An illustration placed on a page in Portrait orientation (upper left), Landscape orientation (lower left), Portrait with Transverse checked (upper right), and Landscape with Transverse checked (lower right)

Understanding Emulsion

Hang out around strippers (at a commercial printing company . . . get your mind out of the gutter), and you will hear them constantly talk about "emulsion up" and "emulsion down." What they are referring to is the black stuff on film. If you have a piece of film from a printer lying around, look at it near a light. One side is shinier than the other side. That side is the side without emulsion. When you are burning plates for presses, the emulsion side (dull side) should always be toward the plate.

In the Separation Setup dialog box, you use the Emulsion option to control which side the emulsion goes on. If you are printing negatives on film, choose Down (right reading) from the Emulsion pop-up menu. For printing on paper, just to see what the separations look like, choose Up (right reading). Always consult with your printer for the correct way to output film.

Note   Although "wrong reading" isn't an option in the Separation Setup dialog box, you can reverse an illustration by choosing the opposite emulsion setting. In other words, Down (right reading) is also Up (wrong reading), and Up (right reading) is also Down (wrong reading).

Reversing text creates the kind of secret code illustrations that you can send to your friends. The only way to understand the illustrations is by viewing them in a mirror. This technique works best with text, of course, and I wouldn't expect to fool really smart people with this type of code.

Thinking of the emulsion as the toner in a laser printer may help you understand this concept better. If the toner is on the top of the paper, you can read it fine, as always (Up emulsion, right reading). If the toner is on the bottom of the paper, and you can read the illustration only when you place the paper in front of a light, the emulsion is Down, right reading. Thinking along these lines helped me back when I was new to the printing industry, and it should help you as well.

Setting Up the Halftone Screen

The halftone screen setting is one of the great mysteries of life to the graphic designer who has not been informed about it. A too-low halftone screen setting renders an illustration terribly, making text and pictures unclear and fuzzy, sometimes even showing the dots that create the tints in the illustration. But if the halftone screen setting is too high, blends and gradations will show banding, and some areas or the entire illustration may look posterized. The halftone setting can be too high for a particular press, resulting in smeary, terrible-looking results. Blends, gradations, and how to avoid banding are discussed in Chapter 10.

Understanding Halftone Line Screens

The most common mistake that graphic designers make is confusing dots-per-inch (dpi) with lines-per-inch (lpi). Lines-per-inch is another way of saying line screen or halftone line screen.

The number of dots-per-inch of the output device controls what the potential lines-per-inch settings are. The higher the dpi, the higher the lpi can be, but the higher the lpi, the lower the possible number of grays.

In bitmap graphics software such as Photoshop, the dpi of the image is also important. In Illustrator, objects that you create are based on locations of points rather than on dots-per-inch. Trust me, dealing with an image's dots-per-inch is no picnic, and the fact that Illustrator can bypass this specification entirely is a great boon. Of course, if you have placed or imported pixel-based images in your file, you haven't learned anything. . . .

Line screens are made up of a combination of halftone cells. Each halftone cell has a certain number of dots within it that can be turned on and off. Usually the dots are turned on and off in a round pattern to create a halftone dot.

As an example, consider a common dpi/lpi ratio, that of a 300-dpi laser printer with a 60-line screen. Each halftone dot is made up of a 5 x 5 halftone cell (300/60 = 5). The number of pixels within each cell is 25. Figure 18-14 shows 5 x 5 halftone cells at different percentages.

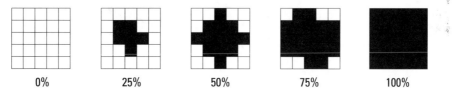

Figure 18-14: 5x5 halftone cells at different percentages

At a 25% tint, 25% of the dots are black. In a halftone cell of 25 dots, 6.25 dots would be black. Because you cannot print a quarter of a dot with this method, 6 dots are black.

Because the halftone cell has 25 pixels, only 26 levels of gray are available when you are using a 300-dpi laser printer with a 60-lpi screen (1 level for each of the 25 pixels plus 1 level for no pixels on at all yields 26). To get more grays, you need to lower the line screen.

Lower line screens seem rougher than higher line screens. The cutoff point for line screens is about 105; anything higher is considered a fine line screen, and anything lower is a coarse line screen.

A 300-dpi laser printer prints 90,000 dots for every square inch ($300 \times 300 = 90,000$). Figure 18-15 shows one square inch blown up 500% so you can see the different dot patterns in a small gradient.

Figure 18-15: Halftone gradients

In deciding on a halftone screen, you need to consider many things, the most important of which are the type of paper or other media that the image will eventually be printed on and the press that it will be printed on.

Common settings for different types of print jobs are: newsprint and photocopiers, 85 lpi; standard magazines, 133 lpi; better quality magazines, 150 lpi; and high-quality book images, 150 or 175 lpi.

Adding Custom Line Screens

In the Separation Setup dialog box, you can specify the line screen only by selecting one of the choices in the Halftone pop-up menu. This restriction can be very limiting, but you can get around it by doing a serious amount of tinkering, as described in the following steps.

1. Make a copy of the PPD file that you want to add halftone screens to and add a suffix, such as *new,* to its name (for example, `Laserwriter.new`). Open the copy with SimpleText, Notepad, or another word processor.

2. Scroll down to a section that looks very similar to what you see in Figure 18-16. Depending on the PPD chosen, the halftone screen numbers may be different from the ones shown in the figure. Select the entire section and copy it. Press the left arrow once and paste.

3. In the copy, change the numbers highlighted in Figure 18-16 to whatever line screen you choose. Paste the copy and repeat this step for every new halftone screen that you want to include in the PPD file.

4. Save the changes.

5. Open the new PPD in the Separation Setup dialog box. If all went well, new pop-up menu items will reflect your recent changes.

```
*%  For  60  lpi / 300 dpi  ================================

*ColorSepScreenAngle ProcessBlack.60lpi.300dpi/60 lpi / 300 dpi: "45"
*ColorSepScreenAngle CustomColor.60lpi.300dpi/60 lpi / 300 dpi: "45"
*ColorSepScreenAngle ProcessCyan.60lpi.300dpi/60 lpi / 300 dpi: "15"
*ColorSepScreenAngle ProcessMagenta.60lpi.300dpi/60 lpi / 300 dpi: "75"
*ColorSepScreenAngle ProcessYellow.60lpi.300dpi/60 lpi / 300 dpi: "0"

*ColorSepScreenFreq ProcessBlack.60lpi.300dpi/60 lpi / 300 dpi: "60"
*ColorSepScreenFreq CustomColor.60lpi.300dpi/60 lpi / 300 dpi: "60"
*ColorSepScreenFreq ProcessCyan.60lpi.300dpi/60 lpi / 300 dpi: "60"
*ColorSepScreenFreq ProcessMagenta.60lpi.300dpi/60 lpi / 300 dpi: "60"
*ColorSepScreenFreq ProcessYellow.60lpi.300dpi/60 lpi / 300 dpi: "60"
```

Figure 18-16: The line screen values that can be changed in a text editor

The final thing to think about when you are choosing a halftone screen is the type of media that the illustration will be output on from an imagesetter. If the output will be on paper, the halftone screen needs to be lower than if the output will be on film.

The Printing Process and Saving $$ with Your Computer

The following brief rundown of the process that a printer goes through when taking a job from start to finish can help you understand some of the choices that you need to make when you are printing out of Separator. Of course, the following is a generalization, and all printers do things a little differently.

First, the printer gathers all of the materials for the print job. These materials may include artwork, logos, photos, and copy. The materials may go to different places, depending on what equipment the printer has. A typical commercial printer has limited prepress equipment in-house.

Color artwork and color photos are sent to a color separation house that specializes in creating film separations from full-color originals. The cost for each piece of artwork can range from $50 to $1,000, depending on the quality desired and the quantity.

Black-and-white artwork is shot with a camera (usually in-house) and resized to fit. Text is sent to a typesetting firm and set.

Black-and-white artwork and text are pasted on to pasteboards, proofed, and then shot with a camera. A stripper takes the resulting film to a light table where any seams in the film are opaqued out.

Film from the separation houses is stripped into the film from the artwork and type. This particular process is the most time-consuming and adds substantially to the prepress portion of the labor bill.

At this point, proofs are created. Printers may use many different proofing methods, but the least expensive and most basic is the *blueline,* so called for the blue color of the text and artwork that appears on the sheets.

After the blueline is approved (or *if,* to be more precise), each piece of film is used to create a printing press plate for each color.

The plates are applied to presses, and the number of copies specified by the customer is run, plus several more copies to account for errors in printing and cutting.

After the ink on the printed paper dries, the copies are cut along crop marks, bound, and folded along fold marks. Depending on the type of product, the printed pieces may be bound, folded, and cut in any order.

The final piece is boxed and shipped to the client.

If you do everything you can with your system, you can save substantial amounts of money in all of the prepress areas. Do as many of the following as possible to save money and avoid problems:

✦ Do as much as you can electronically — this is one rule you should live by.

✦ Have someone else proof your work *before* you output it to film. Objectivity for your own work decreases geometrically in relation to the time you spend working on it. Your subconscious doesn't want to find mistakes.

✦ Get a separation house to scan photos and traditionally created artwork. Have the separation house provide you with the files on disk. Sure, you can buy a flatbed desktop scanner inexpensively, but color pictures from them can look like mush next to scans from a drum scanner at a separation house.

✦ Assemble all your artwork, type, and photos in QuarkXPress, FrameMaker, or PageMaker.

✦ Have all film negatives output by a reputable service bureau. If your job contains a large amount of color artwork or photos, or if you need the artwork and color photos to be of the best possible quality, take everything back to the color separation house to have your job output at a better quality than most imagesetters can produce.

Changing from Positive to Negative to Positive

You use the Image pop-up menu to switch between printing positive and negative images. Usually, you use a negative image for printing film negatives and a positive image for printing on paper. The default for this setting, regardless of the printer chosen or PPD selected, is Negative.

Working with Different Colors

At the lower right of the Separation Setup dialog box, a color list window displays where you can select different colors and set them to print or not print, and set Custom Colors to process separately.

The list of colors contains only the colors that are used in that particular illustration. At the top of the list of separation colors are the four process colors in italic, if they, or spot colors that contain those process colors, are used in the illustration. Below the process colors is a list of all the spot colors in the document.

Caution   If the illustration has any guides in it, their colors are reflected in the color list window. From looking at the preview of the illustration in the Separation Setup dialog box, you can't easily determine that these blank separations will print. The best thing to do is release all guides and delete them.

By default, all process colors are set to print, and all spot colors are set to convert to process colors. Clicking the Convert To Process checkbox at the bottom of the Separation Setup dialog box toggles between converting everything (checked) and spot colors (unchecked).

Each color in the list has its own frequency and angle. Don't change the angle or frequency for process colors because Separator has automatically created the best values for the process colors at the halftone screen you've specified. Instead, make sure that any spot colors that may be printing have different angles from each other so that no patterns develop from them.

As soon as you type new values or check different options using the color list, the changes are applied.

Separations

To print with the settings you've selected, click OK in the Separation Setup dialog box and then choose File ➪ Print (or press ⌘-P [Ctrl+P]). This displays the Print dialog box. On a Mac, select Adobe Illustrator from the pop-up menu and change the Output pop-up to Separate. In Windows, change the Output option to Separations. The separations you've specified will print.

Printing Separations from Other Applications

Many other software programs, particularly page layout software programs, incorporate color-separation capabilities. These programs usually enable you to import Illustrator files that have been saved as Illustrator EPS files.

When you produce color separations from other software, make sure that any custom colors that are in the Illustrator illustration are present and accessible in the document that the illustration is placed within. Usually, you can set the custom colors to process separately or to spot separately.

Caution   You cannot change the colors of an imported Illustrator EPS document in a page layout program, so be sure that the colors are correct for the illustration while it is in Illustrator.

Trapping

Trapping is one of the most important but least understood issues in all of printing. In the past, desktop publishing has been noted for its inefficiency in trapping, but QuarkXPress and a few after-the-fact trapping software packages, such as Luminus TrapWise and Island Trapper, have gradually bettered the trapping capabilities of electronic publishing.

 Caution Illustrator, while it does incorporate a trapping filter, is not a trap-happy piece of software. For detailed illustrations, it usually isn't worth your time to set the trapping inside Illustrator; instead, you'll want to have your printer do the work for you.

Understanding What Trapping Does

Traps solve alignment problems when color separations are produced. The most common problem that occurs from misalignment is the appearance of white space between different colors.

 Note The thought of trapping scares many graphic designers—not just because they don't know how to do it, but also because they aren't sure what trapping is and what purpose it serves. Understanding the concept of trapping is the hard part; trapping objects is easy (though somewhat tedious in Illustrator).

Figure 18-17 shows a spot color illustration with four colors. The top row shows each of the individual colors. The first illustration in the second row shows how the illustration prints if all the separations are aligned perfectly. The second illustration in the second row shows what happens when the colors are misaligned. The third illustration in the second row shows how the illustration looks when trapped, with black indicating where two colors overprint each other.

This example shows extreme misalignment and excessive trapping; I designed it just as a black-and-white illustration for this book. Ordinarily, the overprinting colors may appear a tiny bit darker, but they do not show as black. I used black so that you can see what parts of the illustration overlap when trapping is used. The trapping in this case is more than sufficient to cover any of the white gaps in the second illustration.

Trapping is created by spreading or choking certain colors that touch each other in an illustration. To spread a color, enlarge an object's color so that it takes up more space around the edges of the background area. To choke a color, expand the color of the background until it overlaps the edges of an object.

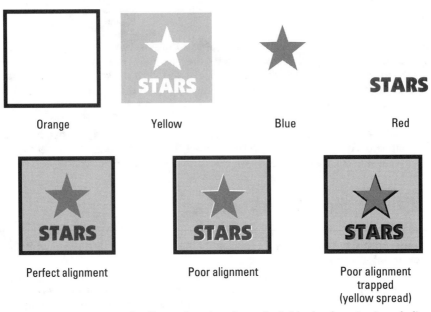

Orange   Yellow   Blue   Red

Perfect alignment   Poor alignment   Poor alignment
trapped
(yellow spread)

Figure 18-17: A Spot Color illustration that shows individual colors (top) and aligned, misaligned, and trapped composites

The major difference between a spread and a choke has to do with which object is considered the background and which object is the foreground. The foreground object is the object that traps. If the foreground object is spread, the color of the foreground object is spread until it overlaps the background by a certain amount. If the foreground object is choked, the color of the background around the foreground object is expanded until it overlaps the foreground object by a certain amount.

Tip   To determine whether to use a choke or a spread on an object, compare the lightness and darkness of the foreground and background objects. The general rule of thumb is that lighter colors expand or contract into darker colors.

Figure 18-18 shows the original misaligned illustration and two ways of fixing it with trapping. The middle star has been spread by 1 point, and the third star has been choked by 1 point.

Original   Blue (star shape)   Blue (star shape)
                     1 pt spread   1 pt choke

Figure 18-18: The original illustration (left), fixing the star by spreading it 1 point (middle), and fixing the star by choking it 1 point (right)

Why Color Separations Do Not Properly Align and Require Trapping

The three reasons why color separations don't align properly are that the negatives are not the same size, the plates on the press are not aligned perfectly when printing, or the gods have decided that a piece is too perfect and needs gaps between abutting colors. Trapping is required because it is a solution for covering gaps that occur when color separations do not properly align.

Negatives can be different sizes for a number of reasons. When the film was output to an imagesetter, the film may have been too near the beginning or the end of a roll, or separations in the same job may have been printed from different rolls. The pull on the rollers, while fairly precise on all but top-of-the-line imagesetters, where it should be perfect, can pull more film through when there is less resistance (at the end of a roll of film), or less film when there is more resistance (at the beginning of a roll of film). The temperature of the film may be different if a new roll is put on in the middle of a job, causing the film to shrink (if it is cold) or expand (if it is warm).

The temperature of the processor may have risen or fallen a degree or two while the film was being processed. Once again, cooler temperatures in the chemical bays and in the air dryer as the film exits the process have an impact on the size of the film.

Film negatives usually don't change drastically in size, but they can vary up to a few points on an 11-inch page. That distance is huge when a page has several abutting colors throughout it. The change in a roll of film is almost always along the length of the roll, not along the width. The quality of the film is another factor that determines how much the film will stretch or shrink.

Most strippers are quite aware of how temperature affects the size of negatives. A common stripper trick is to walk outside with a freshly processed negative during the colder months to shrink a negative that may have enlarged slightly during processing.

Check with your service bureau staff to see how long they warm up the processor before sending jobs through it. If the answer is less than an hour, the chemicals will not be at a consistent temperature, and negatives that are sent through too early will certainly change in size throughout the length of the job. Another question to ask is how often they change their chemicals and check the density from their imagesetter. Once a week is acceptable for a good-quality service bureau, but the best ones will change chemicals and check density once a day.

The plates on a press can be misaligned by either an inexperienced press operator or a faulty press. An experienced press operator knows the press and what to do to get color plates to align properly. A faulty press is one where plates move during printing or are not positioned correctly. An experienced press operator can determine how to compensate for a faulty press.

No press is perfect, but some of the high-end presses are pretty darn close. Even on those presses, the likelihood that a job with colors that abut one another can print perfectly is not very great.

If a job doesn't have some sort of trapping in it, it probably will not print perfectly, no matter how good the negatives, press, and press operator are.

How Much Trap?

The amount of trap that you need in an illustration depends on many things, but the deciding factor is what your commercial printer tells you is the right amount.

The most important thing to consider is the quality of the press that the printer will use. Of course, only the printer knows which press your job will run on, so talking to the printer about trapping is imperative.

Other factors to consider include the colors of ink and types of stock used in the job. Certain inks soak into different stocks differently.

Traps range from $\frac{3}{1,000}$ of an inch to $\frac{6}{1,000}$ of an inch. Most traditional printers refer to traps in thousandths of inches, but Illustrator likes values in points for this sort of thing. Figure 18-19 is a chart with traps in increments of $\frac{1}{1,000}$, from $\frac{1}{1,000}$ of an inch to $\frac{10}{1,000}$ of an inch, and gives their point measurements. The trapped area is represented by black to be more visible in this example.

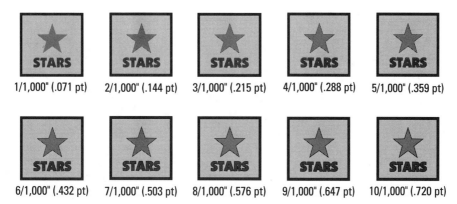

Figure 18-19: Different trap amounts

Remember that the greater the trap, the less chance that any white gaps will appear, but the trap may actually be visible. Visible traps of certain color pairs can look almost as bad as white space.

Trapping Illustrator Files Manually

In Illustrator, you accomplish manual (nonfilter) trapping by selecting a path's Stroke or Fill and setting it to overprint another path's Stroke or Fill. The amount that the two paths' Fills or Strokes overlap and overprint is the amount of trap that is used.

The most basic way to create a trap on an object is by giving it a Stroke that is either the Fill color of the object (to create a spread) or the Fill color of the background (to create a choke).

Be sure to make the width of any Stroke that you use for trapping twice as wide as the intended trap, because only half of the Stroke (one side of the path) actually overprints a different color. In some circumstances, fixing a Stroke that is not wide enough initially can be difficult.

1. Select one path of a pair of overlapping or abutting paths. If possible, select the lighter of the two paths.

2. Give the selected path a Stroke of the same color that the Fill is. Change the weight to the amount of trap you'd like to use. For this example, so it could be seen easily in this book, I've used a 3-point trap.

3. Set the overlapping Stroke to overprint. These steps are shown in Figure 18-20.

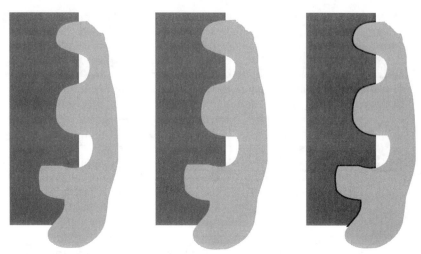

Figure 18-20: Steps for manual trapping

Trapping with Trap

For this example, I'll use the same paths from Figure 18-20 to show how Trap works.

1. Select all pieces of art that are overlapping or abutting.

2. Choose Trap from the Pathfinder palette. (You will find the Trap button when you choose Options from the Pathfinder pop-up menu.) Then enter the width into the Width text field (see Figure 18-21).

3. Click OK and the object has trapping applied instantly (well, if the artwork is complex it won't be instant. . .).

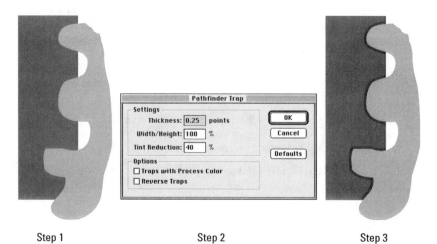

Step 1   Step 2   Step 3

Figure 18-21: Steps for trapping with Trap

Complex Trapping Techniques in Illustrator

The preceding trap illustrations are extremely simplified examples of trapping methods in Illustrator. In reality, objects never seem to be a solid color, and if they are, they are never on a solid background. In addition, most illustrations contain multiple overlapping objects that have their own special trapping needs.

I consider trapping to be complex when I can't just go around selecting paths and applying trap quickly. Complex trapping involves several different techniques:

✦ **Create a separate layer for trapping objects.** By keeping trapping on its own layer, you make myriad options available that are not available if the trapping is intermixed with the rest of the artwork. Place the new layer above the other layers. Lock all the layers but the trapping layer so that the original artwork is not modified. You can turn trapping on and off by hiding the entire layer or turning off the Print option in the Layers Options dialog box.

✦ **Use the round joins and ends options in the Stroke portion of the Paint Style palette for all trapping Strokes.** Round joins and ends are much less conspicuous than the harsh corners and 90-degree angles of other joins and ends, and they blend smoothly into other objects.

✦ **Trap gradations by stroking them with paths that are filled with overprinting gradients.** You cannot Fill Strokes with gradients, but you can Fill paths with gradients. You can make any Stroke into a path by selecting it and choosing Outline from the Pathfinder palette. After you have transformed the Stroke into a path, Fill it with the gradient and check the Overprint Fill box (in the Attributes palette) for that path.

Note

Whenever I start a heavy-duty trapping project, I always work on a copy of the original illustration. Wrecking the original artwork is just too easy when you add trapping.

When Trapping Yourself Isn't Worth It

Before you spend the long amounts of time that complex trapping entails and modify your illustration beyond recognition (at least in Artwork mode), you may want to reconsider whether you should do the trapping yourself.

If you estimate that trapping your job will require several hours of work, the chances of doing it correctly dwindle significantly. If the illustration includes many crisscrossing blends and gradations or multiple placed images, you may not have the patience to get through the entire process with your sanity intact.

If you determine that you cannot do the trapping yourself, you can have it done after the fact with Liminus TrapWise or Island Trapper, or you can have a service bureau with special output devices create trapping automatically. These services will undoubtedly cost more than doing the trapping yourself, but it will get done right, which is the important thing.

Summary

✦ Print separations from within Illustrator.

✦ Choose whether to print a composite or separations from the Print dialog box.

✦ Determine separation information in the Separation Setup dialog box.

✦ Prevent potential white strips that can appear when a printer isn't perfectly aligned with trapping.

✦ Separation Setup lets you specify which colors print, and what angle and frequency they print at.

✦ ✦ ✦

Getting the Most Out of Illustrator

Along with using Illustrator to do all types of incredible artwork is the practical, real-world side of Illustrator where deadlines have to be met and there's little or no time for play. This chapter focuses on real-world applications of Illustrator and on how to get the most out of the software.

What You Can Learn from Existing Artwork

Examples are a wonderful teacher for Illustrator. In light of this, I've included several figures from the color insert of *Illustrator 8 Bible* on the accompanying CD-ROM, so when you see a figure, you'll know exactly how it was created. But just looking at art doesn't tell you too much except that maybe a blend was used where you thought a gradient would be, and, hey, that isn't a pattern, it's really individual paths.

You can learn how to create better artwork by dissecting existing artwork and trying to modify it.

Taking Apart Artwork

Artwork created in Illustrator usually consists of hundreds of paths. Some of those paths are Filled, some are Stroked, others may be Filled and Stroked.

The best way to get started is by looking at the illustration in Artwork mode. This shows the basic framework of the art, and is the best first step in understanding how it was created.

Unfortunately, Artwork mode doesn't show you when paths are perfectly overlapping. For that, you'll need to switch between Artwork and Preview modes, or even delve into Preview Selection mode.

Making Your Art Easy to Understand

Possibly the most frustrating thing about editing artwork occurs when there was a different author of the original work. People have their own way of doing things, and while one way isn't necessarily better than another, there are a few things you can do to make your artwork more editable in the future. After all, it may be you opening up your art in a few months or years, and you'll never remember what screwy grouping methods you used that may have made sense back then.

One thing you can do that will make your art easier to interpret is to use common groupings. Masks should be grouped to the paths they mask. Text converted to outlines should be grouped together. The paths in objects should be grouped together. Related objects can be grouped to each other.

But more important than grouping is to use layers. Proper use of layers will let your artwork be compartmentalized quickly and easily, providing not only easy access for selecting and modifying sets of paths, but also a means for controlling printing of the illustration.

Copyrighting Your Electronic Artwork

This is the opposite of the previous section. Often, you'll have done artwork that you'd rather not have anyone mess with. Unfortunately, there's no foolproof way of doing this, but you can put your "stamp" on any illustration and make it difficult for a wouldbe art thief to abscond with your artwork.

The most basic way of doing this is to put a copyright notice on each object in the document using the Attributes dialog box, which is shown in Figure 19-1.

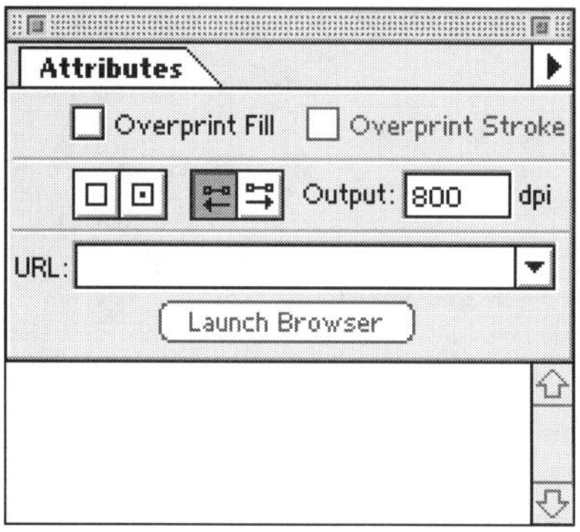

Figure 19-1: Attributes dialog box

1. Select the artwork you wish to copyright.

2. Choose Window ⇨ Show Attributes (F11), which displays the Attributes Palette. To display the note option choose Show Note from the Attributes pop-up menu.

3. Type your copyright notice in the Notes section.

At this point, all the art in the document you selected will have this note attached.

To make the art more secure, create a white box somewhere outside the Illustration (which can't be selected or deleted easily). You can also lock your artwork. Another thing to do is to create a text box with your copyright notice in it and change the text color to None or White.

You could also use layers to secure copyrighted pieces of art by locking or hiding layers with objects that have the copyright in them.

The Link Manager

New to Illustrator 8 is the addition of a Link Manager. Adobe has brought PageMaker's file management capability into Illustrator. Users link files via the Links palette. This wonderful feature alone will save time and money when it comes to printing out files, especially when you send a file to a printer or service bureau.

Using the Link Manager

The Links palette (see Figure 19-2) shows a list of files embedded in an Illustrator file. The linked files will show up with a small thumbnail view of each image. If you see a triangle symbol with an exclamation point inside, that tells you that the original image has changed and was not updated in your file. A stop sign symbol with a question mark inside tells you that the image was moved from its original folder.

The Links palette pop-up menu (see Figure 19-3) enables you to specify how you want to view the linked files and what you want to do with them.

Figure 19-2: Links palette

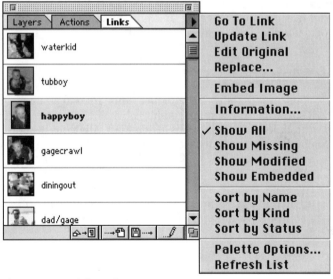

Figure 19-3: Links palette pop-up menu

The options available in the Links palette pop-up menu are:

✦ **Go To Link**: This option shows and selects the link that you have highlighted in the Links palette.

✦ **Update Link**: This option automatically updates the highlighted link to the latest modification of the original file.

✦ **Edit Original**: When you choose Edit Original, the program that created the original image opens so you can make adjustments to the image. The image automatically updates in your Illustrator file.

✦ **Replace**: The Replace option lets you replace the highlighted link with another image.

✦ **Embed Image**: The Embed Image option embeds the linked image to the Illustrator file. When you embed a file, you don't have to include it with the Illustrator file when sending the file to a printer. The Illustrator file has the image's information embedded as part of the file.

✦ **Information**: This option brings up the Link Information dialog box (Figure 19-4). This box tells you the Name, Location, Size, Kind, Creation date, Modification Date, and Transform date.

✦ **Show All**: This displays all of the linked files in the document.

✦ **Show Missing**: This displays the linked files that have been moved and are missing from their original folder.

✦ **Show Modified**: This displays all of the linked files that have been modified in some way.

✦ **Show Embedded**: This displays all of the linked files that are embedded in the document.

✦ **Sort by Name**: This option sorts the linked files alphabetically.

✦ **Sort by Kind**: This option sorts the linked files by file type.

✦ **Sort by Status**: This option sorts the linked files by showing the embedded files first then the linked ones.

✦ **Palette Options**: The palette options let you choose how you want to view your thumbnails. You have the choice of None, Small, Medium, and Large thumbnail views.

✦ **Refresh List**: This option refreshes the screen list of the linked files.

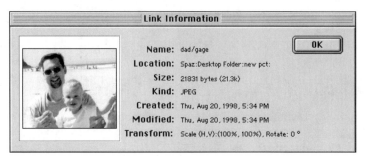

Figure 19-4: Link Information dialog box

The Art in the *Illustrator 8 Bible*

The art in this book was done entirely with Illustrator and Photoshop. The only thing I used Photoshop for was for quickly touching up screen shots. The following sections describe how particular figure types were created.

Paths

One difference between the *Illustrator 8 Bible* and any other Illustrator book is the way I've shown paths in the figures. The easy thing to do is to take screen shots of paths and just use those. Unfortunately, while paths look fine onscreen, they look absolutely hideous on the printed page. So I recreated each path for the artwork views needed in figures, especially those at the front of the book.

Each path is a 0.3-point Stroked Black path; each selected Anchor Point is a 2-point x 2-point Black square with a 0.3 black Stroke (unselected Anchor Points have a White Fill); and each Control Handle is a 2-point x 2-point Black circle with no Stroke. This made the printed paths look the way they do onscreen, but without the jaggies.

1. First draw the path in Illustrator that you want to appear as a path. Change the Stroke to 0.3-point Black.

2. To draw the first point, create one 2-point x 2-point square that is Filled with Black and Stroked with 0.3-point Black.

3. Zoom in to 1600%, and switch to Artwork mode. Drag the center of the square over a point on the path.

4. Option[Alt]-copy the Anchor Point until all the points are properly on the path.

5. Change any Anchor Points to "unselected" Anchor Points by selecting them and Filling them with White.

6. To show Control Handles, first draw a 2-point x 2-point circle and then change the Fill to Black and the Stroke to None.

7. Position the Control Handles over the handles of the original path.

8. Draw lines from the Control Handles to their corresponding Anchor Points.

Of course, for most of my examples that illustrate the Steps procedures, I had to Option[Alt]-copy the objects to the next position and then continue. I often used the Transform palette to accurately control spacing between steps.

Labeled Palettes

To label items within palettes (like the one shown in Figure 19-5), toolboxes, and dialog boxes, I placed a raster image and positioned it on the page. Then I drew one line from the area I wanted to label out of the image, painting the line with a 0.3-point Black Stroke and a Fill of None. I created a label with Point Type, usually using 10-point Futura Book.

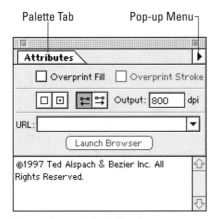

Figure 19-5: Labeled palette

After centering or positioning the type correctly, I Option[Alt]-copied both the label and line, placing the end of the line at the new location on the image. Then I selected the type and the other end of the path with the Direct Selection tool and positioned it accordingly. I repeated that process for each of the labels in a figure.

Color Section Artwork

The artwork in the color section is Illustrator based. To generate the backgrounds, I often selected a portion of the original artwork and scaled it up, and then lightened it with Extensis VectorColor.

Where the background had to be lighter or darker for text, I copied the entire background, placed a path a little larger than the text area on top and masked it, and then lightened or darkened that portion with VectorColor again.

Using Art as Outlines for a Transparency

Use the following steps to create the outlines of the artwork for a transparency. (These steps are similar to the procedure I would use to show the Artwork mode of an Illustration.)

1. Change the Paint Style of the original artwork to a Fill of White and a Stroke of 0.25-point, 100% Black.

2. Release all the masks in the artwork by choosing Edit ⇨ Select All (⌘-A) [Ctrl+A] and then choosing Object ⇨ Mask ⇨ Release (⌘-Option-7) [Ctrl+Alt+7]. Check to see whether all the masks were released by choosing Object ⇨ Mask. If Release is still an option not grayed out, not all the masks have been released. Click Release until the Release option is no longer available.

3. Make any necessary adjustments. After checking the original to determine the weight of the Strokes, change the outline of those paths to that weight and then choose Object ⇨ Path ⇨ Outline ⇨ Path.

If an illustration includes a photograph or imagery created in Photoshop, you'll need to posterize it and outline it in Streamline to produce the outlining you need for a transparency.

Scanning Artwork at the Proper Resolution

By scanning at a high resolution and saving at a lower resolution without changing the file size, you produce an image that you can reduce in Illustrator to much smaller than its blown-up size. You can then use this image for zooming in to high levels of magnification without sacrificing clarity.

The Proper Image Size for Tracing

To produce the best possible image to trace in Illustrator, you have to save the file at the correct size and number of dots-per-inch. As a result, you need to know the original image's size and at what resolution (dpi) it was scanned.

To figure out what dpi to scan at, you first need to decide how much detail you want to be able to see in Illustrator. By *detail*, I am referring to the level at which you want to zoom in and still be able to see the scan clearly. Table 19-1 shows the zoom level as a percentage and the required dpi for scanning to achieve detail at that zoom level. The table also shows how much you need to reduce the image with the Scale tool to return it to the original size.

Table 19-1
Zoom Level Percentages and the DPI for Scanning That's Required to Achieve Detail at a Specified Zoom Level

Zoom	Scan dpi	Scale image	Size (3" x 5" CMYK Color)
100%	72-dpi	100.00%	0.30MB
150%	108-dpi	66.67%	0.68MB
200%	144-dpi	50.00%	1.19MB
300%	216-dpi	33.33%	2.67MB
400%	288-dpi	25.00%	4.75MB
600%	432-dpi	16.67%	10.70MB
800%	576-dpi	12.50%	19.00MB
1200%	864-dpi	8.33%	42.70MB
1600%	1152-dpi	6.25%	75.90MB

If you will be using the image at less than 100%, scanning at 72-dpi is still a good idea.

After you have scanned the image at the proper resolution, open it in Photoshop and select Image ➪ Image Size. In the Image Size dialog box, make sure that the File Size and Proportions checkboxes are checked. Use a setting of 72 in the dpi text field and press OK. Save the file as a raster image format.

In Illustrator, import or place the image and double-click the Scale tool. Enter the reduction amount from the third column of the list in the Uniform text field. You can now trace the image up to and including the zoom specified.

Remember that the size of a pixel-based file may make an Illustrator file unmanageable. A 75MB image requires an enormous amount of time for redrawing and also uses a healthy chunk of the hard drive.

Backgrounds for Illustrations

This section contains examples of backgrounds (see Figure 19-6) and suggestions for creating backgrounds for illustrations. You can create backgrounds in a number of ways. For example, you can use gradients, raster images, blends, and patterns. When you are deciding what type of background to use, remember that you need to consider how well a background will interact with the front artwork.

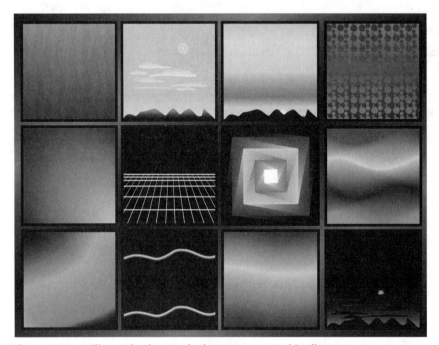

Figure 19-6: Different backgrounds that were created in Illustrator

Using Gradients for Backgrounds

Gradients can be very effective backgrounds all by themselves, providing that they don't detract from the front artwork.

In the following example, I combined linear and radial gradients for an impressive effect.

1. Draw a rectangle to serve as the background area. Create a bottom edge (I used mountains) that will sit in front of the background. For sunsets and other

sky-related backgrounds, try to avoid a flat, horizontal base. Color the mountains or bottom edge with a solid Fill color and then select the background for the rectangle. (You create the gradient after you create the object that it will Fill so that you can instantly see how the gradient will appear in that object in the illustration.)

2. Double-click the Gradient tool to display the Gradient palette (or press F9).

3. In the Gradient palette, make the following color stops: at 0%, White; at 5%, Yellow 100%; at 15%, Yellow 100%; at 25%, Yellow 100% and Magenta 50%; at 35%, Magenta 50%; at 50%, Cyan 15% and Magenta 10%; at 80%, Cyan 25%; and at 100%, Cyan 50%. (The first two 100% Yellow color stops create a solid area of Yellow within the gradient.)

4. Draw a circle in the solid yellow area of the gradient. In the Gradient palette, create a new radial gradient called "Sunset Sun" with the following color stops: at 0%, White; at 5%, Yellow 30%; at 80%, Yellow 60%; at 100%, Yellow 100%. Because the sun blends into the color of the solid band in the sunset gradient, it appears to blend very nicely. In the example, I partially hid the sun behind some of the clouds.

Using the same technique, I created the sun for a blue sky. In the sun gradient, the last color stop is the same color as the sky.

By themselves, gradients can be effective backgrounds. When you combine gradients with patterns, blends, or other objects, they can form a complex, sometimes realistic, backdrop.

Blends and Blend Effects for Backgrounds

You can use several methods to create backgrounds by using blends:

✦ One method is to blend two shapes together, one larger and one smaller. You can achieve different effects by choosing different shapes.

✦ By blending from a large circle to a small circle, you can create a very smooth blend that produces better results than using a radial gradient.

✦ One of the best ways to get a smooth, unobtrusive background when you are using gradients is to blend smoothly curved lines together and mask them in the shape of the background rectangle.

✦ You can achieve interesting highlights between two blend shapes by blending to different points on objects.

✦ You can use the new Gradient Mesh tool.

Using Textures for Backgrounds

There are a variety of ways to create textures in Illustrator, and with version 8, the Ink Pen filter is undoubtedly the most efficient and productive method. With the Ink Pen Effects dialog box, you can quickly change a solid- or gradient-Filled background into a textured background. Several patterns and textures are included on the application CD.

1. Create the background object (typically a rectangle, although you can use any shape) with a gradient Fill. Make sure this object is behind all the other objects. (When using the Pen & Ink filter to create textures, I usually lock all other objects in the document and place the background object on a separate layer. This keeps the typically hundreds or thousands of paths that are generated separate from the rest of the illustration.)

2. Select the background object and choose Filter ➪ Pen & Ink ➪ Hatch Effects. In the dialog box, select Match Objects Color, which makes the texture the same shades as the gradient. Adjust any of the other settings in the Pen & Ink dialog box. Select Preview to view a thumbnail of the effect while the dialog box is still open.

3. Click OK. The texture is generated. If the background is only showing around the edges of your artwork, or takes up less than 50% of the total background area, you may want to ungroup the Fill created with Ink Pen Effects and select and delete the objects that aren't visible. This is much easier if the other objects are locked away on a separate layer.

Another useful texture can be created by modifying a blend somewhat, so that it appears to be textured. With this method of creating a background, you *can't* delete unseen portions of the artwork.

The following steps show one common method of texturizing a blend.

1. Create a blend, either manually or by using the Expand command (Object ➪ Expand) on an existing gradient-Filled object.

2. Select the Blend step—you may want to choose View ➪ Hide Edges (⌘-H) [Ctrl+H] so the mass of selected paths doesn't obscure your view—and choose Filter ➪ Distort ➪ Roughen.

The Actions Palette

A wonderous new addition to Illustrator 8 is the Actions palette (see Figure 19-7). Adobe has borrowed the technology from Photoshop and brought it into Illustrator to ease mundane repetitive tasks. The task of applying color, object transformations, and text functions are easily automated using the Actions palette. Illustrator comes with some prerecorded actions and you can create your own.

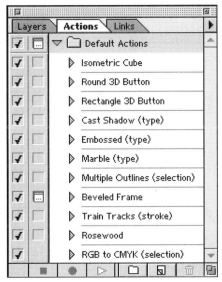

Figure 19-7: The Actions palette

Using a Default Action

The Default Actions are by far the easiest to use. Some Default Actions require a path or type while other Default Actions require nothing. Figure 19-8 shows the result of choosing a few of the Default Actions. To activate a Default Action click on the action to highlight it and then press the Play button.

Figure 19-8: Isometric Cube, Round 3D button, Rectangle 3D button, Cast Shadow (type), Embossed (type), Marble (type), and Train Tracks (Stroke) are a few of the Default Actions

Creating a New Action

If the numerous default actions aren't enough, you can create your own actions. To start recording a new action you need to create a new action. Click on the Create New Action icon at the bottom of the Action palette or choose New Action from the pop-up menu. Hold down the Option [Alt] key to pass up the New Action dialog box to name the action and the action set. After entering a name (I prefer to give it a name so I know what action it does), you hit the Record button and start doing your action. After you are done, you can move the order or delete parts of your action.

Creating a New Set

When you create a new action, it gets put in a folder with a set of actions. You can have multiple actions in a folder, or just one. A new action needs to be a part of a set (or in a folder). It can be an existing set or a new set. Think of actions as packages. To create a new set click on the New Set icon at the bottom of the palette or select New Set from the pop-up menu.

What Is Recordable

In Illustrator, not everything is recordable. As with anything, there are limits. The following list describes what is recordable in the Actions palette:

- ✦ **File**: New, Open, Close, Save, Save as, Save a Copy, Revert, Place, and Export
- ✦ **Edit**: Cut, Copy, Paste, Paste in Front, Paste in Back, Clear, Select All, Deselect All, and Select filters
- ✦ **Object**: Transform Again, Move, Scale, Rotate, Shear, Reflect, Transform Each, Arrange, Group, Ungroup, Lock, Unlock All, Hide Selection, Show All, Expand, Rasterize, Blends, Mask, Compound Path, and Cropmarks
- ✦ **Type**: Block, Wrap, Fit Headline, Create Outlines, Find/Change, Find Font, Change Case, Rows & Columns, Type Orientation, and Glyph Options
- ✦ **Filters**: Colors, Create, Distort, Stylize, and the Photoshop filters
- ✦ **View**: Guides-related only
- ✦ **Palettes**: Color, Gradient, Stroke, Character, MM Design, Paragraph, Tab Ruler, Transform, Pathfinder, Align, Swatch, Brush, Layer, and Attribute
- ✦ **Toolbox tools**: Ellipse, Rectangle, Polygon, Star, Spiral, Move (Selection tool), Rotate, Scale, Shear, and Reflect
- ✦ **Special**: Bounding-box Transform, Insert Select Path, Insert Stop, and Select Objects

Duplicating and Deleting an Action

You can duplicate an action when you want to change something about an existing action and don't want to re-record the whole darn thing. To duplicate an action, first select an action in the Action palette and then choose Duplicate from the pop-up menu. This makes a copy of the action. To change the name of the action double-click on the action to open the Action Options dialog box. You can change the name of an action this way, but not the name of the action set. Deleting an action is pretty easy. Select the action you want to delete and drag it onto the trash icon at the bottom of the palette or use the pop-up menu item.

Starting and Stopping Recording

To start recording, do one of the following:

✦ Create a new action set and action.

✦ Select an existing action and click the Begin Recording icon at the bottom of the palette.

✦ Activate an action and select Start Recording in the pop-up menu.

To stop recording, do one of the following:

✦ Click the Stop Playing/Recording icon button.

✦ Select Stop Recording in the pop-up menu.

Inserting a Menu Item

If you have either duplicated an action, or want to add to an action, you may want to insert an item into the action. To insert a menu item, activate an action, start recording, and select Insert Menu Item from the pop-up menu. This allows you to record most menu items: File, Edit, Object, Type, Filter, and guide-related Views. You don't have to use this to record a menu item.

Inserting a Stop

Insert Stop enables you to stop the play back of an action at a point where you may want to make the action more custom each time you replay it. During your recording select Insert Stop in the pop-up menu. You can have some fun with this one. You are creating your own dialog box. Put in a message just for fun. Always allow the user to continue if they want. This is great for using Actions to partially do the creation, but stops so you can customize it as you wish.

Action Options

The Action Options are where you can name or rename the action, move it to a set, assign a Function Key, or assign a Color to the Action. The Function key is a cool feature that lets you assign an "F" key number to an action so you can just hit the F+number and your action starts.

Playback Options

The Playback Options let you customize your actions even further. You can accelerate, step through, or pause your Actions, as follows:

✦ **Accelerated**: Plays the action all at once, quickly. This is great for monotonous, repetitive actions such as renaming figures or adding a tag line.

✦ **Step by step**: Plays the action one step at a time. This lets you decide whether you want to perform a step or add in-between steps.

✦ **Pause for**: Stops at each step for the specified time. This is a good choice if you want to see closely how something was recorded and would like to stop the recording at a certain spot.

Inserting a Selected Path

You cannot record the Pen tool or the Pencil tool, but you can record a path. First, draw the path, while the path is selected start recording, choose Insert Select Path from the pop-up menu, then stop recording. You have just placed a path in your action.

Selecting an Object

If you want to select an object to use later in your recording, you need to name and select an object or path first, as described in the following steps.

1. Select the object or path.

2. Choose Show Note from the Attributes palette pop-up menu.

3. Enter the name you want to give the object in the bottom field and click the Actions palette to record the new setting.

4. When you need to select the object or path, choose Select Object in the pop-up menu, type in the name you gave it in the Attributes palette, and click OK. The object or path is now selected.

Clearing, Resetting, Loading, Replacing, and Saving Actions

Whew, even after creating a bunch of cool actions, you want more options. You can clear, reset, load, replace, and save actions. Now you can create, delete, load sets, and save to your heart's content. The following describes what each option does:

✦ **Clear Action:** Deletes all the action sets in the Action palette.

✦ **Reset Action:** Resets the palette to the Default Actions.

✦ **Load New or Replace Action:** Lets you navigate to a folder where the action sets are and select one. You can find a ton of prerecorded actions and action sets on the application CD.

✦ **Save Action:** Once you have recorded an action you need to save it just like a file if you want to use it the next time you launch Illustrator. Select Save Action in the pop-up menu and navigate to where you want to save your action set (maybe the Action Sets folder within the application folder?).

Using the Button Mode

Button mode lets you play an action by clicking the button. You can only play — not record — in this mode.

Discovering New Features on Your Own

This book contains many neat tips and techniques. I discovered most of them by doing some really hard playing with Illustrator.

If you are excited and enthusiastic about Illustrator, you will undoubtedly discover things that I didn't include in this book because of a lack of space or a lack of time — or possibly, because I didn't know anything about them.

I have stuffed within these pages all of the best things about Illustrator that other graphic artists who contributed to this book and I could come up with, but I know that in the short time between writing the chapters and having the book appear on bookshelves, I will discover many more things that I could have included.

Illustrator is one of the, if not *the,* most versatile software packages around. There are limits to what you can do with it, but those limits are being pushed farther and farther each time an upgrade appears and every time computer systems become more powerful and cheaper. New technologies will continue to enhance Illustrator's capabilities, but the core of the product will always be the same.

Finding New Features

My observation in the area of finding "new" things that Illustrator can do is that any time I say to myself, "Golly! This sure does take a long time to do!" there is probably a shorter way to do it that I haven't figured out yet.

Note Very rarely do I exclaim "Golly!" but when I do, I take note. Others hearing this outburst take note as well, and, yes, they have recommended counseling.

Like everyone else, I can't just sit and play with Illustrator all day in order to come up with techniques and tips that no one else has yet discovered. But when I do use Illustrator, I make the best use of my time, and I try to use key commands for everything. If I have to pull down a menu because I don't know a key command, it is a sad day in my life.

As I use Illustrator, I try different ways of doing ordinary things. For example, I often select almost everything in an illustration and lock it. The first method that I used for this procedure was to select everything by selecting All, which selected all the objects in the illustration. I then deselected particular objects by Shift-clicking them and choosing Object ➪ Lock (⌘-3) [Ctrl+3]. This method wasn't too productive because I usually had the other items selected (the ones that I didn't want locked) and I had to deselect all of them before I could lock the others.

The second method that I tried was a little better, but I knew that somehow there had to be a better way. Because all the things that I didn't want locked were selected, I chose View ➪ Fit in Window (⌘-0) [Ctrl+0], pressed the Shift key, and dragged a marquee around everything. This action selected all the unselected objects and deselected all the selected objects. I then locked the selected objects.

The third method was the best to that time. Because everything that I wanted to select and lock wasn't selected, I chose Edit ➪ Select ➪ Inverse, which selected everything that wasn't selected and deselected the selected objects. That way I didn't have to select the other objects with the mouse, which always slows me down. Then I locked the selected objects.

Have you noticed that these paragraphs are getting shorter? The method I now use is almost too easy. The objects that I want locked are the only things not selected, so I press Option [Alt] and choose Object ➪ Lock (⌘-Option-3) [Ctrl+Alt+3], which locks everything that isn't selected.

Back when I was Shift-clicking, if I had known that ⌘-Option-3 [Ctrl+Alt+3] locked everything that wasn't selected, I could have avoided a great deal of wasted time and frustration. But because I tried to do this operation so many different ways, I *know* that command and I use it more than ever.

Knowing versus Memorizing

Even if you memorize all the key commands in this book and take the time to memorize all the tips and techniques listed in these pages, you will still not be able to use Illustrator as well as the pros.

To get the most out of Illustrator, you need to use the software until the commands and techniques become intuitive. Memorizing the menus may help you find menu items faster, but knowing in depth what each menu item does will score that information into your subconscious and enable you to use Illustrator better than otherwise possible.

Very few people in the graphic arts industry know Illustrator inside and out; yet the ones who do are producing the best quality illustrations. What does it take to know Illustrator? If you can see in your mind how to create an entire illustration, step by step, you know the software. On the other hand, if you make a mistake in real-life and type a mental ⌘-Z [Ctrl+Z], it's time for therapy.

What You Can Do to Learn More

Read this book inside and out and think to yourself, "Gee, I can do that better *and* faster," and sit down and figure it out. Strangely enough, the first time you discover that you can do something faster than before, doing it will take twice as long as it used to take.

Look at the last three sets of steps in Chapter 17 and figure out how you can reduce the number of steps from 22 to 10. Before I came up with the printed version of the steps for creating a rounded rectangle with reversed corners, I must have thought of five other ways to create it. The method that appears in this book is the fastest, most accurate way to do it. Now if only I could come up with a better, tighter *name* for the darned things.

If you have to Option[Alt]-copy (duplicate a selected object, drag with the Option [Alt] key, and then release the mouse button before the Option [Alt] key) a hundred things, decide whether it would be better to choose Object ➪ Transform ➪ Transform Again (⌘-D) [Ctrl+D] 99 times or to select all the objects 10 times, Option[Alt]-copy *them,* and select Transform Again only 8 more times. Which method is faster for your job? Why?

Is it better to create an object and change the Paint Style information after it is selected or to deselect all (⌘-Shift-A) [Ctrl+Shift+A], change the Paint Style, and then create an object? Or maybe an object on the page already exists, so you can create the object and use the Eyedropper and/or Paintbucket tools to copy the color from one to the other. Or, if an object with that color exists, you can select the object, which changes the Paint Style to that color, and then create the new object.

If you think about all these things as you are drawing, your illustration time will decrease, the quality of your drawings will increase, and you will have more time for using Illustrator to design a solar-powered hang glider, or whatever you do when you aren't using Illustrator for real work.

Getting Answers and Information from Adobe

When you can't find an answer to a problem or want to know whether a way exists to do some tedious task faster, call the Adobe Tech Support line.

Note The main problem with most software company support these days is the "not our fault" answer. (Whatever problem or question you have, it isn't the software company's fault.) You don't find this attitude at Adobe. Most of the support staff are polite and they will help even the most befuddled user along, as well as give additional tips and techniques. The main problem with Adobe Tech Support is the difficulty in reaching a human being. When you call, you get routed through a series of questions ("If you are having trouble designing a hang glider with Adobe Illustrator, press 465") that hardly ever seem to pertain to your particular problem. After a grueling mechanical question-and-answer session, you are put on hold while some tech people argue about who has to answer the call (and other tech people place bets on how long it will be before you hang up). Actually, I'm kidding about the tech support staff's behavior while you are on hold, and I'm sure they jump from one call to the next without pausing to catch a breath. Adobe now has a special support line that you pay a premium for, which the tech people are the first to answer, and most of them pick up within the first movement of the classical music you're forced to listen to.

If you don't need an answer right away, you can fax Adobe. (Check the Adobe Web site or your Illustrator documentation for the correct phone number.) You should get a response within one business day by either phone or return fax. Faxing is great because you can send along your illustration so that the tech people can actually look at it.

In addition, Adobe has a free Bulletin Board Service (BBS) running at 28.8Kbps that anyone can call. Adobe tech people regularly answer posted questions and you can send your Illustrator file along with your questions.

Summary

✦ Taking apart existing artwork is one of the best ways to learn how to create that type of artwork.

✦ To make your art usable and modifiable in the future, create it logically and in an orderly manner; use layers whenever possible.

✦ Use the Links Manager to make outputting your artwork a breeze and hassle-free.

✦ Use gradients, textures, blends, and lightened artwork for quick, effective backgrounds.

✦ Use the Actions palette to streamline repetitive tasks in Illustrator.

✦ Focus on *knowing* Illustrator rather than on memorizing commands and shortcuts.

✦ Talk to other Illustrator users to learn different techniques and to help solve technical snafus.

✦   ✦   ✦

Using the CD-ROM

The CD-ROM that's included with this book is full of surprises:

◆ Trial versions for Adobe Illustrator 8.0, Dimensions 3.0, Streamline 4.0, and Photoshop 5.0

◆ Three new Adobe Plug-Ins from the Illustrator 8 SDK

◆ An exclusive plug-in from Extensis: VectorFrame SE (Mac only)

◆ An exclusive plug-in from Cytopia: Doodle Jr. (Mac only)

◆ Most of the Illustrator artwork that appears in the color section of this book in vector format

◆ LeftyCasual and RansomNote fonts (Mac only)

◆ Demo software and filters

Installing the Trial Versions of Adobe Software

To install the Adobe trial versions on a Macintosh, insert the disc into your CD-ROM drive; go to the specific application's folder and double-click the Install icon; follow the installation instructions.

To install the Adobe trial versions on a PC, insert the disc into your CD-ROM drive; go to the specific application's folder and double-click the `setup.exe` icon; follow the installation instructions.

If you are interested in programming Adobe Illustrator 8 plug-ins, go to Adobe's Web site. The SDK is free and can be obtained from the Web site at: `http://www.adobe.com/supportservice/devrelations`.

Installing and Using VectorFrame SE (Mac Only)

A fully functional trial version of VectorTools is included on your CD-ROM, but it will only work for 30 days before expiring. The VectorFrame SE plug-in we've included on the CD-ROM, on the other hand, is completely self-sufficient, and won't expire. Ever! If you're planning on buying VectorTools, or already have it, then you can ignore the instructions in this section and use VectorFrame with the free trial or as a fully functional package. The only difference is the SE plug-in (on this CD) is chosen from the Windows menu. However, you may want to install VectorFrame SE to take advantage of the five additional presets you'll get from VectorFrame SE in addition to the five in VectorFrame.

To install VectorFrame SE, locate it inside the VectorFrame SE folder on the *Illustrator 8 Bible* CD-ROM. Drag it into your Adobe Illustrator Plug-Ins folder. Restart Illustrator; VectorFrame SE is now accessible from the Windows menu. To display the VectorFrame SE palette, select it from the Windows menu.

Installing and Using Doodle Jr. (Mac Only)

To install Doodle Jr., locate it inside the Doodle Jr. folder on the *Illustrator 8 Bible* CD-ROM. Drag it into your Adobe Illustrator Plug-Ins folder. Restart Illustrator. To display the Doodle Jr. dialog box, select it from the Fun submenu in the Filter menu.

✦   ✦   ✦

Installing Illustrator

The installation of Illustrator is pretty straightforward. If you've installed any software recently on your Macintosh or Windows system, you're already familiar with the installation process. This appendix provides some additional information you may find helpful when installing Illustrator. The first section deals with installing Illustrator for Macintosh, while the second section addresses installing Illustrator for Windows.

System Requirements for Macintosh

To run Adobe Illustrator 8 on a Macintosh, there are certain requirements that your computer system needs to meet. Of these, the CPU and RAM are the most important.

Macintosh Computer Requirements

The following is a list of the Macintosh computers you *can't* use to run Illustrator 8. Don't attempt to load Adobe Illustrator 8 on any of the following systems:

+ Macintosh 128 (the original Mac)
+ Macintosh 512K or 512KE
+ Macintosh Plus
+ Macintosh SE
+ Macintosh Portable
+ Macintosh Classic
+ Macintosh PowerBook 100
+ Macintosh II
+ Macintosh LC

Fortunately, Illustrator can run on all of the Macs sold today, including all members of these classes (or families):

✦ Macintosh Performa (68030 models)

✦ Macintosh PowerBook, including Duos (except PowerBook 100)

✦ Macintosh Centris

✦ Macintosh Quadra

✦ Macintosh SE/30, Classic II, Color Classic

✦ All Power Macintoshes and Mac clones

The rule here is that your system must have a 68030 or greater processor or a PowerPC 6xx processor. The systems that don't make the cut are 68000-based.

RAM

Illustrator 8 needs a minimum of 10MB of memory to run efficiently. What this means is that your system should have *at the very least* 16MB of RAM total. The system software usually takes up between 3 and 4MB of RAM, and more for Mac OS 8 than for System 7.5.

A good way to check how much RAM you have available for Illustrator is to restart your system. After the desktop appears, go to the Apple in the upper-left corner and pull down About This Computer. The number in the Largest Unused Block box needs to be 8000K or larger. If not, then you need to buy some RAM.

Other Attachments

You also need a hard drive with about 25MB of free space on it, a color monitor that can display 640 x 480 (or larger), a keyboard, and a mouse.

Macintosh System Recommendations

If you have the minimum system that Adobe recommends, Illustrator will work — kind of. If you have armloads of patience and plenty to do between certain operations, this minimum setup may work for you.

CPU and FPU

Although a 68030 is fast compared to a 68000, it crawls compared to a 68040, and it stops compared to a PPC 601, 603, or 604. To do color work, investigate your options regarding a 68040 or better. Systems with 68040s include Centris, Quadra, LCIV, and some of the latest PowerBooks and Performas.

There is a catch, however. If you are using KPT Vector Effects or Adobe Dimensions, make sure that your computer has a math coprocessor (also called a floating-point unit or FPU). Dimensions will run, though slowly, without an FPU, but Vector Effects won't run at all. Most computers have an FPU, but some don't. Here is a list of systems with a 68020 or greater processor that do *not* have a math coprocessor:

✦ Macintosh IIsi (FPU comes on the NuBUS adapter card), IIvi

✦ Macintosh, LCII, LCIII (optional)

✦ Macintosh Classic II, Color Classic (optional)

✦ PowerBook 140, 145, 145B, 150, 160

✦ PowerBook Duo 200 series (available on Duo Dock)

✦ Performa 200, 400, 600 (optional), 405, 430, 450 (optional)

✦ Centris 610

✦ Quadra 605

✦ Quadra 610 (base 8/160 model; all others have it)

Note   Power PC computers have FPU functions integrated into their chip. Illustrator, Vector Effects, and Dimensions understand this, and regard PPC systems as having an FPU.

A way to get around this limitation if your computer does not have an FPU is to get Software FPU (available on most online services and many FTP sites), a shareware utility that fools KPT Vector Effects into thinking that there is an FPU installed. Unfortunately, this utility only serves to slow down the FPU version of Dimensions.

Too Much RAM Is Never Enough

Through the Get Info box (in the Finder, select the Illustrator 8 icon and then choose File ➪ Get Info or press ⌘-I), you can allocate as much RAM to Illustrator as you like. If you don't have much RAM available, Illustrator uses as much RAM as it can.

A good setting for the Preferred Memory size of RAM (on the Get Info box) is at least 16,000K. This is more RAM than Adobe recommends, but 16,000K lets you work with medium-sized documents at a pretty fast clip.

No matter how much RAM you add to your system and allocate to Illustrator, there will surely be times when you get out-of-memory errors. One of the most common of these errors is the "Not enough memory for Undo/Redo" error, which occurs when the computer doesn't have enough memory to keep some of the oldest undos in your system. Because different operations take up different amounts of memory and more complex drawings take up more memory than simpler ones, the amount of RAM you need at any one time can vary.

Other areas that need lots of RAM are patterns (especially transparent ones), blends, multicolor gradients, complex masks, compound paths, and the use of some filters (Object Mosaic and Roughen are notorious for RAM usage).

If you are installing additional filter sets, a good rule of thumb is to allocate about 1MB of RAM for every additional third-party filter set.

Caution   Certain KPT Vector Effects filters will generate large numbers of additional paths, which can quickly use up the available RAM. The filters to watch out for are KPT 3D Transform, KPT ShadowLand, and KPT ShatterBox.

Installing Illustrator 8 for Macintosh

Remove all extensions but the ones needed to run your CD-ROM drive (use a startup manager to facilitate this).

Insert and open the Illustrator installation CD and double-click the Install Me icon. Click the Easy Install button, and Illustrator will install itself in a matter of minutes. It's actually faster and easier to install Illustrator this way and then remove items you don't want than to go through and do a Custom Install of Illustrator.

Illustrator will install ATM 4 into your System Folder, requiring you to restart after installation.

After restarting, run Illustrator and enter your serial number at the prompt.

System Requirements for Windows

To run Illustrator 8 on a PC, there are certain requirements that need to be met. Of these, the CPU, installed RAM, and operating system are the most important.

The minimum system requirements for Illustrator 8 for Windows are:

+ Intel 486 processor
+ Windows 95, Windows NT 4.0 Workstation, or Windows NT 4.0 Server operating system
+ VGA display card
+ CD-ROM drive (a 3.5" disk set is available for purchase; however, it doesn't contain all the CD's "goodies")
+ 16MB of RAM installed
+ 25MB of free hard disk space for installation

Adobe, however, recommends:

✦ Pentium or greater processor

✦ High-resolution (24-bit or greater Super VGA) video display card

✦ 32MB or more of RAM installed

Personally, I recommend a 133MHz or better Pentium. Anything slower (even a 90MHz) starts to slow Illustrator down. Also, if you are using lots of placed bitmap images (or rasterizing at high resolution within Illustrator), you want to have more RAM on hand.

Installing Illustrator for Windows

Insert the Adobe Illustrator 8 CD-ROM. Double-click the Setup icon. The Install Wizard will prepare the installation (this takes a while on slower systems). When the Installation screen appears, choose Typical from the list of options and press the Next button. Enter your name, title, and serial number, and continue pressing Next until Illustrator has installed.

After installation, Illustrator provides a method for you to register at that time. This is a good thing to do, as it provides Adobe with your contact information regarding special deals, upgrades, and so on.

After the installation is complete, double-click the Illustrator 8 icon (or choose Illustrator 8 from the Start menu) to run Illustrator.

✦   ✦   ✦

What's New in Illustrator 8

Adobe has come up with an amazing upgrade worthy of shelling out the bucks to update Illustrator to version 8. User requests have been answered with around 300 feature updates in this version. The enhancements, as well as completely new and cool features, make Illustrator 8 a must-have.

This appendix is organized into two sections. First, the new features are listed. Second, the more dramatic of the changes from version 7 are listed by the Illustrator area that they effect (such as menus or paths). Illustrator 8 also includes several changes to keyboard commands. These changes are not covered in this appendix, but rather in Appendix D, which lists all the Illustrator 8 commands and notes the ones that have been changed or added for Macintosh and Windows.

New Features

The following features have been added to Illustrator 8 (the italicized chapter number at the end of each feature description tells you where the feature is covered in this book):

- ✦ **Actions palette**: This wonderful new addition is like Photoshop's Actions palette. The Actions palette lets you automate functions to increase productivity. *Chapter 19*

- ✦ **Link Manager**: Adobe has taken the power of the Link Manager from PageMaker and added it to Illustrator. This great feature keeps track of linked files and images. *Chapter 19*

- ✦ **Smart Guides**: These temporary guides pop up to help align, transform, and move objects with ease. *Chapter 4*

✦ **Live Blends**: Live blends enable Illustrator users to change color, edit, or move a blend, and since it is live, it will update automatically. This incredible feature saves a ton of time when editing and changing colors of a blend. *Chapter 10*

✦ **Navigator palette**: The Navigator Palette enables you to move about your illustration without having to zoom in, zoom out, zoom in, and so on. You can even leave the Navigator Palette in full color so you can see your image while you work in Artwork mode. *Chapter 5*

✦ **Free Transform tool**: The Free Transform tool lets you perform a variety of transformation tasks at one time with mouse control. This tool also lets you create 3D effects with ease. *Chapter 7*

✦ **Registration Color**: A big user request was to add a registration color for printing and registration purposes. *Chapter 18*

✦ **Art Brush**: The Art Brush is one of the three new brush tools added to Illustrator 8. This brush enables you to "paint" out a selected object chosen from the Brushes palette. In the Brush Palette, you specify the particulars of the object, including its color, orientation, and scale factor. *Chapter 3*

✦ **Scatter Brush**: The Scatter Brush is another of the three new brush tools added to Illustrator 8. This particular brush scatters a selected object chosen from the Brushes palette according to a specified size, spacing, dispersion, and randomization. This brush is highly affected by the pressure-sensitive tablet. *Chapter 3*

✦ **Pattern Brush**: The Pattern Brush replaces the Path Patterns option from the Filter menu. This new brush option is much easier to understand and use compared to its predecessor. *Chapter 3*

✦ **Gradient Mesh tool**: The Gradient Mesh tool could possibly be the coolest of all additions to Illustrator 8. This new tool instantly blends more than 1 color in multiple directions. This tool simulates watercolor washes. It can also be used as a light source creation. This fantastic new feature boasts small file size, prints out great, and is quick and easy to use. *Chapter 10*

✦ **Photo Crosshatch filter**: The Photo Crosshatch filter lets you add a crosshatch effect to any photo or rasterized image in Illustrator. *Chapter 11*

✦ **Smoother tool**: The Smoother tool is a new tool added to the Pencil tool's pop-up tool. This tool lets you instantly smooth out any path by selecting the path and dragging the new shape over the top of it. *Chapter 3*

✦ **Erase tool**: The Erase tool is another addition to the Pencil tool's pop-up tools. This tool enables you to erase a portion of a path as if it were an eraser. *Chapter 3*

Changes

In Illustrator 8, several of the menu options, tools, and palettes have been significantly enhanced.

Menu Changes

The Illustrator menus have undergone the following changes in Version 8:

✦ **File ⇨ Open:** Adds the option to specify a start in directory for opening and saving, and enhances the preview capability of version 4.1 files in 8.0.

✦ **File ⇨ Save/Save As:** Adds the capability to delete unused swatches and brushes and the option to save as older Illustrator files to the Export area.

✦ **File ⇨ Close:** Adds the option to close all files by pressing the Option [Alt] key while choosing the Close command.

✦ **File ⇨ Place:** Adds placing and linking of PDF files and PICT files (Mac only).

✦ **File ⇨ Export:** Adds the option to delete unused swatches and brushes.

✦ **File ⇨ Page/Print Setup:** Returns Page Setup/Print Setup to the File menu.

✦ **File ⇨ Separations Setup:** Custom page adds the use of inches and millimeters. Also, the custom page dialog box retains current values.

✦ **File ⇨ Preferences:** Renames Keyboard Increments to Type & Auto Tracing and adds Q in type units to refer to millimeters.

✦ **Edit ⇨ Select:** Adds Select Again, the capability to select Text objects, and to use Select Masks with masked text.

✦ **Object ⇨ Masks:** Adds lock and unlock for masks, Stroke and Fill functions, and visible full Stroke values.

✦ **Object ⇨ Crop Marks:** New Registration color.

✦ **Object ⇨ Blend:** Adds new feature for Blending and Blending options.

✦ **Type ⇨ Tab Ruler:** Returns version 6's keyboard shortcut.

✦ **Type ⇨ Check Spelling:** Now includes all available foreign language and hyphenation dictionaries.

✦ **Type ⇨ Show Hidden Characters:** Adds the visibility of space, nonbreaking space, 2-byte space, tab, hard and soft returns, hyphen, nonprinting characters, and end of text.

✦ **Filter ⇨ Create ⇨ Trim Marks:** Supports large Strokes.

✦ **Filter ⇨ Stylize ⇨ Add Arrowheads**: Now covers large strokes and large arrowheads.

✦ **View ⇨ Zoom In/Zoom Out**: Adds the capability to zoom to 6400%.

✦ **View ⇨ Show/Hide Templates**: Returns the capability to use templates.

✦ **View ⇨ Show/Hide Rulers**: Fixes page shift.

✦ **View ⇨ Clear Guides**: Deletes all guides.

Tools

The following changes have been made to the tools and toolboxes in Illustrator 8 (the italicized chapter number at the end of each description tells you where the tool or toolbox is covered in this book):

✦ The toolbox is reorganized. While most tool positions are evident in the toolbox, hidden tools within each slot are not. *Chapter 1*

✦ The Selection tool works with the Bounding Box. *Chapter 3*

✦ The Group Selection is available from the Direct Selection through the Option [Alt] key. *Chapter 3*

✦ The Type tool adds shortcuts to increase/decrease point size by 10-point increments. For more on keyboard shortcuts, see Appendix D. *Chapter 8*

✦ The Ellipse works with the Bounding Box feature. The Ellipse is movable while drawing by holding the Spacebar down. Although the Center Ellipse tool is removed, holding down the Option [Alt] key while drawing accesses it. *Chapter 2*

✦ Rectangles are movable while drawing by holding down the Spacebar. Although the Center Rectangle tool is removed from the toolbar, holding the down Option [Alt] key while drawing accesses it. Pressing of the ⌘ [Ctrl] key adjusts the roundness of the rectangles corners. *Chapter 2*

✦ The Pen tool adds a feature whereby clicking over an existing path adds or deletes an Anchor Point. Also, when drawing with the Pen tool and dragging to get a smooth point, you can press the Option [Alt] key to convert the direction of the path. *Chapter 3*

✦ The Pencil tool is now fully editable. *Chapter 3*

✦ The Paintbrush tool improves the Calligraphic Brush and adds an Art Brush, a Scatter Brush, and a Pattern Brush. *Chapter 3*

✦ When applying Scissors to a path, only the remaining path is selected so you can see which path has been cut. *Chapter 7*

✦ The Knife tool automatically cuts a straight line from the mouse drag down to up as the default. The Knife is enhanced to include cuts resulting in open path polygons, and cuts affect only the selected object, or if nothing has been selected then every object the Knife tool is dragged over is affected. *Chapter 7*

✦ The Scale dialog box is now radio buttons. *Chapter 7*

✦ The Blend tool now includes editable blends and blend options. *Chapter 10*

✦ The Measure tool adds the capability to change the grid preferences by double-clicking on it and making changes in the Guides and Grids preferences dialog box that appears. *Chapter 4*

✦ The Paint Bucket tool now supports text. *Chapter 8*

✦ The Eyedropper tool now supports text. *Chapter 8*

✦ The Hand tool now moves in 1-pixel increments rather than snapping to 16-pixel increments. *Chapter 5*

✦ The Page tool adds the option to reset the Page Setup defaults by double-clicking the Page tool in the toolbox. *Chapter 1*

✦ The Zoom tool is enhanced so that when you click on the page, the page automatically recenters on the object you clicked on. The Zoom tool adds variable zoom levels up to 6400%. You can also fit all in the window by double-clicking on the Zoom tool. *Chapter 5*

Palettes

The following palettes in Illustrator 8 possess some new features (the italicized chapter number at the end of each description tells you where the tool or toolbox is covered in this book):

✦ **The Color palette**: Adds the Stroke option with the Fill option and the None choice to the palette. *Chapter 2*

✦ **The Gradient palette**: Changes the clicking on a midpoint option. Now clicking a midpoint lets you make any color you want rather than sticking the existing color from the Color palette in it. *Chapter 10*

✦ **The Stroke palette**: Entering 0 means None, choosing Dashed highlights the dash box, and there is a millimeters options to the Stroke weights. *Chapter 2*

✦ **The Swatches palette**: New colors and patterns from opening a file automatically appear in the Swatches palette, and registration color has been added. Also, duplicate swatches are noted. *Chapter 2*

✦ **The Transform palette**: Adds the option to Display information using Stroke weight. *Chapter 7*

✦ **The Layers palette**: Returns the thinner layers option and the capability to drag to hidden layers as in version 6. Also added are a variable scrolling speed and italicized layer name for layers that aren't set to print. *Chapter 7*

✦ **The Character palette**: When you enter a size and Undo, the size box is now highlighted. *Chapter 8*

✦ **The Paragraph palette**: Enhances hanging punctuation for centered text. Also adds the Japanese equivalent to hanging punctuation and support for the Kinsoku Shori. *Chapter 8*

✦ **The Pathfinder palette**: The previous Pathfinder options were found in a menu. Now they are easier to access in the palette form. *Chapter 7*

✦　　✦　　✦

Shortcuts for Illustrator 8

There are more keyboard commands, functions, and shortcuts in Illustrator than ever before. The tables in this appendix give you a quick reference to the commands, functions, and shortcuts for both Macintosh and Windows (as in the rest of the book, the Windows commands are shown in square brackets).

Menu Commands

The File Menu	
Command	*Shortcut*
New Document	⌘[Ctrl]-N
Open Document	⌘[Ctrl]-O
Close Document	⌘[Ctrl]-W
Save Document	⌘[Ctrl]-S
Save As	⌘[Ctrl]-Shift-S
Save a Copy	⌘[Ctrl]-Option[Alt]-S
Revert	F12 (Mac only)
Separation Setup	⌘-Option-P (Mac only)
Document Setup	⌘[Ctrl]-Option[Alt]-P
Page [Print] Setup	⌘[Ctrl]-Shift-P
Print Document [Print]	⌘[Ctrl]-P
General Preferences	⌘[Ctrl]-K
Quit Illustrator	⌘[Ctrl]-Q

The Edit Menu

Command	Shortcut
Undo	⌘[Ctrl]-Z F1 (Mac and Windows)
Redo	⌘[Ctrl]-Shift-Z
Cut	⌘[Ctrl]-X F2 (Mac and Windows)
Copy	⌘[Ctrl]-C F3 (Mac and Windows)
Paste	⌘[Ctrl]-V F4 (Mac and Windows)
Paste in Front	⌘[Ctrl]-F
Paste in Back	⌘[Ctrl]-B
Clear	Delete (Mac and Windows)
Select All	⌘[Ctrl]-A
Deselect All	⌘[Ctrl]-Shift-A
Select Again	⌘[Ctrl]-6

The Object Menu

Command	Shortcut
Transform Again	⌘[Ctrl]-D
Move	Double-click Selection tool (Mac and Windows)
Bring to Front	⌘[Ctrl]-Shift-]
Bring Forward	⌘[Ctrl]-]
Send Backward	⌘[Ctrl]-[
Send to Back	⌘[Ctrl]-Shift-[
Group	⌘[Ctrl]-G
Ungroup	⌘[Ctrl]-Shift-G
Lock	⌘[Ctrl]-2

Command	Shortcut
Lock Unselected	⌘[Ctrl]-Shift-2
Unlock All	⌘[Ctrl]-Option[Alt]-2
Hide Selection	⌘[Ctrl]-3
Hide Unselected	⌘[Ctrl]-Shift-3
Show All	⌘[Ctrl]-Option[Alt]-3
Join	⌘[Ctrl]-J
Average	⌘[Ctrl]-Option[Alt]-J
Join and Average	⌘[Ctrl]-Option[Alt]-Shift-J
Make Blend	⌘[Ctrl]-Option[Alt]-B
Release Blend	⌘[Ctrl]-Option[Alt]-Shift-B
Make Mask	⌘[Ctrl]-7
Release Mask	⌘[Ctrl]-Option[Alt]-7
Make Compound Path	⌘[Ctrl]-8
Release Compound Path	⌘[Ctrl]-Option[Alt]-8

The Type Menu

Command	Shortcut
Font	⌘[Ctrl]-Option[Alt]-Shift-M
Show/Hide Character Palette	⌘[Ctrl]-T (toggle)
Show/Hide Paragraph Palette	⌘[Ctrl]-M (toggle)
Tab Ruler Palette	⌘[Ctrl]-Shift-T
Create Outlines	⌘[Ctrl]-Shift-O

The Filter Menu

Command	Shortcut
Apply Last Filter	⌘-E
Last Filter Dialog Box	⌘[Ctrl]-Shift-E

The View Menu	
Command	*Shortcut*
Artwork/Preview	⌘[Ctrl]-Y (toggle)
Preview Selection	⌘[Ctrl]-Shift-Y
Zoom In	⌘[Ctrl]-+
Zoom Out	⌘[Ctrl]- −
Fit in Window	⌘[Ctrl]-0 Double-click Hand tool (Mac and Windows)
Actual Size (100%)	⌘[Ctrl]-1 Double-click Zoom tool (Mac and Windows)
Hide Edges	⌘[Ctrl]-H (toggle)
Hide Template	⌘[Ctrl]-Shift-W (toggle)
Show/Hide Rulers	⌘[Ctrl]-R (toggle)
Show/Hide Guides	⌘[Ctrl]-; (toggle)
Lock Guides	⌘[Ctrl]-Option[Alt]-;
Make Guides	⌘[Ctrl]-5
Release Guides	⌘[Ctrl]-Option[Alt]-5
Show/Hide Grid	⌘[Ctrl]-' (toggle)
Snap to Grid	⌘[Ctrl]-Shift-'
Snap to Point	⌘[Ctrl]-Option[Alt]-'
Smart Guides	⌘[Ctrl]-U
New View 1	⌘[Ctrl]-Option[Alt]-Shift-1
New View 2	⌘[Ctrl]-Option[Alt]-Shift-2
New View 3	⌘[Ctrl]-Option[Alt]-Shift-3
New View 4	⌘[Ctrl]-Option[Alt]-Shift-4
New View 5	⌘[Ctrl]-Option[Alt]-Shift-5
New View 6	⌘[Ctrl]-Option[Alt]-Shift-6
New View 7	⌘[Ctrl]-Option[Alt]-Shift-7
New View 8	⌘[Ctrl]-Option[Alt]-Shift-8
New View 9	⌘[Ctrl]-Option[Alt]-Shift-9
New View 10	⌘[Ctrl]-Option[Alt]-Shift-0

The Window Menu	
Command	*Shortcut*
Show/Hide All Palettes/Tools	Tab (Mac and Windows; toggle)
Show/Hide Info Palette	F8 (Mac and Windows; toggle)
Show/Hide Transform Palette	none (Mac and Windows)
Show/Hide Pathfinder Palette	none (Mac and Windows)
Show/Hide Align Palette	none (Mac and Windows)
Show/Hide Color Palette	F6 (Mac and Windows; toggle) ⌘[Ctrl]-I (toggle)
Show/Hide Gradient Palette	F9 (Mac and Windows; toggle)
Show/Hide Stroke Palette	F10 (Mac and Windows; toggle)
Show/Hide Swatches Palette	F5 (Mac and Windows; toggle)
Show/Hide Brushes Palette	none (Mac and Windows)
Show/Hide Links Palette	none (Mac and Windows)
Show/Hide Layers Palette	F7 (Mac and Windows; toggle)
Show/Hide Navigator Palette	none (Mac and Windows)
Show/Hide Attributes Palette	F11 (Mac and Windows; toggle) ⌘[Ctrl]-Shift-I (toggle)
Show/Hide Actions Palette	none (Mac and Windows)

Tool Shortcuts

Many of the one-key tool shortcuts may require pressing the key more than once if that tool is hidden within a tool slot. For instance, to access the Auto Trace tool, press **B** if the Auto Trace tool is showing in the Blend tool slot, or **B B** if it is not showing. All one-key tool shortcuts are shown, assuming the tool slots contain the default tools; therefore, the shortcut for the Auto Trace tool is B B.

Toolbox Commands	
Tool	*Shortcut*
Hide/Show toolbox & other palettes	Tab (Mac and Windows)
Hide/Show all palettes except toolbox	Shift-Tab (Mac and Windows)
Reset all tool slots to their default tools	⌘[Ctrl]-Shift-double-click any tool

Selection Tools

Tool	Shortcut
Selection tool	V (Mac and Windows) ⌘[Ctrl]-Tab with Direct Selection tool, then hold ⌘[Ctrl] ⌘[Ctrl] with all other tools if Selection tool was the last tool used
Direct Selection tool	A (Mac and Windows; toggles with Group Selection tool) ⌘[Ctrl]-Tab with Selection tool, then hold ⌘[Ctrl]-Option[Alt] with Group Selection tool ⌘[Ctrl] with all other tools if Direct Selection tool was the last tool used
Group Selection tool	A A (if default Direct Selection tool is in slot in Mac or Windows; toggles with Direct Selection tool) Option[Alt] with Direct Selection tool ⌘[Ctrl]-Option[Alt] with all other tools if Direct Selection tool was the last tool used

Function	Procedure
Select one point	Click with Direct Selection tool (Mac and Windows)
Select one segment	Click with Direct Selection tool (Mac and Windows)
Select one path	Click with Group Selection tool (Mac and Windows)
Select next group up	Click again on selected path with Group Selection tool (Mac and Windows)
Select top-level group	Click with Selection tool (Mac and Windows)
Select additional	Shift-click (Mac and Windows)
Select specific points	Drag with Direct Selection tool (Mac and Windows)
Select specific paths	Drag with Selection tool (Mac and Windows)
Deselect selected	Shift-click on selected (Mac and Windows)
Move selection	Drag (Mac and Windows)
Duplicate selection	Option[Alt]-drag
Constrain to 45° movement	Shift-drag (Mac and Windows)
Duplicate and constrain	Option[Alt]-Shift-drag
Proportionately resize object	Shift-drag-Bounding Box handle (Mac and Windows)
Resize from center	Option[Alt]-drag Bounding Box handle
Resize proportionately from center	Option[Alt]-Shift-drag Bounding Box handle
Select all	⌘[Ctrl]-A
Deselect all	⌘[Ctrl]-Shift-A

Path Tools

Tool	Shortcut
Pen tool	P (Mac and Windows; toggles with Add Anchor Point tool, Delete Anchor Point tool, and Convert Direction Point tool)
Add Anchor Point tool	+ (if default Pen tool is in slot in Mac or Windows; toggles with Pen tool, Delete Anchor Point tool, and Convert Direction Point tool) Option[Alt]-Delete Anchor Point tool Option[Alt]-Scissors tool
Delete Anchor Point tool	– (if default Pen tool is in slot in Mac or Windows; toggles with Pen tool, Add Anchor Point tool, and Convert Direction Point tool) Option[Alt]-Add Anchor Point tool
Convert Direction Point tool	P P (if default Pen tool is in slot in Mac or Windows; toggles with Pen tool, Add Anchor Point tool, and Delete Anchor Point tool) Option[Alt]-Pen tool ⌘[Ctrl]-Option[Alt] with Direct Selection tool ⌘[Ctrl]-Option[Alt] if Direct Selection tool was the last selection tool used
Add Anchor Point to a selected path	Drag over a section of the path (Mac and Windows)
Delete Anchor Point from a selected path	Drag over a point on the path (Mac and Windows)
Pencil tool	N (Mac and Windows)
Smoother tool	N N (Mac and Windows; toggles with Pencil tool)
Erase tool	N N N (Mac and Windows; toggles with Pencil tool)
Paintbrush tool	B (if default Pencil tool is in slot in Mac or Windows; toggles with Paintbrush tool)
Scissors tool	C (Mac and Windows; toggles with Knife tool)
Knife tool	C C (if default Scissors tool is in slot in Mac or Windows; toggles with Scissors tool)
Function	**Procedure**
Create a straight corner point	Click with Pen tool (Mac and Windows)
Create a smooth point	Drag with Pen tool (Mac and Windows)
Continue existing open path	Click/drag with Pen tool on endpoint of existing path (Mac and Windows)

(continued)

Path Tools *(continued)*

Tool	Shortcut
Close open path	While drawing, click/drag with Pen tool on the initial endpoint (Mac and Windows) Click/drag with Pen tool on each endpoint in succession (Mac and Windows) Select path and join (⌘[Ctrl]-J)
Constrain new point to 45° from last point	Shift-click/drag with Pen tool (Mac and Windows)
Constrain control handles to 45°	Shift while dragging with Pen tool (Mac and Windows)
Create a path	Click/drag a succession of points with Pen tool (Mac and Windows)
Add anchor points to existing path	Click with the Pen tool on path (Mac and Windows)
Delete anchor points from existing path	Click with Pen tool on an anchor point (Mac and Windows)
Convert anchor point to smooth point	Drag with Convert Direction Point tool on existing point (Mac and Windows)
Convert smooth point to corner point	Click with Convert Direction Point tool on smooth point (Mac and Windows)
Convert smooth to combination corner	Drag one handle with Direct Selection tool back into the anchor point (Mac and Windows)
Convert smooth to curved corner	Drag one handle with Convert Direction Point tool (Mac and Windows)
Draw freestyle paths	Drag with Pencil tool (Mac and Windows)
Erase Pencil tool path while drawing	⌘[Ctrl]-drag with Pencil tool over area to be erased
View Paintbrush options	Double-click on Paintbrush tool in toolbox (Mac and Windows)
Split path	Click with Scissors tool (Mac and Windows)
Slice multiple paths	Drag with Knife tool (Mac and Windows)
Constrain Knife slice to 45°	Shift-drag with Knife tool (Mac and Windows)
Duplicate section of paths	Option[Alt]-drag with Knife tool
Use selected path to slice	Choose Object ⇨ Path ⇨ Slice (Mac and Windows)

Type Tools

Tool	Shortcut
Type tool	T (Mac and Windows; toggles with all other type tools) Shift-Vertical Type tool (Mac and Windows)
Area Type tool	T T (if default Type tool is in slot in Mac or Windows; toggles with all other type tools) Option[Alt]-Path Type tool Shift-Vertical Area Type tool (Mac and Windows) Option[Alt]-Shift Vertical Path Type tool
Path Type tool	T T T (if default Type tool is in slot in Mac or Windows; toggles with all other type tools) Option[Alt]-Area Type tool Shift-Vertical Path Type tool (Mac and Windows) Option[Alt]-Shift-Vertical Area Type tool
Vertical Type tool	T T T T (if default Type tool is in slot Mac or Windows; toggles with all other type tools) Shift-Type tool (Mac and Windows)
Vertical Area Type tool	T T T T T (if default Type tool is in slot in Mac or Windows; toggles with all other type tools) Option[Alt]-Vertical Path Type tool Shift-Area Type tool (Mac and Windows) Option[Alt]-Shift-Area Type tool
Vertical Path Type tool	T T T T T T (if default Type tool is in slot in Mac or Windows; toggles with all other type tools) Option[Alt]-Vertical Area Type tool Shift-Path Type tool (Mac and Windows) Option[Alt]-Shift -Area Type tool
Function	**Procedure**
Create point type	Click with Type tool (Mac and Windows)
Create rectangle type	Drag with Type tool (Mac and Windows)
Place path type on a closed path	Click on path with Path Type tool (Mac and Windows) Option[Alt]-click on path with Type tool Option[Alt]-click on path with Area Type tool
Place path type on an open path	Click on path with Path Type tool (Mac and Windows) Click on path with Type tool (Mac and Windows) Option[Alt]-click on path with Area Type tool
Place area type on a closed path	Click on path with Area Type tool (Mac and Windows) Click on path with Type tool (Mac and Windows) Option[Alt]-click on path with Path Type tool

(continued)

Type Tools *(continued)*

Function	*Procedure*
Place area type on an open path	Click on path with Area Type tool (Mac and Windows) Option[Alt]-click on path with Type tool Option[Alt]-click on path with Path Type tool
Change vertical type to horizontal type	Choose Type ⇨ Orientation ⇨ Horizontal (Mac and Windows)
Change horizontal type to vertical type	Choose Type ⇨ Orientation ⇨ Vertical (Mac and Windows)
Select entire text block	Click on text block with Selection tool (Mac and Windows)
Select one character	Drag across character with any Type tool (Mac and Windows)
Select one word	Double-click on word with any Type tool (Mac and Windows)
Select one paragraph	Triple-click on paragraph with any Type tool (Mac and Windows)
Select all text in text block	Click in text block with any Type tool, and then press ⌘[Ctrl]-A
Flip type on a path	Double-click the I-bar with any selection tool or just drag it to the opposite side (Mac and Windows)

Shape Tools

Tool	*Shortcut*
Ellipse tool	L (Mac and Windows; toggles with Polygon tool, Star tool, and Spiral tool)
Polygon tool	L L (if default Ellipse tool is in slot in Mac or Windows; toggles with Ellipse tool, Star tool, and Spiral tool)
Star tool	L L L (if default Ellipse tool is in slot; toggles with Ellipse tool, Polygon tool, and Spiral tool)
Spiral tool	L L L L (if default Ellipse tool is in slot in Mac or Windows; toggles with Ellipse tool, Polygon tool, and Star tool)
Rectangle tool	M (Mac and Windows; toggles with Rounded Rectangle tool)
Rounded Rectangle tool	M M (if default Rectangle tool is in slot in Mac or Windows; toggles with Rectangle tool, Centered Rectangle Tool, and Centered Rounded Rectangle tool) Option[Alt]-Centered Rounded Rectangle tool

Function	Procedure
Create ellipse using numbers	Click with Ellipse tool (Mac and Windows)
Draw ellipse	Drag with Ellipse tool (Mac and Windows)
Draw circle	Shift-drag with Ellipse tool (Mac and Windows)
Create centered ellipse using numbers	Option[Alt]-click with Ellipse tool
Draw centered ellipse	Option[Alt]-drag with Ellipse tool
Create polygon using numbers	Click with Polygon tool (Mac and Windows)
Draw polygon	Drag with Polygon tool (Mac and Windows)
Constrain polygon angle	Shift-drag with Polygon tool (Mac and Windows)
Move polygon while drawing	Spacebar-drag with Polygon tool (Mac and Windows)
Create multiple polygons	~-drag with Polygon tool (Mac and Windows)
Increase polygon sides	Up Arrow-drag with Polygon tool (Mac and Windows)
Decrease polygon sides	Down Arrow-drag with Polygon tool (Mac and Windows)
Create star using numbers	Click with Star tool (Mac and Windows)
Draw star	Drag with Star tool (Mac and Windows)
Constrain star angle	Shift-drag with Star tool (Mac and Windows)
Move star while drawing	Spacebar-drag with Star tool (Mac and Windows)
Create multiple stars	~-drag with Star tool (Mac and Windows)
Draw even-shouldered star	Option[Alt]-drag with Star tool
Move outer points only	⌘[Ctrl]-drag with Star tool
Increase star points	Up Arrow-drag with Star tool (Mac and Windows)
Decrease star points	Down Arrow-drag with Star tool (Mac and Windows)
Create spiral using numbers	Click with Spiral tool (Mac and Windows)
Draw spiral	Drag with Spiral tool (Mac and Windows)
Constrain spiral angle	Shift-drag with Spiral tool (Mac and Windows)
Move spiral while drawing	Spacebar-drag with Spiral tool (Mac and Windows)
Create multiple spirals	~-drag with Spiral tool (Mac and Windows)
Decrease spiral decay	⌘[Ctrl]-drag with Spiral tool
Increase spiral length/size	Option[Alt]-drag with Spiral tool (toggle)
Increase spiral length	Up Arrow-drag with Spiral tool (Mac and Windows)

(continued)

Shape Tools *(continued)*

Function	Procedure
Decrease spiral length	Down Arrow-drag with Spiral tool (Mac and Windows)
Create rectangle using numbers	Click with Rectangle tool or Rounded Rectangle tool (Mac and Windows)
Draw rectangle	Drag with Rectangle tool (Mac and Windows)
Draw square	Shift-drag with Rectangle tool (Mac and Windows)
Create rounded rectangle using numbers	Click with Rectangle tool or Rounded Rectangle tool (Mac and Windows)
Draw rounded rectangle	Drag with Rounded Rectangle tool (Mac and Windows)
Create centered rectangle using numbers	Option[Alt]-click with Rectangle tool
Draw centered rectangle	Option[Alt]-drag with Rectangle tool
Create centered rounded rectangle	Option[Alt]-click with Rectangle tool or Rounded Rectangle tool
Draw centered rounded rectangle	Option[Alt]-drag with Rounded Rectangle tool

Transformation Tools

Tool	Shortcut
Rotate tool	R (Mac and Windows; toggles with Twirl tool)
Twirl tool	R R (if default Rotate tool is in slot in Mac or Windows; toggles with Rotate tool)
Scale tool	S (Mac and Windows; toggles with Reshape tool)
Reshape tool	S S (if default Scale tool is in slot in Mac or Windows; toggles with Scale tool)
Reflect tool	O (Mac and Windows)
Skew tool	O O (Mac and Windows)
Free Transform tool	E (Mac and Windows)

Function	Procedure
Rotate using numbers	Option[Alt]-click with Rotate tool
Rotate from center of selection with numbers	Double-click with Rotate tool (Mac and Windows)
Free Rotate (live)	Click with Rotate to set Origin, and then drag with Rotate tool (Mac and Windows)

Function	Procedure
Free Rotate around selection center	Drag with Rotate tool (Mac and Windows)
Constrain rotation to 45°	Shift-drag with Rotate tool (Mac and Windows)
Rotate a copy	Option[Alt]-drag with Rotate tool
Rotate pattern only	~-drag with Rotate tool (Mac and Windows)
Twirl using numbers	Option[Alt]-click with Rotate tool
Free Twirl (live)	Drag with Twirl tool (Mac and Windows)
Scale using numbers	Option[Alt]-click with Scale tool
Scale from center of selection with numbers	Double-click with Scale tool (Mac and Windows)
Free Scale (live)	Click with Scale to set Origin, and then drag with Scale tool (Mac and Windows)
Free Scale around selection center	Drag with Scale tool (Mac and Windows)
Constrain scaling to 45°	Shift-drag with Scale tool (Mac and Windows)
Scale a copy	Option[Alt]-drag with Scale tool
Scale pattern only	~-drag with Scale tool (Mac and Windows)
Reshape a path	Select points with Direct Selection, then drag with Reshape (Mac and Windows)
Reflect using numbers	Option[Alt]-click with Reflect tool
Reflect from center of selection with numbers	Double-click with Reflect tool (Mac and Windows)
Free Reflect (live)	Click with Reflect to set Origin, and then drag with Reflect tool (Mac and Windows)
Free Reflect around selection center	Drag with Reflect tool (Mac and Windows)
Constrain reflecting to 45°	Shift-drag with Reflect tool (Mac and Windows)
Reflect a Copy	Option[Alt]-drag with Reflect tool
Reflect Pattern only	~-drag with Reflect tool (Mac and Windows)
Skew using Numbers	Option[Alt]-click with Skew tool
Skew from Center of Selection with numbers	Double-click with Skew tool (Mac and Windows)
Free Skew (live) with Skew	Click with Skew to set Origin, and then drag (Mac and Windows)

(continued)

Transformation Tools *(continued)*

Function	Procedure
Free Skew around selection center	Drag with Skew (Mac and Windows)
Constrain skewing to 45°	Shift-drag with Skew tool (Mac and Windows)
Skew a copy	Option[Alt]-drag with Skew tool
Skew pattern only	~-drag with Skew tool (Mac and Windows)

Blend/Auto Trace/Graph Tools

Tool	Shortcut
Blend tool	W (Mac and Windows; toggles with Auto Trace tool)
Auto Trace tool	W W (if default Blend tool is in slot in Mac or Windows; toggles with Blend tool)
Column Graph tool	J (Mac and Windows; toggles with all other graph tools)
Stacked Column Graph tool	J J (if default Column Graph tool is in slot in Mac or Windows; toggles with all other graph tools)
Bar Graph tool	J J J (if default Column Graph tool is in slot in Mac or Windows; toggles with all other graph tools)
Stacked Bar Graph tool	J J J J (if default Column Graph tool is in slot in Mac or Windows; toggles with all other graph tools)
Line Graph tool	J J J J J (if default Column Graph tool is in slot in Mac or Windows; toggles with all other graph tools)
Area Graph tool	J J J J J J (if default Column Graph tool is in slot in Mac or Windows; toggles with all other graph tools)
Scatter Graph tool	J J J J J J J (if default Column Graph tool is in slot in Mac or Windows; toggles with all other graph tools)
Pie Graph tool	J J J J J J J J (if default Column Graph tool is in slot in Mac or Windows; toggles with all other graph tools)
Radar Graph tool	J J J J J J J J J (if default Column Graph tool is in slot in Mac or Windows; toggles with all other graph tools)

Function	Procedure
Blend between two paths	Click on corresponding selected points on each path with Blend tool (Mac and Windows)
Auto Trace Images	Click on area to be traced with Auto Trace tool (Mac and Windows)

Function	Procedure
Create a Graph sized by numbers	Click with any Graph tool (Mac and Windows)
Create a Graph sized by dragging	Drag with any Graph tool (Mac and Windows)

Paint Tools

Tool	Shortcut
Gradient tool	G (Mac and Windows)
Gradient Mesh tool	U (Mac and Windows)
Paintbucket tool	K (Mac and Windows) Option[Alt]-Eyedropper tool
Eyedropper tool	I (Mac and Windows) Option[Alt]-Paintbucket tool

Function	Procedure
Measure a distance	Click on the start and end location with the Measure tool (Mac and Windows)
Measure a distance by 45° angles	Shift-click on the start and end location with the Measure tool (Mac and Windows)
Change Linear Gradient direction/length	Drag with Gradient tool (Mac and Windows)
Constrain Gradient Direction to 45° angles	Shift-drag with Gradient tool (Mac and Windows)
Change Radial Gradient size/location	Drag with Gradient tool (Mac and Windows)
Change Radial Gradient origin point	Click with Gradient tool (Mac and Windows)
Sample color to Color palette	Click with Eyedropper tool (Mac and Windows)
Sample Screen color to Color palette	Shift-click with Eyedropper tool (Mac and Windows)
Change Paint Style of selected objects	Double-click with Eyedropper tool on an object with the desired style (Mac and Windows)
Paint unselected objects	Click on objects with the Paintbucket tool (Mac and Windows)

Viewing Tools

Tool	Shortcut
Hand tool	H (Mac and Windows; toggles with Page tool) Spacebar (when not entering text in Mac or Windows)
Page tool	H H (if default Hand tool is in slot in Mac or Windows; toggles with Hand tool)
Measure tool	H H H (Mac and Windows; toggles with Hand tool)
Zoom tool	Z (Mac and Windows) ⌘[Ctrl]-Spacebar
Zoom Out tool	Option[Alt]-Zoom tool

Function	Procedure
Zoom in	Click with the Zoom tool (Mac and Windows) ⌘[Ctrl]-+
Zoom out	Option[Alt]-click with the Zoom tool ⌘[Ctrl]- –
Zoom in to a specific area	Drag with the Zoom tool (Mac and Windows)
Move the Zoom Marquee while drawing	Spacebar while dragging with the Zoom tool (Mac and Windows)
Draw the Zoom Marquee from its center	Control-drag with the Zoom tool (Mac and Windows)

Viewing Shortcuts

Action	Shortcut
Zoom in	⌘[Ctrl]-+ Click with Zoom tool (Mac and Windows)
Zoom out	⌘[Ctrl]- – Option[Alt]-click with Zoom tool
Fit document in Window	⌘[Ctrl]-0 Double-click on Hand tool (Mac and Windows)
View at actual size (100%)	⌘[Ctrl]-1 Double-click on Zoom tool (Mac and Windows)
Artwork/Preview mode	⌘[Ctrl]-Y (toggle)
Preview Selection mode	⌘[Ctrl]-P-Option[Alt]-Y

Action	Shortcut
Custom View recall	⌘[Ctrl]-Option[Alt]-Shift-1 through ⌘[Ctrl]-Option[Alt]-Shift-0
Show/Hide edges	⌘[Ctrl]-H (toggle)
Show/Hide guides	⌘[Ctrl]-;
Show/Hide grid	⌘[Ctrl]-'
Show/Hide rulers	⌘[Ctrl]-R
Hide selected objects	⌘[Ctrl]-3
Hide unselected objects	⌘[Ctrl]-Option[Alt]-3
Show all hidden objects	⌘[Ctrl]-Shift-3
Window mode (normal)	F (when in Full Screen mode in Mac or Windows)
Full Screen mode with menu	F (when in Window mode in Mac or Windows)
Full Screen mode (no menus)	F (when in Full Screen mode with menu in Mac or Windows)

Type Shortcuts

Action	Shortcut
Copy type on a path	Option [Alt]-drag the I-bar using any selection tool. (This shortcut actually creates two paths as well as two text stories.)
Flip type on a path	Double-click the I-bar with any selection tool or just drag it to the opposite side of the path (Mac and Windows)
Move insertion point to next character	Right Arrow (→) (Mac and Windows)
Move insertion point to previous character	Left Arrow (←) (Mac and Windows)
Move insertion point to next line	Down Arrow (↓) (Mac and Windows)
Move insertion point to previous line	Up Arrow (↑) (Mac and Windows)
Move insertion point to next word	⌘[Ctrl]-Right Arrow (→)
Move insertion point to previous word	⌘[Ctrl]-Left Arrow (←)
Move insertion point to next paragraph	⌘[Ctrl]-Down Arrow (↓)

(continued)

Type Shortcuts *(continued)*

Action	*Shortcut*
Move Insertion Point to previous paragraph	⌘[Ctrl]-Up Arrow (↑)
Select (by highlighting) all type in story	⌘[Ctrl]-A when the insertion point is in the story
Select all type in document	⌘[Ctrl]-A when any tool but the Type tools are selected
Select next character	Shift-Right Arrow (→) (Mac and Windows)
Select previous character	Shift-Left Arrow (←) (Mac and Windows)
Select next line	Shift-Down Arrow (↓) (Mac and Windows)
Select previous line	Shift-Up Arrow (↑) (Mac and Windows)
Select next word	⌘[Ctrl]-Shift-Right Arrow (→)
Select previous word	⌘[Ctrl]-Shift-Left Arrow (←)
Select next paragraph	⌘[Ctrl]-Shift-Down Arrow (↓)
Select previous paragraph	⌘[Ctrl]-Shift-Up Arrow (↑)
Select word	Double-click on word (Mac and Windows)
Select paragraph	Triple-click on paragraph (Mac and Windows)
Deselect all type	⌘[Ctrl]-Shift-A
Duplicate column outline and flow text	Option[Alt]-drag column outline with Direct Selection tool
Insert discretionary hyphen	⌘[Ctrl]-Shift-hyphen
Insert line break	Press Return[Enter] (on keypad)

Paragraph Formatting

Action	*Shortcut*
Display Paragraph palette	⌘[Ctrl]-Shift-M
Align paragraph flush left	⌘[Ctrl]-Shift-L
Align paragraph flush right	⌘[Ctrl]-Shift-R
Align paragraph flush center	⌘[Ctrl]-Shift-C
Align paragraph justified	⌘[Ctrl]-Shift-J
Align paragraph force justified	⌘[Ctrl]-Shift-F

Action	Shortcut
Display Tab Ruler palette	⌘[Ctrl]-Shift-T
Align Tab palette to selected paragraph	Click on Tab palette size box (Mac and Windows)
Cycle through tab stops	Option[Alt]-click on tab stop
Move multiple tab stops	Shift-drag tab stops (Mac and Windows)
Cycle tab measurements	Click (Mac and Windows)

Character Formatting

Action	Shortcut
Display Character palette	⌘[Ctrl]-T
Highlight font	⌘[Ctrl]-Option[Alt]-Shift-M
Increase type size*	⌘[Ctrl]-Shift->
Decrease type size*	⌘[Ctrl]-Shift-<
Increase type to next size on menu	⌘[Ctrl]-Option[Alt]->
Decrease type to next size on menu	⌘[Ctrl]-Option[Alt]-<
Highlight size	none (Mac and Windows)
Set leading to Solid (same as pt. size)	Double-click Leading symbol in Character palette (Mac and Windows)
Highlight leading	none (Mac and Windows)
Increase Baseline Shift (Raise)*	Option[Alt]-Shift-Up Arrow (↑)
Decrease Baseline Shift (Lower)*	Option[Alt]-Shift-Down Arrow (↓)
Increase Baseline Shift (Raise) x5*	⌘[Ctrl]-Option[Alt]-Shift-Up Arrow (↑)
Decrease Baseline Shift (Lower) x5*	⌘[Ctrl]-Option[Alt]-Shift-Down Arrow (↓)
Reset Baseline Shift to 0	none (Mac and Windows)
Highlight Baseline Shift	none (Mac and Windows)
Kern/Track closer*	Option[Alt]-Left Arrow (←)
Kern/Track apart*	Option[Alt]-Right Arrow (→)
Kern/Track closer x5*	⌘[Ctrl]-Option[Alt]-Left Arrow (←)
Kern/Track apart x5*	⌘[Ctrl]-Option[Alt]-Right Arrow (→)
Reset Kerning/Tracking to 0	⌘[Ctrl]-Shift-Q
Highlight Kerning/Tracking	⌘[Ctrl]-Option[Alt]-K
Reset Horizontal Scale to 100%	⌘[Ctrl]-Shift-X

*Value/amount set in Preferences

Color Commands

Color Palette	
Action	**Shortcut**
Show/Hide Color palette	F6 (Mac and Windows; toggle) ⌘[Ctrl]-I (toggle)
Revert to default colors	D (White Fill, Black Stroke; Mac and Windows)
Toggle focus between Fill and Stroke	X (Mac and Windows)
Choose current color in Color palette	, (comma; Mac and Windows)
Change paint to None	/ (Mac and Windows)
Apply to inactive Fill/Stroke (Fill when Stroke is active, Stroke when Fill is active)	Option[Alt]-click in color ramp on Color palette
Apply color to unselected object	Drag color swatch from Color palette to object (Mac and Windows)
Apply color to selected object	Click on swatch in Color palette (Mac and Windows)
Copy Paint Style to unselected objects	Click on unselected objects with Paintbucket (Mac and Windows)
Copy Paint Style from any (source) object to all selected objects	Click on source object with Eyedropper (Mac and Windows)
Tint process color	Shift-drag any Color palette slider (Mac and Windows)
Cycle through Color modes	Shift-click on Color Ramp (Grayscale, CMYK, RGB; Mac and Windows)

Swatches Palette	
Action	**Shortcut**
Show/Hide Swatches palette	F5 (Mac and Windows; toggle)
Toggle focus between Fill and Stroke	X (Mac and Windows)
Add swatch	Click the New Swatch icon (Mac and Windows) Drag from Color or Gradient palette into swatches (Mac and Windows)

Action	Shortcut
Replace swatch	Option[Alt]-drag from Color or Gradient palette into swatches
Duplicate swatch	Option[Alt]-drag swatch onto New Swatch icon in Swatches palette
Delete swatch	Drag to Trash icon in Swatches palette (Mac and Windows) Click on Trash icon with swatches selected (Mac and Windows)
Select contiguous swatches	Shift-click on first and last swatches (Mac and Windows)
Select noncontiguous swatches	⌘[Ctrl]-click on each swatch
Switch keyboard focus to Swatches palette (for selecting swatches by name as they are typed)	⌘[Ctrl]-Option[Alt]-click in Swatches palette
Apply color to unselected object	Drag color swatch from Swatches palette to object (Mac and Windows)
Apply color to selected object Windows)	Click on swatch in Swatches palette (Mac and

Gradient Palette

Action	Shortcut
Choose current gradient in Gradient palette	. (period; Mac and Windows)
Show/Hide Gradient palette	F9 (Mac and Windows; toggle)
Apply swatch to selected color stop on gradient palette	Option[Alt]-click on swatch
Add new color stop	Click below gradient ramp (Mac and Windows)
Duplicate color stop	Option[Alt]-drag color stop
Swap color stops	Option[Alt]-drag color stop on top of another
"Suck" color for color stop with Eyedropper	Shift-click with Eyedropper (Mac and Windows)
Reset Gradient to default Black, White	⌘[Ctrl]-click in Gradient swatch
Apply color to unselected object	Drag color swatch from Gradient palette to object (Mac and Windows)
Apply color to selected object	Click on swatch in Gradient palette (Mac and Windows)

Stroke Palette	
Action	*Shortcut*
Show/Hide Stroke palette	F10 (Mac and Windows; toggle)
Increase/decrease Stroke weight	Highlight Stroke field, use Up/Down Arrows, press Return[Enter] when finished
Increase/decrease Miter amount	Highlight Miter field, use Up/Down Arrows, press Return[Enter] when finished

Other Palettes

Miscellaneous Palette Commands	
Action	*Shortcut*
Collapse/display Palette	Click box in upper right (Mac and Windows)
Cycle through Palette views	Double-click palette tab (Mac and Windows)
Apply settings	Return[Enter]
Apply settings while keeping last text field highlighted	Shift-Return[Enter]
Highlight next text field	Tab (Mac and Windows)
Highlight Previous Text field	Shift-Tab (Mac and Windows)
Highlight any text field	Click on label or double-click current value (Mac and Windows)
Increase value by base increment	Highlight field, Up Arrow ($\uparrow$) (Mac and Windows)
Decrease value by base increment	Highlight field, Down Arrow ($\downarrow$) (Mac and Windows)
Increase value by large increment	Highlight field, Shift-Up Arrow ($\uparrow$) (Mac and Windows)
Decrease value by large increment	Highlight field, Shift-Down Arrow ($\downarrow$) (Mac and Windows)
Combine palettes	Drag palette tab within other palette (Mac and Windows)
Dock palette	Drag palette tab to bottom of other palette (Mac and Windows)
Separate palette	Drag palette tab from current palette (Mac and Windows)

Transform Palette

Action	Shortcut
Show/Hide Transform palette	none (Mac and Windows)
Copy object while transforming	Option[Alt]-Return[Enter]
Scale proportionately	⌘[Ctrl]-Return[Enter]
Copy object while scaling proportionately	⌘[Ctrl]-Option[Alt]-Return[Enter]

Layers Palette

Action	Shortcut
Show/Hide Layers palette	F7 (Mac and Windows)
New layer	Click on New Layer icon (Mac and Windows)
New layer with Options dialog box	Option[Alt]-click on New Layer icon
New layer above active layer	⌘[Ctrl]-Option[Alt]-click on New Layer icon
New layer below active layer	⌘[Ctrl]-click on New Layer icon
Duplicate layer(s)	Drag layer(s) to New Layer icon (Mac and Windows)
Change layer order	Drag layers up or down within Layer list (Mac and Windows)
Select all objects on a layer	Option[Alt]-click on that layer
Select all objects on several layers	Shift-Option[Alt]-click on each layer
Select contiguous layers	Shift-click on layers (Mac and Windows)
Select noncontiguous layers	⌘[Ctrl]-click on layers
Move objects to a different layer	Drag colored square to a different layer (Mac and Windows)
Copy objects to a different layer	Option[Alt]-drag color square to a different layer
Hide/Show layer	Click on Eyeball icon (Mac and Windows)
View layer while hiding others	Option[Alt]-click on Eyeball icon
View layer in Artwork mode	⌘[Ctrl]-click on Eyeball icon
View layer in Preview while others are artwork	⌘[Ctrl]-Option[Alt]-click on Eyeball icon
Lock/Unlock layer	Click on Pencil icon (Mac and Windows)
Unlock layer while locking others	Option[Alt]-click on Pencil icon

(continued)

Layers Palette *(continued)*	
Action	*Shortcut*
Delete layer	Drag layer to Trash icon (Mac and Windows) Select layer and click on Trash icon (Mac and Windows)
Delete layer without warning	Option[Alt]-drag layer to Trash icon Select layer and Option[Alt]-click on trash icon

Miscellaneous Commands

Action	*Shortcut*
Nudge selection*	Arrow keys (Mac and Windows)
See special Status Line categories	Option[Alt]-click status bar (lower left)
Cycle through units	⌘-Control-U (Mac only)
Display Illustrator debug screen (CAUTION: This can be dangerous.)	⌘-Option-Control-0 (zero; Mac only)
View anagrams of credits	Option[Alt]-click Illustrator click on toolbox
Speed up credits in About box	Option[Alt]
Display context-sensitive menus	Control-click [Right-click]
Highlight last active text field	⌘[Ctrl]-~ (tilde)

*Value/amount set in Preferences

Generic Dialog Box Commands

Action	*Shortcut*
Cancel	Esc (Mac and Windows)
OK (or dark bordered button)	Return [Enter]
Highlight next text field	Tab (Mac and Windows)
Highlight previous text field	Shift-Tab (Mac and Windows)
Highlight any text field	Click on label or double-click current value (Mac and Windows)

✦   ✦   ✦

Resources

This appendix contains resources for related products, services, and other information that Illustrator users may find useful. All phone numbers, addresses, and version numbers are subject to change without notice, of course.

People and Companies

Jennifer Alspach
jen@bezier.com

Jennifer Alspach is the author of other books on computer-related subjects, including *Photoshop and Illustrator Synergy Studio Secrets, Illustrator 7 Complete*, and *PhotoDeluxe 2.0 Visual Quickstart Guide*. Jennifer is a nationally known artist and writer, with clients all over the United States. Her work has appeared in several books, including *The Illustrator WOW! Book*. Jennifer created many of the figures throughout the Illustrator 8 Bible (and its previous editions). She regularly speaks at various seminars, Macworld Expos, and user groups all over the country. Jennifer also teaches Photoshop and Illustrator for business and everyday users.

Robert Burger
BurgerBobz@aol.com
URL: http://www.voicenet.com/~rbbb

Robert is an award-winning illustrator whose work can be seen in many magazines and books, on magazine and book covers, on album covers, in advertising, and on Web pages. His work has been honored by the Society of Illustrators of Los Angeles, the Society of Illustrators of New York, Graphics Design Annual, Print's Regional Design Annual, The Art Directors Club of Philadelphia, and the Art Directors Club of New Jersey.

K. Daniel Clark
Technical Illustration
3218 Steiner Street
San Francisco, CA 94123
dan@artdude.com
Phone: (415) 922-7761
Fax: (415) 922-7049

Joe Jones
DujaVe@aol.com

Joe Jones has been a professional graphic artist in the Denver area since 1983 and
vice president and art director of his own production screen printing shop, Cotton
Grafix. There, Joe had his multicolor, hand-separated preprint work sold at the
retail level over the entire Mountain region of the United States. He has created
artwork for almost every conceivable application and requirement. Joe's work has
been featured in other texts such as *KPT Studio Secrets, Photoshop and Illustrator
Synergy Studio Secrets*, and *Illustrator 7 Studio Secrets.*

Nikolai Punin
nokolai punin design
311 Greenwich Street #9b
New York, NY 10013
nikolaip@aol.com

Joe Shoulak
JoeCalif1@aol.com
URL: http://users.lanminds.com/~shoulak/
Phone: (510) 450-0298

Marty Smith
mstekart@aol.com

Marty Smith is a freelance Technical Illustrator with an office in Burbank, California.
He is conventionally trained in airbrush and pen and ink, with a background in
circuit board design and mechanical engineering. He transforms blueprints, photos,
or actual parts into digital renderings. He specializes in line art, exploded views,
and photorealistic cutaways. He works exclusively with Adobe Illustrator. His
clients include Apple, Otis Elevators, Sony, Nissan, Accura, Federal Express, Clorox,
GT Bikes, and Disney.

Clark Tate
Tate Studio
PO Box 339
Gridley, IL 61744
tatestudio@aol.com
URL: http://members.aol.com/TATESTUDIO
Phone: (309) 747-3388
Fax: (309) 747-3008

Teeple Graphics
rob@teeple.com
Phone: (717) 944-2034
Middletown, Pennsylvania

Teeple Graphics is a Macintosh VAR and World Wide Web service provider specializing in desktop publishing and high-end graphic systems integration. Teeple Graphics's expertise is unparalleled.

Thomas-Bradley Illustration and Design
tkn@gridley.org
bradneal@gridley.org
Phone: (309) 747-3266
Gridley, Illinois

Tom Neal and Brad Neal are partners in the Illinois-based Thomas-Bradley Illustration and Design firm, considered to be the premier house of vector realism. Established in 1987, the firm has had articles on their work appear in *The Illustrator WOW! Book*, *MacWEEK* magazine, *Computer Artist* magazine, *Adobe Spotlight*, several technical journals, and 13 published books. Their photorealistic Avia sneaker was featured in the last edition of the *Illustrator Bible*. Their clients include Pepsi-Cola, Anheuser-Busch, Nike, State Farm Insurance Company, Deere & Company, Caterpillar Tractor Company, and six major automobile manufacturers. They have also been featured speakers at several conferences and seminars across the country.

Wayne Vincent
wvassoc@aol.com

Wayne Vincent graduated from the Corcoran School of Art in Washington, DC, and has been working as an illustrator in the Washington area for the past 17 years. Trained as an airbrush illustrator, Wayne began working with Macintosh computers 11 years ago and now works exclusively in digital media.

Pamela Drury Wattenmaker
pamela@wattenmaker.com
URL: http://www.wattenmaker.com

Adobe Systems, Inc.
1585 Charleston Road
PO Box 7900
Mountain View, CA 94039-7900
Customer service: (800) 833-6687
Technical support
(available to registered users with a valid serial number only): (206) 628-3953
BBS (First Class software): (206) 623-6984

Publisher of Adobe Illustrator, Adobe Photoshop, Adobe PageMaker, Adobe
Streamline, Adobe Premiere, Adobe Dimensions, and several other products. Demo
versions of Illustrator, Streamline, and Dimensions are included on this book's
CD-ROM.

Extensis Corporation
1800 SW First, Suite 500
Portland, OR 97201
URL: http://www.extensis.com
Phone: (503) 274-2020
Fax: (503) 274-0530

Publisher of Extensis VectorTools, which are plug-ins for Adobe Illustrator and
Micromedia FreeHand. A demo version is available on the CD-ROM that comes with
this book.

hotdoor
40 Nieto Avenue, Suite #17
Long Beach, CA 90803
URL: http://www.hotdoor.com/cadtools/
Phone: (888) 236-9540

hotdoor is the publisher of CADtools plug-ins for Adobe Illustrator 8. A demo of
CADtools is found on the *Illustrator 8 Bible* CD-ROM.

MetaCreations, Inc.
6303 Carpinteria Avenue
Carpinteria, CA 93013
kptsupport@aol.com
Customer service: (805) 566-6200
Fax: (805) 566-6385

Publisher of KPT Vector Effects for Illustrator and FreeHand, Kai's Power Tools, KPT
Convolver, KPT Bryce, and more. A demo version of KPT Vector Effects is included
on the CD-ROM that comes with this book.

Other Illustrator Books

Several books are available on Adobe Illustrator and related topics, but the following books are especially good and come highly recommended. They are books that I have in my Illustrator library, and all are fantastic supplements to the *Illustrator 8 Bible*. Of course, some of these books I've written (I'm certainly not above blatant self-promotion), so naturally I recommend them.

Illustrator 7 Studio Secrets
By Ted Alspach

This full-color book contains all the good stuff about Adobe Illustrator, as well as Macromedia FreeHand, Extensis VectorTools, Adobe Dimensions, and other vector products. It features the world's most talented vector artists. IDG Books Worldwide, Inc.

Photoshop and Illustrator Synergy Studio Secrets
By Jennifer Alspach

This full-color book shows how to use Photoshop and Illustrator together. It also includes using Photoshop with FreeHand, QuarkXPress, PageMaker, 3D programs, and more. The second section of the book displays a fantastic gallery of images and tips on how they were done. IDG Books Worldwide, Inc.

Illustrator 7 Complete
By Jennifer Alspach et al.

Yet another giant entry in Hayden Books' Complete series (which also features a delightful Photoshop volume coauthored by yours truly), *Illustrator Complete* leaves no stone unturned in its exploration of every feature in Illustrator. Graphics gurus Jennifer Alspach and Steve Frank provide a unique perspective and "complete" coverage of Adobe Illustrator. Hayden Books.

Illustrator Filter Finesse
By Ted Alspach and Jennifer Alspach

The best (and only) book devoted to Illustrator and FreeHand plug-ins. Complete coverage of all the native filters, Vector Effects, Socket Sets, and more, combined with an outstanding how-to portion, make this book invaluable for all plug-in users. Random House Electronic Publishing.

The Illustrator WOW! Book
By Sharon Steuer

A fantastic full-color collection of Adobe Illustrator artwork and techniques from the industry's leading artists.

Design Essentials
Imaging Essentials
By Luanne Cohen et al.

These full-color books provide step-by-step examples and techniques for using Adobe Illustrator with Photoshop and Dimensions to produce the cornerstone elements of design. Luanne's wonderful art makes the examples come alive on each page.

FreeHand Books

Huh? What? Well, if you must succumb to using *that other program* because you can't convince your boss and/or spouse to use Illustrator 100% of the time, you'll find these books quite handy:

FreeHand 8 Visual QuickStart
By Sandee Cohen

This is the best way to learn FreeHand. Written by an Illustrator expert, it makes FreeHand's quirkiness understandable and almost usable (hey, it's still FreeHand, after all).

The Macworld FreeHand 8 Bible
By Deke McClelland

The antithesis to the book you're holding (although they do look awful nice sitting on a shelf together), Deke's *FreeHand Bible* has long been the most comprehensive guide to the Dark Side of vector graphics. IDG Books Worldwide, Inc.

Real World FreeHand
By Olav Martin Kvern

Written by FreeHand and PageMaker know-it-all Olav Kvern (I'm not kidding, he knows everything there is to know about both programs, and even wrote the FreeHand tips for Extensis VectorTools), this book explores FreeHand in depth, with all sorts of incredible insights and lengthy explanations you won't find elsewhere.

◆   ◆   ◆

Context-Sensitive Menus

As a Macintosh user, have you ever jealously coveted your Windows-using buddies' right mouse button? Okay, neither have I. And likewise, I doubt that many Windows users have lusted after the Mac's extra modifier key (Windows has Shift, Ctrl, and Alt; Macs have Shift, Control, Command, and Option).

To compensate Macintosh users for the loss of several keyboard commands associated with the Control key (which wouldn't be available on Windows systems), the Control key now works as a "mouse button switcher" between the right mouse button and the left mouse button of Windows users. And what does the right mouse button do for Windows users? It gives them context-sensitive menus, an up-and-coming standard for most Windows software.

What's a Context-Sensitive Menu?

Glad you asked, or this whole appendix wouldn't be necessary. A context-sensitive menu is a menu that pops up at your cursor when you press Control and click (on the Mac) or right-click (on a PC). The menu typically contains several standard options, such as Undo, and other selection-specific ones. For instance, if type is selected, you'll often see the Font and Size submenus in the context-sensitive menu.

The idea behind this is that there's no need to travel up to the menu bar each time you want to select a menu item; chances are many menu items will be available right at your cursor. This can often be faster than pressing a keyboard shortcut. Even so, I'm a bit perplexed as to why Adobe does not list the shortcuts next to each of the pop-up menu's commands; to see the shortcuts, you'll need to look in the real menu or refer to the comprehensive list in Appendix D of this *Illustrator 8 Bible*.

The Context-Sensitive Menus

There are six main context-sensitive menus you'll find in Illustrator 8. Each of them is shown in this section next to explanations for when they appear.

No Selection

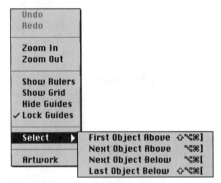

Figure F-1: The context-sensitive menu that appears when no items are selected

Standard Path Selection

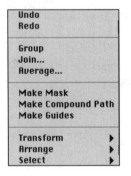

Figure F-2: The context-sensitive menu that appears when regular paths are selected

Group, Mask, or Compound Path Selection

Figure F-3: The context-sensitive menu that appears when a group, a mask, or a compound path is selected

Placed Image Selection

Figure F-4: The context-sensitive menu that appears when a placed image is selected

Type Selection

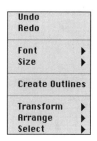

Figure F-5: The context-sensitive menu that appears when type is selected

Graph Selection

Figure F-6: The context-sensitive menu that appears when a graph is selected

✦　　✦　　✦

Index

(continued)

IDG BOOKS WORLDWIDE, INC.
END-USER LICENSE AGREEMENT

READ THIS. You should carefully read these terms and conditions before opening the software packet(s) included with this book ("Book"). This is a license agreement ("Agreement") between you and IDG Books Worldwide, Inc. ("IDGB"). By opening the accompanying software packet(s), you acknowledge that you have read and accept the following terms and conditions. If you do not agree and do not want to be bound by such terms and conditions, promptly return the Book and the unopened software packet(s) to the place you obtained them for a full refund.

1. **License Grant.** IDGB grants to you (either an individual or entity) a nonexclusive license to use one copy of the enclosed software program(s) (collectively, the "Software") solely for your own personal or business purposes on a single computer (whether a standard computer or a workstation component of a multiuser network). The Software is in use on a computer when it is loaded into temporary memory (RAM) or installed into permanent memory (hard disk, CD-ROM, or other storage device). IDGB reserves all rights not expressly granted herein.

2. **Ownership.** IDGB is the owner of all right, title, and interest, including copyright, in and to the compilation of the Software recorded on the disk(s) or CD-ROM ("Software Media"). Copyright to the individual programs recorded on the Software Media is owned by the author or other authorized copyright owner of each program. Ownership of the Software and all proprietary rights relating thereto remain with IDGB and its licensers.

3. **Restrictions on Use and Transfer.**

    (a) You may only (i) make one copy of the Software for backup or archival purposes, or (ii) transfer the Software to a single hard disk, provided that you keep the original for backup or archival purposes. You may not (i) rent or lease the Software, (ii) copy or reproduce the Software through a LAN or other network system or through any computer subscriber system or bulletin-board system, or (iii) modify, adapt, or create derivative works based on the Software.

    (b) You may not reverse engineer, decompile, or disassemble the Software. You may transfer the Software and user documentation on a permanent basis, provided that the transferee agrees to accept the terms and conditions of this Agreement and you retain no copies. If the Software is an update or has been updated, any transfer must include the most recent update and all prior versions.

4. **Restrictions on Use of Individual Programs.** You must follow the individual requirements and restrictions detailed for each individual program in Appendix A of this Book. These limitations are also contained in the individual license agreements recorded on the Software Media. These limitations may include a requirement that after using the program for a specified period of time, the user must pay a registration fee or discontinue use. By opening the Software packet(s), you will be agreeing to abide by the licenses and

restrictions for these individual programs that are detailed in Appendix A and on the Software Media. None of the material on this Software Media or listed in this Book may ever be redistributed, in original or modified form, for commercial purposes.

5. **<u>Limited Warranty</u>.**

   (a) IDGB warrants that the Software and Software Media are free from defects in materials and workmanship under normal use for a period of sixty (60) days from the date of purchase of this Book. If IDGB receives notification within the warranty period of defects in materials or workmanship, IDGB will replace the defective Software Media.

   (b) IDGB AND THE AUTHOR OF THE BOOK DISCLAIM ALL OTHER WARRANTIES, EXPRESS OR IMPLIED, INCLUDING WITHOUT LIMITATION IMPLIED WARRANTIES OF MERCHANTABILITY AND FITNESS FOR A PARTICULAR PURPOSE, WITH RESPECT TO THE SOFTWARE, THE PROGRAMS, THE SOURCE CODE CONTAINED THEREIN, AND/OR THE TECHNIQUES DESCRIBED IN THIS BOOK. IDGB DOES NOT WARRANT THAT THE FUNCTIONS CONTAINED IN THE SOFTWARE WILL MEET YOUR REQUIREMENTS OR THAT THE OPERATION OF THE SOFTWARE WILL BE ERROR FREE.

   (c) This limited warranty gives you specific legal rights, and you may have other rights that vary from jurisdiction to jurisdiction.

6. **<u>Remedies</u>.**

   (a) IDGB's entire liability and your exclusive remedy for defects in materials and workmanship shall be limited to replacement of the Software Media, which may be returned to IDGB with a copy of your receipt at the following address: Software Media Fulfillment Department, Attn.: *Illustrator 8 Bible*, IDG Books Worldwide, Inc., 7260 Shadeland Station, Ste. 100, Indianapolis, IN 46256, or call 1-800-762-2974. Please allow three to four weeks for delivery. This Limited Warranty is void if failure of the Software Media has resulted from accident, abuse, or misapplication. Any replacement Software Media will be warranted for the remainder of the original warranty period or thirty (30) days, whichever is longer.

   (b) In no event shall IDGB or the author be liable for any damages whatsoever (including without limitation damages for loss of business profits, business interruption, loss of business information, or any other pecuniary loss) arising from the use of or inability to use the Book or the Software, even if IDGB has been advised of the possibility of such damages.

   (c) Because some jurisdictions do not allow the exclusion or limitation of liability for consequential or incidental damages, the above limitation or exclusion may not apply to you.

7. **<u>U.S. Government Restricted Rights</u>.** Use, duplication, or disclosure of the Software by the U.S. Government is subject to restrictions stated in paragraph (c)(1)(ii) of the Rights in Technical Data and Computer Software clause of DFARS 252.227-7013, and in subparagraphs (a) through (d) of the Commercial Computer — Restricted Rights clause at FAR 52.227-19, and in similar clauses in the NASA FAR supplement, when applicable.

8. <u>General</u>. This Agreement constitutes the entire understanding of the parties and revokes and supersedes all prior agreements, oral or written, between them and may not be modified or amended except in a writing signed by both parties hereto that specifically refers to this Agreement. This Agreement shall take precedence over any other documents that may be in conflict herewith. If any one or more provisions contained in this Agreement are held by any court or tribunal to be invalid, illegal, or otherwise unenforceable, each and every other provision shall remain in full force and effect.

my2cents.idgbooks.com

CD-ROM Installation Instructions

The CD-ROM located inside the back cover of the book can be used on both Macintosh and Windows 95/NT systems. The CD-ROM includes artwork featured in the color section of the book, product demos, and fonts. Some files are available only for the Macintosh, and some, only for Windows.

To Install Product Demos

Macintosh: Open the product demos folder. Double-click the folder of the product you want to install. Double-click the Installer icon in that window. Follow the prompts during installation. After installation, double-click the program icon to run the demo.

Windows: Open the product demos directory. Double-click the directory of the product you want to install. Double-click the Setup icon in that window. Follow the prompts during installation. After installation, choose that product from the Start menu.

To Install Fonts

Macintosh only: Open the fonts folder. Drag the folders from the CD-ROM to your System Folder. When prompted to allow your Mac to place the fonts in the Font folder, click OK. In order to see your fonts, the application must be started up *after* the fonts are installed.